The Creation of the American Republic
1776-1787

PUBLISHED FOR THE
Institute of Early American History and Culture
AT WILLIAMSBURG, VIRGINIA

THE
CREATION
OF THE
AMERICAN
REPUBLIC
1776-1787

---

by GORDON S. WOOD

W · W · NORTON & COMPANY

New York · London

To My Mother and Father

Books That Live
The Norton imprint on a book means that in the publisher's
estimation it is a book not for a single season but for the years.
W. W. Norton & Company, Inc.

Library of Congress Cataloging in Publication Data

Wood, Gordon S.
  The creation of the American Republic, 1776–1787.

  (The Norton library, N644)
  Includes bibliographical references.
  1. Political science—History—United States.
I. Title.
[JA84.U5W6   1972]   320.9'73'03   72-4595

W. W. Norton & Company, Inc., 500 Fifth Avenue, New York, NY 10110
W. W. Norton & Company Ltd., 10 Coptic Street London WC1A 1PU

PRINTED IN THE UNITED STATES OF AMERICA

9 0

A new science of politics is needed for a new world.
—ALEXIS DE TOCQUEVILLE, 1835

Preface

Joel Barlow, in his *Advice to the Privileged Orders in the Several States of Europe*, published in 1792, suggested that what really separated the free from the oppressed of the world was simply a *"habit of thinking."* Indeed, said Barlow, the mind of man was "the *only* foundation" for any system of politics. Men never submitted to a king because he was stronger or wiser than they were, but because they believed him born to govern. And likewise men have become free and equal when they have thought they were so. When men asserted that nature had established inequalities among themselves, and thus had given to some the right of governing others, what they actually meant, said Barlow, was cultural nature, not physical. Therefore Aristotle was as right in teaching that some were born to command and others to be commanded as the French National Assembly was in declaring that men were born free and equal. What men believed, said Barlow, was what counted. Many "astonishing effects ... are wrought in the world by the *habit of thinking.*" It was custom, mental familiarity, culture, not force, that supported social gradations and distinctions, and even tyranny itself. But "let the people have time to become thoroughly and soberly grounded in the doctrine of *equality*, and there is no danger of oppression either from government or from anarchy." In the final analysis, concluded Barlow, it was the Americans' habit of thinking *"that all men are equal in their rights"* which had created their Revolution and sustained their freedom.

It was a profound insight, and one that I have attempted to exploit in this study of American political culture between 1776 and 1787. It was not, however, an insight with which I originally set out. I began simply with the intention of writing a monographic analysis of constitution-making in the Revolutionary era;

yet I soon found that I could make little or no sense of the various institutional or other devices written into the constitutions until I understood the assumptions from which the constitution-makers acted. I needed, in other words, to steep myself in the political literature of the period to the point where the often unspoken premises of thought became clear and explicit. What I discovered was much more than I anticipated; my reading opened up an intellectual world I had scarcely known existed. Beneath the variety and idiosyncrasies of American opinion there emerged a general pattern of beliefs about the social process—a set of common assumptions about history, society, and politics that connected and made significant seemingly discrete and unrelated ideas. Really for the first time I began to glimpse what late eighteenth-century Americans meant when they talked about living in an enlightened age.

As I explored this pattern of beliefs, it became evident that many of the historiographical problems involved in interpreting the Revolution and the formation of the Constitution stemmed from a failure to appreciate the distinctiveness of the political culture in which the Revolutionary generation operated. The approach of many historians to the American Revolution, it seemed, had too often been deeply ahistorical; there had been too little sense of the irretrievability and differentness of the eighteenth-century world. Although the vocabulary of the period was familiar, I found the meaning of much of that vocabulary strange and peculiar, and I learned that words such as "liberty," "democracy," "virtue," or "republicanism" did not possess a timeless application. Indeed, even within the very brief span of years that I was studying, it soon became clear that the terms and categories of political thought were undergoing rapid change, beset by the strongest kinds of polemical and experiential pressures. When I began to compare the debates surrounding the Revolutionary constitution-making of 1776 with those surrounding the formation of the federal Constitution of 1787, I realized that a fundamental transformation of political culture had taken place.

The Americans of the Revolutionary generation had constructed not simply new forms of government, but an entirely new conception of politics, a conception that took them out of an essentially classical and medieval world of political discussion into one that was recognizably modern. Of course this transformation of political thought had its origins deep in the colonial past; and the formation of the federal Constitution hardly marked the end of the advancement of American political ideas. Yet the decade of Revolutionary constitution-making seemed especially crucial and catalytic in the creation of a new conception of politics. The quarrel with Britain in the 1760's precipitated a comprehensive examination of politics that easily blended into the Americans' efforts to construct their new republican constitutions, as they attempted to put into practice the ideas the imperial debate had brought into focus. This need to institutionalize American experience under the exigencies of a revolutionary situation had the effect of accelerating and telescoping intellectual developments and of exposing the ambiguities and contradictions of American thought. By the 1780's the way was prepared for a resolution of the problems of American politics in a new political theory—a task made possible by the demands of justifying the new federal Constitution. The result, clear to many Americans by 1790, was a truly original formulation of political assumptions and the creation of a distinctly American system of politics. To describe and explain this creation became the aim of the book.

Of all the recent historians contributing to a renewed appreciation of the intellectual character of the American Revolution none has been more important than Bernard Bailyn, and my debt to him is incalculable. I not only benefited from an early reading of his study of the ideological origins of the American Revolution, but I had the advantage of his penetrating criticism of my manuscript at the beginning stages of its preparation. Most important, however, I am grateful to him, as are many others, for making early American history an exciting and vital field of study.

Others—William W. Abbot, Daniel Boorstin, Richard Buel, Jr., W. Frank Craven, William W. Freehling, Wendell and Jane Garrett, Ira Gruber, Stephen G. Kurtz, Arthur Mann, Marise Rogge, and Robert J. Taylor—read the manuscript at various stages of its development, and I am greatly indebted to them for their discerning suggestions and criticisms. Two persons helped me in ways that they are perhaps not fully aware of: Donald Fleming offered encouragement at a crucial time, and Samuel E. Thorne gave me the benefit of his understanding of both English constitutional history and the nature of the historical process; I convey my gratitude to both of them.

I am especially grateful to the Institute of Early American

History and Culture and in particular to its director, Lester J. Cappon, for providing me as a fellow of the Institute with both the time and the congenial atmosphere for completing the manuscript. Working with the staff of the Institute and sharing in its good cheer has been an invaluable personal experience that goes well beyond expert editorial assistance.

To my wife, Louise, I owe the most of all, for she made the whole venture possible and worthwhile.

GORDON S. WOOD

Ann Arbor, Michigan

Contents

[*xi*]

PART ONE

The Ideology of Revolution

I must indulge a hope that Britain's liberty, as well as ours, will eventually be preserved by the virtue of America.
—JOSEPH WARREN, 1775

CHAPTER I

The Whig Science of Politics

1. HISTORY AND REASON

The American Revolution has always seemed to be an extraordinary kind of revolution, and no more so than to the Revolutionaries themselves. To those who took stock at the end of three decades of revolutionary activity, the Revolution was not "one of those events which strikes the public eye in the subversions of laws which have usually attended the revolutions of governments." Because it did not seem to have been a usual revolution, the sources of its force and its momentum appeared strangely unaccountable. "In other revolutions, the sword has been drawn by the arm of offended freedom, under an oppression that threatened the vital powers of society."[1] But this seemed hardly true of the American Revolution. There was none of the legendary tyranny of history that had so often driven desperate people into rebellion. The Americans were not an oppressed people; they had no crushing imperial shackles to throw off. In fact, the Americans knew they were probably freer and less burdened with cumbersome feudal and hierarchical restraints than any part of mankind in the eighteenth century. To its victims, the Tories, the Revolution was truly incomprehensible. Never in history, said Daniel Leonard, had there been so much rebellion with so "little real cause." It was, wrote Peter Oliver, "the most wanton and unnatural rebellion that ever existed." The Americans' response was out of all proportion to the stimuli: "The Annals of no Country can pro-

1. [William Vans Murray], *Political Sketches, Inscribed to His Excellency John Adams* (London, 1787), 21, 48.

[3]

duce an Instance of so virulent a Rebellion, of such implacable madness and Fury, originating from such trivial Causes, as those alledged by these unhappy People." The objective social reality scarcely seemed capable of explaining a revolution.[2]

Yet no American doubted that there had been a revolution. How then was it to be justified and explained? If the American Revolution, lacking "those mad, tumultuous actions which disgraced many of the great revolutions of antiquity," was not a typical revolution, what kind of revolution was it? If the origin of the American Revolution lay not in the usual passions and interests of men, wherein did it lie? Those Americans who looked back at what they had been through could only marvel at the rationality and moderation, "supported by the energies of well-weighed choice," involved in their separation from Britain, a revolution remarkably "without violence or convulsion."[3] It was, said Edmund Randolph, a revolution "without an immediate oppression, without a cause depending so much on hasty feeling as theoretic reasoning." It seemed in fact to be peculiarly "the result of reason." The Americans were fortunate in being born at a time when the principles of government and freedom were better known than at any time in history. By "reading and reasoning" on politics they had learned "how to define the rights of nature,—how to search into, to distinguish, and to comprehend, the principles of physical, moral, religious, and civil liberty," how, in short, to discover and resist the forces of tyranny before they could be applied. "Justly it may be said, 'the present is an age of philosophy, and America the empire of reason.'"[4]

As early as 1775 Edmund Burke had noted in the House of Commons that the colonists' intensive study of law and politics had made them acutely inquisitive and sensitive about their liber-

2. [Daniel Leonard], *The Origin of the American Contest with Great Britain* . . . [*by*] *Massachusettensis* . . . (New York, 1775), 40; Douglass Adair and John A. Schutz, eds., *Peter Oliver's Origin and Progress of the American Rebellion: A Tory View* (San Marino, 1963), 159; Edward H. Tatum, Jr., ed., *The American Journal of Ambrose Serle, Secretary to Lord Howe, 1776–1778* (San Marino, 1940), 46–47.

3. Simeon Baldwin, *An Oration Pronounced before the Citizens of New-Haven, July 4th, 1788* . . . (New Haven, 1788), 10; [Murray], *Political Sketches*, 48; David Ramsay, *The History of the American Revolution* (Philadelphia, 1789), I, 350.

4. Edmund Randolph, MS History of Virginia, quoted in Kate M. Rowland, *The Life of George Mason, 1725–1792* (N.Y., 1892), I, 123; William Pierce, *An Oration, Delivered at Christ Church, Savannah, on the 4th of July, 1788* . . . (Savannah, [1788]), 8, 6; Enos Hitchcock, *An Oration; Delivered July 4th, 1788* . . . (Providence, [1788]), 14.

ties. Where the people of other countries had invoked principles only after they had endured "an actual grievance," the Americans, said Burke, were anticipating their grievances and resorting to principles even before they actually suffered. "They augur misgovernment at a distance and snuff the approach of tyranny in every tainted breeze." The crucial question in the colonists' minds, wrote John Dickinson in 1768, was "not, what evil *has actually attended* particular measures—but, what evil, in the nature of things, *is likely to attend* them." Because "nations, in general, are not apt to *think* until they *feel*, . . . therefore nations in general have lost their liberty." But not the Americans, as the Abbé Raynal observed. They were an "enlightened people" who knew their rights and the limits of power and who, unlike any people before them, aimed to think before they felt.[5]

From the outset the colonists attempted to turn their decade-long controversy with England into a vast exercise in the deciphering and applying of the philosophy of the age. By 1768 they knew that "never was there a People whom it more immediately concerned to search into the Nature and Extent of their Rights and Privileges than it does the People of America at this Day."[6] Believing with the age that "the actions and affairs of men are subject to as regular and uniform laws, as other events," and that "the laws of Mechanics apply in Politics as well as in Philosophy," they sought constantly to recur to those first principles that overlay the workings of politics, agreeing with young Alexander Hamilton that "the best way of determining disputes, and of investigating truth is by ascending to elementary principles."[7] They implored each other to "let a regard to our liberties and privileges more and more prevail," urged each other to in-

5. Edmund Burke, "Speech on Moving His Resolutions for Conciliation with the Colonies," Mar. 22, 1775, *The Works of the Right Honorable Edmund Burke*, rev. ed. (Boston, 1865–66), II, 125; [John Dickinson], *Letters from a Farmer in Pennsylvania to the Inhabitants of the British Colonies* (Phila., 1768) in Paul L. Ford, ed., *The Life and Writings of John Dickinson* (Historical Society of Pennsylvania, *Memoirs*, 14 [Phila., 1895]), 392, 389; [Guillaume Thomas François Raynal], *The Sentiments of a Foreigner on the Disputes of Great-Britain with America* (Phila., 1775), 22–23.

6. Quoted in Clinton Rossiter, *Seedtime of the Republic: The Origin of the American Tradition of Political Liberty* (N. Y., 1953), 362.

7. Samuel Williams, *The Natural and Civil History of Vermont* . . . (Walpole, N. H., 1794), xi; Charleston *South Carolina Gazette*, June 3, 1774; [Alexander Hamilton], *The Farmer Refuted* . . . (N. Y., 1775), in Harold C. Syrett and Jacob E. Cooke, eds., *The Papers of Alexander Hamilton* (N. Y., 1961——), I, 96.

quire into "matters of power and of right, that we may be neither led nor driven blindfolded to irretrievable destruction."[8]

The result was phenomenal: an outpouring of political writings—pamphlets, letters, articles, sermons—that has never been equaled in the nation's history. It was as if "every order and degree among the people" had heeded John Adams's urgent appeal to "become attentive to the grounds and principles of government." To those who watched the flood of Whig literature with increasing apprehension it seemed that "ALMOST EVERY AMERICAN PEN" was at work. Even "peasants and their housewives in every part of the land" had begun "to dispute on politics and positively to determine upon our liberties." True Whigs, however, were hardly surprised at the prevalence of political interest, for they were coming to see that the stakes were high indeed. If the principles of politics could be comprehended by the people, if "the science of man and society, being the most extended in its nature, and the most important in its consequences, of any in the circle of erudition," were made the "object of universal attention and study," then, wrote Josiah Quincy in 1774, the rights and happiness of man would no longer remain buried "under systems of civil and priestly hierarchy."[9]

Because the Americans sought nothing less than "a comprehensive knowledge of history and of mankind" and believed that if they were successfully to resist tyranny "they ought to be well versed in all the various governments of ancient and modern states," it is not surprising that the intellectual sources of their Revolutionary thought were profuse and various. "Let us study the law of nature," said John Adams; "search into the spirit of the British constitution; read the histories of ancient ages; contemplate the great examples of Greece and Rome; set before us the conduct of our own British ancestors, who have defended for us the inherent rights of mankind against foreign and domestic tyrants and usurpers."[10] History was the most obvious source of

8. *Boston Gazette*, Mar. 9, 1767; [John Adams], "Dissertation on the Canon and Feudal Law" (1765), in Charles F. Adams, ed., *The Works of John Adams, Second President of the United States* (Boston, 1850–56), III, 463.

9. [Adams], "Dissertation," Adams, ed., *Works of John Adams*, III, 462; *New-York Journal*, Oct. 30, 1766; Josiah Quincy, Jr., *Observations on the Act of Parliament Commonly Called the . . . Boston Port Bill . . .* (Boston, 1774), in Josiah Quincy, *Memoir of the Life of Josiah Quincy, Junior, of Massachusetts: 1744–1775* (Boston, 1874), 325–26.

10. Sentinel [pseud.], *To the Inhabitants of the City and County of New-York, Apr. 13, 1776* (N. Y., 1776); [Adams], "Dissertation," Adams, ed., *Works of John Adams*, III, 462.

information, for they knew that they must "judge of the future" by the past. "Happy are the men, and *happy the people, who grow wise by the misfortunes of others*."[11] The writings of classical antiquity, as Josiah Quincy told his son, were especially "elegant and instructive," for in the histories of the ancient world they would "imbue a just hatred of tyranny and zeal for freedom."[12] Naturally the history of England was most important for the colonists, for, as Dickinson said, it "abounds with instances" of how a people had protected their liberties against their rulers.[13] Mingled with their historical citations were repeated references to the natural-law writings of Enlightenment philosophers and the common-law writings of English jurists—both contributing to a more obviously rational, rather than an experiential, understanding of the nature of politics. And for those who continued to confront the world in religious terms the revelations of scripture and the mandates of covenant theology possessed a special force that scarcely contradicted but instead supplemented the knowledge about society reached through the use of history and reason. It seemed indeed to be a peculiar moment in history when all knowledge coincided, when classical antiquity, Christian theology, English empiricism, and European rationalism could all be linked. Thus Josiah Quincy, like other Americans, could without any sense of incongruity cite Rousseau, Plutarch, Blackstone, and a seventeenth-century Puritan all on the same page.[14]

However imprecise, confused, and eclectic the colonists' gleanings from history and quotations from philosophers may seem to us, they represented to eighteenth-century Americans

11. Rind's Williamsburg *Virginia Gazette*, Aug. 25, 1774; [Dickinson], *Letters from a Farmer*, Ford, ed., *Writings of Dickinson*, 375.

12. Quincy quoted in Charles F. Mullet, "Classical Influences on the American Revolution," *Classical Journal*, 35 (1939–40), 102; Rind's Wmsbg. *Va. Gazette*, Mar. 3, 1768, quoted in John C. Miller, *The Origins of the American Revolution* (Boston, 1943), 169.

13. [Dickinson], *Letters from a Farmer*, Ford, ed., *Writings of Dickinson*, 365. On history in the 18th century, see J. G. A. Pocock, *The Ancient Constitution and the Feudal Law* (Cambridge, Eng., 1957), 231–32, 246–50; R. N. Stromberg, "History in the Eighteenth Century," *Journal of the History of Ideas*, 12 (1951), 295–304; Herbert Davis, "The Augustan Conception of History," in J. A. Mazzeo, ed., *Reason and the Imagination: Studies in the History of Ideas, 1600–1800* (N. Y., 1962), 213–29; H. Trevor Colbourn, *The Lamp of Experience: Whig History and the Intellectual Origins of the American Revolution* (Chapel Hill, 1965); Hugh Trevor-Roper, "The Historical Philosophy of the Enlightenment," in Theodore Besterman, ed., *Studies on Voltaire and the Eighteenth Century*, 27 (1963), 1667–87.

14. Quincy, *Observations on the Boston Port Bill*, Quincy, *Memoir*, 329.

the experience and reason of the Western world. To most of the Revolutionaries there was no sense of incompatibility in their blending of history, rationalism, and scripture; all were mutually reinforcing ways of arriving at precepts about human and social behavior, ways of discovering those fundamentals "applicable to every Sort of Government, and not contrary to the common Understanding of Mankind." The coherence and significance of the Americans' incredible jumble of references from every conceivable time and place come ultimately from the overriding purpose to which these references were put—the understanding of what John Adams called "the divine science of politics." The records of all peoples in all situations had to be ransacked to verify empirically those constant and universal principles of human nature that natural reason declared were self-evident. Even scriptural truth could be supported by experience and reason, and few American ministers saw any need to deny the Enlightenment for the sake of religion. In all of their apparently offhand and random citations from the whole of Western culture, the Americans were seeking to determine the scientific principles that would explain man's political and social actions, "the principles of Aristotle and Plato, of Livy and Cicero, and Sidney, Harrington and Locke; the principles of nature and eternal reason; the principles on which the whole government over us now stands."

Inevitably such a mixture of intellectual sources and methods produced tensions and conflicts over priority that found expression in the colonists' polemics. It was not always clear to some Calvinists that the lessons of scripture only confirmed what liberal theologians discovered from the "Constitution of Things, in their Respective Natures and Relations."[15] The Americans' blending of empiricism and rationalism, moreover, lent a permissiveness to their use of history that makes it seem to us superficial and desultory; indeed they often appear to be simply selecting from the past examples to buttress generalizations deduced by pure reason. Since it was the constant and universal principles applicable to solving immediate problems that they were really after, there was always

15. Richard Bland, *An Inquiry into the Rights of the British Colonies* . . . (Williamsburg, Va., 1766), quoted in Rossiter, *Seedtime of the Republic*, 270; [John Adams], *Thoughts on Government* . . . (Phila., 1776), in Adams, ed., *Works of John Adams*, IV, 193; [John Adams], "Novanglus" (1775), *ibid.*, 15; Ebenezer Gay, *Natural Religion as Distinguish'd from Revealed* . . . (Boston, 1759), quoted in Alan Heimert, *Religion and the American Mind: From the Great Awakening to the Revolution* (Cambridge, Mass., 1966), 6.

the danger in the delicate balance between historical experience and self-evident truth that the rational needs of the present would overpower the veracity of the past. "The Colonies," as Roger Sherman pointed out in the Continental Congress in 1774, "adopt the common Law, not as the common Law, but as the highest Reason." But if the common law and English institutions should somehow become incompatible with the highest reason, if what had been from time immemorial should become inequitable and irrational, then it was possible and indeed necessary to move onto what Richard Henry Lee called "the broadest Bottom, the Ground of Nature." In the minds of some Americans, like John Rutledge and James Duane in the Continental Congress debates, a conflict between history and reason did eventually emerge, and they resisted efforts to invoke the law of nature alongside the English constitution, fearful of allowing the certainty of what had been, however irrational it may have become, to be replaced by the revolutionary vagueness of what natural reason declared should be.[16] For James Otis, who was as well read as any American in both the English common law and the European theories of natural law, the conflict became especially acute. His frantic attempts to reconcile the two laws—Coke with Vattel—formed the crisis of his life and helped to tear his mind to pieces. Because he knew English history and the common law too well, because he clung too stubbornly to the veracity of seventeenth-century notions of jurisprudence and parliamentary supremacy, he was eventually compelled to sacrifice Vattel for Coke, to deny natural reason for the sake of historical truth, and to miss the Revolution.[17]

Other Americans, however, less well read and perhaps less de-

16. John Adams, Notes of Debates in the Continental Congress, Sept. 8, 1774, in Lyman H. Butterfield *et al.*, eds., *The Diary and Autobiography of John Adams* (Cambridge, Mass., 1961), II, 129, 128. For an extended interpretation of the split between the evangelism of the Calvinist clergy and the rationalism of the liberal clergy, see Heimert, *Religion and the American Mind*. For the conflict between experience, that is, history, and reason a decade later in the Constitutional Convention, see Douglass Adair, " 'Experience Must Be Our Only Guide': History, Democratic Theory, and the United States Constitution," in Ray Allen Billington, ed., *The Reinterpretation of Early American History: Essays in Honor of John Edwin Pomfret* (San Marino, 1966), 129–48, esp. 131–33.

17. On Otis's intellectual career, see Bernard Bailyn, ed., *Pamphlets of the American Revolution, 1750–1776* (Cambridge, 1965——), I, 100–03, 106–07, 121–23, 409–17, 546–52. Bailyn's long general introductory essay to the *Pamphlets*, entitled "The Transforming Radicalism of the American Revolution," has been elaborated and republished separately as *The Ideological Origins of the American Revolution* (Cambridge, Mass., 1967).

voted to the accuracy of the past than Otis, saw no inconsistency between history and reason and brought Coke with ease into the eighteenth century. Indeed, what is truly extraordinary about the Revolution is that few Americans ever felt the need to repudiate their English heritage for the sake of nature or of what ought to be. In their minds natural law and English history were allied. Whatever the universality with which they clothed their rights, those rights remained the common-law rights embedded in the English past, justified not simply by their having existed from time immemorial but by their being as well "the acknowledged rights of human nature."[18] The great appeal for Americans of Blackstone's *Commentaries* stemmed not so much from its particular exposition of English law, which, as Jefferson said, was all "honeyed Mansfieldism," sliding men into Toryism, but from its great effort to extract general principles from the English common law and make of it, as James Iredell said, "a science."[19] The general principles of politics that the colonists sought to discover and apply were not merely abstractions that had to be created anew out of nature and reason. They were in fact already embodied in the historic English constitution—a constitution which was esteemed by the enlightened of the world precisely because of its "agreeableness to the laws of nature."[20] The colonists stood to the very end of their debate with England and even after on these natural and scientific principles of the English constitution. And ultimately such a stand was what made their Revolution seem so unusual, for they revolted not against the English constitution but on behalf of it.

2. THE ENGLISH CONSTITUTION

If any era of modern times found its political ideals incorporated in a particular national institution, it was the eighteenth century. For the Age of Enlightenment was also the classic age

18. John Dickinson, *A Speech Delivered . . . 1764*, in Ford, ed., *Writings of Dickinson*, 34. See Carl Becker, *The Declaration of Independence: A Study in the History of Political Ideas* (N. Y., 1922), 134; Charles F. Mullet, *Fundamental Law and the American Revolution, 1760–1776* (N. Y., 1933), 39, 41.

19. Daniel Boorstin, *The Mysterious Science of the Law . . .* (Boston, 1958, first published 1941), 20, 26, 31, 35, 36; James Iredell to his father, July 31, 1771, Griffith J. McRee, *Life and Correspondence of James Iredell* (N. Y., 1857–58), I, 91.

20. Boston *Independent Chronicle*, Oct. 23, 1777.

of the English constitution. Perhaps never before and surely never since has any single nation's constitution so dominated Western man's theorizing about politics. The Glorious Revolution of 1688, said John Toland, the late seventeenth-century editor of Harrington, had "settl'd the Monarchy for the future . . . under such wise Regulations as are most likely to continue it forever." By the beginning of the eighteenth century the English government was obviously "the most free and best constituted in all the world."[21] By balancing within the confines of Parliament the ancient contending interests of English society and by mixing within a single government the several categories of politics that had been known to the Western world for centuries, the English, it seemed, had concretely achieved what political philosophers from antiquity on had only dreamed of. In the minds of the English colonists, indeed of the enlightened everywhere in the eighteenth century, the English constitution—"this beautiful system," as Montesquieu called it—seemed to possess no national or cultural limitations.[22] It had "its foundation in nature," said Samuel Adams; its principles were from God and were universal, capable of application by all peoples who had the ability to sustain them. It was, declared one American in 1759, "the best model of Government that can be framed by Mortals."[23] For the Americans the English constitution was always "the glorious fabrick of Britain's liberty," "the palladium of civil liberty . . . that firm foundation of the nation's peace," "the monument of accumulated wisdom, and the admiration of the world." Every day for fifty years, wrote John Adams in 1761, men had boasted that the English constitution was the finest under heaven. "No Government that ever existed, was so essentially free." Even members of the Stamp Act Congress gloried in "having been born under the most perfect form of government."[24]

21. Quoted in Zera Fink, *The Classical Republicans: An Essay in the Recovery of a Pattern of Thought in Seventeenth-Century England* (Evanston, Ill., 1945), 188, 189. See also W. H. Greenleaf, *Order, Empiricism and Politics: Two Traditions of English Political Thought, 1500–1700* (N. Y., 1964), 157, 179, 182–83.

22. C. Secondat, Baron de Montesquieu, *The Spirit of the Laws*, ed. Franz Neumann, trans. Thomas Nugent (N. Y., 1949), Bk. XI, Sec. 6, 161.

23. [Samuel Adams], Committee of Correspondence of Boston to the Committee of Correspondence of Littleton, Mar. 31, 1773, Harry A. Cushing, ed., *The Writings of Samuel Adams* (N. Y., 1904–08), III, 15; *New American Magazine* (Jan. 1759), quoted in Rossiter, *Seedtime of the Republic*, 142.

24. [James Wilson], *Considerations on the Nature and Extent of the Legislative Authority of the British Parliament* (Phila., 1774), in Bird Wilson, ed., *The Works of . . . James Wilson* (Phila., 1804), III, 220; [Moses Mather], *America's*

It is when viewed amidst this widespread and enthusiastic acclamation for the English constitution that the American Revolution takes on its tone of irony and incomprehensibility—a tone not lost to the Revolutionaries themselves. "Of all the known parts of the world, and for many ages, Britain hath been the most extolled for the love and protection of liberty." While the "sacred fires" of freedom had been "extinguished in so many other countries," Britain alone had kept them alive. "But alas!" the Revolutionaries could not help exclaiming, "How are the mighty fallen! the gates of hell hath prevailed against her."[25] The English constitution, "heretofore so much the glory and happiness of our own nation, and the envy and terror of foreigners," Americans saw by 1775 gradually undermined, "till at length, under the hands of bribery and corruption, it seems *rotten* to the very core."[26]

It was an amazing transformation and even after the Declaration of Independence Americans continued to express their astonishment at what had happened.[27] As they themselves keenly realized, their interpretation of the English constitution was the point on which their understanding of the Revolution hinged. For it was the principles of the English constitution that the colonists clung to throughout the dozen years of controversy with the mother country. They said over and over again that it was "both the letter and the spirit of the British constitution" which justified their resistance. Even as late as 1776 they assured themselves there was "no room at all to doubt, but we have justice and the British constitution on our side."[28] This repeated insistence that they were the true guardians of the British constitution, even

---

Appeal to the Impartial World . . . (Hartford, 1775), 12, 50; Adams, MS of newspaper communication, Mar. 1761, Butterfield, ed., *Diary of Adams*, I, 205; Stamp Act Congress, Petition to the House of Commons, Oct. 23, 1765, in Hezekiah Niles, ed., *Principles and Acts of the Revolution in America* (N. Y., 1876), 166.

25. John Hurt, *The Love of Our Country* . . . (Phila., 1777), 16; see also Nathan Perkins, *A Sermon* . . . *the 2d of June, 1775* (Hartford, [1775]), 12; Abraham Keteltas, *God Arising and Pleading His People's Cause* . . . (Newburyport, 1777), 22.

26. Enoch Huntington, *A Sermon Delivered at Middleton, July 20th, A.D. 1775* . . . (Hartford, [1775]), 18.

27. See, for example, John Jay, Charge to the Grand Jury of the Supreme Court, New York, Sept. 9, 1777, Niles, ed., *Principles*, 181.

28. James Wilson, "Speech Delivered in the Convention for the Province of Pennsylvania, Held at Philadelphia in January, 1775," in Wilson, ed., *Works of Wilson*, III, 266, 268; Robert Ross, *A Sermon, in Which the Union of the Colonies Is Considered* . . . (N. Y., 1776), 13.

enjoying it "in greater purity and perfection" than Englishmen themselves, lent a curious conservative color to the American Revolution. By recurring constantly to "the fundamental maxims of the British constitution; upon which, as upon a rock, our wise ancestors erected that stable fabrick," by repeatedly invoking those "explaining and controuling principles, which framed the constitution of Britain in its first stages, . . . and which have been her constant companions through all the mutilations and distortions she has suffered in her progress to the present rank she holds in the world"—by language such as this—the Americans could easily conceive of themselves as simply preserving what Englishmen had valued from time immemorial.[29] They sincerely believed they were not creating new rights or new principles prescribed only by what ought to be, but saw themselves claiming "only to keep their old privileges," the traditional rights and principles of all Englishmen, sanctioned by what they thought had always been.[30]

Yet this continual talk of desiring nothing new and wishing only to return to the old system and the essentials of the English constitution was only a superficial gloss. The Americans were rushing into revolution even as they denied it, their progress both obscured and sustained by a powerful revolutionary ideology— an ideology the radicalism of which paradoxically flowed from the very heritage of the English constitution they were rebelling against. They could actually believe they were "contending not only for our privileges as freemen, but for the support of the British constitution," because the historical traditions of the English constitution they invoked were not the "true principles" held by establishment England in the mid-eighteenth century, but were in fact, as the Tories and royal officials tried to indicate, "revolution principles" outside of the mainstream of English thought.[31]

The colonists were hardly aware that they were seeing the

29. [Adams], "Novanglus," Adams, ed., *Works of John Adams*, IV, 117; Wilson, "Speech Delivered in the Convention," Wilson, ed., *Works of Wilson*, III, 259; Boston *Massachusetts Spy*, Feb. 16, 1775. On the regressive aspects of revolution, see Vernon F. Snow, "The Concept of Revolution in Seventeenth-Century England," *Historical Journal*, 5 (1962), 167–74.

30. [Adams], "Novanglus," Adams, ed., *Works of John Adams*, IV, 131; see also [Thomas Jefferson], *A Summary View of the Rights of British America* ... (Williamsburg, [1774]), in Julian P. Boyd *et al.*, eds., *The Papers of Thomas Jefferson* (Princeton, 1950———), I, 131–35.

31. Purdie's Wmsbg. *Va. Gazette*, Dec. 8, 1775; Earl of Hillsborough to the Governors of America, Apr. 21, 1768, in Merrill Jensen, ed., *American Colonial Documents to 1776* (D. C. Douglas, ed., *English Historical Documents*, IX [N. Y., 1955]), 717; [Adams], "Novanglus," Adams, ed., *Works of John Adams*, IV, 15, 84.

English constitution and their heritage differently from other Englishmen. To judge from their broad and varied references to English writers, they seemed to be reading the same literature, the same law books, the same histories as those being read by Englishmen in the mother country. They cited and borrowed promiscuously from almost every conceivable English writer—from Locke, Blackstone, Addison, Swift, Hale, Hume, and James Thompson, from everyone and anyone a good Englishman might read. Yet amidst their breadth of reading and references was a certain engagement of interest, a certain concentration on a particular strain of attitudes and ideas, that more than anything else ultimately implicated the Americans in a peculiar conception of English history and English life and in an extraordinarily radical perspective on the English constitution they were so fervently defending.

It is only now becoming clear how selective the colonists were in their use of British literature and how much they focused on those writings which expressed what may be termed an Opposition view of English politics.[32] Since the full depth and extent of this Opposition thinking remains still unexplored, it is difficult to characterize precisely. Beneath the apparent complacency and stability of the age of Walpole were deep currents of dissatisfaction, both urban and rural, that eventually found political expression in the Wilkesite and county association movements in the 1760's and 1770's.[33] Although the Opposition criticism inevitably tended to be Whiggish, many of the critics were not Whigs at all but old-fashioned Tories voicing in common terms with Whig radicals their alienation from a corrupted England. And while the tone of the dissatisfaction was generally and fervently nonconformist, some of its most articulate spokesmen were Anglicans. Indeed, so transcendent of traditional eighteenth-century political categories was this Opposition thought that it has been suggested that the eighteenth-century English political mind can be best understood in terms of a country-court division—an old

32. For this Opposition literature, see Caroline Robbins, *The Eighteenth-Century Commonwealthman: Studies in the Transmission, Development, and Circumstances of English Liberal Thought from the Restoration of Charles II until the War with the Thirteen Colonies* (Cambridge, Mass., 1959); Bailyn, *Ideological Origins*, Chap. II, and sources cited there.

33. George Rudé, *Wilkes and Liberty* (Oxford, 1962); Ian R. Christie, *Wilkes, Wyvill and Reform: The Parliamentary Reform Movement in British Politics, 1760–1785* (London, 1962).

seventeenth-century categorization which perhaps sums up as well as any other dichotomy the hostility of those who felt estranged from the established centers of power.[34] At the heart of the country outlook was an independent view of politics, a widely shared conception about the way English public life should be organized—where the parts of the constitution were independent of one another, where the Commons were independent of the Crown, where members of Parliament were independent of any connection or party, in short, the kind of society where no man was beholden to another.

While this Opposition thinking can be broadly conceived, ranging from Bolingbroke to Burke, the expressions of it the Americans found most attractive, most relevant to their situation and needs, were precisely those with the least respectability and force in England—those expressions of radical intellectuals writing to the left of the official Whig line. The radicalism of the Real Whigs, as the most self-conscious of these early eighteenth-century writers called themselves, or Commonwealthmen, as they have recently been called, came not from the concrete proposals they offered for the reformation of English politics. For most of these proposals—prohibitions on placemen in the House of Commons, attacks on the increasing debt and the representational system, and recommendations for shorter Parliaments and the right of constituents to instruct their representatives—were the stock reforms of Opposition politicians during the eighteenth century.[35] The revolutionary character of these radical Whigs came more fundamentally from their fierce and total unwillingness to accept the developments of the eighteenth century. They were reacting against the maturation of the empire, with all that this meant in the use of money and bureaucracy in the running of government. They offered their fellow Englishmen a strident and impassioned critique of their society and politics, all set within a comprehensive understanding of centuries of English history and the ancient

34. J. G. A. Pocock, "Machiavelli, Harrington, and English Political Ideologies in the Eighteenth Century," *William and Mary Quarterly*, 3d Ser., 22 (1965), 552. On the country-court division and Bolingbroke, see Perez Zagorin, "The Court and the Country: A Note on Political Terminology in the Earlier Seventeenth Century," *English Historical Review*, 77 (1962), 306–11; H. N. Fieldhouse, "Bolingbroke and the Idea of Non-Party Government," *History*, New Ser., 23 (1938–39), 46; Archibald S. Foord, *His Majesty's Opposition, 1714–1830* (Oxford, 1965), 24–25, 147–48; Bailyn, *Ideological Origins*, 48–50.

35. Herbert Butterfield, *George III, Lord North and the People, 1779–1780* (London, 1949), 14–15; Foord, *His Majesty's Opposition,* 79–80.

constitution, and grounded in the political and social ideals of the liberal writings of the previous century, especially those of the classical republicans—Harrington, Milton, and Sidney. For three generations—from John Trenchard and Thomas Gordon, through Thomas Hollis and Richard Baron, to Richard Price and James Burgh—the English radicals preserved and transmitted these ideals amidst a society which increasingly seemed to be paying only lip service to them. Yet whatever the intensity and stridency with which the radicals voiced their criticism, their thought was never developed systematically, and it easily blended into widely held opinions about the nature of English history and government. In fact, their thought never transcended the common political and social assumptions of the day.

However unrespected and unheeded this heritage of dissident thought was in England itself, it was eagerly received in the colonies across the Atlantic. The Americans too felt themselves alienated from the official world of cosmopolitan London; they too sensed beneath the apparent similarities the world of differences that separated them from established England. As American society had gradually and almost imperceptibly deviated in a century's time from the norms of English social and political life, pressures had been built up, intensified, and focused by the overlying imperial system. This remotely rooted and often arbitrary legal structure only further complicated the lines of authority in a society whose sanctions for political and social superiority were already inherently tenuous. With such a precariously maintained social hierarchy, sensitive to the slightest disturbance, politics necessarily had become an extraordinarily ticklish business; and almost all of the colonies had been continually racked by a bitter and kaleidoscopic factionalism. Since every political move, however small, was believed to have enormous repercussions, the most minor incidents had erupted into major constitutional questions involving the basic liberties of the people. Every accumulation of political power, however tiny and piecemeal, was seen as frighteningly tyrannical, viewed as some sinister plot to upset the delicately maintained relationships of power and esteem. Jealousy and suspicion, concluded Charles Carroll of Maryland in 1773, had become the very basis of American politics.[36]

36. [Charles Carroll], "Letters of First Citizen," May 6, 1773, in Kate M. Rowland, *Life of Charles Carroll of Carrollton, 1737–1832* . . . (N. Y., 1898), I, 287. On the instability of colonial politics, see Bernard Bailyn, "The Origins of American Politics," *Perspectives in American History,* 1 (1967), 47–120.

In such an atmosphere the ideas of radical Whiggism with their heightened language of intense liberalism and paranoiac mistrust of power were found to be a particularly meaningful way of expressing the anxieties Americans felt. Every point of strain, whether it was the clashing of religious groups, or a royal governor's indictment of a colonial printer, had called forth a new articulation of radical beliefs.[37] Throughout the eighteenth century the Americans had published, republished, read, cited, and even plagiarized these radical writings in their search for arguments to counter royal authority, to explain American deviations, or to justify peculiar American freedoms. But, as in the case of Jonathan Mayhew's blatant borrowing from Bishop Hoadly, there could be no sense of shame or need for apology.[38] What the Whig radicals were saying about English government and society had so long been a part of the American mind, had so often been reinforced by their own first-hand observations of London life, and had possessed such an affinity to their own provincial interests and experience that it always seemed to the colonists to be what they had been trying to say all along.

More than any other source this disaffected Whig thought fused and focused the elements that shaped the colonists' conception of the English constitution and English politics. In the years after 1763 when the need for explanation and understanding assumed a new and vital importance, the Americans could only marvel at the "many things much to the present purpose" offered by this Whig literature, which in those eventful years seemed to "look almost like prophecy."[39] By drawing on the evidence of antiquity and their own English past as transmitted to them through the radical Whig tradition the colonists sought to formulate a science of politics and of history that would explain what was happening to England and to themselves—an explanation that when joined with a complicated medley of notions taken from Enlightenment rationalism and New England covenant theology possessed revolutionary implications.

37. William Livingston *et al.*, *The Independent Reflector* . . . , ed. Milton M. Klein (Cambridge, Mass., 1963); James Alexander, *A Brief Narrative of the Case and Trial of John Peter Zenger* . . . , ed. Stanley N. Katz (Cambridge, Mass., 1963). See also Bailyn, *Ideological Origins*, 52–53.

38. On Mayhew's plagiarism of Hoadly, see Bailyn, ed., *Pamphlets*, I, 208, 697–98.

39. Jonathan Mayhew to Thomas Hollis, Aug. 9, 1765, quoted in Colbourn, *Lamp of Experience*, 64.

3. Power against Liberty

The theory of government that the Americans clarified in their reading and discussion possessed a compelling simplicity: politics was nothing more than a perpetual battle between the passions of the rulers, whether one or a few, and the united interest of the people—an opposition that was both inevitable and proportional. "Whatever is good for the People," Thomas Gordon had written, "is bad for their Governors; and what is good for the Governors, is pernicious to the People."[40] This notion of political dualism between rulers and ruled, characteristic of all Western political theories except those during the heyday of nineteenth-century democratic idealism, was at the bottom of the Whigs' beliefs: their conception of a mutual contract, their understanding of allegiance and protection, their notion of a dichotomy between power and liberty, tyranny and licentiousness, their idea of governmental balance, and their theory of revolution.

Englishmen, like most men in the eighteenth century, continued to cling to a medieval conception of society, divided into estates or orders, with the people constituting a single unitary estate alongside the nobility and the Crown. There was as yet little clear understanding of classes or status groups in the modern sense.[41] The aristocracy were of course rigidly separated from the people; their distinction, however, was not one so much of wealth or even of social outlook as it was one of legal and political privilege. The people were generally assumed to be a homogeneous entity, undeniably composed of an infinite number of gradations and ranks, but still an entity whose interests were considered to be connected and for the purposes of politics basically similar.

Each estate possessed certain rights and privileges recognized in law and by custom, the Crown with its prerogatives, however limited by the settlement of 1689, still having the major respon-

40. [John Trenchard and Thomas Gordon], *Cato's Letters: Or, Essays on Liberty, Civil and Religious, and Other Important Subjects*, 5th ed. (London, 1748), II, 249; see also James Otis, *The Rights of the British Colonies Asserted and Proved* (Boston, 1764), in Bailyn, ed., *Pamphlets*, I, 474. For a contemporary summary of the Whig theory of politics, see Charles Lee, "A Political Essay," in *Lee Papers* (New York Historical Society, *Collections*, 4–7 [1871–74]), IV, 100ff. Hereafter cited as *Lee Papers*. For the best modern assessment, see Bailyn, *Ideological Origins*, 55–93.

41. Asa Briggs, "The Language of 'Class' in Early Nineteenth-Century England," in Asa Briggs and John Saville, eds., *Essays in Labour History: In Memory of G. D. H. Cole* (London, 1960), 43–73.

sibility for governing the realm. Indeed, the eighteenth century's discussion of politics can only be understood in the context of this ancient notion of the Crown's prerogatives, the bundle of rights and powers adhering in the King's authority to rule, set against the rights and liberties of the people, or the ruled, represented in the House of Commons. As long as the idea of prerogative remained meaningful, the distinction between rulers and ruled was clear and vital and the rights of each were balanced in tension. "Liberty," said James Wilson in 1775 "is, by the constitution, of equal stability, of equal antiquity, and of equal authority with prerogative. The duties of the king and those of the subject are plainly reciprocal: they can be violated on neither side, unless they be [not] performed on the other." The magistracy, whatever the source of its authority, retained inherent legal rights and remained an independent entity in the society with which the people must bargain and contract in order to protect their own rights and privileges. The peers, "forming a balance of power between the king and the people," gave the state "the benefit of an aristocracy." It was their duty "to trim this boat of common wealth, and to skreen the people against the insults of the Prince, and the Prince against the popularity of the commons, since if either extreme prevails so far as to oppress the other, they are sure to be overwhelmed in their ruin."[42]

Politics, in other words, was still commonly viewed along a classic power spectrum that ranged from absolute power in the hands of one person on one end, to absolute power or liberty in the hands of the people at the other end. The spectrum met in full circle when, it was believed, the disorder of absolute liberty would inevitably lead to the tyranny of the dictator. All the traditional forms of government could be located along this spectrum as they partook more or less of power and liberty measured by the nature and number of those allowed to share political authority. The ideal of politics since Aristotle had been of course to avoid either extreme, the degeneration "into tyranny on the one hand, or anarchy on the other: either of which is directly subversive of the ends of civil government." "The seeming theoretic excellence of the English constitution" consisted precisely in "that equipoise between the respective branches of the legislature," the "balance of power, being so judiciously placed, as to

42. Wilson, "Speech Delivered in the Convention," Wilson, ed., *Works of Wilson*, III, 260; Peter Thacher, *An Oration Delivered at Watertown, March 5, 1776, to Commemorate the Bloody Massacre at Boston* . . . (Watertown, 1776), in Niles, ed., *Principles*, 44; *N.-Y. Journal*, Dec. 11, 1766.

connect the force, and to preserve the rights of . . . each estate, armed with a power of self defense; against the encroachments of the other two."[43]

Since the three social orders were thought to be fully embodied in the state, Parliament consisting "of all the estates, that composed the nation, in epitome, with the supreme sovereignty of the kingdom," eighteenth-century Englishmen generally had not yet made any clear distinction between state and society.[44] Hence politics was still described in terms of these medieval social categories, as a kind of negotiating and maneuvering for political domination among the three estates of the realm; and not, as today, in terms of divisions among the people themselves, as a struggle among various groups for control of a semi-autonomous state in order to advance particular economic or class interests.

In this continuous contest among the estates of the society, a contest that since the seventeenth century had become more and more confined to one between Crown and Commons, the Whigs' loyalty was always with the people. Although the people were but a single estate in the realm it seemed self-evident to the Whigs that the promotion of the people's happiness was the sole purpose of government. The institution of government was of course "a wise, a necessary, and a sacred thing," an essential restraint on the lusts and passions that drove all men. Without it, "the strongest would be master, the weakest go to the wall . . . . Right, justice and property must give way to power." Hence certain men were "exalted, from among the people, to bear rule."[45] Such magistrates explicitly or implicitly agreed to use their superior power to protect the rights of the people. In return the people pledged their obedience, but only, the Whigs continually emphasized, as long as the rulers promoted the public interest. But unhappily in the eyes of the Whigs the history of politics hardly appeared to be what it should have been; the people's welfare had too often been abused by their governors, and they had too often been compelled to surrender their power to the rulers' power.[46]

43. Allyn Mather, *The Character of a Well Accomplished Ruler* . . . (New Haven, 1776), 4; William Tudor, *An Oration Delivered at Boston, March 5, 1779* (Boston, 1779), in Niles, ed., *Principles*, 59; [Mather], *America's Appeal*, 8, 66–67.

44. [Mather], *America's Appeal*, 7–8.

45. Samuel Williams, *A Discourse on the Love of Our Country* . . . (Salem, 1775), 28; John Joachim Zubly, *The Law of Liberty* . . . (Phila., 1775), 6–7; [Mather], *America's Appeal*, 6.

46. Dan Foster, *A Short Essay on Civil Government* . . . (Hartford, 1775),

The acquisition of power, of course, was what politics was all about. "The love of power is natural," said James Burgh quoting Bolingbroke; "it is insatiable; it is whetted, not cloyed, by possession."[47] It was an obsession with the radical Whigs—this "intoxicating" desire by men for domination over others—and, as often with nagging aches, they could not leave it alone; but, however painful the process, they were driven "to enquire into the nature of power."[48] Men struggled constantly, the Whigs believed, to secure power and if possible to aggrandize it at the expense of others, for power relationships were reciprocating: what was one man's increase of power was another's loss. The minimal amount of power a man deserved, because he was a man, the Whigs defined as liberty—"the Power," as Thomas Gordon put it, "which every Man has over his own Actions, and his Right to enjoy the Fruit of his Labour, Art, and Industry." This was personal liberty, "physical liberty," as Richard Price called it: it was individual; it was what gave a man control of his own destiny; it was the inherent right man had to his life and his property.[49] Its instruments and remedies were all those natural rights that were "not the grants of princes or parliaments, but original rights, conditions of original contracts," protected in England by the common law and recognized by the bills and charters exacted from the rulers.[50] Government itself was formed so "that every mem-

---

30, 36–37; Catharine Macaulay, *An Address to the People of England, Scotland, and Ireland, on the Present Important Crisis of Affairs* (N. Y., 1775), 12. On this matriarch of radical Whiggism, see Lucy M. Donnelly, "The Celebrated Mrs. Macaulay," *Wm. and Mary Qtly.*, 3d Ser., 6 (1949), 173–207.

47. James Burgh, *Political Disquisitions: Or, an Enquiry into Public Errors, Defects, and Abuses* ... (London, 1774–75), I, 106. An American edition of the *Disquisitions* was published in Philadelphia in 1774 and endorsed by 75 prominent Americans. See Oscar and Mary Handlin, "James Burgh and American Revolutionary Theory," *Massachusetts Historical Society, Proceedings*, 73 (1961), 38–57.

48. Quincy, *Observations on the Boston Port Bill*, Quincy, *Memoir*, 307; New York *Constitutional Gazette*, Oct. 25, 1775; Philadelphia *Pennsylvania Packet*, Sept. 26, 1774. Since "so large an amount of the opinion" of the English press was "favorable to the American cause," American editors in the years prior to the Revolution borrowed freely from English newspapers. Fred J. Hinkhouse, *The Preliminaries of the American Revolution as Seen in the English Press, 1763–1775* (N. Y., 1926), 20.

49. [Trenchard and Gordon], *Cato's Letters*, II, 245; Richard Price, *Observations on the Nature of Civil Liberty* ... (London, 1778, first published 1776), 3.

50. Adams, "Dissertation," Adams, ed., *Works of John Adams*, III, 463, taken from Bolingbroke: Colbourn, *Lamp of Experience*, 90. See also Charles E. Shattuck, "The True Meaning of the Term 'Liberty' ... in the Federal and State Constitutions ... ," *Harvard Law Review*, 4 (1890–91), 380.

ber of society may be protected and secured in the peaceable, quiet possession and enjoyment of all those liberties and privileges which the Deity has bestowed upon him." The end of government, in sum, was the preservation of liberty.[51]

The greatest diffusion of this personal power or liberty was for the Whigs the ideal society. Hence most Whigs believed nothing as effectually prevented the abuse of power in a society "as an equality in the state."[52] Some radicals were even inclined to limit liberty for its own sake, to restrict the amount of wealth or land a man could acquire in order to prevent its abuse. Most Commonwealthmen, however, were willing to grant the inevitability of differences of power among the people, differences that with the right kind of republican laws could not be perpetuated or made especially dangerous to the liberty of others. Economic and social inequalities among the people seemed slight and insignificant when compared to the differences of power that flowed from the institution of government. For in opposition to the magistracy the people were one. Although some writers were beginning to stress the overriding importance of class distinctions among the people, the only meaningful kind of power in most eighteenth-century thinking was still political. Therefore no men were further separated from the rest of the community, and hence more dangerous, than the rulers of a society.[53]

"Such is the accursed nature of lawless ambition" that the great amount of power held by the political rulers—legitimized as no other power ever was—necessarily corrupted the "men of abilities, and influence" who commanded it. "Men in high stations . . . ," the Whigs knew, "increase their ambition, and study rather to be more powerful than wiser or better." "Voracious like the grave, they can never have enough, *i.e.* of power and wealth," and they thus drove on to pervert their governmental authority, an excessive abuse which the Whigs defined as tyranny or despotism: "Tyranny being nothing else but the government of one man, or a few, over many, against their inclination and

51. Samuel West, *A Sermon Preached . . . May 29th, 1776, Being the Anniversary for the Election of the Honorable Council for the Colony* (Boston, 1776), in John W. Thornton, ed., *The Pulpit of the American Revolution: Or, the Political Sermons of the Period of 1776* (Boston, 1860), 274.

52. Phila. *Pa. Packet*, Oct. 3, 1774.

53. Robbins, *Commonwealthman*, 38–39, 190–92, 207–08, 353; [Trenchard and Gordon], *Cato's Letters*, I, 113, III, 151, 161, 207.

interest." Therefore, as James Burgh had concluded, government by one or a few was "impossible without continual danger to liberty."[54]

Liberty, defined as the power held by the people, was thus the victim and very antithesis of despotism. Yet the people, like the rulers, could abuse their power; such a perversion of liberty was called licentiousness or anarchy. It was not so much a collective as an individual perversion, each man doing what was right in his own eyes, running amuck and ultimately dissolving all social bonds. "Liberty," good Whigs continually emphasized, "does not consist in living without all restraint." For it seemed certain "that nothing next to *slavery* is more to be dreaded, than the anarchy and confusion that will ensue, if proper regard is not paid to the good and wholesome laws of government."[55] Still slavery was the greater dread. As Josiah Quincy noted, "It is much easier to restrain liberty from running into licentiousness than power from swelling into tyranny and oppression." In the minds of the most extreme Commonwealthmen there could be only one peril confronting England: "the danger of the *people's* being enslaved by the servants of the crown." It was only the propaganda of the ministerial party, declared one irate Whig, "that power ought not to be given to the people." Faction, civil disturbance, and rebellion in history had resulted only from responses to acts of oppression by the rulers, not from any excess of liberty in the people. "It was therefore a want of power in the people which made the Revolution [of 1688] necessary, not a fulness of their power."[56]

The ultimate sanction for the protection of the people's liberty, in the case of the ruler's breach of the mutual contract between them, was the people's right of resistance; but revolution was hardly a sanction that could be commonly used, for, as devout Whigs often said, the remedy must not be worse than the disease. "The Injury suffered ought to be so very notorious, that

54. Oliver Noble, *Some Strictures upon the Sacred Story Recorded in the Book of Esther* . . . (Newburyport, 1775), 5; Phila. *Pa. Packet*, Oct. 3, Sept. 12, 1774; Burgh, *Disquisitions*, I, 106–07.
55. Zubly, *Law of Liberty*, 6; John Carmichael, *A Self-Defensive War Lawful* . . . (Phila., 1775), 30.
56. Quincy, *Observations on the Boston Port Bill*, Quincy, *Memoir*, 304; Burgh, *Disquisitions*, I, 116; Phila. *Pa. Packet*, Oct. 16, 1775; N. Y. *Constitutional Gazette*, Oct. 25, 1775.

every eye may see it." Only the most *"extreme necessity"* justified the war and tumult revolution would bring.[57] Another
sanction, another means of protection for the people within the
bounds of the constitution itself, was necessary. "Peace is seldom
made, and never kept," Algernon Sidney had written, "unless the
subject retain such a power in his hands as may oblige the prince
to stand to what is agreed." Thus the people authorized their
rulers to make and to execute laws to govern them, but "always
provided they retain a right and power to choose a sufficient number from among themselves, to be a representative body of the
whole people . . . to have a voice in the making of all such laws,
. . . and in the management of all the most weighty concerns of
the state." "For, deprive us of this barrier of our liberties and
properties, our own consent; and there remains no security
against tyranny and absolute despotism."[58]

This participation by the people in the government was what
the Whigs commonly meant by political or civil liberty, which
Alexander Hamilton along with other Americans defined as the
right of the people "to a *share* in the government." "CIVIL LIB-
ERTY," said Richard Price, "is the power of a *Civil Society* or
State to govern itself by its own discretion; or by laws of its own
making." No Whig conception could have been more relevant
for Americans. Liberty, Benjamin Church told his Boston audience in 1773, was "the happiness of living under laws of our own
making." "Therefore," for Church and all American Whigs, "the
liberty of the people is exactly proportioned to the share the body
of the people have in the legislature; and the check placed in the
constitution, on the executive power."[59]

Public liberty was thus the combining of each man's individual
liberty into a collective governmental authority, the institutionali-
zation of the people's personal liberty, making public or political
liberty equivalent to democracy or government by the people
themselves. "According to the celebrated Dr. Price," declared a

57. *An Essay upon Government, Adopted by the Americans, Wherein, the
Lawfulness of Revolutions, Are Demonstrated in a Chain of Consequences from
the Fundamental Principles of Society* (Phila., 1775), 83–84; Purdie's Wmsbg.
Va. Gazette, July 14, 1775.
  58. [Adams], "Novanglus," Adams, ed., *Works of John Adams,* IV, 80; Foster,
Short Essay on Civil Government, 29–30; [Mather], *America's Appeal,* 48.
  59. [Alexander Hamilton], *A Second Letter from Phocion . . .* (N. Y., 1784),
in Syrett and Cooke, eds., *Hamilton Papers,* III, 545; Price, *Observations on Civil
Liberty,* 3; Benjamin Church, *An Oration Delivered March Fifth, 1773 . . .* (Boston, 1773), in Niles, ed., *Principles,* 35–36.

Boston writer, "liberty in a State is self-government." No government could possibly be free, could possibly protect each man's individual liberty, unless it partook of democracy, unless, in other words, the people participated in it. Without the pooling of each man's liberty into a common body, no property would be secure. "For power is entire and indivisible; and property is single and pointed as an atom." Liberty was therefore more than a helpless victim of the rulers' hunger; collectively the people's liberty became the essential barrier against arbitrary power. Free people, declared an American orator in 1771, were not those who were merely spared actual oppression, "but those who have a *constitutional check upon the power* to oppress."[60]

Of course there were problems, the Whigs realized, in translating the people into the government. Naturally public liberty was most fully realized when the people themselves exercised their role in government. Hence, it was "obvious that *Civil Liberty*, in its most perfect degree, can be enjoyed only in small states"—where the people could meet and conduct public affairs personally. When the state became so large as to make this impossible, the people were compelled to appoint substitutes or representatives, resulting in a necessary "diminution of Liberty."[61] Here arose "the great Point of Nicety and Care in forming the Constitution," said John Trenchard: "that the Persons entrusted and representing, shall either never have any Interest detached from the Persons entrusting and represented, or never the Means to pursue it."[62]

Representation was indeed a delicate point, surely the most confusing and important in the Whig conception of politics, which rested on a rigid distinction between rulers and ruled, magistracy and people. The people's role in the government was confined to the House of Commons; there the representatives should meet frequently and for a short time to correct the laws, returning immediately to private life to experience the consequence of their actions along with other members of the society. Such frequent and short Parliaments could presumably never en-

60. Boston *Continental Journal*, Jan. 15, 1778; [Mather], *America's Appeal*, 48–49; James Lovell, *An Oration Delivered April 2, 1771* . . . (Boston, 1771), in Niles, ed., *Principles*, 18.

61. Price, *Observations on Civil Liberty*, 7. See also Burgh, *Disquisitions*, I, 5; Albemarle County Instructions concerning the Virginia Constitution (1776), Boyd, ed., *Jefferson Papers*, VI, 287.

62. [Trenchard and Gordon], *Cato's Letters*, II, 233.

act legislation contrary to the interests of the whole people. This anachronistic conception of Parliament assumed that the Commons, although the conservators of liberty, had nothing whatever to do with the actual process of governing the realm. Continuous, day-to-day government, including even what we would call the necessary prerogatives of the legislature, was still the responsibility of the Crown or the rulers. To those who thought in such antiquated terms the King was the people's "sovereign and ruler," while the representatives in Parliament were only "fellow subjects." Many independent-minded Englishmen continued to believe that Parliament "had no right to interfere with the executive power," some going so far as to state that "it was the business of Parliament to raise supplies, not to debate on the measures of Government."[63]

Yet eighteenth-century practice was rapidly undermining this old-fashioned theory of the role of Parliament, creating disturbing implications for the way men thought about politics. The people's increased participation in the actual affairs of state, through their participation in the ever-stronger House of Commons, was tending to blur the rigid distinction between rulers and ruled that lay at the heart of the Whig theory of politics. By their added responsibilities, their long tenure in office, and their consequent separation from the body of the people, the members of the Commons were coming to resemble more the character of rulers than representatives of the ruled. Under the pressure of these changes many Englishmen were beginning to describe this quasi-magisterial quality of the representatives as an advantageous way of enabling the wisest and most virtuous men to speak for the populace, making the House of Commons a kind of independent body distinct from the people and "intended as a balance between them and the sovereign." Some such notion was involved in the

63. Rind's Wmsbg. *Va. Gazette*, Sept. 15, 1774; quoted in Sir Lewis Namier and John Brooke, *The House of Commons, 1754–1790 (The History of Parliament* [London, 1964]), I, 183. See also John Adams, *A Defence of the Constitutions of Government of the United States of America* . . . (London, 1787–88), in Adams, ed., *Works of John Adams*, IV, 581: "The executive power is properly the government." For discussion of this old-fashioned view of the relationship between the government and the legislature, see William B. Gwyn, *The Meaning of the Separation of Powers* . . . *(Tulane Studies in Political Science*, IX [New Orleans, 1965]), 10, 29–30, 32, 42, 58, 75, 78, 113–14. For Edmund Burke's struggle with this problem, see Harvey Mansfield, *Statesmanship and Party Government: A Study of Burke and Bolingbroke* (Chicago, 1965), 128–46. See also below, Chap. V, n. 2.

prevailing belief in the detached and virtual representation of the people and the correlative conception of the sovereignty of Parliament, that is, that Parliament was the final and supreme authority for all law even against the wishes of the people whom it supposedly represented. For the members of Parliament were "the Judges, and the only Judges of the Public Good," and unless "we are to submit to their determinations, . . . we will make all our Laws useless, our Constitution and Government precarious."[64]

Although such changes as the Septennial Act, lengthening and regularizing the life of Parliaments, were actually responsible for the Commons' enhanced importance in the eighteenth-century English constitution, most radical Whigs saw little advantage in them, and repeatedly decried the abandonment of the short Parliaments and frequent elections of earlier days. As one critic pointed out, the reformers were, without fully realizing the significance of what they were saying, calling for a revival of those "ages when the House of Commons was an insignificant part of the Constitution," and when legislation was largely an exceptional and remedial matter.[65] Yet to the radical Whigs the emergent independence of long-tenured Parliaments seemed dangerous to the people's liberty. While it might be necessary for the people "to appoint a power in the State, to which they individually transfer their wills, dress it up in the insignia of sovereignty, and arm it with legislative authority," the radicals had no doubt that this "sovereign power" was "no more than the representative of the people declaratory of their will, and bound to act in subservience to their interest." The idea that the representatives could do what they liked was "almost too monstrous to conceive." "Can there be imagined a more striking absurdity than that the trustee should become independent of the person reposing the trust . . . the creature stronger than the creator?" Parliamentary actions, like the expulsion of John Wilkes from the House of Commons despite his repeated election, only aggravated this fear of the arbitrary

64. Phila. *Pa. Packet*, Dec. 25, 1775; *Essay upon Government*, 52. For an analysis of this quasi-magisterial character of the representatives, see Richard Buel, Jr., "Democracy and the American Revolution: A Frame of Reference," *Wm. and Mary Qtly.*, 3d Ser., 21 (1964), 178–79, 189.

65. Earl Nugent, 1780, quoted in Betty Kemp, *King and Commons, 1660–1832* (London, 1957), 46. On the importance of the convention established by the Septennial Act in elevating the Commons to a position of equality and occasional supremacy in the functioning of English government, see in general *ibid.*, 34–46, 142–43.

independence of the House of Commons, a fear that had run through the radical English mind since the seventeenth century, "when," as Catharine Macaulay recalled, "the representatives had affected an intire independency on, or rather an absolute sovereignty over their constitutents."[66]

Despite this fear, however, most Commonwealthmen were not yet ready to give up on the representational process. They realized that government by representation "deviates more or less from Liberty, in proportion as the representation is more or less imperfect." And representation in the House of Commons seemed so imperfect, so antiquated, and cried out so for reform that its evils would have to be remedied before men could clearly explore the implications of representation for their traditional understanding of politics. They thus concentrated not on denying the efficacy of representation itself, but on anchoring the drifting representatives to the people, so that through the institution of certain safeguards and reforms, like more proportional representation, freer elections, and more frequent Parliaments, the interests of the people and their representatives could "be engaged upon the same Bottom, that Principals and Deputies must stand and fall together."[67] Still the deeply rooted mistrust of any body set above the people, the frightening discrepancy between the people and their spokesmen, however equally or frequently elected, always remained (as the Americans exposed fully in the coming years) a point of nagging confusion in the English understanding of politics.[68] Indeed, lack of confidence in the representational system became the most important means of measuring degrees of radicalism among a Whiggish people.

4. ENGLISH CORRUPTION

This Whig theory of politics, assumed by the Americans with varying degrees of precision during their decade-long debate with England, was not simply a series of political maxims or abstrac-

---

66. Phila. *Pa. Packet*, Jan. 15, 1776; Macaulay, *Address to the People*, 11–12.

67. Richard Price, *Additional Observations on the Nature and Value of Civil Liberty, and the War with America* (London, 1778, first published 1777), 7; [Trenchard and Gordon], *Cato's Letters*, II, 232–33.

68. For examples of the independence of the people outside of Parliament, see Burgh, *Disquisitions*, I, 6; [Obadiah Hulme], *Historical Essay on the English Constitution* (London, 1771), 142.

tions isolated from any social or historical context, unrelated to time and place. "As the interests of People vary with their circumstances," declared one early eighteenth-century English pamphlet republished in America in 1775, "so the Form of Government may be various, and yet each be best in its Proper Place, and by consequence one Form of Government may be best for this People, another for that."[69] The common belief of the age that human nature was forever the same referred essentially to the raw biological nature upon which the environment operated. Most thinkers had little doubt that the cultural natures of men varied with the circumstances in which they lived. The Augustan age was scarcely unhistorical, although it was decidedly contemptuous of mere antiquarianism or storytelling. It was not history for its own sake, not even the evolution through time of a particular people or culture, that attracted men of the age, but rather the abstract process of development, the laws or uniformities which applied equally to all peoples. As in politics it was generalizations, scientific principles about the historical process that the age was after, and men were engrossed in discovering the connectedness of things, particularly the relations between governmental institutions and society, and the principles that governed their changes through time. In this sense eighteenth-century English political thought perhaps owed more to Machiavelli and Montesquieu than it did to Locke.[70] Most English colonists did not conceive of society in rational, mechanistic terms; rather society was organic and developmental. The macrocosm was still like the microcosm. "It is with states as it is with men," was a commonplace of the day; "they have their infancy, their manhood, and their decline." The history of particular nations and peoples, whatever may have been the history of mankind in general, was not a linear progression, but a variable organic cycle of birth, maturity, and death, in which states, like the human body, carried within themselves the seeds of their own dissolution, "which ripen faster or slower," depending on the changing spirit of the society.[71]

---

69. *Essay upon Government*, 118.

70. For the influence of these two European intellectuals on English thought, see Felix Raab, *The English Face of Machiavelli* . . . (London, 1964); Frank T. H. Fletcher, *Montesquieu and English Politics, 1750–1800* (London, 1939).

71. [Mather], *America's Appeal*, 68; Phila. *Pa. Packet*, May 29, 1775; Pinkney's Wmsbg. *Va. Gazette*, June 29, 1775; *Providence Gazette*, Apr. 24, 1779. See Stow Persons, "The Cyclical Theory of History in Eighteenth-Century America," *American Quarterly*, 6 (1954), 147–63.

However much American Whigs were convinced that men were "just beginning to emerge from Egyptian darkness, with respect to the rights of human nature," they well knew that in comparison with the past "the present age shews equal absurdities and vices upon the theatre of politicks . . . everything for which we condemn our ancestors."[72] In those troublesome years approaching the Revolution countless American writings, steeped in radical Whig pessimism, sought to expose the regressive tendencies in politics that lay beneath the promising progress in theoretical science. Politics in the jaundiced eyes of the radical Whigs had always been a tale of "bloodshed and slaughter, violence and oppression," where the "Monarchs of every age . . . surrounded by a banditti which they call a standing army" had committed havoc on the liberty, property, and lives of hapless peoples. "Fountains of tears have been shed, and rivers of blood have been spilt at the shrine of arbitrary power. History both antient and modern is but a detail of calamities which have been brought upon mankind from this quarter." Indeed, the present "degenerate age" seemed even worse than the past, since by the middle of the eighteenth century the world had witnessed "a greater annihilation of public freedom than seen a century before." The very idea of liberty was unknown in Africa and Asia; and it seemed to the alienated Whigs that it might soon be only a memory in Europe, for everywhere "liberty is absorbed by monarchy; and the many must be subject to one."[73] In the course of a single year both Sweden and Poland had been enslaved, leaving on the continent only the Swiss cantons and the Dutch provinces free; and their liberty appeared shortlived. "Where is the kingdom," devout Whigs asked, "that does not groan under the calamities of military tyranny?"[74]

But then in every Englishman's eyes it had always been so. Amidst a tyrannical world England had always stood as a solitary bastion in defense of freedom. No people in history, said John Dickinson, had ever been "so constantly watchful of their lib-

72. N. Y. *Constitutional Gazette*, Feb. 24, 1776.

73. Philadelphia *Pennsylvania Journal*, Nov. 29, 1775; Phila. *Pa. Packet*, Sept. 12, 1774; *The Crisis, Number I* . . . (N. Y., [1775]), 3, 5. Cf. Henry Vyverberg, *Historical Pessimism in the French Enlightenment* (Cambridge, Mass., 1958).

74. Jonathan W. Austin, *An Oration, Delivered March 5th, 1778* . . . (Boston, 1778), in Niles, ed., *Principles*, 53. For other examples, see Williams, *Discourse on the Love of Our Country*, 21; Zubly, *Law of Liberty*, 33.

erty, and so successful in their struggles for it, as the *English*."[75]
It had not been easy, since for seven hundred years the English
had struggled with the forces of tyranny. Although some Whigs,
like Joseph Hawley, saw "the origin of the British state ͟. . . too
far sunk in the dark ages of antiquity to investigate the manner,
or trace the means by which it was formed," most presumed the
existence of a Saxon golden age of liberty and equality with a
pristine gothic constitution which had been ruthlessly invaded by
"that barbarous system of despotism imposed by the Norman tyrant." From that time on the English people, as Jefferson described it, had fought vigorously to regain their liberties from the
Crown and to restore "that antient constitution, of which our
ancestors had been defrauded," each clash resulting in landmarks
in the development of English freedom and representative institutions. In this bitter "continued struggle between the prince and
the people" the seventeenth century seemed to be of crucial importance; for the Crown under the Stuarts had made a grand and
desperate effort to snuff out the liberty of the people once and for
all, causing a fierce and bloody civil war and a disruption of the
constitution that had eventually been settled by "that happy establishment" of 1688.[76]

For most radical Whigs the Glorious Revolution had not
marked the end of the struggle. In their aversion to the developments of eighteenth-century England they refused to turn their
backs on the disordered but exhilarating and promising experience
of the seventeenth century and to accept the Revolution of 1688
as a final solution to the problems of English public life. While
few Americans were willing to go so far as to declare that "England was never more happy before, nor much more since, than
after the head of the first Stuart was severed from his body,"[77]
all true Whigs were forced to conclude that the Revolution of 1688
had not after all been able to preserve the liberty that the great
men of the seventeenth century—the Hampdens, the Sidneys—had

75. [Dickinson], *Letters from a Farmer*, Ford, ed., *Writings of Dickinson*,
II, 388.
76. Boston *Mass. Spy*, Feb. 16, 1775; Macaulay, *Address to the People*, 8;
Gilbert Chinard, ed., *The Commonplace Book of Thomas Jefferson* (Baltimore,
1926), 192–93; Otis, *Rights of the British Colonies*, Bailyn, ed., *Pamphlets*, I, 474.
See also Colbourn, *Lamp of Experience*, 21–56, 194–98; Bailyn, *Ideological
Origins*, 64–67, 80–83.
77. Foster, *Short Essay on Civil Government*, 71.

sought. Especially in the decade after the accession of George III there could be no place for confidence in their writings, only pessimism and an agonizing despair for the future of liberty, not only in Europe but in England itself.

The colonists in these prerevolutionary years watched England in bewilderment as what had long been predicted by "her senators and historians" seemed actually to be happening—the English constitution, formerly "the noblest improvement of human reason," was at last succumbing to the forces of tyranny, "shaken to its very basis." England, the Americans said over and over again, "once the land of liberty—the school of patriots—the nurse of heroes, has become the land of slavery—the school of parricides and the nurse of tyrants." By the 1770's the metaphors describing England's course were all despairing: the nation was fast streaming toward a cataract, hanging on the edge of a precipice; the brightest lamp of liberty in all the world was dimming.[78] Internal decay was the most common image. A poison had entered the nation and was turning the people and the government into "one mass of corruption." On the eve of the Revolution the belief that England was "sunk in corruption" and "tottering on the brink of destruction" had become entrenched in the minds of disaffected Englishmen on both sides of the Atlantic.[79]

These widely voiced fears for the fate of the English constitution, "the mighty ruin of a once noble fabrick,"[80] were not simply the bombastic expressions of revolutionary-minded men. They represented the rational and scientific conclusions of considered social analysis. For all of its rhetorical exaggeration, the ideology of Whig radicalism, embraced by Americans of varying political persuasions and at every social level, was grounded in the best, most enlightened knowledge of the eighteenth century; it was this grounding that gave the Whig ideology much of its persuasive force. When the American Whigs described the English nation and government as eaten away by "corruption," they were in fact using a technical term of political science, rooted in the

78. Williams, *Discourse on the Love of Our Country*, 21; [Mather], *America's Appeal*, 50–51; Phila. *Pa. Journal*, Nov. 29, 1775; Phila. *Pa. Packet*, July 4, Aug. 22, 1774; William Hooper to James Iredell, Jan. 6, 1776, McRee, *Life of Iredell*, I, 269; Charleston *South Carolina and American General Gazette*, Jan. 16, 1777.
79. [Adams], "Novanglus," Adams, ed., *Works of John Adams*, IV, 28; Charles Lee to Robert Morris, Jan. 3, 1776, *Lee Papers*, I, 233; *The Crisis, Number V* ... (N. Y., [1775]), 33.
80. Phila. *Pa. Packet*, Aug. 8, 1774.

writings of classical antiquity, made famous by Machiavelli, developed by the classical republicans of seventeenth-century England, and carried into the eighteenth century by nearly everyone who laid claim to knowing anything about politics.[81] And for England it was a pervasive corruption, not only dissolving the original political principles by which the constitution was balanced, but, more alarming, sapping the very spirit of the people by which the constitution was ultimately sustained.

The corruption of the constitution's internal principles was the more obvious and the more superficial danger. The marvelous mixture of the English constitution was dependent, the Whigs believed, on "the three distinct powers, or bodies" of the legislature being "entirely independent of each other." But as the Whigs interpreted the events of the eighteenth century, the Crown had been able to evade the restrictions of the revolutionary settlement of 1688 and had "found means to corrupt the other branches of the legislature," upsetting the delicately maintained balance of the constitution from within. Throughout the eighteenth century the Crown had slyly avoided the blunt and clumsy instrument of prerogative, and instead had resorted to influencing the electoral process and the representatives in Parliament in order to gain its treacherous ends. This seemed in the minds of devout Whigs a far more subtle tyranny than the Stuarts' usurpations of the previous century, because "the very means which were devised to secure and protect" the people had become "the engines of destruction." George III was "now tearing up the constitution by the roots, under the form of law." Nothing angered radicals and independent-minded Englishmen in the eighteenth century more than the attempts by a frustrated ministry to carry out the Crown's supposed responsibility for governing the realm with the necessary but often little understood cooperation of a balky Parliament—a cooperation that was possible only through ministerial management and influencing of the House of Commons. It appeared to those who clung to the original principles of the constitution and the growing tradition of separation of powers that the Crown, in its painful efforts to build majorities through borough-mongering and the distribution of patronage, was in fact bribing its way into tyranny. "It is upon this principle," Ameri-

81. Pocock, "Machiavelli, Harrington, and English Political Ideologies," *Wm. and Mary Qtly.*, 3d Ser., 22 (1965), 549–83.

cans concluded, "that the King of Great-Britain is absolute; for though he doth not act without the parliament, by places, pensions, honours and promises, he obtains the sanction of the parliament for doing as he pleases. The ancient form is preserved, but the spirit of the constitution is evaporated."[82]

Nonetheless, this disruption of the internal workings of the constitution was not profoundly frightening to good Whigs; indeed it was to be expected, for time did not stand still, and men knew they lived in "a changeable world." Had not Machiavelli and Sidney both written that "all human Constitutions are subject to Corruption and must perish, unless they are *timely renewed* by reducing them to their first Principles"? The constitution's disorder should have been an inevitable but temporary aberration, eventually correctable by the people. Yet everyone knew that reducing the constitution to its first principles—"restoring it to its pristine Perfection"—was impossible if the people themselves had become corrupted and sunk in vice. Until the society itself had been infected, until there was "a general depravity of morals, a total alienation from virtue, a people cannot be compleatly enslaved." It was not any inherent weakness in the principles of the British constitution that had made it defective, since "the strongest constitutions are most liable to certain diseases." But if the diseases remained unremedied, if the constitution could not be restored to its first principles, then the fault could only be the people's. For it was the "distinguished happiness" of the British constitution that "when by any means" it became corrupted, "nothing is wanting to a restoration, but the virtue of the people." Indeed, "all men might be free, if they had but virtue enough to be so."[83]

Borrowing pointedly from the relevant writings of history, especially from classical antiquity, eighteenth-century intellectuals —Montesquieu being but the best among many—had worked out

82. Boston *Mass. Spy*, Mar. 23, 1775; Thacher, *Oration, Delivered March 5, 1776*, Niles, ed., *Principles*, 44; Phila. *Pa. Packet*, Aug. 8, 1774; *Crisis, Number I*, 6; Boston *New England Chronicle*, Sept. 5, 1776. See also Namier and Brooke, *House of Commons*, I, 81, 145–46, 183.

83. Joseph Perry, *A Sermon, Preached before the General Assembly of the Colony of Connecticut, at Hartford, on the Day of Their Anniversary Election, May 11, 1775* (Hartford, 1775), 21; [Dickinson], *Letters from a Farmer*, Ford, ed., *Writings of Dickinson*, 386; Demophilus [pseud.], *The Genuine Principles of the Ancient Saxon, or English Constitution . . .* (Phila., 1776), title page; Bland, *Inquiry*, quoted in Rossiter, *Seedtime of the Republic*, 273; Phila. *Pa. Packet*, Oct. 24, 1774; *N.-Y. Journal*, Dec. 11, 1766; [Mather], *America's Appeal*, 67; Phila. *Pa. Packet*, Sept. 5, 1774.

the ambiguous but necessary and mutual relation they believed existed between the moral spirit of a society and its political constitution.[84] It was a fascinating subject, the kind that commencement speakers at American colleges in the 1770's could not resist. "Empires," declared one orator lecturing "On the Fall of Empires," "carry in them their own bane, and proceed, in fatal round, from virtuous industry and valour, to wealth and conquest; next to luxury, then to foul corruption and bloated morals; and, last of all, to sloth, anarchy, slavery and political death." History, as written by Sallust and Plutarch, only too grimly showed the fate of empires grown too fat with riches. While the Romans, for example, maintained their love of virtue, their simplicity of manners, their recognition of true merit, they raised their state to the heights of glory. But they stretched their conquests too far and their Asiatic wars brought them luxuries they had never before known. "From that moment virtue and public spirit sunk apace: dissipation vanished temperance and independence." "From a People accustomed to the Toils of War, and Agriculture, they became a People who no longer piqued themselves on any other Merit than a pretended fine Taste for all the Refinements of a voluptuous Life." They became obsessed with the "Grandeur and Magnificence in Buildings, of Sumptuousness and Delicacy in their Tables, of Richness and Pomp in their Dress, of Variety and Singularity in their Furniture." That corruption "which always begins amongst the Rich and the Great" soon descended to the common people, leaving them "enfeebled and their souls depraved." The gap between rich and poor widened and the society was torn by extortion and violence. "It was no longer virtue that raised men up to the first employments of the state, but the chance of birth, and the caprice of fortune." With the character of the Roman people so corrupted, dissolution had to follow. "The empire tottered on its foundation, and the mighty fabric sunk beneath its own weight."[85]

The analogy with the present was truly frightening. "Those very symptoms which preceded the fall of Rome, appear but too evidently in the British constitution." And as everyone in the eighteenth century knew, "Similar causes must ever produce similar effects." Both John Adams and William Hooper saw venality

84. On Machiavelli's influence on Bolingbroke's understanding of this relationship, see Herbert Butterfield, *The Statecraft of Machiavelli* (London, 1940), esp. 160.

85. Pinkney's Wmsbg. *Va. Gazette*, June 15, 1775; Phila. *Pa. Packet*, May 29, 1775, Aug. 8, 1774; Purdie and Dixon's Wmsbg. *Va. Gazette*, Sept. 5, 1771.

in England at the pitch it was when Jugurtha left Rome. All the
signs of England's economic and social development in the eighteenth century—the increasing capitalization of land and industry, the growing debt, the rising prices and taxes, the intensifying
search for distinctions by more and more people—were counted
as evidence of "its present degeneracy, and its impending destruction."[86] A "long succession of abused prosperity" drawn into
"ruinous operation by the Riches and Luxuries of the East"—
England's very greatness as an empire—had created a poison
which was softening the once hardy character of the English
people, sapping their time-honored will to fight for their liberties, leaving them, as never before in their history, weakened
prey to the designs of the Crown. It seemed to radical Whigs
and Americans alike that "Gangrene has taken too deep Hold to
be eradicated in these Days of Venality." The English people had
at last become too corrupted, too enfeebled, to restore their constitution to its first principles and rejuvenate their country. "The
whole fabric," warned James Burgh, was "ready to come down
in ruins upon our heads."[87]

5. THE PATTERN OF TYRANNY

It was in the context of this frightening diagnosis of the state
of the British constitution and society that the Americans viewed
the attempts of the British government in the years after 1763 to
put its empire on a surer footing. Some, like James Iredell, continued to the very end of the debate to be "far from thinking"
that the English people were "universally corrupt, though too
many, God knows, are." But whatever the degree of corruption
in England may have been, it seemed even to someone as skeptical as Iredell that "this has been the cause of all our present calamity."[88] True Whigs were well aware that in the last stages of

86. Phila. *Pa. Packet*, Aug. 8, 1774; [Adams], "Novanglus," Adams, ed., *Works
of John Adams*, IV, 54–55; William Hooper to James Iredell, Apr. 26, 1776, in
Joseph S. Jones, *A Defense of the Revolutionary History of the State of North
Carolina from the Aspersions of Mr. Jefferson* (Boston, 1834), 314.
87. Macaulay, *Address to the People*, 9; Charleston *S. C. and American
Gazette*, Nov. 14–21, 1776; Bland, *Inquiry*, quoted in Rossiter, *Seedtime of the
Republic*, 273; Burgh, *Disquisitions*, I, 82.
88. Iredell, "To His Majesty, George the Third . . . ," Mar. 1777, McRee,
Life of Iredell, I, 356.

a nation's life "luxury and its never failing attendant corruption, will render easy the attempts of an arbitrary prince, who means to subvert the liberty of his country." Only in such a venal and degenerate climate did tyrants flourish. If indeed England were "on the verge of ruin," as "by the best accounts, we are assured," then events would confirm that the long anticipated crisis of liberty was at hand. It therefore became the responsibility of the colonial leaders to make clear to their fellow subjects what was happening, to disperse "the clouds of obscuring ignorance" and "trace with enquiring minds the principles of government . . . closely investigate the origin of power, and deduce from unvarying laws" the insidious designs of the British King and ministers that lay behind the events of the 1760's and seventies.[89] The result of their efforts in the years leading up to the Revolution was an extraordinary display of the writing of contemporary history—a scientific analysis of the workings of men and events through time that was at once highly refined and yet extremely crude—designed to enable the colonists, as no people before them ever had, to expose and thus resist the forces of tyranny before they were actually enslaved.

Those Whig spokesmen who bothered to go beyond a simple articulation of Whig maxims offered an especially impressive conception of the patterns of culture and history. They knew it would be no simple task to awaken the people to the dangers confronting their liberties. "The experience of all ages" showed that the people were "inattentive to the calamities of others, careless of admonition, and with difficulty roused to repel the most injurious invasions." The Whigs were struck with "the easiness with which the many are governed by the few, . . . the implicit submission with which men resign their own sentiments and passions to those of their rulers." Many could therefore conclude with David Hume that it was on custom or "opinion only that government is founded, and this maxim extends to the most despotic and most military governments, as well as to the most free and most popular."[90] The people through history, Americans noted over and over again, were generally docile and obedient, disposed "to be as submissive and passive and tame under gov-

89. Phila. *Pa. Packet*, Sept. 5, 1774; Rind's Wmsbg. *Va. Gazette*, Aug. 25, 1774; Perry, *Sermon, May 11, 1775*, 18; Phila. *Pa. Packet*, Aug. 8, 1774.

90. Quincy, *Observations on the Boston Port Bill*, Quincy, *Memoir*, 326; Pinkney's Wmsbg. *Va. Gazette*, June 22, 1775; [Dickinson], *Letters from a Farmer*, Ford, ed., *Writings of Dickinson*, 388–89.

ernment as they ought to be." In fact the people were naturally "so gentle that there never was a government yet in which thousands of mistakes were not overlooked." Men were born to be deluded, "to believe whatever is taught, and bear all that is imposed."[91]

This customary deference of the people was really what explained the overweening dominance of the ruling few through so many centuries of history, for it "gradually reconciles us to objects even of dread and detestation." Because of the Whigs' particular conception of politics, their otherwise sophisticated understanding of the historical process took on a primitive cast, and history became the product of self-conscious acts by rulers seeking to extend their power over an unsuspecting populace. Insignificant, piecemeal changes, none of which seemed decisive or unbearable at the time, "spread over the multitude in such a manner, as to touch individuals but slightly."[92] In a variety of metaphors the colonists sought to express their understanding of how the rulers, possessing their own "particular purposes," slyly used the historical process. Every one of their acts of usurpation was "like a small spark [which] if not extinguished in the beginning will soon gain ground and at last blaze out into an irresistible Flame"; or it was "like the rollings of mighty waters over the breach of ancient mounds,—slow and unalarming at the beginning; rapid and terrible in the current; a deluge and devastation at the end"; or it was like "a spot, a speck of decay, however small the limb on which it appears, and however remote it may seem from the vitals," that would grow and corrupt "till at length the inattentive people are compelled to perceive the heaviness of their burthens," usually, however, too late for the people to resist. "They find their oppressors so strengthened by success, and themselves so entangled in examples of express authority on the part of the rulers, and tacit recognition on their own part, that they are quite confounded." All history was therefore an object lesson in the power of the seemingly insignificant. "Innumerable instances might be produced to shew," said John Dickinson in the most

91. Jonathan Mayhew, *A Discourse concerning Unlimited Submission and Non-Resistance to the Higher Powers* (Boston, 1750), in Bailyn, ed., *Pamphlets,* I, 237; Quincy, *Observations on the Boston Port Bill*, Quincy, *Memoir*, 324. See also [John Adams], *Boston Gazette*, Feb. 9, 16, 1767, in Adams, ed., *Works of John Adams*, III, 489; Charles Lee, "A Political Essay," *Lee Papers*, IV, 107.

92. [Dickinson], *Letters from a Farmer*, Ford, ed., *Writings of Dickinson*, 389, 346–47, 353, 393, 382, 389.

acute analysis of the way history and politics worked that was written in these years, "from what slight beginnings the most extensive consequences have flowed."[93]

Yet the power of custom and the habitual deference of the people to established authority also worked to protect the people against wanton civil disturbance and to prevent rebellion for light and transient causes. Most American Whigs were sure that no people could be falsely incited into revolution by sheer demagoguery, as the Tories were charging. No popular leaders, wrote John Adams, had ever been able "to persuade a large people, for any length of time together, to think themselves wronged, injured, and oppressed, unless they really were, and saw and felt it to be so." Only irrefutable proof, only evidence which was "as clear as the sun in its meridian brightness," could convince the people that they were really threatened with enslavement at the hands of their rulers.[94] By the eve of the Revolution most Whigs believed that they possessed that kind of proof.

It was obvious to the Americans that the events of the years after 1763, "these unheard of intolerable calamities, spring not of the dust, come not causeless." "Ought not the PEOPLE therefore," asked John Dickinson in 1768, "to watch? to observe facts? to search into causes? to investigate designs?" And as their search into the causes for what was happening proceeded, the otherwise inexplicable series of events increasingly seemed to be but pieces of a grand design, nothing less than, in Jefferson's words, "a deliberate, systematical plan of reducing us to slavery." By the 1770's there was hardly a piece of Whig writing, whether pamphlet, newspaper essay, letter, or even diary, that did not dwell on this obsessive fear of a "Conspiracy . . . [against the public liberty] first regularly formed, and begun to be executed, in 1763 or 4." It was scarcely believable, said William Henry Drayton in 1776, "but, nothing less *than absolute proof* has convinced us" that the British government had for the past dozen years carried on a "conspiracy against the rights of humanity." Some out of a deep reverence for England had struggled "long against the evi-

93. Richard Bland, *A Fragment on the Pistole Fee* . . . , ed. Worthington C. Ford (Brooklyn, 1891), 37–39; Quincy, *Observations on the Boston Port Bill*, Quincy, *Memoir*, 326–27; [Dickinson], *Letters from a Farmer*, Ford, ed., *Writings of Dickinson*, 401, 390.

94. [Adams], "Novanglus," Adams, ed., *Works of John Adams*, IV, 14; George Washington to Bryan Fairfax, July 4, 1774, John C. Fitzpatrick, ed., *The Writings of George Washington* (Washington, 1931–40), III, 228.

dence of facts" that had by 1775 "become irresistible." The colonists had simply "too many Proofs that a regular System has been formed to bow down the Neck of America to the *Feet* of the *Ministry*."[95] The cumulative momentum of this belief in a British ministerial conspiracy against the colonists' liberties not only was symptomatic of the rising intensity of the Americans' revolutionary fever, but it also formed for the Americans, as has recently and amply been demonstrated, the only frame of mind with which they could justify and explain their revolution.[96] For in the Whig creed no specific acts of the government against the people could sanction revolution. Only "repeated, multiplied oppressions," placing it beyond all doubt "that their rulers had formed settled plans to deprive them of their liberties," could warrant the concerted resistance of the people against their government.[97]

The notion of conspiracy was not new in Western history. From Sallust's description of Catiline through Machiavelli's lengthy discussion men were familiar with the use of conspiracy in politics. Yet the tendency to see events as the result of a calculated plot, especially events in times of public tumult, appears particularly strong in the eighteenth century, a product, it seems, not only of the political realities and assumptions of the age, but of its very enlightenment, a consequence of the popularization of politics and the secularization of knowledge. Those Americans who continued to see themselves as a specially covenanted people could and did look beyond the earth to Providence for an explanation of the events in the years after 1763: a divinely favored people were being justly punished for their sins. But to those captivated by the Enlightenment of the eighteenth century the wonder-working ways of Providence were not satisfying enough. The explanation of human phenomena lay in the ways of man alone, in human purposes, in political and social science. What-

---

95. [Mather], *America's Appeal*, 59; [Dickinson], *Letters from a Farmer*, Ford, ed., *Writings of Dickinson*, 348; [Jefferson], *Summary View*, Boyd, ed., *Jefferson Papers*, I, 125; Adams, entry, Mar. 6, 1774, Butterfield, ed., *Diary of Adams*, II, 90; Drayton, Charge to the Grand Jury, Charleston, Apr. 23, 1776, Niles, ed., *Principles*, 329; letter to Richard Henry Lee, Sept. 22, 1775, "The Aspinwall Papers, Part II," Mass. Hist. Soc., *Collections*, 4th Ser., 10 (1871), 741; [Robert Carter Nicholas], *Considerations on the Present State of Virginia Examined* ([Williamsburg], 1774), in Earl G. Swem, ed., *Virginia and the Revolution: Two Pamphlets, 1774* (N. Y., 1919), 60.

96. Bailyn, *Ideological Origins*, 94–159.

97. [Adams], "Novanglus," Adams, ed., *Works of John Adams*, IV, 17.

ever happened in history was intended by men to have happened. Enlightened rationalists as well as Calvinist clergy were obsessed with the motives that lay hidden behind deceiving, even self-deceiving, statements, and they continually sought to penetrate beneath the surface of events in order to find their real significance in the inner hearts of men.[98] Yet in replacing Providence with human motivation as a source of historical explanation, men still felt the need to discover the design, "the *grand plan*," that lay beneath the otherwise incomprehensible jumble of events. Now it seemed possible to the men of this enlightened age that they would be able, as the scrutinizers of Providence had been unable, "to trace things into their various connections, or to look forward into all their remote and distant consequences," to disclose at last what had always been in darker days "the hidden and . . . uncertain connection of events."[99] It was precisely this task of tracing, predicting, disclosing, and connecting motives and events that American Whig leaders had set for themselves in the debate with Great Britain. And thus their attributing what was happening to the relations between Britain and her colonies to the conspiratorial designs of a few men in high places became another example of their application of science to human affairs, a noble effort to make natural sense of the complexity of phenomena, a humanization of Providence, an impassioned attempt to explain the ways of man to man, the crude beginnings of what has come to be called the Whig interpretation of history.[100]

The pieces all fell into place, as Whig intellectuals on both sides of the Atlantic worked to make clear the nature of English society and the pattern of the Crown's policy for all to see. This clarification, this growing belief that the English government was con-

98. Arthur Lovejoy, *Reflections on Human Nature* (Baltimore, 1961), 15–31; Thomas P. Peardon, *The Transition in English Historical Writing, 1760–1830* (N. Y., 1933), 11; William C. Lehmann, *John Millar of Glasgow, 1735–1801 . . .* (Cambridge, Eng., 1960), 92.

99. Izrahiah Wetmore, *A Sermon, Preached before the Honorable General Assembly of the Colony of Connecticut, at Hartford, on the Day of Their Anniversary Election, May 13th, 1773* (Norwich, Conn., 1775), 8, 11; Henry Cumings, *A Sermon Preached in Billerica, on the 23d of November 1775 . . .* (Worcester, 1776), 7–8.

100. It was against this "dominant characteristic of the historical thought of the age," this "tendency to explain events in terms of conscious action by individuals," that the brilliant group of Scottish social scientists writing at the end of the 18th century directed much of their work. Duncan Forbes, " 'Scientific' Whiggism: Adam Smith and John Millar," *Cambridge Journal*, 7 (1954), 651, 653–54.

spiratorially making "a bold push for our entire subjection," was, it has been argued, more than anything else responsible for the Americans' decision to revolt.[101] Certainly there can be little doubt of the pervasiveness of these revolutionary beliefs in the minds of the American Whigs. It seemed increasingly evident to the colonists that the forces of tyranny, rapacious as they were, were not content with the conquest of Europe, but now had cast their "jealous eye on this new world" and threatened "to involve it in the miseries of the old." Every successive step by the Crown, under the guise of a corrupted and pliant Parliament, only confirmed American fears of a despotic conspiracy against freedom. The multiplication of new government officials was obviously the beginning of the Court's plan "that millions of leading men's dependents shall be provided for in America, for whom places can by no means be found at home." The sending of new troops to America was merely the introduction of despotism's traditional instrument—a standing army. The new admiralty courts were only the first stage in the eventual elimination of trial by jury. The invigoration of the Anglican establishment could only be directed toward the ultimate destruction of America's religious freedom. The Quebec Act was actually an insidious attempt by the ministry to introduce through the colonies' back door the evils of popery, civil law, and eventual absolutism. And in such a mental atmosphere the Coercive Acts could be but flagrant confirmation of the Crown's grand strategy.[102]

Under the pressures of this intensifying controversy the Americans' conception of their place in history—suggested intermittently in their writings since the seventeenth century and deduced from their understanding of the nature of social development—was raised to a new and powerful height of comprehensiveness. While the mother country grew old and haggard, the colonies seemed "as yet a new and uncorrupted people." In the seventeenth century they had carried "the spirit of liberty" from England to

101. N. Y. *Constitutional Gazette*, Feb. 21, 1776; Bailyn, *Ideological Origins*, Chap. IV.

102. Phila. *Pa. Journal*, Nov. 29, 1775; Phila. *Pa. Packet*, Aug. 29, Sept. 12, 26, Oct. 31, 1774; Carl Bridenbaugh, *Mitre and Sceptre: Transatlantic Faiths, Ideas, Personalities, and Politics, 1689–1775* (N. Y., 1962), Chaps. VII–IX. The colonists, wrote the Tory Samuel Seabury in 1774, believe that the ministers of the British government "have laid a regular plan to enslave America; and that they are now deliberately putting it in execution. This point has never been proved, though it has been asserted over, and over, and over again." *A View of the Controversy between Great-Britain and Her Colonies* (N. Y., 1774), 19.

the wilderness "at the time when it was in its greatest purity and perfection"; and in the New World it had flourished. No wonder, then, that "there seldom ever was a nation . . . more violently assaulted, than we have been." America had become a disconcerting obstacle in the Crown's march to absolutism, a shining symbol to oppressed peoples everywhere that freedom still lived. The crisis with England, so "strange," so "unnatural," seemed by 1774 "to foretell some great event," leading Americans "to imagine there is something at hand that shall greatly augment the history of the world."[103] Out of the frenzied thinking of disaffected Englishmen and the scattered writings of European intellectuals—all grounded in the best scientific knowledge of the day—and out of their own ethnocentric traditions, the Americans began piecing together the immense significance of what they were involved in, ultimately creating one of the most coherent and powerful revolutionary ideologies the Western world had yet seen. They could not help believing—all the evidence, all the enlightened everywhere confirmed it—that liberty was fleeing the Old World entirely and "seeking an asylum westward." Out of the tumult that was sure to come they could only hope that "a great and mighty empire may rise up in this western world," an empire peculiarly dedicated to the principles of liberty.[104]

6. The Preservation of Principles

By 1776 there could be no longer any doubt in the Americans' minds that they were "in the very midst of a revolution, the most complete, unexpected, and remarkable, of any in the history of nations." That it was truly a revolution was attested by the very language they used to express their estrangement from the old order and their hope for the new. For their Revolution had become something more than simply liberation from British rule. "A surprising concurrence of incidents, equally out of our knowledge to have foreseen, or our power to have prevented, point us

---

103. Phila. *Pa. Packet*, Aug. 22, Oct. 3, 1774; Cumings, *Sermon Preached on the 23d of November*, 1775, 10; Joseph Lyman, *A Sermon Preached at Hatfield December 15th, 1774* . . . (Boston, 1775), 30; William Bradford to James Madison, Aug. 1, 1774, William T. Hutchinson and William M. E. Rachal, eds., *The Papers of James Madison* (Chicago, 1962——), I, 118.

104. Hooper to Iredell, Jan. 6, 1776, McRee, *Life of Iredell*, I, 269; Carmichael, *Self-Defensive War*, 34.

to some great event."[105] What had begun in the 1760's as outbursts of hostility against specific actions of Parliament and
particular Crown officials had within a decade escalated into a
genuine revolutionary movement, sustained by a powerful, even
millennial, creed by which Americans saw themselves no longer
merely contending for the protection of particular liberties but
on the verge of ushering in a new era of freedom and bliss.

Like all revolutions, it had not been anticipated, since in times
of confusion, as the Americans themselves realized, men are "carried further than they intended at first setting out." Repeatedly
and sincerely, the colonists denied that they desired anything
new, denied that independence was their aim. Yet, like one Marylander in May of 1776, many saw themselves "proceeding by
degrees to that crisis we so much deprecate," fearing that "in the
end" they would find themselves "in a state of separation without averting to the steps by which we have arrived at it." That
they should have groped and changed their thinking, as events
built upon events and implications built upon implications, was
not surprising. As John Adams said, "When a great question is
first started, there are very few, even of the greatest minds, which
suddenly and intuitively comprehend it, in all its consequences."[106]
While struggling to make meaningful the cataclysm of events in
the decade following the peace with France, the Americans had
sought to stay within the confines of the English constitution as
they had come to perceive it. But their perception of the constitution was so colored by a peculiar strain of English thought
that the gap between their position and that of official England
was exposed at the outset. And as the debate unfolded the gulf
only widened, with the divergent positions and perceptions both
shifting and hardening. Yet right to the end an uncorrupted English constitution remained for most Americans the model of what
a constitution should be. The Whigs devoutly believed and enlightened foreigners assured them that the British constitution was
the very source of those liberties and rights they were being compelled to defend.[107] Only when it became generally clear by the

105. John Adams to William Cushing, June 9, 1776, Adams, ed., *Works of
John Adams*, IX, 391; [Mather], *America's Appeal*, 69.
106. Zubly, *Law of Liberty*, xvii; James Hollyday to Thomas Stone, May 26,
1776, quoted in Herbert E. Klingelhofer, "The Cautious Revolution: Maryland
and the Movement toward Independence. Part I," *Maryland Historical Magazine*, 60 (1965), 288–89; [Adams], "Novanglus," Adams, ed., *Works of John
Adams*, IV, 113.
107. [Raynal], *Sentiments of a Foreigner*, 21; Rossiter, *Seedtime of the Republic*, 349.

mid-1770's that the British people were so corrupted that they were unable to reform and renew their constitution and to stop the relentless course of their rulers, did the American Whigs with varying degrees of enthusiasm determine to break from the mother country and seek a revitalization of the principles of the English constitution in the New World.[108] This break from Great Britain was a momentous one, and good Whigs like John Dickinson agonizingly hesitated out of the fear that America was cutting itself off from the source of its own life-blood of liberty. If the "ligament" between Britain and America "be burst asunder," warned John Randolph, "our Strength will be weakened, and our Security at an End."[109]

Yet because it was the science of politics—generalities and uniformities—that the Americans were concerned with, the break from England became possible without abandoning the "free and antient principles" of the English constitution. Even the Declaration of Independence did not deny the principles of the English constitution. The British themselves, said the New Jersey Council in September 1776, "must applaud an action, which accords so eminently with the true spirit of their own constitution." So absorbed were the Americans in the Commonwealth tradition of English radicalism that even the destruction of monarchy and the institution of republicanism did not clearly signify a repudiation of the ancient constitution; for the spirit of republicanism, the spirit of the great men of the seventeenth century, was "so far from being incompatible with the British constitution, that it is the greatest glory of it."[110]

108. On the shift from resistance to revolution, see Pauline Maier, "John Wilkes and American Disillusionment with Britain," *Wm. and Mary Qtly.*, 3d Ser., 20 (1963), 373–95.

109. [Dickinson], *Letters from a Farmer*, Ford, ed., *Writings of Dickinson*, 326; [John Randolph], *Considerations on the Present State of Virginia* ([Williamsburg], 1774), in Swem, ed., *Virginia and the Revolution*, 23.

110. [Jefferson], *Summary View*, Boyd, ed., *Jefferson Papers*, I, 131; Phila. *Pa. Gazette*, Oct. 9, 1776; [Adams], "Novanglus," Adams, ed., *Works of John Adams*, IV, 68–69.

CHAPTER II

Republicanism

1. A NEW PEOPLE FOR A NEW WORLD

It was obviously a most exciting day for young Thomas Shippen, a Philadelphia gentleman of social prominence, when Thomas Jefferson presented him in 1788 to the French Court at Versailles. For Shippen, as a friend cautioned Jefferson, was very socially conscious, apt to "run wild after the tinsel of life," and had eagerly anticipated his Continental tour with all its opportunities for cultivating "the acquaintance of titled men and Ladies of birth," whose names, the friend regretfully observed, "he soon gets and . . . will never forget."[1] And nowhere on earth were there more tinsel and titles than at the Court of Versailles, more indeed than Shippen in his wildest fancies had imagined. So ceremonious, so luxurious was the French Court that this pretentious Philadelphian could only feel himself "a stranger" in its midst. He could not restrain himself from expressing amazement at the "Oriental splendor and magnificence" of it all. The wealth, the sophistication, the pomp dazzled him: the pictures of the royal family were "larger than life"; the members of the Court had "all separate households and distinct portions of the Palace allotted to them" and "between them they expend 36,000,000 of livres a year"; and the royal gardens—"What walks! What groves! What water works!" It was all so "superb" and so "very splendid," filled with ceremony and behavior, said Shippen, as "I had never seen." Overawed, he could only puff with pride on having "received

1. William Stephens Smith to Jefferson, Jan. 9, 1788, Boyd, ed., *Jefferson Papers*, XII, 501.

very uncommon marks of politeness and attention" from the nobility of the Court.

Yet all the time he knew he was being snubbed. He sensed that the "oppressive . . . civilities" of the courtiers were condescending, that their polite questions only "served to shew rather a desire to be attentive to me, than to be informed of what they did not know already." The American, something of an aristocrat in Philadelphia but hardly one at Versailles, could not help feeling his difference; and that difference understandably became the shield for his self-esteem. He was, after all, as he told his father, a republican: geographically and socially he was from another world. The magnificence and elegance both impressed and repulsed him. How many thousands of subjects, Shippen asked, were doomed to want and wretchedness by the King's wasteful efforts "to shroud his person and adorn his reign" with such luxury? He "revolted" at the King's "insufferable arrogance," and was even "more mortified at the suppleness and base complaisance of his attendants." He rejoiced that he was not a subject of such a monarchy, but the citizen of a republic—"more great because more virtuous"—where there were no hereditary distinctions, no "empty ornament and unmeaning grandeur," where only sense, merit, and integrity commanded respect. He observed beneath all the splendor of the courtiers "an uneasiness and ennui in their faces." The whole wonderful and bitter experience only convinced him "that *a certain degree of equality* is essential to human bliss. Happy above all Countries is our Country," he exulted, "where *that equality* is found, without destroying the necessary subordination."[2]

For most Americans, as for Shippen, this was the deeply felt meaning of the Revolution: they had created a new world, a republican world. No one doubted that the new polities would be republics, and, as Thomas Paine pointed out, "What is called a *republic*, is not any *particular form* of government."[3] Republicanism meant more for Americans than simply the elimination of a king and the institution of an elective system. It added a moral dimension, a utopian depth, to the political separation from England—a depth that involved the very character of their society.

2. Thomas Lee Shippen to William Shippen, Feb. 14–Mar. 26, 1788, *ibid.*, 502–04.
3. Thomas Paine, *The Rights of Man* (London, 1791), in Philip S. Foner, ed., *The Complete Writings of Thomas Paine* (N. Y., 1945) I, 369.

"We are now really another people," exclaimed Paine in 1782.

Socially, of course, they were not really another people, despite much economic unsettling and the emigration of thousands of Tories. But intellectually and culturally they were—and this is what Paine meant. "Our style and manner of thinking have undergone a revolution more extraordinary than the political revolution of the country. We see with other eyes; we hear with other ears; and think with other thoughts, than those we formerly used." Republicanism did not signal the immediate collapse of the traditional social organization; but it did possess a profound social significance. The Revolution was intended in fact to "form a new era and give a new turn to human affairs."[4] From the moment in 1774 and 1775 when independence and hence the formation of new governments became a distinct possibility, and continuing throughout the war, nearly every piece of writing concerned with the future of the new republics was filled with extraordinarily idealistic hopes for the social and political transformation of America. The Americans had come to believe that the Revolution would mean nothing less than a reordering of eighteenth-century society and politics as they had known and despised them—a reordering that was summed up by the conception of republicanism.

2. THE APPEAL OF ANTIQUITY

When in 1807 John Adams told Mercy Warren that he had "never understood" what a republic was, and "no other man ever did or ever will," his memory was playing him badly. These repeated statements of his later years that a republic "may signify any thing, every thing, or nothing" represented the bewilderment of a man whom ideas had passed by. Back in 1776 republicanism was not such a confused conception in the minds of Americans. When Adams himself talked of "a Republican Spirit, among the People," and the eradication of "Idolatry to Monarchs, and servility to Aristocratical Pride," he seems to have understood clearly what it denoted, for the events of the 1760's and seventies had, he said, "frequently reminded" him of the "principles and reasonings" of "Sidney, Harrington, Locke, Milton, Nedham, Neville, Burnet, and Hoadly." However scorned by "modern Englishmen," these writers had a particular relevance for Adams and

4. Paine, *Letter to the Abbé Raynal* . . . (Phila., 1782), in *ibid.*, II, 244, 243; Williams, *Love of Our Country*, 26.

countless other Americans in 1776: "they will convince any candid mind, that there is no good government but what is republican."[5]

To the radical Whigs, rooted in the Commonwealth period of the seventeenth century, the perfect government was always republican. Since a republic represented not so much the formal structure of a government as it did its spirit, pure Whigs could even describe the English mixed monarchy as ideally a republic.[6] Consequently the principles of republicanism permeated much of what the colonists read and found attractive. In fact, "the true principles of republicanism are at present so well understood," so much taken for granted, so much a part of the Americans' assumptions about politics, that few felt any need formally to explain their origin.[7] There was, however, for all Whigs, English and American, one historical source of republican inspiration that was everywhere explicitly acknowledged—classical antiquity, where the greatest republics in history had flourished.

For Americans the mid-eighteenth century was truly a neoclassical age—the high point of their classical period. At one time or another almost every Whig patriot took or was given the name of an ancient republican hero, and classical references and allusions run through much of the colonists' writings, both public and private. It was a rare newspaper essayist who did not use a Greek or Latin phrase to enhance an argument or embellish a point and who did not employ a classical signature. John Dickinson lived up to his reputation for "Attic eloquence and Roman spirit" by ending each of his *Farmer's Letters* with an appropriate classical quotation. Such classicism was not only a scholarly ornament of educated Americans; it helped to shape their values and their ideals of behavior. "The Choice of Hercules, as engraved by Gribeline in some Editions of Lord Shaftsburys Works," which John Adams proposed to the Continental Congress as a seal commemorating the British evacuation of Boston, was a commonplace of the age. Man was pictured in classical terms struggling

5. Adams to Warren, July 20, 1807, Mass. Hist. Soc., *Collections*, 5th Ser., 4 (1878), 353; Adams to J. H. Tiffany, Apr. 30, 1819, Adams, ed., *Works of John Adams*, X, 378; Adams, entry, Mar. 12, 1774, Butterfield, ed., *Diary of Adams*, II, 93; Adams to Richard Cranch, Aug. 2, 1776, Lyman H. Butterfield *et al.*, eds., *Adams Family Correspondence* (Cambridge, Mass., 1963), II, 74; [Adams], *Thoughts on Government*, in Adams, ed., *Works of John Adams*, IV, 194.

6. [Trenchard and Gordon], *Cato's Letters*, II, 28.

7. Salus Populi [pseud.], "To the People of North-America on the Different Kinds of Government," Peter Force, ed., *American Archives . . .* , 4th Ser. (Washington, 1837–46), V, 182.

between the forces of virtue and vice, reason and passion. Rural life was celebrated not for its wild or natural beauty but for its simplicity and repose to which in Horatian fashion virtuous men could retire after a lifetime of devotion to duty and country. The traits of character most praised were the classical ones—restraint, temperance, fortitude, dignity, and independence. Washington seemed to his contemporaries to fit the ideal perfectly; and someone like Landon Carter could only lament that everyone was not as Washington was, "not so much in quest of praise and emolument to yourself as of real good to your fellow-creatures."[8]

Yet it was not as scholarly embellishment or as a source of values that antiquity was most important to Americans in these revolutionary years. The Americans' compulsive interest in the ancient republics was in fact crucial to their attempt to understand the moral and social basis of politics: "Half our learning is their epitaph." Because this "treading upon the Republican ground of Greece and Rome," as Edmund Pendleton said of the Virginians in the Convention of 1776, had such a direct political purpose, the Americans' cult of antiquity cannot really be separated from their involvement in the English Commonwealth heritage, for the two were inextricably entwined. The classical world had been the main source of inspiration and knowledge for enlightened politicians at least since Machiavelli, and never more so than to the classical republicans and their heirs of the seventeenth and eighteenth centuries. The Americans therefore did not always possess an original or unglossed antiquity; they often saw a refracted image, saw the classical past as the Western world since the Renaissance had seen it. While some Americans did own and read the ancient authors in Latin and Greek, most generally preferred translations, popularizations, and secondary surveys that were often edited and written by radical Whigs—Thomas Gordon's *Sallust* and *Tacitus*, Basil Kennet's *Roman Antiquities*, Walter Moyle's dabblings in antiquity, and Edward Wortley Montagu's *Reflections on the Rise and Fall of the Antient Republicks*.[9]

8. Richard M. Gummere, *The American Colonial Mind and the Classical Tradition: Essays in Comparative Culture* (Cambridge, Mass., 1963), 1–2, 7, 109; Adams to Abigail Adams, Aug. 14, 1776; Butterfield, ed., *Family Correspondence*, II, 96–97; Landon Carter to George Washington, May 9, 1776, Force, ed., *American Archives*, 4th Ser., VI, 390.

9. Thomas Dawes, Jr., *An Oration Delivered March 5, 1781 . . .* (Boston, 1781), Niles, ed., *Principles*, 69; Gummere, *Colonial Mind and Classical Tradition*, 18; Colbourn, *Lamp of Experience*, 22–23, 200–32.

Since the aim of most of these popularizations and translations was didactic, to discover, in Montagu's words, "the principal causes of that degeneracy of manners, which reduc'd those once brave and free people into the most abject slavery," the Americans' view of antiquity was highly selective, focusing on decline and decadence. "The 'moss-grown' columns and broken arches of those once-renowned empires are full with instruction" for a people attempting to rebuild a republican world. The names of the ancient republics—Athens, Lacedaemon, Sparta—had "grown trite by repetition," and none more than Rome. There was nothing startling about Gibbon's choice of subject. "Rome," he wrote in his *Autobiography*, "is familiar to the schoolboy and the statesman."[10] This familiarity was not simply the consequence of Rome's preeminence in the ancient world and its influence on Western culture but was also the result of the peculiar character of the literary legacy Rome had passed on to the modern world, a body of writing that was obsessed with the same questions about degeneracy that fascinated the eighteenth century. Enlightened men everywhere in the eighteenth century found much of what they wanted to know about antiquity from the period that has been called the Roman Enlightenment—the golden age of Latin literature from the breakdown of the Republic in the middle of the first century B.C. to the establishment of the Empire in the middle of the second century A.D. Writing at a time when the greatest days of the Republic were crumbling or already gone, pessimistic Romans—Cicero, Sallust, Tacitus, Plutarch—contrasted the growing corruption and disorder they saw about them with an imagined earlier republican world of ordered simplicity and acadian virtue and sought continually to explain the transformation. It was as if these Latin writers in their literature of critical lamentation and republican nostalgia had spoken directly to the revolutionary concerns of the eighteenth century.[11]

From these kinds of antique writings, filtered and fused into the eighteenth-century Enlightenment, the Americans had learned "the melancholy truth" about the ancient republics "that were once great and illustrious, but are now no more" and had used

10. Edward W. Montagu, *Reflections on the Rise and Fall of the Antient Republicks* . . . (London, 1759), 14; Gibbon quoted in Peter Gay, *The Enlightenment; An Interpretation: The Rise of Modern Paganism* (N. Y., 1966), 95.

11. Bailyn, *Ideological Origins*, 25; Gay, *Enlightenment: Rise of Paganism*, 109. Cf. Harold T. Parker, *The Cult of Antiquity and the French Revolutionaries* (Chicago, 1937), 22–23.

their knowledge in their diagnosis of the ills of the mother country in the 1760's and 1770's. "Similar causes will forever operate like effects in the political, moral, and physical world: those vices which ruined the illustrious republics of Greece, and the mighty commonwealth of Rome, and which are now ruining Great Britain, so late the first kingdom of Europe, must eventually overturn every state, where their deleterious influence is suffered to prevail." The history of antiquity thus became a kind of laboratory in which autopsies of the dead republics would lead to a science of social sickness and health matching the science of the natural world.[12]

It was not the force of arms which made the ancient republics great or which ultimately destroyed them. It was rather the character and spirit of their people. Frugality, industry, temperance, and simplicity—the rustic traits of the sturdy yeoman—were the stuff that made a society strong. The virile martial qualities—the scorn of ease, the contempt of danger, the love of valor—were what made a nation great. The obsessive term was luxury, both a cause and a symptom of social sickness. This luxury, not mere wealth but that "dull . . . animal enjoyment" which left "minds stupified, and bodies enervated, by wallowing for ever in one continual puddle of voluptuousness," was what corrupted a society: the love of refinement, the desire for distinction and elegance eventually weakened a people and left them soft and effeminate, dissipated cowards, unfit and undesiring to serve the state. "Then slumbers that virtuous jealousy of public men and public measures, which was wont to scrutinize not only actions but motives: then nods that active zeal, which, with eagle eye watched, and with nervous arm defended the constitution. . . . Thus, before a nation is completely deprived of freedom, she must be fitted for

12. Austin, *Oration, Delivered March 5, 1778*, Niles, ed., *Principles*, 52; Tudor, *Oration Delivered March 5, 1779*, in *ibid.*, 57. For extended discussions of this biological analogy see John Warren, *An Oration, Delivered July 4th, 1783* . . . (Boston, 1783), and Joseph Huntington, *A Discourse, Adapted to the Present Day, on the Health and Happiness, or Misery and Ruin, of the Body Politic in Similitude of That of the Natural Body* . . . (Hartford, 1781). The fascinating connection between 18th-century medical science and terminology and Enlightenment thought needs full exploration. For one interesting revelation of this connection see David Ramsay's description of his writing the history of "the predisposing causes of the revolution" "in what I call the medical stile." Ramsay to Benjamin Rush, Aug. 6, 1786, Robert L. Brunhouse, ed. "David Ramsay, 1749–1815, Selections from His Writings," American Philosophical Society, *Transactions*, 55 (1965), 105.

slavery by her vices." Republics died not from invasions from without but from decay from within.[13]

Out of their reading of the Latin classics and of the contemporary histories of the ancient world, like Charles Rollin's popular studies, together with diffuse thoughts drawn from the English classical republican heritage, all set within the framework of Enlightenment science, the Americans put together a conception of the ideal republican society—filled, said John Adams, with "all great, manly, and warlike virtues"—that they would have to have if they would sustain their new republics. The nostalgic image of the Roman Republic became a symbol of all their dissatisfactions with the present and their hopes for the future. "I us'd to regret," Charles Lee told Patrick Henry shortly after Independence, "not being thrown into the World in the glorious third or fourth century of the Romans." But now it seemed to Lee and to other American Whigs that these classical republican dreams "at length bid fair for being realiz'd." No one went as far as Lee did in sketching on paper a utopian plan for a republican world, simple and agrarian, free of a debilitating commerce which could only "emasculate the body, narrow the mind, and in fact corrupt every true republican and manly principle." But many in 1776 necessarily shared some of Lee's desires for a spartan egalitarian society where every man was a soldier and master of his own soul and land, the kind of society, like that of ancient Rome, where the people "instructed from early infancy to deem themselves the property of the State . . . were ever ready to sacrifice their concerns to her interests."[14]

3. THE PUBLIC GOOD

The sacrifice of individual interests to the greater good of the whole formed the essence of republicanism and comprehended for Americans the idealistic goal of their Revolution. From this goal flowed all of the Americans' exhortatory literature and all that made their ideology truly revolutionary. This republican

13. Pinkney's Wmsbg. *Va. Gazette*, June 15, 1775; Tudor, *Oration Delivered March 5, 1779*, Niles ed., *Principles*, 57.

14. [Adams], *Thoughts on Government*, Adams, ed., *Works of John Adams*, IV, 199; Lee to Henry, July 29, 1776, *Lee Papers*, II, 177; Lee, A Sketch of a Plan for the Formation of a Military Colony, *ibid.*, III, 323–30; Warren, *Oration, Delivered July 4th, 1783*, 7–8.

ideology both presumed and helped shape the Americans' conception of the way their society and politics should be structured and operated—a vision so divorced from the realities of American society, so contrary to the previous century of American experience, that it alone was enough to make the Revolution one of the great utopian movements of American history. By 1776 the Revolution came to represent a final attempt, perhaps—given the nature of American society—even a desperate attempt, by many Americans to realize the traditional Commonwealth ideal of a corporate society, in which the common good would be the only objective of government.

It is not surprising that the Tory, Jonathan Boucher, in his 1775 sermon, "On Civil Liberty; Passive Obedience, and Non-resistance," should have questioned the belief that the common good was the end of all government, especially the "vague and loose" belief that the common good was simply a matter of "common feelings" and "common consent." For this conviction that "the Liberty and Happiness of the People is confessedly the End of Government," best defined by the people themselves, was central to all reformist thinking in the eighteenth century and had become crucial to most Americans by 1776. "Though," as Jacob Duché, Boucher's immediate antagonist, remarked, "no particular mode of government is pointed out" by scripture, there could be no doubt that the "gospel is directly opposed to every other form than such as has the common good of mankind for its end and aim." It was self-evident, by "both reason and revelation," said Samuel West, that the welfare and safety of the people was "the supreme law of the state,—being the true standard and measure" by which all laws and governmental actions were to be judged. To eighteenth-century American and European radicals alike, living in a world of monarchies, it seemed only too obvious that the great deficiency of existing governments was precisely their sacrificing of the public good to the private greed of small ruling groups. "Strange as it may seem," said Josiah Quincy in 1774, "what the many through successive ages have desired and sought, the few have found means to baffle and defeat."[15]

15. Jonathan Boucher, *A View of the Causes and Consequences of the American Revolution* . . . (London, 1797), 512–14; Charleston, *S.-C. Gazette*, Sept. 26, 1775; Jacob Duché, *The Duty of Standing Fast in Our Liberties* (Phila., 1775), in Frank Moore, ed., *The Patriot Preachers of the American Revolution, 1750–1776* (N. Y., 1862), 81–82; West, *Sermon Preached May 29th, 1776*, Thornton, ed., *Pulpit*, 297; Quincy, *Observations on the Boston Port Bill*, Quincy, *Memoir*, 323.

To make the people's welfare—the public good—the exclusive end of government became for the Americans, as one general put it, their "Polar Star," the central tenet of the Whig faith, shared not only by Hamilton and Paine at opposite ends of the Whig spectrum, but by any American bitterly opposed to a system which held "that a Part is greater than its Whole; or, in other Words, that some Individuals ought to be considered, even to the Destruction of the Community, which they compose."[16] No phrase except "liberty" was invoked more often by the Revolutionaries than "the public good." It expressed the colonists' deepest hatreds of the old order and their most visionary hopes for the new.

> Here Governments their last perfection take.
> Erected only for the People's sake:
> Founded no more on Conquest or in blood,
> But on the basis of the Public Good.
> No contests then shall mad ambition raise,
> No chieftains quarrel for a sprig of praise,
> No thrones shall rise, provoking lawless sway,
> And not a *King* to cloud the blissful day.[17]

From the logic of belief that "all government . . . is or ought to be, calculated for the general good and safety of the community," for which end "the most effectual means that human wisdom hath ever been able to devise, is frequently appealing to the body of the people," followed the Americans' unhesitating adoption of republicanism in 1776. The peculiar excellence of republican government was that it was "wholly characteristical of the purport, matter, or object for which government ought to be instituted." By definition it had no other end than the welfare of the people: *res publica*, the public affairs, or the public good. "The word *republic*," said Thomas Paine, "means the *public good*, or the good of the whole, in contradistinction to the des-

16. Horatio Gates to Jefferson, Feb. 2, 1781, Boyd, ed., *Jefferson Papers*, IV, 502; Cecelia M. Kenyon, "Alexander Hamilton: Rousseau of the Right," *Political Science Quarterly*, 73, (1958), 161–78, and "Where Paine Went Wrong," *American Political Science Review*, 45 (1951), 1086–99; [Landon Carter], *A Letter to the Right Reverend Father in God, the Lord B——p of L——n* (Williamsburg, 1760), quoted in Jack P. Greene, ed., *The Diary of Colonel Landon Carter of Sabine Hall, 1752–1778* (Charlottesville, 1965), I, 30.

17. Trenton *New-Jersey Gazette*, May 20, 1778, in William Nelson *et al.*, eds., *Documents Relating to the Revolutionary History of the State of New Jersey* (*Archives of the State of New Jersey*, 2d Ser.), II, 225. Hereafter cited as *New Jersey Archives*.

potic form, which makes the good of the sovereign, or of one man, the only object of the government." Its most exact English equivalent was commonwealth, by which was meant, as Edmund Pendleton suggested, a state belonging to the whole people rather than the Crown. While several of the new states, as John Adams urged, took this "most consistent style" of commonwealth manfully and explicitly in 1776, all of the states shared in its meaning.[18]

Since in a free government the public good was identical with the people's welfare, a "matter of COMMON FEELING" and founded on the "COMMON CONSENT" of the people, the best way of realizing it in the Whig mind was to allow the people a maximum voice in the government. "That the great body of the people," as even the Tory William Smith of Philadelphia admitted, "can have any interest separate from their country, or (when fairly understood) pursue any other, is not to be imagined," "unless," as John Sullivan said, "we suppose them idiots or self-murderers." Therefore any government which lacked "a proper representation of the people" or was in any way even "independent of the people" was liable to violate the common good and become tyrannical.[19] Most Whigs had little doubt of the people's honesty or even of their ability to discern what was good for themselves. It was a maxim, declared a New York patriot, "that whatever may be the particular opinions of Individuals, the bulk of the people, both mean, and think right." Was there ever any fear, James Burgh had gone so far as to ask, that the people might be "*too free* to consult the general good?" Of course even the most radical English Whigs admitted that the people might sometimes mistake their own interest and might often be unable to effect it even when they did correctly perceive it. Most Americans therefore assumed that the people, in their representational expression of their collective liberty in the houses of representatives, could not run the whole government. "Liberty, though the most essential requisite in government," Richard Price had written, "is not the only one;

18. George Mason, Fairfax Company Paper, June 1775, in Rowland, *Mason*, I, 431; Paine, *Rights of Man*, and *Dissertations on Government* . . . (Phila., 1786), in Foner, ed., *Writings of Paine*, I, 369, II, 372; Pendleton to Jefferson, Aug. 3, 1776, Boyd, ed., *Jefferson Papers*, I, 484–85; Adams to J. D. Sergeant, July 21, 1776, and to Francis Dana, Aug. 16, 1776, Adams, ed., *Works of John Adams*, IX, 425, 429.

19. Duché, *Duty of Standing Fast*, Moore, ed., *Patriot Preachers*, 82; Phila. *Pa. Packet*, Mar. 25, 1776; John Sullivan to Meshech Weare, Dec. 11, 1775, Force, ed., *American Archives*, 4th Ser., IV, 242; West, *Sermon Preached May 29th, 1776*, Thornton, ed., *Pulpit*, 280–81.

wisdom, union, dispatch, secrecy, and vigour are likewise requisite"—qualities best supplied by a magistracy and a senate.[20]

Yet such governors and upper houses, however necessary, must be electively dependent on the people. Republicanism with its elective magistracy would not eliminate the problems of politics and the threat of power, but it did promise a new era of stability and cooperation between rulers and ruled. The chronic divisiveness of colonial politics ("the denominations of WHIG and TORY . . . distinctions that properly belong only to the subjects of Great Britain") would now disappear in the unhindered and engrossing pursuit of only the people's welfare. For decades, and especially in recent years, the Crown's presence in America had played havoc with the colonists' political life and was the real source of that factious behavior of which royal officials had so repeatedly and unjustly accused them. "Every man that has lived any time in America, under regal government, knows what frequent, and almost continual opposition there is between the country interest and those in power." "By keeping clear of British government," the Americans could at last be rid of those "jars and contentions between Governors and Assemblies." By allowing the people to elect their magistracy, republicanism would work to "blend the interests of the people and their rulers" and thus "put down every animosity among the people." In the kind of states where *their governors shall proceed from the midst of them*" the people could be surer that their interests exclusively would be promoted, and therefore in turn would "pay obedience to officers properly appointed" and maintain "no discontents on account of their advancement."[21]

What made the Whig conception of politics and the republican emphasis on the collective welfare of the people comprehensible was the assumption that the people, especially when set against

20. [Philip Livingston], *To the Inhabitants of the City and County of New-York. March 4, 1775* [N. Y., 1775], 1; Burgh, *Disquisitions*, I, 116; Price, *Additional Observations on Civil Liberty*, 8.

21. Boston *Independent Chronicle*, Apr. 27, 1780; Jacob Green, *Observations: On the Reconciliation of Great Britain, and the Colonies* . . . (Phila., 1776), 24; David Ramsay, *An Oration on the Advantages of American Independence* . . . (Charleston, 1778), in Niles, ed., *Principles*, 379; William Henry Drayton, Charges to the Grand Jury, Charleston, Apr. 23, 1776, *ibid.*, 332–33; Purdie's Wmsbg. *Va Gazette*, July 14, 1775. On this crucial need to connect rulers and people see also West, *Sermon Preached May 29, 1776*, *Thornton*, ed., *Pulpit*, 280; Samuel Adams to John Adams, Dec. 8, 1777, Cushing, ed., *Writings of Samuel Adams*, III, 416; Judah Champion, *Christian and Civil Liberty* . . . (Hartford, 1776), 9.

their rulers, were a homogeneous body whose "interests when candidly considered are one." Since everyone in the community was linked organically to everyone else, what was good for the whole community was ultimately good for all the parts. The people were in fact a single organic piece (*"for God hath so tempered the body that there should be no Schism in the body, but that the Members should have the same care for one another"*) with a unitary concern that was the only legitimate objective of governmental policy. This common interest was not, as we might today think of it, simply the sum or consensus of the particular interests that made up the community. It was rather an entity in itself, prior to and distinct from the various private interests of groups and individuals. As Samuel Adams said in 1776, paraphrasing Vattel, the state was "a moral person, having an interest and will of its own."[22] Because politics was conceived to be not the reconciling but the transcending of the different interests of the society in the search for the single common good, the republican state necessarily had to be small in territory and generally similar in interests.[23] Despite sporadic suggestions in the press for "a simple government" of a strong continental congress chosen "by the people, (not by their representatives)," and uniting all the people "in one great republick," few Americans thought that such an extensive continental republic, as distinct from a league of states, was feasible in 1776—however much they may have differed over the desirable strength of the expected confederation.[24]

No one, of course, denied that the community was filled with different, often clashing combinations of interests. But apart from the basic conflict between governors and people these were not to be dignified by their incorporation into formal political theory or into any serious discussion of what ought to be. In light of the assumption that the state was "to be considered as one moral whole" these interests and parties were regarded as aberrations

22. *Result of the Convention of Delegates Holden at Ipswich in the County of Essex* . . . (Newburyport, 1778), in Theophilus Parsons, *Memoir of Theophilus Parsons* (Boston, 1861), 364; Worcester *Mass. Spy*, Sept. 11, 1777; "Candidus," Feb. 3, 1776, Cushing, ed., *Writings of Samuel Adams*, III, 266.
23. [Charles Inglis], *The True Interest of America* . . . (Phila., 1776), 17, 53; Boston *New England Chronicle*, July 4, 1776.
24. "On the Present States of America," Oct. 10, 1776, in Force, ed., *American Archives*, 5th Ser. (Washington, 1848–53), II, 967–69. On the pervasive "belief in and insistence upon the independence of the individual states" in 1776 see Merrill Jensen, *The Articles of Confederation* . . . (Madison, Wis., 1940), 118–19, and below, Chap. IX, Sec. 2.

or perversions, indeed signs of sickness in the body politic.[25] Although some eighteenth-century thinkers were in fact beginning to perceive the inevitability, even the desirability, of faction in a free state,[26] most continued to regard division among the people as "both dangerous and destructive," arising "from false ambition, avarice, or revenge." Men lost control of their basest passions and were unwilling to sacrifice their immediate desires for the corporate good. Hence, "party differences," however much they may infect the society, could never ideally be admitted into the institutions of government, but "would be dropped at the threshold of the state house." The representatives of the people would not act as spokesmen for private and partial interests, but all would be "disinterested men, who could have no interest of their own to seek," and "would employ their whole time for the public good; then there would be but one interest, the good of the people at large."[27]

There was nothing really new about these republican principles; John Winthrop would have found them congenial. In fact, republicanism as the Americans expressed it in 1776 possessed a decidedly reactionary tone. It embodied the ideal of the good society as it had been set forth from antiquity through the eighteenth century. This traditional conception of the organic community was still a cliché, although an increasingly weakening cliché, of the eighteenth century. Rousseau's "general will" was only one brilliant effort among many more pedestrian attempts to discover somehow above all the diverse and selfish wills the one supreme moral good to which all parts of the body politic must surrender. The very fact that the social basis for such a corporate ideal had long been disintegrating, if it ever existed, only accentuated its desirability in American eyes. Despite, or perhaps because of, the persistence of social incoherence and change in the eighteenth century, Americans creating a new society could not conceive of the state in any other terms than organic unity. Al-

25. *Essex Result*, Parsons, *Memoir*, 366. "For every division in any degree, is in a Political, what we call a disease in a Natural Body, which as it weakens its strength, so it tends to its destruction": *Essay upon Government*, 38.

26. John Adams and [Daniel Leonard], *Novanglus and Massachusettensis* (Boston, 1819), 149. See Caroline Robbins, "'Discordant Parties': A Study of the Acceptance of Party by Englishmen," *Pol. Sci. Qtly.*, 73 (1958), 505–29.

27. Phillips Payson, *A Sermon Preached . . . at Boston, May 27, 1778 . . .* (Boston, 1778), Thornton, ed., *Pulpit*, 342; Paine, *Dissertations on Government*, Foner, ed., *Writings of Paine*, II, 409; Boston *Independent Chronicle*, July 10, 1777.

though by mid-century the peculiar Filmerist emphasis on monarchial paternalism was decidedly moribund (despite Boucher's efforts to revive it), the compelling theory of order characteristic of Western thought for centuries was not.[28] Whatever differences may have existed among the Whigs, all those committed to revolution and republicanism in 1776 necessarily shared an essentially similar vision of the corporate commonwealth—a vision of varying distinctness fed by both millennial Christianity and pagan classicism. Enlightened rationalism and evangelical Calvinism were not at odds in 1776; both when interpreted by Whigs placed revolutionary emphasis on the general will of the community and on the responsibility of the collective people to define it. The contracts, balancing mechanisms, and individual rights so much talked of in 1776 were generally regarded as defenses designed to protect a united people against their rulers and not as devices intended to set off parts of the people against the majority. Few Whigs in 1776 were yet theoretically prepared to repudiate the belief in the corporate welfare as the goal of politics or to accept divisiveness and selfishness as the normative behavior of men. The ideal which republicanism was beautifully designed to express was still a harmonious integration of all parts of the community.[29]

Yet ironically it was precisely internal discord and conflict for which republics were most widely known. Throughout history "free republican governments have been objected to, as if exposed to factions from an excess of liberty." But this was because liberty had been misunderstood and falsely equated with licentiousness or the liberty of man in a state of nature which was "a state of war, rapine and murder." True liberty was "natural liberty restrained in such manner, as to render society one great family; where every one must consult his neighbour's happiness, as well as his own." In a republic "each individual gives up all private interest that is

28. For an important study of this theme in English thought see Greenleaf, *Order, Empiricism and Politics*, Chap. II–VII. As American experience indicates, the transition from medieval organicism to modern empiricism may have been neither as rapid nor as sharp as Greenleaf suggests.

29. Cf. Heimert, *Religion and the American Mind*, esp. 351–453. By his strenuous efforts to place the evangelical clergy in the vanguard of the Revolutionary movement, Heimert has exaggerated the uniqueness of the Calvinist emphasis on the communal character and corporate power of the people. Whig thought at the Revolution was much more unified and yet at the same time much more diverse than Heimert's rigid dichotomy between evangelicalism and rationalism would suggest. See below, Chap. III, n. 68.

not consistent with the general good, the interest of the whole body."[30] For the republican patriots of 1776 the commonweal was all-encompassing—a transcendent object with a unique moral worth that made partial considerations fade into insignificance. "Let regard be had only to the good of the whole" was the constant exhortation by publicists and clergy. Ideally, republicanism obliterated the individual. "A Citizen," said Samuel Adams, "owes everything to the Commonwealth." "Every man in a republic," declared Benjamin Rush, "is public property. His time and talents —his youth—his manhood—his old age—nay more, life, all belong to his country." "No man is a true republican," wrote a Pennsylvanian in 1776, "that will not give up his single voice to that of the public."[31]

Individual liberty and the public good were easily reconcilable because the important liberty in the Whig ideology was public or political liberty. In 1776 the solution to the problems of American politics seemed to rest not so much in emphasizing the private rights of individuals against the general will as it did in stressing the public rights of the collective people against the supposed privileged interests of their rulers. "Civil Liberty," as one colonist put it, was not primarily individual; it was "the freedom of bodies politic, or States." Because, as Josiah Quincy said, the people "as a body" were "never interested to injure themselves," and were "uniformly desirous of the general welfare," there could be no real sense of conflict between public and personal liberty.[32] Indeed, the private liberties of individuals depended upon their collective public liberty. "The security to justice," said one American in 1776, "is the political liberty of the State." "In every state or society of men," declared Benjamin Church in 1773, "personal

30. Payson, *Sermon Preached May 27, 1778*, Thornton, ed., *Pulpit*, 332; Nathaniel Whitaker, *An Antidote against Toryism . . .* (Newburyport, 1777), 11; Boston *Continental Journal*, Apr. 9, 1778; Levi Hart, *Liberty Described and Recommended* (Hartford, 1775), 11. "A *people* is travelling fast to destruction, when *individuals* consider *their* interests as distinct from *those of the public*": [Dickinson], *Letters from a Farmer*, Ford, ed., *Writings of Dickinson*, 397.

31. *Essex Result*, Parsons, *Memoir*, 365; Adams to Caleb Davis, Apr. 3, 1781, Cushing, ed., *Writings of Samuel Adams*, IV, 255; Benjamin Rush, "On the Defects of the Confederation" (1787), Dagobert D. Runes, ed., *The Selected Writings of Benjamin Rush* (N. Y., 1947), 31; *Four Letters on Interesting Subjects* (Phila., 1776), 20.

32. Whitaker, *Antidote against Toryism*, 11; Quincy, *Observations on the Boston Port Bill*, Quincy, *Memoir*, 323.

liberty and security must depend upon the collective power of the whole, acting for the general interest." The people were the best asylum for individual rights. "All property," declared Thomas Paine, "is safe under their protection." Government in which the people had a proper share, wrote Richard Price, "therefore, does not *infringe* liberty, but *establish* it. It does not *take away* the rights of mankind, but *protect* and *confirm* them." Whatever conflict existed was due to selfish individuals who asserted privileges against the common interest of the people. The Americans, wrote Landon Carter in 1760, could never allow a minority of individuals to differ from the majority when the very well-being of the society was at stake. "One or a few" could never "be better Judges" of the communal "Good than was the multitude." In truth, the suspension of "Private Justice" or the suppression of minority rights for the sake of the public good was "a Thing absolutely necessary to be done" and "therefore just in itself."[33] Since the American Whigs, like Locke before them, regarded the people as a unitary, property-holding, homogeneous body—not "the vile populace or rabble of the country, nor the cabal of a small number of factious persons, but," said John Adams quoting Pufendorf, "the greater and more judicious part of the subjects, of all ranks"—few found it necessary or even intelligible to work out any theoretical defense of minority rights against the collective power of the majority of the people.[34] Although some Americans, like the Tory Daniel Leonard, were grappling with the problem before the Revolution, charging that the people were the real source of despotism, their arguments were quickly rebuffed by rabid Whigs. In the Whig conception of politics a tyranny by the people was theoretically inconceivable, because the power held by the people was liberty, whose abuse could only be licentiousness or anarchy, not tyranny. As John Adams indignantly pointed out, the idea of the public liberty's being tyran-

33. "Loose Thoughts on Government" (1776), Force, ed., *American Archives*, 4th Ser., VI, 730; Church, *Oration Delivered March Fifth, 1773*, in Niles, ed., *Principles*, 35–36; "Forester," May 9, 1776, Force, ed., *American Archives*, 4th Ser., VI, 394–95; Price, *Additional Observations on Civil Liberty*, 13; [Carter], *Letter to B——p of L——n*, quoted in Greene, ed., *Diary of Carter*, I, 31.
34. [Adams], "Novanglus," Adams, ed., *Works of John Adams*, IV, 82. On the unity of property and people see C. B. Macpherson, *Political Theory of Possessive Individualism* (Oxford, 1962), 107–36, 222–29; and John Locke, *Two Treatises of Government*, ed. Peter Laslett, rev. ed. (N. Y., 1965), 125–26. "The distinction between personal and political rights is a new invention": James Otis, *A Vindication of the British Colonies . . .* (Boston, 1765), in Bailyn, ed., *Pamphlets*, I, 558.

nical was illogical: "a democratical despotism is a contradiction in terms."[35]

Thus in the minds of most Whigs in 1776 individual rights, even the basic civil liberties that we consider so crucial, possessed little of their modern theoretical relevance when set against the will of the people.[36] This is why, for example, throughout the eighteenth century the Americans could contend for the broadest freedom of speech against the magistracy, while at the same time punishing with a severe strictness any seditious libels against the representatives of the people in the colonial assemblies.[37] Anyone who tried to speak against the interests of the people "should be held in execration. . . . Every word, that tends to weaken the hands of the people is a crime of devilish dye"; indeed, "it is the *unpardonable Sin* in politics." Thus it was "no *Loss of Liberty*, that court-minions can complain of, when they are silenced. No man has a right to say a word, which may lame the liberties of his country." It was conceivable to protect the common law liberties of the people against their rulers, but hardly against the people themselves. "For who could be more free than the People who representatively exercise supreme Power over themselves?"[38]

This same celebration of the public welfare and the safety of the people also justified the very severe restrictions put on private interests and rights throughout the Revolutionary crisis. The coercion and intimidation used by public and quasi-public bodies, conventions and committees, against various individuals and minority groups, the extent of which has never been fully appreciated, was completely sanctioned by these classical Whig beliefs. As David Ramsay later recalled, "the power of these bodies was undefined; but by common consent it was comprehended in the old Roman maxim: 'To take care that the commonwealth should

35. [Adams], "Novanglus," Adams, ed., *Works of John Adams*, IV, 79. In 1775 it seemed to the Tory-minded Robert Beverley that "the Privileges of Freedom" and "the Spirit of Persecution" were "natural Enemies of each other, but by a strange Perversion of Nature and Reason *now* constantly attendant on each other." Robert M. Calhoon, ed., " 'A Sorrowful Spectator of These Tumultuous Times': Robert Beverley Describes the Coming of the Revolution," *Virginia Magazine of History and Biography*, 73 (1965), 51.

36. "Whatever Rights those Laws give any private person, or persons, they are naturally suppos'd to be granted only so far, as they are consisting with the security of the Public": *Essay upon Government*, 49.

37. See Leonard W. Levy, "Did the Zenger Case Really Matter? Freedom of the Press in Colonial New York," *Wm. and Mary Qtly.*, 3d Ser., 17 (1960), 35–50; Alexander, *Brief Narrative*, ed. Katz, 30–31.

38. Charleston *S.-C. Gazette*, Dec. 19, 1774, Sept. 26, 1775.

receive no damage.' "³⁹ But it was not simply a matter of invoking the Ciceronian maxim, *Salus Populi suprema Lex est.* The extensive mercantilist regulation of the economy, the numerous attempts in the early years of the war to suppress prices, control wages, and prevent monopolies, reaching from the Continental Congress down through the states to counties and towns, was in no way inconsistent with the spirit of '76, but in fact was ideally expressive of what republicanism meant.⁴⁰ In the minds of the most devoted Commonwealthmen it was the duty of a republic to control "the selfishness of mankind . . . ; for liberty consists not in the permission to distress fellow citizens, by extorting extravagant advantages from them, in matters of commerce or otherwise."⁴¹ Because it was commonly understood that "the exorbitant wealth of individuals" had a "most baneful influence" on the maintenance of republican governments and "therefore should be carefully guarded against," some Whigs were even willing to go so far as to advocate agrarian legislation limiting the amount of property an individual could hold and "sumptuary laws against luxury, plays, etc. and extravagant expenses in dress, diet, and the like."⁴²

Even at the beginning, however, there were some good Whigs who perceived the inherent conflict between individual liberty and traditional republican theory. Ancient Sparta, William Moore Smith told the members of the Continental Congress in the spring of 1775, had demonstrated the problem. Knowing that luxury was the great enemy of republicanism and liberty, Lycurgus had sought to avoid the evil by eliminating wealth itself. But

39. David Ramsay, *The History of the Revolution of South Carolina* (Trenton, N. J., 1785), I, 251.

40. For the consuming majoritarian character of Revolutionary thought see Bernard Wishy, "John Locke and the Spirit of '76," *Pol. Sci. Qtly.*, 73 (1958), 413–25. On the mercantilist regulation see Allan Nevins, *The American States during and after the Revolution, 1775–1789* (N. Y., 1924), 64–65, 77; Richard B. Morris, "Labor and Mercantilism in the Revolutionary Era," in Richard B. Morris, ed., *The Era of the American Revolution* (N. Y., 1939), 76–139; Oscar and Mary F. Handlin, "Revolutionary Economic Policy in Massachusetts," *Wm. and Mary Qtly.*, 3d Ser., 4 (1947), 3–26.

41. *Charleston S.-C. and American Gazette*, Aug. 14–21, 1776. For other examples of the Whigs' denial that liberty meant "that in a state or society you had a right to do as you pleased," see Cushing, ed., *Writings of Samuel Adams*, II, 5; *Four Letters*, 10; Zabdiel Adams, *A Sermon Preached . . . May 29, 1782 . . .* [Boston, 1782], 16, 17.

42. Payson, *Sermon Preached May 27, 1778*, Thornton, ed., *Pulpit*, 338; Boston *Independent Chronicle*, Mar. 6, 1777. See also Boyd, ed., *Jefferson Papers*, VI, 290; Adams, ed., *Works of John Adams*, IV, 199, IX, 375.

in doing so he undermined the very basis of freedom. "He seems not to have reflected that there can be no true liberty without security of property; and where property is secure, industry begets wealth; and wealth is often productive of a train of evils naturally destructive to virtue and freedom!" "Here, then," said Smith, "is a sad dilemma in politics." If the people "exclude *wealth*, it must be by regulations intrenching too far upon civil *liberty*." But if wealth is allowed to flourish, "the syren *luxury*" soon follows at its heels and gradually contaminates the whole society. "What is to be done in this case?" Must the society, "to secure the first of blessings, *liberty*," strangle wealth, the first offspring of liberty, in its birth and thus in effect destroy liberty as well? "Or, is there no proper use of *wealth* and *civil happiness*, the genuine descendants of *civil liberty*, without abusing them to the nourishment of *luxury* and *corruption*?" Smith, like other Whigs in 1776, thought there was an answer to the dilemma in the more enlightened policy and "purer system of *religion*" of this modern age—"to regulate the use of wealth, but not to exclude it."

The dilemma was not new, but was actually the central issue Americans had wrestled with since the seventeenth century. Nearly every intellectual movement from Puritanism to Quakerism to Arminianism had struggled with the problems involved in the social maturation of the American body politic, in a continuing effort to find the means of controlling the amassing and expenditure of men's wealth without doing violence to their freedom. American intellectual life was an intensive search for an ever-renewed compression of tensions for the aspiring Americans who were allowed prosperity but denied luxury. The republicanism of 1776 actually represented a new, more secular version of this same steel spring, a new mode of confronting and resisting the temptations and luxury of the world, a new social restraint to which, said Smith, "all systems of education, all laws, all the efforts of patriotism, ought to be directed."[43]

4. The Need for Virtue

Perhaps everyone in the eighteenth century could have agreed that in theory no state was more beautiful than a republic, whose whole object by definition was the good of the people. Yet

43. Phila. *Pa. Packet*, May 29, 1775.

everyone also knew that it was a fragile beauty indeed. It was axiomatic that no society could hold together without the obedience of its members to the legally constituted authority. In a monarchy the complicated texture of the society, "the magnificence, costly equipage and dazzling splendors" lavished on the prince, the innumerable titles, the degrees and subordination of ranks, the pervading sense of honor, the "multitude of criminal laws, with severe penalties," the very vigor of the unitary authority often with the aid of a standing army and an established religious hierarchy, all worked to maintain public order, even though in the eyes of a good Commonwealthman it was an order built on show, where "respect and obedience" were derived "only from the passion of fear." But in a republic which possessed none of this complicated social texture, where the elected rulers were merely "in fact the servants of the public" and known by all "to be but men," and where the people themselves shared in a large measure of the governing—in such a state, order, if there was to be any, must come from below.[44] The very greatness of republicanism, its utter dependence on the people, was at the same time its source of weakness. In a republic there was no place for fear; there could be no sustained coercion from above. The state, like no other, rested on the consent of the governed freely given and not compelled. In a free government the laws, as the American clergy never tired of repeating, had to be obeyed by the people for conscience's sake, not for wrath's.

As Jonathan Boucher warned, by resting the whole structure of government on the unmitigated willingness of the people to obey, the Americans were making a truly revolutionary transformation in the structure of authority.[45] In shrill and despairing pamphlets the Tories insisted that the Whig ideas were undermining the very principle of order. If respect and obedience to the established governments were refused and if republicanism were adopted, then, admonished Thomas Bradbury Chandler, "the bands of society would be dissolved, the harmony of the world confounded, and the order of nature subverted." The principles of the Revolutionaries, said Boucher, were directed "clearly and literally against *authority*." They were destroying "not only all authority over us as it now exists, but any and all that it is

44. [Mather], *America's Appeal*, 67, 68; Duché, *Duty of Standing Fast*, Moore, ed., *Patriot Preachers*, 82.
45. Boucher, *View of the Causes*, 520–21.

possible to constitute." The Tory logic was indeed frightening.
Not only was the rebellion rupturing the people's habitual obedience to the constituted government, but by the establishment of
republicanism the Whigs were also founding their new governments solely on the people's voluntary acquiescence. And, as
Blackstone had pointed out, "obedience is an empty name, if
every individual has a right to decide how far he himself shall
obey."[46]

The Whigs were well aware of the hazards involved in the
revolution they were attempting. Many knew with Hamilton that
when the people were "loosened from their attachment to ancient
establishments" they were apt "to grow giddy" and "more or less
to run into anarchy." Even Samuel Adams warned in 1775 that
"there may be Danger of Errors on the Side of *the People*." Sens-
ing the risk of licentiousness in the throwing off of British authority, many Whig leaders urged the people from the outset
to "have their hearts and hands with the magistrates," for as long
as their appointed rulers acted lawfully and for the public good
"they are bound to obey them." But despite Tory charges that
the Whig principles were "cutting asunder the sinews of government, and breaking in pieces the ligament of social life," the
Americans in 1776 did not regard their republican beliefs as inherently anti-authoritarian.[47] The Revolution was designed to
change the flow of authority—indeed the structure of politics
as the colonists had known it—but it was in no way intended to
do away with the principle of authority itself. "There must be,"
said John Adams in 1776, "a Decency, and Respect, and Veneration introduced for Persons in Authority, of every Rank, or We
are undone." The people would naturally be more willing to obey
their new republican rulers; for now "love and not fear will become the spring of their obedience." The elected republican magistrate would be distinguished not by titles or connections but
by his own inherent worth and would necessarily "know no good,

46. [Thomas B. Chandler], *A Friendly Address to All Reasonable Americans*
. . . (N. Y., 1774), 5; Boucher, *View of the Causes*, 552–53; William Blackstone,
Commentaries on the Laws of England (London, 1765–69), I, 251.

47. Hamilton to John Jay, Nov. 26, 1775, Syrett and Cooke, eds., *Hamilton
Papers*, I, 176–77; Samuel Adams to James Warren, Dec. 5, 1775, Worthington C.
Ford, ed., *Warren-Adams Letters* . . . (Mass. Hist. Soc., *Collections*, 72–73 [1917,
1925]), I, 192; Foster, *Short Essay on Civil Government*, 40; West, *Sermon
Preached May 29th, 1776*, Thornton, ed., *Pulpit*, 276; John Adams, quoting
"Massachusettensis" (Daniel Leonard), Adams, ed., *Works of John Adams*,
IV, 75.

separate from that of his subjects."[48] But such a change in the
nature of authority and the magistracy, the Whigs realized, only
mitigated the problem of obedience in a republican system. The
people themselves must change as well.

In a monarchy each man's desire to do what was right in his
own eyes could be restrained by fear or force. In a republic,
however, each man must somehow be persuaded to submerge his
personal wants into the greater good of the whole. This willingness of the individual to sacrifice his private interests for the good
of the community—such patriotism or love of country—the eighteenth century termed "public virtue." A republic was such a
delicate polity precisely because it demanded an extraordinary
moral character in the people. Every state in which the people
participated needed a degree of virtue; but a republic which rested
solely on the people absolutely required it. Although a particular
structural arrangement of the government in a republic might
temper the necessity for public virtue, ultimately "no model of
government whatever can equal the importance of this principle,
nor afford proper safety and security without it." "Without some
portion of this generous principle, anarchy and confusion would
immediately ensue, the jarring interests of individuals, regarding
themselves only, and indifferent to the welfare of others, would
still further heighten the distressing scene, and with the assistance
of the selfish passions, it would end in the ruin and subversion of
the state." The eighteenth-century mind was thoroughly convinced that a popularly based government "cannot be supported
without *Virtue*." Only with a public-spirited, self-sacrificing
people could the authority of a popularly elected ruler be obeyed,
but "more by the virtue of the people, than by the terror of his
power." Because virtue was truly the lifeblood of the republic,
the thoughts and hopes surrounding this concept of public spirit
gave the Revolution its socially radical character—an expected
alteration in the very behavior of the people, "laying the foundation in a constitution, not without or over, but within the subjects."[49]

This public virtue, "this endearing and benevolent passion,"

48. Adams to James Warren, Apr. 22, 1776, Ford, ed., *Warren-Adams Letters*,
I, 234; [Mather], *America's Appeal*, 68.
49. Payson, *Sermon Preached May 27, 1778*, Thornton, ed., *Pulpit*, 337; Jonathan Mason, Jr., *Oration Delivered March 5, 1780* . . . (Boston, 1780), in Niles,
ed., *Principles*, 62; Williams, *Discourse on the Love of Our Country*, 13; [Math-
er], *America's Appeal*, 68.

was "the noblest which can be displayed" and represented all that men of the eighteenth century sought in social behavior. "Its grand source" lay in the attitudes and actions of the individuals who made up the society, "in that charity which forms every social connection."⁵⁰ In other words, public virtue, the willingness of the people to surrender all, even their lives, for the good of the state, was primarily the consequence of men's individual private virtues. While some men of the eighteenth century could see public virtue arising out of the individual's pride and need for approbation, few endorsed Mandeville's paradoxical view that private vices produced public virtue.⁵¹ For most Americans in 1776 vicious behavior by an individual could have only disastrous results for the community. A man racked by the selfish passions of greed, envy, and hate lost his conception of order; "his sense of a connection with the *general* system—his benevolence—his desire and freedom of *doing good*, ceased." It seemed obvious that a republican society could not "be maintained without justice, benevolence and the social virtues." Since at least the seventeenth century, enlightened intellectuals had been fascinated with the attempt to replace the fear of the hereafter as the basis for morality with a more natural scientific psychology. The Earl of Shaftesbury in particular had tried to convince men of the exquisite happiness and pleasure that would flow from self-sacrifice and doing good. Somehow, as a Boston writer argued in the manner of Francis Hutcheson, the individual's widening and traditionally weakening circles of love—from himself to his family to the community—must be broken into; men must be convinced that their fullest satisfaction would come from the subordination of their individual loves to the greater good of the whole. It was man's duty and interest to be benevolent. "The happiness of every individual" depended "on the happiness of society: It follows, that the practice of all the social virtues is the law of our nature, and the law of our nature is the law of God." "Public good is not a term opposed to the good of individuals; on the contrary, it is the good of every individual collected." "The public good is, as it were, a common bank in which every individual has his respective share; and consequently whatever damage that sustains the individual unavoidably partake of that calamity." Once men correctly perceived their relation to the commonwealth they would never

50. Pinkney's Wmsbg. *Va. Gazette*, Feb. 16, 1775.
51. Lovejoy, *Reflections on Human Nature*, Sec. V.

injure what was really their personal interest to protect and sustain.[52]

5. Equality

That the Americans would come to perceive correctly their relation to the state was not simply a matter of faith. The revolutionary change in the structure of political authority involved in their adoption of republicanism was to be matched and indeed ultimately sustained by a basic transformation of their social structure. Henceforth their society would be governed, as it had not been in the past, by the principle of equality—a principle central to republican thinking, the very "life and soul," said David Ramsay, of republicanism.[53]

The doctrine possessed an inherent ambivalence: on one hand it stressed equality of opportunity which implied social differences and distinctions; on the other hand it emphasized equality of condition which denied these same social differences and distinctions. These two meanings were intertwined in the Americans' use of equality and it is difficult to separate them. Many might agree that "if there could be something like an equality of estate and property, it would tend much to preserve civil liberty," since, as everyone knew, "Luxury is always proportional to the inequality of fortune." Yet despite some sporadic suggestions for leveling legislation, most Whigs generally "acknowledged" that it was "a difficult matter to secure a state from evils and mischiefs from . . . wealth and riches." A real equality just "cannot be expected."[54]

Equality was thus not directly conceived of by most Americans in 1776, including even a devout republican like Samuel Adams, as a social leveling; it would not mean, as Thomas Shippen em-

52. Samuel Magaw, *A Discourse Preached . . . on Sunday, October 8th, 1775* (Phila., 1775), 7; Payson, *Sermon Preached May 27, 1778*, Thornton, ed., *Pulpit*, 338; Boston *Independent Chronicle*, Dec. 4, 1777; Paine, *Dissertations on Government*, Foner, ed., *Writings of Paine*, II, 372; Hurt, *Love of Our Country*, 10.
53. Ramsay, *Oration on Advantages of American Independence*, Niles, ed., *Principles*, 375.
54. Chatham *New-Jersey Journal*, May 10, 1780, in Nelson *et al.*, eds., *New Jersey Archives*, 2d Ser., IV, 366; Warren, *Oration, Delivered July 4th, 1783*, 11, quoting Montesquieu; Payson, *Sermon Preached May 27, 1778*, Thornton, ed., *Pulpit*, 338; Chatham *New-Jersey Journal*, May 10, 1780, in Nelson *et al.*, eds., *New Jersey Archives*, 2d Ser., IV, 366.

phasized, the destruction of "the necessary subordination."
Rather it was considered to be an "equality, which is adverse to
every species of subordination beside that which arises from the
difference of capacity, disposition, and virtue." By republicanism
the Americans meant only to change the origin of social and political preeminence, not to do away with such preeminence altogether. "In monarchies," commented David Ramsay, "favor is
the source of preferment; but, in our new forms of government,
no one can command the suffrages of the people, unless by his
superior merit and capacity." In a republican system only talent
would matter. It was now possible "that even the reins of state
may be held by the son of the poorest man, if possessed of abilities
equal to the important station." The ideal, especially in the southern colonies, was the creation and maintenance of a truly natural
aristocracy, based on virtue, temperance, independence, and devotion to the commonwealth. It meant, as John Adams excitedly
put it, that in the choice of rulers "Capacity, Spirit and Zeal in
the Cause, supply the Place of Fortune, Family, and every other
Consideration, which used to have Weight with Mankind." The
republican society, said Charles Lee, would still possess "honour,
property and military glories," but they now would "be obtain'd
without court favour, or the rascally talents of servility." Only
such an egalitarian society, declared young John Laurens, the son
of the famous Charleston merchant, could permit "the fullest
scope for ambition directed in its proper channel, in the only
channel in which it ought to be allowed, . . . for the advancement
of public good,"[55]

Certainly most Revolutionaries had no intention of destroying
the gradations of the social hierarchy by the introduction of republicanism. The Livingstons of New York, for example, were
as acutely conscious of degrees of rank and as sensitive to the
slightest social insult as any family in America; yet, much to the
anger and confusion of William Smith, they took the transformation to republicanism in stride. Smith in frustration pleaded with

55. *Boston Gazette*, Jan. 21, 1771, Cushing, ed., *Writings of Samuel Adams*, II,
142–53; "Loose Thoughts on Government" (1776), Force, ed., *American Archives*, 4th Ser., VI, 730; Ramsay, *Oration on Advantages of American Independence*, Niles, ed., *Principles*, 377, 375; Adams to Abigail Adams, July 10, 1776,
Butterfield, ed., *Family Correspondence*, II, 42; Lee to Patrick Henry, July 29,
1776, *Lee Papers*, II, 177; Laurens quoted in George C. Rogers, Jr., *Evolution of
a Federalist: William Loughton Smith of Charleston, 1758–1812* (Columbia, S. C.,
1962), 79.

them to recognize the consequences of republicanism: "that there would soon be Land Tax and no Room for an Aristocracy." But they only laughed at him and predicted that he would eventually become "a Republican too." Amazingly, Smith noted, the Livingstons "seemed to be reconciled to every Thing" that had been done.[56] Yet Smith should have realized that the only aristocrats the Livingstons expected to see destroyed were those like the De Lanceys—parasitic sycophants of the Crown. The Livingstons, after all, had always been true Whigs, the spokesmen for and defenders of the people.

Even the most radical republicans in 1776 admitted the inevitability of all natural distinctions: weak and strong, wise and foolish—and even of incidental distinctions: rich and poor, learned and unlearned. Yet, of course, in a truly republican society the artificial subsidiary distinctions would never be extreme, not as long as they were based solely on natural distinctions. It was widely believed that equality of opportunity would necessarily result in a rough equality of station, that as long as the social channels of ascent and descent were kept open it would be impossible for any artificial aristocrats or overgrown rich men to maintain themselves for long. With social movement founded only on merit, no distinctions could have time to harden. Since, as Landon Carter said, "Subjects have no Pretence, one more than another," republican laws against entail, primogeniture, and in some states, monopolies, would prevent the perpetuation of privilege and the consequent stifling of talent.[57] And projected public educational systems would open up the advantages of learning and advancement to all.[58]

Great consequences were expected to flow from such an egalitarian society. If every man realized that his associations with

56. William Smith, entry, Dec. 25, 1777, William H. W. Sabine, ed., *Historical Memoirs from 12 July 1776 to 25 July 1778 of William Smith* (N. Y., 1958), 278.
57. Phila. *Pa. Journal*, Mar. 13, 1776; Carter quoted in Greene, ed., *Diary of Carter*, I, 32. See Dumas Malone, *Jefferson the Virginian* (Boston, 1948), 252–57; Nevins, *American States*, 441–45. For the provisions of the Revolutionary constitutions directed against privilege, see Pa. Cons. (1776), Sec. 37; N. C. Decl. of Rts. (1776), XXII, XXIII; N. C. Cons. (1776), XLIII; Ga. Cons. (1777), Art. LI; Maryland Decl. of Rts. (1776), XXXIX, XL. The state constitutions can most conveniently be found in Francis N. Thorpe, ed., *The Federal and State Constitutions . . .* (Washington, 1909).
58. Malone, *Jefferson the Virginian*, 280–85; Nevins, *American States*, 465–69. For the educational provisions in the state constitutions see Pa. Cons. (1776), Sec. 44; N. C. Cons. (1776), XLI; Ga. Cons. (1777), Art. LIV; Mass. Cons. (1780), Chap. V, Sec. II; N. H. Cons. (1784).

other men and the state depended solely on his merit, then, as former Massachusetts Governor Thomas Pownall told the Americans, there would be an end to the jealousy and the contentions for "unequal Dominion" that had beset communities from time immemorial. Indeed, equality represented the social source from which the anticipated harmony and public virtue of the New World would flow. "It is this principle of equality . . . ," wrote one Virginian in 1776, "which alone can inspire and preserve the virtue of its members, by placing them in a relation to the publick and to their fellow-citizens, which has a tendency to engage the heart and affections to both."[59]

It was a beautiful but ambiguous ideal. The Revolutionaries who hoped for so much from equality assumed that republican America would be a community where none would be too rich or too poor, and yet at the same time believed that men would readily accede to such distinctions as emerged as long as they were fairly earned. But ironically their ideal contained the sources of the very bitterness and envy it was designed to eliminate. For if the promised equality was the kind in which "one should consider himself as good a man as another, and not be brow beaten or intimidated by riches or supposed superiority," then their new republican society would be no different from that in which they had lived, and the Revolution would have failed to end precisely what it was supposed to end.[60] Indeed, although few Americans could admit it in 1776, it was the very prevalence of this ambivalent attitude toward equality that had been at the root of much of their squabbling during the eighteenth century.

By the middle of the eighteenth century the peculiarities of social development in the New World had created an extraordinary society, remarkably equal yet simultaneously unequal, a society so contradictory in its nature that it left contemporaries puzzled and later historians divided.[61] It was, as many observers noted, a society strangely in conflict with itself. On one hand,

59. Thomas Pownall, *A Memorial Addressed to the Sovereigns of America* (London, 1783), 21–22; "Loose Thoughts on Government," Force, ed., *American Archives*, 4th Ser., VI, 730. For the social benefits of equality see also [Adams], *Thoughts on Government*, Adams, ed., *Works of John Adams*, IV, 199–200; Dawes, *Oration Delivered March 5th 1781*, Niles, ed., *Principles*, 68.

60. Chatham *New-Jersey Journal*, May 10, 1780, Nelson *et al.*, eds., *New Jersey Archives*, 2d Ser., IV, 366.

61. Jackson T. Main, *The Social Structure of Revolutionary America* (Princeton, 1965), 43; Robert E. and B. Katherine Brown, *Virginia, 1705–1786: Democracy or Aristocracy?* (East Lansing, Mich., 1964), 33, 36.

social distinctions and symbols of status were highly respected and intensely coveted, indeed, said one witness, even more greedily than by the English themselves. Americans, it seemed, were in "one continued Race: in which everyone is endeavoring to distance all behind him; and to overtake or pass by, all before him."[62] Yet, on the other hand, Americans found all of these displays of superiority of status particularly detestable, in fact "more odious than in any other country."[63] Men in both northern and southern colonies, but particularly in New England, repeatedly expressed their disgust with the "certain Airs of Wisdom and superiority" and the "fribbling Affectation of Politeness," of those groups and families, particularly those "insolent minions" surrounding the royal governors. "The insults they, without any provocation under Heaven, offer to every person who passes within their reach, are insufferable."[64]

Such conflict was not simply social; it was often intensely personal: the simultaneous hunger for and hatred of social pretension and distinction could be agonizingly combined in the same persons. Although, as Jefferson later reminded Joel Barlow, "A great deal of the knolege of things [about the Revolution] is not on paper but only within ourselves," some of this personal tension, some of what John Adams called "the secret Springs of this surprizing Revolution," was occasionally revealed in writing.[65] John Dickinson, like Thomas Shippen a generation later, was thoroughly disgusted with the corrupt and foppish nobility he saw in his travels abroad; yet at the same time he, like Shippen, "could not forbear looking on them with veneration." The parvenu minister, Jonathan Mayhew, who had risen from the wilds of Martha's

62. William Eddis, *Letters from America, Historical and Descriptive . . . from 1769, to 1777, Inclusive* (London, 1792), 106, 112–13; Charleston *S.-C. Gazette*, Mar. 1, 1773, quoted in Carl Bridenbaugh, *Myths and Realities: Societies of the Colonial South* (N. Y., 1963), 115. On the eve of the Revolution the competition among the elite for recognition by the governors had become so keen that Joseph Edmundson, the Mowbray herald extraordinary of the English College of Arms, was required to prepare "Rules of Precedency" in which the precise social position of the various officials in the colonies was laid down. Purdie and Dixon's Wmsbg. *Va. Gazette*, May 26, 1774.

63. Letter of John Chalmers, Aug. 20, 1780, "Aspinwall Papers," Mass. Hist. Soc., *Collections*, 4th Ser., 10 (1871), 796. For a similar observation see [Samuel Peters], *A General History of Connecticut . . .*, 2d ed. (London, 1782), 118–20.

64. Butterfield, ed., *Diary of Adams*, I, 250, 358, also 293–94, 355; Pinkney's Wmsbg. *Va. Gazette*, Oct. 19, 1775.

65. Jefferson to Barlow, May 3, 1802, Boyd, ed., *Jefferson Papers*, I, vii; Adams to Abigail Adams, July 10, 1776, Butterfield, ed., *Family Correspondence*, II, 43.

Vineyard to the richest parish in Boston, remained throughout his life a tortured man, garishly displaying his acquired status and boasting of the wealth of his mercantile acquaintances, while simultaneously defending his rankling social obscurity by preferring to be the poor son of a good man than the rich son of a sycophant and flatterer.[66] A New England lawyer and a Virginia planter both could fill their diaries with their private struggles between the attractions and repulsions of the world of prestige and social refinement.[67] This kind of tension and ambivalence of attitude, when widespread, made for a painful disjunction of values and a highly unstable social situation, both of which the ideology of republicanism was designed to mitigate.

6. WHIG RESENTMENT

The American Revolution was actually many revolutions at once, the product of a complicated culmination of many diverse personal grievances and social strains, ranging from land pressures in Connecticut to increasing indebtedness in Virginia.[68] All the colonies, said John Adams in 1776, "differed in Religion, Laws, Customs, and Manners, yet in the great Essentials of Society and Government, they are all alike."[69] What helped to make them alike, what brought together the various endemic strains and focused them, and what in fact worked to transform highly unstable local situations into a continental explosion was the remotely rooted and awkwardly imposed imperial system. Since the provincial governors, and ultimately the distant authority of the English Crown, were the principal source of power and prestige

66. H. Trevor Colbourn, ed., "A Pennsylvania Farmer at the Court of King George: John Dickinson's London Letters, 1754–1756," *Pennsylvania Magazine of History and Biography*, 86 (1962), 259; Charles W. Akers, *Called unto Liberty: A Life of Jonathan Mayhew, 1720–1766* (Cambridge, 1964), 109, 132, 147, 163, 193.

67. Bernard Bailyn, "Butterfield's Adams: Notes for a Sketch," *Wm. and Mary Qtly.*, 3d Ser., 19 (1962), 237–56; Greene, ed., *Diary of Carter*, I, 3–61. On the creative aspects of this unsettling cultural provinciality see John Clive and Bernard Bailyn, "England's Cultural Provinces: Scotland and America," *Wm. and Mary Qtly.*, 3d Ser., 9 (1954), 200–13.

68. See Forrest McDonald, *E Pluribus Unum: The Formation of the American Republic, 1776–1790* (Boston, 1965), 108–09; Emory G. Evans, "Planter Indebtedness and the Coming of the Revolution in Virginia," *Wm. and Mary Qtly.*, 3d Ser., 19 (1962), 511–33.

69. Adams to Abigail Adams, July 10, 1776, Butterfield, ed., *Family Correspondence*, II, 43.

in the society—of preferment and office, of contracts and favors, of support for Anglican orthodoxy, and even of standards of social and cultural refinement—they inevitably had become the focal points for both aspiration and dissatisfaction among the colonists. The resultant political and social divisions were generally not based on class distinctions; indeed they were fomented by feelings of similarity, not difference. The Pinckneys and Leighs of South Carolina, the Carrolls and Dulanys of Maryland, the Livingstons and De Lanceys of New York, or even the Otises and Hutchinsons of Massachusetts scarcely represented distinct social classes. Because the various groups and factions were held together largely by personal and family ties to particular men of influence, politics was very fractionalized and personal. As Charles Carroll told his father in 1763: "Tis impossible for all men to be in place, and those who are out will grumble and strive to thrust themselves in."[70] As long as politics remained such a highly personal business, essentially involving bitter rivalry among small elite groups for the rewards of state authority, wealth, power, and prestige, the Whig distinction between country and court, legislature and executive, people and rulers, remained a meaningful conception for describing American politics.

However, despite the elitist nature of American politics, larger interest groups within the population, both economic and religious, had entered politics sporadically throughout the eighteenth century to mitigate a specific threat or need. By the middle of the century there were increasing signs, even in so stable a colony as Virginia, that more and more groups, with more broadly based grievances and more deeply rooted interests than those of the dominating families, were seeking under the prodding of popular spokesmen a larger share in the wielding of political authority, a process that would in time work to shape a fundamentally new conception of American politics.[71] "Family-Interests," like the

70. Charles Carroll to his father, June 14, 1763, "Extracts from the Carroll Papers," *Md. Hist. Mag.*, 11 (1916), 337.
71. Note the observation in 1742 of Governor William Shirley of Massachusetts: the people "have it in their power upon an extraordinary Emergency to double and almost treble their numbers, which they would not fail to do, if they should be desirous of disputing any point with his Majesty's Governour, which they might suspect their ordinary Members would not carry against his Influence in the House." *Acts and Resolves, Public and Private of the Province of Massachusetts Bay* . . . (Boston, 1878), III, 70. On the changing nature of politics in Virginia see Gordon S. Wood, "Rhetoric and Reality in the American Revolution," *Wm. and Mary Qtly.*, 3d Ser., 23 (1966), 27–28.

Livingstons and De Lanceys in New York, observed Ambrose Serle in 1776, "have been long in a gradual Decay; and perhaps a new arrangement of political affairs may leave them wholly extinct." Yet by freezing factional politics ("the Guelphs and Gibellines") around the issue of British authority, the controversy with the mother country at first tended to obscure these developments and to drown out the quarrels Americans had among themselves. British policy and the Whig ideology worked in tandem to blur America's internal jealousies, jealousies between North and South, between city and country, and "jealousies naturally arising from the variety of private interests in the Planter, the Merchant, and the Mechanic." For a moment in 1774–76 the imperial contest absorbed and polarized the various differing groups as never before in the eighteenth century and made the Americans a remarkably united people. As Lieutenant-Governor William Bull of South Carolina saw, by 1774 the English government had lost all its power to exploit these different interests by "design." The best it could do now was to allow "chance" to "occasion distrust, disunion, confusion, and at last a wish to return to the old established condition of government." Any hint of British "design" would only "put the discontented up on their guard, and prevail on them to suspend any animosities and cement in one common cause those various interests, which are otherwise very apt to break into parties and ruin each other."[72] In the minds of revolutionary Whigs the problem of British authority had become the single problem of colonial politics. In fact by 1776 the English Crown and the imperial system had come to stand for all that was wrong with American society.

Hence it seemed entirely credible to the Revolutionaries that the elimination of this imperial system would decisively change their lives. For too long America had suffered from a pervasive disorder. Its politics, as Jefferson indicated in *A Summary View*, had been repeatedly disrupted by the wanton interference from abroad, the delaying and negativing of laws for the benefit of remote and often unknown interests. Indeed, "the single interposition of an interested individual against a law was scarcely ever known to fail of success, tho' in the opposite scale were placed the interests of a whole country." For too long had the monarch or

72. Tatum, ed., *Journal of Serle*, 149–50; Governor Bull quoted in Richard Walsh, *Charleston's Sons of Liberty: A Study of the Artisans, 1763–1789* (Columbia, S. C., 1959), 66.

governor, as the sole fountain of honors, offices, and privileges, arbitrarily created social distinctions, advancing, said John Jay, "needy and ignorant dependants on great men . . . to the seats of justice, and to other places of trust and importance." But all this, predicted Philip Freneau in 1775, would soon change.

> The time shall come when strangers rule no more,
> Nor cruel mandates vex from Britain's shore.[73]

No longer would a distinguished public office, like that of chief justice in South Carolina, be filled through the influence of some English lord's mistress. No longer would the honors of the state be "at the disposal of a scepter'd knave, thief, fool, or Coward."[74] The exasperating separation of political and social authority at the highest levels of American life would at last be ended.[75] Now merit and virtue would alone determine a man's political position. The rewards of the state would depend only on a man's contribution to the people, not on whom he knew or on whom he married. "There is," said John Adams in May of 1776, "something very unnatural and odious in a Government 1000 Leagues off. An whole Government of our own Choice, managed by Persons whom We love, revere, and can confide in, has charms in it for which Men will fight."[76]

Nothing was more despicable to a Commonwealthman than a "Courtier," defined as "one who applies himself to the Passions and Prejudices, the Follies and Vices of Great Men in order to obtain their Smiles, Esteem and Patronage and consequently their favours and Preferments." And in the eyes of the Whigs America possessed too many of these "fawning parasites and cringing courtiers," too much soothing and flattering of great men—"perhaps the blackest Crimes, that men can commit." It was these courtiers within the colonies, "whether supported by place or

73. [Jefferson], *Summary View*, Boyd, ed., *Jefferson Papers*, I, 130; [John Jay], "Address to the People of Great Britain" (1774), Henry P. Johnston, ed., *The Correspondence and Public Papers of John Jay* (N. Y., 1890–93), I, 26; [Philip Freneau], *The Present Situation of Affairs in North-America* . . . [Phila., 1775], 8.

74. Rogers, *William Loughton Smith*, 45; Charles Lee to Patrick Henry, July 29, 1776, *Lee Papers*, II, 177.

75. On the separation of political and social superiority in 18th-century America see Bailyn, "Origins of American Politics," *Perspectives in American History*, I (1967), 72–76.

76. Adams to Abigail Adams, May 17, 1776, Butterfield, ed., *Family Correspondence*, I, 411.

pension, or only formed to slavish principles by connection and interest," declared a Carolinian in 1774, who were "more to be feared than the arms of Britain herself." Indeed, on the eve of the Revolution it seemed to some Whigs that the Crown's influence was turning the social world upside down: "Virtue, Integrity and Ability" had become "the Objects of the Malice, Hatred and Revenge of the Men in Power," while "folly, Vice, and Villany" were being everywhere "cherished and supported."[77] Whatever the social reality prior to the Revolution may have been—and the evidence indicates that social mobility was considerably lessening —American Whigs sensed a hardening of the social mold, aggravated by the influx of new royal officials since 1763.[78] Many, like Charles Carroll of Maryland, intuitively felt that the avenues to political advancement were becoming clogged; their Whiggish rhetoric voiced their profound fears that "all power might center in *one family*," and that offices of government "like a precious jewel will be handed down from *father* to *son*."[79]

Beneath all the specific constitutional grievances against British authority lay a more elusive social and political rancor that lent passion to the Revolutionary movement and without which the Americans' devotion to republicanism is incomprehensible. The Whigs' language suggests a widespread anger and frustration with the way the relationships of power and esteem seemed to be crystalizing by the middle of the eighteenth century, under the apparent direction of the Crown. Among all the grievances voiced against executive power, what appears to have particularly rankled the colonists, or at least was most directly confronted in their Whig literature, was the abuse of royal authority in creating political and hence social distinctions, the manipulation of official appointments that enabled those creatures with the proper connections, those filled with the most flattery, those "miniature infinitessimal Deities" John Adams called them, to leap ahead of

77. Adams, entry, Feb. 9, 1772, Butterfield, ed., *Diary of Adams*, II, 53; West, *Sermon Preached May 29th, 1776*, Thornton, ed., *Pulpit*, 315; Annapolis *Maryland Gazette*, July 28, 1774; Adams, MS, Aug. 1770, Butterfield, ed., *Diary of Adams*, I, 365.

78. See Jackson Turner Main, "Social Origins of a Political Elite: The Upper House in the Revolutionary Era," *Huntington Library Quarterly*, 27 (1964), 147–58; Charles S. Grant, *Democracy in the Connecticut Frontier Town of Kent* (N. Y., 1961), 141; James A. Henretta, "Economic Development and Social Structure in Colonial Boston," *Wm. and Mary Qtly.*, 3d Ser., 22 (1965), 75–92.

79. [Carroll], "Letters of First Citizen," Feb. 4, 1773, Rowland, *Carroll*, I, 247, 252.

those equally—if not better—qualified into lucrative positions of power and prestige. As one Whig recorder of American complaints charged, too many "improper men, from sinister designs, because of family connexions, and to serve a turn, have been chose, put into, or continued in places of trust or power," while too many "proper ones have been opposed and kept out, . . . because they would not be so the slaves of a party." The American Whig spirit, said George Clinton, who knew what he was speaking of, was a "Spirit of Resentment," an angry hatred of pretentious sycophants who strutted in display of a social superiority nobody believed they deserved.[80] American writings, in both North and South, were filled with outcries against the "insolence of office, and the spurns That patient merit" had to bear at the hands of the "unworthy" who sought "to lord it over all the rest." "None of us, when we grow old," South Carolinians complained bitterly to Josiah Quincy in 1773, "can expect the honours of the State—they are all given away to worthless poor rascals." Young James Otis was incensed by the dignities and grandeur awarded to those in government who had, he said, "no natural or divine right to be above me." John Adams's fury with Thomas Hutchinson knew no bounds: the Hutchinson clan had absorbed almost all the honors and profits of the province—"to the Exclusion of much better Men." Even ten years after the Revolution Americans could not forget how the diffusion of royal authority had affected their social structure: "Every twentieth cousin of an ale-house-keeper who had a right of voting in the election of a member of Parliament," recalled John Gardiner in a Fourth of July oration in 1785, "was cooked up into a *gentleman*, and sent out here, commissioned to insult the hand that gave him daily bread."[81]

William Livingston (about whom John Adams once said there

---

80. Adams, entry, Apr. 20, 1771, Butterfield, ed., *Diary of Adams*, II, 7; William Gordon, *A Sermon Preached before the Honorable House of Representatives* . . . (Watertown, Mass., 1775), 19–20; William Smith, entry, July 12, 1777, Sabine, ed., *Memoirs of Smith*, 417.

81. Pinkney's Wmsbg. *Va. Gazette*, Apr. 20, 1775; [Carroll], "Letters of First Citizen," Feb. 4, 1773, Rowland, *Carroll*, I, 252; Mark De Wolfe Howe, ed., "Journal of Josiah Quincy, Junior, 1773," Mass. Hist. Soc., *Proceedings*, 49 (1915–16), 454–55; Clifford K. Shipton, "James Otis," *Sibley's Harvard Graduates: Biographical Sketches of Those Who Attended Harvard College* (Cambridge and Boston, 1873——), XI, 256; Adams, entry, Mar. 17, 1766, Butterfield, ed., *Diary of Adams*, I, 306; John Gardiner, *An Oration, Delivered July 4, 1785* . . . (Boston, 1785), 23.

was "nothing elegant or genteel")[82] in one of his typically brilliant satires explored the sense of political and social deprivation that lay behind the bitterness of many of the Whigs. Posing as a befuddled Tory, Livingston exposed the personal meaning republican equality possessed for Americans, and he showed as well how little fear most Whigs had of the social forces they were unleashing. Whatever doubts they may have had were smothered in their resentment of what was felt to be an unmerited aristocracy.

Livingston's Tory was confused: "That the vulgar should be flattered by our muggletonian, tatterdemalion governments, is not to be wondered at, considering into what importance those whimsical raggamuffin constitutions have elevated the heretofore dispicable and insignificant mobility." But he was

astonished that men of fashion and spirit should prefer our hotchpotch, oliverian, oligargical anarchies, to the beautiful, the *constitutional*, the *jure divino*, and the heaven-descended monarchy of Britain. For pray how are the better sort amidst our universal *levelism*, to get into offices? During the halcyon days of *royalty* and *loyalty*, if a gentleman was only blessed with a handsome wife or daughter, or would take the trouble of informing the ministry of the disaffection of the colonies, suggesting at the same time the most proper measures for reducing them to parliamentary submission . . . , he was instantly rewarded with some lucrative appointment, his own disqualifications and the maledictions of the rabble notwithstanding. But how is a gentleman of family, who is always entitled to a fortune, to be promoted to a post of profit, or station of eminence in these times of *unsubordination* and *fifth monarchyism*? Why, he must deport himself like a man of virtue and honor. . . . He must moreover pretend to be a patriot, and to love his country, and he must consequently be a hypocrite, and act under perpetual restraint, or he is detected and discarded with infamy. Besides . . . the comparative scarcity of offices themselves . . . must make every man of laudable ambition eternally regret our revolt from the *mother country*: For the present governments being manufactured by the populace, who have worked themselves into a pursuasion of I know not what, of public weal and public virtue, and the interest of one's country, it has been ridiculously imagined that there ought to be no more offices in a state than are absolutely requisite for what these *deluded creatures* call the benefit of the commonwealth. Under the old constitution, on the contrary, whenever the crown was graciously disposed to oblige

82. Adams, entry, Sept. 1, 1774, Butterfield, ed., *Diary of Adams*, II, 119.

a gentleman, ... an office was instantly invented for the purpose; and both land and water, earth and sea should be ransacked, but his Majesty would create a *Surveyor of Woods* and a *Sounder of Coasts*. Thus every humble suitor who had a proper introduction was always sure of being genteely provided for, without either consulting a mob, or losing time about the wild chimera of public utility.

Furthermore, continued Livingston's distraught Tory, America had lost more than offices by separating from Great Britain. No longer could atheism flourish; no longer could women wear their three-foot hats. America had crudely cut off the influx of gallantry and politeness from the Court of London.

While we received our governors and other principal officers immediately from the fountain-head of high life and polish'd manners, it was impossible for us to degenerate into our primitive clownishness and rusticity. But these being now unfortunately excluded, we shall gradually reimmerse into plain hospitality, and downright honest sincerity; than which nothing can be more insipid to a man of breeding and *politesse*.[83]

What was felt by a Livingston, an Adams, or a Carroll at the uppermost levels of American society could be experienced as well throughout varying layers of the social structure, all generally concentrated by 1776, however, into a common detestation of the English imperial system. Thus a justice of the peace or militia officer in some small western New England town, or a petty Virginia rum merchant with a government permit, both far removed from and ignorant of the forces at work in Whitehall, could awake in the heat of the crisis to find himself labeled a parasitic tool of the Crown, the object of long-suffering and varied local resentments.[84] Whatever the actual responsibility of royal authority for the dissatisfactions and frustrations in American society, by 1776 the English Crown had come to bear the full load, and men could believe, although surely not with the same vividness as John Adams, that the whole royal juggernaut was designed to crush them personally.[85] The Crown had become, in a word, a scapegoat for a myriad of American ills.

83. Trenton *N.-J. Gazette*, Sept. 9, 1778, in Nelson *et al.*, eds., *New Jersey Archives*, 2d Ser., II, 416–19.
84. Richard E. Welch, Jr., *Theodore Sedgwick, Federalist: A Political Portrait* (Middletown, Conn., 1965), 21; Robert J. Taylor, *Western Massachusetts in the Revolution* (Providence, 1954), 68; Pinkney's Wmsbg. *Va. Gazette*, Dec. 23, 1775.
85. "I have groped in dark Obscurity, till of late, and had but just become known, and gained a small degree of Reputation, when this execrable Project was set on foot for my Ruin as well as that of America in General, and of Great

7. THE PENNSYLVANIA REVOLUTION

While most Americans in 1776 were able to short-circuit their accumulated grievances and blame them on the presence of the Crown's influence in American society, not all easily could or did. The complicated medley of passions and resentments that fed into the Revolution could not always be controlled and directed solely at the English monarchy, or even at the structure of executive authority in the various colonies; and not all Americans were willing to trust their legislative assemblies as the proper vehicles for satisfying their discontents. Few of the ideas developed in the controversy with England could be limited; they were in fact easily exploited in ways that had not been anticipated. By attempting to claim equality of rights for Americans against the English, "without Respect to the Dignity of the Persons concerned," even the most aristocratic of southern Whig planters, for example, were pushed into creating an egalitarian ideology that could be and even as early as 1776 was being turned against themselves.[86] Because the "cement in one common cause," as Governor Bull of South Carolina termed it, was not always enough to keep the Whigs together, the Revolution became something more than a move for home rule. In 1776 and more intensely in the coming years in different times and places and in varying degrees it broadened into a struggle among Americans themselves for the fruits of independence, becoming in truth a multifaceted affair, with layers below layers, in which men were viewed from very opposite directions on the political and social scale. Thus as the North Carolina royal governor was denouncing the Whig leader, Samuel Johnston, for possessing a "bent to Democracy which he has manifested upon all occasions," Johnston himself was accusing others of disrespect and disorder and was being labeled a Tory and burned in effigy by more extremist Whigs.[87]

Britain": Adams, entry, Dec. 18, 1765, Butterfield, ed., *Diary of Adams*, I, 265; see also *ibid.*, II, 63.

86. [Bland], *Inquiry*, 25; David J. Mays, *Edmund Pendleton* (Cambridge, 1952), II, 121; William Wirt Henry, *Patrick Henry, Life, Correspondence and Speeches* (N. Y., 1891), I, 411. See Bailyn, *Ideological Origins*, 307.

87. Walsh, *Charleston's Sons of Liberty*, 66; Governor Martin to Lord George Germain, May 17, 1777, William L. Saunders, ed., *Colonial Records of North Carolina 1662–1776* (Raleigh, 1886–90), X, 401; Elisha P. Douglass, *Rebels and Democrats: The Struggle for Equal Political Rights and Majority Rule during the American Revolution* (Chapel Hill, 1955), 120–22. Robert Beverley thought he knew what independence and the appearance of Whig unity really signified:

The complexity of the revolutionary movement, the diversity of its sources, and the difficulty of explaining it simply by reference to Whiggish categories of politics are perhaps brought out most vividly in Pennsylvania. Certainly nowhere else were the shadings of meaning of republican equality more manipulated and exploited; nowhere else was there more social antagonism expressed during the Revolution. Pennsylvania hardly experienced a violent social convulsion, but of all the states in the Revolution it saw the most abrupt and complete shift in political power.

The situation in Pennsylvania in the 1760's was very complicated. Because of the peculiarity of proprietary control of the executive, the sources of strain in the society could not easily be symbolized in a Whiggish conflict between Crown and people. Indeed, on the eve of the debate with Britain, the dominant Quaker group in the Assembly led by Benjamin Franklin was attempting to have the Penn family's proprietary charter revoked in order to establish a royal government in the province. Although the Stamp Act and the growing continental nature of the controversy undercut this scheme, the Assembly still found it difficult to adjust to the line of cleavage emerging in the other colonies. Thus the proprietary-Presbyterian group connected to the governor, rather than the supposed representatives of the people in the Assembly, became for a time the popular spokesman for American interests against England. In fact, the Pennsylvania Assembly was so detached from the Revolutionary movement that in the minds of many by 1776 it had become as much an enemy of the people, whom it presumably embodied, as the traditionally feared executive.

While the dominant political and social groups, entrenched in the Assembly, balked at any final separation from the mother country, the growing momentum for independence enabled new aspirants for political leadership to slip past them, resulting in a revolutionary transference of authority that was nowhere in 1776 so sudden and stark. When members of the Whiggish elite were drawn off by military service or, like John Dickinson, stepped

"Ambition, Resentment, and Interest may have united us for a Moment but be assured, when Interests shall interfere and a Dispute shall arise concerning Superiority, a Code of Laws, and all the Concomitants of a new Government, that that Union will soon be converted into Envy, Malevolence, and Faction, and most probably will introduce a greater Degree of Opposition than even now prevails against the Mother Country." Calhoon, ed., "Robert Beverley," *Va. Mag. of Hist. and Biog.*, 73 (1965), 52.

aside rather than be entangled in the drive for independence, their traditional, highly personal control over the structure of Pennsylvania politics disintegrated, and new men, led by James Cannon, Timothy Matlack, Robert Whitehill, George Bryan—all socially outside of the establishment (Matlack, it was said, "does not keep a chariot") and hardly known in Pennsylvania—sought through the Revolutionary movement to pick up the pieces of political power. Through the use of the new Revolutionary organizations—committees, associations and militia—and through intimidation and coercion, and with the sanction of the Continental Congress, these political outsiders eventually circumvented the decaying authority of the much resented Assembly and in the summer of 1776 captured control of the convention that wrote the most radical constitution of the Revolution. Moreover, these inexperienced upstarts, which is what the traditional leaders not inaccurately called them, rode to power clothed with the most extreme Whig rhetoric expressed in the Revolution.[88]

The Constitution was radical; the ideology extreme; the political situation revolutionary. Yet what happened in Pennsylvania was only an extension and exaggeration of what was taking place elsewhere in America. Because of the peculiar abruptness of its internal revolution, Pennsylvania tended to telescope into several months' time changes in ideas that in other states often took years to work out and became in effect a laboratory for the developing of lines of radical Whig thought that elsewhere in 1776 remained generally rudimentary and diffuse.

In the Pennsylvania press of 1776 the typical Whig outbursts against Tories and Crown were overshadowed by expressions of parvenu resentment and social hostility. In fact, to judge solely from the literature the Revolution in Pennsylvania had become a class war between the poor and the rich, between the common people and the privileged few. It is ironic that both the Revolution and the rhetoric should have been so violently extreme in Pennsylvania, for of all the American provinces in the eighteenth century Pennsylvania had become for the enlightened part of the

---

88. On Pennsylvania in the Revolution see Theodore Thayer, *Pennsylvania Politics and the Growth of Democracy, 1740–1776* (Harrisburg, 1953), Chaps. VIII–XIII; William S. Hanna, *Benjamin Franklin and Pennsylvania Politics* (Palo Alto, Cal., 1964), 188–205; J. Paul Selsam, *The Pennsylvania Constitution of 1776: A Study in Revolutionary Democracy* (Phila., 1936); David Hawke, *In the Midst of a Revolution* (Phila., 1961). On the quotation concerning Matlack see Force, ed., *American Archives*, 5th Ser., II, 1154.

world a symbol of what a free and virtuous society should be—
a happy egalitarian land where different religious groups and
nationalities mingled in harmony and where the laws, as it was
"a thousand times acknowledged in Europe," were "the mildest,
and most equitable now in force on the terrestrial globe." By its
blend of natural rusticity and Quaker simplicity, Pennsylvania
had become the epitome of all that was good in the New World;
as William Bradford told Madison in 1774, it was to America
what America was to the rest of the world—a peculiar "land of
freedom."[89] Yet its very elements of freedom bred a revolutionary
situation; for the long-dominant ruling groups both in the executive and the legislature lacked any sustaining sanctions for their
authority. When the brittle structure on which their power rested
began to crumble, the accumulated grievances of upstart outsiders were starkly revealed.

Equality became the great rallying cry of the Pennsylvania
radicals in the spring and summer of 1776. The former rulers, it
was charged, were "a minority of rich men," a few "men of fortune," an "*aristocratical junto*," who had always strained every
nerve "to make the common and middle class of people their
beasts of burden." Such aristocrats derived "no right to power
from their wealth." The Revolution against Britain was on behalf of the people. And who were the people in America, but the
ordinary farmers and mechanics? If they were to be excluded
from politics, especially in the formation of their governments,
then it would be better for them "to acknowledge the jurisdiction
of the British Parliament, which is composed entirely of GENTLE-
MEN." It must be made clear, the radicals argued, "that a freeman
worth only fifty pounds is entitled by the laws of our province to
all the privileges of the first Nabob in the country."[90] Beneath
these claims for legal and political equality lay strong feelings of
social equivalence. Was not one half the property in Philadelphia,
the radical writers asked, owned by men who wore "LEATHERN
APRONS"?—the derisive term that the well-to-do had used. And
"does not the other half belong to men whose fathers or grand-
fathers wore LEATHERN APRONS?" "Talk not, ye pretenders to

89. Daniel Batwell, *A Sermon, Preached at York-Town, . . . on Thursday, July 20, 1775 . . .* (Phila., 1775), 15–16; Bradford to Madison, Mar. 4, 1774, Hutchinson and Rachal, eds., *Madison Papers*, I, 109. On Voltaire's celebration of Pennsyl-vania see Dumond Echeverria, *Mirage in the West: A History of the French Image of American Society to 1815* (Princeton, 1957), 17–18.

90. Phila. *Pa. Packet*, Mar. 18, Apr. 8, June 10, 24, 1776.

rank and gentility, of your elevated stations.—They are derived from those very people whom you treat with so much contempt." It is impossible to know the breadth of appeal such language had in Pennsylvania in 1776, but its very sharp and biting quality suggests that for the authors at least it must have sprung from personal experiences. The egalitarianism of republicanism could now assuage that rankling bitterness against "gentlemen" who for years had not "condescended to look down at them." "Blessed state which brings all so nearly on a level!" And the radicals meant to keep it so in the future. The new government which they formed in the late summer of 1776 was permeated, more so than any other government created in the Revolution, by the principle of rotation of office, in order to prohibit, as the Constitution stated, "the danger of establishing an inconvenient aristocracy," or, as a radical publication more bluntly put it, "to make room for others of equal, or perhaps superior, merit."[91]

Such expressions of egalitarian resentment were not confined to the actually deprived. Even someone as close to the ruling proprietary group as Dr. William Shippen, the father of Thomas Shippen, could rejoice as vigorously as some unestablished and aspiring Philadelphia entrepreneur that those "who have heretofore been at the head of affairs" were now "ousted or at least brought down to a level with their fellow citizens." Their displacement was not surprising since they had "behaved as though they thought they had a sort of fee simple" in the government, "and might dispose of all places of Honour and Profit as pleased them best." Hugh Henry Brackenridge thought that such resentment was the stuff of Pennsylvania society. "The rich man," he observed, "hates him that is richer than himself, because he is unwilling that any one should be equal or superior to him, in the same line of eminence." This envy, malice, and hatred were not rare vices but were present in every breast. "What man is there among us who has not found in himself a sentiment of some revenge against a brother, because he had not submitted to him . . . in a competition for a magistracy, or place of public trust and appointment of some kind or other?"[92]

91. Philadelphia *Pennsylvania Gazette*, Oct. 30, 1776; Phila. *Pa. Packet*, Mar. 18, June 10, 1776; excerpt from Philadelphia *Pennsylvania Evening Post* in N. Y. *Constitutional Gazette*, May 4, 1776; Pa. Cons. (1776), Sec. 8, 19; *Four Letters*, 23.
92. William Shippen to Edward Shippen, July 27, 1776, in *Pa. Mag. of Hist. and Biog.*, 44 (1920), 286; Hugh Henry Brackenridge, *Six Political Discourses* . . . (Lancaster, Pa., 1778), 6–7.

More than in any other colony in 1776 the Revolution in Pennsylvania was viewed as a social conflict between people and aristocracy; yet it was a peculiar kind of aristocracy that was described. The members of the group surrounding the proprietary governor, noted one astute pamphleteer in the late spring of 1776, "despite their affectation of rank," were not really men of consequence. It was difficult to know why America possessed such a different social structure where the aristocracy was so unrespected. Perhaps because of the rapid, desultory, and accidental manner of becoming rich in America, the author suggested, "wealth does not obtain the same degree of influence here, which it does in old countries." The rich aristocrat was so vulnerable to challenge because his wealth and gentility seemed so recent and so insecure. And his pretension to superiority was so galling because "in the line of extraction" he was often "much beneath the generality of the other inhabitants." No man, the radicals urged in the most American of all arguments, ought "to forget the level he came from; when he does, he ought to be led back and shewn the mortifying picture of originality."[93]

These new radical spokesmen for the people, in their eager desire to keep down the established leaders they had bypassed, found themselves compelled to stretch the republican conception of equality to lengths few Revolutionary leaders and perhaps they themselves had ever anticipated. In a widely circulated and acrimonious broadside James Cannon, writing on behalf of the radical associators, warned the people against electing to the convention that was to form the new Constitution "great and overgrown rich Men" and "Gentlemen of the learned Professions" who were "generally filled with the Quirks and Quibbles of the Schools," since "they will be too apt to be framing Distinctions in Society, because they will reap the Benefits of all such Distinctions." The common people, the "virtuous freeholders," whom the radical leaders said were "Men of like Passions and Interests with ourselves," possessed only "Honesty, common Sense, and a plain Understanding," which were fully adequate for the task of constitution-making or governing.[94] So passionate became the de-

93. *Four Letters*, 2–3. See also John F. Roche, *Joseph Reed: A Moderate in the American Revolution* (N. Y., 1957), 187.

94. [James Cannon], *To the Several Battalions of Military Associators in the Province of Pennsylvania, June 26, 1776* (Phila., 1776); Phila. *Pa. Packet*, June 24, 1776. For the identification of Cannon as the author see Phila. *Pa. Journal*, Mar. 17, 1777, and Hawke, *Midst of a Revolution*, 176–77.

sire to destroy the prevailing "aristocratic" structure of economic and social power by some radicals that "it was debated for some time in the Convention, whether the future legislature of this State should have the power of lessening property when it became excessive in individuals." A preliminary draft of Pennsylvania's Declaration of Rights even contained an article stating "that an enormous Proportion of Property vested in a few Individuals is dangerous to the Rights, and destructive of the Common Happiness, of Mankind," and therefore should be discouraged by the laws of the state.[95] Such agrarian laws were known to be an aspect of classical Whig republicanism and were sporadically suggested by Americans throughout the Revolution; but nowhere were they carried as far as they were in Pennsylvania in 1776. Their eventual abandonment by even the most radical Whigs, however, indicates that Americans were willing to trust more in opportunity than in such legislation to bring about a general leveling.

For all of its bitter tones, the egalitarian language of the Pennsylvania radicals in 1776 can be easily misunderstood. However violent and class-conscious the ideology sounded, the Revolution in Pennsylvania could scarcely be regarded as a rising of the masses against the few. The grievances so widely expressed in pamphlets and press were not the sort that went deep into the society. The internal revolution that took place was very much a minority movement; the radicals who claimed to speak for the people, and who manned the instruments of revolution—the committees and the militia companies and wrote the new Constitution actually feared the traditional deference of the people to their established leaders. They were continually hard put to enlarge their support and weaken their opposition, resorting on one hand to exaggerated popular rhetoric and a broadened suffrage in order to attract new groups and on the other hand to military intimidation and test oaths and disfranchisement in order to neutralize their opponents. Such measures, together with overrepresentation of the western counties, were necessary, for, as the radicals complained, "the poorer commonalty" seemed strangely apathetic to their appeals, too habitually accepting of the traditional authority. The ideas of government in the past had too long been "rather aristocratical than popular." "The rich, having

95. Phila. *Pa. Packet*, Nov. 26, 1776; *An Essay of a Declaration of Rights* (Phila., 1776), Art. 16.

been used to govern, seem to think it is their right," while the people, "having hitherto had little or no hand in government, seem to think it does not belong to them to have any."[96] To convince the people that they rightfully had a share in government became the task of the Pennsylvania radicals and of radicals in all the states in the years ahead. Indeed, it became the essence of democratic politics as America came to know it.

96. Phila. *Pa. Evening Post*, July 30, 1776, quoted in Hawke, *Midst of a Revolution*, 187.

CHAPTER III

Moral Reformation

1. The Easy Transition to Republicanism

The changes the Americans intended to make in their politics and society were truly momentous—so momentous in fact that it is difficult to comprehend the swiftness and confidence with which they embraced republicanism. The Revolution was no simple colonial rebellion against English imperialism. It was meant to be a social revolution of the most profound sort. Different men of course participated with different degrees of enthusiasm, and their varying expectations of change were in fact a measure of their willingness to revolt, distinguishing a confident Richard Henry Lee from a more skeptical Robert Morris. There were doubts and apprehensions in 1776, many of them. Running through the correspondence of the Whig leaders are fearful suggestions of what republicanism might mean, of leveling, of licentiousness, of "the race of popularity."[1] Yet what in the last analysis remains extraordinary about 1776 is the faith, not the doubts, of the Revolutionary leaders. All Americans who became committed to independence and republicanism were inevitably compelled to expect or to hope for at least some amount of reformation in American society, and for many the expectations were indeed high. Everyone was intensely aware of the special character of republicanism and the social and moral demands it put

1. Gouverneur Morris to John Penn, May 20, 1774, in Jared Sparks, *The Life of Gouverneur Morris* . . . (Boston, 1832), I, 24; Edward Rutledge to John Jay, June 29, 1776, Edmund C. Burnett, ed., *Letters of Members of the Continental Congress* (Washington, 1921–36), I, 517–18; Samuel Johnston to James Iredell, Apr. 5, 1776, Saunders, ed., *Col. Recs. N. C.*, X, 1032.

upon a people. When American orators quoted the Whig poet laureate, James Thompson, on the blessedness of public virtue, the audiences knew what was meant. That the greatness, indeed the very existence, of a republic depended upon the people's virtue was "a maxim" established by the "universal consent" and the "experience of all ages." All these notions of liberty, equality, and public virtue were indelible sentiments "already graven upon the hearts" of Americans,[2] who realized fully the fragility of the republican polity. Even the ancient republics, virtuous and grand as they were, had eventually crumbled. The only English experiment in republicanism had quickly ended in a predictable failure, capped by the tyranny of a dictator. The eighteenth century, moreover, offered few prototypes for America's grandiose venture: the only modern republics were tiny, insignificant states, in various stages of decline, paralyzed by surrounding absolutism, hardly fit models for this sprawling New World.

Nevertheless, Thomas Paine could exclaim in 1776 that it was only common sense for Americans to become republicans and have Americans heartily agree with him. Despite their keen awareness of the failure of past republics and of the unusual delicacy of republican government, Americans, observed Thomas Jefferson in the summer of 1777, "seem to have deposited the monarchical and taken up the republican government with as much ease as would have attended their throwing off an old and putting on a new suit of clothes." Looking back at the controversy with Britain from 1776, John Adams was likewise "surprized at the Suddenness, as well as the Greatness of this Revolution." "Is not the Change We have seen astonishing? Would any Man, two Years ago have believed it possible, to accomplish such an Alteration in the Prejudices, Passions, Sentiments, and Principles of these thirteen little States as to make every one of them completely republican, and to make them own it? Idolatry to Monarchs, and servility to Aristocratical Pride, was never so totally eradicated, from so many Minds in so short a Time."[3] Whatever the intensity of the Americans' grievances and whatever affinity the tenets of the republican ideology had for them,

2. Jonathan Mason, Jr., *An Oration, Delivered March 5, 1780* . . . (Boston, 1780), and Dawes, *Oration Delivered March 5, 1781,* both in Niles, ed., *Principles,* 61, 69.

3. Jefferson to Benjamin Franklin, Aug. 3, 1777, Boyd, ed., *Jefferson Papers,* II, 26; Adams to Abigail Adams, July 3, 1776, and Adams to Richard Cranch, Aug. 2, 1776, Butterfield, ed., *Family Correspondence,* II, 28, 74.

this ease of transition into republicanism remains remarkable and puzzling even today.[4] For republicanism after all involved the whole character of the society.

But for Americans this social dimension of republicanism was precisely the point of the Revolution. Even the essential question raised in the debates Americans had with themselves in 1776 over the wisdom of independence was social: were Americans the stuff republicans are made of?—surely the most important and most sensitive issue in all of the Revolutionary polemics, for it involved not any particular economic advantages or political rights, but rather the kind of people Americans were and wanted to be. The question was not easily answered. Out of the Americans' investigation of this crucial issue flowed ambiguous and contradictory conclusions about the nature of their social character. On the one hand, they seemed to be a particularly virtuous people, and thus unusually suited for republican government; yet, on the other hand, amidst this prevalence of virtue were appearing dangerous signs of luxury and corruption that suggested their unpreparedness for republicanism. It was the kind of ambiguity and contradiction that should have led to a general bewilderment and hesitation rather than to the astonishingly rapid embrace of republicanism which actually occurred. Yet curiously the Americans' doubts and fears about their social character were not set in opposition to their confidence and hopes, but in fact reinforced them. Such was their enlightened faith in the comprehensive power of republican government itself that their very anxieties and apprehensions about the fitness of the American character for republicanism became in the end the most important element in their sudden determination to become republican. By 1776 republicanism had become not only a matter of suitability. It had become a matter of urgency.

2. The Debate over the Genius of the People

Thomas Paine in his incendiary pamphlet, *Common Sense*, published early in 1776, touched off the argument that burned to the

4. See Cecelia M. Kenyon, "Republicanism and Radicalism in the American Revolution: An Old-Fashioned Interpretation," *Wm. and Mary Qtly.*, 3d Ser., 19 (1962), 166–67: "Within a very short time, Americans developed an ideological attachment to republicanism. . . . What is puzzling is the reason for the sudden and virtually complete revolution in attitude."

heart of the social issue. "The *time hath found us*," he said, and this became his theme. Independence from Britain was not only desirable, it was necessary; and it was necessary now. The youth of America was no argument against independence; in fact, it was the most compelling reason for adopting republicanism. "History sufficiently informs us, that the bravest achievements were always accomplished in the non-age of a nation." If America delayed it would be too late. Fifty years from now, said Paine, trade and population would have increased so much as to make the society incapable of fighting for and sustaining republicanism. Wealth and distinctions would have created divisions and a jarring of interests among the people. "Commerce diminishes the spirit both of patriotism and military defence" and would eventually destroy America's soul, as it had England's. Years from now, "while the proud and foolish gloried in their little distinctions, the wise would lament that the union had not been formed before." The American people were ripe for revolution and republicanism. "It may not always happen that our soldiers are citizens and the multitude a body of reasonable men." "Virtue . . . ," said Paine, "is not hereditary, neither is it perpetual."[5]

But not everyone thought that republicanism for America was a matter of common sense. Paine's argument immediately aroused several spirited and lengthy responses, the most important being Charles Inglis's *The True Interest of America Impartially Stated* . . . and James Chalmer's *Plain Truth*, both published in Philadelphia in the spring of 1776. Both of Paine's critics built their case against independence around a vigorous defense of the English monarchical constitution. Yet both grounded the core of their arguments on the social dangers of republicanism and on the inability of the American people to sustain a republican polity. Republics, they contended, had always been torn to pieces by faction and internal struggles, tumults from which America would never escape. "All our property throughout the continent would be unhinged," warned Inglis; "the greatest confusion, and the most violent convulsions would take place." Chalmers predicted a dreadful anarchy resulting from republicanism, leading to a Cromwellian dictatorship. At the very least America would witness commercial chaos and agrarian laws limiting the possession of property. "A war will ensue between the creditors and their

5. [Thomas Paine], *Common Sense* . . . (Phila., 1776), in Foner, ed., *Writings of Paine*, I, 30, 36, 41, 45.

debtors, which will eventually end in a general spunge or abolition of debts, which has more than once happened in other States on occasions similar."

Paine, they charged, was flagrantly wrong in his estimate of the peculiar nature of American society. America was incapable of supporting republicanism: "A republican form of government would neither suit the genius of the people, nor the extent of America." American society was basically no different from that of the mother country. "The Americans are properly Britons. They have the manners, habits, and ideas of Britons." Hence any American experiment in republicanism would surely end as had the English attempt in the seventeenth century. The best governments and the wisest laws were ineffective "among a corrupt, degenerate people." Paine, they scoffed, had promised Americans the restoration of the golden age if they became republicans. But until Paine could give "some assurance that may be relied on, that ambition, pride, avarice, and all that dark train of passions which usually attend them" were absent from the American soul, his audience could only "doubt the truth of his assertions."[6]

Other Americans also had doubts of the suitability of their society for republicanism. For William Smith of New York it called "for greater Sacrifices of private Liberty" than seemed possible or necessary. Were Americans capable of receiving a republican government? asked an anxious Virginian in June of 1776. "Have we that Industry, Frugality, Economy, that Virtue which is necessary to constitute it?" Laws and constitutions, after all, "must be adapted to the manners of the People." Several months earlier, in the fall of 1775, during the debates in the Continental Congress over the closing of all American ports to British trade, those opposed to the revolutionary course America was on had also brought into question the capacity of Americans to endure the hardships such economic restriction would cause. "A Republican Government is little better than Government of Devils," warned the Swiss-born John Joachim Zubly. "We must have Trade. It is prudent not to put Virtue to too serious a Test." "More Virtue is expected from our People," said Robert R. Livingston of New York, "than any People ever had." This kind of wholesale economic regulation by government would not work,

6. [Inglis], *True Interest of America*, 49, 52–53; [James Chalmers], *Plain Truth*; . . . *Containing, Remarks on a Late Pamphlet, Entitled Common Sense . . .* (Phila., 1776), 63–64, 70.

declared John Jay in an argument that cut the Commonwealth assumptions to the core. "We have more to expect from the Enterprise, Activity and Industry of private Adventurers, than from the Lukewarmness of Assemblies." Americans needed goods, and individual entrepreneurs could best get them. "Public Virtue is not so active as private Love of Gain. Shall We shutt the Door vs. private Enterprise." But the revolutionary-minded in the Congress would hear none of this justification of selfishness. "We can do without Trade," said Samuel Chase. "I have too good an opinion of the Virtue of our People to suppose they will grumble." By closing all the ports "Merchants will not grow rich—there is the Rub. . . . We must give up the Profits of Trade or loose our Liberties." Such profits were no benefit anyway, added Richard Henry Lee, for "Money has debauched States as well as Individuals." Conventions and committees of the people could suppress whatever violations of the public good might arise.[7]

Probably the most trenchant public critique of this kind of Commonwealth thinking was written by one of Lee's enemies in Virginia, Carter Braxton, in his *Address to the Convention of . . . Virginia; on the Subject of Government . . .* published early in 1776. The advocates of republicanism, Braxton maintained, had confused and blended private and public virtue; the two must be separated. Man's happiness no doubt lay in the practice of private virtue: "In this he acts for himself, and with a view of promoting his own particular welfare." On the other hand, public virtue—"a disinterested attachment to the public good, exclusive and independent of all private and selfish interest"—had, said Braxton, "never characterized the mass of the people in any state." To be a true republican a man "must divest himself of all interested motives, and engage in no pursuits which do not ultimately redound to the benefit of society." This meant that ambition, wealth, luxury, influence—all had to be curbed. "To this species of Government everything that looks like elegance and refinement is inimical," resulting in all those sumptuary and agrarian laws for which the ancient republics were so noted. Such schemes, argued Braxton, were inapplicable for America. However sensible they may have been in naturally sterile countries which had only a

7. Smith, entry, Oct. 18, 1776, Sabine, ed., *Memoirs of Smith*, 24; Alexander White to Charles Lee, June 27, 1776, *Lee Papers*, II, 87; Adams, Notes of Debates in the Continental Congress, Oct. 1775, Butterfield, ed., *Diary of Adams*, II, 204, 193, 219, 210, 212, 213.

scanty supply of necessities, "they can never meet with a favorable reception from people who inhabit a country to which Providence has been more bountiful." Americans will always claim the right to enjoy the fruits of their honest labor, "unrestrained by any ideal principles of Governments"; and they will always accumulate property for themselves and their children "without regarding the whimsical impropriety of being richer than their neighbours." "The truth is," concluded Braxton sententiously, "that men will not be poor from choice or compulsion," only "from necessity." Republicanism was an "ideal" principle—"a mere creature of a warm imagination."[8]

These were potent arguments, thrust upon Americans not only by discredited Tories but also by skeptical Whigs equally concerned with the defense of American liberties but convinced that the republican remedy was worse than the disease. Although these anti-republican writings could be casually dismissed (John Adams, for example thought Braxton's pamphlet was "too absurd to be considered twice"),[9] the questions they raised were not the sort that could be ignored. Because of anti-republican arguments like these and because of their own self-doubts, Americans were compelled to explore the nature of their society. From this analysis involved in the Revolutionary polemics and from the Enlightenment portrait drawn of them, Americans fashioned a conglomerate image of themselves as a distinct people with a social character possessed by few, if any, people before them.

3. REPUBLICANS BY NATURE

Some, like a writer in Purdie's *Virginia Gazette*, answered the critics of republicanism by ridiculing their "terrifying ideas" of

8. [Carter Braxton], *An Address to the Convention of . . . Virginia; on the Subject of Government . . .* (Williamsburg, 1776), in Force, ed., *American Archives*, 4th Ser., VI, 748–52.

9. Adams to Patrick Henry, June 3, 1776, Adams, ed., *Works of John Adams*, IX, 387. Adams at first thought that Braxton's pamphlet was symptomatic of the more aristocratic temper of the southern colonies, and that his own pamphlet, *Thoughts on Government*, would be disdained in the South because it was "too popular." Adams to Warren, May 12, 1776, Ford, ed., *Warren-Adams Letters*, I, 242. When Henry assured him that Braxton's piece was a "silly thing" (Adams, ed., *Works of John Adams*, IV, 201–02), Adams became convinced, although still with surprise, that "the pride of the haughty must, I see, come down a little in the south." Adams to Warren, June 16, 1776, *ibid.*, IX, 398.

republican government—"a dreadful train of domestick convulsions, . . . of jealousies, dissensions, wars, and their attendant miseries." The opponents of republicanism seemed to imagine that it bred, in Milton's words,

> All monstrous, all prodigious things,
> Abominable, unutterable, and worse
> Than fables yet have feign'd, or *fear conceived*
> *Gorgons* and *hydras*, and *chimeras* dire![10]

But their fears were only chimeras, empty and unreal fancies of excited minds. They were unreal because what had happened to previous republics could not happen in America. Arguments taken from the experience of other republics were "by no means conclusive with respect to the North-American colonies." The American people were different. By 1776 most Americans had become convinced that they were "aptly circumstanced to form the best republicks, upon the best terms that ever came to the lot of any people before us."[11]

This American confidence did not grow simply out of self-analysis. Throughout the eighteenth century European liberal intellectuals had put together from the diffuse political thought of the day an image of the New World that contrasted sharply with the Old. Mired in what the Enlightenment believed to be a decadent feudal society debilitated by oversophistication and cultivation, the European illuminati came to see in the Americans, "this enlightened people," as Guillaume-Thomas Raynal called them, all those "robust, nay virtuous," qualities their own countries lacked.[12] The New World seemed uniquely free of the constraining distinctions of social rank—a naturally egalitarian society, young, rustic, energetic, sometimes even frighteningly and fascinatingly barbarous, but at any rate without the stifling and corrupting refinement of the Old World. In the minds of many of the French *philosophes* America had become a "mirage in the West," a symbol of their dreamed-of new order, and a tool in their fight against the decadence of the *ancien régime*.[13] And for the alienated English radicals, like Catharine Macaulay, the image

10. Purdie's Wmsbg. *Va. Gazette*, Apr. 12, 1776.
11. Phila. *Pa. Packet*, Feb. 12, 1776; Purdie's Wmsbg. *Va. Gazette*, May 17, 1776.
12. Pinkney's Wmsbg. *Va. Gazette*, Oct. 5, 1775.
13. Echeverria, *Mirage in the West*; Werner Stark, *America: Ideal and Reality: The United States of 1776 in Contemporary European Philosophy* (London, 1947).

and purpose were no different. Britain was in decline, went a typical English radical communication to the Americans, eaten up by selfishness and venality. "But with you, as with most States, when in the infant innocence of their grandeur, the *publick* is everything, and the *individual* nothing, any farther than as he contributes to the importance of the publick." America seemed to consist, wrote Richard Price, "of only a body of yeomanry supported by agriculture, and all independent, and nearly upon a level." The people were "in the vigour of youth, inspired by the noblest of all passions, the passion for being free." England, in contrast, was old and withered; "inflated and irreligious; enervated by luxury; encumbered by debts; and hanging by a thread." American society was peculiarly founded on nature, said Thomas Pownall, with no single ecclesiastical system, no oppressive established church, no aristocracy, no great distinctions of wealth, only "a general equality, not only in the Persons, but in the power of the landed Property of the Inhabitants." The ancient republics had possessed no such social advantages. Their "grand *Desideratum*," as for all republics, had been equality: to relate the manners of the society to the form of government. Yet lacking that necessary social equality in nature, they were compelled to press it artificially upon the society, thus destroying and perverting all personal liberty "in order to force into establishment Political Freedom." "All this was done and suffered," concluded Pownall, "to obtain (which yet they could never obtain) that natural equal level Basis on which Ye, American Citizens, stand."[14]

Americans were acutely aware that they had "many worthy patrons beyond the Atlantic." "The Eyes of Europe, nay of the World," said President John Rutledge of South Carolina, "are on America." "Men of Virtue throughout Europe," observed Samuel Adams in 1777, "heartily wish well to our Cause." And when in the controversy with England, Americans were forced to search their souls to find out the kind of people they were, they could only be dazzled by the portrait, so "very flattering to us," that the Enlightenment had painted of them. Whatever the social reality may have been—and on examination it did not seem inconsistent—they could not help believing that America was what Europe said it was. Everywhere they looked there was confirma-

14. Macaulay, *Address to the People*, 15; Boston *Independent Chronicle*, Feb. 5, 1778; Price, *Observations on Civil Liberty*, 70–71, 98; Pownall, *Memorial to America*, 58–69.

tion of what the Enlightenment and the English radicals had said about them.[15]

All men were republicans by nature and royalists only by fashion, said Thomas Paine in the spring of 1776. And fortunately Americans had not yet succumbed to the allures of fashion. Republicanism was the concomitant of youth. It was, wrote a Virginian essayist, "the most *ancient* form, because it is the most *natural.*" Monarchy and hereditary aristocracy were deviations from nature, the products of oversophistication, of age and decay. A monarchical constitution may have been the best mode for England, but surely not for America—not for "these young agrarian states, where no such being as a Lord exists." No man held his land by feudal tenure, for "every cultivator" was "lord of his soil."[16] The bulk of the people "instead of being sunk into that general licentiousness, profligacy and dissoluteness of manners, of which there is so much complaint in the ancient countries; are, for the most part, industrious, frugal, and honest." And there were "few so corrupted with riches, as to be above all other pursuits but those of luxury, indolence, amusement, and pleasure." Indeed, the society was peculiarly egalitarian: rich and poor, property and people were not, as in Europe, set in opposition, for "the people of *America*, are a people of property; almost every man is a freeholder." "Americans," said Josiah Quincy, "never were destitute of discernment; they have never been grossly deficient in virtue." The American colonists, declared John Dickinson, "in general are more intelligent than any other people whatever, as has been remarked by strangers, and it seems with reason." England was no match for such a people. The mother country may have been the strongest military power in the world, yet "who but a pompous blockhead . . . could expect to conquer a hardy virtuous set of men," men who were "strangers to that luxury which effeminates the mind and body."[17] They

15. Perry, *Sermon, May 11, 1775*, 17; Charleston *S.-C. and American Gazette*, Apr. 10–17, 1776; Adams to Samuel Freeman, Aug. 5, 1777, and to John Langdon, Aug. 7, 1777, Cushing, ed., *Writings of Samuel Adams*, III, 400, 402–03.

16. Phila. *Pa. Gazette*, Apr. 24, 1776; Purdie's Wmsbg. *Va. Gazette*, May 17, 1776; Phila. *Pa. Journal*, Oct. 11, 1775; Phila. *Pa. Packet*, Feb. 12, Apr. 22, 1776.

17. Williams, *Discourse on the Love of Our Country*, 16; Charleston *S.-C. and American Gazette*, Nov. 6, 1777; Quincy, *Observations on the Boston Port Bill*, Quincy, *Memoir*, 320; [Dickinson], *Letters from a Farmer*, Ford, ed., *Writings of Dickinson*, 349; Benjamin Hichborn, *An Oration, Delivered March 5th, 1777 . . .* (Boston, 1777), in Niles, ed., *Principles*, 49; Thacher, *Oration Delivered March 5, 1776*, in *ibid.*, 46.

told themselves over and over again that they were a numerous, sober, and industrious people, and therefore, as history showed, the ablest to contend with and the most successful in opposing tyranny. "Wherever virtue, wisdom, and public spirit prevail among a people," declared a Delaware minister, "that people will be great and prosperous." And for Americans the future looked auspicious indeed. "The Americans," said William Henry Drayton, "now live without luxury. They are habituated to despise their yearly profits by agriculture and trade. They engage in the war from principle. . . . From such a people everything is to be hoped for, nothing is to be doubted of." It was, Thomas Pownall told them, as if Providence had selected them to be "a chosen people, in a New World, separate and removed far from the regions and wretched Politics of the old One."[18]

Americans, it appeared, were meant to be republican. "And is it a crime to be what we can't help but be?" What then could the dreadful predictions of horror and anarchy by the opponents of republicanism be but futile attempts to "quench a martial spirit which has virtue for its spring?"[19] Americans knew history and the nature of republican government; they had inquired "into the causes which have prevented its success in the world." And they had concluded that past experience was no real measure of the "expediency or duration" of republicanism. "There has always been such a mixture of monarchy and aristocracy in republics, they never have had fair play in the world." They had never been constructed from the proper materials—the materials that America now peculiarly possessed. Could such a chosen, blessed people ever suffer the chaos and confusion of previous republics? "Has there not appeared a becoming resolution? Has it not spread surprisingly thro' all America?" One American even thought that his countrymen now "had virtue enough to be happy under any form of government."[20]

There were moments in 1775 and 1776 when the Whig leaders, even the most pessimistic, stood amazed at what the quarrel with

18. Phila. *Pa. Journal*, Feb. 7, 1776; Address of Rev. Samuel Magaw, Dover, Del., May 1776, Force, ed., *American Archives*, 4th Ser., VI, 464; Drayton, Charge to Grand Jury, Charleston, Oct. 15, 1776, Niles, ed., *Principles*, 341–42; Pownall, *Memorial to America*, 69.

19. [Mather], *America's Appeal*, 69; Rusticus [pseud.], *Remarks on a Late Pamphlet Entitled Plain Truth* (Phila., 1776), 13.

20. N. Y. *Constitutional Gazette*, Feb. 24, 1776; Phila. *Pa. Journal*, Mar. 13, 1776; Perry, *Sermon, May 11, 1775*, 10; Phila. *Pa. Packet*, Feb. 19, 1776.

England was bringing. "A remarkable and unexpected union has taken place, throughout all the colonies." All that men had so long yearned for in America seemed to be occurring. As the possibility of a break with England approached, the American mind seemed almost relieved, as though the Revolution would finally do "away with the flimsy excuses suggested by avarice and mistaken self-interest" and bring "the unanimity, the firmness, and wisdom" that had so long seemed lacking in American society. In the eyes of the Whigs the two or three years before the Declaration of Independence always appeared to be the great period of the Revolution, the time of greatest denial and cohesion, when men ceased to extort and abuse one another, when families and communities seemed peculiarly united, when the courts (many of which were closed) were wonderfully free of that constant bickering over land and credit that had dominated their colonial life. At the height of the prerevolutionary crisis with Britain, when it seemed that an internecine struggle that Englishmen had not seen for a century might break out at any moment, the American Whigs appeared strangely happy, feeling "a joy unutterable and an exhultation never felt before."[21] Those few years before the actual conflict marked the time and spirit which best defined the Americans' Revolutionary objectives and to which they clung throughout the war with increasing nostalgia.

Everywhere the colonists were suffering personal injuries and deprivations for the cause of liberty and their country, more so "than in any given term of time before; no threatening quarrels, or animosities have subsisted; but harmony and internal peace have ever reigned, and one soul has inspired the body politic." And all this at a time, John Page told Jefferson, "when they were free from the Restraint of Laws." The nonimportation agreements and resolves of the Continental Congress and provincial conventions, although lacking the force of law, were surprisingly being obeyed. Americans had amply demonstrated "that a spirit of public virtue may transcend every private consideration." To young James Madison it seemed that "a spirit of Liberty and Patriotism animates all degrees and denominations of men"; so great was this prevailing love of virtue and liberty that no power in the world could "put the yoke on us." James Iredell, no fanatic, was

21. Thaddeus Maccarty, *Praise to God, a Duty of Continual Obligation* . . . (Worcester, 1776), 22; Pinkney's Wmsbg. *Va. Gazette*, Dec. 15, 1774; Purdie and Dixon's Wmsbg. *Va. Gazette*, Nov. 25, 1775.

equally astonished at the peace and order of the people during the long suspension of the courts, "an instance of regularity," he believed, "not to be equalled, in similar circumstances, by any other people under heaven." This, he could only hope, was "a happy presage of that virtue which is to support our present government." Even the Reverend John Witherspoon, who disagreed violently with Paine's optimistic view of human nature and set out in a 1776 sermon to expose the passions and depravity of all men, could not refrain from marveling that "so great a degree of public spirit . . . has prevailed among all ranks of men." Although America's ancient forms of government had for a long time been unhinged, there had been, said Witherspoon, "by common consent, a much greater degree of order and public peace, than men of reflection and experience foretold or expected." No wonder that Americans—however pessimistic—were led to "conclude favorably" for the future "of the principles of the friends of liberty."[22]

The Enlightenment image of America had reflected across the Atlantic and had given force and acceptability in American thinking to the peculiarities of their social development, unsettling and shifting the Americans' system of values. What had once been disturbing deviations from the model of the mother country now could be regarded as desirable perfections. What had once been merely anomalously descriptive could now even be viewed as wonderfully prescriptive.[23] Their "want" of "Art and Address" and of "the exterior and superficial Accomplishments of Gentlemen," their neglect of the fine arts, their lack of "Knowledge of the World" and *politesse*, their inability to support a real aristocracy—all these "Deficiencies" could perhaps be advantages, even necessities, for the maintenance of stable republican governments.[24]

22. Isaac Mansfield, Jr., *A Sermon, Preached in the Camp at Roxbury, November 23, 1775* . . . (Boston, 1776), 23; John Page to Jefferson, Apr. 26, 1776, Boyd, ed., *Jefferson Papers*, I, 288; Thacher, *Oration Delivered March 5, 1776*, Niles, ed., *Principles*, 46; Madison to William Bradford, Nov. 26, 1774, June 19, 1775, Hutchinson and Rachal, eds., *Madison Papers*, I, 129, 152; Iredell, Address to Grand Jury, May 1, 1778, McRee, *Life of Iredell*, I, 389; John Witherspoon, *Dominion of Providence* . . . (Phila., 1776), in *Works of John Witherspoon* (Phila., 1802), III, 39.

23. Bernard Bailyn, "Political Experience and Enlightenment Ideas in Eighteenth Century America," *American Historical Review*, 67 (1961–62), 339–51.

24. John Adams to Abigail Adams, Aug. 4, 1776, Butterfield, ed., *Family Correspondence*, II, 76.

The shift in values was neither easy nor complete. For educated Americans were reluctant to believe that "luxury and tyranny" rather than virtue and liberty were "the patrons of science and philosophy" and thus to be compelled to reject the world of taste and refinement by becoming republican.[25] The Revolution therefore precipitated a debate over the place of the fine arts in a republican culture that continued well into the nineteenth century, with repeated and strained efforts throughout the 1780's to discriminate between those didactic arts which would strengthen virtue and those luxurious arts which would only encourage vice.[26] And always the apparent primitiveness of America had to be defended. Although at present the Americans undoubtedly lacked the wealth to contribute greatly to the arts and sciences, many said over and over, they expected much from the future, for no infant country had done as much, and they were as yet a "young and forming people."[27] There was no doubt in the world, said one honest Virginian in 1776, that America's "national character" had been "fixed at a very low standard." "Nothing can be more insipid than a review of the history of these colonies for a century past," where there could be found "no traces of the philosopher, the poet, or the artist." For cultivated Americans "the seat of the empire, of wealth, of literature, and arts, was in Britain." Benjamin West and Patience Wright found "London, and not America, the proper theatre" for their talents. Even Franklin's works were published in London, "and it is among a very few of the learned only that he is called the *American* philosopher." But the "insignificancy, insipidity, and ignorance" of America was not the product of the wilderness; it was rather the result of its "connexion and dependence on Britain." England stood as "an insuperable barrier between us and the polished world, who, dazzled with the view of the primary planet, either knew not, or disregarded, the humble satellites which served to increase her splendor."[28]

25. David Rittenhouse, *An Oration, Delivered February 24, 1775, before the American Philosophical Society, Held at Philadelphia, for Promoting Useful Knowledge* (Phila., 1775), 20.

26. See Neil Harris, *The Artist in American Society: The Formative Years, 1790–1860* (N. Y., 1966).

27. Williams, *Discourse on the Love of Our Country*, 27. See Henry Cumings, *A Sermon Preached ... May 28, 1783* (Boston, 1783), 34; Ezra Stiles, *The United States Elevated to Glory and Honor ...* (New Haven, 1783), in Thornton, ed., *Pulpit*, 460.

28. Purdie's Wmsbg. *Va. Gazette*, May 3, 1776. See Michael Kraus, *The Atlantic Civilization: Eighteenth Century Origins* (N. Y., 1961), 98.

Still the stubborn evidence remained that art and high culture, attractive as they may have been, were symptomatic of a degree of luxury and of decadence that had no place in a vital republic. Paris, John Adams wrote his wife in 1780, possessed everything "that can inform the Understanding, or refine the Taste, and indeed . . . that could purify the Heart. Yet it must be remembered," he added, "there is every thing here, too, which can seduce, betray, deceive, corrupt and debauch it."[29] David Rittenhouse expressed a similar ambivalence, for he could not help "confess indeed, that by our connections with Europe" Americans had made what advances they had "towards the meridian of glory; But by those connections too, in all probability, our fall will be premature."[30] Unless, of course, those connections were severed by, in John Adams's famous words, a radical change "in the minds and hearts" of the people—an act of self-preservation in the most intensely personal sense. The Revolution was thus epitomized by Charles Carroll's rejection of the "high life" of England with all of its "follies, vices and extravagance," by Joseph Warren's preference for the "lonely cottage" over the "gilded palace," by John Trumbull's scorn for Europe's "silks and lace" and "the glare of dress," and by a Carolinian's proud boast that he was but "a plain unlettered Man, and not acquainted with any Thing but what is natural and common."[31] Republicanism was in fact designed to warm a humiliated provincial's heart. For too long the English "have derided and looked down upon us, with utmost scorn and contempt," too often "representing us as savages and barbarians." Now when the Britishers sneered that "the People of America are at least an hundred years behind the old Countries in Refinement," Americans could retort that in temperance, moral virtue, and veneration for the rights of man the Old World was at least as far behind America.[32]

29. John Adams to Abigail Adams, Apr. 1780, quoted in Butterfield, ed., *Family Correspondence*, II, ix–x. See Wendell Garrett, "John Adams and the Limited Role of the Arts," *Winterthur Portfolio*, 1 (1964), 243–55.

30. Rittenhouse, *Oration, Delivered February 24, 1775*, 20.

31. John Adams to Hezekiah Niles, Feb. 13, 1818, Adams, ed., *Works of John Adams*, X, 282–83; Carroll to his father, Mar. 17, 1762, "Extracts from the Carroll Papers," *Md. Hist. Mag.*, 11 (1916), 262; Joseph Warren, *An Oration, Delivered March 5, 1772* . . . (Boston, 1772), in Niles, ed., *Principles*, 24; [John Trumbull], *An Elegy on the Times* . . . (New Haven, 1775), 8; Charleston *S.-C. Gazette*, Apr. 4, 1774.

32. Elijah Fitch, *A Discourse, the Substance of Which Was Delivered at Hopkinton, on the Lord's Day, March 24th, 1776* . . . (Boston, 1776), 22–23; Champion, *Christian and Civil Liberty*, 24; New London *Connecticut Gazette*, Oct. 20, 1775, quoted in Rossiter, *Seedtime of the Republic*, 430–31.

For many, this provincial indignation was not merely an intellectual response, as perhaps it was to Jefferson, to the arrogance of the Old World diffused through scholarly writings three thousand miles across the ocean toward a seemingly wild and uncivilized America. Americans had felt only too deeply and personally the rankling and presumptuous disdain of persons they had known and spoken with. The contempt shown by the royally commissioned officers for the provincial militia officers had angered the colonials and driven a young and ambitious George Washington into a fury. John Adams's "Humphrey Ploughjogger" series in the Boston press in the 1760's—colored by a rural dialect and a phonetic spelling that anticipated an entire school of American humor—was an understandable and a not uncommon reaction to the sense of sophisticated condescension emanating from the urban coteries. In a remarkable series of letters to his parents written from London in the 1750's young John Dickinson (who, as he himself noted, represented as well as anyone whatever the New World possessed of an aristocracy) poignantly revealed what John Adams's definition of the Revolution meant, as he recounted the humiliation felt by an American who imagines himself something of a lordly noble before he arrives in London and learns that he is really nothing. "After his recovery from this mortifying discovery," Dickinson told his father, "he considers the nature of the things which make this difference between himself and others, and since he can't attract the admiration of mankind, the same pride . . . that made him desire it, now prevents his paying it to others. Thus a titled coward, or a gilded scoundrel he laughs at and despises." The experience exemplified the Americans' upheaval in values, since others in various strata of the society were having similar unsettling thoughts and coming, like Dickinson, to "a just notion of things," ceasing "to gaze and stare," and finding "at last that nothing is really admirable but virtue."[33] For every man had his London, and in Philadelphia John Dickinson became someone else's "gilded scoundrel."

It seems very likely that ultimately the persuasiveness of republicanism for Americans had something to do, as it did for Thomas Shippen at the Court of Versailles, with a defense of

33. Marcus Cunliffe, *George Washington: Man and Monument* (N. Y., 1960), 54; Butterfield, ed., *Diary of Adams*, I, 249–51, 264–65, 290, 355, II, 11, 34–35, 38, 61; Dickinson to his father, Aug. 15, 1754, May 25, 1754, in Colbourn, ed., "Pennsylvania Farmer," *Pa. Mag. of Hist. and Biog.*, 86 (1962), 277–78, 269.

their self-respect. Indeed the Revolution itself became the American people's response to unjustified pride, for "never was a people puffed up with a greater conceit" than the English. For James Iredell it was "the pride and arrogance" of America's oppressors that was so "insufferable." Thomas Paine later dwelt on the "species of haughtiness" with which Great Britain had lorded over the Americans. "It was equally as much from her manners as from her injustice that she lost the colonies." By her abuse of American rights, she had provoked American principles; but her arrogance, said Paine, was what had worn out their tempers.[34]

4. AMERICAN CORRUPTION

Of course, all the while Americans were well aware that their colonial society had not been all the Enlightenment believed it to be, that they had not really been free of the vices and luxury of the Old World. It was not enough that many European intellectuals considered them to be an especially egalitarian, virtuous people. Compared to Europe they did seem naturally republican, destined to be out from under a corrupt monarchy. But they could not believe that the future was simply a matter of becoming what nature had decreed, of accommodating a new political form to a society which had already become republican in spirit. Indeed, even to those who dwelt on America's distinctiveness, it appeared quite the contrary. America, declared some on the eve of the Revolution, "never was, perhaps, in a more corrupt and degenerate State than at this Day." "How have animosities been cherished . . . ! How has injustice abounded! And How prevalent has been every kind of iniquity!"[35] In the eyes of many Americans, whether southern planters or New England clergymen, the society was far from virtuous and in fact seemed to be approaching some kind of crisis in its development. This prevalence of vice and corruption that many Americans saw in their midst did not, however, work to restrain their desire to be republican. It became in fact a stimulus, perhaps in the end the most important stimulus, to revolution. What ultimately convinced

34. Fitch, *Discourse, March 24th, 1776*, 22–23; Iredell to Joseph Hewes, Apr. 29, 1776, Saunders, ed., *Col. Recs. of N. C.*, X, 1036; Paine, *Letter to the Abbé Raynal*, Foner, ed., *Writings of Paine*, II, 220.
35. Samuel Buell, *The Best New-Year's Gift For Young People: Or, the Bloom of Youth Immortal by Piety and Glory* (New London, 1775), 53; Mansfield, *Sermon Preached November 23, 1775*, 25.

Americans that they must revolt in 1776 was not that they were naturally and inevitably republican, for if that were truly the case evolution, not revolution, would have been the eventual solution. Rather it was the pervasive fear that they were not pre-destined to be a virtuous and egalitarian people that in the last analysis drove them into revolution in 1776. It was this fear and not their confidence in the peculiarity of their character that made them so readily and so remarkably responsive to Thomas Paine's warning that the time for independence was at hand and that delay would be disastrous. By 1776 it had become increasingly evident that if they were to remain the kind of people they wanted to be they must become free of Britain. The calls for independence thus took on a tone of imperativeness. Only separating from the British monarchy and instituting republicanism, it seemed, could realize the social image the Enlightenment had drawn of them. Only this mingling of urgency and anxiety during their introspective probings at the height of the crisis could have given their revolutionary language the frenzied quality it acquired. Only profound doubts could have created their millennial vision of a new society, their idealized expectation that "on the morrow" there would be a "new thing under the sun, that hath not been already of old time."[36]

When the Americans examined themselves in the years leading up to the Revolution, it became apparent that their society had been undergoing a drastic and frightening transformation. All the signs of the society's development by the middle of the eighteenth century, as described in the language of the day, became symptoms of regression. "To increase in numbers, in wealth, in elegance and refinements, and at the same time to increase in luxury, profaneness, impiety, and a disesteem of things sacred, is to go backward and not forward." Such apprehensions were not new to Americans. Since the seventeenth century they had warned themselves repeatedly against declension and social corruption. But never before had wealth and luxury seemed so prevalent, especially since the end of the war with France. Never before had Americans been so "carried away by the stream of prosperity."[37] Throughout all the colonies and rising to a fever pitch by

---

36. Gordon, *Sermon before House of Representatives*, 22.

37. Nathan Fiske, *Remarkable Providences to Be Gratefully Recollected, Religiously Improved, and Carefully Transmitted to Posterity* (Boston, 1776), 25; Jacob Duché, *The American Vine, a Sermon, Preached before the Honourable Continental Congress, July 20th, 1775* (Phila., 1775), 23.

1775–76 were strident warnings in newspapers, pamphlets, and sermons of the great social changes that seemed to be sweeping the land.

Not only the anxious clergy everywhere but patriots in the northern cities and planters in the southern colonies were alarmed at the seemingly precipitate and uneven maturation of the social body. In Virginia, especially, the public and private literature was filled with fears of the conspicuous consumption and high living of the aristocracy. There the attacks on luxury and extravagance represented not so much the resentful protests of the socially aspiring, as was often the case in the less structured and more egalitarian societies of the North; rather they represented the uneasy introspections of the ruling planters themselves, fearful of what some took to be social corrosion, apparently caused by the fantastic growth of pride, ostentation and debts among the would-be aristocrats. This increase in luxurious living was not only weakening the planters', and especially their heirs', capacity to rule; but because the planters were "the pattern of all behaviour," it was also being copied by "their inferiors" and infecting the whole society. "Hence extravagance, love of gaieties, the taste for modish pleasures, are in a chain of imitation carried down to the lowest people, who would seem to have a notion of what *high life* is, by spending more than they can afford with those they call their betters."[38] Such developments were disrupting the social fabric, leading to an alarming growth of extortion, profiteering, and social antagonism, and an unnerving increase in social mobility where "those who have neither natural nor acquired parts to recommend them" were soliciting and corrupting the electorate, and where a simple storekeeper or petty official was being "made rich, and above his Calling." Indeed, it is not an exaggeration to say that in the minds of many Virginians the colony seemed on the verge of ruin.[39]

While some Americans found the source of these social changes in their own wantonness as a people, others increasingly came to

38. Hunter D. Farish, ed., *Journal and Letters of Philip Vickers Fithian, 1773–1774* . . . (Williamsburg, 1957), 27; Purdie and Dixon's Wmsbg. *Va. Gazette*, Jan. 12, 1769. See Dixon Wecter, *The Saga of American Society: A Record of Social Aspiration, 1607–1937* (N. Y., 1937), 22–23.

39. Alexander White to Richard Henry Lee, 1758, quoted in Jack R. Pole, "Representation and Authority in Virginia from the Revolution to Reform," *Journal of Southern History*, 24 (1958), 23; Purdie and Dixon's Wmsbg. *Va. Gazette*, Nov. 25, 1773. See "The Effects of Simplicity and Luxury on a State, Exemplified from the Roman History," *ibid.*, Sept. 5, 1771.

attribute what was happening in their society to their connection to the English monarchy. "Alas! Great Britain," said one Virginian in 1775, "their vices have even extended to America! . . . The torrent as yet is but small; only a few are involved in it; it must be soon stopped, or it will bear all before it with an impetuous sway." The cancerous corruption of Europe, David Rittenhouse told the members of the American Philosophical Society in 1775, had spanned the Atlantic and had secured a hold in the New World. America, said the Reverend Jacob Duché, trembled for the mother country and "would fain keep off from our own borders, those luxuries, which may perhaps already have impaired her constitutional vigour."[40]

By the 1760's the multiplication of wealth and luxury, the attempts to harden the social hierarchy, particularly the efforts of those who considered themselves socially superior to set themselves off from the rest of American society by aping the "Asiatic amusements" and "fêtes champêtres" of sophisticated English court life—all seemed to be part of the Crown's conspiracy to numb and enervate the spirit of the American people.[41] On the eve of the Revolution, America was displaying all the symptoms (in the lexicon of eighteenth-century political science) of a state attacked by disease. The "Times of Simplicity and Innocence" of their ancestors seemed to be waning; "Elegance, Luxury and Effeminacy begin to be established." "Venality, Servility and Prostitution, eat and spread like a Cancer." England, it seemed, was encouraging American "dissipation and extravagance" both to increase the sale of her manufactures and geegaws and to perpetuate American subordination. "In vain," recalled David Ramsay in 1778, "we sought to check the growth of luxury, by sumptuary laws; every wholesome restraint of this kind was sure to meet with the royal negative." If Americans had not eventually revolted, concluded Ramsay, "our frugality, industry, and simplicity of manners, would have been lost in an imitation of British extravagance, idleness, and false refinements."[42]

40. Pinkney's Wmsbg. *Va. Gazette*, May 25, 1775; Rittenhouse, *Oration, Delivered February 24, 1775*, 20; Jacob Duché, *Duty of Standing Fast*, Moore, ed., *Patriot Preachers*, 85.

41. Phila. *Pa. Packet*, Aug. 1, 1778. "I have long been convinced," wrote Samuel Adams in the spring of 1776, "that our Enemies have made it an Object, to eradicate from the Minds of the People in general a Sense of true Religion and Virtue, in hopes thereby the more easily to carry their Point of enslaving them." Adams to John Scollay, Apr. 30, 1776, Cushing, ed., *Writings of Samuel Adams*, III, 286.

42. John Adams, draft of newspaper communication, Aug. 1770, Butterfield,

The Crown actually seemed to be bent on changing the character of American society. Everywhere men appeared to be seeking the preferment of royal authority, eager to sell their country "for a smile, or some ministerial office."[43] Throughout the society, particularly in the larger cities, an artificial inter-colonial aristocracy—springing ultimately from the honors and dignities bestowed by the Crown—was entrenching itself, consolidating and setting itself apart from the mass of American yeomen by its royal connections and courtier spirit of luxury and dissipation.[44] Any distinction and title, any refinement, was sought by these aspiring aristocrats as long as it separated them from the rabble. "Even being a member of the Church of England," noted Arthur Browne, the famous Anglican minister at Newport and Portsmouth, "gave a kind of distinctive fashion."[45]

Yet the would-be aristocrats themselves felt insecure. Their political and social position was too recent, too accidental, too arbitrary, too much the result of connections or marriage to command respect. It was with apology that Thomas Hutchinson wrote in 1765 that "altho' places and titles in the colonies are not hereditary, yet *caeteris paribus*, the descendants of such as have done worthily have some claim to be distinguished."[46] By the middle of the eighteenth century royal officials on both sides of the Atlantic were anxiously concerned with the instability of American society; and the air was filled with proposals for reorganizing the imperial structure. What was especially needed, it seemed, was a strengthening of the aristocratic element in the society, those "most distinguished for their Wealth, Merit, and Ability," who needed "some few distinctions" annexed to their persons in order to maintain a proper subordination of rank and civil discipline in the colonies. By the 1760's various kinds of reforms were circulating, all generally pointing to the establishment in America of a "Nobility appointed by the King for life,"

ed., *Diary of Adams*, I, 365; Adams to Catharine Macaulay, Dec. 31, 1772, *ibid.*, II, 75; Ramsay, *Oration on Advantages of American Independence*, Niles, ed., *Principles*, 375. For other examples see Cushing, ed., *Writings of Samuel Adams*, III, 230–31; Annapolis *Md. Gazette*, July 7, 1774; Rogers, *William Loughton Smith*, 60.

43. Pinkney's Wmsbg. *Va. Gazette*, May 25, 1775.

44. Carl Bridenbaugh, *Cities in Revolt: Urban Life in America, 1743–1776* (N. Y., 1955), 212, 309, 334–50.

45. Quoted in *ibid.*, 137.

46. Thomas Hutchinson, *The History of the Colony and Province of Massachusetts-Bay*, ed. Lawrence S. Mayo (Cambridge, Mass., 1936), II, 11.

which could eventually become hereditary.[47] These plans seemed to be no idle tinkering by insignificant and uninfluential British officials. Not only were high colonial officials urging the creation of an American aristocracy, but ministers close to the Crown were doing the same. Perhaps nothing better indicates the gulf of thinking separating official England from the colonists than the ministerial pamphlet, *The Address of the People of England to the Inhabitants of America*, written by Sir John Dalrymple, "at the express requisition of lord *North*," said one angry Virginian. "The deluded amongst you," wrote Dalrymple, "think that we assume airs of superiority over you even where they are needless." This was false, continued Dalrymple, in an argument that could not have been more frightening and rankling to Americans than if it had been so intended. Every honor of England was open to Americans. Indeed, said Dalrymple, "we should even be happy to see you ask the establishment of a Nobility, and of ranks amongst yourselves" so that American spirits could be exalted not only by the love of liberty but by the love of family as well.[48]

This sort of suggestion only confirmed American apprehensions about what the Crown was up to, and in reaction the apparent equality of American society seemed more precious than ever. Anyone who read of these English proposals, warned one irate American Whig, "will then find how eagerly they wish to form distinctions amongst us, that they may create a few more tools of oppression. They wish to see us aspire to nobility, and are ready to gratify us whenever we do." At the present the ministry could depend only on the Crown officials and their dependents, plus a few Anglicans "who prefer basking in the sunshine of British royalty and court favour, to the simple practice of the pure religion of their forefathers." If Americans put off separating from the British only a few years longer, "until they raised

47. Sir Egerton Leigh, *Considerations on Certain Political Transactions of the Province of South Carolina* ... (London, 1774), 68–69, 70; Francis Bernard, *Select Letters on the Trade and Government of America* ... (London, 1774), 83. See also *Copy of Letters Sent to Great-Britain, by his Excellency Thomas Hutchinson, the Hon. Andrew Oliver, and Several Other Persons, Born and Educated among Us* (Boston, 1773), 30–32; Adams and [Leonard], *Novanglus and Massachusettensis*, 19, 171. On Bernard's plans for an aristocracy see Edmund S. and Helen M. Morgan, *The Stamp Act Crisis: Prologue to Revolution*, rev. ed. (N. Y., 1963), Chap. II. For a general discussion of the problem of a nobility in America see Bailyn, *Ideological Origins*, 277–81.

48. Purdie's Wmsbg. *Va. Gazette*, Sept. 22, 1775; Sir John Dalrymple, *The Address of the People of Great-Britain to the Inhabitants of America* (London, 1775), 26–27.

a number of our first men to the different ranks of nobility," the society would be thoroughly corrupted. Then, Americans, "preserve your liberties if you can."[49] This kind of American thinking transcended all particular trade or tax grievances: their very existence as a distinctive egalitarian people seemed at stake.

The controversy with Great Britain thus assumed a peculiar timeliness. In August of 1776 Charles Thompson told John Dickinson that he was fully persuaded, from the prevailing "prejudices" and from "the notions of honour, rank and other courtly Ideas so eagerly embraced," that "had time been given for them to strike deeper root, it would have been extremely difficult to have prepared men's minds for the good seed of liberty." The Americans "were running fast into our vices," observed the English radical, Richard Price, in 1776. "But this quarrel gives them a salutary check."[50] "Let our harbours, our doors, our hearts, be shut against luxury," was the common appeal. By 1775 Americans, like David Rittenhouse, were "ready to wish," as vain as it was, "that nature would raise her everlasting bars between the new and old world; and make a voyage to Europe as impracticable as one to the moon."[51]

But it was more than Europe that the Americans rejected in 1776. It was the whole world as it had been, and indeed it was themselves as they had been. When the language of the eighteenth century is translated into modern terms the obsession with luxury, vice, and corruption becomes an obsession with America's social development, the way in which the society was moving and maturing, the distinctions of prestige and status that were arising, the rate and the nature of mobility, and the distribution of power and wealth. In a broad sense republicanism became the Americans' ideological response to the great social changes that had, as they often described them, "crept in unawares among us" by the middle of the eighteenth century—a response that was as varied and complicated as its sources.[52] To the resentful and the socially

49. Phila. *Pa. Journal*, Feb. 14, 1776.

50. Charles Thompson to John Dickinson, Aug. 16, 1776, "Five Letters from the Logan Papers," *Pa. Mag. of Hist. and Biog.*, 35 (1911), 499; Price, *Observations on Civil Liberty*, 103. See also Nathan Strong, *The Agency and Providence of God Acknowledged, in the Preservation of the American States* (Hartford, 1780), 12–13; Zabdiel Adams, *The Evil Designs of Men . . .* (Boston, 1783), 26.

51. Rittenhouse, *Oration, Delivered February 24, 1775*, 20.

52. Gordon, *Sermon before House of Representatives*, 26. For a discussion of this republican ideology as a legacy of Puritanism see Edmund S. Morgan, "The Puritan Ethic and the American Revolution," *Wm. and Mary Qtly.*, 3d Ser., 24 (1967), 3–43.

aspiring, republicanism meant a leveling of "that exuberance of pride which has produced an insolent domination in a few, a very few, opulent, monopolizing families." But to others who feared the disorder, the mobility, and the bitterness of the past, republicanism promised a new stability and contentment and an end to that incessant "squabbling for election" and scrambling for distinction that was threatening to corrupt American society.[53] Even by 1770 many Virginians were remarking that the nonimportation associations were having a beneficial effect on Virginia's society, giving the planters, as Washington pointed out, a pretext to cut back on their extravagant expenses without injuring either their status or their credit—a social effect that republicanism would only more strongly sanction.[54] In their repeated calls to "banish the syren LUXURY with all her train of fascinating pleasures, idle dissipation, and expensive amusements from our borders," and to institute "honest industry, sober frugality, simplicity of manners, plain hospitality and christian benevolence," different Americans found a common panacea for their different social ills.[55] None, however, found more to hope for from the Revolution than did the Calvinist clergy.

5. A CHRISTIAN SPARTA

Thomas Paine in his *Common Sense* had urged "those whose office it is to watch the morals of a nation, of whatsoever sect or denomination ye are of," to recognize the need for independence from Britain, that is, "if ye wish to preserve your native country uncontaminated by European corruption."[56] But the admonition was hardly necessary. The American clergy were already deep in the process of working out—in an elaborate manner congenial to their covenant theology—the concept of the Revolution as an antidote to moral decay.

To a Calvinist clergyman the Enlightenment image of a virtu-

53. John Adams to Patrick Henry, June 3, 1776, Adams, ed., *Works of John Adams*, IX, 387–88; Brackenridge, *Six Political Discourses*, 23.

54. Rind's Wmsbg. *Va. Gazette*, Sept. 15, 1774; Purdie and Dixon's Wmsbg. *Va. Gazette*, Mar. 22, 1770; Farish, ed., *Fithian Journal*, 27; Rowland, *Mason*, I, 139, 143; Washington to George Mason, Apr. 5, 1769, Fitzpatrick, ed., *Writings of Washington*, II, 502.

55. Duché, *American Vine*, 27.

56. [Paine], *Common Sense*, Foner, ed., *Writings of Paine*, I, 41. See also [Adams], "Novanglus," Adams, ed., *Works of John Adams*, IV, 56.

ous society seemed extremely cloudy. "Others may, if they please, treat the corruption of our nature as a chimera: for my part," said John Witherspoon in a notable sermon delivered at Princeton in the spring of 1776, "I see it everywhere, and I feel it every day." All the exposed disorders and unhappiness of American society were rooted in the "envy, malice, covetousness, and the other lusts of man."[57] In their jeremiads the clergy scourged the people for their vices and warned them that England's Coercive Acts and the shedding of American blood were God's just punishments for a sinful people. "Have we not by our universal declensions, manifold offences, abuse of divine blessings provoked God into this severe controversy?" But the Americans, like the Israelites of old, were God's chosen people ("Where?—in what country, was it ever known that a people arose from paucity to populousness so fast?"), and bound to him by a "visible covenant."[58] Their very afflictions were a test of their peculiar blessedness, so that "God may prove us, whether we be wheat or chaff." "Such a season of declension" was their time of trial, the "day of the American Israel's trouble." It had always been the crafty policy of Israel's enemies, said the ministers in sermon after sermon centering particularly on the book of Nehemiah, to fall upon the "professing people" when they had forsaken their God and had sunk in sin. "Would the Britons have dared thus to magnify themselves against this people of the Lord of hosts, had they not been apprised of our declensions and abounding iniquities?"[59]

Everywhere the clergy saw "Sins and Iniquities . . . very visible and apparent." And the sins were the same vices feared by a political scientist—infidelity, intemperance, profaneness, and particularly "pride and luxury in dress, furniture, eating, and drinking." Especially since the end of the French war it seemed that "luxury of every kind has flowed in faster than ever, and spread itself as a deluge all around us." Society appeared topsy-turvy: "Trade has flourished whereby money has flowed in apace, and raised many to the possession of opulent fortunes, whose fathers were glad to

57. Witherspoon, *Dominion of Providence*, in *Works of Witherspoon*, III, 21.
58. Perry, *Sermon, May 11, 1775*, 18; William Stearns, *A View of the Controversy Subsisting between Great Britain and the American Colonies . . .* (Watertown, Mass., 1775), 14; Huntington, *Sermon Delivered at Middleton, July 20th, A.D. 1775*, 15.
59. Lyman, *Sermon Preached December 15th, 1774*, 15–16; Stearns, *View of the Controversy*, 10; Huntington, *Sermon Delivered at Middleton, July 20th, A. D. 1775*, 14–15; Aaron Hutchinson, *A Well Tempered Self-Love . . .* (Dresden, Vt., [1779]), 17.

get their bread by the sweat of the brow." Pretension, ostentation, refinement—"shopkeepers and tradesmens daughters dressed like peeresses of the first rank"—all these were signs of social and moral deterioration.[60]

Out of the language of their traditional covenant theology the ministers fashioned an explanation of the British tyranny as a divine punishment for the abominations of the American people.[61] The prevalence of vices and immoralities among Americans had provoked their God. "Sin alone is the moral and procuring cause of all those evils we either feel or fear." Until the cause was removed the clergy could offer no relief from British oppression. Yet the Americans were still a peculiarly blessed and covenanted people; if they would but mend their ways and humbly acknowledge their God, good might come out of all this suffering. As Isaiah warned, God "sends his judgments abroad in the earth, that men may learn righteousness."[62] In the sermons of the clergy the success of the Revolution thus became dependent on the repentance and reformation of the people. "We are now in an unusual way called upon to wash ourselves, to make ourselves clean, to put away the evil of our doings to do well, and to seek every kind of judgment." "SIN" itself, in bold capital letters, became the enemy. "May our land be purged from all its sins! May we be truly a holy people, and all our towns cities of righteousness!" Only then would God deliver them from the British.[63]

A good Calvinist could never agree that the British connection was the main source of America's degeneration, for the "cause" of these "awful national Calamities . . . will never be removed, nor our Danger be over, 'until the Spirit is poured out from on

60. Ebenezer Baldwin, *The Duty of Rejoicing under Calamities and Afflictions* . . . (N. Y., 1776), 28; Samuel Langdon, *Government Corrupted by Vice* . . . (Watertown, Mass., 1775), Thornton, ed., *Pulpit*, 247; *An Affectionate Address to the Inhabitants of the British Colonies in America* (Phila., 1776), 37, 41, 44; Address of the Convention of the Representatives of the State of New York to Their Constituents, Dec. 1776, Johnston, ed., *Papers of Jay*, I, 103–10.

61. See Perry Miller, "From the Covenant to the Revival," in James Ward Smith and A. Leland Jameson, eds., *The Shaping of American Religion* in *Religion in American Life* (Princeton, 1961), I, 322–68; Heimert, *Religion and the American Mind*, esp. Chaps. VIII, IX; Alice M. Baldwin, *The New England Clergy and the American Revolution* (N. Y., 1958).

62. *Affectionate Address*, iv; Josiah Stearns, *Two Sermons, Preached at Epping in the State of New Hampshire, January 20th, 1777* (Newburyport, 1777), 25, 32; Lyman, *Sermon Preached December 15th, 1774*, 14.

63. Gordon, *Sermon Preached before House of Representatives*, 22; Stearns, *View of the Controversy*, 33; Langdon, *Government Corrupted by Vice*, Thornton, ed., *Pulpit*, 256.

High.' " Yet the clergy, like other colonial leaders, could not but be amazed at the extraordinary virtue and valor displayed by Americans under the British afflictions of 1774–75. Was it possible that this was "the Time, in which Christ's Kingdom is to be thus gloriously set up in the World?" The clergy, like many other Americans, felt the country "to be on the eve of some great and unusual events" and their language, ecstatic but not uniquely religious, took on a millennial tone.[64] By 1776 it seemed to many of the ministers that decades of corrupt and vicious social behavior had at last caught up with the Americans, that now, here in this crisis with Britain, was the providential opportunity, not to be lost, for "a reformation in principles and practices," involving "a change of mind, and our entertaining different thoughts of past conduct." In this sense the Revolution became as much a rejection as an endorsement of previous American experience—raising some aspects of the way Americans had behaved to new heights of moral acceptability while at the same time repudiating the way they had exploited and maligned one another, out of their "vain appetites for wealth and honour," and the way they had bitterly fought to set themselves off one from another, "from a pique and jealousy of rank and place." Now in the midst of the unanimity and resolution of 1775 America appeared to be moving toward "a state of greater perfection and happiness than mankind has yet seen." With God's help they would build a harmonious society of "comprehensive benevolence" and become "the eminent example of every divine and social virtue." Out of the "perishing World round about" them they would create "a new World, a young World, a World of countless Millions, all in the fair Bloom of Piety."[65]

Independence thus became not only political but moral. Revolution, republicanism, and regeneration all blended in American thinking. Further calamity, John Adams told his wife in July 1776, "will have this good Effect, at least: it will inspire Us with many Virtues, which We have not, and correct many Errors, Follies, and Vices, which threaten to disturb, dishonour, and destroy us."[66] The repeated calls of the clergy for a return to the

64. Buell, *Best New-Year's Gift*, 53; Baldwin, *Duty of Rejoicing*, 31, 32, 39, 40; Williams, *Discourse on the Love of Our Country*, 26.

65. Gordon, *Sermon Preached before House of Representatives*, 22; Brackenridge, *Six Political Discourses*, 23; Williams, *Discourse on the Love of Our Country*, 25; Duché, *American Vine*, 29; Buell, *Best New-Year's Gift*, 53.

66. Adams to Abigail Adams, July 3, 1776, Butterfield, ed., *Family Correspondence*, II, 28.

temperance and virtue of their ancestors made sense not only in terms of the conventional covenant theology but also, as many ministers enjoyed noting, in terms of the best political science of the day. As "pride," "prodigality, and extravagance" were vices, "contrary to the spirit of religion, and highly provoking to Heaven, so they also, in the natural course of things, tend to bring poverty and ruin upon a people." "The light of nature and revelation," social science and theology—perhaps for a final moment at the end of the eighteenth century—were firmly united. "Nothing is more certain," observed John Witherspoon in a common analysis of this fusion of piety and politics, "than that a general profligacy and corruption of manners make a people ripe for destruction." Yet when the character of the people was pure, when virtue and frugality were maintained with vigor, "the attempts of the most powerful enemies to oppress them are commonly baffled and disappointed. This will be found equally certain whether we consider the great principles of God's moral government, or the operation and influence of natural causes."[67] The traditional covenant theology of Puritanism combined with the political science of the eighteenth century into an imperatively persuasive argument for revolution. Liberal rationalist sensibility blended with Calvinist Christian love to create an essentially common emphasis on the usefulness and goodness of devotion to the general welfare of the community. Religion and republicanism would work hand in hand to create frugality, honesty, self-denial, and benevolence among the people. The Americans would then "shew to the nations of the earth (what will be a most singular phenomenon) amidst all the jarring interests, subtlety, and rage of politics" that they "had virtue enough to think of, and to practice these things." The city upon the hill assumed a new republican character. It would now hopefully be, in Samuel Adams's revealing words, "the *Christian* Sparta."[68]

6. REPUBLICAN REGENERATION

The Americans' confidence in their republican future, bred from the evils and anxieties of the past, was not as illusory and as

67. Cumings, *Sermon, Preached on the 23d of November 1775*, 26–27; Gordon, *Sermon Preached before House of Representatives*, 20; Witherspoon, *Dominion of Providence*, in *Works of Witherspoon*, III, 41.
68. Williams, *Discourse on the Love of Our Country*, 28; Adams to John

unjustified as it might on the face of it seem. Their new republican governments were to be more than beacons to the oppressed of the world, more than the consequences of revolution. They were themselves to be the agencies of revolution. There was, the eighteenth century believed, a reciprocating relationship between the structure of the government and the spirit of its people. It was this belief in the mutual influence, the feedback and interplay, between government and society that makes eighteenth-century thinkers like Montesquieu so subtle and elusive. On one hand, there was no doubt that the nature of the government must be adapted to the customs and habits of the people. "A good form of government may hold the rotten materials together for some time, but beyond a certain pitch even the best constitution will be ineffectual, and slavery must ensue."[69] Yet, on the other hand, politics was not regarded simply as a matter of social determinism; the form of government was not merely a passive expression of what the spirit of the people dictated. The scheme of government itself had "a natural and powerful bias, both upon those who rule, and upon those who are ruled."[70] Republicanism was therefore not only a response to the character of the American people but as well an instrument of reform. "If there is a form of government, then," John Adams asked of his countrymen in 1776, "whose principle and foundation is virtue, will not every sober man acknowledge it better calculated to promote the general happiness than any other form?" A republican constitution "introduces knowledge among the people, and inspires them with a conscious dignity becoming freemen; a general emulation takes place, which causes good humor, sociability, good manners, and good morals to be general. That elevation of sentiment inspired by such a government, makes the common people brave and enterprising.

Scollay, Dec. 30, 1780, Cushing, ed., *Writings of Samuel Adams,* IV, 238; Heimert, *Religion and American Mind,* 352–56, 379–82, 387, 399–400, 402–03, 405, 411, 438, 443, 447–48. Heimert himself repeatedly notes this coalescing of evangelicalism and rationalism at the time of the Revolution but insists that it was only a "concession to the times" by both liberals and Calvinists. See also Charles Crowe, "Bishop James Madison and the Republic of Virtue," *Journal of Southern History,* 30 (1964), 58–70.

69. Witherspoon, *Dominion of Providence,* in *Works of Witherspoon,* III, 50. See also Payson, *Sermon Preached May 27, 1778,* Thornton, ed., *Pulpit,* 330.

70. James Wilson, "Lectures on Law, Delivered in the College of Philadelphia in the Years 1790–1791," Wilson, ed., *Works of Wilson,* I, 413. For similar views see James Madison, *A Sermon Preached in the County of Botetourt . . .* (Richmond, 1781), 18; J. P. Brissot de Warville, *A Critical Examination of the Marquis de Chattellux's Travels . . .* (Phila., 1788), 65.

That ambition which is inspired by it makes them sober, industrious, and frugal." Adams could thus conclude that "it is the Form of Government which gives the decisive Colour to the Manners of the People, more than any other Thing." Societies differed, said Samuel West in the Massachusetts election sermon of 1776, and "men become virtuous or vicious, good commonwealthsmen or the contrary, generous, noble, and courageous, or base, mean-spirited, and cowardly, according to the impression that they have received from the government that they are under." "The strength and spring of every free government," said Moses Mather in 1775, "is the virtue of the people; virtue grows on knowledge, and knowledge on education."[71] And education, it was believed, was the responsibility and agency of a republican government. So the circle went.

Enlightened men could believe, as Samuel Stanhope Smith told James Madison sometime in 1777 or 1778, that new habitual principles, "the constant authoritative guardians of virtue," could be created and nurtured by republican laws, and that these principles, together with the power of the mind, could give man's "ideas and motives a new direction." By the repeated exertion of reason, by "recalling the lost images of virtue: contemplating them, and using them as motives of action, till they overcome those of vice again and again until after repeated struggles, and many foils they at length acquire the habitual superiority," by such exertions it seemed possible for man to recover his lost innocence and form a society of "habitual virtue."[72] From these premises flowed much of the Americans' republican iconography—the "Pomp and Parade," as John Adams called it, the speeches and orations, the didactic history, even the "Painting, Sculpture, Statuary, and Poetry"—and the republicans' devotion to "the great importance of an early virtuous education."[73]

Only this faith in the regenerative effects of republican govern-

71. [Adams], *Thoughts on Government*, Adams, ed., *Works of John Adams*, IV, 194, 199; Adams to Mercy Warren, Jan. 8, 1776, Ford, ed., *Warren-Adams Letters*, I, 202; West, *Sermon Preached May 29th, 1776*, Thornton, ed., *Pulpit*, 297; [Mather], *America's Appeal*, 66–67.

72. Samuel Stanhope Smith to Madison, Nov. 1777–Aug. 1778, Hutchinson and Rachal, eds., *Madison Papers*, I, 208–09.

73. Adams to Abigail Adams, July 3, 1776, and same, Apr. 27, 1777, Butterfield, ed., *Family Correspondence*, II, 30, 225; Smith to Madison, Nov. 1777–Aug. 1778, Hutchinson and Rachal, eds., *Madison Papers*, I, 209. On the iconography of the Revolution see Arthur M. Schlesinger, *Prelude to Independence: The Newspaper War on Britain, 1764–1776* (N. Y., 1958), 29–37.

ment itself on the character of the people can explain the idealistic fervor of the Revolutionary leaders in 1776.[74] Concentrating on the nicely reasoned constitutional arguments of John Adams or Jefferson in order to prove the moderation of the Revolution not only overlooks the more inflamed expressions of other Whigs but also misses the enthusiastic and visionary extravagance in the thinking of Adams and Jefferson themselves. Adams's hopes in 1776 were mingled with as much doubt and fear as those of any of the Revolutionaries, and he was as aware as anyone of the vices and passions that drove men. Yet he could sincerely believe that the Revolution was "an Enterprise that is and will be an Astonishment to vulgar Minds all over the World, in this and in future Generations"—an intense conviction of success justified in 1776 by his extraordinary reliance, criticized acutely by Landon Carter, on the eventual ameliorating influence of republican laws and government on men's behavior.[75] For Jefferson, faith in the future was always easier than for Adams, and he of all the Revolutionary leaders never seemed to lose heart. Like the Reverend John Joachim Zubly and others he believed that "when millions of free people at once turn their thoughts from trade, and the means of acquiring wealth, to agriculture and frugality, it must cause a most sensible alteration in the state."[76] In Jefferson's mind the Revolution was just beginning in 1776. The extensive reforms that he and other Virginians planned and in fact effected for their new state have never been fully appreciated and explored, even though Jefferson's autobiography clearly indicates that they in-

74. "It is now in the power of our assembly," Samuel Adams told Elbridge Gerry on Oct. 29, 1775, "to establish many wholesome laws and regulations, which could not be done under the former administration of government." Cushing, ed., *Writings of Samuel Adams*, III, 230. A week later Adams informed James Warren that Massachusetts's new government represented "the golden Opportunity of recovering the Virtue and reforming the Manners of our Country." Nov. 4, 1775, Ford, ed., *Warren-Adams Letters*, I, 171.

75. Adams to James Warren, Mar. 31, 1777, Ford, ed., *Warren-Adams Letters*, I, 308; Landon Carter to George Washington, May 9, 1776, Force, ed., *American Archives*, 4th Ser., VI, 391.

76. Zubly, *Law of Liberty*, xv. For the standard statement of Jefferson's agrarian views see his *Notes on the State of Virginia*, ed. William Peden (Chapel Hill, 1955), 164–65. See also Samuel Adams to R. H. Lee, July 15, 1774, Cushing, ed., *Writings of Samuel Adams*, III, 139: "It is the Virtue of the Yeomanry that we are chiefly to depend on." On the celebration of the yeoman see Chester E. Eisinger, "The Influence of Natural Rights and Physiocratic Doctrines on American Agrarian Thought during the Revolutionary Period," *Agricultural History*, 21 (1947), 13–23, and "The Freehold Concept in Eighteenth-Century American Letters," *Wm. and Mary Qtly.*, 3d Ser., 4 (1947), 42–59.

tended to form "a system by which every fibre would be eradicated of ancient or future aristocracy; and a foundation laid for a government truly republican."[77] The Virginians' revision of laws, for example, although it may not have been, as Jefferson proposed to Edmund Pendleton in the summer of 1776, an immediate return to "that happy system of our ancestors, the wisest and most perfect ever yet devised by the wit of man, as it stood before the 8th century," was indeed, as the General Assembly realized, a work "which proposes . . . various and material changes in our legal code."[78] Through extensive changes in inheritance, landowning, education, religion, administration, and law, designed to involve the people more personally in the affairs of government than at any time since the ancient Saxons, the Virginians hoped that their new republican government would create the sources for its own sustenance.[79]

The reforms were often foiled or compromised, the expectations smashed; yet the intentions were very real in 1776. For a young Virginian, who a decade later was to emerge as one of the greatest minds of the Revolutionary generation, the Revolution offered ecstatic prospects for a new kind of politics. In the spring of 1777 James Madison took his republicanism so seriously that he sought to promote by his own example "the proper reform" in the electoral practices of the state by doing away with all the personal soliciting and treating of voters that were corrupting Virginia's politics—practices that were "inconsistent with the purity of moral and of republican principles," but practices that were part of Virginia's experience for decades.[80] That Madison lost the election to the House of Delegates to a former tavern-keeper, that the republican hopes may have proved illusory, does not detract from the existence of these kinds of hopes in 1776, but indeed helps to explain in the years after Independence the increasing disenchantment of Madison and other Whigs with their Revolutionary assumptions and expectations.

77. Jefferson, "Autobiography," Paul L. Ford, ed., *Writings of Thomas Jefferson* (Washington, 1892–99), I, 68–69. For a general discussion of Jefferson's legal reforms see Boyd, ed., *Jefferson Papers*, II, 305–24.

78. Jefferson to Pendleton, Aug. 13, 1776, Boyd, ed., *Jefferson Papers*, I, 492; Va. Assembly quoted in *ibid.*, II, 315.

79. See Jefferson's general discussion of reform in *Notes on Virginia*, ed. Peden, 130–49. On the influence of the Saxons on Jefferson see Colbourn, *Lamp of Experience*, 158–84, and below, 227–28.

80. Hutchinson and Rachal, eds., *Madison Papers*, I, 193. For Edmund Pendleton's similar hopes see Jack R. Pole, *Political Representation in England and the Origins of the American Republic* (London, 1966), 161.

Yet even as the clergy and Revolutionary leaders were filling the air with their visionary and passionate anticipations in 1776, the underlying anxiety was never lost. It was with mingled "Hopes and Fears," as John Adams put it, that the Americans set about the building of their republican polities. Their image of themselves was truly ambivalent. With their eyes and ears turned toward Europe they marveled at their republican mediocrity and simplicity. Yet when they searched inward they saw all the evils the Enlightenment had told them they lacked. Their society seemed strangely both equal and unequal, virtuous and vicious. The erecting of republican governments, therefore, was not only a natural political adjustment to the social reality of the New World, but also (and hopefully) the instrument for reestablishing and preserving the virtue and equality Americans thought they had been losing prior to the Revolution. By 1776 men had come to believe that the controversy with England, "before we are debased by Bribery and Corruption, or enervated by Luxury, may prove the Means of fixing and establishing Liberty upon the most permanent Basis."[81]

It was a grandiose and dangerous experiment, and because it has succeeded so well (although not as the Revolutionaries anticipated), it is difficult to appreciate their sense of the precariousness of what they were attempting. They realized fully the delicacy of the republican polity and the difficulties involved in sustaining it. "The new Governments we are assuming, in every Part," John Adams told his wife in July 1776, "will require a Purification from our Vices, and an Augmentation of our Virtues or they will be no Blessings." Even Thomas Jefferson, sanguine as he was, raised the possibility in August 1776 of "a re-acknolegement of the British tyrant as our king." "Should we not have in contemplation," he asked Edmund Pendleton, "and prepare for an event (however deprecated) which may happen in the possibility of things." "Remember," he warned, "how universally the people run into the idea of recalling Charles the 2d. after living many years under a republican government."[82]

Indeed, it is only in the context of this sense of uncertainty and risk that the Americans' obsessive concern in 1776 with their social character can be properly comprehended. They knew only

81. Adams to Abigail Adams, July 3, 1776, Butterfield, ed., *Family Correspondence*, II, 28; Baldwin, *Duty of Rejoicing*, 31–32.

82. Adams to Abigail Adams, July 3, 1776, Butterfield, ed., *Family Correspondence*, II, 28; Jefferson to Pendleton, Aug. 13, 1776, Boyd, ed., *Jefferson Papers*, I, 492.

too well where the real source of danger lay. "We shall succeed if we are virtuous," Samuel Adams told John Langdon in the summer of 1777. "I am infinitely more apprehensive of the Contagion of Vice than the Power of all other Enemies." Benjamin Rush in 1777 even expressed the hope that the war would not end too soon: "A peace at this time would be the greatest curse that could befall us. . . . Liberty without virtue would be no blessing to us." Several more military campaigns were needed, he said to John Adams, in order "to purge away the monarchical impurity we contracted by laying so long upon the lap of Great Britain." The Revolution with all its evocation of patriotism and the martial spirit would cleanse the American soul of its impurities and introduce "among us the same temperance in pleasure, the same modesty in dress, the same justice in business, and the same veneration for the name of the Deity which distinguished our ancestors."[83]

83. Adams to Langdon, Aug. 7, 1777, Cushing, ed., *Writings of Samuel Adams*, III, 402–03; Rush to Adams, Aug. 8, 1777, Lyman H. Butterfield, ed., *Letters of Benjamin Rush* (Princeton, 1951), I, 152.

PART TWO

The Constitution of the States

The answer to the . . . question, can America be happy under a government of her own, is short and simple, viz. as happy as she pleases; she hath a blank sheet to write upon.
—THOMAS PAINE, 1776

CHAPTER IV

The Restructuring of Power

1. FOUNDATIONS FOR FREEDOM

"Almost all political establishments have been the creatures of chance rather than of wisdom," wrote James Burgh in the first volume of his *Political Disquisitions*. "Therefore it is impossible to say what would be the effect of a perfect commonwealth," since there was in history "no example of such a phenomenon." Here in these common radical Whig sentiments was a provocative challenge that seemed to the Americans of 1776 to be somehow providentially directed at them. Their response was a spine-tingling exhilaration. "How few of the human race," rejoiced John Adams, "have ever enjoyed an opportunity of making an election of government, more than of air, soil, or climate for themselves or their children!" They did not need James Burgh to remind them that all previous nations had been compelled to accept their constitutions from some conqueror or some supreme lawgiver or had found themselves entrapped by a form of government molded by accident, caprice, or violence. They knew—and they told themselves repeatedly—that they were "the first people whom heaven has favoured with an opportunity of deliberating upon, and choosing the forms of government under which they should live."[1]

It is difficult to recapture the intensity of excitement felt by Americans in 1776 over the prospect of forming new republican

1. Burgh, *Disquisitions*, I, 23; [Adams], *Thoughts on Government*, Adams, ed., *Works of John Adams*, IV, 200; John Jay, Charge to the Grand Jury, Kingston, N. Y., Sept. 9, 1777, Niles, ed., *Principles*, 181.

governments. "It is a work," said Thomas Jefferson, "of the most interesting nature and such as every individual would wish to have his voice in." And to some it seemed as if this was precisely the case. Even the business of the Continental Congress was stifled because so many delegates—including Jefferson—left for home to take part in the paramount activity of erecting the new state governments. "*Constitutions*," remarked Francis Lightfoot Lee, "employ every pen." It was as if every American agreed with the New Yorker who declared that establishing new governments "on wise and lasting principles, is the greatest work the mind of man can undertake"—governments that necessarily had to be those of the individual states, since as John Adams recalled, no one then thought "of consolidating this vast Continent under one national Government"; the central union was actually not to be a government at all, but "after the Example of the Greeks, the Dutch and the Swiss, . . . a Confederacy of States, each of which must have a separate Government."[2] Nothing—not the creation of this confederacy, not the Continental Congress, not the war, not the French alliance—in the years surrounding the Declaration of Independence engaged the interests of Americans more than the framing of these separate governments. Only an understanding of the purpose they gave to their Revolution can explain their fascination.

For the American Revolution was not simply a war for independence, for freedom from colonial bondage. A military victory was of course a necessary prerequisite, but it was also the least important aim of the Revolution. "A bare conquest over our enemy is not enough," declared a New Hampshire writer; "and nothing short of a form of government fixed on genuine principles can preserve our liberties inviolate." "In truth," said Jefferson in the spring of 1776, "it is the whole object of the present controversy." Let Americans mold their governments, enjoined William Gordon, "so as not only to exclude kings but tyranny. . . . Now is the golden opportunity for vanishing tyranny as well as royalty out of the American states, and sending them back to Europe from whence they were imported."[3]

2. Jefferson to Thomas Nelson, May 16, 1776, Boyd, ed., *Jefferson Papers*, I, 292; Robert Morris to Horatio Gates, Oct. 27, 1776, and F. L. Lee to Landon Carter, Nov. 9, 1776, Burnett, ed., *Letters of Congress*, I, 135, 149; Sentinel, *To the Inhabitants of New-York*; Butterfield, ed., *Diary of Adams*, III, 352.
3. "The Republican," Jan. 30, 1776, in Frederick Chase, *A History of Dartmouth College . . .* (Cambridge, Mass., 1891), 431; Jefferson to Nelson, May 16,

Their lengthy debate with Great Britain could easily blend into their discussions of the nature of the new governments—indeed often in the same essay or pamphlet—for the whole was subsumed in their search for an understanding of the science of politics. By 1776 they realized, as Timothy Dwight said, that they were forming their independent republics "at a period when every species of knowledge, natural and moral, is arrived to a state of perfection, which the world never before saw." It had become their awesome responsibility, not only for their own "future happiness or misery . . . as a people" but for that of "millions unborn," to apply with "sober reason and cool deliberation" all that they had learned of "the causes of prosperity and misery in other governments." "With the independency of the American States," they told themselves, "a new era in politics has commenced." "From century to century, the forms of Government have been varied, but have ever been calculated to the meridian of the present day." It seemed to be their destiny "boldly to chalk out a new plan, and shew to *reviving* Eastern realms, if *reviving* should ever be their fate, that the true art of government is yet to unfold." The destruction of their various monarchical constitutions would allow them "to erect more eligible systems of government on their ruins." By taking warning "from the folly of others," wrote the American editor of Burgh's *Political Disquisitions,* the Americans could "start fair, for laying a sure foundation that freedom shall last for many generations."[4]

The building of this permanent foundation for freedom thus became the essence of the Revolution. As early as 1775 the most revolutionary-inclined saw the erection of new governments as the best instrument for breaking the ties with England. By the summer of 1775 the brace of Adamses had worked out a program for independence, involving the establishing of foreign alliances, the creation of a confederation, and the framing of new governments. The crucial step, everyone realized, was "to have Governments set up by the people in every Colony." "When this is done

1776, Boyd, ed., *Jefferson Papers*, I, 292; William Gordon, *The Separation of the Jewish Tribes* . . . (Boston, 1777), 33–34.

4. Timothy Dwight, *A Valedictory Address . . . at Yale College, July 25th 1776* . . . (New Haven, 1776), 12; Ebenezer Elmer, Address, Aug. 7, 1776, Nelson *et al.*, eds., *New Jersey Archives*, 2d Ser., I, 173, 174; Ramsay, *Oration on the Advantages of American Independence*, Niles, ed., *Principles*, 379; Phila. *Pa. Packet*, July 4, 1774; Jay, Charge, Sept. 9, 1777, Niles, ed., *Principles*, 181; Phila. *Pa. Journal*, Nov. 22, 1775.

. . . ," predicted Samuel Adams, "the Colonies will feel their Independence."[5]

As the royal governments disintegrated after fighting broke out in the spring of 1775, the need for some sort of new government in several of the colonies became pressing, and radical-minded men made the best of the necessity. "You have no government, no finances, no troops," wrote one Virginian in the summer of 1775. "Turn then your thoughts, I beseech you, to the formation of a constitution." As early as 1774 men in Massachusetts had urged the resumption of the old 1691 Charter by the Provincial Congress. Although desirous of replacing the interim provincial convention with some firmer form of government, the Massachusetts Congress was reluctant "to assume the reins of civil government" on its own authority and perhaps thereby to disrupt the unity of the colonies. Therefore in May 1775 Massachusetts applied to the Continental Congress for the "most explicit advice, respecting the taking up and exercising the powers of civil government." This was ticklish business and the Congress moved cautiously— too cautiously for some like John Adams; but in June it recommended that Massachusetts resume its Charter of 1691. Although this was far from what the radicals in the Congress wanted, it still represented "a Precedent of Advice to the seperate States to institute Governments"—a precedent that was soon amplified when in the fall of 1775 New Hampshire and South Carolina both sought the sanction of the Congress to form governments. By the end of the year the Congress had recommended to both soliciting colonies and to Virginia, although not explicitly requested to, that each call a full and free representation of the people to form whatever government it thought necessary, "during the Continuance of the present dispute between Great Britain and the Colonies."[6]

Even though the revolutionary-minded were hardly satisfied with the wording of these resolutions, they realized that Con-

5. Samuel Adams to Samuel Cooper, Apr. 30, 1776, Cushing, ed., *Writings of Samuel Adams*, III, 283. On John Adams's staged plan for revolution see Adams to Patrick Henry, June 3, 1776, Burnett, ed., *Letters of Congress*, I, 471.

6. Pinkney's Wmsbg. *Va. Gazette*, Aug. 17, 1775; Harry A. Cushing, *History of the Transition from Province to Commonwealth Government in Massachusetts*, (*Columbia University Studies in History, Economics, and Public Law*, VII [N. Y., 1896]), 168–69; William Lincoln, ed., *The Journals of Each Provincial Congress of Massachusetts in 1774 and 1775* (Boston, 1838), 230; Butterfield, ed., *Diary of Adams*, III, 351–57. See Edmund C. Burnett, *The Continental Congress . . .* (N. Y., 1941), 122–24.

gress's action was "a Tryumph and a most important Point gained" in the movement toward independence. "Gentlemen seem more and more to enlarge their views," Samuel Adams wrote to James Warren in December 1775, "and we must be content to wait till the fruit is ripe before we gather it." "To contrive some Method for the Colonies to glide insensibly, from under the old Government, into a peaceable and contented submission to new ones" was, as John Adams said, "the most difficult and dangerous Part of the Business Americans have to do in this mighty Contest."[7] Throughout the fall of 1775 and winter of 1776 discussion of the necessity and advisability "of revolutionizing all the Governments" grew more and more frequent, both within the walls of Congress and even out-of-doors. By April the colonists not only had heard Paine's call for independence but also were reading John Adams's *Thoughts on Government*, which now proved, said Richard Henry Lee, "the business of framing government not to be so difficult a thing as most people imagine." Early in May independence seemed clearly to be just a question of time and manner. On May 4, Rhode Island formally cut its ties to the Crown; within two weeks Virginia began work on a new government and ordered its delegates in Congress to introduce a resolution for independence. At the same time the radicals intensified their pressure on the Congress, as the best—perhaps the only—means of moving the balky proprietary colonies and of bringing about a continental independence. Dissatisfied with the moderate, piecemeal advice given to individual colonies, and aided by the British act declaring America in rebellion, the Whig radicals moved the Congress toward a general and decisive "Recommendation to the People of all the States to institute Governments"—a recommendation that would in effect drag the reluctant colonies into independence. For, as John Adams told his wife, "No Colony, which shall assume a Government under the People, will give it up."[8]

The fruit of their efforts was the congressional resolution of May 10, 1776, advising the colonies to adopt new governments

7. Butterfield, ed., *Diary of Adams*, III, 357; Samuel Adams to James Warren, Dec. 5, 1775, quoted in Burnett, *Continental Congress*, 124; John Adams to Mercy Warren, Ford, ed., *Warren-Adams Letters*, I, 222.

8. Butterfield, ed., *Diary of Adams*, III, 357, 358; R. H. Lee to Patrick Henry, Apr. 20, 1776, James C. Ballagh, ed., *The Letters of Richard Henry Lee* (N. Y., 1914), I, 179; Adams to Abigail Adams, May 17, 1776, Butterfield, ed., *Family Correspondence*, I, 411.

"where no government sufficient to the exigencies of their affairs have been hitherto established." This was capped on May 15 by a preamble declaring "that the exercise of every kind of authority under the . . . Crown should be totally suppressed," and calling for the exertion of "all the powers of government . . . under the authority of the people of the colonies." A momentous step—and many Americans realized it. When the lukewarm James Duane called it "a Machine for the fabrication of Independence," John Adams could jubilantly retort that "it was independence itself." Not all the delegates who voted for the resolution believed they were endorsing independence, noted Carter Braxton of Virginia, but "those out of doors on both sides [of] the question construe it in that manner."[9]

The May 15 resolution was truly, as John Adams called it, "an Epocha, a decisive Event," "the last step" in the long, tortuous march since 1763, marking a "total, absolute independence" from Great Britain. Adams was surely justified in his later complaint voiced in his autobiography that his anxious labors—which more than anyone's were responsible for the May resolutions—were "then little known" and "now forgotten, by all but . . . a very few."[10] For if, as Jefferson and others agreed, the formation of new governments was the whole object of the Revolution, then the May resolution authorizing the drafting of new constitutions was the most important act of the Continental Congress in its history. There in the May 15 resolution was the real declaration of independence, from which the measures of early July could be but derivations.

2. THE TRANSFORMATION OF THE MAGISTRACY

"To form a new Government requires infinite care and unbounded attention," warned George Washington in May 1776; "for if the foundation is badly laid, the superstructure must be bad. . . . A matter of such moment cannot be the Work of a

9. Worthington C. Ford, ed., *Journals of the Continental Congress 1774–1789* (Washington, 1904–37), I, 342, 357; Butterfield, ed., *Diary of Adams*, III, 386; Carter Braxton to Landon Carter, May 17, 1776, Burnett, ed., *Letters of Congress*, I, 453–54. See also R. H. Lee to Charles Lee, May 21, 1776, *Lee Papers*, II, 31–32.
10. Adams to Abigail Adams, May 17, 1776, Butterfield, ed., *Family Correspondence*, I, 411; Butterfield, ed., *Diary of Adams*, III, 335, 386.

day.''[11] Nevertheless, once the path was opened by the Continental Congress, the formation of new governments was remarkably rapid. In response to separate congressional recommendations New Hampshire and South Carolina as early as January 5 and March 26 of 1776 had drawn up preliminary constitutions. Framers in Virginia were likewise already at work on a new government when the general congressional resolutions of May 10 and 15 gave them a new and broader sanction for their Constitution adopted on June 29. And with the May resolves and the Declaration of Independence the other states followed successively: by the end of 1776 New Jersey (July 2), Delaware (September 20), Pennsylvania (September 28), Maryland (November 9), and North Carolina (December 18) had formed new constitutions. Because the corporate colonies, Rhode Island (May 4) and Connecticut (October), even before the Revolution were republics in fact, they simply confined themselves to the elimination of all mention of royal authority in their existing charters. Largely because of the exigencies of war Georgia (February 5, 1777) and New York (April 20, 1777) delayed their constitution-making until the following year. Vermont, whose integrity and independence no other state recognized until the 1780's, framed its government on July 8, 1777. On March 19, 1778, South Carolina revised and more firmly established its Revolutionary Constitution drafted two years earlier. In the summer of 1775 Massachusetts, upon the advice of the Continental Congress, had recovered its abrogated Charter of 1691 but, like the government of New Hampshire, was managing without a governor, the Council acting as the executive. Both states, however, realized at the outset that their governments were only temporary expedients and devoted a good part of their energies throughout the remaining years of the war to the formation of new constitutions.[12]

11. Washington to John Washington, May 31, 1776, Fitzpatrick, ed., *Writings of Washington*, V, 20.

12. For a general discussion of the constitution-making, see Nevins, *American States*, 117–70. Comparative studies of the Revolutionary state constitutions can be found in William C. Morey, "The First State Constitutions," American Academy of Political and Social Science, *Annals*, 4 (1893), 201–32; and in William C. Webster, "Comparative Study of the State Constitutions of the American Revolution," *ibid.*, 9 (1897), 380–420. On the constitutions of the southern states see Fletcher M. Green, *Constitutional Development in the South Atlantic States, 1776–1860* (Chapel Hill, 1930), 47–141. For works on the constitutions of particular states see Charles R. Erdman, Jr., *The New Jersey Constitution of 1776* (Princeton, 1929); J. Paul Selsam, *The Pennsylvania Constitution of 1776: A*

Because of this rapidity, it has been too easy to see the new governments as simply pragmatic adjustments to independence and as essentially carry-overs of the colonial structures. While the corporate colonies did change only the phrasing of their colonial charters, since their magistrates had been elective even under the Crown, the other states rightly regarded their new governments as revolutionary creations, "the vital principles of which," said William Henry Drayton, "are the reverse in every particular" from their former royal governments. Of course the Americans drew greatly on their past experience, as they well knew and as historians have commonly emphasized. As John Adams warned in his *Thoughts on Government*, it was "safest to proceed in all established modes, to which the people have been familiarized by habit." Yet to stress the continuity of the governments with their colonial predecessors, to look for the antecedents of their Revolutionary polities in their colonial experience, is to miss the significance of their achievement and to render incomprehensible the sense of excitement and enthusiasm they expressed in being involved, like so many Lycurguses, in an affair which was "the most important that has been transacted in any nation for some centuries past."[13]

In a most basic sense, however, the Revolutionary governments did maintain a connection with the past. While their constitutions made new and radical changes in the structure of power as the Americans had known it, the assumptions about the nature of politics which underlay these changes remained essentially what they had been under British authority. Even after Independence most Americans still conceived of politics in conventional Whig terms. Republicanism, whatever else it changed, did not alter for Americans the central problem of government. Republican magistrates were no more "representative" of the people than monarchs.

Study in Revolutionary Democracy (Phila., 1936); H. Clay Reed, "The Delaware Constitution of 1776," *Delaware Notes*, 6th Ser. (1930), 7–42; Frank Nash, "The North Carolina Constitution of 1776 and Its Makers," *James Sprunt Historical Publications*, 11 (1912), 7–23.

13. Drayton, Charge to the Grand Jury, Charleston, Apr. 23, 1776, Niles, ed., *Principles*, 333; [Adams], *Thoughts on Government*, Adams, ed., *Works of John Adams*, IV, 195; "The Interest of America" (1776), Force, ed., *American Archives*, 4th Ser., VI, 840. On the similarity and continuity between the colonial and state governments see Benjamin F. Wright, "The Early History of Written Constitutions in America," in *Essays in History and Political Theory in Honor of Charles H. McIlwain* (Cambridge, Mass., 1936), 344–71; and Nevins, *American States*, 118–19.

Power in the hands of an elected ruler, no less than in a hereditary one, was still presumed to exist autonomously. In classical Whig thought all rulers, whether English kings or Venetian doges, supposedly derived their powers ultimately from the people; election only made explicit what was always implicit. Both hereditary and elected rulers were considered clothed with a special authority and "exalted from among the people, to bear rule."[14] The new American governor, although now elected, was still to be "some one whom variety of circumstances may have placed in a singular and conspicuous point of view, and to whom Heaven had given talents to make him the choice of the people to entrust with powers for sudden and decisive execution." Thus mere popular election, in place of royal appointment or hereditary succession, was no substantial guarantee against tyranny, because as history only too clearly showed, many people "may be disposed to worship a creature of their own creation." "Power like wealth, draws many admirers to its possessor," and although "all men will confess" that a gubernatorial power "is dangerous in any community, they often flatter themselves, that the rising Augustus, having smiled upon them, in his early adventures, they (*in particular*) have nothing to fear from him, and therefore will not oppose him." The Americans knew they had among themselves "tyrants enough at heart"; and although their governors would now be elected periodically by the people or their representatives, so intoxicating and corrupting was the power of ruling that an elected magistrate was actually no less to be dreaded than an hereditary one. Their own colonial experience and their Whig theory of politics had taught them only too well where the source of despotism lay. "The executive power," said a Delaware Whig, "is ever restless, ambitious, and ever grasping at encrease of power."[15]

Only this unaltered Whig fear of magisterial power makes comprehensible the radical changes the Americans made in 1776 in the nature of the authority of their now elected governors. They were not content merely to erect higher barriers against encroach-

---

14. [Mather], *America's Appeal*, 6. See also Foster, *Short Essay on Civil Government*, 5–6, 15–17, 20; *Essay upon Government*, 105, 109; Josiah Stearns, *Two Sermons, January 20th, 1777*, 12.

15. William Hooper to North Carolina Congress, Oct. 26, 1776, Saunders, ed., *Col. Recs. of N. C.*, X, 867; John Sullivan to Meshech Weare, Dec. 11, 1775, Force, ed., *American Archives*, 4th Ser., IV, 243; Demophilus, *Genuine Principles*, 17; "The Republican," Jan. 30, 1777, in Chase, *Dartmouth College*, 431; Phila. Pa. *Journal*, Nov. 13, 1776.

ing power or to formulate new and more explicit charters of the people's liberties. In their ambitious desire to root out tyranny once and for all, they went beyond what Englishmen of 1215 or 1688 had attempted: their new constitutions destroyed "the kingly office" outright and "absolutely divested [it] of all it's rights, powers and prerogatives," so that "all other persons whatsoever shall be and for ever remain incapable of the same; and that the said office shall henceforth cease and never more either in name or substance be re-established within this colony."[16] The Americans, in short, made of the gubernatorial magistrate a new kind of creature, a very pale reflection indeed of his regal ancestor. This change in the governor's position meant the effectual elimination of the magistracy's major responsibility for ruling the society—a remarkable and abrupt departure from the English constitutional tradition. The King may have been rigidly confined in the eighteenth-century constitution; but few Englishmen would deny that the principal duties of government still belonged with the Crown.[17] In fact, it was by seriously attempting to shoulder this constitutional responsibility that George III had run into difficulties—difficulties that the English characteristically solved in time not by the abolition of the Crown but by the parliamentary invasion of it. Few in 1776, however, foresaw the nature of this constitutional transformation, least of all the Americans. For them George III was only a transmigrated Stuart bent on tyranny. And only a radical destruction of that kind of magisterial authority could prevent the resurgence of arbitrary power in their land.

Most Americans in 1776 did "by no means object to a Governour," but at the same time they would "by no means consent to lodging too much power in the hands of one person, or suffering an interest in government to exist separate from that of the people, or any man to hold an office, for the execution of which he is not in some way or other answerable to that people to whom he owes his political existence." They agreed with William Hooper of North Carolina that "for the sake of Execution we must have a Magistrate," but it must be a magistrate "solely executive," a governor, as Thomas Jefferson's 1776 draft for the Virginia Constitution explicitly stated, without a voice in legislation,

16. Jefferson's Third Draft of a Virginia Constitution (1776), Boyd, ed., *Jefferson Papers*, I, 357.
17. For a discussion in 1773 by John Adams of the King's prerogatives see Adams, ed., *Works of John Adams*, III, 545, 555, 559. On the responsibility of the executive to govern see above, 26.

without any control over the meeting of the Assembly, without the authority to declare war or make peace, to raise armies, to coin money, to erect courts, offices, corporations, ports, or navigation aids, to lay lengthy embargoes, to retain or recall members of the state arbitrarily, to make denizens, to pardon crimes, to grant dignities or rights of precedence, in sum, a ruler, as John Adams proposed, "stripped of most of those badges of domination, called prerogatives," those supposed "checks upon the licentiousness of the people," as John Sullivan called them, which were "only the children of designing or ambitious men, no such thing being necessary." While the new state constitutions did not follow Jefferson's example and specify all the various powers the governors were prohibited from wielding, they were clear in forbidding the chief magistrates, "under any pretence," as the Maryland and Virginia constitutions declared, from exercising "any power or prerogative by virtue of any Law, statute, or Custom, of England." As the war years were quickly to show, such an enfeebled governor could not be a magisterial ruler in the traditional sense, but could only be, as Jefferson correctly called him, an "Administrator."[18]

In Pennsylvania, where radical Whig thought found its fullest expression, the governor was actually totally eliminated, and replaced by an Executive Council of twelve, who were elected directly by the people and were, together with the members of the Assembly, as Joseph Reed said, "also the Representatives of the people." The Pennsylvania constitution-makers were determined, at least "for the present" (as the Constitution stated), to keep the executive authority in the hands of the people as closely as seemed practicable and thus to establish a government that was as much a democracy, in the eighteenth-century sense of the term, as seemed feasible for a large state. In the thinking of these most extreme Whigs the very "idea" of a governor seemed "too monarchical," and "would imply an advantage in that form of gov-

18. Sullivan to Weare, Dec. 11, 1775, Force, ed., *American Archives*, 4th Ser., IV, 241–43; Hooper to N. C. Congress, Oct. 26, 1776, Saunders, ed., *Col. Recs. of N. C.*, I, 867; Jefferson's Third Draft, Boyd, ed., *Jefferson Papers*, I, 360; [Adams], *Thoughts on Government*, Adams, ed., *Works of John Adams*, IV, 196; Md. Cons. (1776), XXXIII; Va. Cons. (1776), in Boyd, ed., *Jefferson Papers*, I, 380. The Revolutionary Constitution of Virginia was enacted as a single article, preceded by a declaration of rights. For the texts of the Revolutionary state constitutions see Thorpe, ed., *Federal and State Constitutions*. All citations to the constitutions are by article or section except for the Virginia Constitution of 1776.

ernment we have renounced." There was no longer any "need of
a representative of a King, for we have none."[19]

While no other state in 1776 was as vehement as Pennsylvania in
eradicating even the nominal existence of the governor, Pennsylvania's action was extraordinary only in form, since all of the
states destroyed the substance of an independent magistracy. The
title "president" adopted by three other states, besides Pennsylvania in 1776—Delaware, New Hampshire and South Carolina—
only made explicit what other constitution-makers took for
granted. No one in 1776 expected the new republican rulers to
stand alone: councils of state participated in almost all executive
duties and greatly diluted the independence of the governors'
authority, making them (except in South Carolina) little more
than chairmen of their executive boards.[20] The royal governors
had, of course, also been surrounded by councils, but most of the
new privy councils were significantly different from their colonial predecessors. Their membership was now generally smaller
in number and except in the New England states and New Jersey
they were now confined exclusively to executive or judicial functions, the legislative tasks formerly exercised concurrently with
magisterial responsibilities by the colonial councils—a mixture of
duties which had caused controversy[21]—being now conferred on
separate upper houses of the legislatures. Most important, the new
councils were no longer appointed by the magisterial authority,
as all the colonial councils except those in the corporate colonies
and Massachusetts had been; they were now to be elected for
varying terms by the assemblies, or, as in the cases of Pennsylvania
and Vermont, directly by the people. No longer were the coun-

19. Joseph Reed to General Greene, Nov. 5, 1778, in William B. Reed, *Life
and Correspondence of Joseph Reed* (Phila., 1847), II, 39; Pa. Cons. (1776), Sec.
19; *An Essay of a Frame of Government for Pennsylvania* (Phila., 1776), 4; Phila.
Pa. Packet, July 1, 1776, reprinted in Force, ed., *American Archives*, 4th Ser.,
VI, 843.
20. On the powers of the new state governors see in general Margaret B.
Macmillan, *The War Governors in the American Revolution* (N. Y., 1943),
Chaps. IV, V. For a discussion of the powers of the royal governors see Evarts
B. Greene, *The Provincial Governor in the English Colonies of North America*
(Cambridge, Mass., 1898), esp. Chaps. VI, VIII.
21. On disputes over the mixing of magisterial and legislative duties in the
colonial councils see Leigh, *Considerations*, 67; [Oxenbridge Thacher], *Consid-
erations on the Election of Counsellors, Humbly Offered to the Electors* ([Bos-
ton], 1761), 4–6; Lee to Henry, Apr. 20, 1776, Ballagh, ed., *Letters of R. H. Lee*,
I, 179; Ellen E. Brennan, *Plural Office-Holding in Massachusetts, 1760–1780*
(Chapel Hill, 1945), Chaps. II–III.

cilors to be considered, like the Privy Council of the English King, mere creatures and aides of the magistracy. They now became for Americans more controllers than servants of the governors in the business of ruling, since most of the constitutions were emphatic in stating that what executive powers the governors possessed must be exercised with the advice and consent of the councils of state.

The executives in all of the governments framed in the first year of constitution-making (except in the former corporate colonies and Pennsylvania, Vermont, and New York) were to be elected by the legislatures, usually by joint ballot of the two houses. While this electoral procedure met scattered resistance in 1776, which grew in the coming years, because it "would be putting too dangerous a power" in the hands of a possible "majority of designing men" who "might elect a person to answer their own particular purposes, to the great emolument of those individuals, and the oppression of their fellow-subjects," so confident in 1776 were most of the constitution-makers in the representational system that election of the chief magistrate by the people's representatives, rather than by the people themselves, seemed to pose no threat to liberty. Besides, since the governors were not regarded in any sense as "representatives" of the people, it seemed obvious that such legislative election was the best means—along with specially high property qualifications stipulated in many states—to guarantee, as the Maryland Constitution put it, that someone "of wisdom, experience and virtue" would be selected as chief magistrate. That election of the governor by the legislature would make the governor dependent on the legislature was not generally seen in 1776 as an evil, but rather was viewed, as William Tennent of South Carolina declared, as a "benefit," compelling "the President's asking advice of the House on every important measure."[22]

However slight and dependent the authority granted the rulers, it was to be only temporary, for with frequent elections the governors were "again put on a level with their fellow subjects, . . . which is a great means of preventing mismanagement when in power." All of the states in 1776–77, except Pennsylvania, Delaware, New York, and South Carolina, provided for the annual

22. Sullivan to Weare, Dec. 11, 1775, Force, ed., *American Archives*, 4th Ser., IV, 242; Phila. *Pa. Journal*, Nov. 13, 1776; Md. Cons. (1776), Art. XXV; Newton B. Jones, ed., "Writings of the Reverend William Tennent, 1740–1777," *South Carolina Historical Magazine*, 61 (1960), 192.

election of the executive.[23] Moreover seven of the ten new constitutions drafted in 1776–77—Pennsylvania, Delaware, Maryland, Virginia, North Carolina, South Carolina, and Georgia—limited the number of years the magistrate could successively hold office. "A long continuance in the first executive departments of power or trust is dangerous to liberty," declared the Maryland Constitution, echoing the sentiments of American Whigs; "a rotation, therefore, in those departments is one of the best securities of permanent freedom." In Virginia and Maryland, for example, a person elected governor for three successive years was then ineligible for reelection for four years.[24] For some rabid Whigs even this degree of rotation was not sufficient. Charles Lee, who was a kind of American archetype of the Pure Whig, considered himself "so extremely democratical" that he believed the Virginia Constitution defective because the eligibility of the governor for three successive years furnished him "an opportunity of acquiring a very dangerous influence," and even worse, it enabled "a man who is fond of office and has his eye upon re-election" to court "favour and popularity at the expense of his duty."[25] Mandatory rotation of office and prohibitions on reelection could even be regarded by some Americans and enlightened foreigners as important constitutional devices for compelling mobility in a deferential society where men too often felt obliged to reelect their rulers for fear of dishonoring them.[26] Although many Americans

23. Green, *Observations on Reconciliation*, 23. In Pennsylvania, Delaware, and New York the executive's term was three years; in South Carolina it was two years.

24. Md. Decl. of Rts. (1776), XXXI; Va. Cons. (1776), in Boyd, ed., *Jefferson Papers*, I, 380; Md. Cons. (1776), XXXI. The executive councillors in Pennsylvania were similarly limited (Pa. Cons. [1776], Sec. 19). The second South Carolina Constitution (1778) forbade a governor from reelection for four years (S. C. Cons. [1778], VI). In Delaware the wait for reelection was three years (Del. Cons. [1776], Art. 7). The North Carolina governor was not eligible for more than three years out of six, the Georgia governor one out of three (N. C. Cons. [1776], XV; Ga. Cons. [1777], Art. XXIII).

25. Charles Lee to Patrick Henry, July 29, 1776, *Lee Papers*, II, 178.

26. Increased social mobility was not generally the motive behind rotation of office; rotation was usually regarded as a Whiggish means of preventing an abuse of power. However, on the social implications of rotation see "Loose Thoughts on Government," Force, ed., *American Archives*, 4th Ser., VI, 730; J. Paul Selsam, "Brissot de Warville on the Pennsylvania Constitution of 1776," *Pa. Mag. of Hist. and Biog.*, 72 (1948), 38. The Pennsylvania Constitution uniquely extended the principle of rotation to the members of the legislature as well as the executive so that "the danger of establishing an inconvenient aristocracy will be effectually prevented" (Pa. Cons. [1776], Sec. 19).

in the years ahead would become increasingly disillusioned with the political and social effects of rotation, in 1776 it stood as a cardinal tenet of their Whig faith.

With the Americans' revolutionary conception of what the nature of the ruling authority should be, it was almost a foregone conclusion that the new governors would be prohibited from sharing in the lawmaking authority. Even among those who desired a stronger magistrate than most, it seemed abominable that a single person should have a negative over the voice of the whole society: "From the abuses which power in the hand of an Individual is liable to, and the unreasonableness that an individual should abrogate at pleasure the acts of the Representatives of the people," a third branch in the legislature seemed patently unnecessary. Even John Adams's proposal in his *Thoughts on Government* for a negative power in the hands of the governor was made timidly and without much assurance that it would be followed. Adams did not "expect, nor indeed desire that it should be attempted to give the Governor a Negative" in his own state of Massachusetts. Let the chief executive, he said, be only the head of the Council Board. "Our people will never submit to more," and as Adams explained, it was "not clear that it is best they should."[27]

As if these restrictions on the potential abuse of executive power were not enough, most of the constitutions also provided for the impeachment by the representatives of the people of odious state officials, including even the governors themselves. Nothing indicates better how thoroughly Americans were imbued with Whig apprehensions of misapplied ruling power than their rather unthinking adoption of this ancient English procedure enabling "the grand inquest of the Colony," the representatives of the people, to pull "over-grown criminals who are above the reach of ordinary justice" to the ground. Since impeachment in England had not been used since the early years of the eighteenth century, many of the colonists had retained only a vague sense that their legislatures possessed the power. In fact John Adams stunned his

27. Hooper to N. C. Congress, Oct. 26, 1776, Saunders, ed., *Col. Recs. of N. C.*, X, 868; Adams to James Warren, May 12, 1776, Ford, ed., *Warren-Adams Letters*, I, 242; Adams to Francis Dana, Aug. 16, 1776, Adams, ed., *Works of John Adams*, IX, 429. Among the Revolutionary constitutions drafted in 1776 only the early South Carolina Constitution of March 1776 vested legislative authority in the executive. The elimination of this presidential veto was one of the principal changes made in the new Constitution adopted in 1778.

fellow Massachusetts lawyers in 1774 when he proposed that the House of Representatives use impeachment as a constitutional means of getting at the judges.[28] Hence writing the impeachment process into the Revolutionary constitutions was understandably confused, not only in the designation of the officials liable to impeachment but in the determination of the body trying the impeachment. Some suggested that even members of the legislature, or at least members of the upper house, should be impeachable, but most states confined impeachment to the officers of the state which presumably meant magisterial officials. In Virginia and Delaware the governor could be impeached only after he left office—a means of disgrace that indicates the awe in which the first magistrate, although elective, was still held.[29] As James Madison later pointed out, finding a proper court to try the impeachments was "among the most puzzling articles of a republican Constitution. . . . The diversified expedients adopted in the Constitutions of the several States prove how much the compilers were embarrassed on this subject." While some of the states simply allowed the upper house, like the House of Lords, to try the impeachment, others found this procedure full of problems. For Madison it was manifestly unreasonable that "the right to impeach should be united to that of trying the impeachment," or for that matter, "to that of sharing in the appointment of, or influence on the Tribunal to which the trial may belong."[30] Some

28. [Adams], *Thoughts on Government*, Adams, ed., *Works of John Adams*, IV, 198; *N.-Y. Journal*, Dec. 11, 1766; Foord, *His Majesty's Opposition*, 18n; Mary P. Clarke, *Parliamentary Privilege in the American Colonies* (New Haven, 1943), 39–42; Butterfield, ed., *Diary of Adams*, III, 299–302. See David Y. Thomas, "The Law of Impeachment in the United States," *Amer. Pol. Sci. Rev.*, 2 (1907–08), 378–95.

29. For the impeachment provisions in the state constitutions see Pa. Cons. (1776), Sec. 22; N. Y. Cons. (1777), XXXII–XXXIII; Del. Cons. (1776), Art. 23; Va. Cons. (1776), Boyd, ed., *Jefferson Papers*, I, 382; N. J. Cons. (1776), XII; S. C. Cons. (1778), XXIII; Ga. Cons. (1777), Art. XLIX; Mass. Cons. (1780), Chap. I, Sec. II, Art. VIII; N. H. Cons. (1784), Pt. II, Senate.

30. Madison's Observations on Jefferson's Draft of a Constitution for Virginia, Oct. 1788, Boyd, ed., *Jefferson Papers*, VI, 313–15. In Pennsylvania the executive council that was most likely to be impeached was also the court that tried the impeachments. See *The Proceedings Relative to Calling the Conventions of 1776 and 1790* . . . (Harrisburg, 1825), 110, 127. The debate in New York over what officials were impeachable was especially confused, some suggesting that members of the Senate be liable to impeachment. A special court made up of senators and judges was finally devised to hear the impeachment of "all officers for mal and corrupt conduct in their respective offices," thus leaving the question of who was liable to impeachment purposefully unresolved. See Charles Z. Lincoln, *The Constitutional History of New York from the Beginning of the Colonial*

Americans, like Jefferson, moreover, could never quite reconcile themselves to the idea that anyone—high official or not—could be tried by an extraordinary court outside of the regular rules of law.[31]

3. The Power of Appointment

However important these changes in magisterial authority may have been, they did not in Whig philosophy get to the heart of the matter and destroy the most insidious and powerful weapon of eighteenth-century despotism—the power of appointment to offices. Nothing impressed the radical Whig mind more than the subtle means by which modern societies were enslaved by their rulers. "He who has the giving of all places in a government," Americans were convinced, "will always be master," even "if the constitution were in all other respects the best in the world." The weeds of tyranny flourished because they were able to sink their roots deep into the community, spreading corruption throughout the entire society by the clever distribution of places and positions, so that a "great Chain of political Self-Interest was at length formed; and extended from the *lowest Cobler* in a Borough, to the *King's first Minister*." Although "the wings of prerogative have been clipt, the influence of the crown is greater than ever it was in any period of our history." By exploiting its existence as the fountain of honors, offices, and privileges, the English Crown had been able to evade the restrictions the 1688 Revolution had placed on the royal prerogatives and had "contributed every art to debauch and enervate the minds and morals of all ranks of men." That the Crown, wrote Thomas Paine in *Common Sense*, "derives its whole consequence merely from being the giver of places and pensions is self-evident."[32]

Period to the Year 1905 (Rochester, 1906), I, 538–39. See also Boston *Continental Journal*, June 4, 1778; Return of Lenox, May 28, 1778, in Oscar and Mary Handlin, eds., *The Popular Sources of Political Authority: Documents on the Massachusetts Constitution of 1780* (Cambridge, Mass., 1966), 256. On the impeachment of senators see below, Chap. XIII, n. 7.

31. Jefferson to John Rutledge, Jr., Feb. 2, 1788, Boyd, ed., *Jefferson Papers*, XII, 556–57; Return of Petersham, May 29, 1780, Handlin, eds., *Popular Sources*, 859. North Carolina as well as Virginia provided for impeached officials to be tried by the ordinary courts.

32. Phila. *Pa. Journal*, Jan. 24, 1776; Rev. John Brown, *Estimate of the Manners and Principles of the Times*, 7th ed. (London, 1758), and John Douglas, *Season-*

Not all political commentators saw the King's disposal of offices and emoluments with the jaundiced eyes of the radical Whigs, but all emphasized its importance. For David Hume this pervasive influence of the Crown, whether or not called "by the invidious appellations of *corruption* and *dependence*," was a necessity if the Crown was to carry out its responsibility for governing the realm. Without the prerogative of conferring honors and privileges, wrote William Blackstone, the eighteenth-century Crown would soon have been overborne by the power of the people. The entire collection and management of the large hereditary revenue together with the huge perpetual revenue needed to maintain the growing national debt had been placed in the hands of the King; and this, said Blackstone, had "given rise to such a multitude of new officers, created by and removable at the royal pleasure, that they have extended the influence of government to every corner of the nation." Most Englishmen by the mid-eighteenth century realized that this bestowal of favors and offices was the dynamo that converted royal energy into effective, although subtle, governmental power. Only through the organization and manipulation of a vast system of "influence," used to control elections and pressure members of Parliament, could the Crown's ministers create and maintain any government at all. "It is become an established maxim," wrote Catharine Macaulay disgustedly in her *History of England*, "that corruption is a necessary engine of government."[33]

It was not simply a matter of patronage. In an age where politics was still very personal and political offices and emoluments were the major sources of social distinction and financial security, the power of appointment and preferment cannot be exaggerated. "In the present state of human affairs . . . ," wrote Jonathan Boucher, "a man has, or has not, influence, only as he has, or has not, the power of conferring favours." "Honours and

---

able Hints from an Honest Man (London, 1761), in E. Neville Williams, ed., *The Eighteenth-Century Constitution 1688–1815* . . . (Cambridge, Eng., 1960), 140, 141; Charleston *S.-C. Gazette*, Oct. 3, 1775; [Paine], *Common Sense*, Foner, ed., *Writings of Paine*, I, 8. See Jack P. Greene, "The Georgia Commons House of Assembly and the Power of Appointment to Executive Offices, 1765–1775," *Georgia Historical Quarterly*, 46 (1962), 151–61.

33. David Hume, "Of the Independency of Parliament," *Essays and Treatises on Several Subjects* (London, 1793), I, 51–52; Blackstone, *Commentaries*, I, 334–36; Catharine Macaulay, *The History of England from the Accession of James I* . . . (London, 1769), I, xx. See Kemp, *King and Commons*, 87–90.

offices," declared Blackstone, "are in their nature convertible and synonymous"; offices were the principal marks of social rank, "that the people may know and distinguish such as are set over them, in order to yield them their due respect and obedience." The law supposed, contended Blackstone, that no one was a better judge of the merits and rank of the recipients than the King, who was consequently entrusted with "the sole power of conferring dignities and honours, in confidence that he will bestow them upon none, but such as deserve them."[34] With the unforeseen and prodigious multiplication of offices, places, favors, and perquisites, created by the vast increase in revenues, the eighteenth-century Crown, it appeared, had been given nothing less than the power to structure the society as it saw fit.

In the colonies, where the social hierarchy was especially weak, the power of patronage and preferment assumed an added, in fact, crucial, importance. The royal governors, as the Crown's vicegerents in America, throughout the eighteenth century had continually sought to use their authority as the source of honor and privilege in the community to build webs of influence that could match those in effect in England. Since the history of eighteenth-century colonial politics has yet to be written, it is not clear precisely how successful or unsuccessful they were.[35] Nevertheless the language of the Revolutionaries leaves little doubt that such royal manipulation and influence "in the administration of the provinces"—"the multiplication of officers to strengthen the court interest, . . . advancing to the most eminent stations men without education, and of dissolute manners," and "sporting with our persons and estates, by filling the highest seats of justice with bankrupts, bullies, and blockheads"—was a constant source of exasperation and anxiety in American society. In fact, it was against the seemingly arbitrary and unjust attempts by the British Crown to arrange their political and social order, by "depressing the most virtuous and exalting the most profligate," that the American Whigs were at heart protesting.[36]

34. Boucher, *View of the Causes*, 218; Blackstone, *Commentaries*, I, 271–72. See Richard Pares, *King George III and the Politicians* (Oxford, 1953), 5–30.

35. See, however, Bailyn, "Origins of American Politics," *Perspectives in American History*, 1 (1967), 9–122.

36. Phila. *Pa. Packet*, Mar. 4, 1777. On the governors' patronage see Greene, *Provincial Governor*, 113–17, 157–59. For the success of one royal governor in building a hierarchy of power see Jere R. Daniell, "Politics in New Hampshire under Governor Benning Wentworth, 1741–1767," *Wm. and Mary Qtly.*, 3d Ser., 23 (1966), 76–105.

The Americans did not need Sir Lewis Namier to tell them about the structure of eighteenth-century politics. They knew only too well how society was organized by intricate and personal ties to men of power. The authority that stemmed from the King seemed to form a vast network of connections extending to the royal governors, and ramifying from them into almost every part of American society. By the governors' shameless exploitation of the royal prerogative of conferring offices and dignities "a secret poison has been spread thro'out all our Towns and great Multitudes have been secured for the corrupt Designs of an abandoned Administration." Men who drank of "this baneful poison" were enthralled by the ruling hierarchy and lost their concern for their country. In no colony, it seemed, had the royal designs been more perfected than in Massachusetts, where Americans had watched "with amazement, a numerous and powerful party, formed under the direction of a Governor, born and educated among us, labouring and exerting every nerve to subjugate this country to the most abject slavery, to a foreign power." Not only had Thomas Hutchinson grasped the most important offices into his own hands, but his numerous relatives and hirelings had been placed in strategic positions throughout the community—all so connected and interrelated that it could only be a gigantic pattern of conspiracy. It was the Crown authority—and only the Crown authority—that had caused social and political division in America, for wherever the power of disposing of posts of profit and honor was lodged, "there will be the power of forming a numerous party." For John Adams it was only the "Character and Conduct" of Hutchinson and his vast machine that "have been the Cause of laying a Foundation . . . of perpetual Struggles of one Party for Wealth and Power at the Expense of the Liberties of this Country, and of perpetual Contention and Opposition in the other Party to preserve them." "Is not this amazing ascendency of one Family," asked Adams, "Foundation sufficient on which to erect a Tyranny."[37]

"It may be thought a wonder how one man could influence such numbers to become such implacable enemies to the liberties of their native country." Extensive as the revenues and offices

37. Petition of Pittsfield, Dec. 26, 1775, Handlin, eds., *Popular Sources*, 62; Boston *Independent Chronicle*, Mar. 26, 1778; Adams, entries, Aug. 15, 1765, June 13, 1771, Butterfield, ed., *Diary of Adams*, I, 260, II, 34–35; see also [Mather], *America's Appeal*, 60; Green, *Observations on Reconciliation*, 24; Charleston *S.-C. and American Gazette*, May 21, 1778.

might have been, they were not sufficient to bribe an entire community. But tyrants, Americans realized, did not need to control everyone; they needed to corrupt only a few who in their turn "have overawed the rest." And for the smallest trifle—"for a yard of ribband, or for the sake of wearing any bit of finery at his tail"—a man could be influenced. John Adams was struck by the prevalence of ambition even among the smallest, most insignificant Americans. "The Commission of a Subaltern, in the Militia, will tempt these little Minds, as much as Crowns, and Stars and Garters will greater ones." "It matters not how menial those offices may seem," Ambrose Serle, the young secretary of Admiral Howe, learned from American Tories; "for so there be Influence or Profit in them, they are solicited here more eagerly than in any Country upon Earth." Men, it seemed, would sell their liberty "for any little distinction in title or name."

As one Whig viewed the structure of politics, it seemed that only one man in a hundred was needed to keep the rest in sway. In a remarkable analysis—a Namierite interpretation of politics reduced to a pyramidal geometric progression—the writer attempted to make clear to his readers what had happened in England, what had been attempted in the several colonies, how, in short, a modern tyrant subjugated his people. The ruler, he pointed out, had always a half-dozen supporters around him, "accomplices of his cruelty," who in turn each had a hundred connections—six hundred plunderers, bound to the six as the six were to the tyrant. They filled the key posts of the government and formed "the social bond that holds the country together in the tyrant's sway." Under the six hundred were scattered the instruments of their avarice and cruelty—six thousand, who fed on the people and lived under the shadow and protection of their superiors. The entire structure was tied together by the strongest kinds of links and permeated into the whole society. "Whoever will amuse himself in tracing this chain," concluded the analyst, "will see that not only the six thousand, but perhaps an hundred thousand are fastened to the tyrant by it, of which he makes the same use as Jupiter does in Homer, who boasts that if he but touch the end of it, he can draw all the Gods towards him."[38]

38. Boston *Independent Chronicle*, Mar. 26, 1778; Thacher, *Oration Delivered March 5, 1776*, Niles, ed., *Principles*, 43; Phila. *Pa. Packet*, Oct. 3, 1774; Adams, entry, Feb. 4, 1772, Butterfield, ed., *Diary of Adams*, II, 53; Tatum, ed., *Journal of Serle*, 149; N. Y. *Constitutional Gazette*, Feb. 24, 1776.

Americans in 1776 were resolved to destroy the capacity of their rulers ever again to put together such structures of domination or to determine the ranks of the social order. They were keenly aware, as the Pennsylvania Constitution declared in a terse summary of the radical Whig conception of politics, that "offices of profit" had "the usual effects" of creating "dependence and servility, unbecoming freemen, in the possessors and expectants," and in "faction, contention, corruption, and disorder among the people." The constitution-makers in North Carolina and New Jersey decided to eliminate conclusively the springs of modern executive power by wresting every bit of control over appointments away from the governors.[39] Other Americans were not willing to go quite so far, yet in no state did the chief magistrate alone name men to the judicial and executive offices of the government. While some Whig extremists wanted the selection of all magisterial and executive officials to remain with the people at large ("the people who intend or wish to remain free, ought never to give it out of their own hands"),[40] in most of the Revolutionary state constitutions of 1776 the appointing power was lodged in the legislatures, either exclusively, or concurrently with the governor.[41]

"Rulers," the constitution-makers of 1776 realized, "must be

39. Pa. Cons. (1776), Sec. 36; N. C. Cons. (1776), XIII, XIV; N. J. Cons. (1776), X, XII.

40. Phila. *Pa. Journal*, Nov. 13, 1776. See also Petition of Pittsfield, Dec. 26, 1776, Handlin, eds., *Popular Sources*, 63–64; Boston *Continental Journal*, June 4, 1778. The Georgia Constitution provided for the annual election of all civil officers by the people in each county except for justices of the peace and registers of probate, who were to be appointed by the Assembly (Ga. Cons. [1777], Art. LIII). Despite the implication, the other judicial officials were not elected by the people but appointed by the Assembly. Albert B. Saye, *New Viewpoints in Georgia History* (Athens, Ga., 1943), 188–89.

41. In Delaware, for example, the president (as the chief magistrate was called) and the General Assembly in joint ballot appointed the leading justices of the state, while other executive officers and subordinates were chosen by the president and his privy council. The General Assembly singlehandedly, however, selected all the military officers of the state, and nominated candidates for justices of the peace from which the president with the approval of the privy council could commission one-half (Del. Cons. [1776], Art. 12, 14). In Virginia all the chief judges plus the secretary and the attorney-general were appointed by joint ballot of the two houses of the legislature. The governor was given the selection of all justices of the peace and militia offices, but these appointments were hedged by recommendations from the powerful county courts. In Maryland the magistracy was surprisingly free from legislative interference in appointments, but this, as the Constitution ominously stated, was only "for the time

conceived as the creatures of the people, made for their use, accountable to them, and subject to removal as soon as they act inconsistent with the purposes for which they were formed." "With this for a Basis" the Americans were sure they could build "stable and lasting" governments. It is difficult to appreciate the awful fear in which magisterial authority was held in the eighteenth century. Somehow the governors had to be made to know that they were but men, who "without the least difficulty, . . . may be removed and blended in the common mass." So unsure were the Georgian framers of their governor's willingness to step down from his weak but still exalted position that they required him to swear in his oath of office to resign "peaceably and quietly" when his term was expired. Creature of the people or not, the republican governor was still a political and social being to be reckoned with. As impotent as the new Delaware president was made in 1776, he remained in the minds of the most radical Whigs "a very powerful and dangerous Man." The Americans' emasculation of their governors lay at the heart of their constitutional reforms of 1776. It was not simply a conditioned response to their colonial experience, but represented a deliberate and determined effort to apply to the problems of politics what they knew from enlightened science. The changes they made were momentous, with implications for the nature of magisterial authority that they did not foresee. The ruler in American thought would never again be what it had been in English constitutionalism. In most states the governors remained, but they remained, as one Virginian said, "wholly executive of the political Laws of the State."[42] Americans in their early constitutions

---

being"; and even then all nominations by the governor had to receive the consent of the five-man executive council elected annually by the legislature (Md. Cons. [1776], XLVIII). The Pennsylvania executive was likewise granted sole responsibility for appointing the leading judicial and the civil and military officers (XX)—curiously, since the Pennsylvania Constitution was the most radically Whiggish of all, but explicable, because the Pennsylvania constitution-makers regarded their twelve-man executive council as more a representative instrument of the people than a traditional magistracy. See *Frame of Government for Pennsylvania*, 4.

42. Hooper to N. C. Congress, Oct. 26, 1776, Saunders, ed., *Col. Recs. of N. C.*, X, 867; Drayton, Charge to the Grand Jury, Apr. 23, 1776, Niles, ed., *Principles*, 333; Ga. Cons. (1777), Art. XXIV; Thomas McKean to Caesar Rodney, Sept. 19, 1776, George H. Ryden, ed., *Letters to and from Caesar Rodney, 1756–1784* (Phila., 1933), 123; "Loose Thoughts on Government," Force, ed., *American Archives*, 4th Ser., VI, 731.

had so enervated the traditional conception of the magistracy as an independent constituent of the society that it became in time increasingly impossible for them to think of their governors as anything but the repository of the executive functions of government.

4. SEPARATION OF POWERS

"That all power," as the Virginia Bill of Rights put it, "is vested in, and consequently derived from the people," and "that magistrates are their trustees and servants, and at all times amenable to them," summed up constitutionally what republicanism meant to Americans in 1776. But there was more to the disposition of power than simply making it the creature of the people. Since, as a Marylander wrote in 1776, "all men" were "by nature fond of power" and "unwilling to part with the possession of it, . . . no man, or body of men, ought to be intrusted with the united powers of Government, or more command than is absolutely necessary to discharge the particular office committed to him." "It is essential to Liberty that the legislative, judicial and executive Powers of Government be, as nearly as possible, independent of and separate from each other," read the instructions of the town of Boston to its representatives in the General Court in May 1776; "for where they are united in the same Persons, there will be wanting that natural Check, which is the principal Security against the enacting of arbitrary Laws, and a wanton Exercise of Power in the Execution of them." The histories of many nations, the Continental Congress told the people of Quebec in 1774, "demonstrate the truth of this simple position, that to live by the will of one man, or set of men, is the production of misery to all men." The device "of the several powers being separated, and distributed into different hands, for checks, one upon another," declared the Congress, was "the only effectual mode ever invented by the wit of men, to promote their freedom and prosperity." Many Americans in 1776 agreed, and in four states—Virginia, Maryland, North Carolina and Georgia —the principle was written specifically into the 1776-77 constitutions, the Maryland Declaration of Rights, for example, asserting "that the legislative, executive, and judicial powers of government ought to be forever separate and distinct from each other."[43]

Perhaps no principle of American constitutionalism has attracted more attention than that of separation of powers.[44] It has in fact come to define the very character of the American political system. The roots of the notion of distinct powers of government go back to antiquity, but for the Americans its more immediate sources, like so much of their constitutional theory, lay in the creative and tumultuous thinking of seventeenth-century liberalism. Many English radicals had developed a doctrine of separation of powers during the Revolution and Interregnum as a means of isolating the legislative functions of Parliament from the executive functions of the government. Locke had continued the usage by referring somewhat vaguely to a separation of legislative, executive, and federative (or foreign affairs) powers in his *Second Treatise*; and by the early eighteenth century English Commonwealthmen had made separation of powers an important part of their polemics. Yet separation of powers continued to possess many meanings, especially since it easily became combined with the very different theory of mixed government, that is, the balancing of the estates of the society into three parts of the legislature, which was emerging in English thought at the same time. By the 1730's the division of legislative and executive powers was nearly eclipsed by its frequent blending with the more powerful concept of the mixed constitution.[45] While the doctrine of separating functional powers was never lost from English thought and

43. Va. Cons. (1776), in Boyd, ed., *Jefferson Papers*, I, 379; "To the People of Maryland" (1776), Force, ed., *American Archives*, 4th Ser., VI, 1095; Boston's Instructions to Its Representatives, May 30, 1776, Handlin, eds., *Popular Sources*, 95; "Address to the Inhabitants of the Province of Quebec," Oct. 26, 1774, Ford, ed., *Journals of the Congress*, I, 106; Md. Decl. of Rts. (1776), VI.

44. The literature on separation of powers is enormous. For the most important works see John A. Fairlie, "The Separation of Powers," *Michigan Law Review*, 21 (1922–23), 393–436; M. P. Sharpe, "The Classical American Doctrine of Separation of Powers," *Chicago Law Review*, 2 (1934–35), 385–436; B. F. Wright, Jr., "The Origins of the Separation of Powers," *Economica*, 13 (1933), 169–85; William S. Carpenter, "The Separation of Powers in the Eighteenth Century," *Amer. Pol. Sci. Rev.*, 22 (1928), 32–44; Francis G. Wilson, "The Mixed Constitution and the Separation of Powers," *Southwestern Social Science Quarterly*, 15 (1934–35), 14–28. All these have been superseded by M. J. C. Vile, *Constitutionalism and the Separation of Powers* (Oxford, 1967), 1–175; and particularly William B. Gwyn, *The Meaning of the Separation of Powers* . . . (Tulane Studies in Political Science, IX [New Orleans, 1965]).

45. Gwyn, *Separation of Powers*, Chaps. IV–VII, esp. 63–65, 89–90.

continued to be used by those who sought to keep the Commonwealth ideas alive, its modern development owed its impetus, not
to the English radicals, but to a Frenchman, "the immortal Montesquieu," as the Continental Congress called him. "When the legislative and executive powers are united in the same person, or in
the same body of magistrates," Montesquieu had written in his
widely celebrated *Spirit of the Laws*, "there can be no liberty."
While there was nothing novel in this statement, Montesquieu
went further: "Again," he added significantly, "there is no liberty, if the judiciary power be not separated from the legislative
and executive." There were then in every government "three sorts
of power." While Montesquieu also spoke of the mixed constitution of England and came close to confusing the balancing of estates with the separation of powers, he did succeed in distinctly
defining in a modern way the functional powers of government as
three-fold: executive, legislative, and judicial.[46] It was the Americans, however, in 1776 and more emphatically in the subsequent
decade who were to elevate this doctrine of the separation of three
powers into what James Madison called in 1792 "a first principle
of free government."[47] But the elevation did not come easily or
at once. However common the references to the principle of separation of powers were in 1776, it was not at all obvious then
that the doctrine would become as important as Madison said it
was in 1792. For the meaning it came to acquire for Americans
was not the one it possessed for them at the time of Independence.

"GOVERNMENT is generally distinguished into three parts, Executive, Legislative and Judicial," wrote a Pennsylvania pamphleteer in 1776; "but this is more a distinction of words than things.
Every king or governor in giving his assent to laws acts legisla-
tively, and not executively: the House of Lords in England is
both a legislative and judicial body. In short, the distinction is
perplexing"—perplexing not only to this radical writer in 1776
and increasingly to other Americans in subsequent years but also
to historians ever since. It is not a simple matter to understand

46. Montesquieu, *Spirit of the Laws*, ed. Newmann Bk. XI, Sec. 6, 151–52. On
Montesquieu's influence on Anglo-American thought see Frank T. H. Fletcher,
Montesquieu and English Politics, 1750–1800 (London, 1939) and Paul M. Spur-
lin, *Montesquieu in America 1760–1801* (N. Y., 1940). For a careful assessment
of Montesquieu's contribution to the idea of separation of powers see Gwyn,
Separation of Powers, 109–10.
47. [James Madison], Philadelphia *National Gazette*, Feb. 6, 1792, Gaillard
Hunt, ed., *The Writings of James Madison* (N. Y., 1900–10), VI, 91.

what precisely Americans meant in 1776 by their repeated declarations to segregate the three departments of government. They were not generally referring to the theory of mixed or balanced government, although some in 1776 and historians since, like many eighteenth-century Englishmen, understandably confused what were two distinct conceptions, that of separating the functional departments of the legislature, executive, and judiciary with that of mixing the three estates of the society and the three classic kinds of government in the legislature.[48] Because the doctrine of separation of powers was vague and permissive it was easily exploited by different persons for different purposes. One Virginian, for example, employed it to justify removing the magistracy from any share in legislative authority, that is, denying the governors the power of veto over legislation ("for it is a solecism in politicks to invest the different powers of legislation and the execution of the laws in the same hands"); and revolutionary-minded groups in Maryland saw in the maxim of "the justly celebrated Montesquieu" a means of driving a slow-moving convention, which was exercising "not only the legislative, but the judicial and executive authority," into erecting a regular uncombined government in accord with the May 15 congressional resolution, arguing, "that the Legislative, Executive, and Judicial powers should be vested in one man or body of men, is incompatible with and destructive of liberty."[49] But such expanded uses of the concept were not typical in 1776, and do not comprehend the affirmations of separation of powers written into the Revolutionary constitutions. In fact they only add to the ambiguity surrounding the repeated statements of separation of powers in 1776. For what more than anything else makes the use of Montesquieu's maxim in 1776 perplexing is the great discrepancy between the affirmations of the need to separate the several governmental departments and the actual political practice the state governments followed. It seems, as historians have noted, that Americans in 1776 gave only a verbal recognition to the concept of separation of powers in their Revolutionary con-

48. *Four Letters*, 21. On the confusing of separation of powers with the theory of mixed government see Carpenter, "Separation of Powers," *Amer. Pol. Sci. Rev.*, 22 (1928), 37–38; Wright, "Origins of Separation of Powers," *Economica*, 13 (1933), 170, 174–75, 178.
49. "Loose Thoughts on Government," Force, ed., *American Archives*, 4th Ser., VI, 731; "To the People of Maryland," *ibid.*, 1094.

stitutions, since they were apparently not concerned with a real division of departmental functions.[50]

Throughout the eighteenth century the various colonial legislatures had slowly encroached on many of the prerogatives of the royal governors, gradually accumulating pieces of what were clearly traditional magisterial powers, so that by the middle of the century their authority in many areas extended well beyond that of the British House of Commons. With their broad control over finance, the assemblies intruded into the handling and expenditure of public money, even to the point of presuming to share in the determining and implementing of Indian and military policies and of venturing to appoint most officials concerned with public services. In general they continually sought to eat into the governors' patronage powers and magisterial control over the courts and judges.[51] Moreover, the assemblies in the eighteenth century still saw themselves, perhaps even more so than the House of Commons, as a kind of medieval court making private judgments as well as public law. Because the courts themselves were so involved in governmental and administrative duties, it was inevitable that the line between what was political and what was judicatory would be blurred. Both the county sessions courts in Massachusetts and the county courts in Virginia before and after the Revolution remained crucially important governing bodies, assessing taxes, directing expenditures on local projects, issuing licenses, and in general monitoring the counties over which they presided.[52] Although there is some evidence that by the mid-eighteenth century the distinction between legislative and judicial functions was beginning to harden, the assemblies continued to exercise what we would call essentially judicial responsibilities, largely, it appears, because of the political nature of the court system, the fear of royally controlled judges, the dislike of gubernatorial chancery jurisdiction, and the scarcity of trained judges. The assemblies constantly

50. Edward S. Corwin, "The Progress of Political Theory between the Declaration of Independence and the Meeting of the Philadelphia Convention," *Amer. Hist. Rev.*, 30 (1924–25), 514.
51. See Jack P. Greene, *The Quest for Power: The Lower Houses of Assembly in the Southern Royal Colonies 1689–1776* (Chapel Hill, 1963), 50–107, 221–354; Greene, *Provincial Governor*, Chap. X.
52. Taylor, *Western Massachusetts*, 27–38; Charles S. Sydnor, *Gentlemen Freeholders: Political Practices in Washington's Virginia* (Chapel Hill, 1952), 86–90.

heard private petitions, which often were only the complaints of one individual or group against another, and made final judgments on these complaints. They continually tried cases in equity, occasionally extended temporary equity power to some common law court for a select purpose, and often granted appeals, new trials, and other kinds of relief in an effort to do what "is agreeable to Right and Justice." As a committee of the Maryland Assembly declared in 1719, "a legislative body is not tied to common rules, for if the thing be just they make new rules or dispense with old ones as to the manner of doing it."[53] By the middle of the eighteenth century most colonists were convinced that their assemblies, as the embodiment of their public liberty, represented their only protection against magisterial tyranny. Such assumptions of traditional gubernatorial and judicial authority as the assemblies had made or had attempted to make did not seem to be usurpations, but indeed had come to seem to be the only way in which the people's welfare could be properly promoted.

The Revolution scarcely interrupted this development; indeed, it intensified legislative domination of the other parts of the government. The Revolutionary constitution-makers released and institutionalized what had previously been varied and often confused and thwarted attempts by the legislatures to assume magisterial responsibilities, further blurring in fact the none too clear distinctions between governmental departments. The state constitutions of 1776 explicitly granted the legislatures not only tasks that they had claimed with varying degrees of success in the course of the eighteenth century but also functions that in the English constitutional tradition could in no way be justified as anything but executive, such as the proroguing and adjourning of the assembly, the declaring of war and peace, the conduct of foreign relations, and in several cases the exclusive right of pardon. In the judicial area the constitutions and the chaotic conditions of war had the effect of reversing the growing mid-eighteenth-century distinction between legislative and judicial responsibilities, leading during the 1770's and eighties to a heightened involvement of the legislatures in controlling the

53. See in general Clarke, *Parliamentary Privilege*, 14–60, esp. 30, 33, 49–52, 53, 54; the quotation on Maryland is from 58. For examples of legislative interference in judicial affairs see "Judicial Action by the Provincial Legislature of Massachusetts," *Harvard Law Review*, 15 (1901–02), 208–18, quotation from 209.

courts and in deciding the personal affairs of their constituents in private law judgments. In fact, departmental duties were jumbled as never before in the eighteenth century. This endorsement of legislative supremacy and encroachment into traditionally executive and judicial functions, despite the emphatic declarations, as in the Virginia Constitution, asserting that "the legislative, executive, and judiciary departments shall be separate and distinct, so that neither exercise the powers properly belonging to the other," has understandably led historians to believe that the Americans in their 1776 constitutions meant by separation of powers nothing more than a prohibition of plural officeholding, as the sentence following the declaration of the principle of separation of powers in the Virginia Constitution seems to indicate: "Nor shall any person exercise the powers of more than one of them at the same time."[54]

Certainly the Americans, with their republican resentments against the piling of "a multiplicity of posts upon one man," offices that were obviously only a source of wealth and could never be properly exercised, were eager to prevent "any one man—family—or their connections, from engrossing many places of honor and profit." So careful should the people be "never to heap offices or indeed confer more than one on the same person" that one Pennsylvania radical went so far as to suggest that "no governor, counsellor, representative, sheriff, coroner, attorney at law, or clerk of the peace should ever be a justice of the peace." The Americans translated these fears into their constitutions in 1776, striking out against those oligarchies of officeholding by which men had so long selfishly fed their own interests and fattened themselves at the expense of the public, and insisting very explicitly, as in the North Carolina Constitution, "that no person in the State shall hold more than one lucrative office at any one time."[55]

Yet separation of powers had a more precise significance for Americans than simply an abolition of plural officeholding—a significance that flowed from their conception of the way eighteenth-century politics worked. What particularly troubled the colonists was the means by which the governors had used

54. Va. Cons. (1776), Boyd, ed., *Jefferson Papers*, I, 379. On the identification of separation of powers with plural office-holding see in particular Brennan, *Plural Office-Holding*, 5, 9, 61–62, 113–18, 138, 154, 159.

55. Boston *Continental Journal*, Aug. 15, 1776; Boston *Independent Chronicle*, Mar. 6, 1777; Demophilus, *Genuine Principles*, 22; N. C. Cons. (1776), XXXV. See also Md. Decl. of Rts. (1776), XXXII; Ga. Cons. (1777), Art. XVIII.

their power to influence and control the other parts of the constitution, particularly the representatives of the people in the legislature. The chief magistracy had not only attempted to establish electoral districts and apportion representation but, more frightening, had sought to manipulate the representatives of the people by appointing them to executive or judicial posts, or by offering them opportunities for profits through the dispensing of government contracts and public money, thereby buying their support for the government. In this respect, as in others, the royal governors in the colonies actually possessed more formal constitutional powers than the Crown did in England.[56] While several disqualifying acts had absolutely excluded certain officials from seats in the House of Commons, and in particular the succession to the Crown Acts of 1705 and 1707 had required reelection for all members of the Commons appointed to offices of profit, the royal governors acted under few such legal restrictions in their attempts to gain supporters for their governments in the colonial assemblies. Francis Bernard, governor of Massachusetts during the Stamp Act troubles, had been especially blatant in his use of patronage, dismissing even colonels of the militia from their positions for their adverse votes in the House of Representatives in 1766. With such experience the general Opposition cry against Crown influence in the eighteenth century possessed an especially exaggerated significance for the colonists, and there could be little question that their new constitutions would repudiate, more decisively than Englishmen ever had, the means by which "Royal Ministerial, and Parliamentary Managers cajole, tempt, and bribe the people, to commit suicide on their own liberties."[57]

When Americans in 1776 spoke of keeping the several parts of the government separate and distinct, they were primarily thinking of insulating the judiciary and particularly the legislature from executive manipulation. Even though the governors in most of the new constitutions no longer controlled the appointment of executive officials, so infecting and so incompatible with the public liberty or the representation of the people

56. On the incongruity between the formal and informal powers of the royal governors see Bailyn, "Origins of American Politics," *Perspectives in American History*, 1 (1967), 52–69.

57. Phila. *Pa. Journal*, Nov. 22, 1775. On the problems of executive influence and place acts in the colonies see Greene, *Provincial Governor*, 157–59; Greene, *Quest for Power*, 171–204; Brennan, *Plural Office-Holding*, 21, 58, 72, 86–87. For 18th-century English developments see Kemp, *King and Commons*, 51–69, 95–96.

was magisterial power believed to be that the Americans felt compelled to isolate their legislatures from any sort of executive influence or impingement, thus setting American constitutional development in an entirely different direction from that of the former mother country. All the Revolutionary constitutions drafted in 1776 (except South Carolina's) were emphatic in the exclusion from the assemblies, as the New Jersey Constitution stated, of all "persons possessed of any post of profit under the Government," so "that the legislative department of this Government may, as much as possible, be preserved from all suspicion of corruption"; and in the prohibition from the legislature, as the Maryland Constitution declared, of all persons "receiving the profits, or any part of the profits, arising on any agency for the supply of clothing or provisions for the army or navy."58 Such unqualified debarring of the magisterial presence from their legislatures represented for Americans in 1776 the fruits of their knowledge of political science and one of

58. N. J. Cons. (1776), XX; Md. Cons. (1776), XXXVIII. In Delaware the justices of the Supreme Court and courts of common pleas, the members of the privy council, and the leading executive officials, plus "all persons concerned in any army or navy contracts," were ineligible to sit in either house of the assembly. The Maryland Constitution, in addition to prohibiting all government profiteers, also excluded all military officers and congressional officers from seats in the legislature or privy council. In Pennsylvania no member of the single-house legislature could hold any other office except in the militia. Even justices of the peace, which many of the states exempted from their sweeping exclusion of officeholders from the legislatures, were ineligible to sit in the Pennsylvania Assembly. North Carolina painstakingly enumerated in a series of articles all who were barred from a seat in the legislature: all receivers of public monies, members of the privy council, the chief justices, the major executive officers, all regular military officers, and all military contractors. The leading judges and executive officials, "together with all others holding lucrative offices," the Virginia Constitution declared incapable of being elected members of the legislature or the privy council. In Georgia no person "bearing any post of profit under this State, or . . . any military commission" except in the militia could be elected to the House of Representatives. The New York Constitution of 1777 was much less rigid: only the treasurer, chancellor, and judges of the Supreme Court were excluded from both houses of the legislature; the county court justices were merely prohibited from sitting in the lower house. The South Carolina constitutions of 1776 and 1778 were unusual in allowing members of the legislature elected to the privy council to retain their seats—the prerequisite for cabinet government; and although members of the legislature were prohibited from accepting any places of emolument without a new election, once reelected, as in England, they could continue to hold both positions, except when appointed to certain specified offices. Members of the New Hampshire legislature, according to the Constitution of 1784, were also allowed to retain their seats; the practice was criticized and changed in the Constitution of 1792 (I owe this point to Jere Daniell). Many of the states, in order to obviate any suggestion of a religious establishment, prohibited all clergymen from sitting in the legislature. Md. Cons. (1776), XLV, LIII; Va. Cons. (1776), Boyd, ed., *Jefferson Papers*, I, 382; Del.

their great achievements in building truly free governments. Such isolation of the legislatures from magisterial tampering, with its assumption of a strict dichotomy between ruler and people, also represented a stark crystalization of the traditional Whig conception of the nature of politics.

Indeed, so rigid was the dichotomy in some American minds that it was difficult to fit the judiciary into the scheme of government. "However we may refine and define, there is no more than two powers in any government, viz. the power to make laws, and the power to execute them; for the judicial power is only a branch of the executive, the CHIEF of every country being the first magistrate." Even John Adams in 1766, for all of his later assertions of judicial independence and the traditional tripartite balance of the constitution among King, Lords, and Commons, regarded "the first grand division of constitutional powers" as "those of legislation and those of execution," with "the administration of justice" resting in "the executive part of the constitution."[59] Actually such an old-fashioned conception of the King's being "always present, in person or by his judges, in his courts, distributing justice among the people" made more sense of colonial experience in the eighteenth century than it did of English. While the English Privy Council had long since lost its right to hear appeals from the English common law courts, it had remained for the colonists, often to their exasperation, a final court of appeal in important civil cases from the provincial governors and councils who themselves sat as courts of appeal in all civil cases of error within the colonies. In many colonies judges themselves were also members of the council so that they often heard appeals in cases in which they had originally participated. And in all the colonies (except Pennsylvania) the councils in addition to their executive and judicial responsibilities acted as the upper houses of the legislatures.[60] In Massa-

---

Cons. (1776), Art. 18; Pa. Cons. (1776), Sec. 7, 11, 19, 23, 30; N. C. Cons. (1776), XXV, XXVIII-XXI, XXV; Ga. Cons. (1777), Art. XVII, XVIII; N. Y. Cons. (1777), XXII, XXV; S. C. Cons. (1776), V, X, (1778), IX, XX; N. H. Cons. (1784), Pt. II, Council.

59. *Four Letters*, 21; [Adams], *Boston Gazette*, Jan. 27, 1766, Adams, ed., *Works of John Adams*, III, 480–82. Montesquieu had written: "Of the three powers above mentioned, the judiciary is in some measure next to nothing." *Spirit of the Laws*, ed. Neumann, Bk. XI, Sec. 6, 156.

60. Leonard Labaree, *Royal Government in America* . . . (N. Y., 1958), 401–17; Greene, *Provincial Governor*, 140–41. See also Arthur M. Schlesinger, "Colonial Appeals to the Privy Council," *Pol. Sci. Qtly.*, 28 (1913), 279–97, 433–50. The quotation is from Adams, ed., *Works of John Adams*, III, 481.

chusetts, where this blending of persons and duties was especially blatant and resented, opponents of the Hutchinson machine repeatedly invoked Montesquieu on the proper separation of powers, arguing "that where the legislative and executive powers are in the same persons, that is, where the same persons make laws, and judge upon them after they are made, there is no true liberty."[61] In response to this sort of union of officeholding and jumbling of functions almost all of the Revolutionary constitutions not only established distinct upper houses in the legislature from which judges, except generally justices of the peace, were excluded, but also (except in South Carolina, New Jersey, and Delaware) stripped their new governors and privy councils of their former judicial role by setting up separate courts of appeal and chancery.

In the tenure of their offices during the eighteenth century the colonial judges had also seemed to be much more the creatures of the Crown than the English judges. While judges in England since the Glorious Revolution had been granted their commissions during good behavior, the judges in the colonies continued to hold their offices ambiguously at the pleasure of the Crown. Judicial tenure had been one of the searing issues of the imperial debate: "In the colonies," John Dickinson asked, "how fruitless has been every attempt to have the judges appointed '*during good behavior*?'" Since the colonists had become convinced that dependence of the judges on executive caprice was "dangerous to liberty and property of the subject,"[62] their Revolutionary constitutions sought to isolate the judiciary from any future gubernatorial tampering: in most states in 1776 the governors surrendered to the legislatures the traditional magisterial prerogative of appointing judges; in no state did judicial tenure depend on the pleasure of the chief magistrate.[63] These

61. [Oxenbridge Thacher], *Considerations on Counsellors*, 5–6; Brennan, *Plural Office-Holding*, Chap. II, 50, 84, 90–93, 74–106.

62. [Dickinson], *Letters from a Farmer*, Ford, ed., *Writings of Dickinson*, 367; [William Henry Drayton], *A Letter from Freeman of South-Carolina . . .* (Charleston, 1774), 10. See also Milton M. Klein, "Prelude to Revolution in New York: Jury Trials and Judicial Tenure," *Wm. and Mary Qtly.*, 3d Ser., 17 (1960), 439–62; Greene, *Provincial Governor*, 134–38. For a general discussion of the problem of judicial tenure in the colonies see Bailyn, ed., *Pamphlets*, I, 66–68, 249–55, 699.

63. Of the early Revolutionary constitutions only Maryland's and Pennsylvania's excluded the legislature from at least a share in the appointment of judges. See above, n. 41.

efforts to separate the judges from their customary magisterial connection eventually set the judiciary on a path toward a kind of independence in American constitutionalism that few in 1776 ever envisioned.

But in 1776 it was only the beginning of an independence for the judiciary. Despite John Adams's warnings in his *Thoughts on Government* that "an upright and skillful administration of justice" required the judicial power "to be distinct from both the legislative and executive, and independent upon both," most of the early constitution-makers had little sense that judicial independence meant independence from the people.[64] Not only did many of the early constitutions—New Jersey, Pennsylvania, Rhode Island, Connecticut, and Vermont—limit the judges' term to a prescribed number of years, but even those states granting tenure during good behavior weakened any real judicial independence by legislative control over salaries and fees and by the various procedures for removal, including simply the address of the legislature.[65] These constitutional provisions giving control of the courts and judicial tenure to the legislatures actually represented the culmination of what the colonial assemblies had been struggling for in their eighteenth-century contests with the Crown. The Revolutionaries had no intention of curtailing legislative interference in the court structure and in judicial functions, and in fact they meant to increase it. As Jefferson said to Pendleton in 1776, in relation to the legislator the judge must "be a mere machine." The people's making of law would dispense mercy and justice "equally and impartially to every description of men," while, as any radical Whig knew, the dispensations of "the judge, or of the executive power, will be the eccentric impulses of whimsical, capricious designing man."[66] The expanded meaning of separation of powers, as Jefferson and other Americans later came to express it, along with a new conception of judicial independence, had to await the experience of the years ahead.

64. [Adams], *Thoughts on Government*, Adams, ed., *Works of John Adams*, IV, 198.

65. The judges in both Pennsylvania and New Jersey held office for seven years. In Vermont and the former corporate colonies of Connecticut and Rhode Island they were elected annually. In Georgia only the chief justice was appointed annually, while the assistant judges and the justices of the peace held office at the pleasure of the legislature.

66. Jefferson to Pendleton, Aug. 26, 1776, Boyd, ed., *Jefferson Papers*, I, 505.

CHAPTER V

The Nature of Representation

1. THE REPRESENTATIVE LEGISLATURE

Putting the magistracy in its place may have set the corner-stones of the new state constitutions, but it hardly completed the business of building free governments. For the legislatures remained to be constructed, and no one doubted that the legislature was the most important part of any government. "It is in their legislatures," declared a Rhode Islander, echoing Locke and all good Whigs, "that the members of a commonwealth are united and combined together into one coherent, living body. This is the soul that gives form, life and unity to the commonwealth." In fact, the Revolution had begun precisely because the English, by "declaring themselves invested with power to legislate for us in all cases whatsoever," had threatened the Americans' very existence as a free people. To legislate was to make law, and "as a good government is an empire of laws," said John Adams, "the first question is, how shall the laws be made?" One thing, said Alexander Hamilton, was certain: "no laws have any validity or binding force without the consent and approbation of the people."[1]

But to the Americans in 1776 their legislatures represented more than the supreme lawmaking authority in their new states. They were as well the heirs to most of the prerogative powers

1. *Providence Gazette*, Apr. 3, 1779; Declaration of Independence, quoted in Greene, *Quest for Power*, 452; [Adams], *Thoughts on Government*, Adams, ed., *Works of John Adams*, IV, 204; [Hamilton], *Farmer Refuted*, Syrett and Cooke, eds., *Hamilton Papers*, I, 105. See Locke, *Two Treatises of Government*, ed. Laslett, Second Treatise, Sec. 212.

taken away from the governors by the Revolution. Such legislative assumption of traditional magisterial authority, which, as one minister declared in 1774, meant the people's having "a voice in all public discussions concerning peace and war with other states; making alliances with other powers; sending and receiving embassies; entering into natural leagues and compacts; setting and regulating trade and commerce, etc., etc.," was not simply a means of further restraining fearful gubernatorial power, but actually represented a substantial shift in the responsibility of government. The American legislatures, in particular the lower houses of the assemblies, were no longer to be merely adjuncts or checks to magisterial power, but were in fact to be the government—a revolutionary transformation of political authority which led some Americans, like Richard Henry Lee, to observe that their new governments were "very much of the democratic kind," although "a Governor and second branch of legislation are admitted." It was neither the widespread suffrage nor the institution of the electoral process throughout the governments but the appropriation of so much power to the people's representatives in the legislatures that made the new governments in 1776 seem to be so much like democracies.[2]

All of the Revolutionary state constitutions except in Pennsylvania, Georgia, and Vermont divided their legislatures into two houses, in accord with the Americans' colonial experience and their inherited conception of mixed or balanced government. The senates or upper houses (to be considered later) stood for the aristocratic element in their balanced constitutions, and, like the House of Lords in England and yet distinctly different from the Lords, were supposed to embody something other than the people. The real importance of the legislatures came from their being the constitutional repository of the democratic element of the society or, in other words, the people themselves. It was self-evident to all Whigs that "a branch of the legislative power

2. Foster, *Short Essay on Civil Government*, 48–50, quoted in Baldwin, *New England Clergy*, 127; R. H. Lee to Charles Lee, June 29, 1776, Ballagh, ed., *Letters of R. H. Lee*, I, 203. It would be difficult to exaggerate the importance of this shift in the responsibility of government. For centuries the government had been identified with the executive or the Crown; "Legislation was considered exceptional, corrective, and concerned only with the common welfare." Hence even Locke and the radical Whigs "had believed that a representative legislative assembly meeting briefly and subject to frequent popular elections was very unlikely to enact laws adverse to the public interest." Gwyn, *Separation of Powers*, 58, 113. See above, 26, 136.

should reside in the people," since, as the constitutions of Delaware and Maryland declared, "the right of the people to participate in the legislature is the best security of liberty and the
foundation of all free government." Indeed, in the minds of the
enlightened everywhere such popular participation was an absolute necessity, if the people were not to be "sooner or later oppress'd by their own magistrates."[3] Only with the presence of
the democracy in the constitution could any government remain
faithful to the public good. As John Witherspoon lectured his
students at Princeton, "the multitude collectively always are true
in intention to the interest of the public, because it is their own.
They are the public."[4]

That "the Right to legislate is originally in every Member of
the Community," all Americans agreed. And happy were the
people whose members at large could exercise this right; "but,
alas! . . . this equal and perfect system of legislation is seldom
to be found in the world, and can only take place in small communities." Whenever the inhabitants of a state grew numerous,
it became "not only inconvenient, but impracticable *for all* to
meet in One Assembly." Out of the impossibility of convening
the whole people, it was commonly believed, arose the great
English discovery of representation. Through this device of representation—"substituting the few in the room of the many"—the
people "in an extensive Country" could still express their voice
in the making of law and the management of government.[5] No
political conception was more important to Americans in the
entire Revolutionary era than representation. "Representation,"
they told themselves over and over again, "is the feet on which
a free government stands." "If the government be free, the right
of representation must be the basis of it; the preservation of
which sacred right, ought to be the grand object and end of all
government." Only through the just representation of themselves
in their several assemblies could the Americans find "the greatest

3. Phila. *Pa. Journal*, Mar. 8, 1775; Md. Decl. of Rts. (1776), V; Del. Decl. of
Rts. (1776), VI; Baron Van Der Capellen to Richard Price, Dec. 14, 1777, "Price
Letters," Mass. Hist. Soc., *Proceedings*, 2d Ser., 17 (1903), 317. See also [Ray-
nal], *Sentiments of a Foreigner*, 18.
4. Witherspoon, *Works of Witherspoon*, III, 434.
5. Boston's Instructions to Its Representatives, May 30, 1776, Handlin, eds.,
Popular Sources, 95; "Loose Thoughts on Government," Force, ed., *American
Archives*, 4th Ser., VI, 730; Albemarle County Instructions concerning the Vir-
ginia Constitution (1776), Boyd, ed., *Jefferson Papers*, VI, 287; Boston *Mass. Spy*,
Feb. 16, 1775.

security any free people can have for the enjoyment of their just rights."[6]

"The principal difficulty lies, and the greatest care should be employed, in constituting this representative assembly," cautioned John Adams at the outset of the framing of the constitutions. "It should be in miniature an exact portrait of the people at large. It should think, feel, reason, and act like them." Americans, however, needed no warning; they knew that because their governments would be "undoubtedly a Republic or Commonwealth . . . , it therefore becomes more serious and important that every Man should have equal Liberty, and equal right to Representation in the Legislature." They had also been repeatedly told of, and indeed witnessed, the fate of the English people who, said John Jay, had been "betrayed by their own representatives." James Burgh in particular had "exhausted the subject" in the second volume of his *Political Disquisitions*—"a book," said John Adams, "which ought to be in the hands of every American who has learned to read."[7] The English House of Commons had become so unequally, irregularly, and inadequately representative that by the middle of the eighteenth century it had left "little to the real voice of the people," and had become "separated from, and converted into a different interest from the collective." In constituting their representative bodies, Americans urged themselves, they must "view well the defects in other governments, . . . and learn by these examples."[8]

There was no doubt then that "special care should be paid to the plan of representation" in the new constitutions, if the Americans were to avoid the deficiencies of the English system and of their own colonial past. For the "purpose" of securing "the right of the people to participate in the Legislature," declared the Maryland Constitution, "elections ought to be free and frequent." "The long Duration of Parliament," announced

6. [Mather], *America's Appeal*, 70; Portsmouth *New-Hampshire Gazette*, Jan. 4, 1783; Litchfield County Committee, Conn., May 15, 1776, Force, ed., *American Archives*, 4th Ser., VI, 472.

7. [Adams], *Thoughts on Government*, Adams, ed., *Works of John Adams*, IV, 195; Broadside *County of Essex, Colony of Massachusetts*, Apr. 17, 1776 (Salem, 1776); [Jay], Circular Letter from Congress, Sept. 28, 1779, Johnston, ed., *Papers of Jay*, I, 223; [Adams], "Novanglus," Adams, ed., *Works of John Adams*, IV, 21.

8. Iredell, "Causes Leading Up to the American Revolution," June 1776, McRee, *Life of Iredell*, I, 322; Pinkney's Wmsbg. *Va. Gazette*, Nov. 24, 1774; Purdie's Wmsbg. *Va. Gazette*, June 14, 1776.

a New York broadside, "is allowed by all to be the principal Cause of its present corrupt State." Not only were the members "so long in Power" that they "forget their Dependence on the People," but "the Ministry, knowing they are to continue for seven years, think it worth their while to tempt and seduce them with a high Bribe."[9] The colonists also realized from their decades of experience under royal government to what abuses the representation of the people could be put. Throughout the century the governors, except where they had been circumscribed by charters, had allowed compliant legislatures to sit on for years without new elections or had even attempted to carry on government for months and years at a time without calling the assemblies into session. In general, wrote William Douglass in his *Summary* view of the American colonies, the governor "calls, dissolves, prorogues, adjourns, removes, and other ways harasses the General Assembly at Pleasure." In an effort to restrict this kind of gubernatorial manipulation of their legislatures and to regulate the frequency of elections and sessions, all the colonial assemblies at one time or another had tried to pass triennial or septennial acts modeled on those of the English Parliament, but these for the most part, as Richard Henry Lee lamented in 1766, had been unsuccessful. The people's lack of this "one very essential security, namely the Right of their Members being chosen and meeting in a certain time after being dissolved, as in Britain," had placed "the third or democratical part of our legislature . . . totally in the power of the Crown." The issue had been clearly joined in the royal instructions of 1767 which forbade the governors, among other things, to assent to any bills fixing the meeting or duration of assemblies.[10] Short and regular terms for the new assemblies therefore were inevitable in the Revolutionary constitutions. And since Americans were familiar with the radical Whig maxim, "Where ANNUAL ELECTION ends, TYRANNY begins," all the states except South Carolina provided for the yearly election of their houses of representatives—such a rad-

9. Boston *Continental Journal*, Jan. 15, 1778; Md. Decl. of Rts. (1776), V; Publicola [pseud.], *To the Electors of New York* (N. Y., 1776).
10. William Douglass, *A Summary, Historical and Political . . . of the British Settlements in North-America* (Boston and London, 1755), quoted in Greene, *Provincial Governor*, 152; R. H. Lee to Arthur Lee, Dec. 20, 1766, Ballagh, ed., *Letters of R. H. Lee*, I, 21–22; Greene, *Quest for Power*, 386. On the relationship of the royal governors with the colonial assemblies see in general Labaree, *Royal Government*, 211–13; Greene, *Quest for Power*, 199–203, 381–87; Greene, *Provincial Governor*, 145–48, 154–57.

ical departure from their previous experience for all except the New England charter colonies and Pennsylvania that it alone suggests the revolutionary power of their Whig ideology.[11]

Because it seemed obvious to good Whigs that "a small number of electors, or a small number of representatives, are equally dangerous," both the representation and the suffrage were enlarged by the new state governments. "An ample Representation in every Republick," said one South Carolinian, "constitutes the most powerful Protection of Freedom, the strongest Bulwark against the Attacks of Despotism," since corruption—"that almost invincible Assailant of the best formed Constitutions"— could never arrive at "such irresistible Strength in a *full* as in a *nearly empty House*."[12] In response to the repeated attempts of royal officials to control and restrict the creation of new electoral districts and the enlargement of the size of the assemblies— attempts that culminated in the Privy Council's instructions of 1767 prohibiting the governors from assenting to any bills altering the representation in the legislatures—most of the states greatly expanded the membership in their new houses of representatives, in some cases to as much as two or three times the size of the prerevolutionary legislatures—a drastic increase that had profound political and social ramifications in the coming years.[13] In no way was the expansion of the suffrage during the Revolution comparable to this enlargement of the number of representatives, since even before the Revolution, because of widespread property ownership, much of the white male population already possessed the right to vote.[14] Yet perhaps precisely because the Crown had also sought in 1767 to prevent any expansion of the electorate and because the Revolutionaries needed as much support as they could muster, many states in 1776 did perceptibly enlarge the basis of consent, without however elevating the right

11. On this Whig maxim see Colbourn, *Lamp of Experience*, 191. In South Carolina the representatives were elected biennially, as was the governor.

12. [Paine], *Common Sense*, Foner, ed., *Writings of Paine*, I, 37; Charleston *S.-C. and American Gazette*, Dec. 31, 1778.

13. Labaree, *Royal Government*, 179–86; Greene, *Quest for Power*, 172–85. On the increase in size of the legislatures see Jackson T. Main, "Government by the People: The American Revolution and the Democratization of the Legislatures," *Wm. and Mary Qtly.*, 3d Ser., 23 (1966), 391–407.

14. On the breadth of the franchise in two colonies see Robert E. Brown, *Middle-Class Democracy and the Revolution in Massachusetts 1691–1780* (Ithaca, 1955); Robert E. and B. Katherine Brown, *Virginia, 1705–1786: Democracy or Aristocracy?* (East Lansing, Mich., 1964).

to vote into a major theoretical issue of the Revolution. Indeed, the Revolution came in time to mark a decisive turning point in the development of American thinking about voting.[15] Although not as a result of clearly intended theory the right to vote and the electoral process in general were set on a path to becoming identified in American thought with the very essence of American democracy. But at the outset in 1776 it was not at all obvious that voting itself was crucially important, and all of the states retained some sort of tax-paying or property qualification for the suffrage.

Few in 1776 considered such qualifications a denial of the embodiment of democracy in the constitution. If all men were independent and free of temptation, said James Iredell in an expression of traditional eighteenth-century Whig opinion, then everyone could have "an individual vote for a representative." But because they were not, "there must be some restriction as to the right of voting: otherwise the lowest and most ignorant of mankind must associate in this important business with those who it is to be presumed, from their property and other circumstances, are free from influence, and have some knowledge of the great consequence of their trust."[16] Even the most radical English Whigs, like James Burgh and Joseph Priestley, feared the "people in low circumstances" who were especially susceptible "to bribery, or under the power of their superiors." While some Americans, like Samuel Adams, were also alarmed by the possible influence of the rich on men of "a base, degenerate, servile temper of mind," others expressed more mundane reasons for their fears: "For poor, shiftless spendthrifty men and inconsiderate youngsters that have no property are cheap bought (that is) their votes easily procured Choose a Representative to go to

15. On the question of suffrage during the Revolution see Chilton Williamson, *American Suffrage: From Property to Democracy 1760–1860* (Princeton, 1960), esp. 76–116; and the several articles by Jack R. Pole, "Suffrage Reform and the American Revolution in New Jersey," New Jersey Historical Society, *Proceedings*, 74 (1956), 173–94; "Suffrage and Representation in Massachusetts: A Statistical Note," *Wm. and Mary Qtly.*, 3d Ser., 14 (1957), 560–92; "Representation in Virginia," *Jour. of Southern Hist.*, 24 (1958), 16–50; "Suffrage and Representation in Maryland from 1776 to 1810 . . . ," *ibid.*, 218–25. Some of this material has been integrated into his *Political Representation in England.*

16. Iredell, "To the Inhabitants of Great Britain" (1774), McRee, *Life of Iredell*, I, 210. See also [Wilson], *Considerations*, in Wilson, ed., *Works of Wilson*, III, 209; [Hamilton], *Farmer Refuted*, Syrett and Cooke, eds., *Hamilton Papers*, I, 106–07; Blackstone, *Commentaries*, I, 171; Williamson, *Suffrage*, 10–11.

court, to vote away the Money of those that have Estates."[17] Limiting the suffrage of these kinds of men—those who were "supposed to have no will of their own"—was not for most Whigs a violation of the principle of consent. Jefferson's argument with Edmund Pendleton over suffrage in the summer of 1776 was not concerned with whether or not all citizens in a republic should vote, for "the right of suffrage" was one with "the rights of a citizen," but only with what was the proper evidence of citizenship or attachment to the community, Jefferson liberally favoring "either the having resided a certain time, or having a family, or having property, any or all of them," and Pendleton desiring only the owning "of fixed Permanent property." Even the Pennsylvania Constitution which adopted the broadest suffrage qualifications of all the states in 1776—requiring only age, one year's residence, and the paying of public taxes —explicitly endorsed the general maxim, repeated by other states, "that all free men having a sufficient evident common interest with, and attachment to the community, have a right to elect officers."[18] Despite growing voices in many of the states in 1776 expressing dissatisfaction with any sort of monetary restrictions on the suffrage and suggesting new meanings for the principle of consent, most of the constitution-makers in the early years of the Revolution assumed, although with increasing defensiveness, that "sufficient discretion," making a man "*a free agent* in a *political view*," was a prerequisite to the right to vote.[19]

Because the constitution-makers realized that in spite of restrictive qualifications the franchise would be broad, they believed it imperative that the electoral process be protected against all sorts of outside influences, particularly by men in power, which in England, the Americans knew, had been "one of the principal Sources of that Torrent of Corruption and Bribery, which pervades every Part of that falling degenerate Kingdom," and which, they also knew, had been practiced in their own land as well, both by royal officials and by "those who have neither

17. Burgh, *Disquisitions*, I, 47–48, 56, 62–72; Williamson, *Suffrage*, 71–72; Adams to Elbridge Gerry, Jan. 2, 1776, Cushing, ed., *Writings of Samuel Adams*, III, 247; Return of Sutton, May 18, 1778, Handlin, eds., *Popular Sources*, 232.

18. [Wilson], *Considerations*, Wilson, ed., *Works of Wilson*, III, 209; Pendleton to Jefferson, Aug. 10, 1776, and Jefferson to Pendleton, Aug. 26, 1776, Boyd, ed., *Jefferson Papers*, I, 489, 504; Pa. Decl. of Rts. (1776), VII.

19. *Essex Result*, Parsons, *Memoir*, 375; [Hamilton], *Farmer Refuted*, Syrett and Cooke, eds., *Hamilton Papers*, I, 105. See also Thomas C. Amory, *Life of James Sullivan . . .* (Boston, 1859), 96; Williamson, *Suffrage*, 84–88, 108.

natural nor acquired parts to recommend them."[20] Several of the
constitutions thus explicitly declared against undue interference
in elections, by either military overawing or the bribing of electors, the Pennsylvania Constitution going so far as to forbid any
candidate from giving or any voter from receiving any gifts, in
"meat, drink, money, or otherwise." The North Carolina, Georgia, Vermont, and Pennsylvania constitutions and some counties
in New Jersey provided for elections by secret ballot (which had
been used sporadically throughout the colonies in the previous
decades) so that no elector would have "occasion to recur to any
man for advice or assistance." The New York Constitution proposed to try balloting as an experiment, because some in the state
had contended that voting by ballot "would tend more to preserve the liberty and equal freedom of the people than voting
viva voce."[21]

None of these electoral safeguards for the representational system, however, was as important to Americans as equality of representation; "in other words," said John Adams, "equal interests
among the people should have equal interests" in the legislatures.
More than anything else this equality would prevent the "unfair,
partial, and corrupt elections" and the "monstrous irregularity"
of the English representational system whereby over three hundred members of the House of Commons, as the English radicals
never ceased broadcasting, were elected by only a handful of
the English population concentrated in numerous "beggarly
boroughs." To the radical Whig way of thinking nothing seemed
more designed to perpetuate an aristocratic or court dominance
than England's historical hodgepodge of electoral districts that
allowed small depopulated parts of the country to send more
representatives to Parliament than such "considerable places" as
Manchester, Birmingham, and Sheffield.[22] Because the Americans'

20. Charleston *S.-C. and American Gazette*, Jan. 16, 1777; Alexander White
to R. H. Lee, 1758, quoted in Wood, "Rhetoric and Reality," *Wm. and Mary
Qtly.*, 3d Ser., 23 (1966), 28. See Greene, *Provincial Governor*, 148.

21. Pa. Cons. (1776), Sec. 32; Md. Cons. (1776), LIV; Ga. Cons. (1777), Art.
X; Williamson, *Suffrage*, 40–42; Richard P. McCormick, *Experiment in Indepen-
dence: New Jersey in the Critical Period 1781–1789* (New Brunswick, 1950), 73;
Demophilus, *Genuine Principles*, 19; N. Y. Cons. (1777), VI.

22. [Adams], *Thoughts on Government*, Adams, ed., *Works of John Adams*,
IV, 195; Burgh, *Disquisitions*, I, 39–54, 47–48, 56, 62–72; [James Otis], *Considerations on Behalf of the Colonists . . .* (London, 1765), in Charles F. Mullet, ed.,
Some Political Writings of James Otis (University of Missouri Studies, IV [Co-
lumbia, Mo., 1929]), 366.

electoral divisions—more a product of planned and relatively recent creation than long evolutionary accretion—seemed systematic and comparatively equal, Whigs in Maryland, Virginia, North Carolina, and Delaware saw no great need in 1776 for a drastic alteration in the existing representational structure based on counties, irrespective of differences in population. Unequally representative geographical districts were "submitted to in Virginia," Edmund Randolph later recalled, "without a murmur, or even without a proposition to the contrary," despite "the most pointed declamations in the convention, against the inequality of representation in the British house of commons."[23] What was actually feared in these southern states was not so much the disproportion in county representation as the possibility of future rotten boroughs; both the Maryland and Virginia constitutions provided for the withdrawal of the representation given to several cities if in the future their population for seven successive years should be less than one-half that of the smallest county. Even Baltimore, it was thought, might one day become an Old Sarum.[24]

However, for others in 1776 equality of representation had a more rigorous and more pervasive meaning. The plan of several states that "every county is to have an equal voice, although some counties are six times more numerous and twelve times more wealthy" could only be, said John Adams, a blatant violation of "a first principle of liberty." Even before Independence four colonies—South Carolina, Pennsylvania, Massachusetts, and New Hampshire—had attempted to bring representation more into line with the population of their electoral districts, since, as the Pennsylvania Constitution declared, "representation in proportion to the number of taxable inhabitants is the only principle which can at all times secure liberty, and make the voice of a majority of the people the law of the land." In fact, wrote one Pennsylvania

23. Edmund Randolph, "Essay on the Revolutionary History of Virginia," *Va. Mag. of Hist. and Biog.*, 44 (1936), 48. The Maryland Constitution provided for four delegates from each county; the Virginia and North Carolina constitutions, two from each county; and the Delaware Constitution, seven from each of the three counties, regardless of differences in population. Jefferson in his 1776 draft for a Virginia Constitution proposed proportional representation. Boyd, ed., *Jefferson Papers*, I, 296. While the Georgia Constitution allowed ten members for nearly all the counties, some rough attempt was made to adjust representation for the more heavily and more sparsely populated counties. Ga. Cons. (1777), Art. IV.

24. Va. Cons. (1776), Boyd, ed., *Jefferson Papers*, I, 379; Md. Cons. (1776), V. See Kemp, *King and Commons*, 91–93.

pamphleteer, "A CONSTITUTION should lay down some permanent ratio, by which the representation should afterwards increase or decrease with the number of inhabitants." Thus by "taking warning from the unequal representation of Britain, by the growth of one part and decrease of another," and by seeking to preserve equal representation "thro' all ages and changes of time," five states—New Jersey, Pennsylvania, New York, Vermont, and South Carolina—wrote into their constitutions specific plans for periodic adjustments of their representation, so that, as the New York Constitution stated, it "shall for ever remain proportionate and adequate."[25]

With these kinds of protections and reforms built into their constitutions, "with such security, and not otherwise," many Americans in 1776 were hopeful and confident that their representative assemblies, now definitely free from magisterial contamination, could be fair and suitable embodiments of the people-at-large. The elected members would be, in other words, "an exact epitome of the whole people," "an exact miniature of their constituents," men whom the people could trust to represent their interests, for "if we cannot trust to their understanding and integrity, to form a judgment, when we choose them ourselves, whom can we trust?" Even English radicals, like John Cartwright and Burgh, who remained suspicious of any institution set above the people, had conceded that a representative assembly, if it were "elected by the unbribed, and unbiased suffrage of the freeholders," and were "free from all indirect influence" and possessed "no interest separate from the general good of the commonwealth," could obtain every benefit the people could want as effectively as if each of them were to deliberate and vote in person. As men in both North and South repeatedly declared in 1776, when the "Choice is free, and the Representation, equal, 'tis the People's Fault if they are not happy."[26]

25. Adams to Joseph Hawley, Aug. 25, 1776, Adams, ed., *Works of John Adams*, IX, 435; Pa. Cons. (1776), Sec. 17; *Four Letters*, 21–22; Boston *Continental Journal*, Jan. 15, 1778; N. Y. Cons. (1777), IV, V, XVI; N. J. Cons. (1776), III; Pa. Cons. (1776), Sec. 17; S. C. Cons. (1778), XV; Vt. Cons. (1777), Sec. XVI.
26. Boston *Continental Journal*, June 11, 1778; *Essex Result*, Parsons, *Memoir*, 376; Ross, *Sermon, in Which the Union of the Colonies is Considered*, 14; [John Cartwright], *American Independence the Interest and Glory of Great Britain* . . . (Phila., 1776), viii; Burgh, *Disquisitions*, I, 6; Boston's Instructions to Its Representatives, May 30, 1776, Handlin, eds., *Popular Sources*, 95; "A Form of Government Proposed for the Consideration of the People of Anne Arundel County," June 27, 1776, Force, ed., *American Archives*, 4th Ser., VI, 1093.

Representing the people in the legislature was not all that simple, however. As Richard Henry Lee confessed in 1778, "The doctrine of representation is a large subject." It was, as one English radical said, one of those words that are so long in common use they "acquire so many senses that they lose exactness."[27] Representation had been in fact a central, if not the most fundamental, issue between England and America from the very beginning of the controversy, and because it was so important it was to remain a source of contention among Americans themselves in the years following Independence. The imperial debate had compelled the colonists into a comprehensive inquiry into the nature of representation, with the consequent releasing of a jumble of ideas that the Declaration of Independence had by no means brought into order. The various efforts to ensure a free, full, and equal representation embodied in the constitutional documents of 1776 hardly disclosed the amount of confusion about representation present in American thinking.

2. VIRTUAL REPRESENTATION

It had all started with the passage of the Stamp Act in 1765. Once the ministry sensed a stirring of colonial opposition to the Stamp Act, a group of able English pamphleteers connected with the government—the most important being Soame Jenyns, a long-time member of the Board of Trade, and Thomas Whateley, secretary to George Grenville and the chief drafter of the Stamp Act—set out to explain and to justify parliamentary taxation of the colonies. Before they were done they had revealed the assumptions on which the entire English theory of politics was based. Their arguments differed, Jenyns, for example, going so far as to deny the principle of consent as a basis for taxation; yet all eventually centered on the point that the Americans, like all Englishmen who subscribed to "the principles of our Constitution," were comprehended by acts of Parliament through a system of virtual representation, however "imaginary" and however incomprehensible to "common Sense" this conception of representation may have been. Even though the colonists, like "Nine-

---

27. Lee to Hannah Corbin, Mar. 17, 1778, Ballagh, ed., *Letters of R. H. Lee*, I, 392; *An Answer to a Pamphlet, Entitled "Taxation No Tyranny"* ... (London, 1775), in Force, ed., *American Archives*, 4th Ser., I, 1453.

Tenths of the People of *Britain*," did not in fact choose any representatives to the House of Commons, they were undoubtedly "a Part, and an important Part of the Commons of Great Britain: they are represented in Parliament, in the same Manner as those Inhabitants of *Britain* are, who have not Voices in Elections." Representation in the Commons, the English declared, was not a concomitant of election; "for the Right of Election is annexed to certain Species of Property, to peculiar Franchises, and to Inhabitancy in some particular places." Men did not actually have to vote for members of Parliament to be represented there. "Copyholders, Leaseholders, and all Men possessed of personal Property only, chuse no Representatives; *Manchester*, *Birmingham*, and many more of our richest and most flourishing trading Towns send no Members to Parliament . . . ; yet are they not *Englishmen*? or are they not taxed?" And the colonists, it seemed, were in exactly the same situation as those denied the franchise in England. In fact, all British subjects were really in the same situation: "None are actually, all are virtually represented; for every Member of Parliament sits in the House, not as Representative of his own Constituents, but as one of that august Assembly by which all the Commons of *Great Britain* are represented."[28]

What made this conception of virtual representation intelligible, what gave it its force in English thought, was the assumption that the English people, despite great degrees of rank and property, despite even the separation of some by three thousand miles of ocean, were essentially a unitary homogeneous order with a fundamental common interest. What affected nonelectors eventually affected electors; what affected the whole affected the parts; and what affected the empire ultimately affected every Englishman in it. All Englishmen were linked by their heritage, their liberties, and their institutions into a common people that possessed a single transcendent concern. (If representation "can travel three hundred Miles, why not three thousand? if it can jump over Rivers and Mountains, why cannot it sail over the Ocean? If the towns of *Manchester* and *Birmingham*, sending no Representatives to Parliament, are notwithstanding there represented, why are not the cities of *Albany* and *Boston* equally repre-

28. [Thomas Whateley], *The Regulations Lately Made concerning the Colonies and the Taxes Imposed upon Them, Considered* (London, 1765), 108, 112, 109; [Soame Jenyns], *The Objections to the Taxation of Our American Colonies, by the Legislature of Great Britain, Briefly Consider'd* (London, 1765), 8, 7, 8–9. See Bailyn, ed., *Pamphlets*, I, 599–606.

sented in that Assembly? Are they not alike *British* subjects? are they not *Englishmen?*") The assumption lay at the heart of the Englishmen's theory of politics, and without it few of their notions of government could have stood for long. Their dichotomy between rulers and people, their belief in mixed government, the conviction that the Commons was a full and complete embodiment of the people, and the concept of virtual representation itself—all depended on the conception of Englishmen as a single people with one definable interest. As Edmund Burke told his Bristol constituents in 1774 in the most celebrated expression of this assumption in the eighteenth century, Parliament was not "a *congress* of ambassadors from different and hostile interests, which interests each must maintain, as an agent and advocate, against other agents and advocates; but Parliament is a *deliberative* assembly of *one* nation, with *one* interest, that of the whole, where, not local purposes, not local prejudices ought to guide, but the general good, resulting from the general reason of the whole." The significance of such a conception for the role of the representative, as Blackstone and Thomas Whateley summarized it, was clear: every member of the House of Commons, "though chosen by one particular district, when elected and returned serves for the whole realm," and was "not bound . . . to consult with, or take the advice, of his constituents." The general interests of the whole people, however much they may hurt a member's particular constituency, "ought to be the great Objects of his Attention, and the only Rules for his Conduct; and to sacrifice these to a partial Advantage in favour of the Place where he was chosen, would be a Departure from his Duty." The representatives were independent members free to deliberate and decide by their own consciences what was good for the country both because a single autonomous public interest was presumed to exist, and because the representatives, as the Commons of England, contained all of the people's power and were considered to be the very persons of the people they represented.

With such an assumption it is not surprising then that the English defenders of virtual representation should have denigrated the electoral process by which members were sent to Parliament. Election in and by itself was not what gave the member his representative power. That came ultimately from his mutuality of interests with the whole people for whom he spoke. "If it were otherwise," wrote Thomas Whateley, "*Old Sarum* would enjoy

Privileges essential to Liberty, which are denied to *Birmingham* and to *Manchester*." Only this concept of virtual representation ultimately justified the binding of the whole people "by the Consent of the Majority of that House, whether their own particular Representatives consented to or opposed the Measures there taken, or whether they had or had not particular Representatives there."[29] Whatever one may think of the notion of virtual representation as it pertained to the Americans in 1765, no better justification of majority rule has ever been made.

The Americans, however, immediately and emphatically rejected the British claim that they, like the inhabitants of Manchester and Birmingham, were "*virtually* represented" in the House of Commons, "in the same manner with the nonelectors resident in Great Britain." The idea that members of Parliament spoke for their interests struck them at once as "futile and absurd," contrary to everything they knew about politics: "It cannot surely be consistent with British liberty." "That the people of these colonies are not, and from their local circumstances cannot be, represented in the House of Commons in Great Britain" was self-evident to almost all Americans from the beginning of the controversy and was never shaken.[30]

In rejecting the British claim that Americans were virtually represented in the English House of Commons, however, the colonists never decisively repudiated the conception of virtual representation itself, which held that certain people from the society, if their interests were identical with the rest, could justly speak for the whole, and which presumed that electors could comprehend nonelectors, when "the interest and circumstance of those who do not vote for representatives, are the same with those that do." In England, wrote Daniel Dulany, the foremost American antagonist in the debate over representation, a "virtual

29. [Jenyns], *Objections*, 8–9; Edmund Burke, "Speech to the Electors of Bristol" (1774), *Works of Burke*, II, 96; Blackstone, *Commentaries*, I, 159; [Whateley], *Regulations*, 109.

30. [Daniel Dulany], *Considerations on the Propriety of Imposing Taxes in the British Colonies* . . . ([Annapolis], 1765), in Bailyn, ed., *Pamphlets*, I, 611; Church, *Oration Delivered March Fifth, 1773*, in Niles, ed., *Principles*, 36; Maurice Moore, *The Justice and Policy of Taxing the American Colonies* . . . (Wilmington, N. C., 1765), in William K. Boyd, ed., *Some Eighteenth Century Tracts Concerning North Carolina* (Raleigh, 1927), 167; Declaration of the Stamp Act Congress (Oct. 19, 1765), Jensen, ed., *English Historical Documents*, IX, 672.

representation may be reasonably supposed," since the interests of "the nonelectors, the electors, and the representatives are individually the same, to say nothing of the connection among neighbors, friends, and relations. The security of the nonelectors against oppression is that their oppression will fall also upon the electors and the representatives. The one can't be injured and the other indemnified." As late as 1774–75 some American Whigs were still conceding that virtual representation in Parliament had a relevance in England, where "those who are not freeholders are justly bound by the laws of the land, tho' they have no vote in electing members of Parliament," because all—representatives, electors, and nonelectors—were "governed by the same laws." There was no person in England who did not live in some county which sent several members to the House of Commons, just as there was no person in an American colony, whether he could vote or not, "who is not represented in the provincial legislature where he resides."[31]

The fallacy in the British contention that Americans were virtually represented in Parliament rested, in the minds of many Americans, not so much in the necessity of the representatives to be elected by all, but rather in the disparity of interests between mother country and colonies that was inherent in their emerging conception of the empire—grounds of opposition that allowed any proposals for American representation in Parliament to be instantly dismissed by the colonists as "utterly impracticable and vain." The Americans' objection to parliamentary taxation was "not because we have no vote in electing members of Parliament, but because we are not, and from our local situation never can be, *represented* there." The Americans were in fact coming to argue that in their clarifying conception of the British empire the mother country and the colonists did not possess an overriding harmony of interest that made Englishmen on both sides of the Atlantic one common people. Some like John Dickinson could see a sufficient connection of commercial interests between the different parts of the empire to justify "the authority of the *British* parliament to regulate the trade of all her dominions." For without this trade England's "strength must decay; her glory vanish,"

31. Moore, *Justice and Policy*, Boyd, ed., *Eighteenth Century Tracts*, 169; [Dulany], *Considerations*, Bailyn, ed., *Pamphlets*, 612; Phila. *Pa. Packet*, June 12, 1775, Dec. 19, 1774.

and America's with it; England "cannot suffer without our partaking in her misfortune."[32] But such representation in matters of
imperial commerce could not be extended to the colonists' internal affairs. "That any set of men should represent another,
detached from them in situation and interest," was totally inconsistent with the principles of British liberty. Perhaps some could
virtually represent others from the same society, but surely they
could not virtually represent "*a whole people.*" Many Americans
in effect turned the conception of virtual representation against
the English themselves, arguing that the members of Parliament
were "perfect strangers" to Americans, "not bound in interest,
duty, or affection" to preserve their liberties, and thus were able
"to lay upon us what they would not venture to lay upon their
own constituents." By the taxation of American property, said
Richard Henry Lee, English "property would have been exon-
erated in exact proportion to the burthens they laid on ours."
Indeed, the British had violated the very essence of any kind of
representation, virtual or not, by framing laws to bind the people, "without, in the same manner, binding the legislators themselves."[33]

Such arguments did not undercut the theory of virtual representation but reinforced it. By conceiving of themselves as a
whole people distinct from England, because of the "desparity
between the two countries, in respect of situations, numbers, age,
abilities and other circumstances," the Americans could renounce
parliamentary authority over their internal affairs without necessarily denying the particular concept of virtual representation.
And in fact they continued to embrace it even after Indepen-

32. [Mather], *America's Appeal*, 14; Phila. *Pa. Packet*, Dec. 19, 1774; [Dickin-
son], *Letters from a Farmer*, Ford, ed., *Writings of Dickinson*, 348–50. On the
new conception of the empire, see Richard Koebner, *Empire* (London, 1961),
168–69, 205–07, 211–15; Randolph Adams, *Political Ideas of the American Revolution* . . . (Durham, N. C., 1922), 65–85.
33. Moore, *Justice and Policy*, Boyd, ed., *Eighteenth Century Tracts*, 167;
[Richard Wells], *The Middle Line: Or, an Attempt to Furnish Some Hints for
Ending the Differences Subsisting between Great-Britain and the Colonies*
(Phila., 1775), 29; West, *Sermon Preached May 29th, 1776*, Thornton, ed., *Pulpit*,
280; Gouverneur Morris, Speech in New York Convention (1777), Sparks,
Morris, I, 107; Charleston *S.-C. Gazette*, June 20, 1774; Lee to Corbin, Mar. 17,
1778, Ballagh, ed., *Letters of R. H. Lee*, I, 393; [Hamilton], *Farmer Refuted*,
Syrett and Cooke, eds., *Hamilton Papers*, I, 100. For other examples see [Dickin-
son], *Letters from a Farmer*, Ford, ed., *Writings of Dickinson*, 350; [Mather],
America's Appeal, 41; Ross, *Sermon, in Which the Union of the Colonies Is
Considered*, 14; [Wilson], *Considerations*, Wilson, ed., *Works of Wilson*, III, 218.

dence, for as Hamilton said, "the intimate connexion of interest" among electors, nonelectors, and representatives, and not simply the right to vote, was what really made representation viable. This was most obvious of course in the Americans' denial of the franchise to women and young men. And some such notion of virtual representation, a natural identity of interests between electors and nonelectors, lay behind the various property qualifications for suffrage generally required in the new state constitutions. With every demand in 1776 for an extension of the franchise by Americans pressing for the actuality of consent, the constitution-makers were compelled to fall back on reassertions of the doctrine of virtual representation, always emphasizing of course, as Richard Henry Lee did, the "great difference" between the Americans' case against Britain and "that of the unrepresented in this country."[34]

Moreover, because the conception of virtual representation was inevitably and inextricably bound up with the belief in the homogeneous unity of the people—meaning not only "that the parliament cannot tax the non-voters in England without taxing themselves," but also "that the happiness of the whole nation, must eventually include the happiness of every individual"—the Americans in 1776 were necessarily committed to its central premises. Republicanism with its emphasis on devotion to the transcendent public good logically presumed a legislature in which the various groups in the society would realize "the necessary dependence and connection" each had upon the others. "Our situation requires their being firmly united in the same common cause" with "no schism in the body politic." And this kind of legislature presumed a particular sort of representation—"a house of disinterested men" who "would employ their whole time for the public good." Thus independence and the establishment of their new republics, whether or not Americans clearly realized it, only reaffirmed and strengthened the assumptions involved in the concept of virtual representation; and many Americans in 1776 and in the years following continued to stress, in words no less explicit than those of Burke or Blackstone, the proper duties of a good representative: "candidly and impartially to form his own judgment for himself . . . , to detach himself from all local partiali-

34. [Mather], *America's Appeal*, 14; [Hamilton], *Farmer Refuted*, Syrett and Cooke, eds., *Hamilton Papers*, I, 92–93, 97, 100, 105; Lee to Corbin, Mar. 17, 1778, Ballagh, ed., *Letters of R. H. Lee*, I, 392.

ties, and county-interests, inconsistent with the common weal; and ever considering himself as a representative of the whole state, to be assiduous in promoting the interest of the whole, which must ultimately produce the good of every part." Any other view of the representative's role would turn the legislative assembly into a battlefield, where numerous "partial views and county interests" would struggle for preference and in turn destroy the homogeneity and harmony upon which republicanism rested.[35]

A representative legislature conceived in such Burkean terms also possessed a decided social bias that was not easily reconcilable with the replication idea of representation. John Adams, for example, had urged in 1776 that the representatives should be "in miniature an exact portrait" of the people; yet in the same breath he had suggested that they must also be "a few of the most wise and good" who, as the English defenders of virtual representation had implied, would presumably know better than the bulk of the people what was the proper interest of the society. In Virginia, where confidence in the deferential nature of the society was strongest, concern with ensuring by law that only the "best sort" were elected as representatives was slight. But in other states confidence was slipping. Some Americans were suggesting—in an argument that was to be most cogently expressed a decade later by Melancthon Smith in the New York Ratifying Convention—that if an "exact portrait" of the people was what was desired then "choose a man in midling circumstances" who knows better than puffed-up professors and rich lawyers "the wants of the poor, and can judge pretty well what the community can bear of public burdens." In the simple and plain governments of America, "there is required in a Representative of the People, little more than a common sense and an unshaken integrity."[36]

Such anti-elitist sentiments, only a presage of what was to come, were frightening to many concerned with what a revolution might mean for the stability of the social structure. The middling men whom some wanted as representatives were only "common farmers, who . . . are destitute of any artificial acquisitions," men without dignity and learning, hardly fit to understand the science of government. Yet everyone was a good Whig, and lest anyone

35. [Wells], *Middle Line*, 30–31; Boston *Independent Chronicle*, Apr. 3, July 10, Dec. 4, 1777; Trenton, *N.-J. Gazette*, Jan. 7, 1778, in Nelson *et al.*, eds., *New Jersey Archives*, 2d Ser., II, 2–3; Phila. *Pa. Packet*, Sept. 15, 1786.

36. [Adams], *Thoughts on Government*, Adams, ed., *Works of John Adams*, IV, 194–95; Worcester *Mass. Spy*, July 5, 1775; Charleston *S.-C. and American Gazette*, Jan. 14, 1779.

doubt it the defenders of elitism were quick to point out they did "not intend a reflection upon the commonalty—by no means." They had "great veneration for the people." "But at the same time" society was a hierarchy, "some higher and some lower," and those on the bottom were "not to be put in places of the most important trust." Only "great abilities, or considerable property" could produce respect, and without them any men placed in high stations, including the representatives of the people, would only be rendered conspicuously "contemptible and ridiculous." Most of the framers of the constitutions agreed; and since "great abilities" were difficult to assess, then "considerable property" would have to suffice as the criterion of "the most wise and good." Nearly all of the states therefore provided for special property qualifications (exceeding those for the suffrage) for the members of their assemblies.[37]

3. THE EXPLICITNESS OF CONSENT

In just such measures Americans demonstrated how firmly they clasped the notion of virtual representation in 1776. Yet even as they hung on to the assumptions behind virtual representation and attempted to work them out in their constitutional documents, they were burdened with the implications of another conception of representation that pulled them in a very different direction and connoted a very contrary notion of the body politic.

The tension had been exposed at the very outset of the imperial controversy. Some Americans in the debate with England had not been satisfied merely with questioning the claim that the colonists were virtually represented in Parliament but had pushed beyond arguments like those of Daniel Dulany's to challenge the concept of virtual representation itself. "A *supposed* or *implied* assent of the people is not an assent to be regarded or depended on." The people, it seemed obvious to many Americans, "must be represented actually—not 'virtually,' " and not just the colonists but people anywhere. "To what purpose," asked James Otis, "is it to ring everlasting changes to the colonists on the cases of Manchester, Birmingham and Sheffield, who return no mem-

---

37. Worcester *Mass. Spy*, July 12, 26, 1775; Watchman [pseud.], *To the Inhabitants of the City and County of New York, Apr. 15, 1776* (N. Y., 1776). See in general Frank H. Miller, "Legal Qualifications for Office in America, 1619–1899," American Historical Association, *Annual Report, 1899*, I, 87–153.

bers? If those now so considerable places are not represented, they ought to be." "Surely," some Americans were being compelled to conclude, "he is not my delegate in whose nomination or appointment I have no choice." The consent through representation that was so important to the workings of the British constitution seemed increasingly equivalent, even to those who were willing to grant the relevance of virtual representation in England itself, to the people's "actually choosing their own representatives." From their experience in the New World and from the exigencies of the debate it had become to many Americans "plain that the elected are not representatives in their own right, but by virtue of their election." The process of voting was not incidental to representation but was at the heart of it. Indeed, "representation arises entirely from the free election of the people." Therefore, it was evident that the right of the members of Parliament acquired by their election in England "to pass laws binding upon their electors, does not at the same time give them a right to represent and lay on taxes on those who never invested them with any such power, and by whom they neither were nor could be elected." In response to the Stamp Act and in an effort to make clear what had been their previous experience with representation in the New World, the Americans found themselves in their arguments with England putting an emphasis on the suffrage itself as a basic prerequisite of representation—an emphasis that had momentous implications for the development of American political thought. Apparently the interests of the individuals in the community were so peculiar, so personal, that "the only ground and reason why any man should be bound by the actions of another who meddles with his concerns is, that he himself choose that other to office." Such a view could have limitless ramifications. It was axiomatic by 1776 "that the only moral foundation of government is, the consent of the people." But to what extent should the principle be carried? "Shall we say," asked John Adams, "that every individual of the community, old and young, male and female, as well as rich and poor, must consent, expressly, to every act of legislation?"[38]

38. Essay, Phila., June 22, 1774, Force, ed., *American Archives*, 4th Ser., I, 441; [Otis], *Considerations*, Mullet, ed., *Writings of Otis*, 366; Church, *Oration Delivered March Fifth, 1773*, Niles, ed., *Principles*, 36; Moore, *Justice and Policy*, Boyd, ed., *Eighteenth Century Tracts*, 169; [John Joachim Zubly], *An Humble Enquiry into the Nature of the Dependency of the American Colonies . . .* ([Charleston], 1769), 17, 22; *Boston Evening Post*, June 24, 1765; Adams to James Sullivan, May 26, 1776, Adams, ed., *Works of John Adams*, IX, 375.

Once the assumptions lying behind the notion of actual representation were conceded, this conclusion was difficult to resist. And some Americans argued vehemently but still sporadically in the early constitution-making period that the suffrage must be extended to all members of the society if the principle of consent were to remain inviolate. The growing demand for the right to vote—"the *only privilege* which subjects can *rely* on as a *security* for their *liberty* out of their hands"—was (as in the case of the Pennsylvania radicals) often prompted by the desire to attach as many as possible to the Revolutionary movement; but in all cases (as particularly in the arguments against the proposed exclusion of Negroes, Indians, and mulattoes from the suffrage in Massachusetts) it was made possible by the logic of many Americans' commitment against Britain to the actuality of representation. Even the Tories tried to throw the implications of the Revolutionary notion of actual consent into the faces of American Whigs, arguing that if the Whigs were correct, then no man could be bound by a law unless he had personally voted for a representative.[39] Like other of the American positions in the imperial debate, actual representation could lead in directions that few of those who used it intended to follow.

Because the future of American political thought lay with this doctrine of actual representation, in retrospect it is easy, perhaps too easy, to uncover the adumbrations and processes of its development in the colonial period. Right from the beginnings of the settlements in the seventeenth century the colonists had been continually compelled, from the peculiarity of their circumstances, to believe that the people "should be consulted in the most particular manner that can be imagined." New England colonial assemblies had in fact often refrained from taxing towns which had not yet sent their delegates to the legislature. In 1769 when the royal governor denied representation in the Georgia Assembly to four new parishes, the legislature pointedly refused to tax them.[40] As has recently been pointed out, at the very time in the seventeenth and eighteenth centuries that the English conception of virtual representation was hardening and laying the theoretical foundations for parliamentary sovereignty, the Amer-

---

39. Phila. *Pa. Gazette*, May 15, 1, 1776; Boston *Independent Chronicle*, Apr. 9, 1778, Sept. 23, 1779; Boston *Continental Journal*, Jan. 8, 1778; [Hamilton], *Farmer Refuted*, Syrett and Cooke, eds., *Hamilton Papers*, I, 105; *The Triumph of the Whigs: Or, T'Other Congress Convened* (N. Y., 1775), 8.

40. Essay, Phila., June 22, 1774, Force, ed., *American Archives*, 4th Ser., I, 441; Grant, *Democracy in Kent*, 115–16; Greene, *Quest for Power*, 384.

icans' ideas about representation were moving in a different direction, regressing in fact to an older medieval notion of the relationship between constituents and representatives.[41] While the American experience was recreating the English medieval practice of attorneys or delegates specifically empowered by counties or towns to vote supplies to the rulers and present grievances from their constituencies, the English, from sometime in the late fifteenth century, had gradually but increasingly regarded their members in the House of Commons less as delegated deputies from particular districts and more as spokesmen for the entire estate of the people. It is perhaps not an exaggeration to say that these two conceptions of representation passed each other, at least formally, at the time of the American Revolution. In 1774 Parliament finally repealed the decidedly moribund residential requirements for its members and legalized voting by nonresident electors in order to bring the law into line with their conception of representation. At the same time the Americans' new constitutions and governments put a new stress on residential requirements for representatives and electors, in addition to broadening the suffrage and equalizing electoral districts—all of which measures assumed an actuality of representation alien to official eighteenth-century English thought. Thus by 1769 the Reverend John Joachim Zubly could confront the official English conception of virtual representation head on, by arguing that "every representative in Parliament is not a representative for the whole nation, but only for the particular place for which he hath been chosen . . . and as the right of sitting depends entirely upon the election, it seems clear to demonstration, that no member can represent any but those by whom he hath been elected; if not elected he cannot represent them, and of course not consent to any thing in their behalf."[42] Strong words, with dangerous unfore-

41. Bailyn, *Ideological Origins*, 162–64.
42. [Zubly], *Humble Enquiry*, 17. See in general Hubert Phillips, *The Development of a Residential Qualification for Representatives in Colonial Legislatures* (Cincinnati, 1921). The medieval and early modern origins and development of English representation can be traced from a voluminous literature on the subject in Maude V. Clarke, *Medieval Representation and Consent* . . . (London, 1936); Charles H. McIlwain, "Medieval Estates," *Cambridge Medieval History*, 7 (1932), 665–715; J. G. Edwards, "The Plena Potestas of English Parliamentary Representation," in *Oxford Essays in Medieval History Presented to H. E. Salter* (Oxford, 1934), 141–54; J. G. Edwards, "Taxation and Consent in the Court of Common Pleas, 1338," *English Historical Review*, 57 (1942), 473–82; Gaines Post, "Plena Potestas and Consent in Medieval Assemblies: A Study in Romano-Canonical Procedure and the Rise of Representation, 1150–1325," *Tra-*

seen significance; yet Zubly was only drawing out the meaning, implicit if not always explicit, of America's previous experience with the representational process. The Revolutionary debates had the effect of clarifying this previous experience and setting representation off in the direction it eventually reached in the next century.

Since ideas about representation were in fact linked with all kinds of conceptions about the structure of the state and the nature of the political process, the clarification was not easy and did not come at once. Behind every differing statement concerning the right of taxation, the force of law, or the sovereignty of the legislative authority lay a varying idea of representation. Because the doctrine of representation was the foundation of all of men's ideas about their relation to government, explaining it was difficult and complicated; changes in the conception of representation required and eventually demanded all sorts of adjustments that were scarcely predicted and often stoutly resisted even by those who held to ideas that made the adjustments necessary. Despite more than a decade of intense inquiry into the nature of representation, American thinking in 1776 had still not sorted out its various aspects but stocked them all in a confused and contradictory fashion. "It seems strange . . . ," exclaimed one New Englander in 1778, "that after so much has been well said, on the worth and importance of representation, and our blood and treasure lavishly spent to maintain and preserve it," that it should be still such a subject of contention and confusion among Americans.[43]

Nowhere in the years surrounding the Declaration of Independence were the ambiguities and dissensions over representation more disturbingly exposed than in New England. And nowhere

ditio, 1 (1943), 355–408; G. O. Sayles, "Representation of Cities and Boroughs in 1268," *Eng. Hist. Rev.,* 40 (1925), 580–85; H. M. Cam, "The Relation of English Members of Parliament to Their Constituencies in the Fourteenth Century," in her *Liberties and Communities in Medieval England* (Cambridge, Eng., 1944), 223–35; H. M. Cam, "The Legislators of Medieval England," *Proceedings of the British Academy,* 31 (1945), 127–50; T. F. T. Plucknett, "The Lancasterian Constitution," in *Tudor Studies Presented . . . to A. F. Pollard* (London, 1924); S. B. Chrimes, *English Constitutional Ideas in the Fifteenth Century* (Cambridge, Eng., 1936), 66–101, 115–26; E. T. Lampson, "Some New Light on the Growth of Parliamentary Sovereignty: Wimbish versus Taillebois," *Amer. Pol. Sci. Rev.,* 35 (1941), 952–60. On 18th-century English conceptions see Samuel H. Beer, "The Representation of Interests in British Government: Historical Background," *Amer. Pol. Sci. Rev.,* 51 (1957), 613–50.

43. Boston *Continental Journal,* Jan. 15, 1778.

were the connections and continuity between the imperial debate and the domestic squabbles among Americans themselves more starkly revealed. By 1776 it seemed clear to numerous inhabitants of the western areas of the Connecticut River valley that the fight against tyranny had assumed a two-fold character: "We are contending against the same enemy within, that is also without." In both struggles they saw themselves "pursuing the same general cause . . . that there cannot be any legislation or taxation without representation." As war began and independence from Britain became imminent, men in New Hampshire and Massachusetts abandoned their concern with the colonists' relationship to Parliament and became preoccupied with the precise nature of their connection to their own state legislatures. So engrossed in fact did they become that the problem of representation emerged as a major obstacle to the establishing of new constitutions in both states. "Till this Matter is Remedied about the Representation," the Massachusetts town of Sutton in Worcester County declared in 1778, the state would "never have a court to the satisfaction of the People." Because newly articulated ideas were highly permissive and could be wielded by different men for different purposes, equality of representation could become the rallying cry of various groups, whether farmers in the Berkshires or merchants in Boston, who sought different kinds of legislatures. The heightening Revolutionary sense that representation had to be proportioned to the population somehow had to be reconciled with the long-standing tradition in New England of each town's sending at least one delegate to the legislature.[44]

At the very outset of the Revolution, Massachusetts and New Hampshire had precipitated the issue by attempts to bring representation in the legislatures more in line with the population of the various towns, the Massachusetts act of May 1776, for example, allowing each town an additional representative for every 100 voters it possessed over the base figure of 120; towns with fewer than the base number might combine with others to send a representative. Moreover, each town was to pay for the costs of

44. An Address of the Inhabitants of the Towns of [Grafton County] . . . (Norwich, Vt., 1776), in Nathaniel Bouton et al., eds., The Provincial and State Papers of New Hampshire (Concord, 1867–1943), X, 234; Return of Sutton, May 18, 1778, Handlin, eds., Popular Sources, 233. On the problems of representation in western New England see Pole, Political Representation in England, 172–204; Richard F. Upton, Revolutionary New Hampshire (Hanover, N. H., 1936), 67, 177–78. See also James Warren to John Adams, May 8, 1776, Ford, ed., Warren-Adams Letters, I, 240–41; Boston Independent Chronicle, Sept. 26, 1776.

sending its representatives to the legislature. These acts provoked vigorous opposition by small rural towns, particularly in the Connecticut River valley, which feared either a total elimination or a dangerous dilution of their political power in the states' legislatures. To these small towns with their strong sense of local town autonomy ("for every body politic incorporated with the same powers and privileges, whether large or small, are legally the same"), such representational schemes seemed "very unequal and unsafe," and put the western towns, far removed from the capital, "in the same situation, with reference to the State, that America is to Britain." But to large towns like Boston and to many Americans elsewhere it was obvious that "representation ought to be conformable to some rule, either *property* or *numbers*, or both." It was undoubtedly true, an anonymous spokesman for the Connecticut River valley towns admitted, that "a well-regulated representation is the only security of our liberties." Yet representation could not depend on either taxes or population "without being subject to changes and innovations," or on both together without being "intirely capricious." What was needed was something concrete and permanent, "as is the case with our townships." This proposal of equal representation for all towns regardless of size was, for those familiar with the radical Whig rhetoric, "far from returning a *fair* and *equal* representation. . . . Where," asked William Gordon, English-born chaplain of the Massachusetts legislature, "is the equity of fifty or a hundred Electors returning the same number of Representatives, as a thousand or two thousand?" "The objection is trifling," answered the anonymous defender of town representation; and in an astonishing and tortured argument (subsequently repeated by several towns) he went on to state that "every government is an entire body politic, and therefore each particular member in the legislature does not represent any distinct part, but the whole of the said body." The legislatures of Massachusetts and New Hampshire were supposed to be like the Parliament Edmund Burke had envisioned, and equal representation of every town or every independent "body corporate" would help to make it that way. And Blackstone, of all people, with his description of English virtual representation, was called in to support this justification for the most extreme kind of actual representation voiced in the first year of the Revolution.[45]

45. *Address of the Inhabitants of the Towns of [Grafton County]*, Bouton et al., eds., *State Papers of N. H.*, X, 231; Resolution of Worcester County

In just such a way could Americans blend both actual and virtual representation and thus make conspicuous what had been a basic ambiguity in their thinking about representation from the very beginning of the controversy with England. Indeed, if men were compelled to think about it, some sort of conception of virtual representation was a necessary concomitant of their republican ideology and their Whig belief in the homogeneity of the people's interest. Yet ironically those who were most radically Whiggish, most devotedly republican, were at the same time most committed to the characteristics of the concept of actual representation—equal electoral districts, the particularity of consent through broadened suffrage, residence requirements for both the elected and the electors, the strict accountability of representatives to the local electorate, indeed, the closest possible ties between members and their particular constituents—characteristics that ran directly counter to the central premises of virtual representation and all that they implied about the nature of the body politic. In the years after 1776, without necessarily or clearly grasping the implications of what they were saying, many Americans would increasingly press for a fuller realization of these characteristics of actual representation and thereby threaten not only to undo the intellectual foundations of their theory of politics and their republican experiments but also to expose the whole representational process for the fiction that it was.

4. Ambassadors to an Extraneous Power

As one Whig noted in 1774, the conception of virtual representation, with its assumption that the representatives were in truth the entire people, presumed a more representative legislature, a closer identity between constituents and members, than did the belief that the representatives were only agents, or as

Towns, Nov. 26, 1776, Handlin, eds., *Popular Sources*, 165; Worcester *Mass. Spy*, Jan. 16, 1777; Boston *Independent Chronicle*, June 4, 1778; *The People the Best Governors: Or a Plan of Government Founded on the Just Principles of Natural Freedom* ([Hartford], 1776), in Chase, *Dartmouth College*, 658–59; Boston *Independent Chronicle*, Sept. 26, 1776. On the use of virtual representation, see also Chase, *Dartmouth College*, 552; Samuel Eliot Morison, "The Struggle over the Adoption of the Constitution of Massachusetts, 1780," Mass. Hist. Soc., *Proceedings*, 50 (1916–17), 408; Return of Topsfield, Oct. 22, 1776, Handlin, eds., *Popular Sources*, 154.

Josiah Tucker, cantankerous dean of Gloucester, snorted, "mere attornies of those who elected them" who "ought to do as they are bid" and who "ought not to prefer their own private opinions to the judgments of their constituents."[46] Indeed, it was this breakdown in the sense of mutuality of interests, this mistrust of the representational system, that gave meaning to the notion of actual representation, most clearly seen in the expanded use of instructions by constituents to their delegates in the legislatures.

The Whigs in Delaware in May of 1776 sensed the changes taking place in American ideas about representation, sensed in fact where the Revolutionary movement and arguments were going. Desiring to press the Delaware Assembly into declaring independence, a group of radicals led by Caesar and Thomas Rodney first thought "it was best to present petitions to the Assembly"; but then realizing that "there seems some impropriety in a petition" they "changed the mode into Instructions. . . ."[47] This change of form was actually one of substance, for the petitioning and the instructing of representatives were rapidly becoming symbols of two quite different attitudes toward representation, indeed between virtual and actual representation. Petitioning implied that the representative was a superior so completely possessed of the full authority of all the people that he must be solicited, never commanded, by his particular electors and must speak only for the general good and not merely for the interests of his local constituents. Instructing, on the other hand, implied that the delegate represented no one but the people who elected him and that he was simply a mistrusted agent of his electors, bound to follow their directions.

The use of instructions—directions drawn up by a body of constituents to their particular representatives—had long been common in colonial politics, especially in New England. From the first years of settlement the Massachusetts towns had given mandates to their deputies in a continuing effort to ensure that their local interests were heard and promoted in the General Court. In the other colonies, with less continuity and regularity, instructions had also been used whenever constituents felt the need to press their local views upon their representatives in the

46. Phila. *Pa. Packet*, Sept. 4, 1775; Josiah Tucker, *The True Interest of Britain* . . . (Phila., 1776), 26.

47. Thomas Rodney to Caesar Rodney, May 26, 1776, Ryden, ed., *Rodney Letters*, 84.

legislatures. The elected representatives, read the instructions from Orange County, North Carolina, in 1773, were expected to "speak our Sense in every case when we shall expressly declare it, or when you can by any other means discover it."[48] Because of this long experience with instructions, few Americans in the imperial debate, even those uncommitted to a rigid conception of actual representation, could deny "that the constituent can bind his representative by instructions." "Though the obligatory force of these instructions is not insisted upon," wrote Dulany, "yet their persuasive influence in most cases may be, for a representative who should act against the explicit recommendation of his constituents would most deservedly forfeit their regard and all pretension to their future confidence." Although even the most radical English Whigs had expressed some doubts ("the obeying every mandate of constituents may, in some very extraordinary conjuncture of opinions and circumstances, be wrong," wrote Catharine Macaulay), in the eyes of most patriots the instructing of representatives had become "an undoubted right." And several of the states explicitly provided for this right in their new constitutions. "No apology is necessary," wrote the freemen of Arundel County in Maryland to their representatives in the provincial congress in 1776; "neither is any, we presume, expected of us. From the very nature of the trust, and the relation subsisting between constituent and representative, the former is entitled to express his sentiments, and to instruct the latter upon all points that may come under his consideration as representative."[49]

Instructions by themselves, however, did not necessarily connote a theory of actual representation. As long as instructions were confined largely to parochial and local concerns, they were not really incompatible with the conception of virtual representation. Even the most independent-minded could agree that "where the matter related particularly to the interest of the Con-

48. Kenneth Colegrove, "New England Town Mandates," Colonial Society of Massachusetts, *Publications*, 21 (1919), 411–49; Instructions to the Representatives from Orange County (1773), Saunders, ed., *Col. Recs. of N. C.*, IX, 699–700. On the novel use of instructions in North Carolina see John S. Bassett, "The Regulators of North Carolina (1765–71)," Amer. Hist. Assoc., *Annual Report, 1894*, 161–62.

49. [Dulany], *Considerations*, Bailyn, ed., *Pamphlets*, I, 608; Macaulay, *Address to the People*, 11–12; Charleston *S.-C. and American Gazette*, Dec. 31, 1778; Instructions of the Freemen of Anne Arundel County, 1776, Force, ed., *American Archives*, 4th Ser., VI, 1091–92. The North Carolina, Pennsylvania, and Vermont constitutions provided explicitly for instructions.

stituents alone," then "implicit obedience" by the representative to the will of his constituents "ought to Govern." But where the matter "was to affect the whole Community, Reason and Good Conscience should direct, for it must be absurd to Suppose one part of the Community could be apprized of the good of the whole without Consulting the whole." Such a distinction could be tenuously maintained, as long as questions involving the whole community did not seriously seem to affect local interests or vice versa. The problem in eighteenth-century America was that the bestowal of local and private benefits was so common and wide ranging, because of the newness of the society, that what was private and what was public inevitably blurred—a blurring that the Revolutionary crisis only intensified. Thus constituents who had tended to construe as public matters the disposal of lands or the building of bridges in their locality now saw no incongruity in instructing their delegates in affairs of more obvious general interest. It was through the Revolution's expansion of the use of instructions into those areas of clearly communal concern that the implications of binding directions by local constituencies were brought more sharply and more alarmingly into focus. When in 1776 some Marylanders instructed their representatives about the constitution of the new government, three delegates resigned, "extremely against their inclinations," rather than "adhere to points in their opinion incompatible with good government and the public peace and happiness."[50] Yet some Americans had come to believe that it was precisely on these "great and leading questions" of public policy, such as the formation of governments or the disestablishment of religion, rather than on the more parochial questions, that binding instructions were most necessary. While the freeholders of Augusta County, Virginia, were generally willing to leave their delegates free "as individuals or members of the same community, to use your best endeavours to promote the general good," on certain important issues, however much these involved communal and not local concerns, they felt they must "most solemnly require" and "positively command"

50. Debates of Virginia House of Burgesses, Oct. 1754, Greene, ed., *Diary of Carter*, I, 117; *Proceedings of the Conventions of the Province of Maryland ...* (Baltimore, 1836), 228. On the broadening of instructions into areas of general public policy during the Revolutionary crisis see Pole, *Political Representation in England*, 72–73. On the pervasive public character of private legislative activity in the colonies see Bailyn, "Origins of American Politics," *Perspectives in American History*, 1 (1967), 76–78.

their delegates, "as our representatives," to follow the "opinion of your constituents." And in America's elective politics, as men rapidly saw it intensifying, "no member will venture to counteract the declared sentiments of his constituents; as, besides its being a breach of trust, it would infallibly ruin his interest among them."[51]

Where such a close attachment to local interests could lead, even on questions of supposedly general concern, is perhaps most graphically illustrated in New England. There the reliance on instructions and residential requirements for both electors and elected had the longest history. There the mistrust of any central authority, legislative or magisterial, was most pervasive. New Englanders, particularly in the western areas, in fact considered their towns, and not the legislature, as the real loci of authority and objects of concern. The rebellious inhabitants of the Connecticut River valley in their vigorous opposition to representational schemes blurring town lines only voiced what many in all states of the region assumed to be the nature of the town. "To unite half a dozen or more towns together, equally privileged, in order to make them equal to some one other town, is a new practice in politics. We may as well take the souls of a number of different persons and say they make but one, while yet they remain separate and different." It was crucially important, the western inhabitants of New Hampshire argued in 1776, that every town have at least one representative in the legislature, "as it may be much questioned, if any one distinct corporate body be neglected, or deprived of actual representation, whether, in that case, they are any ways bound, or included by what the others may do." With this kind of stark emphasis on town autonomy and the actuality of representation, these New Englanders were turning the body politic, the single homogeneous unity of the people, into an *"infinite number of jarring, disunited factions."* Since the obstructionist towns of western Massachusetts were "now erecting little democracies," wrote William Whiting in a frightened pamphlet of 1778 challenging the developments taking place in New England, then they ought to withdraw all their

51. Instructions of the Freeholders of Buckingham County, Va. (May 1776), Force, ed., *American Archives*, 4th Ser., VI, 458–59; Purdie's Wmsbg. *Va. Gazette*, June 14, Oct. 18, 1778; Boston *Continental Journal*, Oct. 15, 1778. On the rash of Virginia county instructions in 1776 over the issue of religion see Boyd, ed., *Jefferson Papers*, I, 525–29.

representatives from the General Court; "for," he added in sarcasm, "it is highly unreasonable they should sit there as spies." The towns could then "send them as ambassadors, or commissioners plenipotentiary, and in that character they ought to be received, if received at all, and not as representatives."[52]

While Whiting was in fact writing about the total breakdown of communication between the central and local authorities in western Massachusetts, his criticisms were grounded in a sensitive perception of what was happening elsewhere to the representational process in the new republics. By the mid-1780's the Reverend Levi Hart, minister of Preston, Connecticut, conceded that the members of the Connecticut General Assembly represented only their respective corporations: "The interest of each corporation is to be regarded individually, and as connected with that of the state." The requirement in Pennsylvania that electors be residents of the districts in which they voted, complained one critic in 1786, was turning the counties of the state into "independent hostile republics, with discordant objects of pursuit, uniting merely through necessity and dividing with the cessation of danger." The failure of virtual representation to take effect in the New Jersey legislature, warned Governor William Livingston, was threatening the state with "anarchy and confusion."[53]

By the 1780's even the "Nabob"-dominated state of South Carolina (which had been less susceptible to much of radical Whig thought before the Revolution) was torn with controversy over the right of instructing representatives, "the most invaluable privilege of a free people." If the doctrine of binding instructions be denied, wrote William Hornby, a brewer and a leading critic of the planter aristocracy, "it will at one stroke transform us into *legal* SLAVES to our *lordly* SERVANTS." Yet, wrote Christopher Gadsden, defending the independence and integrity of the legislature and the "old *friendly* habits" of South Carolina, this "fettering" of the representatives "with absolute instructions" had "a great *tendency* in our circumstances, *not only* at times of hindering and embarrassing public business, but *very probably*, of being the *means* of setting up a *directing* club

---

52. *Address of the Inhabitants of the Towns of* [*Grafton County*], Bouton et al., eds., *State Papers of N. H.*, X, 233; [William Whiting], *An Address to the Inhabitants of the County of Berkshire* . . . (Hartford, 1778), 24, 27.

53. Levi Hart, *The Description of a Good Character* . . . (Hartford, [1786]), 16; Phila. *Pa. Packet*, Sept. 15, 1786; Trenton *N.-J. Gazette*, Jan. 7, 1778, Nelson et al., eds., *New Jersey Archives*, 2d Ser., II, 2–3.

or committee, in the city or district where the legislature may sit, which may . . . serve to put the legislature into *leading* strings, and make them as a *body* contemptible, and their members *as individuals* obsequious to the great men of the club." Unless the members were left "*untrammeled*, to act by their own best judgments, upon any point of importance, after it has undergone a thorough discussion *in* the house," the legislature would never be able to "attend to the *general combined* interest of *all* the state *put together.*" But this was not really the way the people should legislate for themselves, wrote an anonymous Carolinian in 1783, in terms that disclosed just how far Americans were willing to carry their concept of actual representation. "Whatever difficulty there may be in convening and taking the sense of all the members of a society at once; there is none in assembling parishes separately." After such deliberation and voting in the separate districts, then "a final issue may be taken in General Assembly on a certain majority of vouched and recorded parochial decisions." The representatives were in effect agents elected and controlled by quasi-independent constituencies. If they were otherwise, "if, after election, the members are free to act of their own accord, instead of abiding by the direction of their constituents," then election by districts was meaningless, for "it would be a matter of indifference from what part of a Republic the Legislative body was taken." "What nation in their senses," concluded the writer in a revealing statement, "ever sent ambassadors to another without limiting them by instructions."[54]

So far then had the legislature become detached from the local constituencies that it was not absurd to conceive of it as "an *extraneous power*," as "a body formed from the combination of pre-existing parts," each with different and clashing interests. Inconsistent as it may have been with their republican assumptions about the nature of the state and the homogeneity of the people, this was increasingly what many Americans in the 1780's were coming to see their legislatures had always been, and would apparently always be: an assembly, as William Smith of New York had complained in the 1750's, composed "of plain, illiterate husbandmen, whose views seldom extended farther than to the reg-

54. Charleston *Gazette of the State of South Carolina*, Aug. 19, July 17, 1784; *Rudiments of Law and Government Deduced from the Law of Nature . . .* (Charleston, 1783), 33–34. Gadsden's newspaper essays during the 1780's can be conveniently found in Richard Walsh, ed., *The Writings of Christopher Gadsden, 1746–1805* (Columbia, S. C., 1966), 200–38.

ulation of highways, the destruction of wolves, wild cats, and foxes, and the advancement of the other little interests of the particular counties, which they were chosen to represent"; or an assembly, as the Tory Samuel Peters of Connecticut described a generation later, composed "of contending factions, whose different interests and pursuits it is generally found necessary mutually to consult, in order to produce a sufficient coalition to proceed on the business of the state." The inhabitants of the towns or districts of a state generally saw "the common interest only through the eyes of their deputies," who in turn proposed "private or particular advantages to their own towns or persons, to the prejudice of other towns and the rest of their fellow subjects." Indeed, perhaps there was no common interest to be found at all: "Legislators can only perceive so many different interests in a confused manner." Each representative, said Ezra Stiles, president of Yale College, in 1783, was concerned only with the parochial interests of his electors. Whenever a bill was read in the legislature, "every one instantly thinks how it will affect his constituents." By 1788 James Madison had also concluded that "a spirit of *locality*" permeated American politics and was "inseparable" from elections by small districts or towns. The members of the various state assemblies were "everywhere observed to lose sight of the aggregate interests of the Community, and even to sacrifice them to the interests or prejudices of their respective constituents." As long as the deputies thought of themselves as spokesmen for special interests in their constituencies, whether farmers, merchants or tradesmen, "so far from being the Representatives of the people, they are only an assembly of private men, securing their own interest to the ruin of the Commonwealth."[55]

Throughout the years of the war and after, Americans in almost all the states mounted increasing attacks on the tendencies of the American representational system, voicing a broadening awareness of what excessive localism, binding instructions, and acutely actual representation signified for their assumptions about

55. Boston *Independent Chronicle*, Mar. 23, 1780; Phila. *Pa. Packet*, Sept. 18, 1786; William Smith, *History of the Late Province New York, from Its Discovery to . . . 1762*, I (N. Y. Hist. Soc., *Collections*, 4 [1829]), 309; [Peters], *History of Connecticut*, 284; Boston *Independent Chronicle*, June 11, 1778; Stiles, *United States Elevated*, in Thornton, ed., *Pulpit*, 420; Madison's Observations on Jefferson's Draft of a Constitution for Virginia (1788), Boyd, ed., *Jefferson Papers*, VI, 308–09; Boston *Independent Chronicle*, Apr. 19, 1787.

the nature of republican politics. The ideal of an independent and deliberative legislature, attending to the common interests of the whole state, would not die. The traditional conception of virtual representation, or at least all that it signified for the nature of the representative's business, lingered on in American thinking, for it was too much bound up with desirable republican notions about the moral oneness of the state and the homogeneity of the people to be easily abandoned. However weak the foundation of this conception in American experience was, few Americans in the 1780's were willing to face up boldly to the far-reaching implications their clarifying ideas of representation had for their image of a transcendent common good that made republicanism what it was. Submerge all particular and partial interests into the general good was still the common cry. James Winthrop was very daring and unusual indeed but very honest in 1787 when he impatiently retorted that "it is vain to tell us that we ought to overlook local interests," for no free government could disregard them. "No man when he enters into society does it from a view to promote the good of others, but he does it for his own good."[56]

56. [James Winthrop], "Agrippa Letters" (1787–88), in Paul L. Ford, ed., *Essays on the Constitution of the United States* (Brooklyn, 1892), 73.

CHAPTER VI

Mixed Government and Bicameralism

1. THE AMERICAN DEFENSE OF THE MIXED STATE

The participation of the people in the government, through their elected representatives, said Alexander Hamilton, "constitutes the democratical part of the government." This was true of the English constitution; it was equally true of the colonists' "little models of the English constitution"; and it was also to be true of the Revolutionary constitutions drafted in 1776. Although the assemblies, representing the people, were undoubtedly the most important parts of the new governments, in most of the states they were not to be the only parts. While it was clear to most Americans that "a free, popular model of government—of the republican kind—may be judged the most friendly to the rights and liberties of the people, and the most conducive to the public welfare," nevertheless, "on account of the infinite diversity of opinions and interests, as well as for other weighty reasons, a government altogether popular, so as to have the decision of cases by assemblies of the body of the people, cannot be thought so eligible." A mixed or balanced government was far preferable.[1]

The theory of mixed government was as old as the Greeks and had dominated Western political thinking for centuries. It was based on the ancient categorization of forms of government into three ideal types, monarchy, aristocracy, and democracy—a classical scheme derived from the number and character of the ruling

1. [Hamilton], *Farmer Refuted*, Syrett and Cooke, eds., *Hamilton Papers*, I, 105; [Adams], "Novanglus," Adams, ed., *Works of John Adams*, IV, 117; Payson, *Sermon Preached May 27, 1778*, Thornton, ed., *Pulpit*, 330.

power. "There are only Three simple Forms of Government," said John Adams in an oration delivered at Braintree in 1772. When the entire ruling power was entrusted to the discretion of a single person, the government was called a monarchy, or the rule of one. When it was placed in the hands of a "few great, rich, wise Men," the government was an aristocracy, or the rule of the few. And when the whole power of the society was lodged with all the people, the government was termed a democracy, or the rule of the many. Each of these simple forms possessed a certain quality of excellence: for monarchy, it was order or energy; for aristocracy, it was wisdom; and for democracy, it was honesty or goodness. But the maintenance of these peculiar qualities depended on the forms of government standing fast on the imagined spectrum of power. Yet men being what they were, experience had tragically taught that none of these simple forms of government by itself could remain stable. Left alone each ran headlong into perversion in the eager search by the rulers, whether one, few, or many, for more power. Monarchy lunged toward its extremity and ended in a cruel despotism. Aristocracy, located midway on the band of power, pulled in both directions and created "faction and multiplied usurpation." Democracy, seeking more power in the hands of the people, degenerated into anarchy and tumult. The mixed or balanced polity was designed to prevent these perversions. By including each of the classic simple forms of government in the same constitution, political fluctuations would cease. The forces pulling in one direction would be counterbalanced by opposing forces. Monarchy and democracy would each prevent the other from sliding off toward an extremity on the power spectrum; and to keep the government from oscillating like a pendulum the aristocracy would act as a centering stabilizer. Only through this reciprocal sharing of political power by the one, the few, and the many, could the desirable qualities of each be preserved. As John Adams told his Braintree audience, "Liberty depends upon an exact Ballance, a nice Counterpoise of all the Powers of the state. . . . The best Governments of the World have been mixed."[2]

2. Adams, Notes for an Oration at Braintree, 1772, Butterfield, ed., *Diary of Adams*, II, 57–60; Blackstone, *Commentaries*, I, 48; Adams and [Leonard], *Novanglus and Massachusettensis*, 169; John Witherspoon, "Lecture on Moral Philosophy," *Works of Witherspoon*, III, 432–35. For discussions of the theory of mixed government see Stanley Pargellis, "The Theory of Balanced Government," in Conyers Read, ed., *The Constitution Reconsidered* (N. Y., 1938), 37–49; Leonard W. Labaree, *Conservatism in Early American History* (N. Y., 1948), 119–42; Bailyn, *Ideological Origins*, 70–77, 273–80.

Yet simple as it seems, the theory of mixture was complicated and comprehensive, concerned not merely with the ruling powers of government but as well with the elements of the society expressing itself in these powers. It was its ability to relate the government to the society, to involve in the government all of the social orders of the body politic—the monarch, the nobility, and the people—which was ultimately responsible for the persuasiveness of the theory. The social or psychological qualities that men used to characterize each particular form of government— "honor, virtue and fear," Edmund Pendleton described them in 1776—had significance because the mixed government was not an institutional abstraction set apart from the society but indeed was the very embodiment of the society.[3]

Although by the nineteenth century the theory had lost its relevance for Western political thought because the state and government had become detached from what was seen as an increasingly complicated social structure, in the previous century through its expression in the English constitution it attained a vitality and prominence it had not had since antiquity. "The British constitution . . . ," said Joseph Warren in Boston in 1772, "is a happy compound of the three forms . . . , monarchy, aristocracy, and democracy; of these three the British legislature is composed." In the polemics accompanying the seventeenth-century convulsions, particularly in Charles I's *Answer to the XIX. Propositions of Both Houses of Parliament*, the King had become identified in English thought as a distinct social being, as a separate estate of the realm. At the same time the clergy had gradually lost their status as a separate estate and were blended in with the other two social entities, the nobility and the people, so that the three estates of the realm had come to correspond exactly to the classic forms of government, monarchy, aristocracy, and democracy. Together these three orders constituted all of English society, and "the meeting of these three estates in Parliament is what we call our government." This marvelous coincidence between the society and the government, together with its relation to the three simple governments of antiquity, gave the English constitution its awesomeness and Parliament its sovereignty. No wonder then that Englishmen, even colonials, could describe the

---

3. Pendleton quoted in Margaret V. Smith, *Virginia 1492–1892 . . . with a History of the Executives . . . of Virginia* (Washington, 1893), 214. Montesquieu of course was the most famous 18th-century exponent of the relation between cultural traits and the form of government. See Werner Stark, *Montesquieu: Pioneer of the Sociology of Knowledge* (London, 1960), 73–78, 124–33.

English constitution as "a system that approached as near to perfection as any could within the compass of human abilities."[4]

The Americans were thoroughly familiar with the theory.
Descriptions of the mixed character of the English constitution,
wrote Robert Carter Nicholas in 1774, were "so many *trite* Observations . . . so repeatedly rung in our Ears, that . . . the veri-
est Smatterer in Politicks must long since have had them all by
Rote." And the Revolution was not intended to erase their memory of it. The English constitution, properly understood and balanced, remained for the Americans at the time of Independence
the model of how a government should be structured, "not so
much from attachment by habit to such a plan of power . . . , as
from conviction that it was founded in nature and reason."[5]

The colonists' proper understanding of the English constitution came largely from the English radical Whig tradition. However alienated this tradition was from official English thought, it
was not so estranged that it had repudiated the mixed form of
government. Harrington, Sidney, and Milton had after all proposed various sorts of mixed states. While some extreme radicals
did emphasize a golden age of a simpler government that lay in a
distant Saxon past, which had been corrupted by a mixture with
Norman tyranny, most Commonwealthmen hesitated to attack
the eighteenth-century constitution head on. Under pressure
Richard Price denied that he cared only for piling up power in
the hands of the people and admitted the need for other qualities
in the government besides liberty. Even James Burgh, although at
times verging on a repudiation of the mixed polity, stated at the
outset of his *Political Disquisitions* that "the present form of government by king, lords, and commons, if it could be restored to
its true spirit and efficiency, might be made to yield all the liberty, and all the happiness, of which a great and good people are
capable in this world."[6]

It was the degeneration of the English constitution from "its

4. Warren, *Oration Delivered March 5, 1772*, Niles, ed., *Principles*, 21; *N.-Y.
Journal*, Dec. 11, 1766; Hooper to N. C. Congress, Oct. 26, 1776, Saunders, ed.,
Col. Recs. of N. C., X, 866. On the origins and development of the theory of the
mixed English constitution see Corinne C. Weston, *English Constitutional
Theory and the House of Lords, 1556–1832* (N. Y., 1965), Chaps. I–IV.

5. [Nicholas], *Considerations*, in Swem, ed., *Virginia and the Revolution*, 40;
Adams, *Defence of the Constitutions*, Adams, ed., *Works of John Adams*, IV,
300.

6. Richard Price, *Additional Observations on Civil Liberty*, 8–9; Burgh, *Disquisitions*, I, 9. See Weston, *English Constitutional Theory*, 143–60.

purity (for what is at present stiled the British Constitution is an apostate)," its "practice," not its theory which was "on many accounts excellent," that the Americans and English radicals were quarreling with. The "fine design" of the English constitution, as Richard Henry Lee wrote in 1776, had been "spoiled in the execution." The Crown's power to create peers and boroughs had "effectually destroyed the equipoise" and had enabled the ministry to apply "that corruption which has now swallowed up every thing but the forms of freedom in Great Britain." Even Carter Braxton, as much as he admired the mixed system of England, admitted that it had not worked properly. The Crown, he said, had "found means to break down those barriers which the Constitution had assigned to each branch of the Legislature, and effectually destroyed the independence of both Lords and Commons"—upsetting the balance of the constitution not only in England but in the colonies as well, through the encroachments of the royal governors on the colonists' assemblies within the colonies and through the extension of parliamentary authority into their internal affairs. "However imperfect the English plan was," Lee reminded Edmund Pendleton, "yet our late Government in Virginia was infinitely worse. With us 2 thirds of the Legislature, and all the executive and judiciary Powers were in the same hands—in truth it was very near a Tyranny." The Americans, in fact, had not even possessed as "good a pattern as the English constitution," for most of their colonial constitutions had been "exceptionally contrived." The royal governors had often been stronger than even the King, dismissing officials, vetoing acts, and prolonging the legislatures in ways that the English Crown since 1688 had been prohibited from doing.[7]

In fact, the Americans to the very end of the imperial controversy justified their constitutional opposition to English policy not by abjuring the theory of mixed government but by using and affirming it. It was the British government's attempt to upset the balance of the colonial constitutions that was "indeed the point now in agitation . . . by the numerous and respectable inhabitants of this extensive continent." "It is Popular Power," said John Adams, "the democratical Branch of our Constitution that

---

7. Hooper to N. C. Congress, Oct. 26, 1776, Saunders, ed., *Col. Recs. of N. C.*, X, 866; Thacher, *Oration Delivered March 5, 1776*, Niles, ed., *Principles*, 44; R. H. Lee to Edmund Pendleton, May 12, 1776, and to Arthur Lee, Dec. 20, 1766, Ballagh, ed., *Letters of R. H. Lee*, I, 190–91, 21.

is invaded." If the King, Lords, and Commons could make laws binding on Americans in all cases whatsoever, "the People here will have no Influence, no Check, no Power, no Controul, no Negative." The English program, it was clear to Samuel Adams, was designed "only to lop off the exuberant Branches of Democracy" in the colonists' mixed constitutions. The long wrangle with England, for all that it touched in the realm of politics, had scarcely contested, and indeed for most Americans had only endorsed, the benefits that flowed from a correctly balanced government.[8]

2. MIXED REPUBLICS

Not surprisingly, then, most Americans set about the building of their new states in 1776 within the confines of this theory of mixed government, for independence and the abolition of monarchy had not altered the basic postulates of the science of politics. "The Constitution of Britain had for its object the union of the three grand qualities of virtue, wisdom, and power as the characteristicks of perfect Government," William Hooper informed the North Carolina Congress framing a constitution in the fall of 1776. "Might not this or something like this serve as a Model for us." Since the English had obviously not been able to sustain a proper balance, "altho' it was the professed aim of that System," it remained for the Americans in their new republics to "correct those errors and defects which are to be found in the most perfect constitution of government which ever the world has yet been blessed with." In fact, in most of the states the theory of mixed government was so axiomatic, so much a part of the Whig science of politics, that it went largely unquestioned, particularly since the colonists' debate with England had not compelled them to explore it comprehensively. As John Witherspoon observed in 1776, the Americans had spent most of their energy in the imperial debate explaining and defending the rights of man and the cause of liberty in general. "The nature of

8. Rusticus, *Remarks on a Late Pamphlet*, 6–7; Adams, Notes for an Oration at Braintree, 1772, Butterfield, ed., *Diary of Adams*, II, 60; Adams to Arthur Lee, Apr. 4, 1774, and to R. H. Lee, July 15, 1774, Cushing, ed., *Writings of Samuel Adams*, III, 100, 138. See also [Dickinson], *Letters from a Farmer*, Ford, ed., *Writings of Dickinson*, 356, 364; Warren, *Oration Delivered March 5, 1772*, Niles, ed., *Principles*, 21; [Adams], "Novanglus," Adams, ed., *Works of John Adams*, IV, 101–02.

government and method of balancing a civil constitution" had not "been handled either with so much fulness or propriety as the other topics." Yet this did not mean that the constitution-makers were unaware of what the theory of mixed government was all about. "If it has not been much reasoned on, it seems nevertheless to be both felt and understood in almost every corner of the continent."[9]

John Adams later suggested that it was he alone who had made the theory of mixed government both felt and understood in all corners of the continent, since (he recalled in his autobiography) as late as November 1775 "every one of my friends, and all those who were the most zealous for assuming Government, had at that time no Idea of any other Government but a Contemptible Legislature in one assembly, with Committees for Executive Magistrates and Judges." Although such a characteristically bold and exaggerated statement can be explained as an attempt by a defeated president and an apparently forgotten Revolutionary to assuage his wounded pride, there can be no doubt that Adams's *Thoughts on Government*, published in 1776 and widely circulated among the leading Revolutionaries in several states, was the most influential pamphlet in the early constitution-making period.

Adams immediately raised the central problem the constitution-makers faced in devising a balanced government in their new republics. In Adams's mind, as in the minds of most of the framers in 1776, it was not a question of whether there would be a mixture or not, but rather a question of what sort of mixture. "Of republics," he wrote, "there is an inexhaustible variety, because the possible combinations of the powers of society are capable of innumerable variations." Whatever their general agreement on the theory of mixed government, Americans in 1776 at once found themselves arguing over these "innumerable variations," in the search for "that particular arrangement of the powers of society" which would guarantee both stability and liberty in their new republics.[10]

9. Hooper to N. C. Congress, Oct. 26, 1776, Saunders, ed., *Col. Recs. of N. C.*, X, 867; Lee to Pendleton, May 12, 1776, Ballagh, ed., *Letters of R. H. Lee*, I, 190–91; Phila. *Pa. Journal*, Dec. 27, 1775; [John Witherspoon], "The Druid, No. II," *Pennsylvania Magazine*, 1 (June 1776), 253.

10. Butterfield, ed., *Diary of Adams*, III, 358; [Adams], *Thoughts on Government*, Adams, ed., *Works of John Adams*, IV, 194. On the circumstances of Adams's writing of the pamphlet see Butterfield, ed., *Diary of Adams*, III, 331–32; Adams, ed., *Works of John Adams*, IV, 181–91; Boyd, ed., *Jefferson Papers*, I, 333–34.

The issue separating a conservative Whig, like Carter Braxton, from a Revolutionary Whig, like Richard Henry Lee, was not the theory of mixed government itself, but the proportion of power to be allotted to each of the elements in the constitution. Braxton in his plan of government for Virginia suggested that the governor hold office during good behavior in order to give him "the dignity to command necessary respect and authority," and "to enable him to execute the laws without being deterred by the fear of giving offence." He also proposed that twenty-four persons be chosen by the Assembly "to constitute a Council of State, who should form a distinct or intermediate Branch of the Legislature, and hold their places for life, in order that they might possess all the weight, stability, and dignity, due to the importance of their office." Richard Henry Lee dismissed Braxton's pamphlet as a "Contemptible little Tract"; yet in the very same breath he defined the problem facing the constitution-makers in 1776 as consisting "certainly in a blending of the three simple forms of Government in such a manner as to prevent the inordinate views of either from unduly affecting the others." What angered Lee and other radical Whigs about Braxton's governmental proposals was not the idea of balance, but the emphasis Braxton had put on the monarchical and aristocratical element in his suggested mixed constitution—an expression, said Lee, of Braxton's "aristocratic pride," betraying "the little Knot or Junto from whence it proceeded." Indeed, most of the numerous drafts for the constitutions of the new governments proposed in debates, pamphlets, and newspapers in 1776, like Lee's and Braxton's, were only variations, although decidedly important variations, on Adams's theme of "a balance between . . . contending powers." For the mixed governments of the American states did not have to be, indeed should not be, replicas of the eighteenth-century English constitution in order to be considered mixed. There could in fact be nearly as many possible blends and balances of the social powers as there were differences in social outlook.[11]

"Some talk of having two councils, one legislative, and the other executive: some of a small executive council only; which

---

11. [Braxton], *Address to the Convention*, in Force, ed., *American Archives*, 4th Ser., VI, 752–53; Lee to Pendleton, May 12, 1776, Ballagh, ed., *Letters of R. H. Lee*, I, 190–91; [Adams], *Thoughts on Government*, Adams, ed., *Works of John Adams*, IV, 196.

should have nothing to do with framing the laws. Some would have the Governor, an integral part of the legislature: others, only president of the council with a casting voice." All were reflections of the gradations of radicalism among the Whigs, differences that were ultimately measured by each man's confidence in the people and thus by the degrees of power to be allotted the several elements—monarchical, aristocratic and democratic—in the new republics. In many states apprehensions over too much power in the hands of the people, in the hands of "Men without Character and without Fortune," fed into the Americans' plans for the new constitutions, creating a division, as Gouverneur Morris remarked of New York, over the character of the mixture in the new republics, "whether it should be founded upon Aristocratic or Democratic principles." The ideal, said one New Jerseyite, was to avoid the two extremes implicit in republicanism: "the one is, that noble birth, or wealth and riches, should be considered as an hereditary title to the government of the republic . . . the other extreme is, that the government be managed by the *promiscuous multitude of the community*," who "though honest, yet from many natural defects, are generally in the execution of government, violent, changeable and liable to many fatal errors." In establishing "the internal Police" of their states, as even Samuel Adams admitted, the Americans had "Scilla and Charybdis to avoid."[12]

While some like John Dickinson despaired of independence and the establishment of any republic, fearing that if the counterpoise of monarchy were taken away the democratic power would carry all before it and destroy all possibility of balanced government, most Whigs in 1776 remained confident that even without a king they could still maintain the right equilibrium and mixture of the powers of the society. Republicanism itself was no obstacle to the institution of the mixed polity. The American states, observed Thomas Pownall in his *Memorial Addressed to the Sovereigns of America*, had preserved the traditional balanced structure of their former colonial governments; "Nor are they less Commonwealths or Republics for taking this mixed form." After

12. Demophilus, *Genuine Principles*, 36; Edward Rutledge to John Jay, June 29, 1776, Burnett, ed., *Letters of Congress*, I, 517–17; Rutledge to Jay, Nov. 24, 1776, Johnston, ed., *Papers of Jay*, I, 94; Morris to John Penn, May 20, 1774, Sparks, *Morris*, I, 25; Trenton *N.-J. Gazette*, May 12, 1779, Nelson *et al.*, eds., *New Jersey Archives*, 2d Ser., III, 351; Samuel Adams to James Warren, Dec. 5, 1775, Ford, ed., *Warren-Adams Letters*, I, 192.

all, said John Adams in 1772, "the Republics of Greece, Rome, Carthage were all mixed Governments." And, as James Burgh had remarked, this mixture had never been an objection against their being republican. Had not the English classical republicans, through the influence of both Polybius and Machiavelli, demonstrated that a republic was superior to a monarchy in realizing the ideal of a mixed state? Having the governors elected frequently by the people—making them, as William Hooper said, "the creatures of the people"—was entirely compatible with the theory of mixed government. In other words, it was possible, as Milton had argued, that the monarchical element might be present in a constitution without there being any king. It was this Commonwealth understanding of the mixed polity, perceived through "Aristotle, Livy and Harrington," that enabled John Adams in 1775 to argue that the uncorrupted "British constitution is nothing more nor less than a republic, in which the king is first magistrate." Even though the upper houses and the governors were now to be periodically selected by the people, no one clearly foresaw in 1776 that their essential nature was to be thereby changed. The upper houses, elective or not, were still the embodiment of "the few," or the aristocratic element; and the governors, elective or not, were still the embodiment of "the one," or the monarchical element in the mixed republics.[13]

3. THE SENATORIAL PART OF THE SOCIETY

"That a mixed government is the best that can be accepted in the respective Colonies" was thus the common sentiment of most constitution-makers in 1776. "The people will naturally be inclined to that which is most like what they have always been used to," that is, a magisterial order together with "two orders in the body of legislation." Yet obviously since the orders of their new republics "now are to derive their authority from the people

13. Pownall, *Memorial to America*, 102; Adams, Notes for an Oration at Braintree, 1772, Butterfield, ed., *Diary of Adams*, II, 58; Burgh, *Disquisitions*, I, 9, 12–14; Hooper to N. C. Congress, Oct. 26, 1776, Saunders, ed., *Col. Recs. of N. C.*, X, 866; [Adams], "Novanglus," Adams, ed., *Works of John Adams*, IV, 106. On the compatibility of republicanism with the theory of mixed government see Fink, *Classical Republicans*, 102–03, 109–10. See also Gilbert Chinard, "Polybius and the American Constitution," *Journal of the History of Ideas*, 1 (1940), 38–58.

only, and in a different manner from what has been usual; it therefore requires the utmost wisdom . . . to constitute them, so to balance their powers as effectually to secure the liberty and happiness of the people forever."[14] Indeed, it required more wisdom than most Americans at first apprehended, for, however confident the Commonwealthmen had been over the possibility of erecting a mixed republic, it was not to be a simple matter to realize in the American environment; and the Revolutionaries, without clearly perceiving the consequences of what they were doing, were soon compelled to make changes in the constituents of their mixed polities that would have enormous repercussions on their understanding of politics.

The most evident yet the least discussed change in the mixed form was the elimination of the governor's role in legislation by all of the states in 1776, except South Carolina. Only President John Rutledge's message accompanying his veto of the 1778 act establishing a new South Carolina Constitution, which abolished the executive's voice in legislation, directly confronted the meaning the governor's legislative power had for the theory of mixed government. "To lop off one branch of the legislature" as the new Constitution did, said Rutledge, was to destroy "a compound or mixed government," which the people had preferred in 1776, and to set up "a simple democracy, or one verging towards it." In 1776 John Adams, less clearly, had also sensed the importance of the governor's role in the legislature for the conception of mixed government. If it was "the powers of society" and not simply governmental functions that were being combined in the state, then it seemed logical to Adams that the governor "be made also an integral part of the legislature"; otherwise his consent to the laws would presumably be lacking. Jefferson in his draft proposal for the Virginia Constitution of 1776 likewise glimpsed the anomaly of the governor's lack of a legislative voice in a mixed state by specifically providing that his administrator "be bound by acts of legislation though not expressly named." Precisely what was the governor in the new republics to be? Was he, as the King of England was, a constituent of the society whose consent to be bound by the laws must be explicit and individual, or was he merely an official whose consent to the laws, like any other person's, was expressed through the people's rep-

14. "On the Present State of Affairs in America," Nov. 5, 1776, Force, ed., *American Archives*, 5th Ser., III, 518.

resentatives in the lower houses? The difference was subtle but momentous, for as an English writer in 1730 had declared, the monarchical element was supposed to be one essential order of the society. "Had the King no more than the executive power, he would not, properly speaking, be any part of the Government at all; but a person entrusted by the Government to execute the laws of it."[15]

While the implications for the theory of mixed government of depriving the governors of a role in legislation went largely unexamined by the Americans, the institution of the aristocratic order in their new balanced constitutions did not. With the Americans' emphasis on republican equality the creation of a hereditary privileged order was out of the question. Not only was the society incapable of sustaining such a nobility, but it was no more necessary for the maintenance of a mixed polity than a king was. The republicanism of the Revolution was not for most Americans directed at aristocracy per se, but only at an artificial Crown-created aristocracy which owed its position not to merit but to connections and influence. That some sort of aristocracy, "consisting of a small number of the ablest men in the nation," was necessary for the stability of their mixed republics few Whigs denied. The history of politics, wrote Adams in his *Thoughts on Government*, had tragically demonstrated that a constitution must embody more than the ruler and the people, for "these two powers will oppose and encroach upon each other, until the contest shall end in war, and the whole power, legislative and executive, be usurped by the strongest." Unfolding the conventional theory of a mixed state very accurately, Adams proposed the erection of another distinct assembly, "as a mediator between the two extreme branches of the legislature, that which represents the people, and that which is vested with the executive power." Although several of Adams's suggestions in his pamphlet were provisional and speculative, the proposal for an upper house in the legislature was not. That "a people cannot be long free, nor ever happy, whose government is in one assem-

15. Ramsay, *History of Revolution of South Carolina*, I, 133–37; [Adams], *Thoughts on Government*, Adams, ed., *Works of John Adams*, IV, 194, 196; Jefferson's Third Draft of a Virginia Constitution, Boyd, ed., *Jefferson Papers*, I, 360; *London Journal*, Sept. 19, 1730, quoted in Robert Shackleton, "Montesquieu, Bolingbroke and the Separation of Powers," *French Studies*, 3 (1949), 34. For anticipations of this change in the concept of the magistracy among radical 18th-century Whigs see Gwyn, *Separation of Powers*, 85–86, 89.

bly," he was as sure of as anything in his life. And so too were most of the constitution-makers of 1776; almost all of the new governments contained upper houses or senates, embodying the aristocratic element of the mixed polity.[16]

The Revolutionaries were generally confident that there existed in the community a "Senatorial part," a natural social and intellectual elite who, now that the Crown was gone, would find their rightful place in the upper houses of the legislatures. These new second branches of the legislature, as their common designation of "senate" indicated, were to be the repositories of classical republican honor and wisdom, where superior talent and devotion to the common good would be recognized and rewarded by the people. Such senates, several Americans noted, would enable "many men of great worth . . . not possessing popular qualities" to find a place in the governments. It was not surprising that compound governments had received the praise of writers from Thucydides down to the present. "To conduct the affairs of a community in a safe and successful way, requires all the *wisdom* of the most learned and experienced members of the state, as well as the *vigilance* and particular attention of the peculiar deputies of the whole people." The body of the people no doubt possessed common sense, honesty, and virtue; yet "few of them [are] much read in the history, laws or politics, even of their own, not to mention other states, from whose rises, revolutions and declensions the great landmarks of legislations and government are taken." To prevent the bulk of the people from being burdened with taxes in order "to furnish livings for hosts of placemen and pensioners, which a government of great men would soon saddle them with, a proper number of guardians from their own class is indispensably necessary." But to this house of representatives, who would guard the purse strings of the people, must be added a senate, which could embody "the wisdom and foresight of persons, who have a long acquaintance with the history and manners of mankind," where "the contemplative and well informed" of the community could revise and correct the well-intentioned but often careless measures of the people and where the power of the ruler and the integrity of the people could be balanced by the wisdom of "the wise and learned." The senate, "behaving as may

16. "Loose Thoughts on Government" (1776), Force, ed., *American Archives*, 4th Ser., VI, 731; [Adams], *Thoughts on Government*, Adams, ed., *Works of John Adams*, IV, 196, 195.

rationally be expected, will command the respect of the people, [and] give a firmness to the government." As young Alexander Hamilton noted in his jottings from Plutarch's *Lives*, "The senate was to the commonwealth what ballast is to a ship."[17]

To presume the existence of this "senatorial part" in American society was one thing; to distinguish it and isolate it from the rest of the community was another, indeed a matter that had distressed royal officials in the eighteenth century as much as it was to disturb Americans in the years following Independence. Every Tory or Crown official who set his mind and pen to the problems of the New World, especially as the imperial crisis began unfolding, perceived at once that the lack of a real nobility in America to fill the councils, "so necessary to preserve the true Political Balance" in the colonists' miniature mixed governments, was "the grand flaw in our Civil Establishment." In none of the royal governments, wrote Thomas Hutchinson in the second volume of his *History of Massachusetts-Bay*, did the upper house possess "that glorious independence, which makes the house of Lords, the bulwark of the British constitution," mediating between the liberty of the people and the prerogative of the Crown. "Our council boards," wrote Daniel Leonard in 1775, "are destitute of the noble independence and splendid appendages of peerages." The upper houses apparently possessed no interests distinct from those of the bulk of the people and were too easily cowed by the force of numbers in the lower houses. No wonder the colonial assemblies were "the favorite institution of the people," George Johnstone, former governor of West Florida and later a member of the Carlisle Commission, told the House of Commons in 1775, for they were "their only barrier . . . against the exactions, oppressions, and extortions of governors," there being in America "no middle institution, as in this country, to balance between the people and the Crown."[18]

The colonial councils were truly in a "precarious situation": being caught between the houses of representatives and the royal

17. Charles Lee to Washington, May 10, 1776, *Lee Papers*, II, 19; *Frame of Government for Pennsylvania*, 3; John Adams to Francis Dana, June 12, 1776, Adams, ed., *Works of John Adams*, IX, 395; Phila. Pa. *Journal*, Sept. 25, 1776; Hamilton, Pay Book of the State Company of Artillery (1777), Syrett and Cooke, eds., *Hamilton Papers*, I, 397.

18. Leigh, *Considerations*, 57, 60; Hutchinson, *History of Massachusetts*, ed. Mayo, II, 7; Adams and [Leonard], *Novanglus and Massachusettensis*, 91, 155, 193; Speech of George Johnstone, House of Commons, Oct. 25, 1775, printed in Boston *Continental Journal*, Aug. 22, 1776; Bailyn, *Ideological Origins*, 275–79.

governors made their "conduct, fickle, uncertain and inconsistent," not only in the eyes of British officials but in the eyes of American Whigs as well. The pathetic public appeal by the Virginia Council in May 1775 to the people of the colony that the councilors "be considered not as a separate body of men, and having a distinct interest from the rest of the countrymen and fellow subjects" revealed the dilemma of men caught in a revolutionary polarization. The councilors, they pleaded, were "the watchful guardians of the rights of the people, as well as of the prerogative of the Crown. They are, most of them, natives of this country, they have families, they have property, and they trust they have integrity too." Yet to Virginia radicals these "twelve private gentlemen, called Counsellors, whose sanction to our laws is merely farcical," were only "creatures of the crown . . . removeable at pleasure" who "never can be considered as a separate branch of government from the crown." From whatever direction it was regarded the council was helplessly dependent. John Adams could quite agree with his antagonist, Daniel Leonard, that the American councilors were destitute of the noble independence of the English peers. "Most certainly!" exclaimed Adams. They were "the meanest creatures and tools in the political creation, dependent every moment for their existence on the tainted breath of a prime minister." The American colonies had no balanced constitution at all. What if the House of Lords were removable at the King's pleasure? What then, asked Adams, would become of the glorious British constitution? The American upper houses possessed all the authority of the English House of Lords but without its independence; "and it is this which makes them so great a grievance." "The crown," said Adams, "has really two branches of our legislature in its power." And yet Americans were being "perpetually insulted by being told, that making our council by mandamus brings us nearer to the British constitution."[19]

On the eve of the Revolution both royal officials and American Whigs proposed solutions for this commonly but differently perceived weakness in the middle branches of the colonial legislatures. The result of the growing concern among imperial ruling circles

19. Andrew Eliot to Thomas Holles, Jan. 29, 1769, Mass. Hist. Soc., *Collections*, 4th Ser., 4 (1858), 438; Dixon and Hunter's Wmsbg. *Va. Gazette*, May 20, 1775; Purdie's Wmsbg. *Va. Gazette*, May 17, 1776; [Adams], "Novanglus," Adams, ed., *Works of John Adams*, IV, 117.

with the instability of the American governments was a series of proposals, as John Adams charged, "to new-model the whole continent of North America," centering on a change in the colonial councils. Governor Francis Bernard of Massachusetts was tireless in his suggestions for reform, filling letter after letter with proposals for the establishment of a nobility, a nobility for life, since Bernard, like others, believed that America had not aged sufficiently to sustain a hereditary aristocracy. Somehow or other, advised Massachusetts Lieutenant-Governor Andrew Oliver, "the honors of government" must be extended in order to "afford opportunity of distinguishing men of character and reputation, the expectation of which wou'd make government more respectable." With real aristocratic titles and distinctions, "as an inducement to Men of Family and Fortune to accept the trust" of councilor, Sir Egerton Leigh of South Carolina hoped that the middle branch of the legislature could shed "its present *impotent* state." The only product, however, of these proposals for constitutional reform was the ill-fated Coercive Act, which brought the Massachusetts Council, formerly elected annually by the General Court, into line with the other royal colonies by providing for appointment at the pleasure of the King.[20]

William Henry Drayton knew very well from his experience in South Carolina what such mandamus councilors, indeed what a council "entirely dependent upon the pleasure even of the Governor," would produce—mere placemen, "strangers destitute of property and natural alliance in the Colonies," legislating on the affairs of a country "in which they have *no interest but their commissions*." Instead, realizing that Americans did "not yet desire Dignities, Lordships, and Dukedoms," Drayton proposed, as many royal officials were doing, councilors appointed for life, who would be drawn only "out of American families . . . connected with the colonies by fortune" in order to create a truly independent middle branch in the provincial legislature. For others, however, like John Adams, the elective Council of Massachusetts—the very Council which royal officials had considered the most irregular and feeble—continued to be the most indepen-

20. [Adams], "Novanglus," Adams, ed., *Works of John Adams*, IV, 24; Brennan, *Plural Office-Holding*, 94–98; Morgan, *Stamp Act Crisis*, Chap. II; Bernard, *Select Letters*, 89; *Copy of Letters Sent to Great-Britain*, 29–32; Leigh, *Considerations*, 68–70. See also Dalrymple, *Address of the People of Great-Britain*, 26–27, 50–51; Anthony Stokes, *A View of the Constitution of the British Colonies . . .* (London, 1783), 137–38. Cf. above, 111–12.

dent and the nearest resemblance to the English House of Lords of any council in America.[21]

As desirous as Adams was in 1776 for a strong, independent upper house, he retained his commitment to periodic elections as the best means of recruiting the upper houses, and readily dismissed proposals still being made by some Whigs even after Independence that the new republican senators hold their offices for life. The controversy over the recruitment of the upper houses thus did not end in 1776 but indeed was amplified and carried into the making of the constitutions. Jefferson, like so many other Whigs, had no doubt in 1776 that there was a group of "wisest men" in the community who should be selected to the senate and be "(when chosen) perfectly independent of their electors." But how? Experience had taught him, he told Edmund Pendleton in August 1776, "that a choice by the people themselves is not generally distinguished for it's wisdom. This first secretion from them is usually crude and heterogeneous." He had thus proposed in his draft for the Virginia Constitution that the senators be elected by the House of Delegates, and not the people, for a nine-year unrenewable term, so that they would not forever "be casting their eyes forward to the period of election (however distant) and be currying favor with the electors, and consequently dependent on them." He could also concur in George Mason's plan for a system of electors to select the upper house. He could even submit to Pendleton's suggestion, "to an appointment for life, or to any thing rather than a mere creation by and dependance on the people." Most of Jefferson's fellow Virginians, however, possessed more confidence in the capacity of the people to pick out their best men than he, Pendleton, or Mason did, for the Virginia Constitution drafted in 1776 provided for a Senate of twenty-four elected by the people directly out of county districts. No special qualifications either for the electors or for the senatorial candidates were felt necessary.[22]

21. [Drayton], *Letter from Freeman*, 9, 18–19, 32; [Adams], "Novanglus," Adams, ed., *Works of John Adams*, IV, 117.

22. Adams to Patrick Henry, June 3, 1776, Adams, ed., *Works of John Adams*, IX, 387–88; Jefferson to Pendleton, Aug. 26, 1776, Boyd, ed., *Jefferson Papers*, I, 503–04. Both Carter Braxton and Pendleton proposed senates for life. [Braxton], *Address to the Convention*, Force, ed., *American Archives*, 4th Ser., VI, 752; Pendleton to Jefferson, Aug. 10, 1776, Boyd, ed., *Jefferson Papers*, I, 489. For Jefferson's and Mason's constitutional plans and the final Virginia Constitution see *ibid.*, 358–59, 366, 379–80. Cf. discussion in Bailyn, *Ideological Origins*, 291–93.

Other states faced the same difficulties in distinguishing "the men of the most wisdom, experience and virtue" (as the Maryland Constitution put it) and sought through various constitutional devices to guarantee that a distinctive upper house filled with the senatorial order of the community would be selected. Nearly all of the states provided for special property qualifications for senatorial candidates exceeding those for candidates for the lower houses. Only in Virginia and Delaware were no differences in qualifications made between the two houses. In North Carolina and New York higher property qualifications were required for the senatorial electorate, a means of distinction which James Madison believed superior to attaching property qualifications to the candidates. The Maryland Constitution provided for a unique system of indirect election of the fifteen senators by a body of electors, two from each county chosen by the people—a scheme that soon came to represent for many the best method of isolating the social elite. To help ensure the senates' independence all of the other states which established upper houses in 1776-77—except Massachusetts, New Hampshire, and South Carolina, all of which soon changed in the constitutional revisions of the late seventies and early eighties—provided for election by the people-at-large rather than by the lower houses. The senates, moreover, were a great deal smaller in size than the lower houses, and were generally granted a longer tenure of office, with staggered terms to lend more stability to this middle branch of the mixed polity.[23]

4. Persons and Property

Despite this general commitment by the constitution-makers to "the propriety of a compound legislature," recalled David Ramsay, "the mode of creating two branches" in the American social environment proved to be "a matter of difficulty." Since in America "none were entitled to any rights, but such as were common to all," how could the framers of the constitutions, as one essayist proposed, "erect different orders of men" in the state to form two distinct houses of the legislature and at the same time ensure that "all government be ultimately in the hands of the people, whose right it is?" Having the people select both houses

23. Md. Cons. (1776), XV; Madison's Observations on Jefferson's Draft of a Constitution for Virginia (1788), Boyd, ed., *Jefferson Papers*, VI, 310, 316; Madison to Caleb Wallace, Aug. 23, 1785, Hunt, ed., *Writings of Madison*, II, 167.

"out of a homogeneous mass of people" was no solution, noted Ramsay, for "this rather made two coordinate houses of representatives than a check on a single one, by the moderation of a select few." At the very beginning of the Revolution, William Smith of New York also put his finger on this discrepancy between the American governments and the society they were supposed to embody. If both houses of the Legislature were equally elected by the people, he asked in 1776, what then was the advantage of constituting two houses? "Unless the Law givers are a compound of distinct Classes of Men really as well as nominally they will have but one Spirit and can therefore neither check nor aid each other." Two homogeneous branches would not make a truly mixed government at all. "They are only two Houses of Assemblymen."[24]

By the 1780's Jefferson believed, as he had feared in 1776, that this was precisely what was happening to the Virginia legislature. The Senate, he wrote in his *Notes on Virginia,* had become too similar to the House of Delegates. "Being chosen by the same electors, at the same time, and out of the same subjects, the choice falls of course on men of the same description." Yet if the theory of mixed government were to be meaningful, the two houses could not embody the same interests, could not contain the same kinds of men with similar education and social standing. "The purpose of establishing different houses of legislation," wrote Jefferson, "is to introduce the influence of different interests or different principles." The British constitution supposedly relied on the House of Commons for honesty and the House of Lords for wisdom ("which would be a rational reliance if honesty were to be bought with money, and if wisdom were hereditary"). But how could America isolate different principles in the legislative branches? In some of the states, Jefferson noted, the legislature was chosen so that the lower house represented the persons and the upper house the property of the state. But with the Virginians "wealth and wisdom have equal chance for admission into both houses." Virginia thus could not derive "those benefits which a proper complication of principles is capable of producing," which alone compensated for the evil of dissensions between the two houses.[25]

24. Ramsay, *American Revolution,* I, 351–52; "Loose Thoughts on Government" (1776), Force, ed., *American Archives,* 4th Ser., VI, 731; William Smith, entry, Oct. 14, 1776, Sabine, ed., *Memoirs of Smith,* 18.
25. Jefferson, *Notes on Virginia,* ed. Peden, 119–20.

The meaning of mixed government, it seemed, was being thwarted in Virginia. For Charles Lee by 1781 the omnipotence of Parliament with its three distinct branches had become less dangerous than the two houses of the Virginia legislature, which, said Lee, "consists of only one, for from the constitution of the Senate, (as it is ridiculously called,) they must be made up of the self-same clay." By 1785 James Madison had concluded that the conception of the balanced polity was breaking down in all of the states. The inability of the senates to "give *wisdom* and *steadiness* to legislation," he told Caleb Wallace of Kentucky, was "the grievance complained of in all our republics." Because "the want of *fidelity* in the administration of power" had been the principal evil felt by most peoples in history and by the Americans under British rule, it was natural, said Madison, for the constitution-makers in 1776 "to give too exclusive attention" to the houses of representatives and to the government's faithfulness to the people. Madison agreed with Jefferson that the right kind of persons was not being elected to the senates. A worse senate than Virginia's could hardly have been constructed. He too endorsed George Mason's scheme of an electoral college to select the senators, a plan which the Virginia Convention's "inexperience and jealousy" had rejected in 1776. If the senates were to be useful bits in the impetuous and inexperienced mouths of the houses of representatives, they had to be constructed on a different basis from the lower houses—composed of a different, better and wiser, sort of people with longer and firmer tenure.[26]

The dilemma that had confronted the royal officials was coming back to haunt the Revolutionaries. The people in the new states seemed to be electing the same kinds of persons to both houses of the legislatures, thus creating a homogeneity of interest between the two branches and destroying the purpose for instituting a mixed polity. One, but not the only, solution to the problem lay in the special qualifications that most of the framers had provided for members of the senates, and it was soon exploited. Senators, William Hooper had said in 1776, should be

---

26. Charles Lee to R. H. Lee, Apr. 12, 1782, *Lee Papers*, IV, 2; Madison to Wallace, Aug. 23, 1785, Hunt, ed., *Writings of Madison*, II, 167; Madison's Observations on Jefferson's Draft of a Constitution for Virginia (1788), Boyd, ed., *Jefferson Papers*, VI, 308. These contemporary observations of the social constituency of the new senates are backed up by Main, "Social Origins of a Political Elite," *Huntington Lib. Qtly.*, 27 (1964), 147–58, and more fully in his *The Upper House in Revolutionary America, 1763–1788* (Madison, Wis., 1967).

"selected for their Wisdom, remarkable Integrity, or that Weight which arises from property and gives Independence and Impartiality to the human mind." Although wisdom and integrity were difficult to measure, property was not. And in property Americans saw a criterion by which their "senatorial part" could be more rigidly distinguished, even though in doing so the meaning many intended to give to the mixed polity in 1776 was set off in a radically altered direction.[27]

Nowhere was this alteration of the meaning of mixed government more baldly exposed than in Massachusetts, first by Theophilus Parsons in the *Essex Result*, the publication of the Essex County Convention which met to consider the proposed Constitution of 1778, and later and more explicitly in the Massachusetts Constitution of 1780. It was clear to Parsons, as to other Americans, that when deducing a constitution from "the established principles" of a mixed state, "we are to look further than to the bulk of the people, for the greatest wisdom, firmness, consistency, and perseverance." To ensure the selection of such a wise and stable elite in the upper house, however, was not easy. Election by the House of Representatives was out of the question: it would make the Senate too dependent on the lower house. But neither were the people as a whole qualified to select the Senate. The proposed Massachusetts Constitution of 1778 was defective because it provided for the selection of the upper house by all the freemen: "a trust is reposed in the people which they are unequal to." This method would make the people too dependent on their representatives for recommendations, and thus the House would in fact choose the senators, making the Senate's independence from the House "visionary" and the benefits expected from a senate, "as one distinct branch of the legislative body," unrealized. But just what were the discriminating marks of the senatorial order? While honesty, probity, and regard for the public good, qualities "that result from a democracy," would be found among the body of the people, it seemed obvious to Parsons that the qualities "that result from an aristocracy"—wisdom and firmness —"will most probably be found amongst men of education and fortune," particularly fortune. It was not, admitted Parsons, that all men of property at present were men of learning and wisdom; but it seemed to Parsons and the Essex Convention that among

27. Hooper to N. C. Congress, Oct. 26, 1776, Saunders, ed., *Col. Recs. of N. C.*, X, 867. Cf. discussion in Pole, *Political Representation in England*, 172–204.

the wealthy there were the largest number of men possessed of education and stability of character.[28]

This emphasis on wealth and property was symptomatic of the Americans' frustration in segregating their natural aristocracy. Many agreed that "riches and ability were not always associated," that the propertied were not necessarily identical with the natural elite. "Integrity," said Jefferson, was not in his experience "the characteristic of wealth." But both Madison and Jefferson were baffled by the apparent inability of the people to perceive the truly talented and were thus compelled reluctantly to endorse property as the best possible source of distinction in the new republics. Yet by focusing on property as the criterion for membership in the senates Americans were being pushed toward a basic shift in their assumptions about the nature of their society that had a disturbing significance for their ideology of republicanism. Property in the minds of the Essex Convention in 1778 and in the minds of other Americans in these and subsequent years was to be more than a crude measure of the best and wisest men in the society. It was becoming an interest in its own right, to be specially represented in the legislature. "No law affecting the person and property of the members of the state," declared the Essex Convention in its recommendation for a new constitution for Massachusetts, "ought to be enacted, without the consent of the majority of the members, and of those also who hold a major part of the property." The Massachusetts Convention of 1780 incorporated this sentiment into its new Constitution: representation in the upper house was based on the proportion of public taxes paid by each senatorial district. And if this was not clear enough, the Convention in its address to its constituents spelled out in the most explicit language the difference between the two houses: "The House of Representatives is intended as the Representatives of the Persons, and the Senate of the property of the Common Wealth."[29]

This isolation of property as a distinct ingredient of the society that must be separately embodied in the government marked an extraordinary change in American thinking, reflective of a general

28. *Essex Result*, Parsons, *Memoir*, 385–86, 369–70.

29. Ramsay, *American Revolution*, I, 351–52; Jefferson to Pendleton, Aug. 26, 1776, Boyd, ed., *Jefferson Papers*, I, 504; Madison's Observations on Jefferson's Draft of a Constitution for Virginia (1788), *ibid.*, VI, 310; *Essex Result*, Parsons, *Memoir*, 389–90; Mass. Cons. (1780), Pt. 2, Chap. I, Sec. II, Art. I; Address of the Convention, Mar. 1780, Handlin, eds., *Popular Sources*, 437. See Pole, *Political Representation in England*, 342.

reappreciation of the nature of American society taking place in the 1780's. Eighteenth-century Whiggism had made no rigid distinction between people and property. Property had been defined not simply as material possessions but, following Locke, as the attributes of a man's personality that gave him a political character: "that estate or substance which a man has and possesses, exclusive of the right and power of all the world besides." It had been thought of generally in political terms, as an individual dominion—a dominion possessed by all politically significant men, the "people" of the society. Property was not set in opposition to individual rights but was of a piece with them. "The Freedom and Liberties of America," said Robert Carter Nicholas in 1774, "are pretty essential Parts of their *Property*." Although differences of property or estates existed, the interests of all property-holders were considered to be essentially identical, and the interest of the people as a whole, as Blackstone said, was generally coincident with the interest of each property-holder.[30] But by the 1780's Americans were emphasizing more and more the "different and discordant interests" existing "in all societies," the various groups and parties—creditors, debtors, farmers, manufacturers, merchants, professionals—who could "for convenience" all be subsumed under "names, invented long ago, the democratic and aristocratic factions," or better, those who possess "the rights of persons" and those who possess "the rights of property."[31]

The implications for the conventional theory of politics of such an old, yet because of the expectations of the Revolution, of such a new, comprehension of the character of American society were at once grasped by some who warned that "attempts of this nature in *our Republic* should be particularly guarded against, its existence as a free government depending on a general unanimity." Yet as early as 1784 Benjamin Lincoln, the Revolutionary general, set out, in a series of articles extraordinary for the boldness of their constitutional suggestions and of their interpretation of American society, a justification for bicameralism in the 1780 Massachusetts Constitution that directly confronted the Revolu-

30. Stearns, *View of the Controversy*, 16; Locke, *Two Treatises*, ed. Laslett, 114–20; [Nicholas], *Considerations*, Swem, ed., *Virginia and the Revolution*, 52; Blackstone, *Commentaries*, I, 139. See Richard Schlatter, *Private Property: The History of an Idea* (New Brunswick, N. J., 1951), 170–71; Pole, *Political Representation in England*, 11–12, 25.

31. Boston *Independent Chronicle*, Dec. 8, 22, 1785, Oct. 18, 1787; Madison's Observations on Jefferson's Draft of a Constitution for Virginia (1788), Boyd, ed., *Jefferson Papers*, VI, 310.

tionary assumptions of 1776. There were, wrote Lincoln, as yet "but few, who are apprehensive of danger or difficulty, from any discordant interests existing within the Commonwealth. With no distinctions in honors or in rank, it is generally supposed, that the old idea of the few, and the many, is unfitly applied. Placed on a common level in point of honorary distinctions, a trifling difference in the distribution of property, can never in general estimation, occasion so great a diversity in views, as to endanger the safety, or peace of the community." But in ten articles partially published in the *Boston Magazine* in 1784 and republished and expanded in the *Independent Chronicle* in 1785 and 1786 Lincoln hammered out "the fallacy of these sentiments," stressing throughout that there was "a difference of interests existing in all governments at the very moment of their institution; and these differing interests are those seeds of destruction which grow with their growth, encrease with their strength, ripen with their age, and end in their dissolution. In republics they may all of them be easily and directly traced to the rights of persons and of property." To prevent such a dissolution the rich must be specially protected in the constitution; indeed, "men possessed of property are entitled to a greater share in political authority than those who are destitute of it." Since property would always have "influence" which "in a government where each citizen has an equality of power, is totally repugnant to its principles, and must be productive of its ruin," such equality of power must be abandoned. The society, said Lincoln, in a remarkable anticipation of the arguments John Adams was shortly to make, must contain what it could not prevent and control this influence of the propertied by segregating them in a separate house of the legislature in order to forestall the rich from using "cunning and corruption" to secure "the power they cannot constitutionally obtain." Therefore, Lincoln concluded, the principle of the Massachusetts government was not equality, as the Revolutionaries of 1776 had thought, "but a species of honour, or a respect for that distinction, which the constitution acknowledges to exist."[32]

32. Charleston *S.-C. and American Gazette*, Feb. 4, 1779; Boston *Independent Chronicle*, Jan. 26, Feb. 9, 1786, Dec. 22, 1785. The ten articles by "The Free Republican" in the *Independent Chronicle* ran from Nov. 24, 1785, to Feb. 9, 1786. The first six had been earlier published in the *Boston Magazine*, 1 (1784), 138–40, 192–95, 271–74, 375–78, 420–23, 546–49. Lincoln was identified as the author from James Freeman's copy of the *Boston Magazine* in the Massachusetts Historical Society.

While such a stark dichotomy between persons and property found its fullest expression in Massachusetts in the 1780's, it was expressed everywhere there was concern with "the rights of the minority . . . in danger" from "a majority . . . united by a common interest or passion." There was, said James Madison in the Philadelphia Convention of 1787, a "diversity of Interest in every Country" between the rich and the poor, creditors and debtors, property and persons, the few and the many. "Persons and property being both essential objects of Government, the most that either can claim, is such a structure of it as will leave a reasonable security for the other. And the most obvious provision of this double character, seems to be that of confining to the holders of property, the object deemed least secure in popular Governments, the right of suffrage for one of the two Legislative branches." Although Madison had doubts whether such a constitutional balance between persons and property was as yet possible given the immature nature of American society, there was no question in his mind what such a conception of the community had done to the 1776 assumptions about the nature of republicanism; and he above all attempted to expose and to resolve the pressing incongruities in American thinking. For such a division between persons and property, as many soon pointed out, was a clear violation of republican equality and homogeneity; "for sure both branches make but one General Court, and each Branch aught Equally to consult the safty, Prosperity, and the happiness of the Whole." "To annex privileges and immunities to men of certain fortunes, is to allow of different ranks and different interests among us, which is the subversion of a free system." After all, republicanism, liberty itself, "depends on a unity of interests."[33]

By separating "the two cardinal objects of Government, the rights of persons, and the rights of property," rights that most Americans in 1776 had assumed "would be more and more identified," and by assigning each to a single house of the legislature, the Americans in a fashion had solved the nagging problem of constituting their bicameral legislatures; but in so doing they had perverted the classic meaning of mixed government, which had placed honor and wisdom, not wealth and property, in the middle

---

33. Madison, in Max Farrand, ed., *The Records of the Federal Convention of 1787*, rev. ed. (New Haven, 1911, 1937), I, 135, 108, II, 204; Return of Mansfield, May 1780, Handlin, eds., *Popular Sources*, 519; *Rudiments of Law and Government*, 20, 25.

branch of the legislature, and had explicitly violated the homogeneity of interests on which republicanism was based. Indeed, by tending, as Madison predicted, to "offend the sense of equality which reigns in a free Country," the rigid distinction between persons and property had only made conspicuous what some from the very beginning had found disturbing in the theory of mixed government. Because republicanism depended so thoroughly on a unity of interests in the society, some Americans as early as 1776 had questioned the possibility of accommodating republican principles with the existence of upper houses—any kind of upper houses, whether embodying property or simply the wisdom of the society—and had moved to challenge directly the applicability of the entire theory of mixed government for the new American states. Such a challenge represented a glaring departure from the eighteenth-century English, even the radical Whig, tradition of political thought and a return to theories of government that had not been seen in England since the days of Lilburne and the Levellers. The denial of bicameralism in any form and the advocacy of an "unmixed" democracy, a government solely by the people, expressed in fact the most politically radical impulse of the American Revolution.[34]

5. SIMPLE DEMOCRACY

For most constitution-makers in 1776, republicanism was not equated with democracy. Indeed, most Americans regarded a pure or simple democracy, as the eighteenth century commonly understood the term, as impractical for any state as large and as populous as the American states were. Had not Sidney written he had known of "no such thing" as, "in the strict sense, . . . a pure democracy, where the people in themselves and by themselves, perform all that belongs to government," and if any had existed in the world he had "nothing to say for it?" For democracy meant government literally by the social estate of the people, that is, not simply a government electively derived from the people, which was a republic, but a government actually administered

34. Madison's Observations on Jefferson's Draft of a Constitution for Virginia (1788), Boyd, ed., *Jefferson Papers*, VI, 310; Madison to Wallace, Aug. 23, 1785, Hunt, ed., *Writings of Madison*, II, 172; Weston, *English Constitutional Theory*, 180.

by the people; it was, as James Otis said, "a government of all over all," in which the ruled became the rulers and the rulers the ruled. While such a democracy, it was thought, had been approximated in the Greek city-states and in the New England towns, most Americans, even the most radical-minded, could not conceive of a scheme of government for their states that would dissolve "the GREAT GOLDEN LINE between the Rulers and Ruled."[35] Governors and senators, like the elders in the Congregational churches, did not cease to be such merely because of their election by the people. Although all Americans in 1776 were certain that the people through their houses of representatives must participate in a large share of the governing of the state, most considered their new states to be, however close, something other than pure democracies. In fact, as the Tories and conservative Whigs realized, democracy, unless incorporated in a mixed polity, was a vituperative term that could be indiscriminately used to discredit the new mixed republics.[36]

There were some in 1776, however, who pushed beyond a mere recomposition of the mixture and actually rejected the entire conception of balance in government, openly celebrating their rejection. There could be, wrote Thomas Paine in *Common Sense*, no consistency between a government whose people "mutually and naturally support each other" and a government which resembled in any way "the so much boasted Constitution of England." That "exceedingly complex" constitution may have been suited "for the dark and slavish times in which it was erected" but not for the new American republics. The English constitution was actually composed of "the base remains of two ancient tyrannies . . . monarchical tyranny in the person of the king," and "aristocratical tyranny in the persons of the peers," mingled with

---

35. Phila. *Pa. Gazette*, Apr. 24, 1776; Otis, *Rights of the British Colonies*, in Bailyn, ed., *Pamphlets*, I, 427; Additional Instructions from the Inhabitants of Albemarle (1776), Boyd, ed., *Jefferson Papers*, VI, 292. See Roy N. Lokken, "The Concept of Democracy in Colonial Political Thought," *Wm. and Mary Qtly.*, 3d Ser., 16 (1959), 570–80; Gaetano Salvemini, "The Concepts of Democracy and Liberty in the Eighteenth Century," in Read, ed., *Constitution Reconsidered*, 105–20. Cf. Merrill Jensen, "Democracy and the American Revolution," *Huntington Lib. Qtly.*, 20 (1956–57), 321–42.

36. [Chalmers], *Plain Truth*, 17; William Smith, entry, Sept. 28, 1776, Sabine, ed., *Memoirs of Smith*, 9; Tucker, *True Interest of Britain*, 21. See Robert R. Palmer, "Notes on the Use of the Word 'Democracy,' 1789–1799," *Pol. Sci. Qtly.*, 68 (1953), 203–26. Cf. Bailyn, *Ideological Origins*, 282–84.

some "new Republican materials, in the persons of the Commons, on whose virtue depends the freedom of England." Only these republican materials belonged in the American constitutions, for the other two, being "independent of the people . . . contribute nothing towards the freedom of the State." In the mixed constitution of England, "the different parts, by unnaturally opposing and destroying each other, prove the whole character to be absurd and useless."[37]

Others in 1776 agreed, arguing like some Massachusetts radicals, that Americans had been blindly led to believe that something similar to the English mixed constitution was "the best we could have." Had not "the best writers on liberty" acknowledged "that the origin and essence of government and power is in the people?" "Let *us then keep the staff in our own hands.*" "The offices of Governor and Lieutenant-Governor" were "entirely unnecessary; their prerogatives will infringe our liberty." Nor was a council or senate needed, for its members were "mostly chosen out of the House, and why they should not be as wise in the lower as the upper House" was incomprehensible. They were "said to be a *check* upon the House," which unfortunately was only too true: "they have formerly been a check and clog to business of consequence, requiring dispatch." What was needed was a "plain and simple" government, in other words, just a single house of representatives.[38]

While much of this criticism of mixed government expressed at the time of the Revolution came from the most radically estranged groups, like the inhabitants of Mecklenburg County, North Carolina, who in 1775 proposed "that Legislation be not a divided right, and that no man or body of men be invested with a negative on the voice of the People duly collected," even such a person as Alexander Hamilton, for all of his fears of the people, sensed in the spring of 1777 the anomaly implicit in the mixed republics Americans were erecting. It was "very disputable," he told Gouverneur Morris in a remarkable letter, "that instability is inherent in the nature of popular governments." He knew that "unstable democracy" was "an epithet frequently in the mouths of politicians"; yet he was sure that "a strict examination of his-

---

37. [Paine], *Common Sense*, Foner, ed., *Writings of Paine*, I, 6–8. "Paine may well have been the first Englishman during the classical age of the constitution to ridicule its maxims publicly." Weston, *English Constitutional Theory*, 192.

38. Boston *Independent Chronicle*, July 10, Mar. 6, 1777.

tory" would show that all the fluctuations of excessively popular governments had flowed from their being mixed with other elements. "Compound governments," said Hamilton, "though they may be harmonious in the beginning, will introduce distinct interests; and these interests will clash, throw the state into convulsion and produce a change or dissolution." If the whole body of the people were to govern directly, "error, confusion and instability," of course, must be expected, but not in a "representative democracy" where the people's power was vested in their elected delegates. A complex legislature would only cause "delay and dilatoriness." Yet this was only a minor evil. The "much greater evil" was that in time the senate, "from the very name and from the mere circumstances of its being a separate member of the legislature, will be liable to degenerate into a body purely aristocratical." For Hamilton, in 1777 at least, there was little "danger of an abuse of power from a simple legislature," especially where "equality and fulness of popular representation" was provided for.[39]

But Hamilton was not speaking the sentiments of most New Yorkers in 1777. Indeed, the debate in the New York Convention forming the Constitution in the spring of 1777 was not over the inclusion of a second chamber or senate—which was taken for granted, but over the incorporation of the governor as a third "separate and distinct" branch of the legislature, a proposal that was later compromised into a separate Council of Revision of which the governor was made a member. The cries up and down the continent in 1776 for a simple legislature were generally intermittent and isolated, and were easily smothered by the Americans' overwhelming preoccupation with the balanced mechanism. However attractive Paine's call for independence and republicanism was in 1776, he was surely not speaking common American sense with his proposals for the simple form the new governments should take. Paine may have been a very keen writer, said John Adams; but he was also "very ignorant of the Science of Government."[40] Nearly all of the states in 1776 worked within the broad

39. Instructions of Mecklenburg County, Aug. 1775, Saunders, ed., *Col. Recs. of N. C.*, X, 239; Hamilton to Gouverneur Morris, May 19, 1777, Syrett and Cooke, eds., *Hamilton Papers*, I, 255.

40. *Journals of the Provincial Congress, Provincial Convention, Committees of Safety and Council of Safety of the State of New York, 1775, 1776, and 1777* (Albany, 1842), I, 834, 836, 843, 853, 860, 862, 891; Adams to James Warren, May 12, 1776, Ford, ed., *Warren-Adams Letters*, I, 243.

theory of mixed government without serious challenge. Pennsylvania of course was the great exception.[41]

6. A RADICAL EXPERIMENT IN POLITICS

All American Whig writing in the spring of 1776 was filled with a spirit of adventure, but it was in Pennsylvania that the sense of excitement and experimentation attained its greatest intensity. And it was in Pennsylvania that the most radical ideas about politics and constitutional authority voiced in the Revolution found expression, resulting in a comprehensive examination of assumptions about government that elsewhere were generally taken for granted.

The charge made by the established elite, displaced by new aspirants for political power, that the Convention which framed the Constitution of 1776 was stocked with "novices" who had "never spent an hour of their lives in the investigation of the principles of law and government" was hardly fair. Social upstarts the members of the Convention may have been, but they surely were not unacquainted with the principles of government. They not only absorbed and fed upon the Revolutionary political thinking that was all around them, but they undoubtedly wrote much of it. The Constitution they framed in the summer of 1776 was no mere carry-over of the provincial charter. The Convention, said one delegate, was "determined not to pay the least regard to the former Constitutions"; in fact it was resolved "to reject every thing . . . to clear away every part of the old rubbish

41. Georgia and Vermont of course also rejected the theory of mixed government, but because of their peripheral location and their delay in drafting, their constitutions had none of the impact Pennsylvania's did on American opinion. Moreover, their unicameralism, or their attempt at simple democracy, was more imperfect than Pennsylvania's. Vermont's Constitution was consciously copied from Pennsylvania's. See Dr. Thomas Young to the Inhabitants of Vermont, Apr. 11, 1777, Eliakim P. Walton, ed., *Records of the Council of Safety and Governor and Council of the State of Vermont* (Montpelier, 1873–80), I, 395. But Young significantly recommended an alteration in the Pennsylvania model which was accepted by Vermont, mitigating the elimination of an upper house: all public bills were to be laid before the governor and Council "for their perusal and proposals of amendment" before the last reading in the assembly. Vt. Cons. (1777), Sec. XIV. The Georgia Constitution also retained the shadow of an upper house by giving the Executive Council power to review legislation, to propose amendments, and to delay the final enactment of laws by the Assembly for five days. Ga. Cons. (1777), Art. XXVII.

out of the way and begin upon a clean foundation." "We must come as near a new form of Government as we can, without destroying private property." The new constitution must be no mere patchwork, but must be begun again, "just as if we had never any form of Government before." The result was the most radical constitution of the Revolutionary era, which everyone—supporters and critics alike—regarded as a monumental experiment in politics.[42]

It was "a radical reformation"[43] in Pennsylvania's government that found its ideals in a golden Anglo-Saxon age before the Norman yoke destroyed "that natural, wise and equal government, which has deservedly obtained the admiration of every civilized age and country." No writing better indicates the kind of Whig radicalism the Revolutionaries in Pennsylvania grasped in order to express the fierceness of their estrangement from the old order than the anonymous pamphlet, *The Genuine Principles of the Ancient Saxon, or English Constitution*, published in Philadelphia in the late spring of 1776.[44] The pamphlet, pointedly addressed to the approaching Convention that would draw up a constitution, contained engrossed extracts of "some sentiments from a certain very scarce book," an *Historical Essay on the English Constitution*, written by an obscure English radical, Obadiah Hulme, and published in London in 1771—a pamphlet expressive of the most alienated strain of English Whiggism that decidedly influenced not only the Pennsylvania constitution-makers but Thomas Jefferson as well.[45]

The *Historical Essay* and its Pennsylvania extraction both stressed the politics of localism. The "peculiar excellence" of the "beautiful system" of the Anglo-Saxon government "consisted in its incorporating small parcels of the people into little communities by themselves." For the Saxons, government obviously had been close to the people. "In their small republics they often met in council upon their common concerns: and being all equally in-

42. General Persifor Frazer to Polly Frazer, Oct. 2, 1776, *Pa. Mag. of Hist. and Biog.*, 31 (1907), 315; Phila. *Pa. Journal*, June 11, 1777; Thomas Smith to Arthur St. Clair, Aug. 3, 22, 1776, William Henry Smith, ed., *The St. Clair Papers* (Cincinnati, 1882), I, 371, 374; Phila. *Pa. Packet*, July 1, 1776.

43. Phila. *Pa. Packet*, Apr. 29, 1776.

44. Demophilus, *Genuine Principles*, 15. H. Trevor Colbourn has suggested that Demophilus may have been George Bryan. See his *Lamp of Experience*, 191.

45. On Hulme see Robbins, *Commonwealthman*, 363–64. For Hulme's influence on Jefferson's Saxon thought see Colbourn, *Lamp of Experience*, Chap. VIII, esp. 170–71; Chinard, ed., *Commonplace Book*, 296–98.

terested in every question . . . they must of course be drawn in to consider, and offer their sentiments on many occasions." This intimate involvement by the ancient Saxons of the common people in politics was what most impressed the Pennsylvania radicals and Jefferson. Men became concerned about government because they participated daily in the affairs of their tithings and towns, not only by paying taxes but by performing public duties and by personally making laws. When these tasks were taken out of the people's hands and given to superior bodies to perform, "men fell into a political stupor, and have never, to this day, thoroughly awakened, to a sense of the necessity there is, to watch over both legislative and executive departments in the state. If they have now and then opened their eyes, it is only to survey, with silent indignation, a state from whence they despair of being able to recover themselves. Fixed establishments on the one hand, rooted habits and prejudices on the other, are not easily got over." It became the responsibility of the Pennsylvania radicals "to convince the bulk of an understanding people, that . . . the old Saxon model of government, will be the best model, that human wisdom, improved by experience, has left them to copy." Hopefully the new widespread communication of sentiments flowing from local committees and town meetings "will give such a new face to the affairs of this colony, and raise up so many able men to improve its internal police; that . . . the principal science that ever rendered mankind happy and glorious, the science of *just* and *equal* government, will shine conspicuous in Pennsylvania."[46]

Larger government, when it had been needed by the Saxons, had not been imposed from above, but had grown out of their small communities, out of their continuous consent, pieced together by their cautious delegation of power, never granted "to any man for a longer time than one year." Indeed, the Saxons made annual elections the "quintessence" of their constitution, "the basis of the whole fabric of their government." "From this view of the gradual progression of the Saxon government, from the smallest combinations of meer neighborhoods to the most extensive Commonwealth of United Colonies they ever possessed, they conceived the power of all civil government as derived only from the voluntary delegations of the whole People." They had delegated all power through election, legislative as well as exec-

46. Demophilus, *Genuine Principles*, 4, 15, 17, 39–40; Phila. *Pa. Packet*, Apr. 29, May 20, Nov. 19, 1776.

utive, for it was all power that was dangerous, "whether it be lodged in the hands of one man, one hundred or one thousand"— including even the power lodged in the representatives of the people. "No country can be called *free* which is governed by an absolute power; and it matters not whether it be an absolute royal power or an absolute legislative power, as the consequences will be the same to the people." "In most states," the radicals warned in essays and pamphlets reflective of the peculiarities of the Pennsylvania revolution, "men have been too careless in the delegation of their governmental power; and not only disposed of it in an improper manner, but suffered it to continue so long in the same hands, that the *deputies* have, like the King and Lords of Great Britain, at length become *possessors in their own right*; and instead of *public servants*, are in fact the *makers* of the public."[47]

These were the sentiments of men hostile not only to the executive authority of the colony but to the entire provincial government. Their radicalism was the expression of men unaccustomed to dominance in provincial politics, men whose rancor was as much directed against the "*great men*" and "the Aristocratic party" controlling the Assembly as against the traditional ruling authority of the proprietary governor. Pennsylvania, in fact, was worse off than the other colonies, because the "House of Assembly is a part of that power from which we are trying to break away." The radicals intended to bring the entire government— legislature and executive—within the control of the people, whom they naturally identified with themselves. In their minds "the more simple, and the more immediately dependent the authority is upon the people, the better; . . . because it must be allowed that they are the best guardians of their own liberties." For such men the mixed polity offered no safety, since "the wisdom and goodness of a constitution" consisted only in delegating and controlling all governmental power in such a way that no one, legislators as well as executive, could abuse it. The people could be protected not by attempting to perfect a legislature out of "any combination of assemblies, for that is impossible, but by forming it in such a manner that its frailties may continually be corrected by its interest."[48]

47. Demophilus, *Genuine Principles*, 5–6, 9, 3; Phila. *Pa. Packet*, May 20, 1776; *Four Letters*, 19.

48. Phila. *Pa. Evening Post*, May 21, 1776; Phila. *Pa. Journal*, Oct. 2, 1776; Phila. *Pa. Gazette*, Nov. 20, 1776, June 11, 1777.

The new government was thus to have only a single legislative house, not because Pennsylvania had possessed as a colony a uni-cameral Assembly but because "the Ancient Saxon constitution, which has commanded universal applause was just as simple." The Pennsylvania radicals, in clear and unmistakable terms, echoed Thomas Paine in repudiating the theory of mixed government. Americans, they said, had an opportunity unknown to previous societies, which had never been able to form an equitable plan of government. Because the people of other societies had not been equal, they had been compelled to incorporate great social distinctions into their constitutions, thereby recognizing an "interest separate and distinct from, and inconsistent with, the general welfare of the people." All history had proved the defectiveness of such complicated and mixed governments. "Had the *Romans* been a true Democracy, without a Senate, or body different from the Plebians, they might have avoided those jars and contentions which continually subsisted between those two bodies." Such irreconcilable distinctions had also destroyed the English experiment with republicanism in the seventeenth century. Then in 1688 the English had tried another balance in order to "secure the rights of the three distinct classes, King, Lords and Commons; and it was thought they had effected it; but later experience has proved the contrary." The mixture could not hold, for "two or more distinct interests can never exist in society without finally destroying the liberties of the people." The result of such a mixture was always a bitter struggle—a struggle that could be avoided only by the recognized presence of a single order in the community. "A nation must consist of all Kings, all nobles, or all simple freemen, to prevent such confusions, and preserve its privileges."

America was at present blessedly different from all other nations. "Having no rank above that of freeman, she has but one interest to consult" and thus should have but a single body representing this "one order of people" in each of the states. In the thinking of these Pennsylvania radicals, republicanism had become identified with democracy. "Popular Government—sometimes termed Democracy, Republick, or Commonwealth—is the plan of civil society wherein the community at large take the care of its own welfare." The erection of governors and upper chambers in the legislatures would only be "setting-up distinctions, and creating *separate*, and *jarring interests* in a society" which should possess "but one *common interest*." "Men, naturally on a level, ought to remain so by the constitution of the society," and ought not to be distinguished by the institution of socio-political orders. Just as there was "no need for a representative of a King, for we have none," so there could be no need of senates "to represent the House of Lords, for we have not, and hope never shall have, a hereditary nobility, different from the general body of the people; but if we admit different branches of the Legislature, there is danger there may be in time."[49] Bicameralism would only breed distinctions and lead to "a perpetual and dangerous opposition," opening "a door for ill-disposed aspiring men to destroy the State." "To say, there ought to be two houses, because there are two sorts of interests, is the very reason why there ought to be but one, and *that one* to consist of every sort." Only a single-house legislature could make "the interest of the legislator and the common interest perfectly coincident."[50]

This unicameral legislature, indeed all institutions set above the people, must be closely circumscribed. "Annual elections, strengthened by some kind of periodical exclusion, seems the best guard against the encroachments of power." Rotation of office, even for the legislators (and in this the Pennsylvania Constitution was unique), would keep the channels of political and social mobility open. The legislators after four annual terms would have to give way to a new set, and thus must "return to mix with the mass of the people and feel at their leisure the effects of the laws which they have made." The legislature, moreover, should be chosen by the free voice of the people in every part of the state. Since everyone, as one radical put it, "who *has a will and understanding of his own* capable to manage his affairs" should vote by ballot, the Constitution provided for the broadest rights of suffrage of any drafted in 1776. To keep the legislature continually dependent upon the people and the people aware of every aspect of government, the doors of the Assembly were to remain open, its votes published weekly, and the press free to examine its proceedings or the proceedings of any part of the government.[51]

49. Phila. *Pa. Packet*, Oct. 22, Apr. 22, July 1, 1776; Phila. *Pa. Journal*, Mar. 13, 1776.

50. *Four Letters*, 20; Phila. *Pa. Packet*, July 1, 1776; Phila. *Pa. Gazette*, June 11, 1777.

51. *Four Letters*, 23; Phila. *Pa. Journal*, Sept. 27, 1775; Phila. *Pa. Packet*, May 20, 1776. On the provisions for rotation and open assemblies see Pa. Cons. (1776), Sec. 8, 13, 14, 35.

When the author of *The Genuine Principles of the Ancient Saxon . . . Constitution* predicted that "in the future . . . *all debates will undoubtedly be held in public,*" it was no exaggeration, for the radicals were intent on carrying the principle of consent to its extremity. In its extraordinary Section 15 the Constitution provided for every bill passed by the General Assembly to be printed for the consideration of the people at large before it could become law in the next legislative session. This part of the Constitution represented all that the radicals wanted in bringing the affairs of government intimately into the hands of the people. "You have the perusal, and consequent approbation of every law before it binds you; so that you must consent to be slaves before you can be made such."[52]

Yet even these safeguards were not enough. Some additional instrument was needed to curb the legislature and protect the Constitution. "If once the legislative power breaks in upon it, the effect will be the same as if a kingly power did it. The Constitution, in either case, will receive its death wound." Therefore, several pamphleteers proposed "that at the expiration of every seven or any other number of years a *Provincial Jury* shall be elected, to inquire if any inroads have been made in the Constitution, and to have power to remove them." Such a distinct inquisitory body would, as Machiavelli recommended, help to keep "the constitution in health and vigor, by having an opportunity to see that it did not depart from its first principles." The suggestion appeared in the Pennsylvania Constitution as the Council of Censors, an organ dragged up from the classical past, modeled on the Spartan Ephori and the Roman Censors, a separate body of men elected septennially by the people to prevent their regularly elected delegates from becoming their own masters. The resort to such a Council illustrates as well as any part of the extraordinary Pennsylvania Constitution the ideological radicalism of its framers, with their "scholastic predilection for the antique in liberty."[53]

To Americans everywhere steeped in the theory of mixed government, and especially to the bypassed gentry of Pennsylvania,

---

52. Demophilus, *Genuine Principles*, 20; Phila. *Pa. Packet*, Nov. 26, 1776.

53. *Four Letters*, 24; Demophilus, *Genuine Principles*, 38; Alexander Graydon, *Memoirs of His Own Time*, ed. John S. Littell (Phila., 1846), 288, and in general 279–80, 285–88. Graydon attributed the Council of Censors to James Cannon and George Bryan which may suggest that Cannon was the author of *Four Letters*. See also Lewis H. Meader, "The Council of Censors," *Pa. Mag. of Hist. and Biog.*, 22 (1898), 265–300.

the Constitution born of the 1776 Pennsylvania Convention was a political monster deserving only to be mercifully put to death. "The whole constitution is intolerable," exclaimed one critic. "It is . . . singular in its kind, confused, inconsistent, deficient in sense and grammar, and the ridicule of all *America* but our selves, who blush too much to laugh." Benjamin Rush thought the people must have been drunk with liberty to have produced such an "absurd" Constitution, which had, he said, "substituted a mob government to one of the happiest governments of the world." To the irascible William Hooper writing from Pennsylvania, the new Constitution was a "motley mixture of limited monarchy, and an execrable democracy—a Beast without a head." He could only hope that no one in North Carolina would give any currency to this monstrosity. "It is truly the Excrement of expiring Genius and political Phrenzy. It has made more Tories than Lord North; deserves more Imprecations than the Devil and all his Angels. It will shake the very being of this once flourishing Country."[54]

Hooper was not wrong, for Pennsylvania was badly shaken. Displaced political groups soon coalesced in opposition to the new Constitution, and for the most part refused to cooperate with the constitution-makers in organizing and running the Revolutionary government. These anti-Constitutionalists were determined to undermine the new government in any way possible. By abstention and by obstruction the established social leaders immobilized a government that could not function without their participation, and thus with self-fulfilling prophecy they realized their own dire predictions of its unworkability.[55] The supporters of the Constitution were helpless. They admitted that obviously "there is a defect existing somewhere," but blamed the opponents of the Constitution rather than the Constitution itself. "We conceive there to be something childishly fallacious and ungenerous, in creating trouble and weakness on purpose to complain thereof." The responsibility for the feebleness of the new government rested on those "who have, by their backwardness, discouraged, and by their opposition endeavoured to prevent the execution of the wholesome laws now in being." They pleaded with their an-

54. Phila. *Pa. Journal*, Oct. 16, 1776; Rush to Anthony Wayne, Sept. 24, 1776, Apr. 2, May 19, 1777, Butterfield, ed., *Rush Letters*, I, 114–15, 137, 148; Hooper to Samuel Johnston, Sept. 26, 1776, Saunders, ed., *Col. Recs. of N. C.*, X, 819–20.
55. Phila. *Pa. Journal*, Apr. 23, 1777; Selsam, *Pennsylvania Constitution*, Chap. VI; Hawke, *Midst of a Revolution*, 183–86, 191–96.

tagonists to close ranks against an imminent British invasion and support the new government.[56]

But the chasm in social standing and political thinking between the supporters and opponents of the Constitution seemed for many too great to bridge. The theory of mixed government had been flagrantly violated; but this was understandable, said the anti-Constitutionalists, considering the kind of people who had written the Constitution. The opponents of the Constitution ("our gentry" as the radicals contemptuously called them) saw only that "many men of excellent characters" had been turned out by "upstarts," who were "totally unacquainted with the principles of government." Too many ignorant persons, it seemed, were meddling in business that was over their heads, "deviating from that line of conduct allotted to every one, and undertaking things beyond their reach," and unsettling the social order by advising the people to avoid electing gentlemen of the learned professions. The new men being thrown up by the Revolution, said one distraught opponent of the Constitution, were like the barbarians who overran Rome.[57]

The anti-Constitutionalists, or the Republicans as they came to call themselves, began at once a determined campaign to overturn the new Pennsylvania Constitution, filling the press with hostile arguments directed particularly against the single-house legislature. The framers of the Constitution, "a few quacks," they charged, had unnecessarily deviated from the old charter government, from the habits and inclinations of the people, and had attached to the Constitution all sorts of "strange innovations." In fact the new Constitution differed "from EVERY Government that has lately been established in *America* on the authority of the people . . . and from those of the most distinguished authors, who have deliberately considered the subject." These innovators "have given us one full of whimsies—a government with only one legislative branch, which never yet failed to end in tyranny."[58] What was most needed was a senate or upper chamber, which

56. Phila. *Pa. Journal*, May 21, 1777; Phila. *Pa. Gazette*, Nov. 13, 1776; Address of the Pennsylvania Convention, Sept. 28, 1776, Force, ed., *American Archives*, 5th Ser., II, 581–82.

57. Phila. *Pa. Packet*, Oct. 22, 1776; Phila. *Pa. Journal*, Apr. 9, June 11, 18, 1777; Thomas Smith to Arthur St. Clair, Aug. 3, 1776, Smith, ed., *St. Clair Papers*, I, 371; Phila. *Pa. Journal*, Mar. 17, Apr. 9, 1777. See Selsam, *Pennsylvania Constitution*, 209–10.

58. Phila. *Pa. Journal*, Oct. 16, Nov. 13, 1776, May 21, 1777; Phila. *Pa. Gazette*, Oct. 23, 1776; Phila. *Pa. Packet*, Nov. 5, 1776.

could balance the basic honesty of the people with the knowledge and experience of the few men of education and leisure in the society. "All political writers ascribe integrity to *plebeans,* i.e. commons; wisdom to *Senators,* men better educated in the general and particular history of mankind." A government to endure must contain each of these elements, segregated in separate branches of the legislature. But why, the defenders of the Pennsylvania Constitution had repeatedly asked, "can we not put the wise and learned man into the House of Assembly, as well as into a Legislative Council? and shall we not have all the benefits of his great talents in the one case that we should in the other?" "By no means," answered the supporters of mixed government in an argument that was to gain great currency with many Americans. The great and wise men would only overawe and beguile the common people with their influence and learned rhetoric. Fifteen men of this senatorial type could probably control a legislature of one hundred common representatives if they sat with them. They therefore must be isolated in a separate chamber among their own class where such deception and influence would never work so efficiently.[59]

There was nothing really new in this justification for a mixed constitution; it was the conventional explanation assumed by most of the constitution-makers in 1776. But its proponents in Pennsylvania, because of the particular exigencies of the state's Revolutionary politics, were compelled to lay out the social basis for a balanced constitution with unusual starkness and comprehensiveness and thus were even driven to call into question the egalitarian nature of American society. A simple republic, the opponents of the 1776 Constitution argued, was impossible in America because of "the great distinction of persons, and differences in their estates or property." "A people who could be free and happy with one legislature might be equally free and happy without any government. Both situations suppose equal degrees of virtue in a people." A single-house legislature representing the people only was not "calculated to the genius, manners, habits and prejudices of the people of Pennsylvania." Too many Americans possessed "a monarchical spirit" which was "natural from the government they have lived under"—all of which made it obvious that "a mixed government is the best that can be adopted in

59. Phila. *Pa. Journal,* Sept. 25, Nov. 13, 1776.

the respective colonies; and most of them have adopted such."[60]

These were unsettling thoughts. Was a mixed form of government incompatible with republicanism? Would it inevitably prevent Americans from becoming an egalitarian and virtuous society? Most Americans in 1776 had not thought so, yet the revelation of the social assumptions implicit in the theory of mixed government was creating doubts and disturbing second thoughts that observations from Europe seemed only to reinforce. The French philosophes, as they gradually became aware of the nature of the new state governments, tempered their initial excitement at watching republics being created with their amazement at seeing the institution of upper houses in the new states. They could only conclude that the new American constitutions were too much the children of the parent, too much influenced by the English form of government—and unreasonably so, for the English mixed constitution, they believed, had no relevance for America. "What is well adapted to England," remarked Mirabeau, "is ill calculated for America." The Americans had uncritically imitated the English constitution, attempting to balance different bodies, "as if," said Turgot in the most pointed and most famous foreign criticism of the American constitutions, "the same equilibrium of powers which has been thought necessary to balance the enormous preponderance of royalty, could be of any use in republics, formed upon the equality of all the citizens." For the philosophes the nation could have only a single interest. Indeed this was the assumption of republicanism. The people, it seemed, could hardly have at the same time two different wills on the same subject. Since, as Condorcet pointed out, "the representatives of a single nation naturally form a single body," there was no place for a senate in an egalitarian republic.[61]

Such foreign criticisms, together with the radical Constitution

60. Phila. *Pa. Packet*, Nov. 5, Oct. 8, 1776; Phila. *Pa. Journal*, Oct. 16, Nov. 13, 1776. "A pure democracy may possibly do, when patriotism is the ruling passion," wrote Edward Rutledge to John Jay from Philadelphia on Nov. 24, 1776; "but when the State abounds with rascals, as is the case with too many at this day, you must suppress a little of that popular spirit." Johnston, ed., *Papers of Jay*, I, 94.

61. Honoré Gabriel de Riquette, Comte de Mirabeau, *Reflections on the Observations of the Importance of the American Revolution . . . [of] Richard Price* (Phila., 1786), 17; Turgot to Richard Price, Mar. 22, 1778, in Adams, ed., *Works of John Adams*, IV, 279; J. Paul Selsam and Joseph G. Rayback, "French Comment on the Pennsylvania Constitution of 1776," *Pa. Mag. of Hist. and Biog.*, 76 (1952), 324. See also Robert R. Palmer, *The Age of the Democratic Revolution . . .* (Princeton, 1959–64), I, 238–82.

of Pennsylvania, brought into focus an apparent inconsistency between the theory of balanced government and the ideology of republicanism. The persuasive egalitarian image of America dazzled and confused American defenders of the senates and at once brought into question what had been taken for granted in 1776. The Revolutionary resentment against aristocracy and the social equality of republicanism soon became serious intellectual obstacles in the assumed and inherited explanation of an upper house designed to embody a distinct social and intellectual group. This kind of pressure demanded a new explanation of the position of the senate.

7. THE HOMOGENEITY OF ORDERS

Most American believers in the theory of mixed government in 1776, like Jefferson, had anticipated senates composed only of an aristocracy of talent, the wisest and best men of the community selected directly or indirectly by the people to fill the upper houses of the legislature. They had seen no incompatibility between a senate possessing interests different from those of the representatives of the people and the basic assumptions of republicanism. Indeed, Jefferson and others believed that the senate had to embody principles distinct from those of the house of representatives if the balance or mixture were to be viable and the elusive public good of republicanism were to be found and properly promoted. Wisdom and sufficient independence in the senators would correct the honest and well-meaning blunderings of the people's representatives in the lower houses and find what was really good for the society. Such senates were by no means to be a European aristocracy, a hereditary nobility artificially protected by law and distinguished by titles. The American aristocracy would be a natural one, made up of men of proven merit, arising temporarily out of the community. Certainly they were to constitute no House of Lords.[62]

62. Even the radically anti-aristocratic author of *Four Letters* (pp. 23-24) admitted the usefulness of "modest and decent honorary titles" in a state, for "they are, when properly conferred, the badges of merit." However, such titles must "be neither hereditary, nor convey legislative authority." His quarrel with the defenders of bicameralism was not over the existence of such men of superior honor and merit but over their embodiment in a separate house of the legislature.

However, there were those like John Sullivan who as early as 1775 perceived a potential and ruinous inconsistency between "that government which admits of contrary or clashing interests" and a republic which could have "but one object . . . , namely, the good of the whole." Yet Sullivan like other devoted republicans in 1776 was not at all opposed to the existence of two houses within the legislature (as long as "one interest should unite the several governing branches") and therefore, without being compelled to think about it, could reconcile bicameralism with republicanism with no embarrassment.[63] But wherever and whenever men began probing critically and strenuously into the social significance of the constitutional balance in the legislature all sorts of incongruities between republicanism and mixed government could be exposed, particularly as more and more Americans began taking seriously and expanding the republican emphasis on equality. Indeed, wherever and whenever the fear of aristocracy and disparate interests was intense but the attraction of bicameralism too strong, the nature and function of the senates were compelled to change, ultimately making intelligible what Sullivan had left obscure.

At the outset of the Revolution premature and scattered expressions by the most radically minded anticipated the central direction American thinking about the upper house was to take in the decade following the Declaration of Independence. In November 1776 Mecklenburg County in North Carolina continued the tone of its instructions of the previous year, urging its delegates to the Constitutional Convention to form a government which would "be a simple Democracy or as near it as possible," and to oppose anything that leaned toward aristocracy or power in the hands of the rich. Yet by 1776 the county had become reconciled to bicameralism—but not to the theory of mixed government, since it instructed its delegates to allow every person to have an equal right to vote for both houses of the legislature so "that the good people of this State shall be justly and equally represented in the two houses."[64] In the traditional lexicon of the

63. John Sullivan to Meshech Weare, Dec. 11, 1775, Force, ed., *American Archives*, 4th Ser., IV, 241–43.

64. Instructions of Mecklenburg County to Its Delegates in the N. C. Congress, Nov. 1776, Saunders, ed., *Col. Recs. of N. C.*, X, 870a, c. Cf. above, XXX. The North Carolina Constitution itself recognized the representative character of the upper house. Both branches, it declared, were to be "dependent on the people," the Senate "composed of Representatives, annually chosen by ballot,

eighteenth century a bicameral legislature in simple democracy was a self-evident contradiction; but not, of course, if somehow the people participated in both houses of the legislature. But then what happened to the theory of mixed government?

Another writer in Massachusetts in 1776 was amazed that the members of the House of Representatives should think "that they were more the Representatives of the people than the Council." Perhaps it was because the Council was elected by the House. But how could the Council be "less the Representatives of the people, than a *Committee* chosen by the House?" The way out of this dilemma, urged the writer, was to have the Council elected directly by the people; "and then the House can't say that the Counsellors are less the Representatives of the people than themselves." In order to reach this conclusion the writer had to believe that election by the people, no matter what the supposed nature of the office, destroyed any distinction between the officeholders. Governor John Rutledge of South Carolina thought that it did, and in his veto of the 1778 South Carolina Constitution he warned that making the upper house directly elective by the people rather than by the lower house, as in the 1776 Constitution, would in effect create the incongruity of "two representative bodies." By 1784 a South Carolina pamphleteer was contending that the senators were just that, another representative body, which like the lower house was bound to obey the instructions of its constituents. In fact the senators' position in the legislature possessed no social significance and would be "entirely useless" if it were not that "the division in the legislative power seems necessary to furnish a proper check to our too hasty proceedings." By these kinds of arguments mere election was becoming the criterion of representation, thereby creating momentous implications for men's understanding of politics.[65]

But most Americans at first hesitated to draw them and, like a radical New England pamphleteer, continued to try to reconcile traditional governmental forms with what they believed to be the desired guarantees for the people's liberty. If there had to be an

---

one for each county in the State," the House of Commons "composed of Representatives annually chosen by ballot, two for each county, and one for each of the [specified] towns." N. C. Cons. (1776), I, II, III.

65. Boston *New England Chronicle*, Aug. 29, 1776; Ramsay, *History of Revolution of South Carolina*, I, 136–37; [Thomas Tudor Tucker], *Conciliatory Hints, Attempting by a Fair State of Matters, to Remove Party Prejudice* (Charleston, 1784), 7.

upper house, argued the anonymous author of *The People the Best Governors*, it must not be elected by the house of representatives. "By chusing representatives to make laws for them" the people put their "power out of their own hands; yet they do not deposit it into the hands of their representatives to give to others, but to exercise it in their room and stead." There was, however, "no real absurdity" in the people's directly electing another body or council with a negative on the house of representatives. But it must be made clear that the house of representatives would then possess only a partial right of representation and legislation, since "this said negative body are likewise virtually the representatives of the people, and derive just so much authority from them as will make up the defect of the others, viz., that of confirming." Yet even with this tortured effort to make the council as equally responsible to the people as the house of representatives, this radical author could not finally bring himself to admit the expediency of a senate with a negative power. Equally representative or not, an upper house had overtones of aristocracy. Would not a mere council of advice after all be preferable? he concluded in a confused and anguished question. It would prevent, would it not, that inequality "which is sometimes occasioned by two destinct fountains of power."[66]

The profusion of constitutional proposals for the Virginia upper house in the summer of 1776 did not begin to expose the confusion Virginians would experience over the place of their Senate in their new commonwealth. As early as the fall of 1776 the people of Albemarle County voiced their bewilderment over the position of the upper house in the new Virginia Constitution. The Senate as constructed seemed "totally unnecessary," and the county feared "several great inconveniences, if the people should ever happen not to make choice of their very best, most sensible, and most able men." But even if the people should elect the best men, the county continued in perplexity, it appeared that from "a defect" in the powers of the Senate (which could originate no bills), "they would be so many valuable Members almost entirely lost to the Community." But the Albemarle inhabitants saw a way out of their confusion: increase the number of senators, put their election "upon a different method," and invest them "with

66. *People the Best Governors*, in Chase, *Dartmouth College*, 656–57. See also *Address of the Inhabitants of the Towns of* [*Grafton County*], Bouton et al., eds., *N. H. State Papers*, X, 232–33.

the same powers entirely as the other members of the Legislature." There "would then be in fact two houses of Representatives, every one endeavouring to promote what they would think advantageous to the Community." Now there could be "no reason for granting less power to one, than the other, none of them being hereditary, and both having the same concerns at stake."[67]

It was not long before such views gained some official sanction. The 1776 Constitution had prohibited the Virginia Senate from altering, let alone initiating any money bills, since supposedly, like the House of Lords, its members did not represent the people and thus could not tamper with the people's money. But when in 1777 an attempt by the Virginia Senate to change a money bill was met by objections by the House of Delegates, the Senate prepared an elaborate and significant explanation of its violation of the Constitution. The House of Delegates, the Senate argued, could not use the precedents of the British Parliament to justify its objection to the Senate's interference with money bills. "The great outlines of the British Constitution," the Senate admitted, "are to be discerned in the frame of our government; yet, when the constituent parts of our Legislatures are compared, so faint is the resemblance, that no ground remains for those jealousies, which have continually prompted the attempts of the Commons against the other House." In England the representatives of the people retained exclusive control of money bills as a barrier to the encroachments of the arbitrary power of the Lords who were "an order of men distinct from their fellow subjects, possessing titles and dignities which flowed to them from the crown, and which therefore inclined them to the side of royalty." But this exclusive control over money bills had no relevance in the Commonwealth of Virginia. The Virginia legislature was in fact quite different from the English Parliament. "In our legislature," declared the Senate, "can be perceived only the representatives of the people, separated into two bodies, and mutually endeavoring to exercise faithfully their delegated power." Thus the constitutional restriction on their equality of authority was unintended and meaningless.[68]

67. Albemarle County Instructions concerning the Virginia Constitution (1776), Boyd, ed., *Jefferson Papers*, VI, 287.

68. Reply of Senate to House of Delegates concerning Money Bills (Dec. 9, 1777), and Communication from House of Delegates to Senate concerning Money Bills (Jan. 9, 1778), Boyd, ed., *Jefferson Papers*, II, 49, 54. "The senate of Virginia is purely a *legislative* body," wrote St. George Tucker several decades

This difference of authority over money bills soon became a focal point for other Americans wrestling with the problem of distinguishing between the two houses of their various legislatures. Throughout the eighteenth century the colonial assemblies had fought long and hard against royal authority and the colonial councils to gain, like the House of Commons, the exclusive right to control money bills.[69] It was therefore understandable that their successors in the new republican states should have remained sensitive to any threats against this traditional right of the representatives of the people. Yet in the decade after Independence upper houses in Maryland, South Carolina, and New Jersey increasingly saw the peculiarity of the restrictions put on their power over money bills by the Revolutionary constitutions and stoutly resisted them, implicitly if not explicitly rejecting any analogy with the House of Lords.[70] In Massachusetts the upper house did more than protest; it actually overrode the Constitution.

In Massachusetts the confusion over the Senate's role in money bills was complicated by the upper chamber's designation as the representative of the property of the state, a designation that may have contributed to the strengthening of the Senate's authority over financial matters in the second proposed Constitution of 1780. For while the rejected 1778 Constitution had followed English practice in allowing the upper house only the power to approve or reject money bills as a whole, the 1780 Constitution

---

later; "they are chosen immediately by the people, in the same manner as their delegates; they have perfectly the same common interest with their constituents, and with the delegates in every respect. Why then not *originate* any bill, nor alter an *iota* of a money-bill?" St. George Tucker, ed., *Blackstone's Commentaries: With Notes of Reference, to the Constitution and Laws, of the Federal Government of the United States; and of the Commonwealth of Virginia* (Phila., 1803), I, Pt. 1, appendix, 111.

69. Greene, *Quest for Power*, Chap. III; Edward McCrady, *The History of South Carolina under the Royal Government, 1719–1776* (N. Y., 1899), 169, 176, 181, 281–86; Lincoln, *Constitutional History of New York*, I, 445–47. North Carolina was the only state in 1776 that made no distinction between the two houses' rights over money bills. Cf. above, n. 64. Although the New York Constitution of 1777 said nothing about the Senate's role in money matters, the lower house in 1778–79 attempted to limit the Senate's authority to originate and amend money bills, an attempt which the upper house successfully withstood. Jackson T. Main, *The Upper House in Revolutionary America, 1763–1788* (Madison, Wis., 1967), 140.

70. Rowland, *Carroll*, II, 62–64, 92; S. C. Senate Journals, Mar. 21, 22, 1785, Mar. 14, 15, 17, 25, 1787; Farrand, ed., *Records of the Federal Convention*, I, 234, 527; Main, *Upper House*, 107–08, 118, 147.

granted the Senate the power to amend but not the power to originate money bills. However, even this restriction proved too much for the Senate. Almost immediately after the establishment of the new Constitution of 1780 the Senate began usurping the exclusive constitutional authority of the House of Representatives to originate money bills. By 1783 the issue came to a head, and after long wrangles between the two branches the House of Representatives was compelled to admit, sixty-two out of ninety-five representatives agreeing, to the Senate's nearly unanimous claim of equality with the lower house in the initiating of money bills. In 1785 the Senate, piqued by the executive's sending a message on a money matter to only the House of Representatives and fearful that "the silence of the Senate on this subject might be construed as a relinquishment of the privilege," declared that "the said message ought to have been directed to both branches of the legislature" and reaffirmed "*the undoubted and acknowledged privilege of the Senate equally with the House of Representatives to originate grants of money*," notwithstanding the explicit prohibition of such a privilege in the Constitution.[71]

The anomaly of the Senate's constitutional disability had been clearly brought out earlier in 1778 by the town of Sutton. Confused by the inconsistency in the proposed Constitution of 1778 between the particular qualification of the Senate's electorate to those with sixty pounds clear estate (the suffrage for the lower house being open to all town taxpayers) and the limitations placed on the Senate's power over money bills, the town argued that "if men of no Property might vote for any part of the Legislature and not the whole; it ought to be that part of the Legislature which are under the greatest Restraints as to Money Bills Acts or Resolves." It just did not make sense to make the Senate the representative of property and then inhibit its authority to protect that property. The elimination of the property distinction between the electorates of the two houses in the Constitution of 1780 did not help matters, but indeed by accentuating the similarity of the two houses made the Senate's position even more bewildering. The truth was, as Benjamin Lincoln argued in 1785, Massachusetts's daring attempt to reformulate the theory of mixed government by distinguishing between persons and property was not working properly. Despite the avowed intention of

71. Robert C. Pitman, *Can the Senate of Massachusetts Originate Grants of Money?* (Boston, 1869), 6–11, in the Massachusetts Historical Society.

the Massachusetts Constitution, the senators could not represent
the property of the state but could really represent only the persons of the particular districts who voted for them. The houses
consequently were too much alike: "a body intended to check
the encroachment of the people are chosen and appointed by the
very men they are instituted to control."[72]

Lincoln in effect was saying, as Jefferson had apprehended in
1776, that no governmental body, whatever its constitutional
function, could represent more than the will of its electors, a conclusion about the nature of American politics being reached by
others in the 1780's. "If a senator, as in Delaware, stands on the
election of only the same district as a deputy," said Ezra Stiles
in 1783, "the Upper House is only the repetition of the lower."
The same was true of New Jersey: it had a "Legislature of one
order only; for although in Jersey it seemeth otherwise, yet that
interest which will determine a vote in one, will determine it in
both Houses." Such beliefs led logically not to a republican rein-
carnation of the House of Lords but to the conclusion repeatedly
expressed by William Gordon in the late 1770's. "However
some in time past might be of the mind that the General Court
should have consisted only of a House of Representatives, the
people in common are now fully convinced, that the two legislative branches are more eligible, and suited to the perpetuating
of liberty than one." But this acceptance of bicameralism did not
signify that the people endorsed any sort of theory of mixed government. For "it should be observed," said Gordon, "that the
Senate will be as much a representative body as the House of Assembly"—a title for the lower branch "more proper than 'House
of *Representatives.*'"[73]

8. A DOUBLE REPRESENTATION OF THE PEOPLE

All of these expressions of confusion and distortion of the role
of the senates in America were sporadic, lacking continuity and

72. Return of Sutton, May 18, 1778, Handlin, eds., *Popular Sources*, 232;
Boston *Independent Chronicle*, Dec. 29, 1785.

73. Stiles, *United States Elevated*, Thornton, ed., *Pulpit*, 420; Boston *New
England Chronicle*, Sept. 5, 1776; Boston *Independent Chronicle*, Mar. 27, 1777,
Apr. 9, 1778; Boston *Continental Journal*, Apr. 9, 1778. See also Madison's Ob-
servations on Jefferson's Draft of a Constitution for Virginia (1788), Boyd, ed.,
Jefferson Papers, VI, 308–10, 316.

fullness of development. Their influence however was not unimportant, as men's minds were changed all the more easily by the disconnectedness and unknowingness of the changes. Yet in one state the development of ideas was clear, continuous, and unmistakable in its direction. Pennsylvania was the only state which consciously and deliberately rejected the mixed polity and which at the same time possessed a sizable and articulate opposition compelled to defend comprehensively, as no other Americans quite had to do, the merits of a mixed republic. The result was the most lengthy and expanded argument over the nature of the upper house in American history, an argument that began with the traditional defense of the mixed British constitution and ended with an entirely new and revolutionary conception of politics.

The spirited defense of the British monarchy and its mixed form in the Philadelphia press throughout the spring of 1776 by those at odds with the Revolution—Charles Inglis, James Chalmers, and William Smith—immediately left those Whigs who favored resistance to English tyranny but who were violently opposed to the democratic Constitution of 1776 peculiarly vulnerable to charges of Toryism and of a desire to create aristocratic distinctions in the society. "Once grant that a government by Kings, Lords and Commons, is without exception, in all states and circumstances, the best of all possible governments, and then, certainly we can have no rational objection to a convenient number of Lords being created in America." No matter that the opponents of unicameralism in the fall of 1776 wanted their proposed upper house to incorporate not a traditional hereditary aristocracy but only the wisdom of the natural elite of the society. The difference seemed so clear to the anti-Constitutionalists, yet so difficult to put into words that would satisfy a people who seemed particularly sensitive about equality. Bold public expression of the view that the senate embodied any sort of aristocracy —natural or not—was liable to misinterpretation or to political manipulation by discontented or socially and politically aspiring groups. Had not the members of the Pennsylvania Convention that framed the Constitution called a legislative council "a House of Lords and twenty other unpopular names" in order to frighten the people? Had not the Pennsylvania radicals exhorted the people against electing educated gentlemen? warning them, "you will have an Aristocracy, or Government of the Great, if improper Persons are to form your Constitution," for they would inevitably frame "Distinctions in Society" and create a negative on the people's will.[74]

In 1777 Benjamin Rush, in the most comprehensive criticism of the Pennsylvania Constitution of 1776, categorically denied that the Republicans' proposal for an upper house in Pennsylvania meant foisting a House of Lords on the people. The English nobility, he argued, had no "application in the present controversy." The House of Lords derived its power from the Crown, not from the people, and possessed privileges which did not belong to the House of Commons. No wonder then the Lords consulted their own interests in preference to those of the people. But in Pennsylvania, said Rush, the case was different; the Republicans wanted an upper house "with *no one* exclusive privilege, and we disclaim every idea of their possessing the smallest degree of power, but what is derived from the *annual* suffrages of the People." A body so chosen could have only the happiness of its constituents as an object. It was ridiculous to argue that a compound legislature would create an aristocratical power in the community. "Who would believe," asked Rush in questions that were filled with significance that he scarcely perceived, "that the same fountain of pure water should send forth, at the same time, wholesome and deadly streams? Are not the Council and Assembly both formed alike by the *annual* breath of the people?"

Rush, however, had no intention of repudiating the traditional conception of the mixed polity. In answering the Constitutionalists' argument "that there is but one rank of men in America, and therefore, that there should be only one representation of them in a government," Rush admitted that America had "no artificial distinctions of men into noblemen and commoners"; but he contended that superior degrees of ability and energy had produced inequalities of property among Americans, and "these have introduced natural distinctions of rank in Pennsylvania, as certain and general as the artificial distinctions of men in Europe." Indeed, said Rush, an upper house was necessary in order to isolate the rich and to enable the middling people to collect "their *whole* strength . . . against the influence of wealth."

Rush's attack on the Pennsylvania Constitution was many-sided, and he offered several diverse justifications for the necessity of an upper house in the legislature. One of these assorted

74. Phila. *Pa. Packet*, Apr. 22, Nov. 26, 1776.

arguments, however, was to gain in time a special, even a unique, importance in the Republicans' case against the Constitution of 1776. A single legislature, said Rush, was dangerous to liberty precisely because it was unrestrained. The supporters of a single house may have told the people that there could be no danger of its becoming tyrannical, since the representatives had to partake of all the burdens they laid upon their constituents. But what about all those examples in history, asked Rush, where even *"annual* Assemblies . . . refused to share with their constituents in the burdens which they had imposed upon them." With his prediction that a single unchecked assembly would become a frightening "arbitrary power" Rush was raising a bogey that could strike terror into the heart of a radical Whig. Power anywhere, even in the hands of the people's elected representatives, was dangerous to the people and their liberty. The Pennsylvania radicals themselves, after all, had written into their Constitution all sorts of curbs on the power of the legislature. "But why all these arguments in favor of checks for the Assembly?" asked Rush pointedly. Was there then not justification for another, more formidable and more effective, check on the Assembly? Was there not a Whiggish need for an upper house, "a double representation of the people," as Rush called it?[75]

Here were points buried in the jumble of Rush's arguments that the opponents of the Pennsylvania Constitution were to develop and sharpen to use against the Constitutionalists, forcing them intellectually onto the defensive. The Republicans began turning the radicals' own Whiggish thinking back upon them. By 1779 an address by the Republican Society, attributed to James Wilson, stated that the principal weakness of the 1776 Constitution was its vesting "the whole legislative authority in a single body without any controul." In the judging of law, argued Wilson, men had appeals from decisions; but in the making of law there was none. A single legislature naturally tended toward despotism, which fact the Constitution itself with its numerous checks on the Assembly apparently had recognized.[76]

Absent now from the anti-Constitutionalist argument was any reference to the upper house as an embodiment of a special social

75. [Benjamin Rush], *Observations upon the Present Government of Pennsylvania in Four Letters* (Phila., 1777), in Runes, ed., *Writings of Rush*, 61, 62, 63, 60, 65, 66, 68.

76. Phila. *Pa. Gazette*, Mar. 24, 1779. Timothy Matlack identified Wilson as the author of the address of the Republican Society. *Ibid.*, Mar. 31, 1779.

or intellectual group in the community. Any suggestion of this sort smelled too much of aristocracy. And it was on the charge of fomenting an aristocracy that the Republicans had felt most vulnerable. Not only had the Constitutionalists phrased the recent election issue over the Constitution in a simple question to the people: "Are you for a House of Lords or against one?" but they had told the people that the opponents of the Constitution were only "a junto of gentlemen in Philadelphia, who wished to trample upon the farmers and mechanics, to establish a wicked aristocracy, and to introduce a House of Lords, hoping to become members of it." Such a charge of plotting a House of Lords was false and absurd, said Wilson. The Republicans had no intention of setting up two distinct orders of men. "We disavow the injurious imputation: it is replete with malice and slander. May merit and the unbiassed voice of the people be the only titles to distinction ever known in Pennsylvania." Indeed the legislative Council chosen by the people was no more a House of Lords than was an assembly chosen by the people. The two houses, moreover, could never wrangle and deadlock. "The Council and Assembly," wrote Wilson on behalf of the Republicans, "would both draw their power from the same source—from the people, the fountain of all authority. They could not have opposite interests, which are the causes of frequent contests. As both would be dependent on the people, both would be cautious not to neglect or oppose the public welfare." This reply met the radicals' objection to the presence of clashing interests in a republican state. But what did it do to the theory of mixed government? The homogeneity of interests between the two houses here promoted by Wilson was precisely the deficiency of the American mixed governments that men like Jefferson and Madison were worried about. What then was the purpose of another house?

The upper house was in fact to be only a Whiggish rein on unchecked power. "Surely," said Wilson, "an Assembly and a Council, mutually controuled by each other, are less dangerous and have less resemblance to a despotic Aristocracy, than a single Assembly, without any constitutional controul." The checks on the single legislature provided in the 1776 Constitution were really inadequate; "for if the Assembly choose to disregard them, to whom shall we apply for relief?"[77] Such Republican arguments left the Constitutionalists hard pressed for an answer. Since the

77. Phila. *Pa. Gazette*, Mar. 24, 1779.

creation of the Constitution, its opponents had hammered at the
necessity of controlling the power of a single house, until by the
1780's the Republicans' entire justification for an upper house
had come to rest on the view that the Constitution and the people's
liberty could be preserved only "if the legislative power of the
State were divided between two branches, who might mutually
restrain and inform each other."[78] Because this Whiggish argument was the basis of all the Constitutionalists' thinking, it was
one they could hardly contest. At the outset of the polemics they
therefore conceded their opponents' premise and agreed with the
need for a check on the possible dangerous usurpations of a single
legislature. But what kind of check? "The enemies of the constitution," remarked one commentator, "wish to see the check
placed in the hands of a Council—the friends of the constitution
wish to see it in the hands of the people at large." Section 15 of
the Constitution, the right of the whole people to peruse and dis-
cuss all bills before they became law, became for the radicals a
justification for their omission of an upper house, and a peculiar
kind of defense—in terms of the mixed polity—of the 1776 Constitution. Pennsylvania, said one writer, now had no need for an
upper house, since by Section 15, "the whole State becomes its
own council, and every freeman in it is a counsellor, and the
negative lies in the whole body politic, and not in a few grandees."
This sort of council of the people was "as much to be preferred
to the legislative council of these gentlemen, as the wisdom and
virtue of the whole State is to be preferred to that of twenty or
thirty of our gentry."

This argument outraged the proponents of an upper house.
Section 15, they said, was only a ridiculous contrivance to avoid
the obvious need for another branch in the legislature, and only
made the single assembly "indeed supreme and absolute." Such
supposed discussion among the people would never truly express
the sense of the people, since only the persons who frequented
public houses where the laws were posted would participate.
"Taverns and beer houses," said the Republicans contemptuously,
"were to form the second branch of our legislature." Because their
opinions could never be gathered in this absurd way, the people
out of necessity must elect delegates to express their will. There-

78. Phila. *Pa. Journal*, June 19, 1784. See also the 1784 report of the first session of the Council of Censors dominated by the Republicans. *Conventions of
1776 and 1790*, 69–70.

fore, "would not" an upper house composed of members elected from each county "be properly the representatives?" There would then be two houses equally representing the people.[79]

When in the arguments of the Republicans the upper house became merely a device to check an otherwise unrestrained legislative power, it lost at the same time its embodiment of any kind of aristocracy in the society. Indeed, as Arthur St. Clair, a leading Republican, insisted in 1784, "It is because I abhor every species of aristocracy, that I object to a single branch in a legislature." The proposed upper house, he told the people, "will be your representatives, the breath of your nostrils ... chosen by you from amongst yourselves, without distinction either in the electors or elected." The proposed legislative Council was to be merely another kind of representation of the people, a "double representation" of the people as many had come to call it. "A Citizen of Pennsylvania" writing in the *Pennsylvania Journal* of July 7, 1784, carried this line of thinking into unmistakable clarity. He began, as all defenders of bicameralism in Pennsylvania were now doing, by denying any desire of introducing "an aristocracy" or "a House of Lords," and by claiming that a unicameral legislature held greater danger "to liberty from an aristocracy" than "a different distribution of power." He proposed to divide the present total representation of the people in half, delegating half to each house of the legislature. The qualifications of the electors and the elected would be identical for both houses. "The powers of these two bodies," he argued, were "to be the same, except the originating of money bills [was to] be reserved to the House of Representatives; tho' this ... seems not necessary in this plan, where the two bodies are to be chosen *at the same time*, and in the *same manner*, by *the same persons*, and when *their numbers will be so nearly the same*."[80]

For the Pennsylvania Republicans the justification of an upper house no longer had any relation to the incorporation of an aristocracy, whether of talent or of wealth. Rather the two houses were designed only to prevent hasty, impetuous action, both branches "endeavouring to justify their conduct in the judgment of their constituents upon whom they are equally dependent."[81]

79. Phila. *Pa. Packet*, Nov. 26, 1776; Phila. *Pa. Journal*, Mar. 12, 26, 1777; Phila. *Pa. Packet*, Oct. 15, 1776.
80. Phila. *Pa. Journal*, Feb. 14, 1784; Phila. *Pa. Gazette*, Feb. 11, 1784; Phila. *Pa. Journal*, July 7, 1784.
81. Phila. *Pa. Journal*, July 7, 1784.

Their interests were to be identical since they flowed from the same source. Indeed, the Republicans in their polemics had stressed and praised the homogeneity of interests between the proposed two branches—a homogeneity which other Americans had anxiously identified as the principal fault in America's bicameral system. In order to justify the existence of an upper house, the Republicans had been compelled by the exigencies of Pennsylvania politics to disavow completely the traditional social foundations of mixed government.

Although the future clarification of American politics lay in this direction, most men in the 1780's only vaguely glimpsed where their thinking about the senates was taking them. The model of the British constitution and the presumed social basis of the mixed polity still remained strong. Everywhere men spent "their important time in disputing the distinct privileges, or determining with mathematical exactness, the peculiar rights of each house"; and everywhere they felt compelled to affirm that they were "no longer under the British constitution," and to demonstrate, "from our former prejudices in favor of it, and from the idea, almost become universal, of its perfection," that it was "a tyranny, a jumble of contradictions, and an incongruity with the law of nature." While many therefore found it difficult to divest themselves of "inculcated prejudices" in favor of the British mixed system, ultimately not even the strongest senate in America could resist the intellectual momentum that often indeliberately and unevenly but relentlessly carried men into a new conception of their upper houses.[82]

No senate in all of the states was more favorably regarded by those who clung desperately to the traditional meaning of the mixed government than that of Maryland. With its small membership, its five-year term of office, and its unique indirect method of election by an electoral college, it seemed to many to be the most successful republican expedient for accomplishing the end of a hereditary nobility in a balanced constitution. For James Madison, writing in *The Federalist*, the Maryland Senate by itself appeared to be giving the Maryland Constitution "a reputation in which it will probably not be rivalled by that of any State in the Union." It was therefore especially appropriate that the position of the

---

82. Trenton *N.-J. Gazette*, Mar. 4, 1778, Nelson *et al.*, eds., *New Jersey Archives*, 2d Ser., II, 89; *Rudiments of Law and Government*, xiii; [Tucker], *Conciliatory Hints*, 16, 23.

Maryland Senate should have been cogently challenged in the 1780's. Indeed, in no state was the ambiguous place of the upper house in the American republics brought into more dramatic focus than in Maryland on the eve of the federal Constitutional Convention.[83]

As early as 1777, Daniel of St. Thomas Jenifer, one of Maryland's fifteen senators, had warned of the precarious nature of Maryland's aristocratic Senate. He questioned first whether, because of "so many gradations and Exclusions," enough men of superior abilities could be found to run the government. The Senate, moreover, did "not appear . . . to be a Child of the people at Large, and therefore will not be Supported by them longer than there subsists the most perfect Union between the different Legislative branches." How long harmony could be preserved, said Jenifer, was anyone's guess. "The two houses are composed of 89 members, 8 of whom have it in their power to counteract 81. Will they submit?"[84]

The issue was faced early in 1787. The Maryland Senate had turned down a series of paper money bills passed by the lower house. The House of Delegates in a formal appeal then urged the people at large to make their sense known on the money emissions "to both branches of the legislature." The lower house argued that both houses of the legislature were bound by the instructions of the people whenever they pleased to give them. "On a diversity in sentiment between us and the senate," the delegates told the people, "you alone are to decide, and to you only can there be any appeal."[85] This remarkable action was to raise the most significant constitutional debate of the entire Confederation period.

The Senate, realizing that a wrong step could lead to a constitutional disaster, made a cautious reply and anxiously pointed out the serious consequences of the unprecedented doctrine espoused by the House of Delegates. "Every man of reflection will readily perceive, if this practice should prevail, that the public

83. *The Federalist*, No. 63. On the celebration of the Maryland Senate see Ramsay, *American Revolution*, I, 445; Farrand, ed., *Records of the Federal Convention*, I, 27, 56, 218–19, II, 291; Jonathan Elliot, ed., *The Debates of the State Conventions, on the Adoption of the Federal Constitution* . . . (Washington, 1854), IV, 325; William Loughton Smith, *A Comparative View of the Constitutions of the Several States with Each Other, and with That of the United States* . . . (Phila., 1796), 15–16.

84. Quoted in Philip A. Crowl, *Maryland during and after the Revolution* (Baltimore, 1943), 39–40.

85. Baltimore *Maryland Journal*, Feb. 2, 1787.

business will no longer be conducted by a select legislature, consisting of two branches, equally free and independent, calmly deliberating and determining on the propriety of public measures." Since the delegates were more numerous and more dispersed throughout the state, they would obviously have a greater opportunity of influencing the people in drawing up instructions. "Once . . . appeal is made from the dictates of judgment to the voice of numbers," declared the Senate, that "freedom of discussion and decision" which the Constitution had explicitly intended for the upper house would be taken away. The senators secured their rear by a categorical denial that they had any interest separate from that of the people. The reelection of so many senators over the previous ten years, they stated, assured them that they must have the confidence of the people.[86]

Mild as the Senate's reply was, polemicists jumped on it as insidiously and subtly asserting that the Senate was "independent *of the people*, and not bound by their instructions *in any case*." The whole issue seemed dangerously close to getting out of hand. Petitions to be presented to the legislature had been circulating throughout all the counties, calling for a clear understanding once and for all of the position of the Senate in the government. "Since the Revolution, and the Establishment of our present Form of Government," declared the petition, "it cannot be questioned, that both Branches of our Legislature are the Representatives and Trustees of the People," and that from the political relation between representative and constituent, the representative must always speak and execute the sense of the constituent whenever it was collected and communicated to him.[87]

Samuel Chase, who by the 1780's had become something of a demagogue in Maryland, joined the popular side of the debate. "Both branches of our legislature," Chase argued, "derive *all* their power from the people, and *equally* hold their *commissions* to legislate, or make laws, from the *grant* of the people; and there is no difference between them but *only* in the *duration of their commission*. Their authority proceeds from the same source, and is co-equal, and co-extensive." The indirect method of electing the Senate made no difference in its political relation to the people. "*Both* branches," said Chase, "must be equally the *representatives, trustees*, and *servants* of the people, and the people are

86. *Ibid.*, Feb. 6, 1787.
87. *Ibid.*, Feb. 13, Jan. 23, 1787.

equally the *constituents* of both." The legislature was divided into
"*two* distinct bodies of men" only that they might "operate as
checks upon each other."[88]

These were new thoughts for Maryland, and they bore no
resemblance, as one writer pointed out, to the assumptions of the
framers of the Constitution, Samuel Chase included, who in 1776
had intended the Senate to represent "the aristocratical part of the
government."[89] No one, however, dared defend the Senate on
those grounds now. If the senators, said Thomas Stone, the drafter
of the Senate's reply to the House of Delegates, ever "set themselves in opposition to the great body of the people of this State,"
they would undoubtedly be "objects to be confined for insanity
[rather] than dreaded as tyrants." The supporters of the Senate
thus unfortunately but understandably avoided any probing discussion of the distinctive character of the upper house. They tacit-
ly admitted that the Senate was as representative of the people as
the lower house, and instead concentrated on the problem of instructions, denying that either branch of the legislature could be
commanded by the people. Consequently (as will be seen) the
debate which ran on for six months is perhaps more interesting
for its expression of shifting American views of representation.
Yet the wrangle had exposed the incongruity of a traditional upper house in the America of the 1780's. As one Maryland querist
put it, "If both branches of the legislature are co-equal, is not the
Senate then a nullity? Then why the institution?"[90]

It was a pointed question, and men continued to wrestle with
it while the federal Constitution was being created. Madison in
The Federalist was still trying to find a way of distinguishing the
two houses of the legislature from each other "by every circumstance which will consist with a due harmony in all proper measures, and with the genuine principles of republican government,"
for the advantage of bicameralism still seemed to be "in proportion to the dissimilarity in the genius of the two bodies." Yet the
genuine principles of republicanism were necessarily leading
others to disavow any suggestion of a different social basis for the
upper houses, and were in fact turning them into another kind of
representation of the people, often of course differently recruited,
and with their organization and tenure emphasizing stability and

88. *Ibid.*, Feb. 13, 1787.
89. *Ibid.*, Nov. 8, 1785, May 1, 1787.
90. *Ibid.*, Apr. 6, Feb. 23, May 1, 1787.

continuity, but with their existence justified publicly if not always privately almost solely in terms of a functional Whiggish division of mistrusted legislative power.[91] The apparent inability of the American people to distinguish readily their social elite only made the justification of the upper house easier for those who stressed the identity of interests between the two representative houses.

Moreover, the change in the meaning of the senates that Americans were making in these years could not be simply verbal, since it suggested a startling new conception of the people's relationship to the government—a relationship whose implications were often only dimly perceived even by those who described the senate as only another kind of representation of the people. Picturing the people as partaking equally in both branches of the legislature not only destroyed the conventional theory of mixed government but it necessarily involved a major adjustment in the conception of representation; for it was now somehow possible for the people, simply through the electoral process, to have two different agents speaking for them at the same time. Other developments in political thought were at work in these years that would not only make such an idea of "double representation" of the people intelligible but would in time fundamentally alter the Americans' understanding of politics.

91. *The Federalist*, No. 62. Cf. Pelatiah Webster, *A Dissertation on the Political Union and Constitution of the Thirteen United States* (Phila., 1783), 20: "These two houses will be governed by the same natural motives and interests, viz. the good of the commonwealth and the approbation of the people."

PART THREE

The People against the Legislatures

———————————

It has become absolutely necessary, that the "majority of persons" should be cautioned against acquiescing in the sentiment of placing implicit confidence in their Representatives.
—BENJAMIN AUSTIN, 1786

CHAPTER VII

Law and Contracts

1. WRITTEN AND UNWRITTEN LAW

As a result of the American Revolution, wrote Thomas Paine in his *Rights of Man*, a constitution had become "a political bible" for the Americans, possessed by every family and every member of the government. "Nothing was more common when any debate arose on the principle of a bill, or on the extent of any species of authority, than for the members to take the printed Constitution out of their pocket, and read the chapter with which such matter in debate was connected." It was as he had predicted in 1776: in America the law had become king.[1] But the development of the Americans' peculiar conception of a constitution was not as simple as Paine implied. Under the pressure of the debate with England in the 1760's and seventies the Americans had molded the basic form their ideas of a constitution would assume; yet the implications of the new ideas were only drawn in the years of actual constitution-making. The idolatry of a constitution that Paine expressed so nicely in 1791 was the product of a complicated series of changes in American thinking about politics that took place in the Revolutionary years, no one of which was isolated. The idea of a constitution revealed and clarified by 1776 was not only explored and expanded in the subsequent years but the metaphors and analogies that underlay the Americans' constitutional conceptions were radically altered as well—all contributing by the late 1780's to an often unsurely grasped but decisively new

1. Paine, *Rights of Man*, and *Common Sense*, Foner, ed., *Writings of Paine*, I, 378, 29.

interpretation of the character of constitutional restraints on political power.

So important to the imperial debate was the conception of a constitution that the word became by 1776 for Tories and Whigs alike "so little understood—so much perverted," so "bandied about without any determinate sense being affixed thereto," that it eventually seemed "absolutely necessary that we should have a new dictionary" to interpret it. It was during this controversy that the crucial divergence in the constitutional tradition of the English-speaking world was made.[2] By 1776 the Americans had produced out of the polemics of the previous decade a notion of a constitution very different from what eighteenth-century Englishmen were used to—a notion of a constitution that has come to characterize the very distinctiveness of American political thought. So enthralled have Americans become with their idea of a constitution as a written superior law set above the entire government against which all other law is to be measured that it is difficult to appreciate a contrary conception.

Although Englishmen in the seventeenth century had anticipated the American Revolutionary experience by creating a written constitution which was believed to be the foundation of the government, their experiment in constituting fundamental law had not been lasting. By the eighteenth century the growing sense of the omnipotence of Parliament had made the notion of a single written instrument of government creating and limiting the government decidedly obsolete. Although the idea of fundamental law or of natural law underlying all governmental actions and positive law was scarcely forgotten (Blackstone himself spoke of "the law of nature and the law of revelation" as the "two foundations" of all human law), by the last quarter of the eighteenth century it seemed clearer than ever before to most Englishmen that all such moral and natural law limitations on the Parliament were strictly theoretical, without legal meaning, and relevant only in so far as they impinged on the minds of the lawmakers.[3]

The English constitution therefore could not be any sort of fundamental law. Most eighteenth-century writers, from Boling-broke in 1733 to Charles Inglis, the American Tory, in 1776 (in almost identical terms) could not conceive of the constitution as

2. [Inglis], *True Interest of America*, 18; *Four Letters*, 18; Boston *Independent Chronicle*, Oct. 23, 1777. See Bailyn, *Ideological Origins*, 175–84.

3. Blackstone, *Commentaries*, I, 40–44. See in general John W. Gough, *Fundamental Law in English Constitutional History* (Oxford, 1961), Chaps. XI, XII.

anything anterior and superior to government and ordinary law, but rather regarded it as the government and ordinary law itself, as "*that assemblage of laws, customs and institutions which form the general system; according to which the several powers of the state are distributed, and their respective rights are secured to the different members of the community.*" The English constitution was not, as the Americans eventually came to see with condescension, committed to parchment. For Blackstone and for Englishmen generally there could be no distinction between the "constitution or frame of government" and the "system of laws." All were one: every act of Parliament was in a sense a part of the constitution, and all law, customary and statutory, was thus constitutional. "The constitution," wrote William Paley, that summarizer of common eighteenth-century English thought, "is one principal division, head, section, or title of the code of publick laws, distinguished from the rest only by the particular nature, or superiour importance of the subject, of which it treats. Therefore the terms *constitutional* and *unconstitutional*, mean *legal* and *illegal.*"[4]

It was precisely on this point that the Americans came to differ with the English. A major difficulty in the debate with England, said John Adams in 1773, lay in the "different ideas" men received "from the words *legally and constitutionally.*" However legal the actions of the Parliament in the 1760's and seventies were, that is, however much they conformed to the accepted way of making law, it seemed absurd to most American Whigs that such actions were thereby automatically constitutional, or in accord with those basic principles of right and justice that made the English constitution what it was. Security of life, liberty and property—"these," said Joseph Hawley in 1775, "were the fundamental, the explaining and controuling principles, which framed the constitution of Britain in its first stages, . . . and which have been her constant companions through all the mutilations and distortions she has suf-

---

4. [Inglis], *True Interest of America*, 18; Blackstone, *Commentaries*, I, 126; William Paley, *The Principles of Moral and Political Philosophy* (Phila., 1788), quoted in Wilson, "Lectures on Law," Wilson, ed., *Works of Wilson*, I, 310. On these points see Charles H. McIlwain, *Constitutionalism: Ancient and Modern*, 2d ed. (Ithaca, 1947), 3; Edward S. Corwin, *The "Higher Law" Background of American Constitutional Law* (Ithaca, 1959), 81; Ernest Barker, *Essays on Government* (Oxford, 1945), 126. The English constitution, wrote Noah Webster, was not a single document; "It consists rather of practice, or of common law, with some statutes of Parliament." "Government . . . ," *American Magazine*, 1 (1787–88), 77.

fered in her progress to the present rank she holds in the world."
Throughout the entire debate with England the colonists continually sought to define those "fundamental principles," those
"true, certain, and universal principles," and those "sacred Laws
of Justice" of the English constitution. The isolating of these fundamentals from the rest of the constitution was eventually what
marked the Americans' peculiar conception of a constitution, but
it was an isolation not easily achieved.[5]

As early as 1761, James Otis argued that the writs of assistance
were "against the fundamental Principles of Law." In fact, said
Otis, any act of Parliament "against the Constitution is void: an
Act against natural Equity is void," and the courts "must pass
such Acts into disuse." These were strong prophetic words that
were not forgotten. Yet, as has been nicely shown, Otis's position was not as modern as it sounds, and was indeed curiously
complicated, indicating just how indeliberately and haltingly the
Americans' eventual conception of constitutional restraints on
public power came into being. Otis in his forthright language of
1761 and later was not distinguishing between fundamental and
statutory law and measuring one against the other, thereby repudiating the traditional eighteenth-century conception of the English constitution. Indeed, as Otis's arguments unfolded in the
1760's, it became clear that far from rejecting the conventional
English understanding of a constitution, he was endorsing it with
as much vehemence as Englishmen themselves.[6]

Throughout all his mental wanderings in the 1760's Otis stead-
fastly identified, as strongly as Paley later did, constitutionality
with legality and continually assumed that English rights, government, laws, and constitution were all of a piece, all bound together
and "fixed in judgment, righteousness, and truth," permeated by
common principles of equity and justice and by a common respect
for the "natural, essential, inherent, and inseparable rights" of the
people, rights that "no man or body of men, not excepting the
Parliament, justly, equitably, and consistently with their own

5. *Boston Gazette*, Feb. 8, 1773, in Adams, ed., *Works of John Adams*, III, 556;
Boston *Mass. Spy*, Feb. 16, 1775; [Adams], "Novanglus" (1775), Adams, ed.,
Works of John Adams, IV, 60, 88; Rossiter, *Seedtime of the Republic*, 270;
[Nicholas], *Considerations*, Swem, ed., *Virginia and the Revolution*, 66. See
Ernest Barker, "Natural Law and the American Revolution" in his *Traditions of
Civility* (Oxford, 1948), 263–355.
6. Josiah Quincy, Jr., *Reports of Cases Argued and Adjudged in the Superior
Court of Judicature of . . . Massachusetts Bay, between 1761 and 1772* (Boston,
1865), 471, 474. For an explanation of Otis's complexity and apparent inconsis-
tency see Bailyn, ed., *Pamphlets*, I, 100–03, 106–07, 121–23, 409–17, 546–52.

rights and the constitution can take away." Yet as fundamental as Otis believed these principles and rights were, he never conceived their being so fundamental that they had to be differentiated and separated from the institutions of government and the ordinary statutes of Parliament. Indeed, such principles and rights were dependent upon and protected by the very workings of the government, particularly Parliament, the bulwark of popular liberty. Acts of Parliament could never be set in opposition to the adjudications and procedures of the common law courts; they were identified with them. The custom and principles of the common law were therefore not restrictive of Parliament's power but were "subordinate and controulable at pleasure of, and created, for the most part, by, parliament." Since the rights of Englishmen and the principles of the constitution were "part of the common law" and since "the greatest part of what is now called common law, is held by the sages to have been originally enacted by parliament," it was logically impossible for the power of Parliament to work against the constitution or the rights of the colonists; for " 'tis from and under this very power and its acts, and from the common law, that the political and civil rights of the colonists are derived."[7]

Basic to all of Otis's beliefs and what made his seemingly contradictory remarks in the 1760's intelligible was his old-fashioned, even medieval, presumption that the whole purpose of law, if it would be truly law, was the preservation of men's rights and that all judgments in all courts, including the highest court of Parliament, would always attempt to interpret the law so as to do justice for all men. By viewing law not as the enacted will of the legislature but more in the nature of a judgment declaratory of the moral principles of the law by the high court of Parliament ("the supreme judicature") that must be inherently just and equitable—as determined and construed by the artificial reason of the common law that animated all courts—Otis could see no need to deny the obvious legal supremacy of Parliament. It was true, said Otis, quoting Jeremiah Dummer, former Massachusetts agent, from a pamphlet written in 1721, that " 'the legislative power is absolute and unaccountable, and King, Lords, and Commons may do what they please; but the question here is not about *power* but *right*' (or rather equity) 'and shall not the su-

7. Otis, *Rights of the British Colonies*, in Bailyn, ed., *Pamphlets*, I, 456, 444, 475, 466, 443; [James Otis], *Brief Remarks on the Defence of the Halifax Libel on the British-American-Colonies* (Boston, 1765), in Mullett, ed., *Writings of Otis*, 165.

preme judicature of all the nation do right?'" In fact, "'what the Parliament cannot do justly they cannot do at all'"; the intrinsic workings of the institutions of government would see to it. "If the reasons that can be given against an act are such as plainly demonstrate that it is against *natural* equity, the executive courts will adjudge such act void," just as Coke had done in the previous century, not because such an act violated some fundamental higher law separated from and set over the government, but because such an act, being "contrary to eternal truth, equity, and justice," would not really be law and would be declared so by the courts, including the highest court of all, "the Parliament itself when convinced of their mistake." Therefore, to say that Parliament was "absolute" was not to say that "Parliament might make itself arbitrary, which it is conceived it cannot by the constitution." Indeed, "it would be a most manifest contradiction. ... The Parliament cannot make 2 and 2, 5: omnipotency cannot do it. The supreme power in a state is *jus dicere* only: *jus dare*, strictly speaking, belongs only to GOD." Parliament therefore only interpreted and declared the existing law as preserved in the law reports and precedents of the common law; it would not actually create new law.[8]

By the middle of the eighteenth century, in the face of Parliament's sovereign power ("if the parliament will positively enact a thing to be done which is unreasonable," wrote Blackstone, "I know of no power that can control it"), Otis's position, to say the least, was a difficult one to maintain, a remarkable attempt to apply the assumptions of previous centuries of English jurisprudence, particularly as they had lingered in the mind of Coke, to the new age of Blackstone. Otis's fellow Americans, more keenly aware of the altered political and constitutional circumstances of the eighteenth century, could not fully accept his presumption that law had to be intrinsically just and reasonable in order to be law. To many Americans, particularly by the late sixties and early seventies when the British argument was reinforced by the publication of Blackstone's *Commentaries*, it became more and

8. Otis, *Rights of the British Colonies*, Bailyn, ed., *Pamphlets*, I, 466, 449, 454, 450, 446, 454. See Bailyn's discussion (pp. cited in n. 6) on which these paragraphs are based. Bailyn's account is very much indebted to the interpretation of Coke and of medieval jurisprudence by Samuel E. Thorne, in his "The Constitution and the Courts: A Re-Examination of the Famous Case of Dr. Bonham," in Read, ed., *Constitution Reconsidered*, 15–24; and in his edition of *A Discourse upon the Exposicion and Understandinge of Statutes* (San Marino, 1942). See the discussion in Gough, *Fundamental Law*, Chaps. II–III; also Pocock, *Ancient Constitution*, 35–37, 173–77.

more obvious that law was something more than a judgment, more than simply the acts of a supreme court that could be interpreted, adjusted, or voided by other courts when required by the principles of reason and equity that supposedly adhered in all law. Parliament, as events, the British debate, and Blackstone had made evident, was no longer simply the highest court among others in the land, but had in truth become the sovereign lawmaker of the realm, whose power, however arbitrary and unreasonable, was uncontrollable. Parliament could now actually create new law whose binding force came not from its intrinsic justice and conformity to the principles of the common law, but from its embodiment of the will of the social constituents of the nation or from simply its sovereign authority. This new parliamentary law was now, as it had not been in medieval times, considered to be manifestly distinct and separate from the customary common law, whose binding force came not from enactment but, as Blackstone said, from long and immemorial usage preserved in the law books and court decisions from ancient times.[9]

There were essentially then two kinds of law in the eighteenth century, written and unwritten, both equally binding, but for very different reasons. They could in fact, as most Americans but not Otis believed, be set in opposition to one another. It was Parliament's attempts in the 1760's and seventies, as Jefferson said, "to make law where they found none, and to submit us at one stroke to a whole system no particle of which has it's foundation in the Common law" that Americans were resisting. To Jefferson and to others it was obvious that acts of Parliament, although law, were not declaratory of the ancient principles of the common law. The common law in fact was no longer any part of Parliament's preserve, "for we know that the Common law is that system of law which was introduced by the Saxons on their settlement in England, and altered from time to time by proper legislative authority from that to the date of the Magna charta which terminates the period of the Common law, or *Lex non scripta*, and commences that of the Statute law, or *Lex scripta*."[10]

Such a sharp and rigid dichotomy between custom and statute,

9. Blackstone, *Commentaries*, I, 91, 67. See Gough, *Fundamental Law*, 21, 27, Chap. XI.

10. Chinard, ed., *Commonplace Book*, 354. See [Richard Bland], *The Colonel Dismounted . . .* (Williamsburg, 1764), in Bailyn, ed., *Pamphlets*, I, 321; Blackstone, *Commentaries*, I, 67–70, 85–86; Tucker, ed., *Blackstone's Commentaries*, I, pt. 1, appdx., 386–87; Wilson, "Lectures on Law," Wilson, ed., *Works of Wilson*, II, 37–38, 43–44.

unwritten and written law, was thoroughly modern, and came to correspond in American thought with the distinction between constitutional and legal. If the arbitrary actions of the Crown and the Parliament could not be restrained from violating the fundamental principles and rights embedded in the ancient common law and the constitution by the inner workings of the institutions of government, then somehow these principles and rights must be protected and guaranteed by lifting them out of the government. "Something must exist in a free state, which no part of it can be authorised to alter or destroy, otherwise the idea of a constitution cannot subsist." The English bill of rights and acts of settlement confirming the liberties of the people were, it was true, only statutes of Parliament, but they were "undoubtedly of a nature more sacred than those which established a turnpike road." It seemed inconceivable that the liberties of the people should depend "upon nothing more permanent or established than the vague, rapacious, or interested inclination of a majority of five hundred and fifty eight men, open to the insidious attacks of a weak or designing Prince, and his ministers." And yet their English ancestors had apparently made no provision for limiting the power of the people's representatives, probably because "they never imagined that the representative could ever possess an interest distinct from that of his constituent, or that pecuniary advantage could outweigh the public good in his breast."[11]

Under the pressure of events in the 1760's and seventies, many Americans were determined to provide for the protection of these fundamental rights and moved, as their English ancestors had in the seventeenth century, toward a definition of a constitution as something distinct from and superior to the entire government including even the legislative representatives of the people. It seemed clear, as Samuel Adams wrote in the Massachusetts Circular Letter of 1768, "that in all free States the Constitution is fixed; and as the supreme Legislative derives its Power and Authority from the Constitution, it cannot overleap the Bounds of it without destroying its own foundation." Indeed, if the people were to be truly free they must "fix on certain regulations, which if we please we may call a *constitution*, as the standing measure of the proceedings of government." With this kind of clarification the basic principles were being taken out of the complex array

11. *The Crisis, Number XI* (N. Y., [1775]), 81–87. See [Hulme], *Historical Essay*, 141–47.

of institutions, laws and rights that made up the English constitution and being considered "only as a line which marks out the enclosure." So "that not a single point may be subject to the least ambiguity," it was important that these principles, "the fundamental Pillars of the Constitution should be comprised in one act or instrument." To devout Whigs "vague and uncertain laws, and more especially constitutions, are the very instruments of slavery." Magna Carta, after all, said Samuel Adams, had been "very explicit." Power could be limited only "by some certain terms of agreement." Expressly written documents were the best security against "the danger of an indefinite dependence upon an undetermined power."[12]

By 1776 the emerging logic of separating principles from government, constitutional from legal, seemed conclusive to some. "A Constitution, and a form of government," wrote the anonymous Pennsylvania author of *Four Letters on Interesting Subjects*, "are frequently confounded together, and spoken of as synonimous things; whereas they are not only different, but are established for different purposes: All countries have some form of government, but few, or perhaps none, have truly a Constitution." The English certainly had none, for the people had given up all their power to the legislature, allowing whatever it enacted to be both legal and constitutional. They had no constitution "which says to the legislative powers, 'Thus far shalt thou go, and no farther.' " By October 1776 the town of Concord, Massachusetts, had fully described this emerging conception. "A Constitution in its proper Idea intends a System of Principles Established to Secure the Subject In the Possession and enjoyment of their Rights and Privileges, against any Encroachments of the Governing Part," including even "the Supreme Legislature."[13]

It is not coincidence that the clearest, most advanced thinking was expressed by groups in those areas where confidence in the existing legislative assemblies was weakest, since their defini-

12. Mass. House of Representatives to the Speakers of Other Houses of Representatives, Feb. 11, 1768, Cushing, ed., *Writings of Samuel Adams*, I, 185; Charles Turner, *A Sermon Preached before His Excellency Thomas Hutchinson* . . . (Boston, 1773), 16; Samuel Cooke, *A Sermon Preached at Cambridge* . . . *May 30th, 1770* . . . (Boston, 1770), in Thornton, ed., *Pulpit*, 160–61; Albemarle County Instructions concerning the Virginia Constitution (1776), Boyd, ed., *Jefferson Papers*, VI, 286–87; "Candidus," Feb. 3, 1776, Cushing, ed., *Writings of Samuel Adams*, III, 262. See Bailyn, *Ideological Origins*, 181–84.

13. *Four Letters*, 18–19; Return of Concord, Oct. 22, 1776, Handlin, eds., *Popular Sources*, 153.

tion of a constitution as a "*sett of fundamental rules* by which even the supreme power of the state shall be governed," legislature as well as executive, was compelled by a pervading suspicion of all governmental authority set above the people, including their elected representatives—a suspicion that was not fully comprehended by all Americans in 1776, thus producing variations and confusion in their attempts to create their new constitutions. It was clear to Americans in 1776 that "all constitutions should be contained in some written Charter," as their remarkable constitution-writing experience demonstrated. But it was not yet clear to many what these written charters actually represented or against what kind of political power they were to be directed.[14]

2. The Contract of Rulers and Ruled

Like all Englishmen the colonists were familiar with written documents as barriers to encroaching power. "Anxious to preserve and transmit" their liberties "unimpaired to posterity," the English people had repeatedly "caused them to be reduced to writing, and in the most solemn manner to be recognized, ratified and confirmed," first by King John, then Henry III and Edward I, and "afterwards by a multitude of corroborating acts, reckoned in all, by Lord Cook, to be thirty-two, from Edw. 1st. to Hen. 4th. and since, in a great variety of instances, by the bills of right and acts of settlement."[15] Moreover, America's own past was filled with written charters to which the colonists had continually appealed in imperial disputes—charters or grants from the Crown which by the time of the Revolution had taken on an extraordinary importance in American eyes.

By 1775 or earlier the colonists' various historical charters, royal, corporate, and proprietary, had become transformed into what, "from their subject matter and the reality of things, can only operate as the evidence of a compact between an English King and the American subjects." This was the most prominent, although not the only contractual image of the day—that of a mutual bargain between two parties drawn from the legal and mercantile world, more specifically, the political agreement between ruler and people in which protection and allegiance be-

14. Demophilus, *Genuine Principles*, 4; *Four Letters*, 15.
15. [Mather], *America's Appeal*, 8–9.

came the considerations. Back in the seventeenth century the Americans' ancestors in each colony "either before, or soon after their emigration, entered into particual compacts with the Kings of England," involving their several forms of government which were "by charters, royal proclamations, and the laws and regulations in each colony . . . made by the mutual consent of the King and the People."[16] These charters were not franchises or grants from the Crown that could be unilaterally recalled or forfeited, as the Tories claimed: "Their running in the stile of a grant is mere matter of form and not of substance." They were reciprocal agreements, "made and executed between the King of England, and our predecessors," and like Magna Carta, they were the recognition, not the source, of the people's liberties. Their charters had become for Americans the way to bring the English constitution into view, "to reduce to a certainty the rights and privileges we were entitled to" and "to point out and circumscribe the prerogatives of the crown," so that "these prerogatives are as much limited and confined in the colonies as they are in England."[17]

This contract between rulers and people was an impressive image, and the Whig theory of politics was built upon it, even though such a notion of a legal bargain borrowed from the mercantile world assumed a mutuality of interests and good will between the parties that the most radical Whigs doubted existed. Although the prerogatives of the magistracy derived originally from the people, when the people consented to the compact "the Power they had once, is given away, so long as that Union continues"; and the prerogatives of the magistracy became as much its right as the privileges reserved by the people were theirs. The compact like any legal bargain thereby bound the people to respect these prerogatives and "to yield all due obedience to their civil rulers, both supreme and subordinate," as long as the terms of the contract were in effect. The rulers on their part were obliged to secure the people in their rights and to promote only the public good. When the magistracy perverted the proper end of government for its own selfish ends, it then broke the con-

16. Worcester *Mass. Spy*, Apr. 6, 1775; Phila. *Pa. Packet*, June 12, 1775. On the notion of a contract between rulers and ruled see Leonard Krieger, *The Politics of Discretion: Pufendorf and the Acceptance of Natural Law* (Chicago, 1965), 121. On the emergence of a new contractual theory of political obligation see John Gough, *The Social Contract: A Critical Study of Its Development*, 2d ed. (Oxford, 1957), 135, 147–63.

17. Adams and [Leonard], *Novanglus and Massachusettensis*, 194; Worcester *Mass. Spy*, Feb. 23, Apr. 6, 1775.

tract and released the people from their duty of obedience, throwing both parties back into a state of nature.[18]

Clumsy as this contractual conception was, it made comprehensible the always perplexing problem of obedience by the ruled to the rulers. Obedience by the people to acts of the legislature was explicable in terms of consent, because the people presumably participated in the legislature and thereby bound themselves to the laws. But obedience to the prerogative acts of the rulers involved no such consent and needed some other justification, which the notion of contract supplied. This is why, for example, John Dickinson in his *Letters from a Farmer in Pennsylvania* argued that Americans could constitutionally accept the royal governor's suspension of the New York legislature through the legal act of his prerogative, but that they could never accept such a suspension by act of Parliament, for that "gives the suspension a consequence vastly more affecting," involving a legislative action to which the New York colonists had not consented. This distinction and the contractual image that accompanied it helped contribute to the Americans' notion, reached by 1774, that they were distinct peoples related solely to the Crown in a "private bargain" to which the British people and their Parliament were "total strangers," even though "they have in some instances strangely intermedled." Finally, the contractual notion explained, however crudely, the right of the people to throw off oppressive rulers who had broken the agreement. Everyone in the eighteenth century knew that the English had justified their Glorious Revolution by a violation of the assumed contract by James II. And by 1776 Americans had in a like way come to describe their Revolution as resulting from a similar break in "the original contract between king and people." "The King by withdrawing his protection and levying war upon us, has discharged us of our allegiance, and of all obligations to obedience: For protection and subjection are mutual, and cannot subsist a part."[19]

18. *Essay upon Government*, 109; Foster, *Short Essay on Civil Government*, 37, also 70. See Noble, *Some Strictures*, 21–22; [Wilson], *Considerations*, and Wilson, "Speech Delivered in the Convention," in Wilson, ed., *Works of Wilson*, III, 241, 261; [Adams], "Novanglus," Adams, ed., *Works of John Adams*, IV, 16, 84, 128.

19. [Dickinson], *Letters from a Farmer*, Ford, ed., *Writings of Dickinson*, 310; Boston *Mass. Spy*, Feb. 23, 1775; William Henry Drayton, Charge to the Grand Jury, Charleston, Apr. 23, 1776, Niles, ed., *Principles*, 332; [Mather], *America's Appeal*, 68–69. See also McRee, *Life of Iredell*, I, 351; Whitaker, *Antidote against Toryism*, 17–18.

With the deep impression this contractual image had on their minds it is not surprising that the Americans carried it into their constitution-making in 1776, since Independence and republicanism had not substantially altered the problems of politics as the Whigs saw them. "The origin of all civil government, justly established," said Hamilton in 1775, "must be a voluntary compact, between the rulers and the ruled." God had ordained for all people "that there shall be magistracy among them; and when a Community have, regularly and orderly settled this authority upon particular men, they have a divine right to execute just that authority over the people, that is thus committed into their hands, but no more." It was thus still necessary "that certain great first principles be settled and established, determining and bounding the power and prerogative of the ruler, ascertaining and securing the rights and liberties of the subjects, as the foundation stamina of the government; which in all civil states is called the constitution, on the certainty and permanency of which, the rights of both the ruler and the subjects depend."[20] Although the constitutions were now to be firmly fixed and established, they were still identified in the minds of many with their old colonial charters, as contracts between magistrates and people, defining and delimiting the powers and rights of each. It is in the context of this contractual image that the Americans' sporadic and confused adoption of bills of rights can best be seen.

Because many believed that the people's liberties, trial by jury, liberty of conscience, security against arbitrary imprisonment, freedom of the press, "in short, all the great rights which man never mean, nor ever ought, to lose, should be *guaranteed*, not *granted*, by the Constitution," five states in 1776— Virginia, Pennsylvania, Maryland, Delaware, and North Carolina—prefaced these rights to their constitutions in a jarring but exciting combination of ringing declarations of universal principles with a motley collection of common law procedures in order to fence them off from the rulers' power.[21] Yet precisely because the power

20. [Hamilton], *Farmer Refuted*, Syrett and Cooke, eds., *Hamilton Papers*, I, 88; Stearns, *Two Sermons, January 20, 1777*, 12; [Mather], *America's Appeal*, 22–23.

21. *Four Letters*, 22. The later constitutions of Vermont (1777), Massachusetts (1780), and New Hampshire (1784) were also preceded by declarations of rights. Many of the other constitutions, although lacking a separate bill of rights, contained guarantees for common law liberties in the body of the constitution. N. J. Cons. (1776), XVIII–XIX, XXII; N. Y. Cons. (1777), XXXVIII, XLI; S. C. Cons. (1778), XXXVIII, XLI–XLIII; Ga. Cons. (1777), Art. I, LVI, LIX–LXI.

of the rulers or governors was so circumscribed by the body of
the constitutions, men in other states saw no need for any such
lengthy and separate delineations of the people's liberties—indicating just how narrowly focused on the magistracy their fear of
political power in 1776 was. Indeed, it was only the pressure of
instructions from constituents that compelled the North Carolina
Congress meeting in the fall of 1776 to add a bill of rights to its
Constitution; the earlier Congress of April 1776 in its prematurely
drafted Constitution had felt no necessity for any.[22]

What after all did a bill of rights mean? Although, as Albemarle
County in Virginia stated, the "Bill of Rights will be an honorable
monument to the memory of its Compilers," it still seemed evident "that the true sense of it is not generally understood." For
what was really needed was "a proper and clear line . . . drawn
between the powers necessary to be conferred by the Constituents to their Delegates, and what ought prudently to remain in
their hands." Yet bills of rights in English history had traditionally
been designed to delineate the people's rights against the Crown
or the ruler, not against Parliament which presumably represented
the people.[23] Nevertheless, for some Americans in some states the
bills of rights were assuming a broader significance, reflective of
their experience with Parliament and their incipient anxiety, expressed by Jefferson in his *Summary View*, that "bodies of men
as well as individuals are susceptible of the spirit of tyranny."[24]

Consequently, several of the constitutions drafted in 1776—
Delaware, New Jersey, North Carolina, and to a lesser extent,
Maryland—sought to insure the permanence of these individual
liberties, whether embodied in a separate bill of rights or incorporated in the constitution, not only from magisterial but from
legislative encroachment as well, by stating that they "ought
never to be violated on any pretence whatsoever." These were
simple admonitions, rudimentary efforts to restrain the legislatures and important largely because of later developments. It was
the most radical states—Pennsylvania, Georgia, and Vermont
where the possibility of legislative, as distinct from magisterial,
usurpation was most keenly felt—that most emphatically ex-

22. Enoch W. Sikes, *The Transition of North Carolina from Colony to Commonwealth* (*Johns Hopkins University Studies in Historical and Political Science*, Ser. XVI, Nos. 10–11 [Baltimore, 1898]), 68.
23. Albemarle County Instructions concerning the Virginia Constitution
(1776), Boyd, ed., *Jefferson Papers*, VI, 286.
24. [Jefferson], *Summary View*, Boyd, ed., *Jefferson Papers*, I, 124. See also
Essex Result, Parsons, *Memoir*, 367.

panded such prohibitory statements to include the entire constitution, not only declaring the bills of rights inviolable but also insisting that the legislators "shall have no power to add to, alter, abolish, or infringe any part of this Constitution."[25] Americans were to spend the following years in expanding such prohibitions and in attempting to make them effective.

3. THE CONSTITUTION AS FUNDAMENTAL LAW

The movement of thought in the Revolutionary era was not linear and the emergence of new and original ideas was often uneven and disconnected, not so much the result of borrowed thoughts as the consequence of varied political and social realities pushing and pulling commonly held ideas into new shapes and forms. Hence radical and mature positions anticipated by some groups as early as 1776 were not reached by others until the 1780's. It was difficult for many in 1776, for example, to envision the constitutions they were drafting, fundamental as they may have been in theory, as any sort of "check on the Representatives of the people, to prevent their assuming more power than would be consistent with the liberties of the people." While Orange and Mecklenburg counties in North Carolina had by 1776 already worked out a sophisticated conception of a constitution designed to limit the entire government, representatives included, the only means of constraint on the legislature which the prominent North Carolina Whig, Samuel Johnston, could conceive of was the counterbalancing force of the magistracy. Moreover, since the American governments were so weighted in favor of the assemblies, Johnston believed this traditional inhibition of a properly mixed government would probably have little effect. "After all," he concluded in a despairing letter to James Iredell in April 1776, "it appears to me that there can be no check on the Representatives of the people in a democracy, but the people themselves"; and this, as Johnston and others agreed, was best effected "by having their elections very frequent, at least, once in a year."[26]

Elsewhere there was the same confusion. The experience with

25. N. C. Cons. (1776), XLIV; Md. Decl. of Rts. (1776), XLII; Md. Cons. (1776), LIX; N. J. Cons. (1776), XXII, XXIII; Del. Cons. (1776), Art. 30; Pa. Cons. (1776), Sec. 9; Ga. Cons. (1777), Art. VII; Vt. Cons. (1777), Sec. VIII.

26. Johnston to Iredell, Apr. 20, 1776, Saunders, ed., *Col. Recs. of N. C.*, X, 498–99; Peter Whitney, *American Independence Vindicated . . .* (Boston, 1777), 49.

Parliament in the 1760's and seventies and the reiterated statements of English radicals like "Junius" and Enlightenment philosophers like Vattel—declaring that "the power of the legislature is *limited* ... by the FORMS and PRINCIPLES of the constitution" and denying that it "extends so far as to change the constitution of the state"—had convinced most Americans by 1776 that the constitution was something fundamental, something other than ordinary law. "A charter," as Bryan Fairfax had told Washington at the time of the British alteration of the Massachusetts Charter, "should not be altered without the Consent, or Consulting with the Majority of the people, or upon some very flagrant or violent Occasion wherever the good of the whole is endangered." It was the people who made the form of government, and therefore "they ought to be the best Judges of the Conveniences or Inconveniences attending it."[27] But since the legislatures, as the legitimate representatives, were the spokesmen for the people in the society, it was difficult, if not impossible, without a new conception of representation to deny them the right to alter or to construe the constitutions as they saw fit when the needs of the society demanded.

Throughout the following years therefore the distinction between fundamental and statutory law remained for many somewhat theoretical—not very different from the experience of eighteenth-century Englishmen who continued to mouth platitudes about the fundamental laws of the constitution while all the time making Parliament the judge of those fundamental laws.[28] Like Parliament, the American legislatures in the seventies and eighties, even in some states which had provided for some rudimentary devices to protect the constitution against legislative encroachment, acted as the principal interpreters of the fundamental laws they sat under and, as many increasingly complained, violated the constitutions "upon any Occasion to serve a purpose." The New Jersey legislature never questioned its ability to alter the fundamental law, in 1777 changing by simple act the very wording of the Constitution. Despite elaborate provisions for constitutional change written into the Georgia Constitution of 1777, the Georgia legislature at least three times throughout the eighties assumed the authority to explain portions of the fundamental law.

27. Phila. *Pa. Journal*, May 7, 1777; Fairfax to Washington, Aug. 5, 1774, Fitzpatrick, ed., *Writings of Washington*, III, 238n. See West, *Sermon Preached May 29, 1776*, Thornton, ed., *Pulpit*, 278.
28. Gough, *Fundamental Law*, Chap. XII, esp. 194.

The South Carolina legislature seemed especially flagrant in its repeated "irregularities" and suspensions of the Constitution, so much so, said Aedanus Burke in 1783, "that the very name of a democracy, or government of the people, now begins to be hateful and offensive." Under the exigencies of war many of the states were forced to set aside the constitution; an emergency act of the North Carolina legislature in 1780, for example, compelled the governor, who was without a veto, to resign rather than submit to an abrogation of his power over the military granted to him by the Constitution. "If it were possible it would be well to define the extent of the Legislative power but," concluded James Madison regretfully in 1785, "the nature of it seems in many respects to be indefinite."[29]

The problem for Americans in the 1780's then was to refine and to make effective the distinction between fundamental and statutory law that all in 1776 had at least paid lip service to, and this essentially involved making clear the precise nature of a constitution. Probably no one in the years after Independence wrestled more persistently with this problem than did Thomas Jefferson, beginning with his frustrated attempts in 1776 to get the Virginia Convention to recognize in some way the fundamentality of the constitution it was drafting. By 1779 Jefferson's concern with separating fundamental principles and "the natural rights of mankind" from ordinary statutory law had intensified, notably revealed in his Article for Establishing Religious Freedom. Because from experience it was now clear to Jefferson that no assembly, "elected by the people for the ordinary purposes of legislation only," could restrain the acts of succeeding assemblies, he knew that "to declare this act irrevocable would be of no effect in law; yet we are free," he insisted, "to declare, and do declare, that . . . if any act shall be hereafter passed to repeal the present or to narrow its operation, such act will be an infringement of natural right." Such a declaration was only a symptom of his frustration, and in the 1780's both he and James Madison fought "to form a real constitution" for Virginia, Madison citing as one of the Constitution's many defects "the doubts and im-

29. James Warren to John Adams, June 24, 1783, *Warren-Adams Letters*, II, 219; Erdman, *New Jersey Constitution*, 76–77; Kenneth Coleman, *The American Revolution in Georgia, 1763–1789* (Athens, Ga., 1958), 196; *Rudiments of Law and Government*, 53; [Aedanus Burke], *Considerations on the Society or Order of Cincinnati . . .* (Charleston, 1783), 27; Sikes, *Transition of North Carolina*, 71; Madison to Wallace, Aug. 23, 1785, Hunt, ed., *Writings of Madison*, II, 168.

putations under which it now labours," since, as Jefferson wrote in his *Notes on the State of Virginia*, "the ordinary legislature may alter the constitution itself." The body that drew up the Constitution possessed "no powers but what were given to every legislature before and since." And because no legislature could pass an act transcendent of the power of other legislatures, the Constitution was merely an "ordinance" with "no higher authority than the other ordinances of the same session." It could be neither "perpetual" nor "unalterable by other legislatures." In fact, the succeeding assemblies had continued to pass acts "in contradiction to their ordinance of government." Regardless of the people's acquiescence in the Constitution, Jefferson was sure, as his own 1783 draft for a new Virginia Constitution demonstrated, that some means—a separate constituting body and a council of revision—must be used to make the Constitution "permanent" and to deny the legislature "the power to infringe this constitution."[30]

Similar kinds of ideas about a constitution spread throughout all of the states in these years. The fundamental nature of a constitution that had been dormantly present in the assumptions of 1776 was now vitalized and drawn out by the growing dissatisfaction with legislative activity, a dissatisfaction with the fairest and fullest representative legislatures in the world that most Americans at the time of the Revolution had not really anticipated, however much they had been aware of Parliament's abuses. The logic of the emerging meaning of a constitution as something *"sacred and inviolate,"* which "no Legislature ought to presume to alter or amend" in the slightest way, was such that few who increasingly felt the need to limit their legislatures could resist it.[31] Thus groups outside of the main stream of constitutional development in the Revolution suddenly found themselves questioning what in 1776 had been taken for granted.

At Independence neither one of the corporate colonies had felt any need to frame new constitutions and both had simply retained their existing charters with minor verbal changes. But by

30. A Bill for Establishing Religious Freedom (1779), Boyd, ed., *Jefferson Papers*, II, 546–47; Jefferson to Démeunier, Jan. 24, 1786, quoted in *ibid.*, VI, 280; Madison's Notes of Speech on Proposed Amendment to Constitution of Virginia, June 1784, Hunt, ed., *Writings of Madison*, II, 55; Jefferson, *Notes on Virginia*, ed. Peden, 121–22; Jefferson's Draft of a Constitution for Virginia (1783), Boyd, ed., *Jefferson Papers*, VI, 298, also 281–82.

31. Trenton *N.-J. Gazette*, May 12, 1779, in Nelson *et al.*, eds., *New Jersey Archives*, 2d Ser., III, 352.

the late 1770's and early eighties some inhabitants of Rhode Island and Connecticut began doubting whether either state had a constitution after all, since their assemblies had simply endorsed and altered their former corporate charters, which "in their legislative capacity," it now seemed, they had "no right or authority" to do. Only the people by either "persons *legally authorized* by them or themselves" could create or alter a constitution. "If we suffer our Representatives to assume powers never committed to their trust unnoticed *once*," wrote Benjamin Gale in 1782 in a lengthy analysis of Connecticut's lack of a real constitution, "we may not be surprized to have it done a *second time*." By 1786–87 when a bill reducing the representation from two members to one from each town was introduced in the Connecticut General Assembly the new ideas of what a constitution was had become firmly grasped polemical tools. When opponents of the bill contended that the legislature could not change the constitutional right of representation, for "the people are the fountain of power, and must agree if the mode is altered, the assembly cannot do it," the supporters of the bill changing the representation were driven to argue that Connecticut had actually "no constitution but the laws of the state" which like any statute could be altered at pleasure by the legislature. When the bill's opponents stood firm, contending that "it is a ruling principle, that what is established by the constitution, cannot be altered by the General Assembly," the sponsors retreated, admitting, as all American Whigs found themselves doing, that the people alone could tamper with the Constitution. But their resort to instructions from the towns to the legislature as a means of satisfying the need for popular endorsement of constitutional change was still unacceptable to those with a newly refined understanding of constitution-making. "If all the towns in the state but one should give instructions to lessen the representation, the assembly would not be impowered to make the alteration." The legislature, however representative and however instructed, simply had no business meddling with the Constitution. There were "certain established rights, which no Assembly can touch."[32]

32. *Providence Gazette*, Mar. 20, Apr. 24, 1779; [Benjamin Gale], *Brief, Decent, but Free Remarks and Observations, on Several Laws Passed by the Honorable Legislature of the State of Connecticut, since the Year 1775* (Hartford, 1782), 24–28; Hartford *Connecticut Courant*, Nov. 13, 1786, June 4, 1787. See Richard J. Purcell, *Connecticut in Transition, 1775–1818* (Washington, 1918), 174–80. On Gale's tortured world see George C. Groce, Jr., "Benjamin Gale," *New England Quarterly*, 10 (1937), 697–716.

The people of Connecticut could never again be complacent about their Constitution. They remained haunted by the belief that they possessed no real constitution, compelling writers time and again to explain that despite its enactment by an ordinary legislature the old charter had become a Constitution through the tacit consent of the people. Although many were convinced that their Constitution was "a very bad one" and needed alteration, it now seemed evident that reform could no longer be "accomplished in the ordinary course of legislation," "not because the legislature *cannot* reform it," Noah Webster told Jefferson in 1790, "but because they *dare* not," largely due to the prevailing "idea" that there existed "some constitutional powers paramount to their own in the government." By the early 1790's some were questioning whether the need for constitutional change "will not justify a departure from that strict political principle, on which the legislature would claim all the powers of the community."[33] What Connecticut continued to struggle with as late as the second decade of the nineteenth century, the other states succumbed to, perhaps nowhere in the 1780's more abruptly and vividly than in South Carolina.

Some Carolinians in March of 1776 had objected to the Revolutionary Congress's adoption of a new Constitution without a new election; but this opposition represented more of a tactical resistance to independence than any comprehension of the Constitution's being beyond legislative enactment. When the legislature in 1778 sought to replace the earlier Constitution with a new one, however, Governor John Rutledge did veto the enacted Constitution, partly on the grounds, as he explained, that the legislative authority was "fixed and limited" and therefore could not change its character (as it was attempting to do by eliminating the governor's voice in legislation and by transforming the legislative Council into a Senate elected directly by the people) "without subverting the constitution from which it is derived." Yet Rutledge's objection was isolated and overridden, and the Constitution eventually passed as an ordinary legislative act when Rutledge resigned.[34] It was only after the crisis with Britain had

33. Noah Webster to Jefferson, Dec. 12, 1790, Harry R. Warfel, ed., *Letters of Noah Webster* (N. Y., 1953), 64; [William Pitt Beers], *An Address to the Legislature and People of . . . Connecticut* (New Haven, 1791), 36–37. See Zephaniah Swift, *System of the Laws of the State of Connecticut* (Windham, Conn., 1795–96), I, 55–62; Purcell, *Connecticut in Transition*, 265–66, 366.

34. Nevins, *American States*, 126, 129; Edward McCrady, *The History of South Carolina in the Revolution, 1775–1780* (N. Y., 1901), 235–41; Ramsay, *History of Revolution of South-Carolina*, I, 133.

passed that the doubts about this legislative enactment of the Constitution exploded. Only when South Carolina attempted a political reconstruction in the wake of a disruptive war and revolution did the earlier confidence in the legislature disintegrate, driving Carolinians to turn on each other with a viciousness that was unmatched in any other state in the 1780's. In the process, among other things, they rapidly developed an understanding of what a constitution should be.

By the mid-1780's those South Carolinians antagonistic to the existing legislature, filled with "the rankest aristocracy that any set of people were ever curst with," charged that "we have no such thing as a Constitution"; the document of 1778 was "a mere cobweb," since "the principles of the Constitution are, at present established no otherwise than by a simple Act of the Legislature."[35] And because it was but "an ENACTED LAW," "subsequent Assemblies have paid very little attention to it"; even "a partial repeal of the said Act has been made in several instances," without the least regard to Article XLIV of the Constitution which required ninety days' notice and the consent of a majority of both houses for any change. That any body of men should possess such power in a republic was unthinkable, for "if any over-grown influence should be ever permitted to encroach so far as to sap the foundation of Public Freedom, and by that means dethrone the Majesty of the People; the usurpers will then have it in their power to subjugate both Civil and Religious Liberty, to the arbitrary, whimsical, and capricious *Edicts*, of a few domineering Tyrants, to which the Laws of *Draco*, said to be written in blood, may be supposed to bear no comparison." These seemed to be no inflated fears, as the Jacksonboro legislature, with its arbitrary confiscation of property and its discriminatory amercement of nearly three hundred supposed Tories, had recently demonstrated. As long as the Constitution remained "nothing more than an act of the General Assembly made by a former Legislature, it will be found impracticable *without a greater solemnity being made use of*, to prevent a future one from new modelling our government to that shape, which the majority present shall be of opinion will best answer their own private purpose."[36]

35. Charleston *State Gazette of South Carolina*, Aug. 10, Oct. 5, Sept. 28, 21, 1786.
36. Charleston *Gazette of the St. of S. C.*, Jan. 24, 1785; Charleston *St. Gazette of S. C.*, Sept. 28, 21, Aug. 10, 1786.

These were the fulminations of several newspaper writers, necessarily brief and inchoate. But, as one of them noted, the ideas
and assumptions they were using had been fully developed earlier,
in 1784, by Thomas Tudor Tucker in one of the most prescient
and remarkable pamphlets written in the Confederation period,
entitled *Conciliatory Hints, Attempting by a Fair State of Matters, to Remove Party Prejudice.*[37] No other piece of writing prior
to 1787 revealed as clearly and cogently as Tucker's just how far
Americans had departed from the English conception of politics.
In Tucker's opinion "the political language" of Great Britain
had long since lost its relevance for Americans, and they should
immediately realize it. "The mysterious doctrine of undefinable
privileges, transcendent power, and political omnipotence, so
pompously ascribed to the British parliament, may do very well
in a government where all authority is founded in usurpation,
but ought certainly to be for ever banished from a country that
would preserve the freedom of a commonwealth." There were
good reasons why the privileges and power of the British Parliament were undefinable, reasons that were in no way applicable
to the South Carolina legislature. "Their constitution is established only on precedents, or compulsory concessions," "upon
a compromise of differences betwixt two or more contending
parties, each according to the means it possesses, extorting from
the others every concession that can possibly be obtained, without the smallest regard to justice or the common rights of mankind." Whatever stability there was in the English government
was a kind of "truce," for it naturally was and always has been "a
state of warfare," "a government of contention, in which the
opposite parties have been for a length of time by chance so
nearly balanced as not yet to have destroyed each other." True,
the King, Lords, and Commons were "limited, though in an uncertain way, with respect to each other; but the three together are
without any check in the constitution, although neither can be
properly called the Representatives of the people. It is for this
reason that this transcendent power or omnipotence is ascribed
to the Parliament." The only remedy the people possessed against
this unlimited power was rising in "a tumultuous opposition or
civil war."

37. Charleston *St. Gazette of S. C.*, Sept. 21, 1786. For the identification of
Tucker as the author of the pamphlet see Tucker, ed., *Blackstone's Commentaries*, I, Pt. 1, appdx., 60.

South Carolina, like the other American republics, had no need for this kind of tumultuous opposition, for the state was not, and should not be considered to be, a combination of contesting interests at war with one another, even though its legislature resembled the English Parliament. "Bred up in the erroneous notion of the freedom and excellence of the English constitution, we have unthinkingly adopted many of its faults." "In a true commonwealth or democratical government," such as the American states were, there was no place for an omnipotent legislature. "All authority is derived from the people at large, held only during their pleasure, and exercised only for their benefit. . . . No man has any privilege above his fellow-citizens, except whilst in office, and even then, none but what they have thought proper to vest in him, solely for the purpose of supporting him in the effectual performance of his duty to the public." Therefore, "the privileges of the legislative branches ought to be defined by the constitution and should be fixed as low as is consistent with the public welfare." South Carolina needed a new Constitution. The old one "(if such it may be called)" should be amended by convening the people in accord with "the true principles of equal freedom" that were being accepted by almost all Americans in the 1780's, thereby fixing the Constitution "on the firm and proper foundation of the express consent of the people, unalterable by the legislature, or any other authority but that by which it is to be framed." Only such a constitution based on this "undeniable authority" of the collective people would be something "more than the will of the legislature" and therefore "would have the most promising chance of stability." Then, in a brilliant passage, Tucker summed up what Americans had done in two decades to the conception of a constitution: "The constitution should be the avowed act of the people at large. It should be the first and fundamental law of the State, and should prescribe the limits of all delegated power. It should be declared to be paramount to all acts of the Legislature, and irrepealable and unalterable by any authority but the express consent of a majority of the citizens collected by such regular mode as may be therein provided."[38]

It was a conclusive statement that has not essentially changed in two hundred years. But it was not as easily arrived at as its proliferation in these years might indicate, for, as Tucker's elabo-

38. [Tucker], *Conciliatory Hints*, 10–11, 14, 15, 11, 12, 20, 12, 11, 10, 22, 28, 22, 30–31.

rate analysis of the Englishmen's assumptions about politics indicated, the new understanding of a constitution involved all sorts of adjustments and changes in other areas of political thought. The rush of new and unforeseen events in the years after Independence drove Americans in search of new ways of describing and dealing with a rapidly changing political reality. In the process old ideas, old images, were twisted and eventually shattered.

4. THE SOCIAL CONTRACT

When many Americans in 1776 and after identified "a proper and clear line" between rulers and ruled with that between representatives and constituents, and quoted *Cato's Letters* against a society's trusting "to the sole management, mere mercy, and absolute discretion of its own magistrates" to justify restrictions on the legislature, they were, whether they fully realized it or not, profoundly shifting the basis for their Whig understanding of politics.[39] Trenchard and Gordon and most radical Whigs had not generally equated the magistrates or rulers with the representatives of the people or ruled. Such an equation would have made nonsense of their theory of politics, just as it was doing for the Americans in the years after Independence, most obviously revealed in the pressure being put on the contractual metaphor that had been designed to explain the people's obedience to the prerogatives of their rulers. Although some writers in the eighteenth century were hesitantly and ambiguously ascribing a magisterial character to the elected representatives of the people, no one had clearly attempted to describe the relationship between representatives and constituents in terms of the traditional contract theory, that is, as a mutual bargain in which protection and allegiance were the considerations, since the people's obedience to Parliament still commonly rested on representational consent, however virtual it may have become. Thus when the Americans began conceiving of their written constitution as something more than a Magna Carta, indeed, as a set of fundamental principles circumscribing all parts of the government, representatives included, the constitution's imaginary characterization as a charter or reciprocal agreement between rulers and people lost its meaning.

39. Albemarle County Instructions, Boyd, ed., *Jefferson Papers*, VI, 286; *Rudiments of Law and Government*, 32.

The mutual contract between rulers and ruled began to seem inoperable once the character and the obligations of the two parties overlapped and combined and became indistinguishable. Unless the idea of representational consent was abandoned, this contractual image was bound to blur.

There was, however, another contractual analogy that ran through the Whig mind of the eighteenth century. This was the idea of the social compact, the conception John Locke had developed in his *Second Treatise on Civil Government*, not a governmental contract between magistrates and people, rulers and ruled, but an agreement among isolated individuals in a state of nature to combine in a society—a social compact which by its very character was anterior to the formation of government. Although this Lockean notion of a social contract was not generally drawn upon by Americans in their dispute with Great Britain, for it had little relevance in explaining either the nature of their colonial charters or their relationship to the empire, it became increasingly meaningful in the years after 1776. Under the changing exigencies of their polemics and politics, Americans needed some new contractual analogy to explain their evolving relationships among themselves and with the state. Only a social agreement among the people, only such a Lockean contract, seemed to make sense of their rapidly developing idea of a constitution as a fundamental law designed by the people to be separate from and controlling of all the institutions of government.[40]

Pennsylvania in 1776, with its remarkably advanced theories of a constitution, witnessed some of the earliest struggles to describe what was new in the traditional contractual language. The constitution was obviously not simply an old-fashioned colonial charter republicanized, not just the form of government, not merely a document separating power and liberty. A constitution did not contain the division and distribution of the state's power; rather it "*describes* the portions of power with which the people invest the legislative and executive bodies, and the portions which they *retain* for themselves." Indeed, it was "the particular business of a Constitution to mark out *how much* they shall

---

40. On Locke's contract see John W. Gough, *John Locke's Political Philosophy* (Oxford, 1956), 121. Cf. Thad W. Tate, "The Social Contract in America, 1774–1787: Revolutionary Theory as a Conservative Instrument," *Wm. and Mary Qtly.*, 3d Ser., 22 (1965), 375–91.

give up." Thus if it were a charter, "*that* Charter should be the act of *all* and not of *one man.*" The constitution seemed in fact to be the basis of the society itself—"the *charter* or *compact* of the whole people, and the LIMITATION of all *legislative* and *executive* powers." There actually seemed to be in one writer's mind two distinct stages involved in the constitution-making process. First, a special delegation of the people must form a "Social Compact" which "should be unalterable in every point, except by a delegation of the same kind of that which originally framed it, appointed for that purpose." But then "what should be done after this compact is finally agreed upon?" Another charter, "a *charter of delegation*" was needed, which would be "a clear and full description of the quantity and degree of power and authority, with which the society vests the persons intrusted with the powers of the society, whether civil or military, legislative, executive or judicial."[41]

Others elsewhere were also grappling with the nature of the contracts that supposedly lay behind the existence of government. A Rhode Islander in 1779, citing Locke and Sidney and quoting extensively from Pufendorf, described what he thought were three covenants involved in the creation of a body politic. "1. To unite in the establishment of a commonwealth. 2. To submit to the form of government agreed upon by the majority. 3. To support and maintain the government established by the constitution, and to preserve all the rights and privileges of the rulers and subjects agreeable thereto."[42] Yet elaborate as such a description was it lacked depth and development. It was in western Massachusetts and New Hampshire that the conception of a social contract was most fully worked out. For the towns of the Connecticut River valley the contractual nature of the body politic came to possess more than an intellectual meaning; it emerged not simply out of quotations from enlightened thinkers but out of their experience.

Throughout the entire Revolutionary era the Massachusetts towns west of the Connecticut River were in a state of virtual rebellion from the governing authorities in the East. Popular uprisings and mob violence were continual and extraordinarily ef-

41. [Paine], "Candid and Critical Remarks on a Letter Signed Ludlow," June 4, 1777, Foner, ed., *Writings of Paine*, II, 275; *Four Letters*, 19, 15; Phila. *Pa. Gazette*, Oct. 30, 1776; Phila. *Pa. Journal*, May 22, 1776.
42. *Providence Gazette*, Apr. 3, 1779.

fective. The courts were closed in 1774 and did not open again in Hampshire County until 1778 and in Berkshire County until after the Massachusetts Constitution of 1780 was put into effect, and even through the eighties mob outbursts periodically forced the courts to suspend judication. "Those unhappy Tumults and Disorders which both so much prevailed in this part of the State" were not the fancies of overwrought minds; the threat of "a Total Subversion of Government among us" was continuously real.[43] Shays's uprising in 1786 was only the climactic episode in one long insurrection, where the dissolution of government and the state of nature became an everyday fact of life. Indeed, it was as if all the imaginings of political philosophers for centuries were being lived out in a matter of years in the hills of New England.

As early as 1774 the Berkshire Constitutionalists, led by Thomas Allen of Pittsfield, began an attack on the royal court structure that led in the following years to a full-fledged assault on the patriot authorities in the East; for if these westerners could not control their own town and county governments, particularly the courts, "we are indifferent who assumes it whether any particular persons on this or on the other side of the water." By 1775 their antagonism was focused on "that Constitution now adopting in this province," the old 1691 Charter being resumed by the Whig government in Boston. They would prefer to remain in a state of nature than to have that "antient Mode of Government among us which we so much detest and abhor." Only the establishment of a constitution "De novo" could preserve the people's liberties. From these negative beginnings the Berkshire Constitutionalists moved swiftly toward a fuller understanding of how governments should actually be constituted. By May 1776 they were convinced that the Revolution had thrown the people "into a state of Nature," where they would remain until "the formation of a fundamental Constitution as the Basis and ground work of Legislation." Changing the wording of the judges' commissions, reducing the legal fee tables—"all is to us Nothing whilst the foundation is unfixed the Corner stone of Government unlaid." This could be done only by the people themselves, not by the representatives of the people—"they being but servants of the people cannot be greater than their Masters."

43. Towns of Goshen and Chesterfield (1784), quoted in Taylor, *Western Massachusetts*, 121.

To contend, as some had, that the representatives of the people in the legislature, however often elected, could impose on the society whatever constitution pleased them was "the rankest kind of Toryism, the self-same Monster we are now fighting against." The American people had heard much of "Governments being founded in Compact," but none existed in Massachusetts; that is, no "Barrier" between rulers and people had been established. "What is the fundamental Constitution of this province, what are the unalienable Rights of the people the power of the Rulers, how often to be elected by the people etc. have any of these things been as yet ascertained."[44]

So far the Berkshire Constitutionalists had used only the absence of the traditional Whig contract between rulers and people to justify their being in a state of nature. Seizing on this point, William Whiting, in his 1778 *Address to the Inhabitants of the County of Berkshire. Respecting Their Present Opposition to Civil Government*, sought to undercut the Constitutionalists' claim that they were free of all obligation to obey the temporary political authority that possessed the acquiescence of the majority of the society. Although the Declaration of Independence may have destroyed the political constitution of Massachusetts, said Whiting, it had not annihilated the social compact and thrown the people into a state of nature. "No revolution in, or dissolution of, particular constitutions or forms of government, can absolve the members of the society from their allegiance to the major part of the community." Forming a society was one thing and framing a government or constitution was another—two separate and distinct stages which the Berkshire inhabitants had hopelessly confused, rendering their justification for civil disobedience "altogether groundless."[45]

Yet Whiting's argument depended upon equating the constitution with the form of government, an identification most Americans were rapidly abandoning, since the government must clearly be only the creature of the constitution. By November 1778 the Berkshire Constitutionalists perceived the difference and now

44. Pittsfield Memorial, Dec. 26, 1775, and Pittsfield Petitions, May 29, 1776, Handlin, eds., *Popular Sources*, 64, 61, 64, 90, 92, 91, 92, 91–92. See also Taylor, *Western Massachusetts*, 86.

45. [Whiting], *Address to Inhabitants*, 10–16, 25–26. See Stephen T. Riley, "Dr. William Whiting and Shays' Rebellion," American Antiquarian Society, *Proceedings*, 66 (1956), 119–66.

subtly shifted their emphasis away from a purely political contract, a "sacred Barrier" against the rulers' oppression, like Magna Carta or the Bill of Rights, which were but "imperfect Emblems of the Securities of the present grand period." What was now needed was a "social Compact," uniting men one to another and justifying majority rule; for in all free states the "social Tie" itself was "founded in Compact." Only such a truly fundamental, social constitution could make intelligible the important distinction between a constitution and the acts of the legislators, "it being the foundation on which they themselves stand and from which the Legislature derives its Authority."[46]

The towns of western New Hampshire reached similar conclusions about the contractual nature of the constitution with even more explicitness. Because of their strong conviction that every town in the state should be equally represented in the legislature, the towns, in an *Address* written in July 1776, completely denied the legitimacy of the existing government established by the temporary Constitution in January 1776, "a little horn, growing up in the place where the other was broken off." In truth, they said, there was "no legal power subsisting in the Colony. . . . It is still in the hands of the people." By 1777 it appeared even clearer that the Declaration of Independence had nullified all governmental authority; "by that act the people of the different colonies slid back into a state of nature, and in that condition they were to begin anew." Whatever doubts there may have been about what happened to the people of the other colonies, there could be no question that the people of these western towns had "reverted to a state of nature." Because this Green Mountain territory had been disputed in the middle of the eighteenth century by both New York and New Hampshire, Governor Benning Wentworth of New Hampshire had issued royal charters to new towns in the Connecticut River valley pending the resolution of the contested land. Now with the Revolution these towns of the New Hampshire Grants saw themselves in a unique situation: since they had been joined to New Hampshire only through the royal governor's commissions the voiding of all royal authority had left them "unconnected with the former Government of New

---

46. Pittsfield Address to the General Court, Nov. 1778, Robert J. Taylor, ed., *Massachusetts, Colony to Commonwealth: Documents on the Formation of Its Constitution, 1775–1780* (Chapel Hill, 1961), 98, 99, 100.

Hampshire or any other incorporated State." They were free, they declared, to join with whatever state they wished.[47]

In a 1778 reply Timothy Walker, a member of the governing Council, pointed out the dangerous consequences of the westerners' principles "that the Declaration of Independence dissolves all political relations and connections." If all the provincial lines were eliminated by Independence and the people truly "reduced to a State of Nature," as the towns claimed, then all the subordinate corporations, all the town lines, were likewise void. The society then became a jumbled "heap of sand, without any cement to hold it together," leading only to chaos and civil war. For what then could compel all those minorities who wished to tie themselves to the state of New Hampshire to obey the majorities in each of the rebellious towns?[48]

The New Hampshire Grant towns backed away from this logic, arguing that the people in the old provinces of New Hampshire did not by the Declaration of Independence revert to a complete state of nature after all. When the Crown's authority was rejected, "*the people made a stand at the first legal stage*, viz. *their town incorporations*," miniature constitutions that made every one of the towns "a State by itself," able to justify binding its minority by the majority. So convinced now were these rebellious westerners that a corporate charter was needed to establish and make legal a body politic that they recommended in 1778 to all towns not already incorporated that they "forthwith incorporate themselves."[49]

By now the decisive conclusion was being drawn: the existence of society itself depended upon a concrete charter or constitution. In fact, the western radicals argued, it was precisely the lack of such a charter that had differentiated New Hampshire from her sister colonies in New England. Charters alone had made the people of Massachusetts and Connecticut "a body corporate

47. *Address of the Inhabitants of the Towns* [*of Grafton County*], Bouton et al., eds., *State Papers of N. H.*, X, 233–34; Letter of the Republican, Jan. 30, 1777, in Chase, *Dartmouth College*, 431–32; Address of the Towns of the New Hampshire Grants to the Assembly, June 11, 1777, *ibid.*, 455–56. See also *Observations on the Right of Jurisdiction . . . over the New Hampshire Grants . . .* (Danvers, Vt., 1778), in Bouton et al., eds., *State Papers of N. H.*, X, 259–67.

48. [Timothy Walker], An Address to the Inhabitants of the New Hampshire Grants, July 18, 1778, in Bouton et al., eds., *State Papers of N. H.*, X, 270.

49. *A Public Defence of the Right of the New-Hampshire Grants . . . to Associate Together, and Form Themselves into an Independent State* (Dresden, Vt., 1779), *ibid.*, 312–13; Chase, *Dartmouth College*, 460, 461, 485.

and politic in name and fact," and through these social compacts the people "hold themselves indissolubly connected together." But the inhabitants of New Hampshire possessed no such compact, "for take away the royal prerogative power which alone held them together, and what have they left? Nothing but a number of little town incorporations. . . . In short, *they never were a body politic in any legal sense whatever.*" It had long since become evident that a body politic could rest only on a constitution, a "compact or agreement of the People whereby they became united . . . into a new and distinct State."[50]

Although other Americans never quite experienced the state of nature and the Lockean contract so vitally as these dissident New Englanders, they could not resist the appeal of the contractual analogy. The Massachusetts Constitution of 1780 declared itself to be "a social compact, by which the whole people covenants with each citizen, and each citizen with the whole people, that all shall be governed by certain laws for the common good." Since in the forming of such a compact or in the changing of a constitution, as the New Hampshire rebels suggested as early as 1776, "it is absolutely necessary that the whole should be active in the matter, in order to surrender their privileges in this case, as they cannot be curtailed without," every adult male, regardless of his property-holding or the suffrage restrictions provided in the Constitution being established, was entitled to participate—since it was the society itself that was being constituted, as Thomas Dawes exclaimed in a Boston oration celebrating the new Constitution. "We often read of the original contract, and of mankind, in the early ages, passing from a state of nature to immediate civilization"—a time so distant, so far removed that no eyes had ever penetrated to it. "And yet," said Dawes, "the people of Massachusetts have reduced to practice the wonderful theory." The people had "convened in a state of nature, and, like our ideas of the patriarchs," had actually drawn and signed "a glorious covenant."[51]

What was explicitly stated in Massachusetts was less officially but no less conclusively being reached elsewhere in the 1780's.

50. *Public Defence*, Bouton *et al.*, eds., *State Papers of N. H.*, X, 314–15; *Observations on the Right of Jurisdiction*, in *ibid.*, 264.
51. Mass. Cons. (1780), Handlin, eds., *Popular Sources*, 441; *Address of the Inhabitants of the Towns of* [*Grafton County*], Bouton *et al.*, eds., *State Papers of N. H.*, X, 233–34; Dawes, *Oration Delivered March 5th 1781*, in Niles, ed., *Principles*, 71.

From South Carolina to New Jersey the constitution had become "a social covenant entered into by express consent of the people," "that original compact entered into by every individual of a society, whereby a certain form of government is chalked out and established unalterably, except by the people themselves: thus by a constitution then, . . . we do not mean government itself, but the manner of its formation and existence."[52] Although many continued to refer to the constitution as that *"civil compact"* which "points out the manner in which we chuse to be governed, the *privileges* of the people, and the *prerogatives* of the governing body," once the changes Americans were making in the nature of politics were grasped, the constitution could no longer be intelligibly regarded as a contract, like Magna Carta, between rulers and people. All authority in all parts of the government was equivalently derived from the people, "through the medium of that constitutional compact, which binds them together in one body." The constitution was not a bargain between two parties but had become the very basis of the society, and because "established by the people, it is stronger than any law the assembly can make, it being the foundation whereon they stand."[53]

So crucial was this conception of a constitution to the Americans' interpretation of government and their relationship to it that it could easily become the focal point of wide-ranging political arguments, as it did in Maryland in 1787 in the debate over the right of the people to instruct the Senate. "The question between us," Judge Alexander Hanson told his antagonist William Paca, "depends on the construction of the compact." Since the people of Maryland, Hanson argued, had not retained in their Constitution the right of instructing their legislators, they did not and could not possess it, for "it is plain they can have no rights *'paramount'* the compact." This Paca denied, insisting that the people's rights belonged to them in a state of nature, "before compact, and therefore, if not transferred by compact, might be exercised, although not mentioned therein, defined or ascertained." When Hanson questioned the existence of any such state of nature, Paca exploded with quotations from Locke and Sidney,

---

52. [Tucker], *Conciliatory Hints*, 12; [John Stevens], *Observations on Government, Including Some Animadversions on Mr. Adams' Defence of the Constitutions* . . . (N. Y., 1787), 44.

53. Adams, *Sermon Preached May 29, 1782*, 21; Cumings, *Sermon Preached May 28, 1783*, 16; [Isaac Backus], *A Door Opened for Equal Christian Liberty* . . . (Boston, [1783]), 5.

contending that the Americans' understanding of government and a constitution absolutely depended on a state of nature. Hanson conceded that there may have been at one time such a hypothetical state of nature; yet "when the people entered into a compact of government" they "thereby parted with the whole legislative power." Therefore since this so-called natural right of the people to instruct their legislators, although not explicitly denied in the Constitution, "is incompatible with the exercise of the legislative power, conferred on a body, or bodies of men, common sense must decide, that it is given up, as clearly, as if it had been mentioned." But, replied Paca, a constitution and the delegation of legislative power by the people did not work that way. It was not a wholesale surrender of power; it was piecemeal and controlled. None of the rights of the people were "parted with or transferred by any compact that we have made." In fact, said Paca, the constitution was not inclusive of the people's rights; it did not and could not define them. When the colonists resisted the tyranny of Great Britain they also had referred to charters, compacts, and constitutions. Yet, asked Paca, did they "rest the rights of America upon these charters or compacts? Or did they deduce them from a higher source, *the laws of God and nature?*" With such questions Paca had stumbled into the most perplexing problem of American constitutional law.[54]

5. The Ambiguity of American Law

Important as this development of the constitution as a fundamental law superior to ordinary legislative acts was to American constitutionalism, it ultimately was not the most important source of the peculiarly effective nature of American constitutional restrictions on legislative power. What in the final analysis gave meaning to the Americans' conception of a constitution was not its fundamentality or its creation by the people, but rather its implementation in the ordinary courts of law. The idea of fundamental law was, after all, a continuing one in Western political thought, especially among Englishmen in the seventeenth century who likewise had experimented with a written constitution. And despite its precipitous decline in the eighteenth century, the con-

54. Baltimore *Md. Journal*, Aug. 3, 31, 1787; Annapolis *Md. Gazette*, June 28, Aug. 2, 16, 1787.

cept of fundamental law had never entirely lost its attractiveness for Englishmen. Blackstone, as well as Locke and Bolingbroke before him, continued to see Parliament limited by an overriding natural law. Yet for all English Whigs, Trenchard and Gordon as well as Burgh, the fundamental law they believed in was one enforceable only by the people's right of revolution, a final sanction that dissolved the contract of government, leaving the people free to do as they would in the future. There was therefore no logical or necessary reason why the notion of fundamental law, so common to Englishmen for over a century, should lead to the American invocation of it in the ordinary courts of law. Indeed, in an important sense the idea of fundamental law actually worked to prohibit any such development, for it was dependent on such a distinct conception of public law in contrast to private law as to be hardly enforceable in the regular court system. The Americans' development of what came to be called judicial review was not simply the product of their conception of a constitution as a higher law embodied in a written document. Other states since the eighteenth century have resorted to formal, rigid constitutions without at the same time allowing the judges of their courts to set aside legislative acts in conflict with the constitution.[55] Different circumstances, different ideas ultimately made the practice of judicial review possible and justifiable in America.

The Americans' preoccupation in the early seventies with written restraints on political power actually masked a peculiar confusion in the American mind about the nature of law—a confusion that only gradually became evident in the years after Independence. On the surface the colonists' resort to written documents and charters as the best means of defending liberties against an encroaching parliamentary power signified an acceptance of the modern definition of law as the command of a sovereign will against which the only protection of the people's rights and the basic principles of the constitution were their written specification. The Americans' idea of a written fundamental constitution was, in other words, a consequence of presumptions about the nature of law held by most Englishmen in the mid-eighteenth century. No Whig more clearly realized the implications of this reliance on written documents than did James Otis. The colonists' "essential rights," he frantically warned, were guaranteed not by pieces of paper but "by the laws of God and nature as well as

55. On these points see Gough, *Fundamental Law*, 186–90, 206, 214.

by the common law and by the constitution of their country." If an act of Parliament should "annihilate all those charters" it could not in any way "shake one of the essential, natural, civil, or religious rights of the colonists." "Codes, pandects, novels, decretals of popes" may have been suitable for other peoples but not for Englishmen who could "rest content with the laws, customs, and usages of our ancestors." But Otis's anachronistic conception of law which underlay his aversion to written documents and his faith in the inner workings of the English constitution as the best defense of American liberties were eventually drowned out by the colonists' increasing awareness of the modern nature of law made evident by the examples of and the arguments over the sovereign power of Parliament in the late 1760's. In a world of arbitrary legislative power where law could be *"de jure"* as well as *"de facto"* unjust, reliance on the intrinsic justness of the law itself seemed patently and frighteningly insufficient. "To deduce our rights from the principles of equity, justice, and the Constitution, is very well; but equity and justice are no defence against power," wrote that little-known but important framer of the Pennsylvania Constitution, James Cannon, in a quotation from *An Historical Essay on the English Constitution* directly antithetical to the thought of Otis. "Constitutional rights" must be protected and defended "as the apple of your eye" from danger "or they will be lost forever." They must be established "on a foundation never more to be shaken," that is, they must be specified and written down in immutable documents.[56]

Nevertheless, with all of the Americans' misunderstanding of Otis, with all of their emphasis on written documents in the 1770's and its implied concession to the modern definition of law, many Whigs, as Paca reminded Hanson in 1787, had not thereby conceded that their charters and codifications by themselves were the source of their rights and liberties. Such rights and liberties, said John Dickinson in 1766, were "not annexed to us by parchments and seals. They are created in us by the decrees of Providence, which establish the laws of our nature. They are born with us; exist with us; and cannot be taken from us by any human power, without taking our lives. In short, they are founded on the immutable maxims of reason and justice." When Tories tried

56. [Otis], *Vindication of the British Colonies*, Bailyn, ed., *Pamphlets*, I, 558, 579; Otis, *Rights of the British Colonies*, in *ibid.*, 443, 444; [James Cannon], "Cassandra," Apr. 1776, Force, ed., *American Archives*, 4th Ser., V, 1094, quoting from [Hulme], *Historical Essay*, 143–44.

to draw out the implications of the colonists' dependence on written documents, arguing, for example, that as New Yorkers had no charter, they could have no charter rights, Whigs like Hamilton and Philip Livingston resisted with vehemence, denying that "the sacred rights of mankind" were "to be rummaged for, among old parchments, or musty records." The Americans would never concede "that any right . . . if it be not confirmed by some statute law, is not a legal right." Legal rights, wrote Livingston in 1774 in words that Otis would have agreed with, were "those rights which we are entitled to by the eternal laws of right reason."[57] Putting them on parchment did not create them; it only affirmed their natural existence. Yet as often as such statements were made, their significance was not fully appreciated, and a pervasive confusion about law remained. If codification did not create but only declared what was the already existing law and the rights of the people, then it followed, as Otis had so strongly argued, that the rights and principles of the constitution did not actually have to be specified and written down in order to be in force.

The debate in 1773 between John Adams and William Brattle, a member of the Massachusetts Council, over the tenure of judges in the colonies hinged precisely on this question, "whether," as Adams put it, "by the common law of England, the judges of the king's bench and common bench had estates for life in their offices." Brattle thought they had, and following Chief Justice Holt who at the beginning of the century had attempted to affirm the unity of English law by denying any distinction between parliamentary and common law, he argued that the parliamentary act of 1701 establishing judicial tenure during good behavior was not actually the creation of any "new law" but only an "affirmance of the old law, that which was really law before." Thus there was no necessity, said Brattle, for the colonial justices to have "*quamdiu bene se gesserint* in their commissions; for they have their commissions now by that tenure as truly as if said words were in," because their tenure was settled by "the common law of England, the birthright of every man here as well as at home."[58]

57. [John Dickinson], *An Address to the Committee of Correspondence in Barbados* . . . (Phila., 1766), Ford, ed., *Writings of Dickinson*, 262; [Hamilton], *Farmer Refuted*, Syrett and Cooke, eds., *Hamilton Papers*, I, 122; [Philip Livingston], *The Other Side of the Question* . . . (N. Y., 1774), 9.
58. *Boston Gazette*, Feb. 1, 1773, and Boston *Massachusetts Gazette*, Jan. 4, 1773, in Adams, ed., *Works of John Adams*, III, 540, 518, 517, 518. On Holt's views see Gough, *Fundamental Law*, 177–79.

It was a strained and obsolescent argument, as Adams delighted in showing by a dazzling array of citations; but it was not as foolish or as unusual as Adams made it out to be. Brattle's argument had actually been used by other colonists in an earlier dispute over judicial tenure, in 1760 in Pennsylvania, when Joseph Galloway as the spokesman for the antiproprietary party contended that Parliament's Act of Settlement in 1701 had "created no innovation of the ancient constitution," since "Parliament had no design to change but only to restore the ancient laws and customs of the realm, which were the true and indubitable rights and liberties of the people of *England*." In fact, Brattle's position (as he acutely emphasized by labeling Adams as an upholder of "tory principles") was not essentially different from that of all those Whigs who argued that an Englishman's rights existed in the maxims of the common law and nature, whatever Parliament said or did not say. Law, in other words, was basically what the principles of right reason declared to be law, the codification of which was hardly inclusive. Indeed when pressed, few Americans would admit that the codification of the fundamental principles of law and justice was the actual source of those principles and the only means of their implementation.[59]

The consequence was the creation of a basic ambiguity in the American mind about the nature of law that was carried into the Revolution. The Americans were firmly committed to the modern notion of statute law based on legislative enactment—a commitment implicit in their resort to fundamental law and written charters. Yet at the same time they were never willing to acknowledge that "the obligation of the ruled to obey" depended "solely upon, '*Be it enacted, Etc.*'" and thus continued to retain something of Otis's conviction that "righteousness should be the basis of law." From the time in 1646 when the Massachusetts General Court declared that the fundamental basis of all laws is the law of God and right reason and that "if anything hath been otherwise established, it was an error, and not a law . . . , how-

---

59. *A Letter to the People of Pennsylvania; Occasioned by the Assembly's Passing That Important Act, for Constituting the Judges . . . during Good Behaviour* (Phila., 1760), in Bailyn, ed., *Pamphlets*, I, 266–67; *Boston Gazette*, Jan. 25, 1773, Adams, ed., *Works of John Adams*, III, 531. For a similar argument in New York over whether the privileges of Englishmen have to be enacted in order to be in force see William Smith, *History of New York*, I, 313–14. For a modern version of Brattle's argument concerning judicial tenure see Charles H. McIlwain, *Constitutionalism and the Changing World* (Cambridge, Eng., 1939), 294–307. Cf. Bailyn, ed., *Pamphlets*, I, 249–55.

ever it may bear the form of a law," such a belief in the morality of law had been a central part of the Americans' legal history in the New World. Their law had existed in such a confused and chaotic state that the only criterion for its authority had seemed to be its intrinsic justice—a justice, however, that had not been set in opposition to legislative will but indeed had depended upon it.[60]

Although the history of American law remains to be written, it does seem evident that the colonists' legal development, despite attempts in the mid-eighteenth century to bring it more into line with the mother country, remained decidedly different from that of England. "The complex subtleties" of English legal practice, Peter Van Schaack, the knowledgeable reviser of New York's eighteenth-century laws, declared in 1786, were as unsuited to "the simplicity of our courts" as "the appendages of an old dowager's toilette ornamental to the bloom of nineteen."[61] It was a common observation, and it went to the heart of America's legal difficulties. Paradoxically it was the very "simplicity" of American jurisprudence that created the ambiguities and complexities of colonial law, a simplicity both intentionally and necessarily bred from their provinciality. Much of the colonists' law (and no one was sure quite how much) came from outside their society, in English statutes, legal authorities, and court precedents, and mingled confusedly with their own colonial law in court systems that were, relative to the English courts, remarkably undifferentiated. In such circumstances—where there were "two Fountains of their Law," where the courts exercised "A SOVEREIGN AUTHORITY, in determining *what parts of the common and statute law* ought to be extended"—judicial discretion so abounded that "the issues of a cause depended not so much on the right of a Client, as on the breath of the Judge, and what was looked upon as a very good plea in one circuit was disallowed in another."[62] The

60. John Devotion, *The Duty and Interest* . . . (Hartford, 1777), 29–30; Mass. General Court, quoted in Richard B. Morris, *Studies in the History of American Law* . . . (N. Y., 1930), 19.

61. Peter Van Schaack to Robert Yates, 1786, quoted in Richard B. Morris, ed., *Select Cases of the Mayor's Court of New York City, 1674–1784 (American Legal Records*, 2 [Washington, 1935]), 56.

62. Henry Hartwell, James Blair, and Edward Chilton, *The Present State of Virginia, and the College*, ed. Hunter D. Farish (Williamsburg, 1940), 40; [Dickinson], *Letters from a Farmer*, Ford, ed., *Writings of Dickinson*, 369–70; Governor Henry Moore of New York, Feb. 26, 1768, quoted in Irving Mark, *Agrarian Conflicts in Colonial New York 1711–1775* (N. Y., 1940), 77. For additional

consequence for colonial jurisprudence was both flexibility and uncertainty. With no printed indigenous decisions there could be little reliance on local precedents other than those in memory, and although English authorities were cited constantly they appear to have expanded rather than restricted judicial discretion. Because of the very perplexities of colonial law the judges were free, indeed were driven, to select and to innovate in order to adjust continually to local circumstances. "I never presumed to call myself a Lawyer," wrote Thomas Hutchinson of his experiences as chief justice of the Massachusetts Superior Court from 1760–69. "The most I could pretend to was when I heard the Law laid on both sides to judge which was right."[63]

Although a legally untrained judge, like Associate Justice John Dudley of New Hampshire, could charge a jury "to do justice between the parties not by any quirks of the law out of Coke or Blackstone—books that I never read and never will—but by common sense as between man and man," colonial adjudication was not simply a matter of applying some kind of crude, untechnical law to achieve common-sense "frontier" justice. There is much evidence to suggest that even as early as the late seventeenth century in new back-country counties the quality of legal procedures was remarkably sophisticated; and by the middle of the eighteenth century, in Massachusetts and New York at least, colonial jurisprudence approached very closely that of the English.[64] In fact, approximating without really duplicating the English common law procedures was responsible for the colonists' legal confusion.

comments on the complexity of American law in the 18th century see Smith, *History of New York*, I, 309–10; Robert Beverley, *The History and Present State of Virginia*, ed. Louis B. Wright (Chapel Hill, 1947), 255–56; Wilson, "Lectures on Law," Wilson, ed., *Works of Wilson*, II, 54; James Kent to Simeon Baldwin, July 18, 1786, quoted in Julius Goebel, Jr., *et al.*, eds., *The Law Practice of Alexander Hamilton* (N. Y., 1964——), I, 50; Tucker, ed., *Blackstone's Commentaries*, I, Pt. 1, appdx., 384–412; Elizabeth G. Brown, *British Statutes in American Law 1776–1836* (Ann Arbor, 1964), 1–22; William W. Crosskey, *Politics and the Constitution in the History of the United States* (Chicago, 1953), I, 585–93, 600–02.

63. Thomas Hutchinson to John Sullivan, Mar. 29, 1771, in L. Kinvin Wroth and Hiller B. Zobel, eds., *Legal Papers of John Adams* (Cambridge, Mass., 1965), I, xli, also l. For the "selection," "adaptation," and "experimentation" of colonial law in New York see Goebel, ed., *Hamilton's Law Practice*, I, 42.

64. Dudley quoted in Daniel J. Boorstin, *The Americans: The Colonial Experience* (N. Y., 1958), 201. On the sophistication of jurisprudence in a frontier county of Maryland at the end of the 17th century see Joseph H. Smith and Philip A. Crowl, eds., *Court Records of Prince Georges County, Maryland 1696–1699* (*American Legal Records*, 9 [Washington, 1964]), cxv.

Many of the English common law forms were present but often with defects and irregularities. The use of some writs and not others, the corrupting and blending of forms of action, the avoidance of special pleading and the insufficiency and inaccuracy of pleading in general—pleading lying at the heart of common law jurisprudence—helped to create an atmosphere of permissiveness and uncertainty which a sharp lawyer with a collection of English precedents no one had ever heard of could often turn to advantage. The overlapping and blurring of different, even contrary jurisdictions like those of probate and common law, and the absence of chancery jurisdiction in many of the colonies, compelling the common law to apply equitable procedures "to moderate the rigour of the law," added to the colonists' legal disorder. Although there was no court of equity in Pennsylvania, wrote John Dickinson during his training at the Inns of Court, "it woud be much properer to say every court there is a court of equity, for both judges and juries think it hard to deny a man that relief which he can obtain no where else, and without reflecting that equity never intermeddles but where law denies *all manner* of assistance, every judgment, every verdict is a confused mixture of private passions and popular error, and every court assumes the power of legislation."[65]

Such experience bred among the colonists a profound fear of judicial independence and discretion, reflected in their repeated resort to written charters and to legislative intervention either by direct interference in the process of adjudication or by the correction and amendment of court-administered law by statute. Yet ironically the same legal complexities that were responsible for the much resented abuses of magisterial will were also responsible for the colonists' central concern for reason and equity in their law, in effect leading the colonists into a reversion to a kind of medieval English jurisprudence, where the right reason of the common law, as accumulated and passed on in the law reports and minds of the English judges, had constructed and controlled the declarations of what was properly and equitably the

65. Wroth and Zobel, eds., *Adams Legal Papers*, I, xliv, xlv, 27–29, 32, 36, 37, 44, 49, 61, 66, 71, 116, 231, 233, 237, 245, 255, 261; the quotation on moderation of the law is from the Mass. act of 1698 granting the common-law courts powers of equity, cited 231; Goebel, ed., *Hamilton's Law Practice*, I, 10, 16, 83, 109; Dickinson to father, Aug. 2, 1756, Colbourn, ed., "Pennsylvania Farmer," *Pa. Mag. of Hist. and Biog.*, 86 (1962), 450–51.

law in every particular case.[66] Amidst the confusion and disorder of colonial law, lawyers and judges had really no other basis but reason and equity for clarifying their law and for justifying the deviations in their jurisprudence from that of the English. "There seems to be no Reason for this," wrote Alexander Hamilton in explanation of the absence of a particular English form in New York's legal practice. The haphazard and piecemeal introduction of the common law into the colonies and the Americans' adoption of only those laws, as they often stated, "which from a similarity of genius and local situation suited this country" strengthened their idea that the authority of law came not from its being old or being English, "but as being founded in the nature and fitness of things," for "though the reporters of adjudged cases have been read and attended to in our courts, yet where the injustice of them could be pointed out they were rejected."[67] The problem was: could this emphasis on reason and equity in their law be maintained without judicial discretion?

At the Revolution most of the state constitutions provided for

66. See Gough, *Fundamental Law*, 18–19, 27, 38–39, 225, Pocock, *Ancient Constitution*, 35–37; Wilson, "Lectures on Law," Wilson, ed., *Works of Wilson*, II, 29; Goebel, ed., *Hamilton's Law Practice*, 43. Because of the scarcity of law books and law reports, American lawyers tended to rely heavily in their legal education on the medieval and early modern classics of English law, thus accentuating their old-fashioned interpretation of jurisprudence. So John Adams, lacking copies of the English Statutes and Trials, read as much as he could in the likes of Bracton and Glanville. Butterfield, ed., *Diary of Adams*, III, 274. To Jefferson there was no "profounder learning in the orthodox doctrines of British liberties" than *Coke on Littleton*, The "young brood of lawyers" brought up on "the honeyed Mansfieldism of *Blackstone* . . . no longer know what whiggism or republicanism means." Even as late as 1798 young Joseph Story "breathed a purer air" and "acquired a new power" after reading the crabbed medieval intricacies of Coke. Charles Warren, *A History of the American Bar* (Boston, 1911), 174, 175–76, and in general 157–87. See also Paul M. Hamlin, *Legal Education in Colonial New York* (N. Y., 1939), 65–66.

67. Hamilton's Practice Manual, Goebel, ed., *Hamilton's Law Practice*, 59, 51; Boston *Independent Chronicle*, Apr. 17, 1777. See also Wilson, "Lectures on Law," Wilson, ed., *Works of Wilson*, II, 29; Tucker, ed., *Blackstone's Commentaries*, I, Pt. 1, appdx., 393. "All Lawyers agree," wrote Hamilton, "that the *spirit* and *reason* of a law, is one of the principal rules of interpretation." [Hamilton], *Farmer Refuted*, Syrett and Cooke, eds., *Hamilton Papers*, I, 137. To William Livingston it was "a monstrous Absurdity to suppose, that the Law is to be learnt by a perpetual copying of Precedents," for "Time immemorial can never give a Sanctum to what is against Reason and common Sense." Hamlin, *Legal Education*, 169. For a 1772 Virginia argument for voiding legislation "contrary to right and justice" see T. F. T. Plucknett, "Bonham's Case and Judicial Review," *Harvard Law Review*, 40 (1926–27), 65.

the retention of as much of the English statute and common law as was applicable to the local circumstance, until it should be altered by future legislative acts—thus perpetuating the problem but promising the remedy. Already some Americans were protesting against the mid-eighteenth-century maturation of legal development that touched off a debate on American law that carried well into the following century. Because laws had become "complicated to an unwieldly size," "equity and justice have been nearly banished from the world." While some simply expressed amazement at the complex mixture of English and American law, which involved lawyers and jurists in "so much splendid and useful as well as so much tedious and antiquated Learning" and made ordinary laymen so "much addicted to Quirks in the Law," others launched vicious attacks on "the whole bundle of perplexities" and "jumble of intricacies" in the existing legal structure and the "want of a proper system of laws, adapted to our particular state and circumstances: The numerous precedents brought from *Old English Authorities*, serve to embarrass all our judiciary causes, and answer no other purpose than to increase the influence of lawyers, as from such authorities they can cull and select precedents to answer every purpose." Society needed "but a few laws, and these simple, clear, sensible, and easy in their application to the actions of men."[68]

Beccarian sentiments like these, although not always so vehemently expressed, were widely felt and resulted in increasing attacks on lawyers and demands for the weeding out of British law and the codification and simplification of American law. "Now that we had no negatives of Councils, Governors and Kings to restrain us from doing right," Jefferson later said of his efforts at legal reformation in Virginia, it was at last possible for the whole legal system to be "reviewed, adapted to our republican form of government, and . . . corrected, in all it's parts, with a single eye to reason, and the good of those for whose government

68. "On the Present States of America," Oct. 10, 1776, Force, ed., *American Archives*, 5th Ser., II, 969; Kent to Baldwin, July 18, 1786, in Goebel, ed., *Hamilton's Law Practice*, I, 50; Douglass, *Summary of the British Settlements*, I, 520; [Benjamin Austin], *Observations on the Pernicious Practice of the Law* (Boston, 1786), 38, 12; "On the Present States of America," Oct. 10, 1776, Force, ed., *American Archives*, 5th Ser., II, 969. On the status of the common law at the Revolution see Tucker, ed., *Blackstone's Commentaries*, I, Pt. 1, appdx., 410; Crosskey, *Politics and the Constitution*, I, 593–99. On the "multitude of mischivious and unnecessary Laws" which plagued ancient Rome (" 'twas a complaint of *Tacitus*") see *Essay upon Government*, 56.

it was framed."[69] Although the story is still untold, there were similar, although perhaps less comprehensive, attempts in all of the states to eliminate *"useless British statutes"* and to systematize and put into statute form parts of the common law in order to make the judge "a mere machine" and to ensure that "the laws may be executed upon the strictest principles of *equity*." As Beccaria had written, and William Henry Drayton quoted in 1778 with approval, "in republics, the very nature of the constitution requires the judges to follow the letter of the law." "Let the rule of right be not matter of controversy, but of fact" through codification and strict judicial observance so that the people did not become "slaves to the magistrates."[70] Such codification assumed that equity and "the *fair principles of law*" could be precisely defined and "adapted to every man's information," since, as Jefferson wrote in his *Summary View*, "the great principles of right and wrong are legible to every reader: to pursue them requires not the aid of many counsellors."[71]

Reform-minded Americans were thus committed to equity as the basis of law, but by resting their plans on legislative enactment they at the same time denied the judicial discretion that made equitable interpretations necessary and possible. While a writer in 1777 could in one breath assert that "right, not power, is the source of law," he could in the next argue in Beccarian terms that "no axiom is more dangerous than that the spirit of the law ought to be considered, and not the letter; if this is adopted, the same laws that condemn today, will acquit tomorrow, according to different opinions which different judges may form of its spirit." If the spirit of the law had to be considered, said the author of *The People the Best Governors*, then it should

69. Jefferson, Autobiography, Ford, ed., *Writings of Jefferson*, I, 66–67. On legal reform in Virginia see Boyd, ed., *Jefferson Papers*, II, 305–24.

70. [Austin], *Observations on the Pernicious Practice of the Law*, 37, 24; Jefferson to Pendleton, Aug. 26, 1776, Boyd, ed., *Jefferson Papers*, I, 505; William Henry Drayton, Speech to General Assembly of South Carolina, Jan. 20, 1778, Niles, ed., *Principles*, 359. On the means used to clarify American law at the time of the Revolution see Brown, *British Statutes*, 23–45.

71. [Austin], *Observations on the Pernicious Practice of the Law*, 22, 37, also 34–35; [Jefferson], *Summary View*, Boyd, ed., *Jefferson Papers*, I, 134. "Men who have but a superficial knowledge of law, and take it for a rule of conduct," argued one victim of legal injustice in 1784, "oftener transgress the very LAW they take for their rule, than men of a tolerable degree of understanding, who know nothing of law, but govern their conduct by the justice and fitness of things." Jonathan Parsons, *A Consideration of Some Unconstitutional Measures, Adopted and Practiced in This State* (Newburyport, 1784), 8.

be done only on appeal to the representatives of the people. If the judges "put such a construction on matters as they think most agreeable to the spirit and reason of the law . . . , they assume what is in fact the prerogative of the legislature, for those that made the laws ought to give them a meaning when they are doubtful." Not the courts but only the legislatures could redress the grievances of the people, said a New Jerseyite in 1781, "because they are the representatives of the people." The courts "must take the law as it is, and by all due and proper means execute it, without any pretense to judge of its right or wrong." Legislatures should be the sole source of law.[72]

The promise of codification and precise legislative enactment was never lost and continued strong into the nineteenth century. Yet as early as the mid-1780's some began to perceive that codification was not working out as had been anticipated. There were many statutes and much printing of laws but not always in the way reformers like Jefferson and Madison had wanted. Comprehensive codes were being mutilated and broken apart through piecemeal enactment that was defeating the very purpose of clarification, resulting in "strong apprehensions that the work may never be systematically perfected." As St. George Tucker later observed, every attempt by Virginians to form a complete digest of statute law "seems to have been the parent of new perplexities, by the introduction of new laws; and the re-enaction, omission, or suspension of former acts, whose operation is thus rendered *doubtful*, even in the most important cases." "As far as laws are necessary to mark with precision the duties of those who are to obey them, and to take from those who are to administer them a discretion which might be abused, their number is the price of liberty." But, wrote Madison in a notable summary of a decade of experience with codification, when they exceeded this necessity they became "a nuisance of the most pestilent kind."[73] "What then is to be done?" asked an agonized South Carolinian in 1783, perplexed by the dilemma being brought to a head in the years after Independence. "What people in their senses would make the

72. Boston *Independent Chronicle*, Sept. 4, 1777; *People the Best Governors*, Chase, *Dartmouth College*, 662; Trenton *N.-J. Gazette*, Apr. 18, 1781, Nelson *et al.*, eds., *New Jersey Archives*, 2d Ser., V, 232–34.
73. Madison to Edmund Pendleton, Jan. 9, 1787, and to Jefferson, Feb. 15, 1787, Hunt, ed., *Writings of Madison*, II, 304–05, 309; Tucker, ed., *Blackstone's Commentaries*, I, Pt. 1, xiii; Madison, "Vices of the Political System of the United States" (Apr. 1787), Hunt, ed., *Writings of Madison*, II, 365.

judges, who are fallible men, depositaries of the law; when the easy, reasonable method of printing, at once secures its perpetuity, and divulges it to those who ought in justice to be made acquainted with it." Yet it had become obvious that "no number of statutes will comprehend every particular case; so indefinite is the variety from changes of circumstances." In fact, the attempt by codification to explode all "law from precedent," as the multiplicity of legislation in the 1780's was demonstrating, made the attaining of simplicity and equity more difficult; "for every new law . . . acts as rubbish, under which we bury the former." Therefore if the people were not to be inundated by confusing and contradictory laws, some judicial discretion was necessary: "When there is a contrariety between law and reason," as Otis would have said, "the judges *must be* embarrassed." It began to seem to some that Americans could not have specific legislative enactment and equity at the same time, or, contrary to the Beccarian belief, that codification and simplification of the law demanded an increase, not a lessening, of judicial interpretation and discretion. When particular statutes had to be enacted for every circumstance, said Moses Mather in a Connecticut election sermon in 1781, the laws proliferated and resulted in a confusion that wicked men turned to their private advantage. What was needed was simply the enactment of a few plain general rules of equity, leaving their interpretation to the courts. "Indeed," said Mather, "where civil justice is to be administered not by particular statutes, but by the application of general rules of equity, much will depend upon the wisdom and integrity of the judges."[74]

At the heart of the problem lay the Americans' ambivalent attitude toward law in confrontation with the new circumstances of the 1780's. In their new republics it was more imperative than ever before in the eighteenth century that their laws "be founded on the Principles of JUSTICE AND EQUITY," if they were to avoid "introducing such Penalties to enforce Obedience as would disgrace the Courts of Tripoli or Algiers." Morality was the basis of a republic. But now it was becoming all too evident to some that

74. *Rudiments of Law and Government*, 35–37; Moses Mather, *Sermon, Preached in the Audience of the General Assembly . . . on the Day of Their Anniversary Election, May 10, 1781* (New London, 1781), 7–8. Note the concern of the town of Braintree (1780) over the inability of written law alone to legitimate the property confiscations of the Revolution. Only *"natural Law (which in old Countries have obtained the name of common Law)"* could justify such confiscations. Handlin, eds., *Popular Sources*, 765–66.

the legislatures "(*the very fountain from whence justice must necessarily flow*)" were not always able to guarantee equity by their enactments, and in fact seemed to be becoming the greatest source of injustice in the society. Yet most Americans were too fully aware of the modern conception of statutory law, too deeply committed to consent as a basis for law, and from their colonial experience too apprehensive of the possible arbitrariness and uncertainties of judicial discretion to permit themselves easily to allow "Judges to set aside the law" made by the representatives of the people. "This," said James Madison in 1788, "makes the Judiciary Department paramount in fact to the Legislature, which was never intended and can never be proper." In a republican government there seemed no remedy for the making of bad laws except remonstrances by the people to their legislators to rescind or alter them. "If they do not, the people are to reject such legislators as traitors, and elect more faithful and honest in their places." If "the interpretation of the law" was dependent on "the will of the Judge," then "the government is very emphatically a despotism." "If the law is wrong," it seemed clear to many, "the Legislator only can alter it."[75]

To bring their abiding belief in the intrinsic equitableness of all law into harmony with their commitment to legislative supremacy, without doing violence to either, became the task of the 1780's. The concept of the constitution as fundamental law was not by itself a sufficient check on legislative will, unless it possessed some other sanction than the people's right of resistance. Even if the constitution could be invoked by the courts, as James Wilson remarked in the Constitutional Convention, it might not be adequate to the problems emerging in the 1780's. "Laws may be unjust, may be unwise, may be dangerous, may be destructive; and yet not be so unconstitutional as to justify the Judges in re-

---

75. *Providence Gazette*, July 8, 1786; Charleston *St. Gazette of S. C.*, Sept. 8, 1784; Farrand, ed., *Records of the Federal Convention*, II, 298–99; Madison's Observations on Jefferson's Draft of a Constitution for Virginia, Boyd, ed., *Jefferson Papers*, VI, 315; Trenton *N.-J. Gazette*, June 10, 1778, in Erdman, *New Jersey Constitution*, 90; Boston *Independent Chronicle*, Jan. 26, 1786. To Jefferson in 1785 judicial discretion in the administration of justice was still the great evil and codification the great remedy. "Relieve the judges from the rigour of text law, and permit them, with pretorian discretion, to wander into it's equity, and the whole legal system becomes incertain." Nothing could be worse than to allow, as England seemed to be doing under Mansfield and as America was soon to surpass, "the courts of Common law to revive the practice of construing their text equitably." Jefferson to Philip Mazzei, Nov. 1785, Boyd, ed., *Jefferson Papers*, IX, 68–71.

fusing to give them effect." Somehow the principles of justice and equity that made law what it was to Americans must be enforced in the ordinary courts, without at the same time conferring "upon the judicial department a power superior, in its general nature, to that of the legislature."[76] What was needed in fact was a revolutionary clarification in the Americans' understanding of law and of politics.

76. Farrand, ed., *Records of the Federal Convention*, II, 73; Wilson, "Lectures on Law," Wilson, ed., *Works of Wilson*, I, 460–62.

CHAPTER VIII

Conventions of the People

1. The Novelty of Constitutional Conventions

"A new sett of ideas," noted Oliver Ellsworth of Connecticut in the Philadelphia Convention of 1787, "seemed to have crept in since the articles of Confederation were established. Conventions of the people, or with power derived expressly from the people, were not then thought of." The legislatures, said Ellsworth, had at one time been considered "competent" to devise or revise a constitution. But now in the minds of most Americans, like James Madison, it had become "clear that the Legislatures were incompetent" for such tasks, so clear in fact that now "it would be a novel and dangerous doctrine that a Legislature could change the constitution under which it held its existence." This new set of ideas that Ellsworth spoke of, remarkable as it was, had indeed become so much a part of the Americans' thinking by 1787, so closely tied to their emergent notion of a fundamental constitution, that perhaps only an inhabitant of Connecticut, where the new thought was particularly slow in acceptance, could have realized its newness and the fact that it had not always prevailed. Although the idea of a convention of the people existing outside of the legislature was far more important than the concept of a higher law in indicating the direction American political thought was taking in the years after Independence, the two ideas were inextricably linked, and developed in tandem; for if the constitution were to be made truly immune from legislative alteration, it soon became obvious that it would have to be created "by a power superior to that of the ordinary legislature."[1] But just as the Ameri-

1. Farrand, ed., *Records of the Federal Convention*, II, 91–93; Jefferson's

cans' refined conception of a constitution did not at once spring into being everywhere with Independence, so too was the institution of the constitutional convention only awkwardly and unevenly developed.

Most Americans in 1776 had as yet no real modern appreciation of the permanent and unalterable nature of the constitution, or if they did, they possessed little knowledge of the means by which it was to be made permanent and fundamental. It was obvious to all, said Samuel West in the Massachusetts election sermon of 1776, that "it is the major part of a community that have the sole right of establishing a constitution and authorizing magistrates; and consequently it is only the major part of the community that can claim the right of altering the constitution, and displacing the magistrates." But how was the will of the major part of the community determined? Undoubtedly, said West, the community could not all meet together; "hence comes the necessity of appointing delegates to represent the people in general assembly." Thus it followed that it was the assemblies representing the community that had the right to establish or alter a constitution. And most in 1776 agreed. In all of the states in 1776 therefore (except in Pennsylvania where the circumstances were peculiar) the constitutions were created by the legislatures, when they were still sitting, or by Revolutionary congresses considered to be legally imperfect legislatures, although still representative of the people. Some colonies did not even bother with new elections to bolster the authority of their existing representative bodies for such important business. In Virginia only Jefferson among the leading planters raised an outcry against the existing convention's right to frame a constitution without a new election.[2] The New Jersey Revolutionary convention also assumed a new constitution without a new election and never doubted that the Constitution (except for certain specified articles) was amendable by the ordinary legislature. In South Carolina only a minority questioned the capacity of the Revolutionary congress to frame a constitution or the right of the legislature to replace it two years later. The Revolutionary convention that created the Vermont Constitution of 1777 never acquired any special importance in the eyes of Ver-

Draft of a Constitution for Virginia (1783), Boyd, ed., *Jefferson Papers*, VI, 295.

2. Samuel West, *Sermon Preached May 29th, 1776* (Boston, 1776), in Thornton, ed., *Pulpit*, 278–79. On Jefferson's call for a special election see Randolph, "Essay on Virginia," *Va. Mag. of Hist. and Biog.*, 44 (1936), 43. There is some doubt however about Jefferson's reasons for a new election; see Irving Brant, *James Madison*, (N. Y., 1941–61), I, 252–54.

monters and indeed seemed to have left the legality of their Constitution in doubt. In 1779 and again in 1782 the Vermont legislature felt compelled to reenact the Constitution, declaring that "in order to prevent disputes respecting the legal force of the constitution of this State," the Constitution "shall be forever considered, held, and maintained, as part of the laws of this State."[3]

Yet the distinction between the fundamental law of the constitution and ordinary statutory law was strong enough in 1776 to drive others into wrestling with devices to put their constitutions beyond the reach of mere legislative acts. The Delaware Constitution declared the Declaration of Rights and certain specified articles immune from any alteration, and, drawing upon William Penn's old charter of government, made the consent of five-sevenths of the Assembly and seven members of the legislative Council necessary for any amendment of the remainder of the Constitution. The Maryland Constitution could be altered only by the acts of two successive separately elected legislatures. In Georgia the Constitution could not be changed except by a special convention called by the Assembly after receiving petitions from the voters in a majority of the counties in the state. The second South Carolina Constitution, that of 1778, provided that no part could be altered without ninety days' notice and the approval of a majority of both houses. In Pennsylvania where the distinction between constitutional and legislative law was most sharply appreciated, elaborate machinery for amending the Constitution was adopted (and copied by Vermont), including a strange new body, a Council of Censors, to inquire periodically into violations of the Constitution by the government.[4] Although a few groups in scattered areas—those most fearful of and estranged from the Whigs' assuming power in the new governments, like the freeholders of Orange and Mecklenburg counties in North Carolina, the inhabitants of some New England towns, and the mechanics of New York City—were already in 1776 contending that only the people-at-large through their personal consent could truly create or amend a constitution, their views, rapidly as they be-

3. Erdman, *New Jersey Constitution*, 39–40, 58; Edward McCrady, *South Carolina in the Revolution*, 235–41; Ramsay, *History of Revolution of South Carolina*, I, 133; William Slade, ed., *Vermont State Papers* (Middlebury, Vt., 1823), 288, 449.

4. Del. Cons. (1776), Art. 30; Md. Cons. (1776), LIX; Ga. Cons. (1777), Art. LXIII; S. C. Cons. (1778), XLIV; Pa. Cons. (1776), Sec. 47. See Walter F. Dodd, *Revision and Amendment of State Constitutions* (*Johns Hopkins University Studies in Historical and Political Science*, New Ser., 1 [Baltimore, 1910]), 120–22.

came accepted in the coming years, were still too advanced for the legislatures and congresses of 1776. Even Jefferson, anxious as he was to insure the fundamental character of his 1776 proposed Constitution for Virginia, could only suggest in his first draft that the Constitution be unrepealable except "by the unanimous consent of both legislative houses." By his second and third drafts, however, he had refined his thinking, now proposing that the Constitution or "bill" be referred "to the people to be assembled in their respective counties and that the suffrages of two thirds of the counties shall be requisite to establish it," the Constitution then being unalterable "but by the personal consent of the people on summons to meet in their respective counties."[5]

These were beginnings, rudimentary efforts to make effective the distinction between the fundamental principles of the constitution and positive law. And if the concept of the constitution as higher law had been the only ingredient in the American Revolution, these beginnings by themselves might well have sufficed. But the concept of fundamental law was not the only ingredient. Other elements, other institutions and thoughts, contributed to the conclusion reached by almost all states by the early eighties, as Jefferson observed in his *Notes on the State of Virginia*, "that to render a form of government unalterable by ordinary acts of assembly, the people must delegate persons with special powers. They have accordingly chosen special conventions to form and fix their governments."[6] To justify and to make intelligible the presence of the constitutional convention in the American political system required more than simply the desire to distinguish between higher law and statute law. For in the context of eighteenth-century thought the idea of a legal body existing outside of the representative legislature and making law which the legislature could not make was such a radical innovation in politics that the concept of fundamental law by itself hardly explains it. The rise of the constitutional convention was actually a symptom of a larger, more significant development of the period, of a transformation taking place in the people's traditional relationship to the government. It was not that conventions of the people were new institutions in 1776. Americans were very used to them; in

---

5. Jefferson's Drafts of the Virginia Constitution (1776), Boyd, ed., *Jefferson Papers*, I, 345, 354, 364. On the N. C. counties see Saunders, ed., *Col. Recs. of N. C.*, X, 870a-g; on the New England towns see below, Sec. 4; on the N. Y. mechanics see Niles, ed., *Principles*, 174–76. Cf. Tate, "Social Contract in America," *Wm. and Mary Qtly.*, 3d Ser., 22 (1965), 380.
6. Jefferson, *Notes on Virginia*, ed. Peden, 125.

fact for most they had been the instruments of revolution. But such conventions did not generally mean then what they soon came to mean in the following years.

2. THE DEFICIENCY OF CONVENTIONS

Convention was an ancient term in English history, dating back at least to early medieval times. Literally a convention was a meeting, an act of coming together, used to refer to all sorts of assemblies, especially formal assemblies, convened for deliberation on important matters, whether ecclesiastical, political, or social. Meetings of the clergy or of the barons, or of both, together with spokesmen for the people, outside of the established Crown institutions, were commonly called conventions. It was just such an assembly of the barons, prelates, and people—a convention of the estates of the realm—that accepted Edward II's abdication in 1327, and a similar convention of estates participated in a more ambiguous manner in the accession of Henry IV in 1399. Throughout the medieval period such conventions of the estates of the realm were regarded as quite distinct from the Parliament and in fact were thought to embody the nation more completely than Parliament did, since Parliament was more the King's instrument for receiving taxes and petitions and for governing the realm than it was a full representation or spokesman of the society. This medieval Parliament of the King thus did not legislate in the modern sense; rather it made judgments as the King's high court, judgments whose binding authority came not from any sort of consent by the constituents of the Parliament but from the sanction of the King in his capacity as justiciar for the nation. But by the end of the fourteenth century and the beginning of the fifteenth the conventions of the estates—barons, clergy, and the people—which had hitherto been extraordinary meetings outside of the Parliament were increasingly being identified with the Parliament itself, so that Englishmen in time came to believe that their whole society was constitutionally encased in the King's High Court of Parliament—a momentous identification that separates medieval from modern English constitutionalism.[7]

Indeed, so identified did the estates of the realm become with Parliament that Englishmen eventually found it impossible to con-

7. See May McKisack, *The Fourteenth Century 1307-1399* (Oxford, 1959), 91-92, 494-96; Chrimes, *English Constitutional Ideas*, 106-17.

ceive of any convention of the estates existing outside of Parliament except in a legally deficient manner. Therefore by the end of the sixteenth century meetings of the Parliament in which no bills were assented to by the King had become technically "but a Convention, and no Parliament, or Session." While all kinds of other conventions or meetings of groups continued to be held, conventions of the estates or of the whole society could now be conceived of only in terms of Parliament. It is not surprising then that during the constitutional struggles of the seventeenth century, when the Commons and Lords were forced to convene without the King, Englishmen struggled with the proper terms to describe the meetings, with convention being commonly used by those who considered the bodies legally irregular. When Charles II was restored to the throne in 1660 by such a body, men were hard pressed to answer "whether anything done by this convention can be obliging to the nation, seeing they have not the right constitution of a parliament, according to the fundamental laws of the Kingdom?" In 1688 the body of Lords and Commons likewise called itself a convention until it had conferred the Crown on William and Mary at which time it became a Parliament. Thus by the early eighteenth century a convention, when applied to the representatives of the nation, was widely regarded as some sort of defective Parliament, an imperfect or partial embodiment of the estates of the realm, considered by most Englishmen to be inferior in legal authority to the Parliament because of the absence of the King, especially since the King in the course of the previous century had become a distinct estate in the society.[8] Even the radical James Burgh, proud as he was of the "convention-parliament" of 1688, since it was responsible for "the greatest thing that ever was done for this island," admitted that it was "irregular in its construction."[9]

8. See in general J. Franklin Jameson, "The Early Political Uses of the Word Convention," *Amer. Hist. Rev.*, 3 (1897–98), 477–87; the quotations are from 480, 481. On Noah Webster's distinction between a convention and a parliament see his *Collection of Essays and Fugitive Writings on Moral, Historical, Political and Literary Subjects* (Boston, 1790), 51–52: "The assembly of Lords and Commons which restored Charles II, and that which raised the Prince of Orange to the throne, were called Conventions, or *parliamentary Conventions* . . . a *Convention* being an assembly or meeting of Lords and Commons, on an emergency, without the King's writ, which is the regular constitutional mode of summoning them, and by custom necessary to render the meeting a *Parliament*." Webster also goes on to describe the new meaning of a convention as it had emerged in American thought by 1790.

9. Burgh, *Disquisitions*, I, 297–98.

The American colonists were familiar with the term convention and used it to denote all sorts of meetings for quasi-public
purposes, whether of New England Congregational ministers in
the early eighteenth century or of delegates discussing plans for
continental union in 1754. During their own versions of the Glorious Revolution in 1689 the colonists had also fallen back upon
conventions, convocations of the representatives of the people, in
the absence of legally constituted authority. In fact throughout
the eighteenth century whenever the governor or council was not
present or the legality of the writs electing the lower house was in
question, the representatives of the people declared, as did the
South Carolina Assembly in 1719, "that we cannot Act as an Assembly, but as a Convention, delegated by the People, . . . until
His Majesty's Pleasure be known."[10]

Eighteenth-century Americans, like the English, thus generally
regarded conventions as legally deficient bodies existing outside of
the regularly constituted authority. Not that such conventions
or meetings of the people were necessarily illegal, for they were
closely allied in English thought with the people's right to assemble and to present grievances to the government. It was this
right of assembly that justified the numerous associations and congresses that sprang up during the Stamp Act crisis, all of which
were generally regarded as adjuncts rather than as replacements
of the constituted governments. But the increasing difficulty in
the 1760's of the people's using their legislatures to express their
will, because of the governors' speedy and arbitrary prorogations, was making "excusable" the belief, said Thomas Hutchinson, "that, in other ways, the minds of the people collected together should be known, though perhaps, in ordinary times, not
strictly regular."[11] The first major attempt by the colonists to im-
plement this belief and actually to supplant rather than merely aid
the existing legislature with a convention of the representatives—
that of the Massachusetts Whigs in 1768—was a distinct failure.
"Calling of an Assembly by private persons only" was a flagrant

10. John A. Jameson, *The Constitutional Convention: Its History, Powers,
and Modes of Proceeding* (Chicago, 1867), 8–9; S. C. Assembly quoted in Jameson, "Early Political Uses," *Amer. Hist. Rev.*, 3 (1897–98), 478. Other works on
conventions include Roger Hoar, *Constitutional Conventions* . . . (Boston, 1917),
and Charles S. Lobingier, *The People's Law or Popular Participation in Law-
Making* . . . (N. Y., 1909). See also the brief discussion in Handlin, eds., *Popular
Sources*, 5.
11. Hutchinson, *History of Massachusetts*, ed. Mayo, III, 145, 152, 149.

attack on constituted authority, warned Governor Francis Bernard; and changing the name of this purported representation of the people to a convention did not "alter the Nature of the Thing." Bernard made a strong constitutional stand and many of the members of the Convention, "fearful of the legality of their proceedings," immediately recognized their meeting's doubtful legal status by renouncing "all pretence to any authoritative or governmental acts," and the Convention went on "with less spirit than was expected." Nevertheless, as Hutchinson remarked, this attempt by the people to convene on their own authority an assembly "which, in everything but in name, would be a house of representatives," had "a greater tendency towards a revolution in government, than any preceding measures in any of the colonies."[12]

By the early 1770's circumstances had changed. What had been premature and doubtful in 1768 was now becoming essential and hence more acceptable. The crisis had so deepened that the colonists felt they no longer could rely on the existing governmental institutions to organize the people. "The people at large, when they lose their constitutional guard," English radicals were writing, "are like a rope of sand, easily divided asunder; and therefore when the acting parts of the constitution shall abuse their trust, and counteract the end for which they were established, there is no way of obtaining redress but by associating together, in order to form a new chain of union and strength in defence of their constitutional rights." By 1773 not only had local committees of correspondence assumed governmental duties in the towns and counties, but nearly all the colonies had established provincial bodies to act as standing committees of the legislatures, which in effect, as Hutchinson told Lord Dartmouth in July 1773, "defeats and counteracts the power reserved to the governors . . . of proroguing or dissolving the assembly at pleasure."[13] This prerogative power was such that the Whigs in the assemblies had found themselves driven by the governors' hasty dissolutions of the legislatures "to the unhappy dilemma of either sacrificing the most es-

12. Governor Francis Bernard quoted in John C. Miller, "The Massachusetts Convention, 1768," *New Eng. Qtly.*, 7 (1934), 465–66; Hutchinson, *History of Massachusetts*, ed. Mayo, III, 152, 149.
13. [Hulme], *Historical Essay*, 151, also 161; Burgh, *Disquisitions*, I, 6; Hutchinson to Lord Dartmouth, July 10, 1773, in Edward D. Collins, "Committees of Correspondence of the American Revolution," in Amer. Hist. Assoc., *Annual Report, 1901*, I, 255.

sential interests of their constituents, or of meeting in General Convention to assert and preserve them." If the governor would not call the legislature, said the speaker of the North Carolina Assembly in March 1774, "then the people will convene themselves," since as Joseph Hawley wrote, "The people will have some government or other." The royal governors stood helpless as they watched para-governments grow up around them, a rapid piecing together from the bottom up of a hierarchy of committees and congresses that reached from the counties and towns through the provincial conventions to the Continental Congress.[14]

The convening of these conventions and congresses, "without the Governor, by the meer act of the People," immediately touched off a debate on their constitutionality. Tories and royal officials warned the people against supporting such "popular and tumultuous associations," whose "leaders in vain seek by attentions and courtesies that compliance with their commands" which the regular representative legislatures "derive from established undisputed authority." The resort to congresses and committees at the time of the Stamp Act, for all of the commotion and disorder it occasioned, was still, the Tories admitted, justifiable and eventually successful because the colonists never denied the legality of British authority. Now, however, "the case is altered. The grand Congress, the *piddling* Committees through the continent, have *all* disclaimed their subjection to the sovereign authority of the empire." It was the recognized privilege of Englishmen to meet together and to settle upon the substance and forms of petitions for the redress of grievances. But the present congresses and committees had gone beyond these legitimate bounds, setting up powers that were "foreign and unconstitutional," and subverting the existing legislatures. Undoubtedly the people had a right to participate in government. "This right they exercise by choosing *representatives*. . . . But when they have chosen their representatives, that right, which was before diffused through the whole people, centers in their *Representatives alone*; and can legally be exercised by *none but them*." Dangerous repercussions could only follow from attempts to delegate the trust placed in the legitimate repre-

14. Purdie's Wmsbg. *Va. Gazette*, Sept. 8, 1775; Sikes, *Transition of North Carolina*, 35–36; Joseph Hawley, "Broken Hints to be Communicated to the Committee of Congress for the Massachusetts," Niles, ed., *Principles*, 108. See Rowland, *Mason*, I, 208; Macmillan, *War Governors*, 20–21; Collins, "Committees of Correspondence," Amer. Hist. Assoc., *Annual Report, 1901*, I, 256; Nevins, *American States*, 28–43.

sentatives "to any body of men, whose powers are circumscribed by no law, and their existence unknown to the constitution." Governor Josiah Martin of North Carolina saw the implications only too clearly in his confrontation with the most impudent form of revolutionary convention: in April 1775 the North Carolina Congress convened simultaneously with the legislature, met in the same room, with the same person presiding, and with largely the same personnel as the legal Assembly. Such illegal action, Martin warned the legislature, only wounded the dignity of the representatives, and created "a belief in the people that they are capable of electing representatives of superior powers to the members of your House; which if it can possibly obtain, must lead by obvious consequences to the destruction of the essence, if not the very being, of an assembly in this Province, and finally to the utter dissolution and overthrow of its established happy constitution."[15]

The Whigs' answers to this criticism were generally defensive, since they realized they were moving into revolutionary ground. "Whenever we have departed from the Forms of the Constitution, . . . and if in any Instances we have assumed powers which the laws invest in the Sovereign or his representatives," explained the North Carolina Provincial Congress in a public apology to the mother country in September 1775, "it has been only in defence of our persons, properties and those rights which God and the Constitution have made Unalienably ours." Such congresses were to be only temporary. "As soon as the cause of our Fears and Apprehensions are removed, with joy will we return these powers to their regular channels; and such Institutions formed from mere necessity, shall end with that necessity that created them." The Maryland Convention was "introduced as a temporary expedient—a child of necessity—to supply, in some measure, a want of Government." Even the Tories were joining in the provincial

15. Thomas Hutchinson, *Strictures upon the Declaration of the Congress at Philadelphia; In a Letter to a Noble Lord* . . . (London, 1776), in *Old South Leaflets*, No. 227, ed. Malcolm Freiberg (Boston, 1958), 15; [Henry Barry], *The Strictures on the Friendly Address Examined* . . . ([Boston], 1775), 5; [Seabury], *View of the Controversy*, 23, 31; [Thomas B. Chandler], *What Think Ye of the Congress Now?* . . . (N. Y., 1775), 8–9, 43; [Samuel Seabury], *An Alarm to the Legislature of the Province of New York* . . . (N. Y., 1775), 4; [Crean Brush], *Speech of a Member of the General Assembly of New York, at Their Session, in 1775* (N. Y., 1775), 7–8; Martin quoted in Phila. *Pa. Journal*, Apr. 26, 1775. On N. C. see also Nevins, *American States*, 77–78; Sikes, *Transition of North Carolina*, 38–39. For the Assembly's answer to Martin see Niles, ed., *Principles*, 312.

congresses, noted Governor William Franklin of New Jersey, because the congresses were "the only expedient, in such an exigency, for the preservation of Peace and good order and the security of private property."[16]

Up and down the continent the colonial conventions and Whig spokesmen contended that the people had no alternative to the calling of such bodies, since "their General Assemblys were subject to the adjournments Prorogations and Dissolutions of Governors." When the people's ordinary means of defense against "arbitrary impositions" failed, declared the South Carolina Congress in June 1775, "mankind generally have had recourse to those that are extraordinary." Such bodies, declared James Wilson, "if not authorized by the forms, because that was rendered impossible by our enemies, are nevertheless authorized by that which weighs much more in the scale of reason—by the spirit of our constitutions," indeed by the strongest precedents in English history itself. Whigs like Wilson could not "conceal" their "emotions of pleasure" when they realized "that the objections of our adversaries cannot be urged against us" without denying the legality of the proceedings of the Revolution of 1688. When the English people were similarly subjected to despotism, "they assembled by their representatives in 1688, not in Parliament, but in Convention (or Congress if you will) and determined to banish the tyrant STUART from the throne." Even if such conventions were illegal, wrote Alexander Hamilton, it would not matter, for "there are some events in society, to which human laws cannot extend." "This is a time," the Whigs stated in an argument from which there could be no further appeal, "when we must have recourse to original principles; when no longer fettered by human institutions, we obey the unchangeable laws of nature." It was undoubtedly true, wrote Jefferson in a concise summary of the general Whig view, that as long as the assemblies "to whom the people have delegated the powers of legislation" were in existence, "they alone possess and may exercise those powers. But when they are dissolved by the lopping off one or more of their branches, the power reverts to the people, who may use it to unlimited extent, either assembling together in person, sending deputies, or in any other way they may think proper."[17]

16. "Address to the Inhabitants of the British Empire," Sept. 8, 1775, Saunders, ed., *Col. Recs. of N. C.*, X, 202; "To the People of Maryland," June 1776, Force, ed., *American Archives*, 4th Ser., VI, 1095; Governor William Franklin to the Earl of Dartmouth, May 6, 1775, in Erdman, *New Jersey Constitution*, 15.
17. Thomas Waldron to the Congress or General Assembly of New Hamp-

Since these congresses were not actually equivalent in authority to the regular constituted legislatures but only "instituted on principles of public necessity," their proceedings had to be in the form of resolves or recommendations. "We have no coercive or legislative Authority," declared John Rutledge in 1774 in the Continental Congress. "Our Constituents are bound only in Honour, to observe our Determinations." Despite the fact that the "*Recommendations*" of these conventions, to the amazement of Whigs and royal officials alike, "have the same regard paid to them by the body of the people, as used to be paid to laws enacted in form," most Americans doubted the efficacy of operating government under such tentative circumstances.[18] By the summer of 1775 the Virginia Congress was putting all its actions "through all the formalities of a bill in the House of Burgesses," said George Mason, in order to have them as much as possible wear "the face of law—Resolves as recommendations being no longer trusted to in matters of importance." Indeed, it was the precarious legal position of these conventions, where "Resolves and Recommendations of Congresses and Committees are put in place of the commands of a Legislature," that persuaded many Whigs of the need to institute governments even before independence was publicly mentioned.[19] The people of Massachusetts, Samuel Adams told Joseph Warren in September 1774, would probably be better united in a house of representatives under their old Charter than in a provincial congress, for they would then more easily see themselves in "a constitutional opposition to tyranny." Thus when Massachusetts resumed its Charter in the summer of 1775, the first act of the re-established General Court was to confirm all the resolutions of the

shire, Jan. 16, 1776, Bouton *et al.*, eds., *State Papers of N. H.*, VIII, 28; Address of the Provincial Congress of South Carolina, June 20, 1775, Niles, ed., *Principles*, 320; Wilson, "Speech Delivered in the Convention," Wilson, ed., *Works of Wilson*, III, 256; Purdie's Wmsbg. *Va. Gazette*, Mar. 8, 1776; [Hamilton], *Farmer Refuted*, Syrett and Cooke, eds., *Hamilton Papers*, I, 136; Rind's Wmsbg. *Va. Gazette*, July 21, 1774; [Jefferson], *Summary View*, Boyd, ed., *Jefferson Papers*, I, 132.

18. Dixon and Hunter's Wmsbg. *Va. Gazette*, Aug. 5, 1775; Adams, Notes on Debates in the Continental Congress, Sept. 6, 1774, Butterfield, ed., *Diary of Adams*, II, 125; John Winthrop to Richard Price, Apr. 10, 1775, "Price Letters," Mass. Hist. Soc., *Proceedings*, 2d Ser., 17 (1903), 284. See also Lord Dunmore to the Earl of Dartmouth, Dec. 24, 1774, Fitzpatrick, ed., *Writings of Washington*, III, 249n.

19. George Mason to Martin Cockburn, Aug. 22, 1775, Rowland, *Mason*, I, 208; Phila. *Pa. Packet*, Apr. 15, 1776. On the pressure to establish regular governments see R. H. Lee to Robert Carter Nicholas, Apr. 30, 1776, Ballagh, ed., *Letters of R. H. Lee*, I, 184; Francis Lightfoot Lee to Landon Carter, Apr. 9, 1776, Burnett, ed., *Letters of Congress*, I, 417.

provincial congresses as lawful and of as much force as if they had
been passed by a legitimate legislature. As justifiable by expediency, nature, or history as the Americans' Revolutionary conventions and congresses were "in these very Critical and Alarming
Times," still they were no substitute for properly constituted representations of the people in regular legislatures.[20]

Yet the convention in American thinking eventually became
something more than a legally deficient legislature, indeed became an extraordinary constitution-making body that was considered to be something very different from and even superior to the
ordinary legislature—all so rapidly and so suddenly that it is difficult to recapture its origins. It was perhaps inevitable that the
Americans' conventions of 1774–75, as the instruments of revolution and constitution-making, should have eventually assumed
an unusual importance in their eyes. Some Englishmen at the time
of their own Revolution in 1688 had also been unable to avoid the
significance of what their Convention, defective as it was, had
done. In 1689 a few pamphleteers, in a distinctly minority opinion, had argued that the Convention placing William and Mary
on the throne, although made up of the same Lords and Commons
that usually composed a Parliament, "yet being the Representatives of the whole Kingdom gathered together in an extraordinary
case and manner, and for extraordinary ends, . . . seemeth to be
something greater, and of greater power than a Parliament." An
early eighteenth-century English pamphlet, republished in Philadelphia in 1775, echoed this view of the 1688 Convention, arguing
that when a society was thrown into a state of nature by revolution it had "an Inherent Right" to put itself under any form of

---

20. Samuel Adams to Joseph Warren, Sept. 1774, Cushing, ed., *Writings of
Samuel Adams*, III, 157; Cushing, *Transition in Massachusetts*, 179; Address of
the Georgia Provincial Congress to the Governor, July 17, 1775, in "Proceedings
and Minutes of the Governor and Council . . . ," *Ga. Hist. Qtly.*, 34 (1950), 295.
See in this regard the opinion of St. George Tucker in *Kamper* v. *Hawkins* in
1793: the Revolutionary conventions "were the *people*, assembled by their deputies, not a *legal*, or *constitutional assembly*, or *part* of the *government* as then organized. Hence they were not, nor could be deemed the ordinary legislature;
that body being composed of the governor, council, and burgesses, who sat in
several distinct chambers and *characters*: while the other was composed of a
single body, having neither the character of governor, council, or legitimate
representatives among them: they were, in effect, *the people themselves*, assembled by their delegates, to whom the care of the commonwealth was especially, as well as unboundedly confided." Judges Brockenbrough and Holmes, eds.,
*A Collection of Cases Decided by the General Court of Virginia . . . Commenc-
ing in the Year 1789 . . .* (Phila., 1815), I, 69.

government it chooses. "Yet it cannot be regularly said to be done by the Society, unless it be done by such Persons only as are appointed by the Society for that purpose." In 1764 James Otis voiced a similar impression of the Glorious Revolution, implying that the Convention of 1688 in some curious way had actually created the government anew and thus was not less but in fact more than an ordinary Parliament.[21]

The Americans with a similar heritage and confronted with similar situations during their own constitution-making experience would approximate and elaborate these sporadically expressed ideas about the English Convention-Parliament. But they would do more. They would make the conventions that created their constitutions something more than simply extraordinary constituent bodies isolated in time without duplication before or since. The conventions of the people would become for Americans permanent continuing institutions, integral parts of their political system, essential for its working, and always available for the people's use. It was as if the revolution the Americans had begun in the early 1770's never ceased, as if the government dissolved in those years, throwing "back, into the hands of the people the powers they had delegated," and leaving them "as individuals to shift for themselves," was never really resumed.[22] Indeed, all the developments and creations of the period, including the idea of a constitution and the institution of a constitutional convention, were ultimately grounded in the increasing difficulty Americans had in sustaining representative legislatures which could satisfactorily speak for the people. Beginning with the Revolutionary movement (but with roots deep in American history) the American people came to rely more and more on their ability to organize themselves and to act "out-of-doors," whether as "mobs," as political clubs, or as conventions.

3. THE PEOPLE OUT-OF-DOORS

America had a long tradition of extra-legislative action by the people, action that more often than not had taken the form of mob violence and crowd disturbance. From the time of the first

21. Jameson, "Early Political Uses," *Amer. Hist. Rev.*, 3 (1897–98), 479; *Essay upon Government*, 113–14; Otis, *Rights of the British Colonies*, Bailyn, ed., *Pamphlets*, I, 421–22.
22. Jefferson, *Notes on Virginia*, ed. Peden, 127.

settlements on through the eighteenth century rioting at one time or another paralyzed all the major cities; in the countryside outbursts of angry farmers and frontier settlers periodically destroyed property, closed courts, and brought government to a halt. These were not the anarchic uprisings of the poor and destitute; rather they represented a common form of political protest and political action in both England and the colonies during the eighteenth century by groups who could find no alternative institutional expression for their demands and grievances, which were more often than not political.[23] The South Carolina Regulators of 1767–68, for example, formed extralegal associations composed largely of back-country property-holders in order to bring some measure of order and stability to a chaotic area that the existing government in Charleston had ignored. Although the Regulators' vigilante movement, because it posed no direct threat to the constituted authorities in the East, gained a kind of legitimacy that other contemporary mob uprisings did not, its composition, its resort to formal association and written articles, and its discrimination in the choice of victims and force were not essentially different in character from the North Carolina disturbances in 1769–70, or from the Paxton uprisings in Pennsylvania in 1763–64, or even from the numerous mobs that erupted in the cities during the 1760's. All were efforts by discontented groups to use violence and intimidation to redress diverse grievances unsatisfied by weak and unresponsive governments.[24] In fact it seemed at times that the governments were so weak that they had to be bypassed in dealing with such mobs. Counter-mob elements were often compelled to organize their own extralegal associations to put down the insurrectionist movements in the defense of order.[25]

Good Whigs, particularly those in the Commonwealth tradition, recognized and appreciated the political existence of the people "out-of-doors," that is, outside of the legal representative

23. See Bailyn, ed., *Pamphlets*, I, 581–84; Gordon S. Wood, "A Note on Mobs in the American Revolution," *Wm. and Mary Qtly.*, 3d Ser., 23 (1966), 635–42; and sources cited in these.

24. Richard M. Brown, *The South Carolina Regulators* (Cambridge, Mass., 1963); Basset, "The Regulators of North Carolina," Amer. Hist. Assoc., *Annual Report, 1894,* 141–212; Brooke Hindle, "The March of the Paxton Boys," *Wm. and Mary Qtly.*, 3d Ser., 3 (1946), 461–86; Bridenbaugh, *Cities in Revolt*, 113–18, 305–14; Morgan, *Stamp Act Crisis*, Chap. VIII.

25. Brown, *South Carolina Regulators*, Chap. VIII; Basset, "Regulators of North Carolina," Amer. Hist. Assoc., *Annual Report, 1894,* 197; Hindle, "Paxton Boys," *Wm. and Mary Qtly.*, 3d Ser., 3 (1946), 475.

institutions, and under certain circumstances were even willing to grant a measure of legitimacy to their actions. "I love a mob," the Duke of Newcastle was supposed to have said, or so Bostonians read in their newspapers in the early seventies. "We owe the Hanoverian succession to a mob." Popular demonstrations were often condoned and even led by "better sorts" in the society when they could be turned to political advantage. The Regulator movements in the Carolinas contained many men of wealth and status. The march of the Paxton Boys in 1764, noted one observer, was "invited and Encouraged by many Considerable persons in Philadelphia" who shared the westerners' hostility to the Pennsylvania legislature. Even John Adams, as much as he detested "private mobs," was cautiously willing to justify "Popular Commotions . . . in Opposition to attacks upon the Constitution," but "only when Fundamentals are invaded." It was in this spirit that many Whig leaders instigated or permitted the mob violence of the sixties and early seventies. Riots and mobbing, threatening royal officials, enforcing nonimportation agreements, intimidating Tories, persecuting printers, were not only excused but often directed and abetted by respectable members of the community—planters, merchants, lawyers—like Christopher Gadsden of South Carolina, or Robert Morris of Pennsylvania, or John Ashe of North Carolina. The Sons of Liberty became in effect organized mobs, "a necessary ingredient," said the Tories, in fomenting the American Revolution.[26]

The disintegration of royal authority in the early seventies and the corresponding growth of revolutionary organizations intensified the Whigs' reliance on extralegal popular action. Clubs and associations that had in the 1760's been organized as extralegal pressure groups for particular and limited purposes, whether for the intimidation of stamp collectors or for the enforcement of nonimportation agreements, now began to assume the actual functions of government. Many of the groups that had hitherto used or participated in mobs or other loosely organized "popular assemblies," as Lieutenant-Governor William Bull of South Caro-

26. Newcastle citation, in Bridenbaugh, *Cities in Revolt*, 309; Hindle, "Paxton Boys," *Wm. and Mary Qtly.*, 3d Ser., 3 (1946), 477; Adams to Abigail Adams, July 7, 1774, Butterfield, ed., *Family Correspondence*, I, 131; Arthur M. Schlesinger, "Political Mobs and the American Revolution, 1765–1776," American Philosophical Society, *Proceedings*, 99 (1955), 244. On the respectability of the leaders of the mobs see Morgan, *Stamp Act Crisis*, 231–37; Walsh, *Charleston's Sons of Liberty*, 32–33, 46, 48, 71; Bridenbaugh, *Cities in Revolt*, 114, 307.

lina called them, now joined in the committees and conventions
that were fast springing up everywhere, and thereby gained a
quasi-legitimacy that they had not had before. Mob violence as
such, with the exception of the tea parties, rapidly declined in the
two years before the Revolution, since in effect it had been institutionalized by the new revolutionary associations. By 1775 committees and conventions in nearly all of the colonies were controlling and regulating all aspects of American life, more completely
perhaps than ever before in the eighteenth century: overawing
voters, dictating appointments, disposing of the militia, regulating
trade, levying taxes, supervising courts, and in fact, as the Tories
protested, even directing "what we shall eat, drink, wear, speak,
and think."[27]

The "dangers" of thus throwing all power back into the hands
of the people were "conspicuous," wrote Jefferson in 1774, but,
as Jefferson had intended, much more conspicuous to the Tories
than to the Whigs. Royal officials saw only too well what the multiplication of committees and conventions, where "a private man
take upon him to summon a whole province," might lead to:
"There will be nothing but cabals and combinations, and the
peace of the Province, and minds of the people, continually heated, disturbed, and distracted." Some Whigs too, "men of property," it was claimed, began to sense "that the many headed power
the People, who have hitherto been obediently made use of by
their numbers and occasional riots to support the claims set up in
America, have discovered their own strength and importance, and
are not now so easily governed by their former leaders." Just as
the Sons of Liberty had become a cloak for all sorts of brigandage
and lawlessness in the mid-sixties, so the more numerous and more
legitimate committees and associations of 1774–75 became a cover
for various extensions into public areas, even in some cases for

---

27. Walsh, *Charleston's Sons of Liberty*, 46; [Seabury], *View of the Controversy*, 37. On the powers assumed by the committees and conventions see *To
the Privates of the Several Battalions of Military Associators in the Province of
Pennsylvania* (Phila., 1776), 2–3; *To the Freeholders and Freemen of the City
and County of New-York* ([N. Y., 1775]), 1–2; Ramsay, *History of Revolution
of South Carolina*, I, 60; Walsh, *Charleston's Sons of Liberty*, 60, 64, 65, 71–73;
Collins, "Committees of Correspondence," Amer. Hist. Assoc., *Annual Report,
1901*, I, 264–67. On "the Introduction of Anarchy and Oppression" caused by
the new institutions see Calhoon, ed., "Robert Beverly," *Va. Mag. of Hist. and
Biog.*, 73 (1965), 50–51. For examples of mob persecution in the Revolution see
Wallace Brown, *The King's Friends: The Composition and Motives of the
American Loyalist Claimants* (Providence, 1966), 47–48, 64–65, 78, 135, 212.

purely private purposes, by "warm People," as Joseph Galloway complained, "of neither Property nor significance among us."[28] As early as May 1774, Gouverneur Morris warned that it was becoming "impossible to curb" the "mobility" exercising "tribuntial powers" through numerous extralegal committees and associations. "How to keep them down" became a central question not only to Tories in the years before Independence but increasingly to the Whigs themselves in the decade after Independence.[29]

"In planning a government by representation," James Burgh wrote in his *Political Disquisitions*, "the people ought to provide against their own *annihilation*. They ought to establish a regular and constitutional method of acting by and from *themselves*, without, or even in opposition to their *representatives*, if necessary"—surely the most disruptive yet the most creative idea expressed in the entire Revolutionary era, since it meant that the final and full embodiment of the people in the government was impossible. As the English radicals observed with approval, the Americans had successfully acted upon this idea in the sixties and seventies when their constitutional legislatures had been prevented from sitting. Now with Independence and with popular governments of their "own establishment, equal to all the purposes for which government is instituted, and laws of our own making," some Americans continued to act upon this idea, continued to assemble in committees and conventions outside of the legal governments and "to consult and debate upon the degree of submission due the constitutional government"—actions which increasingly seemed to others to "lead, if in the first instance they do not amount, to a reassumption of the power to govern into the hands of the people."[30]

Interstate and regional conventions and committees for the purpose of regulating the economy began meeting at the very out-

---

28. [Jefferson], *Summary View*, Boyd, ed., *Jefferson Papers*, I, 132; Governor Wright to the Earl of Dartmouth, Aug. 24, 1774, Force, ed., *American Archives*, 4th Ser., I, 731; Governor Bull to the Earl of Dartmouth, Mar. 28, 1775, quoted in Rogers, *William Loughton Smith*, 78; Galloway to Samuel Verplanck, Jan. 14, 1775, quoted in Julian P. Boyd, *Anglo-American Union: Joseph Galloway's Plans to Preserve the British Empire 1774–1788* (Phila., 1941), 40. For examples of private committees see Northumberland County (Pa.) Committee, May 24, 1776, Force, ed., *American Archives*, 4th Ser., VI, 562; Selsam, *Pennsylvania Constitution*, 125–26.
29. Gouverneur Morris to John Penn, May 20, 1774, Force, ed., *American Archives*, 4th Ser., I, 342.
30. Burgh, *Disquisitions*, I, 6; *Providence Gazette*, Sept. 9, 2, 1786.

break of war, at first under congressional and state auspices, then less officially, justified, as Samuel Adams said in 1777, by the right of the people "to assemble upon all occasions to consult measures for promoting liberty and happiness." When by the late seventies Congress and the state legislatures began to turn against these efforts to control prices and wages and to stabilize credit, local committees and county conventions in the New England and middle states became more and more spontaneous, springing up without legislative authorization to take action against monetary depreciation, engrossing, and profiteering, often relying on crude force and intimidation for enforcement. The very failure of the states' penal laws to restrain rising prices became a justification for the resort to voluntary associations which military companies offered to support by arms. Whenever goods seemed short or prices seemed exorbitant men proposed committees for investigation and control. By 1779 groups in Philadelphia were parading the streets in search of forestallers and monopolizers. In fact to some the entire mercantilist system of committees had become simply "a Mob . . . assembled to regulate prices."[31]

Organization of the people outside of the government was not confined to the regulation of the economy. Committees and associations of the people, given form and sanction by the experience of the Revolutionary movement, were spilling out everywhere to voice grievances or to realize political goals. "I am afraid," said Christopher Gadsden in 1778, the former tribune of the people of Charleston, "we have too many amongst us who want again to be running upon every fancy to the Meeting of [the] liberty tree."[32] Serious rioting under the direction of radical committees recurred in all of the major cities and formed the background for the incorporation movements in Boston, New Haven, Philadelphia, and Charleston in the 1780's.[33] Electioneering and attempts to influ-

31. Adams, quoted in Benjamin Rush's Diary, Feb. 4, 1777, and Daniel of St. Thomas Jenifer to Gov. Thomas Johnson, Jr., May 24, 1779, both in Burnett, ed., Letters of Congress, II, 234, IV, 232. On the mercantilist regulation see Morris, "Labor and Mercantilism," in Morris, ed., Era of the Revolution, 76–139; Robert L. Brunhouse, The Counterrevolution in Pennsylvania 1776–1790 (Harrisburg, 1942), 70–74; Walsh, Charleston's Sons of Liberty, 64–65, 73–74, 77; Oscar and Mary Handlin, "Revolutionary Economic Policy in Massachusetts," Wm. and Mary Qtly., 3d Ser., 4 (1947), 3–26.

32. Walsh, Charleston's Sons of Liberty, 87.

33. Merrill Jensen, The New Nation: A History of the United States during the Confederation, 1781–1789 (N. Y., 1958), 118–22.

ence town meetings and legislative bodies—citizens threatening "their fellows with loss of property for voting according to their own judgment"—had never seemed so prevalent. "A POLITICAL PHALANX" was always ready to be used "on *all* favorite mob or electioneering occasions."[34] The Whig and Republican societies of Philadelphia and the Marine Anti-Britannic Society of Charleston were only the most famous of many such self-constituted bodies organized for quasi-public purposes. In fact more such groups sprang up in the dozen years after Independence than in the entire colonial period.[35] The people's representatives in the legislature seemed "so far out of our Reach" that men felt pressed to fill "this wide Step and Vacancy" between themselves and their delegates either, as one pamphlet in 1782 suggested, by the establishment of regular county assemblies, or more commonly, by the spontaneous constitution of separate organizations of the people to watch over "that which they had gained by wisdom and fortitude" and did not want to lose by "remissness and inattention."[36] Western Massachusetts never really resumed a constitutional government after its dissolution in 1774, but lived under a series of mob-like committees and conventions. Even after the establishment of the 1780 Constitution, mobs calling themselves Regulators continued to close courts and intimidate public officials, culminating with the Shays movement in 1786. These rioters were not rabble, as one observer noted. They were country farmers under strong economic pressures, prompted by "a certain jealousy of government, first imbibed in the beginning of our controversy with Britain, fed by our publications against the British government, and now by length of time became in a manner habitual and ready to rise whenever burthens press, at once concluding, that *burthens* must be *grievances*." By the middle eighties the whole of New England was beset by conventions voicing not only local grievances and resentments against the impost and commutation measures of the Confederation Congress, but contesting the aims of other conventions. In the summer of 1787 even counties in Virginia were rising in spontaneous association, burning courthouses and stopping tax

---

34. Nathaniel Whitaker, *The Reward of Toryism* . . . (Newburyport, 1783), 31; Charleston *Extra Gazette of the St. of S.-C.*, July 12, 1784.

35. Jensen, *New Nation*, 141.

36. *Proposals to Amend and Perfect the Policy of the Government* . . . ([Phila.], 1782), 8; *Principles and Articles Agreed On by the Members of the Constitutional Society* . . . (Phila., 1780).

collections. In those states in the 1780's, particularly Massachusetts, Connecticut, and South Carolina, where large groups were unable to satisfy their grievances through ordinary legislative politics, "defiance of law, and resistance to its authority, was everywhere breathed."[37]

To the participants such associations of the people outside of the regularly constituted government seemed as necessary under their new republican governments as they did under the British government, "for," as Suffolk County, Massachusetts, declared in 1784, "whenever any measures are adopted . . . destructive to the Commonwealth, the people must either submit to them, or (if they proceed with decency and regularity) must take this method for relief." Did the present opponents of such extralegal organizations of the people, it was repeatedly and pointedly asked, "at the time of the Stamp Act, stickle so for Government? . . . Did they give the opprobrious epithet of MOBS to the leaders of the measures in those days?" The Revolution was fought precisely because government had acted contrary to the interests of the people. "Do not the fears and jealousies of the good people of the State at this day spring from the *like source?*"[38]

So prevalent did the usurpation of governmental functions by conventions and associations become that some Americans began to fear that the whole society would "shortly be overrun by committees." "The original ostensible design of them was laudable, and under proper regulations might, perhaps, produce good effects." But now they seemed to be merely "Instruments in the Hands of designing Men" who wish "to place the Government again in the Hands of the People" for their own selfish purposes. "The interference of clubs and private societies" in politics and lawmaking, "instead of being of any public use, *only* serves, if attended to, to embarrass the assembly, and split the members into parties. If one club meddles, may not another, and a third, and so on, with *equal* right and propriety." In reaction some of the once fervent Whig leaders began to sound like the Tories of 1775. There were legitimate channels for public expression in the town meetings, warned Governor John Sullivan of New Hampshire; assemblies of private orders of men "under the cover of conven-

37. Taylor, *Western Massachusetts*, Chaps. V–VII, quotation from 119; Brant, *Madison*, III, 116; Charleston *St. Gazette of S.-C.*, Feb. 22, 1787.
38. Boston *Independent Chronicle*, May 20, 1784; Charleston *Gazette of the St. of S.-C.*, May 13, 1784.

tion authority" would only undermine the constitution of the
state. Even the old Son of Liberty, Samuel Adams, by 1784 had
come to believe that "popular Committees and County Conventions are not only useless but dangerous." When they were used
in place of the royal legislatures, they had served "an excellent
Purpose," but "as we now have constitutional and regular Governments and all our Men in Authority depend upon the annual and
free Elections of the People, we are safe without them. . . . Bodies
of Men, under any Denomination whatever, who convene themselves for the Purpose of deliberating upon and adopting Measures which are cognizable by Legislatures only will, if continued,
bring Legislatures to Contempt and Dissolution."[39] "Where
will this capricious *retail tyranny* end?" men asked. Organized
mobs and unconstitutional combinations were "continually starting up here or there, and carried on merely as the gnawing worm
of malice or resentment may bite individuals." In Connecticut the
apprehensions became so great that the Assembly refused to recognize the legitimacy of any convention and on those grounds declined to send any delegates to Annapolis in 1786.[40] The press,
especially in New England, was filled with confused and anxious
pleas for the people to recognize the difference between 1774 and
1784. With Independence "the reason and necessity of the Convention ceased." Despite guarantees of the people's right of assembly in the Massachusetts Constitution, the framers had never
intended "to institute a subordinate representative body to act for
the people." The English people's organizing of themselves outside of Parliament was justified, but the Americans' was not. "In
a government constituted like that of Great-Britain, the attention
of the Representatives are turned wholly to the Ministry, or men
in power, unless where disappointed ambition throws it into the
scale of opposition." But in the American republics the legislatures
faced entirely toward the people: "The pleasure or displeasure of
the people, rests with great weight upon their Deputies in the legislatures." If the people "cannot trust representatives who have a

39. Meriwether Smith to Jefferson, June 25, July 30, 1779, William Fleming
to Jefferson, July 13, 1779, Boyd, ed., *Jefferson Papers*, III, 16, 33, 59; Charleston
Gazette Extra. of the St. of S.-C., July 17, 1784; Sullivan quoted in Phila. *Pa.
Packet*, Oct. 21, 1786; Samuel Adams to John Adams, Apr. 16, 1784, Adams to
Noah Webster, Apr. 30, 1784, Cushing, ed., *Writings of Samuel Adams*, IV, 296,
305-06.
40. Charleston *South-Carolina Gazette and General Advertiser*, May 11-13,
1784; Madison to Jefferson, Aug. 12, 1786, Boyd, ed., *Jefferson Papers*, X, 232.

common interest with us, . . . what greater reason is there to expect that our county conventions will be more faithful?"[41]

4. A POWER SUPERIOR TO THE ORDINARY LEGISLATURE

The mistrust of all men and all institutions set above the people-at-large was precisely the point. No legislative assembly, however representative, seemed capable of satisfying the demands and grievances of large numbers of Americans. And it was this dissatisfaction and the suspicion it engendered, as much as the idea of fundamental law, that explained the prominence that one kind of convention existing outside of the normal representative legislature gained in American thought. The unique position of legitimacy that the constitutional convention eventually attained, together with its close connection with the new conception of a constitution, has tended to obscure the disruptive forces that made such an extralegislative body possible and comprehensible—forces that had been laid bare at the very beginning of the Revolutionary movement. "Some step forth and tell you," said Philip Livingston in 1775 in answer to New York Tories, "you ought to support your Representatives—what! right or wrong!"[42] Out of just such exhortations to civil disobedience and such pervasive mistrust of the representational process was the conception of the constituent convention essentially formed.

As early as 1775 some Whigs were observing that the people in their revolutionary conventions had never been more fully and fairly represented in any legislatures in their history.[43] "The more just and equal representations of the people in the Colony Congresses," wrote Ezra Stiles, "acquire more and more weight, and feel more liberty to act for the public good unchecked by an arbitrary Governor." When the South Carolina Congress in March 1775 admonished the New York legislature, which was still sit-

---

41. Response of the Worcester Committee of Correspondence to Pittsfield, Oct. 8, 1778, Handlin, eds., *Popular Sources*, 372; Boston *Independent Chronicle*, Sept. 14, 1786, Apr. 8, 1784, Mar. 25, 1784.

42. [Livingston], *To the Inhabitants of New-York*, 2.

43. Thus the Georgia Convention told Gov. Wright in 1775 that "the Province never was more fully represented in any Assembly"; and the Virginia Convention declared in the same year that their body was "the most numerous assembly that had ever been known in this colony." Address of the Ga. Provincial Congress, July 11, 1775, in *Ga. Hist. Qtly.*, 34 (1950), 295; "A Declaration of the Delegates . . . in General Convention," in Purdie's *Wmsbg. Va. Gazette*, Sept. 8, 1775.

ting, for not joining in the general association of the colonies, it did so with an argument that had radical implications for the place of the convention and the people's relation to the institutions of government that few Whigs then envisioned. Perhaps the New York Assembly's refusal to act, suggested the South Carolina Congress, stemmed from a doubt of its authority, having been chosen prior to the present dispute. Surely "the legal representatives" of the people of New York were not really representing "the opinion of their constituents," but only intended to leave the voicing of that opinion "to another representation, not so much according to the letter of the law, but equally respectable, and as much to be depended on." The constituted legislature of New York must realize that it was not "the definitive voice of the colony." As the experience of the other colonies was demonstrating, other bodies, conventions or congresses, could perhaps better reflect the people's will than the regular legislatures. Yet precisely because the conventions were irregular bodies, "extraordinary perhaps in their nature, but warranted by necessity," dissatisfied groups could contend that even they were unequal to the "new affairs of the utmost importance." In fact simply to infer that the people's will was being fully represented by any institution, to infer that "the acts of those Representatives are the acts of their constituents," was not enough for some in these years, and in the years ahead it was to become never enough. "Why should such an inference be made? Where is the necessity for it? Cannot an appeal be made to the people? Their sentiments taken—be from themselves, and not guessed at? If they have not wisdom and virtue enough to become agents in promoting their own temporal salvation, it is vain for others to attempt it."[44]

No American in a responsible position by 1775 challenged the purity of the people in the contest with the Crown; all by then were good Whigs, with some, of course, more radical than others. John Adams's ideas that the people were the "Source of all Authority and Original of all Power" were not, as he recalled in his autobiography, "new, strange and terrible Doctrines, to the greatest Part of the Members" of the Continental Congress, although Adams's suggested timing and methods for their implementation perhaps were. Even the Tory, Daniel Leonard, writing as "Massa-

44. Ezra Stiles to Richard Price, Apr. 10, 1775, "Price Letters," Mass. Hist. Soc., *Proceedings*, 2d Ser., 17 (1903), 283; Phila. *Pa. Journal*, Apr. 12, 1775; Address of the Assembly of N. C. to Gov. Josiah Martin, Apr. 1775, Niles, ed., *Principles*, 312; Essay, June 22, 1774, Force, ed., *American Archives*, 4th Ser., I, 441.

chusettensis," agreed that "the rights of the people" were "sacred" and admitted that the people had "an inherent right to change their form of government." The difficulty was in applying this right "to the cause of the whigs," since the Tories stoutly denied that the rebel leaders spoke for the whole people. "That all Government originates from the People," as James Wilson pointed out in an argument resisting the pull toward independence, was "A Maxim," widely accepted by almost everyone.[45] The people were the undisputed, ubiquitous source that was appealed to by both the advocates and the opponents of independence. But who were the people? What institutions expressed their will?

In the confused manipulations of politics leading up to the May 15, 1776, resolution of the Continental Congress and to the Declaration of Independence, the Whigs groped awkwardly for some institutional representation of the people with which to justify the erection of new governments. Many advocates of new governments were unwilling to have their colony stand alone, and argued, like one New Jersey writer, that they "would by no means have this step taken without consulting the Continental Congress" and begging its "advice and approbation." Throughout 1774-75 the Massachusetts Provincial Congress continually sought to bolster its doubtful authority by connecting itself with the Congress in Philadelphia. Others, like James Sullivan, saw no need for congressional sanctions, having "many doubts whether the Congress has, or ought to have, power to regulate the internal police of the different Colonies." A similar argument was made by those resisting the drive toward independence, some congressional delegates pleading that they could not endorse the May resolutions or a Declaration of Independence without opposing the will of their constituents. The difficulty was, as Richard Henry Lee pointed out, that "those who wish delay, and want nothing done, say, let the people in the colonies begin, we must not go before them— Tho' they well know the language in the Country to be, Let the Congress advise."[46]

"There never was a time," as one writer told the people of

45. Butterfield, ed., *Diary of Adams*, III, 352; Adams and [Leonard], *Novanglus and Massachusettensis*, 225; Adams, Notes of Debates in the Continental Congress, May 13-15, 1776, Butterfield, ed., *Diary of Adams*, II, 238-39.
46. Phila. *Pa. Packet*, Apr. 15, 1776; Cushing, *Transition in Massachusetts*, 160-62; James Sullivan to John Adams, May 9, 1776, in Amory, *Sullivan*, I, 76-77; Adams, Notes of Debates in the Continental Congress, May 13-15, 1776, Butterfield, ed., *Diary of Adams*, II, 238-39; Klingelhofer, "Maryland and Independence," *Md. Hist. Mag.*, 60 (1965), 295; R. H. Lee to Charles Lee, May 11, 1776, *Lee Papers*, II, 26.

Maryland in June 1776, "in which it was more necessary for you to inquire into the conduct of your Representatives." The press was filled with claims and counterclaims by both those who desired and those who opposed independence, each questioning the representative character of particular bodies—Congress, conventions, legislatures, committees—and each calling for new and renewed mandates from the people. Wherever the provincial congresses or legislatures were slow to join in the Revolutionary movement, as in the middle colonies, men argued that another elective body, a new convention, would be more expressive of the people's will. Many of the delegates themselves, either realizing that they were involved in subjects "of the greatest importance" or hoping to postpone precipitate action, urged the collection of "the opinion of the people at large, in some manner or other."[47] In the late spring of 1776 the New York Convention found itself confronted with rising "doubts" whether it was "invested with the sufficient power and authority to deliberate and determine on so important a subject as the necessity of erecting and constituting a new form of Government." Since it was incontestable "that the right of framing, creating, or remodelling Civil Government is and ought to be in the People," the divided Convention decided to leave the question of its authority to the people, either to authorize their existing representatives or to choose a new body. Yet when suddenly in early June independence rather than new governments became the pressing issue, the New York Convention could turn its doubtful representative authority back upon the independence-minded radicals and plead in its instructions to its delegates in Philadelphia that it had not been vested by its constituents "with a power to deliberate and determine on that question." The people were rapidly becoming a permutable force whose will could never be embodied by any representative institution.[48]

47. "To the People of Maryland," June 1776, Force, ed., *American Archives*, 4th Ser., VI, 1096; N. H. Delegates to the President of N. H., June 11, 1776, Burnett, ed., *Letters of Congress*, I, 483; Md. Delegates to Md. Council of Safety, June 11, 1776, Force, ed., *American Archives*, 4th Ser., VI, 807. See also Phila. *Pa. Packet*, June 10, 1776; Klingelhofer, "Maryland and Independence," *Md. Hist. Mag.*, 60 (1965), 286.

48. Resolution of N. Y. Congress, May 31, 1776, Debates in N. Y. Congress, May 24, 1776, Report of Committee of N. Y. Congress, May 27, 1776, N. Y. Congress to Its Delegates in the Continental Congress, July 1, 1776, all in Force, ed., *American Archives*, 4th Ser., VI, 1351–52, 1332, 1338, 814. See Carl Becker, *History of Political Parties in the Province of New York, 1760 to 1776* (Madison, Wis., 1909), 267–72.

In this revolutionary atmosphere it is not surprising that special elections were held in seven of the colonies prior to the framing of new constitutions and the Declaration of Independence.[49] These new elections or mandates from the people, considering that they involved "business of the highest consequence for the government and welfare of the people," scarcely signified a general comprehension that a special representative body was needed to create a constitution. These newly elected bodies were simply newer and hence perhaps truer representations of the people, but they were as yet still traditional conventions, legally imperfect bodies, although designed, as Maryland stated, "for the express purpose of forming a new government, by the authority of the people only, and enacting and ordering all things for the preservation, safety, and general weal of this colony" until regular legislatures could be established. Printing of the constitution for "consideration" by the people for a two-week period before passage, as was done in Maryland, North Carolina, and Pennsylvania, was not the equivalent of ratification. Nevertheless these extraordinary appeals to the people did serve as the germ of the idea that somehow for certain "matters of such momentous concern" the existing representative body was not sufficiently representative to speak conclusively for the people.[50] Once conceded, the idea could have both troublesome and creative ramifications—ramifications that perhaps can be followed most vividly in Delaware and Pennsylvania, since their proprietary legislatures, possessing autonomous control over their capacity to meet, were still sitting in the spring of 1776.

In Delaware this inability to institutionalize the people in any final or complete form lent a permissiveness to politics that dramatically shaped new ideas about institutions. The most revolutionary-minded Delaware Whigs, faced with the congressional resolution of May 15, actually saw themselves free to choose between alternative means of representing the people. Since neighboring Pennsylvania's experience with a convention seemed cumbersome and divisive, the Whig leaders agreed that

49. New elections were held in New Hampshire, Pennsylvania, Delaware, Maryland, North Carolina, and Georgia. See Nevins, *American States*, 129.

50. President Archibald Bullock of Georgia, quoted in Nevins, *American States*, 130; Resolution of Md. Convention, July 3, 1776, *Proceedings of Convention of Maryland*, 184; Md. Delegates to Md. Council of Safety, June 11, 1776, Force, ed., *American Archives*, 4th Ser., VI, 807. See Dodd, *Revision of State Constitutions*, 10–23.

"the Recommendation of Congress was certainly meant to go to the Assemblies, where there were such who had authority to Set." Yet should the Delaware Assembly prove intractable there was still "time enough for the people to take the matter up in another way" by calling a convention. From then on the radical Whigs found themselves in a continual process of defining and redefining the people's will, playing off the people-at-large against the institutions that supposedly represented them. Unable to control the Assembly, they eventually resorted to the "other way" of a convention despite the heated objections of conservative Whigs that the May 15 resolve was being misinterpreted, "as if the Congress had intended another mode of representation and government, than by Assemblies," which in Delaware's case at least was "competent and adequate" to do the job of establishing new governments.[51] Yet when the people, so "blinded that they could not see their true interests," elected a "T[or]y Convention," the radicals ("the undesigning Patriotick part") were determined to circumscribe what they could not dominate by setting the people-at-large against their representatives and preventing "the Convention taking upon them, or concerning with, the least Iota Except the barely frameing a plan of Government." The Convention had not been "vested with the legislative power," the radicals argued, but only with the authority to frame a constitution, "which if we exceeded we were usurpers and tyrants."[52] The argument, isolated and premature, was ignored by the Convention which proceeded to conduct all the business of legislation and government in addition to forming a constitution. The distinction between constituent and legislative authority was left to be more fully explored in the neighboring state of Pennsylvania.

In Pennsylvania the development of optional institutions for expressing the people's will, which was often irregularly and confusedly worked out in other states, was compressed into a matter of months, beginning effectively with the debate between William Smith ("Cato") and a group of radicals led by James Cannon ("Cassandra") in the early spring of 1776. Smith, as the spokes-

51. Caesar Rodney to Thomas Rodney, May 29, 1776, George H. Ryden, ed., *Rodney Letters*, 85; Phila. *Pa. Journal*, Aug. 14, 1776.

52. Caesar Rodney to Thomas Rodney, Aug. 3, 18, 1776, Thomas Rodney to Caesar Rodney, Aug. 30, 1776, Caesar Rodney to John Haslet, Sept. 12, 1776, Thomas McKean to Caesar Rodney, Sept. 19, 1776, Ryden, ed., *Rodney Letters*, 100, 105, 107, 116, 124. See also Reed, "Delaware Constitution," *Delaware Notes*, 6th Ser. (1930), 7–36.

man for the conservative Whigs in the province resisting the push toward independence, rested his case on the maintenance of the Pennsylvania Charter and the continued existence of the Pennsylvania Assembly "vested with the authority of the people," whose members "can meet when they please, and sit as long as they judge necessary." This legislative independence, said Smith, had made Pennsylvania the envy of the other colonies, "who, enjoying no such perfection in their civil constitutions, have been driven into the measure of conventions," which of course lacked the full legal standing of legislatures. "Does any other colony, whose Assemblies can exercise their authority, ever think of committing the conduct of affairs to Conventions?" The attempt by committees to call a convention when "the constitutional body" still sits only wounds "the majesty of the people . . . in the persons of their legal Representatives." America in fact, declared Smith, had more than enough of "Committees and Conventions." Proposals that the delegates to the Continental Congress should merely echo the sentiments of the committees that chose them and declare independence would eventually result in our being "echoed and re-echoed out of our liberties, our property, our happiness, and plunged deeper and deeper into all the growing horrors of war and bloodshed, without ever being consulted," since obviously "no Committees were ever entrusted with any authority to speak the sense of the people of *Pennsylvania* on this question." Your liberties, Smith told the people, "can nowhere be so safe as in the hands of your Representatives in Assembly."[53]

This kind of argument, replied James Cannon, was designed only to reconcile us to the colonists' former dependence on Great Britain. The royal governors in all the provinces where they had the power "not only refused to concur in our measures, but also prevented us from making use of our Representatives, that we might not have the shadow of a Legislature to support us." This legislative reliance on the governors was "a capital defect" in all the American constitutions and its remedy certainly did not lie in a return to those constitutions. "The Continent has had a twelve years' constant experience that the Constitution of the Colonies could not protect them from *British* oppression." The day the first committee or convention was formed was proof enough "that our Constitutions were not equal to the task of protecting

53. Phila. *Pa. Packet*, Mar. 18, 25, 1776. The articles can also be found in Force, ed., *American Archives*, 4th Ser., V, 125–27, 443–46.

themselves." Since even the Pennsylvania Assembly, autonomous as it was, "can do nothing legal without the governor," it was not surprising that "Cato" was "fiery hot" for "confining" the people of Pennsylvania to the Assembly, instead of favoring "a Convention, which is under no such restrictions." Indeed, added Thomas Paine in one of his typically radical ultimatums that smashed the terms of a previous argument, "If the body of the people had thought, or should still think, that the Assembly, or any of their Delegates in Congress, by sitting under the embarrassment of oaths, and entangled with Government and Governours, are not so perfectly free as·they ought to be, they undoubtedly had, and still have, both the right and the power to place even the whole authority of the Assembly in any body of men they please; and whoever is hardy enough to say to the contrary is an enemy to mankind."[54]

Events ultimately broke the deadlock between the Assembly and the proposed convention. With the May 15 resolution of the Continental Congress the Pennsylvania radicals believed they possessed the necessary sanction for finally destroying the old charter government. At a meeting of a Committee of the City and Liberties of Philadelphia on May 20, 1776, a group of radicals drew up a Protest to the Pennsylvania Assembly renouncing "the authority and qualifications of this House from framing a new Government" in accord with the terms of the congressional resolution. The members of the legislature were so bound to America's enemy, by oaths of allegiance or by "connections" and "pecuniary employments," that the Assembly could scarcely fall within the description of the congressional resolve "as an 'Assembly under the authority of the people' only." Yet the Assembly, the radicals added, was not thereby disqualified from exercising its ordinary powers of legislation. It simply lacked the authority to frame a new government, which only a provincial convention chosen for that "express purpose" could do. The meeting concluded with directions for the county committees throughout the colony to hold a Provincial Conference in order to determine the plans for the election of such a convention.

The Protest was answered on May 22, 1776, with a Remonstrance to the Assembly drawn up by a group of conservative Whigs opposed to the abandonment of the Pennsylvania Charter.

54. Phila. *Pa. Packet*, Apr. 8, Mar. 25, 1776; Phila. *Pa. Gazette*, Apr. 3, 1776; also found in Force, ed., *American Archives*, 4th Ser., V, 921–26, 431–34, 529–32.

The congressional resolve of May 15, they argued, had been mis-understood, since Congress obviously intended "that wherever Assemblies exist, and can meet as the ancient constitutional bodies," as in Pennsylvania, Connecticut, and Rhode Island, "the publick business is to be carried on by them." Conventions were to be called "only in those urgent cases where arbitrary Gover-nors, by prorogations and dissolutions, prevent the Representa-tives of the people from sitting to deliberate on their own affairs, or have subverted the Constitution by abdicating their offices." Such was not the case in Pennsylvania: its Assembly was still meeting; its courts were still open; and like the two corporate colonies of New England its ancient form of government was capable of functioning without recourse to an expedient and legal-ly defective convention. The authority for any changes that might have to be made in the Constitution was by the Charter "fully vested in our Representatives in Assembly freely and annually chosen."[55]

This defense of the Assembly was smothered by a barrage of petitions from all kinds of meetings and groups, protesting the legislature's authority and denying the people's confidence in it. The Assembly, the radicals charged, remained too closely tied to the old regime, as its votes still entitled with the governor's name indicated, and it did not really represent the people of Penn-sylvania, stocked as it was with men connected to the proprietary and the Crown, "persons so inconsistently circumstanced" that no free government could possibly be drawn up by them. The Assembly, torn by party rivalry and the repeated withdrawal of members, watched its authority in June 1776 simply erode away. It had become a body, the radicals said, as much to be feared as the English Parliament itself. "May not *constitutional power* (as it is called) sometimes become dangerous to a state?"[56]

With this for a premise—the assumption that the representative body of the people was a "power that might become ten thousand times more dangerous to the elective rights of the People than the Crown could ever possibly be"—new ideas about the people's relationship to the institutions of government followed rapidly. All power and authority "did in a whole and entire manner orig-inate from the people at large," and with the "dissolution of gov-

55. Phila. *Pa. Gazette*, May 22, 1776; also in Force, ed., *American Archives*, 4th Ser., VI, 519–20, 522–23. See also Selsam, *Pennsylvania Constitution*, 116–26.
56. Phila. *Pa. Gazette*, May 22, 29, 1776; Phila. *Pa. Packet*, June 24, Mar. 18, 1776.

ernment" recognized by the May 15 resolution of Congress they "in the same whole and entire condition" returned "to the people at large again." Consequently, the radicals argued, the Assembly had no right to form a new government, for "the people at large never delegated the least power to the Assembly, much less to the lower House of Assembly in its *separate capacity*, to frame constitutions: They only gave power to them, as one constituent part of the legislature, to make laws agreeable to the constitution." Those who argued that three-fourths, or six-sevenths, or any proportion of the Assembly should be allowed to alter the constitution had missed the point. "For it is three fourths of those who are to reap the advantages, and he must be endowed with uncommon virtue and self-denial, who would oppose his own elevation." "Legislative bodies of men," declared the author of a pointed little four-page pamphlet entitled *The Alarm*, have no power to destroy or create "the authority they sit by." "Otherwise every legislative body would have the power of suppressing a constitution at will; it is an act which can be done *to them*, but cannot be done *by them*." If the Assembly could legally alter the old constitution, then it "might afterwards suppress the *new* authority received from the people, and thus by continually making and unmaking themselves at pleasure, leave the people at last *no* rights at all." If the constitution were to be a "*sett of fundamental rules* by which even the supreme power of the state shall be governed," declared the author of *The Genuine Principles of the Ancient Saxon, or English Constitution*, it must "be formed by a convention of the delegates of the people, appointed for the express purpose." Only then would it be unalterable "in any respect by any power besides the power which first framed it. By this means an effectual bar will be opposed to those enterprising spirits, who have told us with much assurance, that after the people had made their annual or septennial *offering*, they had no more to do with government than their cattle."[57]

It was the very historical and legal inferiority of a convention to a legislature that compelled the radicals to argue that a convention was "in a special manner the epitome of the People," that, in fact, only a convention could make the people of Pennsylvania "*a legal people*." The constitution formed by a special convention

57. Phila. *Pa. Packet*, Apr. 29, 1776, quoting [Hulme], *Historical Essay*, 142; Phila. *Pa. Journal*, June 12, 1776; Phila. *Pa. Packet*, Nov. 12, 1776; *The Alarm: Or, an Address to the People of Pennsylvania on the Late Resolve . . .* (Phila., 1776), 1; Demophilus, *Genuine Principles*, 4.

was as much an act of the people, "indeed more so," the radicals told the people, "than any law that was ever made by your former Assembly; for in this establishment you had no partner in the case, you had no King, no Lord Proprietor, no *during pleasure*, Councillor of my Lord's chusing, to bias your deliberations: you were absolutely free." Under the pressure of protests by growing numbers of opponents to the new Constitution, the Pennsylvania radicals, led by James Cannon, David Rittenhouse, Timothy Matlack, and Thomas Young, were driven to the same conclusions about the nature of their Convention that had been reached by some Englishmen in 1689. What was once considered to be a legally deficient body because of the absence of the magistrates or rulers was now for the same reason seen to be "the most important body that ever convened on the affairs of this State," an extraordinary representation of the people actually superior in authority to the ordinary legislature.[58]

Yet in the opinion of some even this special convention was not supposed to possess the full authority of the people. Its members were to be "invested with powers to form a plan of government *only*, and not to execute it after it *is* framed; for nothing can be a greater violation of reason and natural rights, than for men to give authority to themselves." The people's authority was in fact to be divided up. "CONVENTIONS . . . are the only proper bodies to *form* a Constitution, and Assemblies are the proper bodies to make Laws agreeable to *that* Constitution." So strongly did the radicals emphasize "that *especial* purpose" for which the Convention was called that when in the late summer of 1776 the Convention was unable, because of the disintegration of the Assembly and the urgencies of war, to confine itself solely to constitution-making, the opponents of the Convention were able to charge that it had exceeded its authority. It was an effective argument and it sorely embarrassed the radical framers, since they had written this "just distinction" between constitution-making and legislating into the Constitution itself, with a separate body, also representative of the people, designated as its guardian, "well knowing that if they entrusted the power of altering one punctillio of that constitution to any body of men they should appoint to act within its express limitation, they thereby should have made the legislature their

58. Phila. *Pa. Packet*, Sept. 17, 1776; *Alarm*, 3; Phila. *Pa. Packet*, Oct. 22, 1776; Remarks on the Meeting of Oct. 21–22, Force, ed., *American Archives*, 5th Ser., II, 1154.

own carvers, and in a convenient time had them as independent, nay indeed, as absolute masters of the lives and fortunes of their constituents in Pennsylvania as they now are in Great-Britain." In order to determine "whether the constitution has been preserved inviolate in every part; and whether the legislative and executive branches of government have . . . exercised other or greater powers than they are intitled to by the constitution," a distinct inquisitory body, a Council of Censors, was to be elected by the people every seven years to meet for no longer than a year and "to pass public censures, to order impeachments, and to recommend to the legislature the repealing such laws as appear to them to have been enacted contrary to the principles of the constitution." If this Council of Censors thought that amendments or additions to the Constitution were necessary, it was to have the power to call a convention to meet within two years; any proposed changes, however, were to be "promulgated at least six months before the day appointed for the election of such convention, for the previous consideration of the people, that they may have an opportunity of instructing their delegates on the subject."[59]

Although this Council of Censors proved to be a clumsy device in Pennsylvania, simply a political instrument of the contending parties, it did represent the first and only provision in 1776 for calling a body distinct from legislature to amend a constitution, and as such was used effectively in 1786 by the Vermonters who had in 1777 copied almost verbatim the Pennsylvania Constitution of 1776.[60] It was in two other New England states, however, Massachusetts and New Hampshire, that the modern conception of the people's creating and amending their constitution through special institutional representation and through personal ratification was most fully developed. Both states had regarded their constitutions adopted in 1775–76 as temporary and had almost immediately laid plans for more permanent governments, plans

59. *Alarm*, 3; "To the Freemen of the Commonwealth of Pennsylvania," Sept. 1776, Force, ed., *American Archives*, 5th Ser., II, 582; *Alarm*, 3; Phila. *Pa. Packet*, Nov. 5, 1776; Pa. Cons. (1776), Sec. 47. See Lewis H. Meader, "Council of Censors," *Pa. Mag. of Hist. and Biog.*, 22 (1898), 265–300.

60. The result of the Vermont Council of Censors meeting in 1785–86 was the first instance of a written constitution being amended by a special constitutional convention. See Lewis H. Meader, "Council of Censors in Vermont," *Essays in the Early History of Vermont* (Vermont Historical Society, *Collections*, 6 [1943]), 255–87; Daniel B. Carroll, *The Unicameral Legislature of Vermont* (Montpelier, 1933), 14–15.

that eventually took a half dozen years or more to realize. The result was to draw out and elaborate what had in Pennsylvania prematurely crystalized in only a few short months. Pennsylvania's experience was not precisely duplicated, yet the premise that underlay that experience was the same in Massachusetts and New Hampshire: a heightening suspicion and fear of representative legislative authority that soon came to equal the former suspicion and fear of Crown authority.

In the fall of 1776 three-fourths of the Massachusetts towns that responded to an appeal by the House of Representatives favored granting authority to the General Court to form a new constitution for the state. For some dissidents, however, the idea that the General Court could by itself "enact" a constitution which was supposed to be its controller was intolerable. The form of government, said the town of Boston, "includes our all—it effects every Individual, every Individual therefore ought to be consulting, aiding and assisting." Such an important business ought not to be "restricted or confined to any particular Assembly however respectable." This extraordinary description of the legitimate representation of the people was made comprehensible by the growing claims that the present General Court was not in fact equally or fairly representative of the people. The people, various towns argued in their returns of October 1776, could be better represented in another body—perhaps a pooling of the local authority of the towns in county conventions and then ultimately in a state convention ("whereby the Wisdom of the whole State may be collected").[61] Already, as early as August 1776, the inferior Revolutionary conventions resorted to from expediency by many of the other colonies had come to assume an extraordinary character that made them seem to some to be an intentionally designed superior "mode" of constitution-making, by "electing persons for the expressed purpose of forming the Plan of Government." The House of Representatives specifically rejected these sporadic calls for a special convention but gave in to the desire of the people themselves to assent to any new constitution. Thus in April 1777 the House of Representatives requested the electorate in the towns to vest the General Court with

---

61. Return of Boston, Oct. 11, 1776, Return of Attleborough, Oct. 28, 1776, Handlin, eds., *Popular Sources*, 136, 144. See also the returns of Rehobeth, Norton, Lexington, Concord, Topsfield, Acton, Sutton, and the resolution of the Worcester County towns, in *ibid.*, 117, 124, 149–51, 152–53, 154, 158, 163, 164–66.

"full powers" to form a constitution "in addition to the Common and ordinary powers of Representation," conceding, however, the right of approval "by at least two thirds of those who are Free and twenty one years of age" before the constitution took effect. This was a significant concession, since the legislature had admitted that at least for the purpose of ratifying the constitution it was not a full embodiment of the people. By 1778 such personal ratification was no longer sufficient and the Constitution enacted by the General Court in 1778 was rejected by a five to one majority of towns, partly because it had not been drafted by a separate body. Boston was now convinced that the legislature had no business at all in making a constitution. "A Convention for *this* and *this alone*, whose existence is known no longer than the Constitution is forming, can have no prepossessions in their own favour." The representatives in the General Court "upon a matter of this kind" could hardly "divest themselves of the idea of their being *members*" of the government, and this "may induce them to form the government, with particular reference to themselves," which would mean that they would probably "monopolize to themselves a variety of offices." What the people wanted, said William Gordon, was a special state convention, "whose members will not be of the General Court." The General Court finally capitulated and in June 1779 issued a call to the towns for every male inhabitant over twenty-one to elect representatives "to form a Convention for the sole purpose of framing a new Constitution" which was to be ratified by two-thirds of the same electorate.[62]

In New Hampshire the assumption by the Provincial Congress of even a temporary government in January 1776 provoked opposition from all sides. While easterners in Portsmouth objected to the precipitate move toward independence by the Congress without having "the minds of the People fully Taken on Such a Momentous Concernment," westerners in the New Hampshire Grants, fearful of the representational scheme, denied the existence of any legitimate government at all. The same intense mistrust of the existing legislature that was leading other Americans

---

62. Boston *New England Chronicle*, Aug. 29, 1776; Resolution of the House of Representatives, Apr. 4, 1777, Handlin, eds., *Popular Sources*, 172; Boston *Independent Chronicle*, June 4, Apr. 16, 1778; Call for a Convention, June 1779, Handlin, eds., *Popular Sources*, 402–03. For analyses of the convention and ratification see Samuel E. Morison, "Vote of Massachusetts on Summoning a Constitutional Convention, 1776–1916," and "Struggle over the Adoption," Mass. Hist. Soc., *Proceedings*, 50 (1916–17), 241–46, 353–411.

to the convocation of separate bodies eventually compelled the New Hampshire Assembly in February 1778 to call for a special convention to form a permanent constitution, which was to be approved by three-fourths of the inhabitants in their town meetings. Partly because the Constitution submitted to the voters in 1779 was too similar to the existing government, it was overwhelmingly rejected. A new Constitution, modeled on the recently established Massachusetts Constitution, was framed by another Convention in 1781 and submitted to the people for a necessary two-thirds approval. The people in their town meetings rejected this 1781 Constitution, and another in 1782, before the Convention, empowered to continue in session until an acceptable constitution was framed, devised a form of government in 1783 that was finally ratified by the requisite majority of the people. It was a long, drawn-out process, acutely embarrassing to some in the state; yet it illustrated for all Americans to see the way in which a constitution should properly be put into effect.[63]

By the 1780's it had become such a firmly established way of creating or changing a constitution that governments formed by other means actually seemed to have no constitution at all, "not founded on the free and unanimous choice of the people."[64] Only "a Convention of Delegates chosen by the people for that express purpose and no other," as the South Carolina legislature after four years of bitter contention finally admitted in 1787, could establish or alter a constitution. It was an extraordinary invention, the most distinctive institutional contribution, it has been said, the American Revolutionaries made to Western politics.[65] It not only enabled the constitution to rest on an authority different from the legislature's, but it actually seemed to have legitimized revolution. Without a constitution based on convention authority, as Jefferson had complained, the people must "rise in rebellion" every time they wished to prevent legislative encroachment on their

63. Memorial of Portsmouth, Jan. 10, 1776, Bouton *et al.*, eds., *State Papers of N. H.*, VIII, 16; Dodd, *Revision of State Constitutions*, 6–7; Upton, *Revolutionary New Hampshire*, 180–86; Jeremy Belknap to Ebenezer Hazard, Nov. 10, 1782, Jan. 8, 1783, *Belknap Papers* (Mass. Hist. Soc., *Collections*, 5th Ser., 2 [1877]), 161–62, 175.

64. *The Political Establishments of the United States* (Phila., 1784), 16. This pamphlet has been edited by Edmund S. Morgan and conveniently printed in *Wm. and Mary Qtly.*, 3d Ser., 23 (1966), 286–308. See also the reprint in Crosskey, *Politics and the Constitution*, II, 1179–1205.

65. Journal of the Senate of S. C., Mar. 16, 1787, 211; Palmer, *Age of the Democratic Revolution*, I, 214.

liberties or to revise their constitution. But now in America, wrote Thomas Tudor Tucker, "tumultuous proceedings are as unnecessary as they would be improper and ineffectual. Other means are in our hands, as much preferable as good order is to confusion, as peace to discord, as efficacy and security to disappointment and ruin." If it were the sense of a majority of the people of the society to change the constitution, "it is entirely in their power to effect it without the smallest disturbance."[66]

66. Jefferson, *Notes on Virginia*, ed. Peden, 125; [Tucker], *Conciliatory Hints*, 21.

CHAPTER IX

The Sovereignty of the People

1. THE ANGLO-AMERICAN DEBATE OVER SOVEREIGNTY

For Lieutenant-Governor Thomas Hutchinson of Massachusetts, as for almost everyone by the early 1770's, the constitutional issue dividing Britain and America had become very clear. "I know of no line," he told the Massachusetts General Court in well-reasoned tones early in 1773, "that can be drawn between the supreme authority of Parliament and the total independence of the colonies: it is impossible there should be two independent Legislatures in one and the same state; for . . . two Legislative bodies will make two governments as distinct as the Kingdoms of England and Scotland before the Union." The lieutenant-governor's logic seemed so unassailable; yet, declared the Massachusetts Council, "as all human authority is, in the nature of it, and ought to be, limited," there had to be some restriction on the authority of Parliament, some liberties protected by the constitution, some discernible line between right and wrong. "To fix them with precision," however, the Council conceded, was both difficult and presumptuous. The House of Representatives was both more bold and less courageous, for in its revolutionary reply it decided to accept Hutchinson's logic and not attempt to fix any limits. "If there be no such line" between the supreme authority of Parliament and the total independence of the colonies, said the House, "the consequence is, either that the colonies are the vassals of the Parliament, or that they are totally independent." And, as it could not be supposed that the parties to the constitutional compact intended Americans to be "reduced to a state of vassalage," the conclusion in the eyes of the members of the House of Representatives was unmistakable: "that it was their sense, that we were thus independent." Since two independent legislatures in the same state were, as Hutchinson said, impossible, the colonies had to be in fact "distinct states from the mother country," united and connected only through the King "in one head and common sovereign."[1]

The essence of the imperial debate between Britain and the colonies was capsulated in this heated exchange between the Massachusetts lieutenant-governor and the General Court. They had deadlocked, wrote John Adams in his diary, "upon the greatest Question ever yet agitated." The idea of sovereignty, that "in all civil states it is necessary, there should some where be lodged a supreme power over the whole," was at the heart of the Anglo-American argument that led to the Revolution. Almost every writer, British or American, who groped for an acceptable compromise that would prevent the breach had sooner or later stumbled over this problem of sovereignty. The doctrine of sovereignty almost by itself compelled the imperial debate to be conducted in the most theoretical terms of political science. It was the single most important abstraction of politics in the entire Revolutionary era. Every new institution and new idea sooner or later had to be reconciled with this powerfully persuasive assumption that there could be but one final, indivisible, and incontestable supreme authority in every state to which all other authorities must be ultimately subordinate; "for otherwise, there could be no supremacy, or subordination, that is no government at all." The theory of sovereignty pervaded the arguments of the whole Revolutionary generation from the moment in the 1760's when it was first raised through the adoption of the federal Constitution in 1787.[2]

The eighteenth century's conviction that there must be in every state, if it were to be a state, an indissoluble supreme power from which there could be no appeal was a necessary concomitant of the growth of the nation-state with its emphasis on centralization of authority and its obsession with order. A state with more than

1. Alden Bradford, ed., *Speeches of the Governors of Massachusetts from 1765 to 1775* (Boston, 1818), 340, 351, 363.

2. Adams, entry, Mar. 4, 1773, Butterfield, ed., *Diary of Adams*, II, 77; [Mather], *America's Appeal*, 46; [Hamilton], *Farmer Refuted*, Syrett and Cooke, eds., *Hamilton Papers*, I, 98. See the discussion in Bailyn, *Ideological Origins*, 198–229; Adams, *Political Ideas*, Chap. VIII.

one independent sovereign power within its boundaries was a violation of the unity of nature; it would be like a monster with more than one head, continually at war with itself, an absurd chaotic condition that could result only in the dissolution of the state.[3] By adapting the Roman law notion of the *imperium* to the medieval institutions of the emerging nation-states, Continental theorists led by Jean Bodin in the late sixteenth century had given the doctrine its modern beginnings. Since many of these theorists considered the classic conception of mixed government to be incompatible with the notion of sovereignty, they had generally attempted to apply this final, independent power to the king, the sovereign, the only conceivable unitary authority in the early modern states. In England the location of sovereignty was more difficult. Although Robert Filmer with his correspondence between family and state could see no alternative to depositing the sovereign power in the monarchy, his patriarchal doctrine was too detached from the realities of seventeenth-century English politics to be lasting.[4] But neither could this sovereignty be placed for long in the people or House of Commons without destroying the monarchy. While some theorists well into the eighteenth century continued to speak of the ultimate sovereignty of the people, it seemed obvious that such a popular sovereignty was but a vague abstraction of politics, meaningful only during those rare moments of revolution when the people took back all power into their hands. In the day-to-day workings of the state it was impossible for the people themselves to exert sovereign power, for the essence of sovereignty was the making of law: the sovereignty had to be concretely legal, not simply theoretically political.[5] Somehow this final supreme lawmaking power had to be shared among the three constituents of the English state.

Thus for the English, as the seventeenth-century upheavals had made clear, this legal sovereignty could reside only in Parliament where the three estates of the realm were wonderfully combined. The basis for this modern legislative sovereignty had been laid in the sixteenth century, when the King's High Court of Parliament was gradually becoming the representative body of the nation. The famous case of *Wimbish* v. *Taillebois* in 1553 marks an im-

3. Isaac Hunt, *The Political Family* . . . (Phila., 1775), 6–7.
4. Greenleaf, *Order, Empiricism and Politics*, 87–93.
5. Gough, *Fundamental Law*, 174–76, and in general Chaps. XI, XII; C. H. McIlwain, "Sovereignty in the World Today," *Measure*, 1 (1950), 109–17.

portant and revealing point in the transition of Parliament from a judicial to a legislative body. In this case involving the right of Parliament in the Statutes of Uses and Wills to transfer property from its owners by a judgment in direct violation of the private rights of the common law, Chief Justice Montague struggled to maintain the judicial nature of Parliament in spite of its modern and arbitrary legislative action. Parliament, said Montague, could not actually take the property since it was itself "nothing but a court." Rather the legal owners or "the feoffees to uses" themselves were the donors, "for when a gift is made by parliament every person in the realm is privy to it and assents to it, but the thing shall pass from him that has the most right and authority to give it. . . . For if it should be adjudged the gift of any other, then parliament would do a wrong to the feoffees, in taking a thing from them and making another a donor to it." In other words, Parliament was not actually taking the property in violation of the common law, for as the highest court in the realm it could do only what was right by the law. Parliament instead had simply registered the private conveyances of the property by the owners who were presumed to be sitting in the Parliament. Once this rudimentary idea of consent was merged with Parliament's judgments as the High Court there could be little conceivable limit to its authority.[6]

It was this combination of representation with Parliament's judicial character that led eventually to the modern conception of legislative sovereignty in the seventeenth century. In the polemics of the 1640's, particularly after the appearance in 1642 of *His Majesties Answers to the XIX. Propositions of Both Houses of Parliament*, the King increasingly came to be identified as an estate or constituent of the society along with the Commons and Peers, at last making it possible to conceive of the King in Parliament, or a mixed government, actually sharing an indivisible sovereignty.[7] This notion that the entire society was represented in Parliament persisted into the eighteenth century and formed the foundation, although an increasingly weakening foundation, for parliamentary sovereignty. The whole of English society was obliged to obey the laws of Parliament because every part of the society had presumably consented to them. As James Wilson de-

6. Lampson, "Some New Light," *Amer. Pol. Sci. Rev.*, 35 (1941), 952–60. See also Gough, *Fundamental Law*, 26.
7. Weston, *English Constitutional Theory*, Chap. II.

clared, "The king is bound, because he assented to them. The lords are bound, because they voted for them. The representatives of the commons, for the same reason, bind themselves, and those whom they represent." This representational explanation of parliamentary sovereignty was comprehensible to Americans and they rarely disputed it. "In the Infancy of the British empire, when every considerable part of it could be represented in one parliament," said one South Carolinian in 1775, "that Parliament was the Bulwark against every Encroachment; in such a Case, to talk of Slavery by Parliament, was the same as to talk of the People being enslaved by themselves; hence originated the Idea of its unlimited Supremacy, as being favourable to Liberty; for who could be more free than the People who representatively exercise supreme Power over themselves?"[8]

Yet in the development of the idea of sovereignty its representational basis was always in danger of being forgotten and falling away, leaving the sovereign authority simply as the stark power to command—a frightening notion made famous by Hobbes in the seventeenth century and denounced but never really repudiated by almost all eighteenth-century thinkers. Sovereignty in the eighteenth century was coming to be too closely associated with the need for order and authority to require a representational substance. "The great capital Argument . . . that no *Englishman* is, or can be taxed, but by his own Consent," Soame Jenyns could write in 1765, was "so far from being true, that it is the very Reverse of the Truth." Even if it could be shown, as the Americans so forcefully did in 1765–66, that the representational basis of Parliament's sovereignty was a fiction, still, as the Declaratory Act of 1766 made clear, it remained an axiom of eighteenth-century English thought that Parliament "had, hath, and of right ought to have, full power and authority to make laws and statutes of sufficient force and validity to bind the colonies and people of America, subjects of the crown of Great Britain, in all cases whatsoever." Once the Americans, led by Dulany, had exposed the weakness of virtual representation as a justification for taxing America, the Britons put less and less emphasis on American representation in Parliament, virtual or otherwise, and instead stressed the logic of sovereignty itself. "In sovereignty," wrote Samuel Johnson in 1775 in a culmination of this tendency of the

8. [Wilson]. *Considerations*, in Wilson, ed., *Works of Wilson*, III, 220–21; Charleston *S.-C. Gazette*, Sept. 26, 1775. For the classic description of this view of parliamentary sovereignty see Blackstone, *Commentaries*, I, 48–49, 50, 184.

British argument, "there can be no gradations. There may be limited Royalty. . . ; but there can be no limited Government. There must, in every society, be some power or other from which there is no appeal; which admits no restrictions; which pervades the whole mass of the community; regulates and adjusts all subordination; enacts laws or repeals them; erects or annuls judicatures; extends or contracts privileges; exempts itself from question or control; and bounded only by physical necessity." Such a sovereignty needed no representational justification. It was one of those "fundamental principles" of political science, "comprising the primary and essential condition of all political society," that no one had ever had the effrontery before to doubt "til it became disputed by those zealots of anarchy, who have denied to the Parliament of *Britain* the right of taxing the *American* Colonies."[9]

Americans had begun the imperial debate by groping to make sense of their past experience in the empire. With the Stamp Act some had awkwardly and hesitantly drawn a distinction between external and internal taxes in an effort to delimit the separate spheres of authority the colonies and Parliament had held during the eighteenth century. When it soon became obvious, particularly with the Townshend duties, that "external" taxation was as much designed to collect revenue as the "internal" Stamp Act, the distinction, never surely grasped, at once dissolved, to be replaced by John Dickinson's original efforts to distinguish between the colonists' power to tax themselves and Parliament's superintending power to regulate imperial trade, the measure of Parliament's authority for any imposition becoming its relation to the preservation of "the connection between the several parts of the *British* empire." Others too, while doubting that the Americans could be "doubly taxed, as well as doubly represented," were struggling to prove what they knew from experience to be "different degrees of dependency on the mother state." However, to the British, unable to conceive of the empire as anything but a single community with a final undivided authority located somewhere, all such distinctions were absurd and ultimately would lead to the dissolution of the union between England and America. If Parliament even "in one instance" was as supreme over the colonists as over the people of England, then, wrote William Knox in 1769, the Americans were members "of the same community

---

9. [Jenyns], *Objections*, 4, 5, 6; Morgan, *Stamp Act Crisis*, 347, 361; [Samuel Johnson], *Taxation No Tyranny* . . . (London, 1775), in Force, ed., *American Archives*, 4th Ser., I, 1436, 1431–32.

with the people of England." But if Parliament's authority over the colonists were denied "in any particular" then it must be denied in "all instances" and the union dissolved. "There is no alternative: either the Colonies are part of the community of Great Britain or they are in a state of nature with respect to her, and in no case can be subject to the jurisdiction of that legislative power which represents her community, which is the British Parliament." Everywhere the colonists turned they faced these "trite" but "captivating" assertions of parliamentary sovereignty based on "the well known necessity of one central, supreme power, being somewhere lodged in every empire."[10] The Americans' efforts to divide and limit this sovereignty were so new, so original, and so contrary to the prevailing maxims of political science that they could not be sustained.

By the early 1770's, particularly with the introduction of Blackstone's *Commentaries* into the colonies, the doctrine that there must be in every form of government "a supreme, irresistible, absolute, uncontrolled authority, in which the *jura summi imperii*, or the rights of sovereignty, reside," had gained such overwhelming currency that its "truth," many Americans were compelled to admit, could no longer "be contested." While some like Dickinson continued to "assert, a line there must be" between Parliament and the colonial legislatures and to argue that "sovereignty over these colonies must be limited," others, despairing of breaking the unbreakable and separating the inseparable, began rapidly in 1773–74 to concede, like the Massachusetts House of Representatives, the terms of the British argument as phrased by Thomas Hutchinson: that America must be either totally under parliamentary authority or under no parliamentary authority at all. Apparently there was no middle ground. James Wilson said in 1774 that he had entered upon his *Considerations on the Nature and Extent of the Legislative Authority of the British Parliament* with an "expectation of being able to trace some constitutional line between those cases in which we ought, and those in which we ought not, to acknowledge the power of parliament over us." But in the process Wilson, like many other Americans, "became fully convinced that such a line does not exist; and that there can

10. [Dickinson], *Letters from a Farmer*, Ford, ed., *Writings of Dickinson*, 349; [Zubly], *Humble Enquiry*, 11, 16; [William Knox], *The Controversy between Great Britain and Her Colonies Reviewed* . . . (London, 1769), 50–51; Boston *Continental Journal*, Aug. 29, 1775; Pinkney's Wmsbg. *Va. Gazette*, Feb. 23, 1775. See Edmund S. Morgan, "Colonial Ideas of Parliamentary Power, 1764–1766," *Wm. and Mary Qtly.*, 3d Ser., 5 (1948), 311–41.

be no medium between acknowledging and denying that power in *all* cases." As early as 1768 Benjamin Franklin had questioned the American arguments that admitted some subordination to Parliament, while at the same time denying Parliament's power to make laws for the colonies. The more he thought on the subject, said Franklin, the more convinced he became "that no middle doctrine can be well maintained, I mean not clearly and with intelligible arguments." It was either one or the other of the extremes: "That Parliament has a right to make *all laws* for us, or that it has a power to make *no laws* for us."[11]

The distinction between taxation and legislation, which some Americans and Chatham and Camden had earlier tried to maintain, was by 1775 seen to be "vain and groundless." "Taxation can differ from legislation (to speak logically) only as the species differ from the *genus*. . . . Nothing but uncommon sense could have split such a hair as to divide what is indivisible." If Americans had a right to consent to taxation, then they had a stronger right to consent to all legislation, for the whole, of course, was greater than the part. When the Tory, Daniel Leonard, writing as "Massachusettensis," declared that "two supreme or independent authorities cannot exist in the same state," since "it would be what is called *imperium in imperio*, the height of political absurdity," John Adams, as "Novanglus," could only acknowledge his agreement. Two supreme authorities could obviously not exist in the same state, said Adams, "any more than two supreme beings in one universe." Therefore it was clear, concluded Adams, "that our provincial legislatures are the only supreme authorities in our colonies." The basis of Joseph Galloway's entire argument in his *A Candid Examination of the Mutual Claims of Great Britain and Her Colonies*, remarked John Dickinson and Charles Thompson in a Pennsylvania newspaper, was the principle that "there must be in every state a supreme legislative authority universal in its extent over every member." Galloway's mistake lay in his application of this principle, not in his assumption of it. If America admitted Parliament to be the supreme power, as Galloway contended, then "there is no such thing as a colonial legislature in existence." But Galloway had mislocated the supreme power. It

11. Blackstone, *Commentaries*, I, 48–49; [Mather], *America's Appeal*, 46; [John Dickinson], *An Essay on the Constitutional Power of Great Britain over the Colonies in America* (Phila., 1774), in *Pennsylvania Archives*, 2d Ser., III, 569, 603; [Wilson], *Considerations*, Wilson, ed., *Works of Wilson*, III, 201; Benjamin Franklin to William Franklin, Mar. 13, 1768, Albert Henry Smyth, ed., *The Writings of Benjamin Franklin* (N. Y., 1905–07), V, 115.

was rightfully in the Pennsylvania Assembly. "And of course the legislature of Great Britain is not the legislature of Pennsylvania; for it would be irregular and monstrous to suppose us subject to two legislatures." Two legislatures in the same state, said Hamilton, "can not be supposed, without falling into that solecism, in politics, of *imperium* in *imperio*."[12]

The result was a fundamental shift in the American position. By 1774 the colonists, like Jefferson, were contending that Parliament's acts over America were void not because they were unjust, as Otis had argued in the 1760's, but because "the British parliament has no right to exercise authority over us." The Americans in effect accepted the irresistible logic of the concept of legislative sovereignty and turned it against the British to justify their legislatures' independence from all parliamentary control. Their connection with the British empire, it was now claimed, was solely through the King, in his personal not his political capacity, said John Adams, for it was with the natural person of the King that the American people had made their several contracts. The colonial legislatures had thus become miniature parliaments, each headed by the same royal authority of the King, together forming a loosely federated empire of independent states which did no violence to the principle of sovereignty. "By the charter of this province," said Samuel Adams of Massachusetts, "the legislative power is in the Governor, who is appointed by the King, the Council and House of Representatives." The legislative authority of Parliament was disavowed, but the concept of legislative sovereignty was not; it was only transplanted. "The legislative of any commonwealth," conceded Adams, "must be the supreme power." The Americans thus acknowledged their "submission to the authority of our Provincial Legislatures in the same manner as the people in Great-Britain acknowledge the power of parliament over them; because the assemblies here and the parliament there are composed in part of persons elected by the people ... as their representatives."[13]

12. Boston *Mass. Spy*, Feb. 23, 1775; Adams and [Leonard], *Novanglus and Massachusettensis*, 170, see also 88–89; Phila. *Pa. Journal*, Mar. 8, 1775; [Hamilton], *Farmer Refuted*, Syrett and Cooke, eds., *Hamilton Papers*, I, 164.

13. [Jefferson], *Summary View*, Boyd, ed., *Jefferson Papers*, I, 125; [Adams], "Novanglus," Adams, ed., *Works of John Adams*, IV, 114, 141–47, 176–77; *Boston Gazette*, Oct. 28, 1771, in Cushing, ed., *Writings of Samuel Adams*, II, 260. On the clarification of the colonies' relation to the empire see Adams, *Political Ideas*, 65–85.

This all-or-nothing acceptance of one of two alternatives was not of course a very satisfactory explanation of past American experience in the empire, as John Adams, for one, frankly admitted. This surrender to the concept of legislative sovereignty made it difficult for Americans to explain Parliament's previous and acknowledged regulation of colonial trade, the "only power we can, with justice to ourselves," said Hamilton, "permit the British parliament to exercise." The best Americans could do by 1774 was allow Parliament's power of external commercial regulation, as the Declaration of Colonial Rights and Grievances put it, "from the necessity of the case, and a regard to the mutual interest of both countries."[14]

The Americans' fascinating probes into the nature of sovereignty which had marked the imperial debate of the 1760's had thus been stifled in the early 1770's by their eventual submission to the logic of the doctrine of legislative sovereignty. They had picked away at the unity of the empire and had sought to make all sorts of exemptions from the imperial power of Parliament. But in the end they found the doctrine of sovereignty unassailable and made it in fact a major weapon in their argument. Therefore, when the Americans came in 1776 to erect their own confederated empire, most did so with an overwhelming conviction, as Samuel Adams told the Carlisle Commission in 1778, "that in every kingdom, state, or empire there must be, from the necessity of the thing, one supreme legislative power, with authority to bind every part in all cases the proper object of human laws." Despite the original contributions to political thought in the 1760's made by the Americans and despite their long experience with different spheres of authority, there was in 1776 little theoretical comprehension among most Whig leaders of any possibility of a divided sovereignty, of any possibility, in other words, of two legislatures' existing in the same state. "The same collective Body," said James Wilson in 1776, "cannot delegate the same Powers to distinct representative Bodies." It was "incongruous and absurd that the same Property should be liable to be taxed by two Bodies independent of each other" and that "the same Offense" should be "subjected to different and perhaps inconsistent Punishments." Before Amer-

14. [Adams], "Novanglus," Adams, ed., *Works of John Adams*, IV, 130; [Hamilton], *Farmer Refuted*, Syrett and Cooke, eds., *Hamilton Papers*, I, 133; Declaration of Colonial Rights and Grievances. Oct. 1, 1774, in Jensen, ed., *American Colonial Documents*, IX, 807. See also McRee, *Life of Iredell*, I, 350.

icans like Wilson could conceive of, let alone justify, two legislatures' existing in the same state they had to rethink the character
of legislative authority and the nature of representation. Indeed,
they eventually had to conceive of the structure of politics in a
way entirely different from what any other people ever had.[15]

2. THE ARTICLES OF CONFEDERATION

The problem of sovereignty was not solved by the Declaration
of Independence. It continued to be the most important theoretical question of politics throughout the following decade, the ultimate abstract principle to which nearly all arguments were sooner
or later reduced. Curiously, however, sovereignty was not as ex-
plosive and as wide-ranging an issue in the formation of the Americans' confederation as might have been expected from the experience of the debate of the previous decade.

With Independence it became obvious that the Continental
Congress, not really a governmental body and created simply out
of the exigency of events in 1774, needed some more solid basis;
the congressional delegates immediately began working on an
agreement that would more permanently connect the new states
in a central union. But the creation of these Articles of Confederation sparked no extensive exploration into the problems of politics.
Throughout the 1770's there was remarkably little discussion in
the press or pamphlets of the nature of the union being formed.
What debate there was was largely confined within the walls of
Congress and was very limited and intellectually insignificant in
comparison with the exciting and sweeping debates over the formation of the state constitutions—a graphic indication of the relative importance Americans attributed to their central and state
governments. The principle of sovereignty was not probed and
analyzed by Americans in 1776–77 the way it had been in the
sixties, because whatever the limitations the Confederation may
have placed in fact on the individual sovereignty of the states, few

15. "An American" to the Earl of Carlisle and others, July 16, 1778, Cushing,
ed., *Writings of Samuel Adams*, IV, 37; Wilson, "An Address to the Inhabitants
of the Colonies Submitted to the Continental Congress" (Feb. 1776), in Randolph
G. Adams, ed., *Selected Political Essays of James Wilson* (N. Y., 1930), 106–07.
Cf. Andrew C. McLaughlin, "The Background of American Federalism," *Amer.
Pol. Sci. Rev.*, 12 (1918), 215–40.

believed that their union in any theoretical sense contravened that sovereignty. As Vattel, whom many Americans read, had written in his *Law of Nations*, "several sovereign and independent states may unite themselves together by a perpetual confederacy without each in particular ceasing to be a perfect state. . . . The deliberations in common will offer no violence to the sovereignty of each member."[16] It was this kind of confederation that the Revolutionaries intended to make in 1776, a "league of friendship," a "Treaty of Confederation," "a council of nations," similar to the plans for a Christian European union conceived of by Henry IV and the patriot Sully of France in the late sixteenth century. It was not, as Ezra Stiles remarked in 1783, meant to be "a body in which resides authoritative sovereignty; for there is no real cession of dominion, no surrender or transfer of sovereignty to the national council, as each state in the confederacy is an independent sovereignty."[17]

There were nationalistic sentiments in 1776, brought to the fore by the events of the previous decade—perhaps more of a feeling of oneness among thirteen disparate states than at any time in history. And this sense of union had assumed institutional form. Not only had the Continental Congress since 1774 exercised an extraordinary degree of political, military, and economic power over the colonists—adopting commercial codes, establishing and maintaining an army, issuing a continental currency, erecting a military code of law, defining crimes against the Union, and negotiating abroad. It also through its encouragement and resolves was centrally responsible for the colonies' assumption of new governments and the final break from England. The authority of the Continental Congress and the Continental Army was in fact so great during the critical years of Independence and the war as to provoke a continuing if fruitless debate from the nineteenth century to the present over the priority of the union or the states.[18]

16. Emmerich de Vattel, *The Law of Nations; Or Principles of the Law of Nature* . . . (London, 1759, 1760), Bk. I, Chap. I, Sec. 10, 67. See Adams, *Defence of the Constitutions*, in Adams, ed., *Works of John Adams*, IV, 579–80.

17. The Articles of Confederation and Perpetual Union. . . (1777), Art. 3, in Jensen, *Articles of Confederation*, 263; Governor Cooke of Rhode Island, quoted in Claude H. Van Tyne, "Sovereignty in the American Revolution: An Historical Study," *Amer. Hist. Rev.*, 12 (1906–07), 538; Stiles, *United States Elevated*, in Thornton, ed., *Pulpit*, 418–19.

18. On the early idea of union see Curtis P. Nettels, "The Origins of the Union and of the States," Mass. Hist. Soc., *Proceedings*, 72 (1957–60), 68–83.

Yet for all this exercise of continental authority, for all of the colonists' sense of being "Americans," for all of their talk of choosing between "a sovereign state, or a number of confederated sovereign states,"[19] few in 1776 conceived of the thirteen states' becoming a single republic, one community with one pervasive public interest.

Americans were well aware of the prevailing maxim, made famous by Montesquieu—indeed it was basic to their thought in 1776—that only a small homogeneous society whose interests were essentially similar could properly sustain a republican government. But the climate and the economic and social interests of the separate states, as the Americans themselves emphasized and foreign observers verified, seemed so varied, the habits and character of the people, particularly between North and South, appeared so different, that a continental republic with a single government coalescing all the states was as nearly impossible of establishment in 1776 as the erection of a monarchy. A man's "country" was still his state; for John Adams the Massachusetts delegation in Congress was "our embassy." As late as 1787 Marylanders still called their state "the nation."[20] The Declaration of Independence, drawn up by the Continental Congress, was actually a declaration by "thirteen united States of America" proclaiming that as "Free and Independent States they have full power to levy war, conclude peace, contract alliances, establish commerce, and to do all other acts and things which independent States may of right do." And the Articles of Confederation, for all the powers it theoretically gave to the Congress, did not in fact alter this independence. Commercial regulation and taxing power, indeed all final governmental, lawmaking power remained with the states. Seven of the states even felt it necessary to enact the Declaration of Independence to give it the obligation of law within the state. Congressional resolutions continued to be mere recommendations which the states were left to enforce. The states not only jealously guarded their independence and sovereignty by repeated assertions and declarations, but in fact assumed the powers of a sovereign state that Independence had given them, even in violation of the Articles of Confederation, making war, providing for armies, laying

19. John Adams to Patrick Henry, June 3, 1776, Burnett, ed., *Letters of Congress*, I, 471.
20. John Adams to Abigail Adams, Sept. 18, 1774, *ibid.*, I, 35; Baltimore, *Md. Journal*, May 18, 1787.

embargoes, even in some cases carrying on separate diplomatic correspondence and negotiations abroad. The Confederation was intended to be, and remained, a Confederation of sovereign states.[21]

The debates that took place in the Continental Congress in 1776–77 over the formation of the Confederation were essentially involved with concrete state interests, the apportionment of taxes and the disposition of western lands. Only the debates over representation, whether the same for each state or proportional to population or wealth, touched on the nature of the union and the problem of sovereignty, and even here the polemics were tied closely to particular state interests: the larger states "threatened they would not confederate at all if their weight in congress should not be equal to the numbers of people they added to the confederacy; while the smaller ones declared against an union if they did not retain an equal vote for the protection of their rights." Nevertheless, the debate did lead some congressional delegates, James Wilson, Benjamin Rush, and John Adams, to argue that in "those matters which are referred to Congress, we are not so many states; we are one large state." "The confederacy," said John Adams, "is to make us one individual only; it is to form us, like separate parcels of metal, into one common mass. We shall no longer retain our separate individuality, but become a single individual as to all questions submitted to the Confederacy." The spokesmen for the small states, John Witherspoon, Roger Sherman, and Stephen Hopkins, argued, on the contrary, that "every Colony is a distinct Person," and "that as such in all disputes they should have an equal vote." Since only that business relating to the states and "nothing relating to individuals could ever come before Congress," there was no need of an "incorporating" union. No confederacy in history, the Germanic, the Helvetic, the Dutch, had ever dissolved the parts into one common mass. "The Safety of the whole," said Hopkins of Rhode Island, "depends upon the distinctions of Colonies."[22]

21. Van Tyne, "Sovereignty in the American Revolution," *Amer. Hist. Rev.*, 12 (1906–07), 529–45; Jensen, *Articles of Confederation*, 117–18, 162–63; Daniel Boorstin, *The Americans: The National Experience* (N.Y., 1965), 402–05.

22. Jefferson, Notes of Proceedings in the Continental Congress, June 7 to Aug. 1, 1776, Boyd, ed., *Jefferson Papers*, I, 323, 327, 325, 324, 325, 326; Adams, Notes of Debates on the Articles of Confederation, July 30–Aug. 1, 1776, Butterfield, ed., *Diary of Adams*, II, 245–48.

There was something specious about the arguments of the large-state advocates, for it is problematic just how consolidated they either wanted or expected the Confederation to be in 1776–77. John Adams, for example, had said only a few months earlier that he saw "no occasion" for any central government "but a Congress." Their arguments seem to represent more expedient rationalizations for protecting large-state interests than the beginnings of any grand design, only sporadically being suggested in the press, for a "simple government" in "one great *American* republick" with Congress filled with "representatives of all *America*" and "the supreme power of all our affairs."[23] Yet just these sorts of suggestions for a continental republic, isolated, undeveloped, and contrary to the best political science of the day as they were, together with the nature of the arguments used by large-state delegates, inevitably raised the suspicions of devout republicans and of small-state delegates, particularly Thomas Burke of North Carolina, who repeatedly challenged every move to aggrandize congressional authority. Burke found Article III of the Dickinson draft of the proposed Confederation, which "expressed only a reservation of the power of regulating the internal police, and consequently resigned every other power," especially dangerous, and he moved for its amendment, which eventually became Article 2 of the Confederation: "Each State retains its sovereignty, freedom and independence, and every power, jurisdiction, and right, which is not by this confederation expressly delegated to the United States, in Congress assembled." Burke's amendment was "at first so little understood," perhaps because it was so much taken for granted, that "it was some time before it was seconded." Wilson of Pennsylvania and Lee of Virginia voiced some opposition, but the amendment easily carried, eleven states to one, Virginia being opposed and New Hampshire divided. Burke should not have been, but he seemed surprised "to find the opinion of accumulating powers to Congress so little supported." Even as early as 1776 it was clear to some that any confederation as strong as even the Dickinson plan envisioned "can never pass." The attempts of the centralist-minded to destroy "all Provincial Distinctions" and to make "every thing of the minute kind bend to what they call the good of the whole" bred too many fears of large-state

23. John Adams, quoted in Nevins, *American States*, 624; "On the Present States of America," Oct. 10, 1776, Force ed., *American Archives*, 5th Ser., II, 967–69.

or northern domination and led delegates, like Edward Rutledge of South Carolina, to resolve "to vest the Congress with no more Power than is absolutely necessary."[24]

What is truly remarkable about the Confederation is the degree of union that was achieved. The equality of the citizens of all states in privileges and immunities, the reciprocity of extradition and judicial proceedings among the states (which pointed up their quasi-international relationship), the elimination of travel and discriminatory trade restrictions between states, and the substantial grant of powers to the Congress in Article 9 made the league of states as cohesive and strong as any similar sort of republican confederation in history—stronger in fact than some Americans had expected. Many of the delegates, Samuel Chase told Richard Henry Lee in July 1776, did not even "see the importance, nay the necessity, of a Confederacy." If the Articles could not be formed in 1776–77, Roger Sherman feared that a union might never be formed. Some saw the Confederation as only a temporary combination of the states, for the sole purpose of waging war, that with peace should be allowed to lapse. By December 1783 the Congress in Jefferson's opinion had lost much of its usefulness. "The constant session of Congress can not be necessary in time of peace." After clearing up the most urgent business the delegates should "separate and return to our respective states, leaving only a Committee of the states," and thus "destroy the strange idea of their being a permanent body, which has unaccountably taken possession of the heads of their constituents, and occasions jealousies injurious to the public good." Congressional power, which had been substantial during the war years, now began precipitously to disintegrate, and delegates increasingly complained of the difficulty of gathering even a quorum. By the middle eighties Congress had virtually ceased trying to govern.[25]

24. Thomas Burke to Gov. Richard Caswell, Apr. 29, 1777, Burnett, ed., *Letters of Congress*, II, 345–46; Articles of Confederation, Art. 2, in Jensen, *Articles of Confederation*, 263; Edward Rutledge to John Jay, June 29, 1776, Burnett, ed., *Letters of Congress*, I, 517–18.

25. Samuel Chase to R. H. Lee, July 30, 1776, Force, ed., *American Archives*, 5th Ser., I, 672; Roger Sherman, Aug. 25, 1777, cited in Van Tyne, "Sovereignty in the American Revolution," *Amer. Hist. Rev.*, 12 (1906–07), 538; Jefferson to Marbois, Dec. 5, 1783, Boyd, ed., *Jefferson Papers*, VI, 374. On the quasi-international relationship of the states see Andrew C. McLaughlin, *A Constitutional History of the United States* (N. Y., 1935), 127, still the best survey of the constitutionalism of this period. For a comparison with the contemporary Swiss Confederacy see Palmer, *Age of Democratic Revolution*, II, 395–98. On

Beginning in the early 1780's there were some Americans, increasingly concerned with the weakness of the confederacy, who sought by every possible means to strengthen the Congress, by direct amendment, by broad interpretation of the Articles, or even by military force and dictatorship.[26] Only with the multiplication of these proposals for reform was the problem of sovereignty as it related to the Confederation seriously and widely confronted; but the issue was decided even before it was raised. Despite all of their fulminations against "the present futile and senseless confederation" and their frantic denials of "the *Complete Sovereignty of each State*," the advocates of a stronger central government could not escape from the basic confederate nature of the union and the principle of sovereignty. "There was in nature no middle way between a federal and a corporate union," opponents of centralization repeatedly retorted. "Each party to the confederation must possess a sovereignty, for without that they are no longer States, and while they possess a sovereignty, that sovereignty must be independent: For a dependent sovereignty is nonsense."[27] The clumsy efforts of the nationalist-minded to devise schemes for enforcing the measures of Congress, by distraining the property and interdicting the trade of the delinquent states—in effect levying war on the states—emphasized their frustration in dealing with such independent, sovereign states, "each with a government completely organized within itself, having all the means to draw its subjects to a close dependence on itself."[28] So fundamentally malconstructed was the Confederation that some actually feared the ratification of the Articles and the ending of the war with Britain out of the belief that the resultant complacency would prevent further strengthening of the Union.[29] Despite the growing senti-

the near collapse of the Confederation in the 1780's see McDonald, *E Pluribus Unum*, 8, 134–54. For an emphasis on the stabilizing effect of subordinate institutions of the Confederation and for a call for a broader constitutional history of the period see Herbert A. Johnson, "Toward a Reappraisal of the 'Federal' Government: 1783–1789," *American Journal of Legal History*, 8 (1964), 314–25.

26. Merrill Jensen, "The Idea of a National Government during the American Revolution," *Pol. Sci. Qtly.*, 58 (1943), 368.

27. Hamilton to Robert Morris, Apr. 30, 1781, Syrett and Cooke, eds., *Hamilton Papers*, II, 630; Charleston *S.-C. Gazette and General Advertiser*, Apr. 12, 1783; Boston *Independent Chronicle*, Oct. 20, 1785.

28. Hamilton to James Duane, Sept. 3, 1780, Syrett and Cooke, eds., *Hamilton Papers*, II, 403. On the problem of enforcing congressional authority see Madison to Jefferson, Apr. 16, 1781, Boyd, ed., *Jefferson Papers*, V, 473–74; George Bancroft, *History of the Formation of the Constitution of the United States of America* (N. Y., 1883), I, 27.

29. Jensen, "Idea of a National Government," *Pol. Sci. Qtly.*, 58 (1943), 372–

ment, as voiced by the Massachusetts legislature in July 1785, that the Articles were "not adequate to the great purpose they were originally designed to effect," every effort to change them was defeated. Even a continental impost, it was claimed, would bring into question not only the very existence of the state legislatures but the whole purpose of the Revolution.[30]

As vigorous as these efforts to increase the strength of the central government in the early eighties were, they were not at the heart of the problems of politics in the Confederation period. It was the exigencies of the financial and war situation in 1780, more than the logic of Hamilton's *Continentalist* essays, that had prompted what nearly successful attempts there were to add a limited taxing power to Congress. And with the coming of peace the temporary ascendancy of those "who think continentally" rapidly declined and the chances of reforming the Confederation piecemeal with them. Simply to assert, as one writer in 1783 did, that Congress was "a tribunal to which all subordinate powers must appeal, and whose decision is conclusive and compulsory," or to urge, as Pelatiah Webster did in the same year, that the states part with as much of their sovereignty as necessary for an effectual central government was to fly in the face of the realities of American politics in the 1780's.[31] With peace Americans were now more eager than ever before "to oppose all encroachments of the American Congress upon the sovereignty and jurisdiction of the separate states." The states had become increasingly jealous of their power and in fact through their handling of public lands and public debts were fast moving to absorb the major political and economic groups, creating a vested interest in state sovereignty. It had become obvious from the early eighties that no substantial reform of the Confederation was possible as long as each state retained "the idea of an uncontrollable sovereignty . . . over its internal police."[32]

73; E. James Ferguson, *The Power of the Purse: A History of American Public Finance, 1776–1790* (Chapel Hill, 1961), 171.

30. Bancroft, *Formation of the Constitution*, I, 190; Boston *Independent Chronicle*, Feb. 6, 1783.

31. Hamilton to Washington, Apr. 8, 1783; Syrett and Cooke, eds., *Hamilton Papers*, III, 321; ̄ ullius [pseud.], *Three Letters Addressed to the Public* (Phila., 1783), 15; Webster, *Dissertation*.

32. Address and Instructions of Fairfax County, May 30, 1783, in Rowland, *Mason*, II, 50; Hamilton to Duane, Sept. 3, 1780, Syrett and Cooke, eds., *Hamilton Papers*, II, 402. On the vested interest being created in state sovereignty see McDonald, *E Pluribus Unum*, 30, 56.

Ironically, however, it was the very "JEALOUSY OF POWER" so much deplored by the proponents of centralization that was to be the eventual source of their success.[33] The most significant political developments of these years lay not in the attempts by a dynamic minority of nationalists to weaken the idea of the sovereignty of the states from above, that is, by adding powers to Congress. Rather they lay in the widespread attacks on the idea of state sovereignty from below, that is, by the repeated and intensifying denials by various groups that the state legislatures adequately spoke for the people. Sovereignty was still the issue, but in the struggles between the legislatures and the people-at-large the state governments were put on the defensive as they had not been with the Congress. In the contest between the states and the Congress the ideological momentum of the Revolution lay with the states; but in the contest between the people and the state governments it decidedly lay with the people.

"It is a Maxim," proclaimed the Massachusetts General Court in January 1776, "that, in every Government, there must exist, Somewhere, a Supreme, Sovereign, absolute, and uncontroulable Power; But this Power resides, always in the body of the People, and it never was, or can be delegated, to one Man, or a few."[34] In one sense this was a traditional utterance, for no one doubted, even most Tories, that all power ultimately resided in the people. But it was in another intensely real sense that many Americans in the years after 1776 were to interpret the sovereignty of the people. It was to become no vague abstraction of political science to which all could pay lip service. The trite theory of popular sovereignty gained a verity in American hands that European radicals with all of their talk of all power in the people had scarcely considered imaginable except at those rare times of revolution. "Civil liberty" became for Americans "not 'a government of laws,' made agreeable to charters, bills of rights or compacts, but a power existing in the people at large, at any time, for any cause, or for no cause, but their own sovereign pleasure, to alter or annihilate both the mode and essence of any former government, and adopt a new one in its stead." American liberty seemed in fact to have made revolution perpetual and civil disorder legitimate.[35]

33. [Hamilton], "The Continentalist No. 1," July 12, 1781, Syrett and Cooke, eds., *Hamilton Papers*, II, 652.

34. Proclamation of the General Court, Jan. 23, 1776, Handlin, eds., *Popular Sources*, 65.

35. Hichborn, *Oration, March 5th, 1777*, in Niles, ed., *Principles*, 47.

All the developments of the period pointed to this conclusion. The growing participation of the people "out-of-doors" in mobbing and electioneering, the rise of extra-legislative organizations, including constitutional conventions, the elaboration of various constitutional restraints on legislative authority, and the heightening insistence on the extreme actuality of representation, were all symptomatic of a profound change taking place in the Americans' comprehension of the people's proper role in the affairs of government. It was in these ripening ideas about the people's relation to the government and in their implications for the traditional concept of representation, and not in the proposals for establishing or reforming the Confederation, that the Americans of the 1780's most directly confronted the orthodox doctrine of legislative sovereignty, eventually making sensible their intensifying claims that such final and absolute lawmaking power lay not in any particular body of men but in the people-at-large.

3. THE DISINTEGRATION OF REPRESENTATION

Because both the English and the colonists had "seen the representative power of the people separated from and converted into a different interest from the collective," the radical Whig mind never did possess full confidence in the representational process. "It is incontestable," declared the inhabitants of Albemarle County, Virginia, in 1776, "that the freedom of a Community is reduced in proportion to the power conferred to a small number of its Members, and that such reduction of freedom is a necessary evil in an extensive Country, where all the people cannot meet at one place to transact their public concerns." Under such circumstances, said Samuel Adams, it was essential for the people "to acquaint themselves with the Character and Conduct of those who represent them at the Distance of four hundred Miles. . . . What do frequent Elections avail, without that Spirit of Jealousy and Strict Inquiry which alone can render such Elections any Security to the People?" Paradoxically the intensity of a Whig's radicalism was measured not by his confidence in the representatives of the people but by his suspicion of them. Those in 1776 who voiced fears of the representative bodies' forming interests separate from those of the people constituted the most alienated and radical groups in America. Yet such suspicion and jealousy was

always relative: a radical Whig might distrust the elected assembly compared to the people themselves, but he surely distrusted
the executive or magistracy more. Since the degree of a radical
Whig's faith in the legislative representatives depended on whom
he was pitting them against, the people-at-large or the rulers, the
representatives could somehow be both the people and not the
people. The elected representatives, Joseph Hawley admitted in
1775, were vested by election with the full authority of the people: "Their constituents, are in speculation, virtually present, acting themselves, by the votes and suffrages of their Representatives.
This is what gives universal obligation to their proceeding." However, the elected deputies did not always speak as the people.
Whenever they deviated from the fundamental principles of government, "they act in their private capacity, and not as the substitute of the people."³⁶ Such ambivalence was common in 1776, and
was to grow more intense in the years ahead, as the Revolution,
begun against Crown and magisterial authority, moved into new
stages, with the Americans scrambling among themselves to see
who was to dominate their new republican legislatures. It was
these secondary stages of the Revolution occurring at different
times in different places—when the Whig representative legislatures themselves were brought into question—that put the most
serious kinds of strains on the inherited body of Whig thought
used to explain and justify the Americans' original revolt against
magisterial authority.

Wherever there were groups in 1776 deeply mistrustful of the
legislatures, a gap between the people-at-large and the representatives was opened that had momentous implications for Whig
political thought. The radical counties of Orange and Mecklenburg, North Carolina, as suspicious of the dominant Whig leaders
as they were of the royal officials, expressed this distinction in a
most explicit way. "Political power," they informed their delegates in the North Carolina Convention of 1776, "is of two kinds,
one principal and superior, the other derived and inferior.... The
principal supreme power is possessed by the people at large, the
derived and inferior power by the servants which they employ."
With this crucial distinction between the people and all elected
officials in hand radical groups were able to make intelligible all

36. Pinkney's Wmsbg. *Va. Gazette*, Nov. 24, 1774; Albemarle County Instruc-
tions concerning the Virginia Constitution (1776), Boyd, ed., *Jefferson Papers*,
VI, 287; Samuel Adams to John Adams, Dec. 8, 1777, Cushing, ed., *Writings of
Samuel Adams*, III, 416; Worcester *Mass. Spy*, Mar. 9, 1775.

sorts of restrictions on governmental, even legislative, authority, and to make comprehensible every important constitutional innovation of the Revolutionary era. For "no authority can exist or be exercised but what shall appear to be ordained and created by the principal supreme power," and "whatever is constituted and ordained by the principal supreme power cannot be altered, suspended or abrogated by any other power."[37] This vivid discrepancy between the people and all officials, representatives of the people included, was not perceived by all Whigs in 1776, and even when it was, its significance was not always readily appreciated. Yet the discrepancy was implicit in the Whigs' fear of all political power and was always liable under the pressure of circumstances to be exposed.

Indeed, as early as 1775–76 during the drive for independence many Whigs were pushed into arguments whose consequences for the reconstruction of independent governments they could scarcely have foreseen. The dissolution of the ordinary legislatures and the continued appeals to alternative bodies and to the nebulous will of the people in a state of nature rendered all institutions set above the people precarious and made representation itself suspect. Wherever revolutionary-minded Whigs found existing representative bodies, whether legislatures or conventions, reluctant to move with them, they entered a wedge between the people and those who supposedly spoke for them, even to the point of urging that the people in the hesitant middle colonies be instigated to rise against their representatives, arguing that the people were so much in favor of "a total and final separation" from England that they would support independence "even if the Conventions and Delegates of those Colonies vote against it."[38] It seemed obvious to some radicals in the Continental Congress "that the voice of the representatives is not alwais consonant with the voice of the people."[39] While most Whigs were not yet able or willing to unravel the implications of this idea in their new state governments, some in 1776 were.

Within various states in 1776 different groups, those most alien-

37. Instructions of Mecklenburg and Orange Counties, 1776, Saunders, ed., *Col. Recs. of N.C.*, X, 870 b, f.

38. Elbridge Gerry to James Warren, June 25, 1776, Burnett, ed., *Letters of Congress*, I, 508. See also Md. Delegates to Md. Council of Safety, June 11, 1776, Force, ed., *American Archives*, 4th Ser., VI, 806–07; Klingelhofer, "Maryland and Independence," *Md. Hist. Mag.*, 60 (1965), 305.

39. Jefferson, Notes of Proceedings in the Continental Congress, June 7–Aug. 1, 1776, Boyd, ed., *Jefferson Papers*, I, 312.

ated from the existing centers of authority and least hopeful of controlling the legislatures of the newly constituted governments, expressed doubts of the ability of any representative body to speak conclusively for them. Both the freeholders of Albemarle County, Virginia, and the mechanics of New York City went so far as to deny the efficacy of representation altogether, arguing that the power of "approving, or disapproving, their own laws . . . ought forever to remain with the whole body of the people." Not only in the ratifying of their constitution but even in the making of their laws, declared the New York mechanics in a notable address of June 14, 1776, every man out-of-doors "is, or ought to be by inadmissible right, a co-legislator with all the other members of that community." Only the people-at-large were "the sole lawful legislature"; they could never really divest themselves completely of their "co-legislative power" to any set of representatives, "which, if repeatedly declared by us, to have been freely granted, would only proclaim our insanity, and for that reason, be void of themselves." The provincial congresses with their resolves in place of laws seemed in fact more properly aware of their own limitations than previous legislatures had been, and were thus to be commended for "so nobly asserting the rights which the people at large have to legislation. . . . Their laws, issued in the style of recommendations, leave inviolate, in the conventions, the committees, and finally the people at large, the right of rejection or ratification." The radicals in Pennsylvania actually carried this right of the people-at-large to legislate into constitutional form. In the 1776 Constitution the representative assembly became a kind of upper house, while the people "out-of-doors" retained all their original power of legislation. This turned the elected representatives into an aristocracy of sorts, which was to be restrained by "the grand legislative Council the People who had a right to approve or disapprove every bill" passed by the Assembly. "In a word," said one perceptive critic, "the new system of government for Pennsylvania destroys all ideas of representation."[40]

This disintegration of the concept of representation begun by the most suspicious and estranged groups in 1776 increasingly spread in the years after Independence, all the while being justified by an extension of republican Whig principles. "It has be-

40. Albemarle County Instructions, *ibid.*, VI, 286–87; Address of the Mechanics of New York City, June 14, 1776, in Niles, ed., *Principles*, 174–76; Phila. *Pa. Journal*, Mar. 12, 1776; Phila. *Pa. Packet*, Oct. 15, 1776.

come absolutely necessary," wrote Benjamin Austin of Massachusetts, a typical example of the new radical politician being vaulted into prominence by the developments of the 1780's, "that the 'majority of persons' should be cautioned against *acquiescing* in the sentiment of placing *implicit confidence* in their Representatives." Only "an *aristocratical party*" could desire to inculcate such confidence, in an effort "to persuade the *people*, that a *few men* know the things belonging to their political welfare much better than *themselves*." In South Carolina where the presence of an aristocratic party was as real as anywhere in America in the 1780's the calls for a "virtuous jealousy" and "resentment" of all "the Nabob members of the legislature" by emerging radical politicians, like William Hornby and Alexander Gillon, attained an intensity and breadth new to Carolinians; and the representativeness and the integrity of the legislature were brought into question as never before. Suspicion and jealousy by the people of their legislators, it was claimed, had been made essential by the Revolution and the institution of republics; without such popular opposition "free governments soon become absolute, and the *people ruined* and *enslaved*, by the FEW whom *they have* CREATED." The postwar actions of the South Carolina legislature were but "specimens" indicating "*a settled plan of ruling by a few, with a rod of iron*" over "the *middling* and the *poor*" of the state. In the eyes of some Carolinians the 1784 case of William Thompson, a tavern-keeper threatened with banishment and reprimanded by the House of Representatives for allegedly insulting one of its "Nabob" members, John Rutledge, became as notorious an example of an abuse of legislative privilege as the *Ashby* v. *White* and Wilkes cases had been to many eighteenth-century Englishmen. All such assumptions of power by the legislature were "with republicans, unconstitutional" and "more alarming" and "more intolerable" than any previous actions of the British monarchy, since the usurpation "of 40 *tyrants* at our doors, exceeds that of *one* at 3000 miles." The press of South Carolina in the 1780's sounded very much like the press of Pennsylvania in 1776.[41]

Because of this kind of abuse of their representative authority by legislators, the people were increasingly urged to take back into their own hands the power they had delegated. The orthodox conviction that it was impossible to convene the people of a large

41. [Austin], *Observations on the Pernicious Practice of the Law*, 44–45; Charleston *Gazette of the St. of S.-C.*, July 29, Aug. 19, 1784.

state in the aggregate was, as one South Carolinian pamphleteer suggested, being proved wrong by the Americans. The people themselves in their mobbings, in their district committees and conventions, and in their explicit directions to their elected deputies seemed in fact to be replacing their representatives in the legislatures as the deliberative bodies for the states. "Yes, *they legislate at home!*"[42] There is scarcely a newspaper, pamphlet, or sermon of the 1780's that does not dwell on this breakdown of confidence between the people-at-large and their representative governments. The people, it appeared to those alarmed by these developments, were only pretending to give up their authority to their representatives, since they "afterwards reserve the right of making and of judging of all their laws themselves." In Massachusetts in particular "the confidence of the people has been transferred from their Representatives in Court, to county *Conventions*, and from thence to a *mob*." The Americans, it seemed, were being once again "LITERALLY placed on the broad field of nature."[43] Presumably the society had "never vested any body of men with any such power or authority, as bind the people to obedience or subjection." The acts of the legislature had to be in the nature of tentative recommendations, since it was assumed "that as the people had all power originally in themselves; so they still retain it, to such a degree, that a majority of the people at large, have a right to reverse and annul every act and contract of all the legislatures on the continent." They were everywhere forming "combinations within the State in opposition to their own laws and government." The extreme actuality of representation being honed and extended in the decade after Independence, with its concomitant weakening of the binding character of law, was leading, it seemed to many, "to anarchy and confusion," and tending "to dissolve and render nugatory every civil compact."[44]

It was not simply a problem of the breakdown of governmental

42. *Rudiments of Law and Government*, 33; [Noah Webster], "Government," *American Magazine*, 1 (1787–88), 207.

43. [Rush], *Observations on the Government of Pennsylvania*, in Runes, ed., *Writings of Rush*, 71; Boston *Independent Chronicle*, Jan. 18, 1787; Benjamin Hichborn, *An Oration Delivered July 5th, 1784* . . . (Boston, 1784), 13.

44. Boston *Independent Chronicle*, Jan. 24, 1782; Hartford *Conn. Courant*, Oct. 21, 1783; Samuel Macclintock, *A Sermon Preached . . . June 3, 1784. On the Commencement of the New Constitution* . . . (Portsmouth, 1784), 43; Mather, *Sermon Preached May 10, 1781*, 11; [David Cooper], *An Enquiry into Public Abuses, Arising for Want of a Due Execution of Laws* (Phila., 1784), 3.

authority. Not only were the people ignoring and disobeying the laws "meerly because such measures do not coincide with their private views and separate interests," but the lawmakers in the legislatures were being bandied about and intimidated by electoral combinations and instructions in their local districts, pressured into thinking only of that "little circle with which they are immediately connected," out of a desire for "popular applause and their own advancement in office."[45] Self-appointed leaders of the people, *"demagogues,"* "with the *vox populi vox Dei* in their mouths," men who were "at the bottom, *whether of yesterday or the day before,* who under plausible pretences, ... for dark, ambitious, or (not unlikely) speculative purposes, which they dare not own," were "disturbing the peace of the public, and causing the government to be bullied." The legislatures, it was repeatedly claimed, were becoming simply the instruments and victims of parties and private combinations, puppets in the hands of narrow-minded, designing men. And no wonder, for "so long as the people shall be impressed with the idea, that they can, at any time, *constitutionally* control and direct the legislature, ... they will be appealed to for that purpose, whenever men of popular talents shall be disappointed in their favourite schemes."[46]

It was at bottom a problem of representation, of the proper relationship between the people-at-large and their elected representatives, brought out most vehemently and fully in those states like Massachusetts and South Carolina where large numbers felt themselves unable to satisfy their desires in the legislatures. It was in the seemingly most stable of the revolutionary states, however, in Maryland on the eve of the formation of the federal Constitution, that the issue of representation underlying the politics of the decade was most pointedly and illuminatingly joined. The attempt by the Maryland House of Delegates in the winter of 1786–87 to bring pressure on the Senate by urging the people-at-large to instruct the members of the upper house to pass paper money bills precipitated the longest and most important constitutional debate of the Confederation period prior to the meeting of the Philadel-

45. Henry Cumings, *Sermon Preached May 28, 1783,* 13; Macclintock, *Sermon, June 3, 1784,* 43; Samuel Wales, *The Dangers of Our National Prosperity . . .* (Hartford, 1785), 22.
46. Adams, *Sermon Preached May 29, 1782,* 25; Boston *Independent Chronicle,* Dec. 1, 1785; Charleston *S.-C. Gazette and General Advertiser,* May 11–13, 1784; Baltimore *Md. Journal,* Apr. 13, 1787.

phia Convention. As described earlier, the bills' opponents wisely avoided any attempt to define the upper house as a body distinctive from the lower house, that is, as an aristocracy immune from popular dictation.[47] Conceding that the Senate was equally representative of the people, they instead concentrated on a denial of the right of the people to instruct either representative branch of the legislature. Since the expanded use of binding instructions was an important symptom of what was happening to the relation between the people and their legislative delegates in the 1780's, this debate over instructions had the effect of laying bare fomenting changes in American thinking about representation.

The opponents of instructions began in February 1787 with a conventional statement of the notion of virtual representation. The people, they readily admitted, were the source of all political power; but the people could express this power only through periodic elections, not through binding instructions to their representatives. "The supreme power of legislation, is in the people— but when they choose representatives to make laws, . . . they are bound by the laws that shall be so made." All the people's original powers "are invested in the legislature, and are not reserved in the people." Representation was not "limited, confined, or imperfect." Instead the representative had a full and general power to transact business for his constituent: "Whatever he may do, will be binding on the principal; notwithstanding the business was not done agreeable to his opinion and sentiments; and he has no remedy, but to appoint another representative to do his business in future." Judge Alexander Hanson, emerging as the principal opponent of legislative instructions, repeated this same line of argument throughout the spring and summer of 1787. "All power indeed flows from the people," conceded Hanson; "but the doctrine that the power, actually, at all times, resides in the people, is subversive of all government and law." As Locke and other Whigs had shown, in all representative governments "the legislative possesses the only power of making laws," a power which lasted until the next election or the dissolution of the government. Instructions to delegates from a particular county on some special parochial concern, Hanson admitted, may be allowable, but surely not in this case where "national" instructions from all counties simultaneously were to be directed at both branches of the legislature. This in effect, said Hanson, gave the people-at-large a lawmaking

47. See above, 251–54.

capacity outside of the legislature, making them literally "masters" of their "servants" in the legislature, an idea that was "one of the most incongruous and absurd, that ever entered into a human brain." The representatives were to be independent legislators, once elected, free to deliberate on the public good; they thus could not be "mere tools" of the people. Yet those who believed in binding instructions must "erroneously imagine, the constitutional legislature to be nothing more than agents, deputies, or trustees."[48]

Erroneous or not, this was precisely what many Americans believed their representatives to be—mere agents or tools of the people who could give binding directions "whenever they please to give them." The people's power, declared Samuel Chase, in an image borrowed from James Burgh, "is like the light of the sun, native, original, inherent, and unlimited by human authority. Power in the rulers or governors of the people is like the reflected light of the moon, and is only borrowed, delegated and limited by the grant of the people." Every elected official was equally a representative of the people. "From the nature of a government by *representation*, the *deputies* must be subject to the will of their *principals* or this manifest absurdity and plain consequence must follow, that a *few* men would be *greater* than the *whole* community, and might act in *opposition* to the *declared* sense of *all their constituents*." "The *legislature* are the *trustees* of the people and *accountable* to them," asserted William Paca, who assumed the principal burden of defending the instructions. All the great Whigs—Locke, Molesworth, Trenchard, Hampden, and Sidney—had upheld this trusteeship relation between constituents and representatives. Therefore, the "people only" could be "the *constitutional judges* of *legislative* or *public* oppressions," best exercised through their right of instructing. The "question" being debated here in Maryland, said Paca, was "not upon the *right* or *force* of instruction from a *particular* county, city, or borough, but upon the *right* and *force* of the *national voice* communicated and declared to the legislature by memorial, remonstrance, or INSTRUCTION, from *every* county, city, and borough, or the *majority* of the nation." Thus, Paca concluded, the people-at-large through this broadened use of positive instructions on general questions of public interest were in fact capable of doing what no eighteenth-

48. Baltimore *Md. Journal*, Feb. 23, June 22, Aug. 3, 1787.

century thinker considered possible for so large a society, to participate in the exercise of legislative authority *"personally"* as well
as *"representationally."*[49]

4. THE TRANSFERAL OF SOVEREIGNTY

It was inevitable that the orthodox notion of sovereignty, the
most important doctrine of eighteenth-century political science,
would be thrust in the way of these radical constitutional developments; for this denigration of the legislature's authority, this
"reservation of any power in the hands of the people" in order to
"interfere with the power of the Legislature to consult the public
interest, and prevent its exercise," more directly violated the concept of sovereignty than did any of the Americans' efforts prior to
1787 to erect or strengthen the Confederation. "Sovereignty . . . ,"
went the conventional doctrine, "consists in the understanding
and will of the political society," which admittedly was originally
in the people. When the government was formed, however, the
people vested the sovereignty "where and in what manner" they
pleased; "he or they to whom it is delegated is the sovereign, and
is thus vested with the political understanding and will of the people, for their good and advantage solely." Since "the power of
making rules or laws to govern or protect the society is the essence
of sovereignty," the legislatures of the states had become the sovereign powers in America. There thus could be no power in the
states existing outside of the legislatures, because "this sovereignty
can never be a subordinate power, or be amenable to any other
power."[50]

Hence beginning in the late seventies and continuing on
through the eighties opponents of all of these radical extensions
of Whiggism—the mobbing and electioneering, the proliferation
of conventions, the broadened use of instructions, the acute actualization of representation—repeatedly fell back upon this doctrine of sovereignty as the final, best rebuttal they could offer.
"The idea of Committees forming County Conventions, and these

49. *Ibid.*, Feb. 13, 20, May 18, Aug. 31, 1787. Burgh used the image of the sun
and moon in *Disquisitions*, I, 3–4.

50. [Noah Webster], "Government," *American Magazine*, 1 (1787–88), 76;
Phila. *Independent Gazetteer*, Apr. 22, 1788, in John B. McMaster and Frederick
D. Stone, eds., *Pennsylvania and the Federal Constitution 1787–1788* (Phila.,
1888), 532; Boston *Independent Chronicle*, Oct. 20, 1785.

County Conventions advising State Conventions to act in opposition to, or in conformity with the General Court, the supreme authority of the State, ... the supposition of two different powers in a State assuming the right of controling the people," seemed to the people of Worcester, Massachusetts, "to be intirely inconsistent with the best and most established maxims of government," forming "that great political solecism imperium in imperio, a head within a head." In every state, legislative authority was "placed in an assembly, that is annually and fully chosen by the people." These representative assemblies, as those alarmed by the growing disrespect of legislative actions repeated over and over, were no distant Parliament; they were the people's own elected representatives, in whom the sovereignty had been deposited. "The people resign their own authority to their representatives—the acts of these deputies are in effect the acts of the people. ... It is as wrong to refuse obedience to the laws made by our *representatives*, as it would be to break laws made by *ourselves*." If a law was bad, then the people could elect new deputies to repeal it; "but while it is a law, it is the act and will of the sovereign power and ought to be obeyed."[51] As every good republican should know, "the Legislature have an undoubted right to make the interest of the State forego that of individuals, and that our duty is to acquiesce." The representative legislature must be "considered as the greatest power on earth," since "*there cannot be two wills in the same public body*." The resort to binding instructions from local districts fomented by "a *directing* club or committee" would prove to be "a dangerous Jesuitical imperium in imperio" and make the legislature "as a *body* contemptible." The concept of sovereignty was as essential to a republic as to any state. "This kind of sovereignty is the *power that enacts laws*," which in every state was "lodged in the *General Assembly*." The people retained elective powers, but "the deliberative powers" of lawmaking belonged to the sovereign legislature. "A right to *instruct* the sovereignty places the *deliberative power in the people*, and brings everything back to that chaos which existed before the compact." The point was, as Benjamin Rush said in 1787 summing up the arguments of those resisting this popular radicalism, "the people of America have mistaken the meaning of the word sovereignty." "It is often said that

51. Response of the Worcester Committee of Correspondence to Pittsfield, Oct. 8, 1778, Handlin, eds., *Popular Sources*, 371; Boston *Independent Chronicle*, Aug. 31, 1786; "Principles of Government and Commerce," *American Magazine*, 1 (1787–88), 9.

'the sovereign and all other power is seated *in* the people.' This idea is unhappily expressed. It should be—'all power is derived *from* the people.' They possess it only on the days of their elections. After this, it is the property of their rulers, nor can they exercise it or resume it, unless it is abused."⁵²

But this common distinction "between power being *derived* from the people, and being *seated* in the people" was rapidly being dissolved in the years after Independence, as radical writers "in the transition from monarchy to a republic" expanded and indeed "bastardized" the principles of the Revolution. The people, it was argued, "must not only retain the right of delegating, but of resuming power, at stated periods, if they will be free. . . . If power sufficient to controul the Officers of Government is *not seated* in the people," then the Revolution had been meaningless. "Who have we . . . besides the people? and if they are not to be trusted with the care of their own interests who can?" The Americans, it was claimed at the outset by the freeholders of Augusta County, Virginia, were "neither guided, nor will ever be influenced by that slavish maxim in politicks, 'that whatever is enacted by that body of men in whom the supreme power of the state is vested must in all cases be implicitly obeyed.' " Those who iterated such a view, realizing the dangerous logic of it, could "disclaim the construction . . . and the application some have made of it" and disavow the anarchy it could induce. Yet Americans, being good Whigs, could never deny the sentiment itself: "Is it possible," asked the Augusta freeholders, "that they should *believe* the contrary?" Yet a decade later men were still compelled to contend "that the boasted *omnipotence* of the Legislature is but a gingle of words, and literally understood is but little short of blasphemy. . . . If there is *no* bound to the Legislature, we are no longer in a free country, but governed by an oligarchical tyranny."⁵³

Many thus found themselves by the 1780's increasingly pressed to determine these bounds and to distinguish between lawful and unlawful resistance to legislative authority. Writer after writer

52. Charleston *Gazette of the St. of S.-C.*, Oct. 7, 1784; [Whiting], *Address to Inhabitants*, 27; Boston *Independent Chronicle*, Apr. 5, 1787; Charleston *Extra Gazette of the St. of S.-C.*, July 17, 1784; Baltimore *Md. Journal*, Mar. 2, 16, 1784; Rush, "Defects of the Confederation," Runes, ed., *Writings of Rush*, 28.
53. Charleston *S.C. Weekly Gazette*, July 21–24, 1784; Charleston *S.-C. Gazette and General Advertiser* Aug. 9, 1783; Phila. *Pa. Packet*, June 10, 1777; Dixon and Hunter's Wmsbg. *Va. Gazette*, Dec. 20, 1776; *Providence Gazette*, Aug. 5, 1786.

began with a defense of the Revolutionary lesson of the "need of vigilancy on the side of the people" but ended with a warning that "suspicion may be carried too far." If the "assembly stretch their prerogatives beyond constitutional bounds, they may lawfully be opposed," asserted Zabdiel Adams in 1782. Such legitimate opposition, however, was no justification for forming dangerous combinations. For after all, said Adams in obvious confusion, the legislatures were now the people's own freely elected representatives. "As the choice of the people is the only rational source of power, so it makes obedience the most rational act." The laws enacted by "the ordinary representatives of the state," declared Moses Hemmenway in the Massachusetts Election Sermon of 1784, should be considered "as the will and law of the state, when the contrary does not appear." But who was to decide when the contrary appeared? The answer was inevitably the people-at-large, since "surely such laws ought not to stand in force against the manifest will and interest of the community. For a people to be so enslaved, either to their *rulers*, or even their *own laws*, as not to be able to exercise their essential right of sovereignty for their own safety and welfare, is as inconsistent with civil liberty, as if they were enslaved to an army, or to any foreign power." Still, added Hemmenway, pointing up the perplexing dilemma of American politics, the right to exercise this sovereignty was no excuse for abusing it and becoming licentious. Indeed, "this caution against the abuse of liberty ought to sink deep into our hearts; for here seems to be our greatest danger." Even those most mistrustful of legislative authority, like an anonymous author of a 1783 South Carolina pamphlet entitled *Rudiments of Law and Government, Deduced from the Law of Nature*, admitted that "in free governments and equal representations, the levy of taxes, or other State transactions, do not imply compulsion; for how can that be compulsion, which reason has suggested, his delegate advised, and his self permitted." Yet at the same time, as many were coming to realize, "no sufficient reason can be assigned, why the representatives of a country should not be restricted in their power. It ought to be a maxim that their authority extends not to doing wrong." The opposite nonsense was accepted only in England, where "the supposition of the law," as Blackstone had stated, "is that neither the king nor either House of Parliament, collectively taken, is capable of doing any wrong.—Since in such cases, the law feels itself incapable of furnishing an adequate remedy." But, asked this

South Carolinian of his fellow Americans, "shall not our prudence supply a remedy?"[54]

The search for this remedy—a way to control and restrict the elected representatives in their power—dominated the politics and constitutionalism of the Confederation period. Yet the devices to limit legislative omnipotence being discovered or implemented in these years—the idea of a written constitution as fundamental law, the resort to special constituting bodies, and the actualization of representation through the growing use of instructions and local residence requirements—were all products of the very breakdown of confidence between people and representatives and the atmosphere of suspicion and jealousy so much condemned. It seemed that once it was conceded that the legislature did not possess the full power of the people to do anything it wished for the good of the state, then there could be no logical way of restraining the slippage of nearly all authority away from the legislature to the people-at-large.

No one saw this more clearly, no one grasped more fully the interconnectedness of all the political and constitutional developments of the 1780's, than did Noah Webster, writing in 1787–88 as "Giles Hickory" in an extraordinary series of articles published in his own *American Magazine*.[55] In these honest and penetrating papers Webster argued with great persuasiveness that Americans could not have their constitutional remedies without the evils, that all of the developments and devices of the decade since Independence were inextricably bound together, leading eventually, if not totally repudiated, to a subversion of all government. Webster challenged directly what had become, he ruefully admitted, "the opinions and prejudices of my countrymen." By boldly confronting every major advance the American Revolution had made in

54. Adams, *Sermon Preached May 29, 1782*, 24, 20; Cumings, *Sermon Preached May 28, 1783*, 17; Moses Hemmenway, *A Sermon, Preached before His Excellency John Hancock . . .* (Boston, 1784), 20, 39; *Rudiments of Law and Government*, 17, 36.

55. The articles were entitled "On Bills of Rights"; "Government. Whether, in a Free State, There Ought to Be Any Distinction between the Powers of the People or Electors, and the Powers of the Representatives in the Legislature"; "Government. Mr. Jefferson's Arguments in Favor of an Unalterable Constitution, Considered"; "Government. The Practice of Instructing Representatives Absurd and Contrary to the True Principles of Liberty," in *American Magazine*, 1 (1787–88), 13–15, 75–80, 137–45, 204–10. Noah Webster republished the essays without substantial change in *Collection of Essays* and *Fugitive Writings on Moral, Historical, Political and Literary Subjects* (Boston, 1790), 45–48, 49–58, 59–71, 72–80.

constitutional thought, by denying the need for bills of rights, unalterable forms of government, perpetual constitutions, and special conventions with powers not given to the representative legislatures, and by indicting the conception of actual representation more comprehensively than any Tory or even Burke had, Webster in effect called into question what he saw to be by 1788 "a fundamental maxim of American politics, which is, that 'the sovereign power resides in the people.' "[56]

Written constitutions and bills of rights, said Webster, could never be effective guarantees of freedom. "Liberty is never secured by such paper declarations; nor lost for want of them." The truth is, declared Webster, in the most traditional and powerful argument of eighteenth-century political science, government "takes its form and structure from the genius and habits of the people; and if on paper a form is not accommodated to those habits, it will assume a new form, in spite of all the formal sanctions of the supreme authority of a State." The people of the United Netherlands lost their liberties to "a rich aristocracy" almost as soon as they had won them. "There was no compulsion—no external force in producing this revolution; but the form of government, which had been established on paper, and solemnly ratified, was not suited to the genius of the subjects." The Dutch burghers had a right to elect their rulers, but they voluntarily neglected it. "A *bill of rights*, and a *perpetual constitution* on parchment guaranteeing that right, was a useless form of words, because opposed to the temper of the people." Americans had become too enamored with such artificial devices. "Unless the advocates for unalterable constitutions of government, can prevent all changes in the wants, the inclinations, the habits and the circumstances of people, they will find it difficult, even with all their declarations of unalterable rights, to prevent changes in government. A paper-declaration is a very feeble barrier against the force of national habits, and inclinations."[57]

The Americans, wrote Webster, had gone wrong in assuming that their experience was like "the experience of other nations"; all their constitutional devices had rested on this false assumption. The Europeans in fact had never "possessed the true principles of liberty. . . . There has been, from time immemorial, some rights of government—some prerogatives vested in some man or body of

56. Webster, "Government," *American Magazine,* 1 (1787–88), 75, 204.
57. *Ibid.,* 141, 140.

men, independent of the suffrages of the body of the subjects," and this is what "distinguishes the governments of Europe and of all the world, from those of America." Every European nation had thus been torn by "an incessant struggle" between the rights of the people and hereditary prerogatives. "The Americans have seen the records of their struggles; and without considering that the objects of the contest *do not exist in this country*; they are laboring to guard rights which there is no party to attack. They are as jealous of their rights, as if there existed here a King's prerogatives or the powers of nobles, independent of their own will and choice, and ever eager to swallow up their liberties." "A Bill of Rights against the encroachments of Kings and Barons, or against any power independent of the people, is perfectly intelligible; but a Bill of Rights against the encroachments of an elective Legislature, that is, against our *own* encroachments on ourselves, is a curiosity in government." In English history Magna Carta, indeed "every law or statute that defines the powers of the crown, and circumscribes them within determinate limits, must be considered as a barrier to guard popular liberty." Such documents recognized and established the people's rights in order to prevent their resumption "by the crown under pretence of ancient prerogative." These bills or statutes, like the seventeenth-century habeas corpus act, were esteemed by the English not because they were thought to be unalterable by Parliament, "for the same power that enacted them, can at any moment repeal them; but they are esteemed, because they are barriers erected by the Representatives of the nation, against a power that exists independent of their own choice." In America such declaratory documents had none of the same relevance. There were no prerogatives, no rights or powers, "but what are common to *every man*." Americans with their perpetual bills of rights and unalterable paper constitutions thus resembled "Don Quixotes fighting windmills." "The jealousy of the people in this country has no proper object against which it can rationally arm them—it is therefore directed *against themselves*, or against an invasion which they *imagine* may happen in future ages."[58]

This fear of themselves actually underlay all of the Americans' foolish contrivances—their perpetual constitutions, their special conventions, and their use of instructions—and was involving them in all sorts of tangled contradictions. In a free government, said Webster, no political or civil regulation should be perpetual,

58. *Ibid.*, 140, 142, 13, 142.

for the people "have no right to make laws for those who are not in existence." Jefferson's conviction that the Constitution of Virginia was defective because it was not created by a special convention and was thus alterable by the ordinary legislature was foolish, said Webster, and indeed, although Webster did not draw the connection, did violence to Jefferson's own concern with the tyranny of the past. Americans' efforts to fix a form of government in "perpetuity," Webster argued, supposed a *"perfect wisdom and probity* in the framers; which is both arrogant and impudent." Indeed, "the very attempt to make *perpetual* constitutions, is the assumption of a right to control the opinions of future generations; and to legislate for those over whom we have as little authority as we have over a nation in Asia." Why should the Americans be "so jealous of future Legislatures" and at the same time be so confident of the infallibility of present conventions? "What was a convention" anyway? "Why a body of men chosen by the people in the manner they choose the members of the Legislature, and commonly composed of the same men; but at any rate they are neither wiser nor better. The sense of the people is no better known in a convention, than in a Legislature." The distinction between the two bodies was thus "without a difference," "useless and trifling." Since the people had to be represented in one body or the other, "of what consequence is it whether we call it a *Convention* or a *Legislature*? or why is not the assembly of the representatives of [the] people, at all times a Convention, as well as a Legislature?" "A convention can therefore have no more power, and differs no more from an ordinary Legislature, than one Legislature does from another." Americans must realize, as the people of Connecticut had, that "the Legislature is a part of the people, and has the same *interest*." And this *"union of interests"* between the people and their representatives, and not any artificial devices or *"empty things,"* was not only "the *best*, but the *only* security" for the people's liberties. "The people will choose their Legislature from their own body—that Legislature will have an interest inseparable from that of the people—and therefore an act to restrain their power in any article of legislation, is as unnecessary as an act to prevent them from committing suicide."[59]

At the heart of America's problems, said Webster, lay this misconception of the nature of representation, most vividly revealed in the absurd and persistent resort to instructions from local con-

59. *Ibid.*, 76, 138–39, 14, 77, 78, 80, 144, 142.

stituencies. All of the profuse, hastily drawn, capricious, confused, and unjust legislation of the 1780's—"most of the destructive measures which have been pursued by the states" since the war —had "originated in towns and counties, and been carried by positive instructions from constituents to Representatives." The practice of giving binding instructions to representatives, said Webster, rested on the belief "that the constituents, on a view of their local interests, and either with none, or very imperfect information, are better judges of the propriety of a law, and of the general good, than the most judicious men are (for such generally are the Representatives) after attending to the best official information from every quarter, and after a full discussion of the subject in an assembly, where clashing interests conspire to detect error and suggest improvements." In truth, said Webster, instructions "dictated by local interests" negated the very idea of representation: "They make the opinions of a small part of the state a rule for the whole—they imply a decision of a question, before it is heard— they reduce a Representative to a mere machine, by restraining the exercise of his reason—they subvert the very principles of republican government." Since all laws were designed for "the true interest of the whole state," and not merely for "a particular part," they "must be founded on the best *general* information: the people themselves have no right to consent to a law, without this general information," or "on a view of a local interest," or "without hearing the objections and arguments suggested by every part of the community, which is to be affected by that law." Therefore, "if the collective sense of a state is the basis of law, and that sense can be known officially no where but in an assembly of all the people or of their Representatives . . . , where is the right of *instructing Representatives?*" The local sense of the people, "taken in small meetings, without a general knowledge of the objections, and reasonings of the whole state," can never produce the general good; each district is but "part of the state, and not competent to judge fully of the interest of the whole."[60]

Americans did not understand the proper role and duty of a representative. Those who believed in binding instructions appar-

---

60. *Ibid.*, 206, 205, 207. Webster's ideal representative was Thomas Bourne of Sandwich, Massachusetts, who resigned as representative to that state's Ratifying Convention rather than be instructed by the town, declaring that with instructions "the greatest ideot may answer your purpose as well as the greatest man." *Ibid.*, 208. Cf. Samuel B. Harding, *The Contest over the Ratification of the Federal Constitution in the State of Massachusetts* (N. Y., 1896), 57.

ently thought "that a Deputy chosen by a certain number of free-men, is their Representative only or particularly," and that as merely "an agent for a town or small society" he was "bound to attend to the *particular interest of the men who elect him*, rather than to the *general interest*." If this were the representative's true role, Webster admitted, "it would obviate, in some measure, the objections against instructions." But it was "*clearly false*," for "the constituents of every Representative are not solely those who vot-ed for him, but the *whole state*, and the man that acts from a local interest, and attends merely to the wishes of those men who elect-ed him, violates his oath, and abuses his trust." Unless the represen-tatives were free of partial interests and binding instructions the public good that made republicanism viable would never be pro-moted, and "the local views and attachments which now embar-rass government"—more fatally in America, said Webster, than in any other country—would never be eliminated.[61]

Again and again throughout all of his rambling criticisms of America's recent constitutional developments Webster kept com-ing back to this question of the representativeness of the people in their assemblies: "Whether, in a free State, there ought to be any distinction between the powers of the people or electors, and the powers of the Representatives in the Legislature." All of Web-ster's attacks on the right of instructions, on unalterable constitu-tions, and on special constitutional conventions, were eventually grounded on his conviction, the basic conviction of orthodox eighteenth-century political science, that "*the Legislature has all the power, of all the people*," and that there could be in no state "a pretended power paramount to the legislature." Representation should not be actual or partial; "the powers of a Legislature should be co-extensive with those of the people," for "the collective body of Representatives is the collective sense and authority of the peo-ple." There could thus be "no power residing in the State at large, which does not reside in the legislature." If some power was with-held from the representatives and left with the people-at-large, then the way was opened to a full denial of legislative power. "Unless the Legislature is the supreme power, and invested with *all* the authority of the State, its acts are not laws, obligatory upon the whole State." The principle of sovereignty required that if the legislature had an "unlimited power to do *right*" for the state, then

61. Webster, "Government," *American Magazine*, 1 (1787–88), 209, 207, 209, 206.

it must also have "an unlimited power to do *wrong*." There was
no other choice. If the representation of the people in the legislature was not full and "virtual," then, as Webster saw as acutely as
anyone, the various state legislatures were in theory no more sovereign, no more lawmaking bodies, than was the Confederation
Congress.[62]

However "repugnant to the principles received by my countrymen and recognized by some of the state constitutions" Webster's
sentiments were, the logic of his central argument was compelling—the same logic that the British had used against the Americans in the late sixties and early seventies: there must be in every
state a supreme, absolute, indivisible, sovereign power.[63] If the
Americans in the 1780's were forced to choose between their legislatures and the people-at-large as the repository of this sovereignty, just as they had been forced in the early seventies to choose
between Parliament and their legislatures, there could be no doubt
now as there had been no doubt then where they would place the
final supreme power. "For," as one Connecticut town declared in
1783, "there is an original, underived and incommunicable authority and supremacy, in the collective body of the people, to
whom all delegated power must submit, and from whom there is
no appeal." Rather than disavow the powerful conception of sovereignty when confronted with it, many now, as earlier, chose to
relocate it. If sovereignty had to reside somewhere in the state—
and the best political science of the eighteenth century said it did
—then many Americans concluded that it must reside only in the
people-at-large. The legislatures could never be sovereign; no set
of men, representatives or not, could "set themselves up against
the general voice of the people." "The community, however represented, ought to remain the supreme authority and ultimate judicature." In the people alone "that plenary power rests and abides
which all agree should rest somewhere."[64]

To someone steeped in British legal thought this explicit reten-

---

62. *Ibid.*, 75, 78, 80, 76, 75, 79, 75, 76.
63. *Ibid.*, 209. Compare Webster's thinking in 1787–88 with his earlier views
expressed in his *Sketches of American Policy* (Hartford, 1785), esp. 6. Webster,
even as the *Sketches* was being published, expressed doubts of its ideas and in
time repudiated much of what he had written in the early eighties as "chimerical"
and "too democratic," unwarranted by experience. "We grow wiser with age."
See the introduction to the Harry R. Warfel edition of the *Sketches* (N. Y.,
1937), ii–iii.
64. Hartford *Conn. Courant*, Aug. 12, 1783; [Tucker], *Conciliatory Hints*, 21;
Rudiments of Law and Government, 30.

tion of legal sovereignty in the people was preposterous. It could only signify a repudiation of the concept and an eventual breakdown of all governmental order. But developments in America since 1776 had infused an extraordinary meaning into the idea of the sovereignty of the people. The Americans were not simply making the people a nebulous and unsubstantial source of all political authority. The new conception of a constitution, the development of extralegal conventions, the reliance on instructions, the participation of the people in politics out-of-doors, the clarification of the nature of representation, the never-ending appeals to the people by competing public officials—all gave coherence and reality, even a legal reality, to the hackneyed phrase, the sovereignty of the people.

5. THE DISEMBODIMENT OF GOVERNMENT

Transferring sovereignty from the legislative bodies to the people-at-large outside of all governmental institutions represented far more than simply an intellectual shift of a political conception. It had consequences and implications that were at first only vaguely perceived, but when sparked into illumination by debates and the logic of arguments became confusing and often frightening indications of the changes Americans were making in their inherited political theory. By weakening the representativeness of the people in the legislatures through the resort to conventions, instructions, and other out-of-doors action, by expressing as much fear and suspicion of their elected representatives as of their senators and governors, the Americans were fundamentally unsettling the traditional understanding of how the people in a republic were to participate in the government. The logic of the principles of the Revolution was being spun out with such rapidity in these years, impelled by the strongest kinds of polemical pressures and political and social circumstances, that most scarcely sensed the enormity of the intellectual changes they were participating in. All that had begun in the 1760's with the debate with England was now being brought to a head. A series of tiny, piecemeal changes in thought, no one of which seemed immensely consequential, was preparing Americans for a revolution in their conceptions of law, constitutionalism, and politics.

If the people were not actually voicing their will in the representative assemblies, then no law enacted by the legislatures could be considered fully binding. Some almost immediately in the 1780's began drawing that conclusion, arguing that it was "impossible" for the representatives "to impose an irrevocable act contrary to the majority of the people, from whom they received their power." Horrified opponents retorted that this made the people "not subject to law" and indeed destroyed the idea of law itself. "If an act of a representative is not the act of his constituents, it is nothing; it is only the act of an individual—of Tom, Dick, or Harry." For some this was precisely what the laws in the 1780's seemed to be: acts of mistrusted individuals that were in the nature of temporary recommendations to the people, standing only so far as "the vote of the community does not oppose." And such communal opposition, as the proliferation of committees and conventions demonstrated, was even considered by some to be legitimate. No legislature, said a New Jerseyite, could ignore the voice of the people out-of-doors, for "the plain definition of republican government is that every elector has a voice in every law which is made to govern him the same as if he personally sat in council." The state legislatures, it was claimed, contained no more of the inherent power of the American people than the British Parliament ever had. With the repeated complaints in the press and pamphlets that the legislatures were violating the bounds of justice and all that made law what it was, the people were increasingly advised from the 1770's on through the eighties never to accept that "plausible nonsense 'that nothing is beyond the reach of the Supreme Legislature.' " With the resort to conventions and extra-legislative organizations it was now realistically possible to deny "that the will of the people is properly known from the Representatives." The legislators must realize that they merely possessed "a trust from the people for their good, and in several instances so far from possessing an absolute power, they ought to acknowledge that they have no power at all." Representation of the people could therefore never be full and inclusive. "It is a vain and weak argument," wrote Thomas Tudor Tucker of South Carolina in 1784, "that, the legislature being the representatives of the people, the act of the former is therefore always to be considered as the act of the latter. They are the representatives of the people for certain purposes only, not to all intents and purposes whatever." The significance for men's understanding of law of this change in the conception of representation was immense. If law made by a legislature was not really a reflection of the will of the people, not the command of a superior sovereign, but only the act of the people's suspected agents, then some sanction other than consent would have to be emphasized in order to make law obligatory.[65]

The implications of these changes in the nature of the people's role in the government were as important for men's understanding of politics as they were for their understanding of law. They were in fact tending not only to a radical redistribution of the powers of society within the government but to a total destruction of these powers and a shattering of the categories of government that had dominated Western thinking for centuries. Already by the middle eighties the senates in several states were being regarded as a kind of double representation of the people with disturbing but not always clearly perceived consequences for the theory of mixed government. In Maryland in 1787 this admission that the Senate had become simply another representation of the people was accompanied by an intensive examination of the nature of representation, thus resulting in a particularly illuminating expression of the transformation of thought taking place.

The right of the people to instruct their representatives was an old tradition in Maryland, said Samuel Chase; Marylanders had frequently exercised this right of instructing their delegates in the former proprietary government and had in fact instructed Chase himself in the Convention of 1776. Of course, admitted Chase, the people had previously never claimed any right to instruct the members of the upper house, since they had been appointed by the proprietor and thus in fact had been his representatives and not the people's. But now under the new republican government the situation was different: "By our constitution," Chase told the people, "*you* do appoint the Senate, and they are, and have *uniformly* claimed themselves to be, your *representatives*." And as "your representatives, they are bound by your instructions, or you destroy the very idea of *election* and of *delegating* power"— but only if election and the delegation of power by the people had become, as they had for Chase and for other Americans in these years, the sole criteria of representation.[66]

65. Hartford *Conn. Courant*, Sept. 30, 1783; Elizabethtown *Political Intelligencer*, Jan. 4, 1786, in McCormick, *New Jersey in the Critical Period*, 73; Boston *Independent Chronicle*, June 19, 1777; Charleston *S. C. Weekly Gazette*, Mar. 22, 1783; [Tucker], *Conciliatory Hints*, 25.
66. Baltimore *Md. Journal*, Feb. 13, 1787.

If logically carried out, this electoral basis of representation would turn every elected official into a kind of representative of the people. Those opposed to instructing the Maryland Senate saw the implications and tried to resist them. Suppose, said Alexander Hanson, the people of Maryland had instituted a different form of government in 1776. "It was debated in convention, whether there should not be three distinct branches of the legislature. Had the proposition been adopted, would you have called them all agents, deputies, or trustees, subject to the order of their principal?" Would the governor simply by being elected by the people become their representative capable of being instructed by them? Yet once it was admitted that the Senate because elective was as equally representative of the people as the lower house, it was difficult to deny the pervasion of representation in a republic. "If the people who have a common right of suffrage claim a right to instruct the Senate, as ultimately chosen by them," cried one Marylander, "by a parity in reasoning, the Governor and Council, Delegates to Congress, and Judges of our Courts are liable to be instructed by them."[67]

Hanson in particular wrestled with the troublesome implications of his concession that the Senate was a representation of the people and fumbled with the new and peculiar problems of politics being created in America. It was quite explicable, he said, that "writing on so important a subject" he had had "no recourse to authority" or quotations to buttress his arguments. For nowhere could he find a writer before himself who had examined "the case of a legislature, consisting of two distinct bodies of men, deriving their authority immediately or ultimately, from the act of the people." The classical categories of government were of little help in untangling the knotted lines of American political thinking, since America no longer seemed governed by the one, the few, or the many, or even by all together. "When the legitimate power is in the people at large," wrote Hanson in an attempt at a clarification useful for his purposes, "it is truly the government of the people, or a strict democracy." However, "when society enters into a solemn compact, prescribing modes of election by the people, whereby a select body or two, or more select bodies, shall be for ever kept up, to legislate for the people, this is another form of government. This is the government by representation." The proponents of national instructions, by urging the people at

67. *Ibid.*, Aug. 3, May 1, 1787.

large to "deliberate for themselves, and prescribe laws," had turned Maryland's Constitution into a "government of the people, confounded with the government of representation, or properly no regular government at all." Government by representation was thus all-pervasive, and excluded the presence of democracy from the constitution entirely. Squeezed between his admission of the representative character of the Senate and his desire to maintain the independence of the legislature from continuous popular dictation, Hanson, like others in the same years for different reasons, found himself inventing a new category of politics. The American states were neither simple democracies nor traditional mixed governments. They had become in all branches governments by representation.[68]

The use of binding instructions and the growing sense that the representative was merely a limited agent or spokesman for the local interests of his constituents in the decade after Independence ate away the independent authority of the representative and distorted, even destroyed, the traditional character of representation. Evidently the people could never be fully embodied in their houses of representatives; sovereignty and the ultimate power to make law, as the extra-legislative devices developing in this period illustrated, remained with the collective people. The logic of these developments was to take the people out of the government altogether, and to blur the previous distinction among representatives, senators, and magistrates. Once the supposed representatives of the people (the democratic elements) in the lower houses of the legislature were regarded with the same suspicion and uneasiness as the traditional rulers and upper houses (the monarchical and aristocratic elements) had been (representation was after all, said one Virginian, "at best, but a species of aristocracy"),[69] it became a much simpler matter to view the rulers and senators in the same light as the supposed representatives were viewed. Once the mutuality of interests between representatives and people that made representation what it was to most eighteenth-century Englishmen was broken down by the American atmosphere of suspicion and jealousy, the only criterion of representation left was election, which helps explain the Americans' increasing concern with the right to vote as a measure of

68. *Ibid.*, Apr. 13, 1787.
69. "Loose Thoughts on Government" (1776), Force, ed., *American Archives*, 4th Ser., VI, 731.

representation. With election or simply the derivation of authority from the people becoming the sole basis and measure of representation, the several branches of the government began to seem indistinguishable. All elected officials could be considered as kinds of representatives of the people, as equally trusted or mistrusted agents of the people. "In our republican government," the people could now be told, "not only our *Deputies*, but our *Governor* and *Council* may in a good sense be esteemed our representatives, as they are annually chosen by you, to manage our public affairs." After all, "who have we in America but the people? Members of congress, of assemblies, or councils, are still a part of the people. Their honours do not take them out of the aggregate body." It was not unreasonable now to argue that "the principle for Representation" should be extended "throughout every public body" so that all elected, hence representative, officials—senators or others—should be elected in proportion to the population, the logic of which it has taken us nearly two centuries to realize.[70] "In a free state," wrote Thomas Tudor Tucker of South Carolina in 1784, "every officer, from the Governor to the constable, is, so far as the powers of his office extend, as truly the representative of the people, as a member of the legislature; and his act, within the appointed limitation, is the act of the people; for he is their agent, and derives his authority from them."

The people no longer actually shared in a part of the government (as, for example, the people of England participated in their government through the House of Commons), but they remained outside the entire government, watching, controlling, pulling the strings for all their agents in every branch or part of the government. They embraced the whole government, and no branch or part could speak with the complete authority of the people. Indeed, not even all parts of the government collectively incorporated the full powers of the people. "With us it would be an absurd surrender of liberty to delegate full powers to any set of men whatever." Conventions, assemblies, senates, magistracy were all agents of the people for certain limited purposes. Only such a conception of representation made sense of the developments of the Confederation period—the use of instructions, the electioneering, and the extra-legislative organizations, in particular the special

70. Hartford *Conn. Courant*, Apr. 2, 1787; Boston *Independent Chronicle*, Dec. 19, 1782, Jan. 16, 1783; Frederick Muhlenberg, 1784, in Oswald Seidensticker, "Frederick Augustus Conrad Muhlenberg . . . ," *Pa. Mag. of Hist. and Biog.*, 13 (1889–90), 199–200.

constituting conventions creating a superior law ratifiable by the people themselves in their sovereign capacity and hence unalterable by the people's provisional agents in the legislatures. "Delegates may be sent to a convention with powers, under certain restrictions, to frame a constitution. Delegates are sent to the General Assembly with powers, under certain restrictions prescribed . . . by a previously established compact or constitution, to make salutary laws." Yet neither the convention nor the assembly possessed the total authority of the people. "If either one or the other should exceed the powers vested in them, their act is no longer the act of their constituents." The power of the people outside of the government was always absolute and untrammeled; that of their various delegates in the government could never be.[71]

These were revolutionary ideas that had unfolded rapidly in the decade after Independence, but not deliberately or evenly. Men were always only half aware of where their thought was going, for these new ideas about politics were not the products of extended reasoned analysis but were rather numerous responses of different Americans to a swiftly changing reality, of men involved in endless polemics compelled to contort and draw out from the prevailing assumptions the latent logic few had forseen. Rarely before 1787 were these new thoughts comprehended by anyone as a whole. They were bits and pieces thrown up by the necessities of argument and condition, without broad design or significance. But if crystalized by sufficient pressures they could result in a mosaic of an entirely new conception of politics to those who would attempt to describe it.

71. [Tucker], *Conciliatory Hints*, 25–26.

PART FOUR

The Critical Period

Republics, in their very constitution, are shorter lifed than other governments.

—SAMUEL MACCLINTOCK, 1784

CHAPTER X

Vices of the System

1. THE INCONGRUITY OF THE CRISIS

In his commencement address at Harvard College in July 1787, John Quincy Adams spoke of "this critical period," when, it seemed to Adams, the whole country was "groaning under the intolerable burden of . . . accumulated evils." It was an apt phrase —"critical period"—as John Fiske a century later was to discover. But it was hardly an original one, either with Fiske or with Adams. The belief that the 1780's, the years after the peace with Britain, had become the really critical period of the entire Revolution was prevalent everywhere during the decade. By the mid-eighties the oratory and writings were filled with talk of crisis to the point of redundancy: "The present crisis is critical in the extreme." "That a kind of despondency has gone through the continent, is evident from the public prints of every State." Americans suddenly seemed to have lost their nerve. "A foreigner could hardly believe we were that brave people who so nobly struggled for our Independence." Increasingly the events of the 1780's seemed to point toward "a crisis of the most delicate nature taking place," leading to "some crisis, some revolution" that could not be predicted. Many like John Jay found themselves uneasy, "more so than during the war." Then there had been a "fixed object," and although the means and timing were questionable few had had doubts of the ultimate victory. But with the coming of peace "the case is now altered." Men saw ahead of them "evils and calamities, but without being able to guess at the instrument, nature, or measure of them."[1] The evidence is overwhelming from every source —newspapers, sermons, and correspondence—that in the minds of many Americans the course of the Revolution had arrived at a crucial juncture.

With the problems of war and reconstruction it is unquestionable that the period was unsettled—a time of financial confusion and social flux, of great expansion and contraction when fortunes were made and lost. New governments had to be erected and made secure; new economic patterns outside of the empire had to be found; and the void left by the emigration of thousands of Tories, many in high political and economic positions, had to be filled—all resulting in political, social, and economic dislocations that have never been adequately measured. On the face of it, however, this dislocation, this unsettlement, hardly seems to warrant the desperate sense of crisis voiced by so many.[2] On the surface at least the American states appeared remarkably stable and prosperous. The political leaders at the uppermost levels remained essentially unchanged throughout the period. Both the Confederation government and the governments of the separate states had done much to stabilize the finances and the economy of the country. The states had already moved to assume payment of the public debt, and the Confederation deficit could not be considered serious. Despite a temporary depression in the middle eighties the commercial outlook was not bleak. As historians have emphasized, the period was marked by extraordinary economic growth.[3]

1. Quoted in Robert A. East, *John Quincy Adams: The Critical Years, 1785–1794* (N. Y., 1962), 85; Boston *Independent Chronicle*, Aug. 31, 1786; *Providence Gazette*, Oct. 6, 1787; Charleston *S.-C. Gazette and General Advertiser*, Aug. 9, 1783; John Jay to George Washington, June 27, 1786, Johnston, ed., *Papers of Jay*, III, 204–05.

2. Historians who have minimized the criticalness of conditions in the 1780's have naturally tended to see the movement for the Constitution as something in the nature of a conspiracy by a few without widespread justification in the social and economic realities of the period. The "critical period," wrote Charles Beard, was perhaps not so critical after all, "but a phantom of the imagination produced by some undoubted evils which could have been remedied without a political revolution." Charles A. Beard, *An Economic Interpretation of the Constitution of the United States* (N. Y., 1935), 48. For similar views see Ferguson, *Power of the Purse*, 337; Jackson T. Main, *The Antifederalists: Critics of the Constitution 1781–1788* (Chapel Hill, 1961), 177–78; Jensen, *New Nation*, 348–49; E. Wilder Spaulding, *New York in the Critical Period 1783–1789* (N. Y., 1932), 27; for an analysis of the historical debate see Richard B. Morris, "The Confederation Period and the American Historian," *Wm. and Mary Qtly.*, 3d Ser., 13 (1956), 139–56.

3. Jensen, *New Nation*, 256, 339–40, 423–24; Ferguson, *Power of the Purse*, 336.

In fact, as contemporaries noticed, it was a decade of very high expectations, clearly reflected in the rapid rate of population growth which despite little immigration was the fastest of any decade in American history.[4]

It is thus difficult to look back at the period and not feel that the pessimism and apprehension so widely expressed did not in some way exaggerate the real problems of the 1780's. Some of the contemporaries themselves saw an incongruity between the alarms and the situation. "In reality," said one South Carolinian, "though there never was a period in which calamity was so much talked of, I do not believe there ever was a period in which it was so little experienced by the people of this State. If we are undone, we are the most splendidly ruined of any nation in the universe." Although "many people appear to be uneasy and to prognosticate revolutions," David Humphreys wrote to Jefferson in 1786, "they hardly know how or why." True, there was a scarcity of money, "but to judge by the face of the country; by the appearance of ease and plenty which are to be seen every where, one would believe a great portion of the poverty and evils complained of, must be imaginary."[5]

But the complaints were far from imaginary. They were real, intensely real, rooted, however, not in poverty or in real deprivation but rather in prosperity and in the very unintended promises the Revolution seemed to be offering large numbers of Americans. From the vantage of two hundred years later the Revolution by the 1780's seems to have been a glorious success. The war had been won and independence achieved; the peace with Britain was as much as could have been hoped for in 1775. Yet because the Revolution represented much more than a colonial rebellion, represented in fact a utopian effort to reform the character of American society and to establish truly free governments, men in the 1780's could actually believe that it was failing. Nothing more vividly indicates the intensity of the Americans' Revolutionary expectations than the depth of their disillusionment in the eighties. "What astonishing changes a few years are capable of producing," said Washington in a common exclamation of these years. "Have

4. Madison (Va.), in Elliot, ed., *Debates*, III, 394; J. Potter, "The Growth of Population in America, 1700–1860," in D. V. Glass and D. E. C. Eversley, eds., *Population in History: Essays in Historical Demography* (Chicago, 1965), 640.

5. Charleston *South Carolina Gazette and Public Advertiser*, May 18–21, 1785; David Humphreys to Jefferson, June 5, 1786, Boyd, ed., *Jefferson Papers*, IX, 609. See also Charles Thompson to Jefferson, Apr. 6, 1786, *ibid.*, 380.

we fought for this?" was the repeated question. "Was it with these expectations that we launched into a sea of trouble, and have bravely struggled through the most threatening dangers?" All the fervent hopes of 1776 were going awry. Perhaps, as Charles Backus said in 1788, Americans "have had too high expectations from the world." The outset of the Revolution had given "unusual scope to all our wishes." Almost everyone had joined the war against Britain with glowing enthusiasm. "Their motives indeed were very different; but happening to fix upon the same general object, a very great apparent union existed. In the day when our hopes were brightest, the imagination of the Poet knew no bounds, in describing what America *would* be." Thus "we raised our expectation of happiness from the world, beyond what it can afford." If these expectations should prove illusory, if America would not become what men in 1776 had hoped, then, as Richard Price told the Americans in 1785, "the consequence will be, that the fairest experiment ever tried in human affairs will miscarry; and that a REVOLUTION which had revived the hopes of good men and promised an opening to better times, will become a discouragement to all future efforts in favour of liberty, and prove only an opening to a new scene of human degeneracy and misery."[6]

2. THE PERVERSION OF REPUBLICANISM

Almost immediately after the war began the Americans' doubts and anxieties, never far below the surface in 1776, began to emerge with increasing frequency. As early as 1778 Benjamin Rush could write that "the time is now past when the least danger is to be apprehended to our liberties from the power of Britain, the arts of commissioners, or the machinations of tories. Tyranny can now enter our country only in the shape of a whig. All our jealousy should be of ourselves." Americans now had more to dread from "our whigs" than they had "from a host of Governor Johnsons, Dr. Berkenhouts, Hutchinsons, or Galloways." Other Americans agreed, and well before the contest with England was settled they began turning on each other with a jealousy and a fierceness

6. Washington to Jay, Aug. 15, 1786, Johnston ed., *Papers of Jay*, III, 208–09; Phila. *Pa. Packet*, Oct. 14, 1786; Charles Backus, *A Sermon Preached at Long Meadow, April 17th* . . . (Springfield, 1788), 7; Richard Price, *Observations on the Importance of the American Revolution* . . . (Dublin, 1785), 85.

that Rush could scarcely have anticipated. In 1782 Samuel Otis was writing to Theodore Sedgwick that he had expected "bloody noses" before the new Massachusetts Constitution was firmly established. "Indeed almost all revolutions are founded in blood." But he had never expected to see the likes of what was happening in Massachusetts in these past several years. The Whigs realized there were "extravagancies that usually accompany" the "blessings of freedom," but not what they were witnessing. The British and the Tories had warned in the 1770's that the moment a separation from Britain had taken effect "intestine quarrels will begin," and Americans would "split into parties." Now it seemed that such dire prophesies were being fulfilled. The Revolution, it became more and more obvious, was turning upon itself in ways that had not been foreseen, and men were emphasizing with renewed intensity that "unless a proper education of the rising generation is adopted, a new way of thinking and new principles can be introduced among the People of America, there are little hopes of the present republican Governments or anything like republican Governments being of any duration."[7]

It was ironic but undeniable: by the 1780's the Revolutionary ideals seemed to be breeding the sources of their own miscarriage. "The people," said Fisher Ames in 1787, "have turned against their teachers the doctrines which were inculcated in order to effect the late revolution." All the evils which the Revolution was designed to eliminate were instead being aggravated. "It is a favorite maxim of despotick power, that *mankind are not made to govern themselves*"—a maxim which the Americans had spurned in 1776. "But alas!" many were now saying, "the experience of ages too highly favours the truth of the maxim; and what renders the reflection still more melancholy is, that the people themselves have, in almost every instance, been the ready instruments of their own ruin." It had become all too evident to many that "in times of public confusion, and in the demolition of ancient institutions, blustering, haughty, licentious, self-seeking men" were gaining "the ear of the people," exploiting republican ideol-

7. Rush to William Gordon, Dec. 10, 1778, Butterfield, ed., *Rush Letters*, I, 221; Samuel A. Otis to Theodore Sedgwick, July 30, 1782, Theodore Sedgwick Papers, A. 55, Massachusetts Historical Society, Boston; David Ramsay to Benjamin Rush, July 11, 1783, in Rogers, *William Loughton Smith*, 105; Phila. *Independent Gazetteer*, Sept. 27, 1787, in McMaster and Stone, eds., *Pennsylvania and the Federal Constitution*, 127; Charles Lee to Benjamin Rush, Sept. 26, 1779, *Lee Papers*, III, 372.

ogy and disrupting the social fabric. Authority had been challenged in 1776 by appeals to the people that now seemed limitless. The right to rule, the Whigs had said, existed only so long as the people's good was promoted. But who could judge the people's good better than the people themselves? What do "those who are continually declaiming about *the people, the people . . .* mean by the people?" it was asked in exasperation. No part of the government, even their representatives, seemed capable of embodying them. By the 1780's the people had become simply the collective community standing outside of the entire government—a final court of appeal to which every aggrieved group took its case.[8]

The republican emphasis on talent and merit in place of connections and favor now seemed perverted, becoming identified simply with the ability to garner votes, thus enabling "the most unfit men to shove themselves into stations of influence, where they soon gave way to the unrestrained inclination of bad habits." Republicanism was supposed to unleash men's ambitions to serve the state. But what was praiseworthy ambition and what was spurious? "An emulation to excel in virtue is laudable, it gives vigor to every political nerve, advances the meritorious, and produces the most happy effects in a community; but a desire of excelling in power, grandeur and popularity, tends to the certain ruin of a society." Who was to distinguish? Who else but the people? But were they any more capable than the Crown had been?[9]

Equality was not creating harmony and contentment after all. Indeed, it was noted, equality had become the very cause of the evils it was designed to eliminate. In a free and independent republic "the idea of equality breathes through the whole and every individual feels ambitious, to be in a situation not inferior

8. Boston *Independent Chronicle*, Mar. 1, 1787, in Seth Ames, ed., *Works of Fisher Ames with a Selection from His Speeches and Correspondence* (Boston, 1854), II, 101; Boston *Independent Chronicle*, Aug. 31, 1786, Mar. 29, 1787; Baltimore *Md. Journal*, Aug. 3, 1787. John Trumbull's poem, *McFingal*, offers an interesting barometer for measuring the shift of attitude toward the Revolution that occurred among many Whiggishly patriotic Americans in the years after Independence. The poem was written piecemeal throughout the Revolutionary era, and while the early cantos emphasize a typical Whig confidence in the people, the third and fourth cantos, written in 1782, stress the abuses of liberty and a social structure turned topsy-turvy by the excesses of the Revolution. See Alexander Cowie, *John Trumbull, Connecticut Wit* (Chapel Hill, 1936), 167, 172–73, 192–93.

9. Baltimore *Md. Journal*, Sept. 4, 1787; Portsmouth *N.-H. Gazette*, May 10, 1783.

to his neighbour." Among Americans, "the idea of inferiority, as of pursuing a mean employment or occupation . . . mortifies the feelings, and sours the minds of those who feel themselves inferior." Consequently, everyone strives to be equal with those above him, "in dress, if in nothing else." Although the Revolution had placed government almost wholly in the hands of the people, the people were still suspicious and jealous, "the offspring of envy and disappointed ambition." "What stronger proof can we possibly have," it was said, "of an uneasy querulous disposition in the people." It was in the people's blood. Despite the success of the war against Britain the people remained possessed by a "general uneasiness, . . . without the least apparent cause." Instead of a community of placid yeomen, celebrated in Crèvecoeur's *Letters from an American Farmer*, the society appeared filled with inveterate grumblers. "Every man wants to be a judge, a justice, a sheriff, a deputy, or something else which will bring him a little money, or what is better, a little authority."[10]

In all of the states, from New England to South Carolina, the egalitarian atmosphere spread by the Revolution made "superiority from incidental circumstances not annexed to merit . . . galling and insufferable." The Revolution seemed to many simply to have replaced one obnoxious elite with another. "There are some among *us* who call *themselves* persons of quality," declared a typical diatribe from Massachusetts in the mid-eighties. But in fact they were no different from that "set of mushroom gentry" of a few years back who, dignified with imperial offices and connected with those "whom they condescended to admit into their circle," attempted to assume "the character of the *better sort of people*." So manifestly absurd was this appellation "that the very terms became thoroughly contemptible and odious in the estimation of the people." The warning was now out against any repetition of their behavior, against any further attempt "to introduce scenes of pleasure and dissipation," against any efforts to instruct America's youth in becoming fine gentlemen and ladies by the use of plays, operas, music, Venetian balls, and the entire courtier system of English elegance. The ferocious attacks on the Order of the Cincinnati in the 1780's actually represented only the most notable expression of these egalitarian resentments. Because this

10. "On Hard Times," *American Museum*, 1 (1787), 462; Cumings, *Sermon Preached May 28, 1783*, 17–18; Boston *Independent Chronicle*, Mar. 23, 1787; "To the Good People of America," *American Museum*, 1 (1787), 305–07; Hartford *Conn. Courant*, Nov. 20, Apr. 24, 1786.

"Barefaced and Arrogant" attempt by former Revolutionary army officers to perpetuate their honor was considered by men like Aedanus Burke, James Warren, and Samuel Adams to be "as rapid a Stride towards an hereditary Military Nobility as was ever made in so short a Time," it had little chance of maintaining itself as a hereditary body.[11] In vain did supporters of the Cincinnati argue that America lacked the wealth and means for supporting the kind of aristocracy the critics talked of. Under the pressure of the public outcry and Washington's disavowal the Order was quickly forced to renounce its original hereditary character and to become simply another one of the numerous political and social organizations emerging in a country which, as the governor of South Carolina said in 1784, had gone "Society mad."[12]

The republican aversion to artificial distinctions was being broadened into a general denunciation of all differences, whether economic, social, intellectual, or professional. Writers scoffed at the "academical education" of their aristocratic enemies and boasted that they were "plain, unlettered" men better able to communicate with the people. "Overgrown wealth" itself was attacked: "A certain excess of fortune sets a man above the public opinion, and in equal proportion makes him despise those who are poor." The emergent professionalization of careers became more intensely suspect, and even those fearful of too much leveling satirized the "jargon" and the "peculiarities" of the medical profession as it sought to establish itself by "technical terms" and by prescribing "what is new and uncommon."[13]

Naturally it was Pennsylvania that witnessed the most emphatic expression of this republican hatred of distinction and privilege. Throughout the late seventies and early eighties privilege assumed

11. *Rudiments of Law and Government*, 20; Boston *Independent Chronicle*, July 21, 1785; James Warren to John Adams, May 18, 1787, Ford, ed., *Warren-Adams Letters*, II, 291; Samuel Adams to Elbridge Gerry, Apr. 23, 1784, Cushing, ed., *Writings of Samuel Adams*, IV, 301. See [Burke], *Considerations on the Cincinnati*; and Wallace E. Davies, "The Society of the Cincinnati in New England in 1783–1800," *Wm. and Mary Qtly.*, 3d Ser., 5 (1948), 3–25.

12. *Observations on a Late Pamphlet, Entitled, "Considerations upon the Society or Order of the Cincinnati"* . . . (Phila., 1783), 8, 20–21; Boston *Independent Chronicle*, June 17, Apr. 8, 1784.

13. Charleston *Gazette of the St. of S.-C.*, Aug. 19, 1784; *To the Inhabitants of Pennsylvania* ([Phila., 1782]), 2; Hugh Henry Brackenridge, *Modern Chivalry*, ed. Claude M. Newlin (N. Y., 1937), 10–12. On the problems of the emergent professions in the Revolutionary era and after see Daniel H. Calhoun, *Professional Lives in America: Structure and Aspiration, 1750–1850* (Cambridge, Mass., 1965).

a special pointedness for the Scotch-Irish Presbyterian defenders of the 1776 Constitution confronted with a Philadelphia establishment of gentlemen with tight family and mercantile connections who carried their heads *"so very high."* For the Constitutionalists equality became the great ideological weapon to be used not only against would-be social superiors, but against any sort of privilege that stood apart from the equal rights of the people. It was heatedly contended in the press and in the legislature in the sort of argument that carried well into the next century that all corporate grants, even when their public purpose was obvious, like those for the College of Philadelphia, the Bank of America, or the city of Philadelphia, were repugnant to the spirit of the American republics, "which does not admit of granting peculiar privileges to any body of men." "Equal liberty and equal privileges are the happy effect of a free government. They are, in fact, convertible terms: neither can subsist without the other. A popular government (that is, a genuine republic) holds out *this equality* to its citizens; and it is *this*, which gives it the pre-eminence over monarchies, and aristocracies; in *this* consists its excellence. The unequal or partial distribution of public benefits within a state, creates distinctions of interest, influence and power, which lead to the establishment of an aristocracy, the very worst species of government." Such immunities and privileged grants to groups may have made sense in European monarchical governments as devices serving "to circumscribe and limit absolute power." But in America where only the people wielded power "all such combinations of men and property" were irrelevant and harmful, for "as much as the combination of citizens enjoying corporation immunities may be calculated, even at this day, to relieve from the weight of monarchical sway, to the same degree are they contrary to the equal and common liberty which ought to pervade a republic." Because it was "the characteristic of freemen" and "the object of the present revolution" that the people "cannot be affected in their rights of personal security, personal liberty and private property, but by the laws and regulations of their representatives in general assembly," no extra-legislative corporate bodies ought to be established. The Assembly "ought carefully to retain their full exercise of legislative power over every part of the commonwealth," the city of Philadelphia included. Since "the state was one great family: and the laws are our common inheritance," said William Findley, in an argument

in 1786 against the rechartering of the Bank of North America,
the legislature had no right "to give monopolies of legal privilege
—to bestow unequal portions of our common inheritance on fa-
vourites." It was true, Findley admitted, that Pennsylvanians,
like the other Americans, were "too unequal in wealth to render
a perfect democracy suitable to our circumstances: yet we are
so equal in wealth, power, etc. that we have no counterpoise sufficient to check or control an institution of such vast influence
and magnitude" as the Bank of North America. Since Pennsylvania had "no kingly prerogatives—no wealthy nobles, with vastly
great estates and numerous dependents—no feudal laws to support
family dignity, by keeping landed estates undivided," there was
no security to set "against the eventual influence of such wealth,
conducted under the direction of such a boundless charter." It
was obvious then that wealth in America must not be allowed
to concentrate in a few hands, for "wealth in many hands operates as many checks." "An equal circulation of the signs of
wealth, tends to promote equal interests—equal manners—and
equal designs." This equal circulation so necessary for a republic
was difficult enough to maintain when wealth was "in the hands
of jarring individuals" but it would be impossible "when in the
hands of a permanent society, congregated by special privilege,
and actuated by the principles of united avarice."[14]

Precisely because of the existence of these kinds of privileges
republicanism had not brought the commonwealth consensus that
had been anticipated. In fact party strife in all of the states seemed
as bitter as before the war. Only now, with the elimination of
royal authority and the reduction of magisterial power, the Whig
conception of politics could not easily explain or justify the divisiveness. The Tories were gone. "The success of the war, and
the establishment of legal government, has necessarily coalesced
all party distinctions." The parties that were emerging were not
those of the people against the rulers, the country against the
court; they were instead parties among the people themselves,

14. Phila. *Pa. Gazette*, Mar. 31, 1779; Mathew Carey, ed., *Debates and Proceedings of the General Assembly of Pennsylvania* (Phila., 1786), 77; Phila.
Pa. Packet, Mar. 31, 1785, Sept. 2, 1783, Aug. 23, 1786, Sept. 20, 1783; Carey, ed.,
Debates of the General Assembly of Pennsylvania, 65, 66, 126, 125. The best account of the political and social division between the Pennsylvania Constitutionalists and Republicans in the 1780's is Owen S. Ireland, The Ratification of the
Federal Constitution in Pennsylvania (unpubl. Ph.D. diss., University of Pitts-
burgh, 1967).

each aiming "at its own aggrandizement." "Formerly, political distinctions originated in the prevailing sentiment of patriotism—in the present times, they seem only relative to particular principles of interest," to occupations, credit, debt, or religion. Such divisions among the people, it was argued, were obvious indications of selfishness and infirmity in the society. "Parties are the dangerous diseases of civil freedom; they are only the first stage of anarchy, cloathed in mild language." Unless they were "cramped in embrio," they would grow and eventually tear the state apart. Factionalism in a republic "should be particularly guarded against, its existence as a free government depending on a general unanimity."[15]

3. THE ABUSES OF LEGISLATIVE POWER

Traditional eighteenth-century political theory offered a ready explanation for what was happening. The political pendulum was swinging back: the British rulers had perverted their power; now the people were perverting their liberty. "Power abused ceases to be lawful authority, and degenerates into tyranny. Liberty abused, or carried to excess, is licentiousness." "This revolution," David Ramsay told Benjamin Rush in 1783, "has introduced so much anarchy that it will take half a century to eradicate the licentiousness of the people." "The pulling down of government," men now saw, "*tends to produce a settled and habitual contempt of authority in the people*," and to make liberty "a popular *idol*." All the mobbing, the conventioneering, all the actions of popular legislatures, seemed to indicate that the people were fast running wild into "anarchy and licentiousness." "Never," it was claimed, "was there greater danger of these evils, in this land, since the first settlement of it than now."[16]

Nevertheless, for some observers, the conventional abuses of the people's liberty, licentiousness and anarchy, no longer seemed to be the only terrors to be feared from the popular end of the political spectrum. By the 1780's some Americans began to

15. Worcester *Mass. Spy*, June 21, 1780; *Providence Gazette*, Aug. 5, 1786; Feb. 24, 1779; Charleston *S.-C. and American Gazette*, Feb. 4, 1779.

16. Cumings, *Sermon Preached May 28, 1783*, 12; Ramsay to Rush, July 11, 1783, in Rogers, *William Loughton Smith*, 105; Boston *Independent Chronicle*, Mar. 29, 1787; Hemmenway, *Sermon Preached before Hancock*, 40; Mather, *Sermon Preached May 10, 1781*, 10–11.

perceive a new political phenomenon unfolding in American experience that made nonsense of the traditional conception of politics. True, there were sufficient examples of the people's licentiousness: western Massachusetts was a valley of horrors. But anarchy and the breakdown of government that it connoted no longer seemed an accurate way to describe all of what was happening in the 1780's. An excess of power in the people was leading not simply to licentiousness but to a new kind of tyranny, not by the traditional rulers, but by the people themselves—what John Adams in 1776 had called a theoretical contradiction, a democratic despotism. It was too much government, not the lack of it, that was so frightening to some. Instead of falling into pieces, as could have been anticipated from the conventional theory of politics, the people appeared more capable of oppression.

The confiscation of property, the paper money schemes, the tender laws, and the various devices suspending the ordinary means for the recovery of debts, despite their "open and outrageous . . . violation of every principle of justice,"[17] were not the decrees of a tyrannical and irresponsible magistracy, but laws enacted by legislatures which were probably as equally and fairly representative of the people as any legislatures in history. Property admittedly could be taken from an individual with his consent or with the consent of his elected representative. Yet increasingly in the decade after Independence those who felt victimized by the actions of the various popular assemblies argued that men surrendered their natural rights to property only in so far as the surrender promoted the welfare of the whole society or conformed to what were variously and ambiguously referred to as the "eternal principles of social justice." The legislature whose laws or acts violated "those fundamental principles which first induced men to come into civil compact" thereby substituted "*power* for *right*" and destroyed free government. "The representative body . . . are not authorized to ascertain the value of the property of individuals; and to decide on what terms (excepting by equal taxation) they shall part with it. In that case there could be no private property; but all property would in fact be a joint stock, and the property of the representative body." "Have the people, or those to whom they have delegated the *legislative power*," it was confusedly asked, "the right to suspend, supercede,

17. Charleston *St. Gazette of S.-C.*, Mar. 5, 1787.

or render void by *extemporary decrees*, the established standing laws, by which the payment of debts were secured?" Acts which took property and denied men's rights without equivalent compensation, whatever the legality of the procedure by which they were passed, "could not have the force of law."[18]

The people's will as expressed in their representative legislatures and so much trusted throughout the colonial period suddenly seemed capricious and arbitrary. It was not surprising now for good Whigs to declare that "a popular assembly not governed by fundamental laws, but under the bias of anger, malice, or a thirst for revenge, will commit more excess than an arbitrary monarch."[19] The economic and social instability engendered by the Revolution was finding political expression in the state legislatures at the very time they were larger, more representative, and more powerful than ever before in American history. "We have been constantly changing our assembly," it was commonly charged, "repealing old laws, and substituting new ones."[20] The result in almost all the states was that few acts went without alteration in the succeeding sessions of the legislatures. "The revised laws have been altered—realtered—made better—made worse; and kept in such a fluctuating position, that persons in civil commission scarce know what is law." This lack of "*wisdom* and *steadiness*" in legislation, said Madison in 1786, was "the grievance complained of in all our republics." The laws had become so profuse and complicated that, as one Vermont minister charged, the very means appointed to preserve order had become the source of irregularity and confusion.[21]

18. [Hamilton], *Second Letter from Phocion*, Syrett and Cooke, eds., *Hamilton Papers*, III, 550; *Providence Gazette*, Aug. 5, Oct. 21, 1786; Boston *Independent Chronicle*, Jan. 29, 1778; Parsons, *Consideration of Some Unconstitutional Measures*, 10.

19. [Aedanus Burke], *An Address to the Freemen of the State of South-Carolina* . . . (Phila., 1783), 23.

20. Hartford *Conn. Courant*, Sept. 30, 1783. In 1778, for example, 83 members of the Massachusetts House of Representatives had not sat in the General Court the previous year. Boston *Continental Journal*, May 28, 1778. In Virginia during the 1780's the average annual rate of turnover in the House of Burgesses, according to Forrest McDonald, was 44.8 per cent. *E Pluribus Unum*, 258.

21. "Address of the Council of Censors," Feb. 14, 1786, Slade, ed., *Vt. State Papers*, 540; Madison to Caleb Wallace, Aug. 23, 1785, Hunt, ed., *Writings of Madison*, II, 167; Gershom C. Lyman, *A Sermon, Preached at Manchester . . . on the Day of the Anniversary Election, October 10, 1782* (Windsor, Vt., 1784), 7–8. On complaints about the confusion of the Virginia laws in the 1780's see Boyd, ed., *Jefferson Papers*, II, 324.

Paradoxical as it seemed, it was the very force of the laws of the states, not anarchy or the absence of law, that was vitiating the new republics. All the states with no exceptions were being smothered by a multiplicity of laws, wrote Madison in a comprehensive indictment of the 1780's entitled "Vices of the Political System of the United States," written in 1787 for private circulation and later publicly incorporated into *The Federalist* papers. "The short period of independency has filled as many pages as the century which proceeded it" with laws that were hopelessly mutable. "We daily see laws repealed or suspended, before any trial can have been made of their merits, and even before a knowledge of them can have reached the remoter districts within which they were to operate." Most alarming of all, the laws were repeatedly unjust. "The want of a decided tone in our government in favor of the general principles of justice" was a continuing complaint in the press throughout the eighties. Debtor relief legislation, declared one New Jersey town in typical terms, was "founded not upon the principles of Justice, but upon the Right of the Sword; because no other Reason can be given why the Act . . . was passed than because the Legislature had the Power and Will to enact such a Law." Public faith and private confidence were being destroyed by paper money and *ex post facto* legislation. Who would lend money, it was repeatedly asked, "if an omnipotent legislature can set aside contracts ratified by the sanction of law?" Right and justice seemed in the thinking of many to have lost all connection with law. "Woe to that people, whose laws legitimate crimes and vice!"[22]

Consequently, law was becoming contemptible in the eyes of those from whom it traditionally should have commanded the greatest respect. "The acts of almost every legislature," charged Judge Alexander Hanson in 1784, "have uniformly tended to disgust its citizens, and to annihilate its credit." The North Carolina laws of 1780 were to Attorney-General James Iredell "the vilest collection of trash ever formed by a legislative body." The New York legislature, remarked Chancellor Robert Livingston, was "daily committing the most flagrant acts of injustice." In 1787 a

22. Madison, "Vices of the Political System of the United States" (1787), Hunt, ed., *Writings of Madison*, II, 365–66; Boston *Independent Chronicle*, May 31, 1787; Petition of Salem, Oct. 12, 1784, quoted in McCormick, *New Jersey in the Critical Period*, 183; Rusticus, "On Ex Post Facto Laws," *American Museum*, 2 (1787), 169–70; *Providence Gazette*, Aug. 5, 1786.

group of Germantown, Pennsylvania, inhabitants announced they were banding together as "a shield against the rapacity of the law," resolving to settle all cases among themselves by arbitration in order "to prevent the people from wasting their property by the chicane of the law."[23]

But the representative assembly in the several states was not only corrupting the law; it was, as Madison put it in 1788, "drawing all power into its impetuous vortex." All the functions of government, legislative, executive, and judicial, warned Jefferson as early as 1783, were ending up in the legislative body. The diminution of executive authority in the new constitutions, the closing or general breakdown of the courts, the popular fear of magistrates—all reinforced legislative predominance in the governments. The governors were mere ciphers, almost totally dependent on the legislatures, with little or no power to resist or control the political and social instability. The appointing authority which in most constitutions had been granted to the assemblies had become the principal source of division and faction in the states. The legislature, charged the Vermont Council of Censors, was reaching for "uncontrolled dominion" in the administration of justice: becoming a court of chancery in all cases over £4,000, interfering in causes between parties, reversing court judgments, staying executions after judgments, and even prohibiting court actions in matters pertaining to land titles or private contracts involving bonds or debts, consequently stopping nine-tenths of all causes in the state. In their assumption of judicial power the legislators had determined every cause, said the Council, guided by no rules of law but only by their crude notions of equity, "or in other words, according to their sovereign will and pleasure."[24]

Although the Pennsylvania Council of Censors in its second

23. [Alexander C. Hanson], *Political Schemes and Calculations, Addressed to the Citizens of Maryland* (Annapolis, 1784), v; James Iredell to Mrs. Iredell, May 18, 1780, McRee, *Life of Iredell*, I, 446; George Dangerfield, *Chancellor Robert R. Livingston of New York, 1746–1813* (N. Y., 1960), 107; "Resolutions Entered Into by a Respectable Number of the Inhabitants of Germantown, March 1, 1787," *American Museum*, 2 (1787), 166.

24. *The Federalist*, No. 48; Jefferson, *Notes on Virginia*, ed. Peden, 120; "Address of the Council of Censors," Feb. 14, 1786, Slade, ed., *Vt. State Papers*, 537. Benjamin Gale likewise complained that the Connecticut Assembly was getting too involved in private controversies, even in some instances in private cases involving decisions in equity. [Gale], *Brief, Decent, but Free Remarks*, 31–32. See also Taylor, *Western Massachusetts*, 151.

session was dominated by supporters of the 1776 Constitution, its 1784 report was filled with similar complaints about rash resolutions and interference in the execution of the laws by the legislature. Apologetically the Constitutionalist majority of the Censors explained that this legislative confusion and usurpation stemmed from the people's experience under the proprietary government, "when every increase of power, obtained by their representatives from the executive, and every instance in which the force of law could be obtained to a resolve of the house, seemed at least to be favorable to the public interest." Thus every effort had been made by former legislatures to acquire power at the expense of the proprietor, who had possessed "an interest opposed to that of the people." This legislative arrogation "unfortunately acquired too great a sanction with the people from custom." The people "have been taught to consider an application to the legislature as a shorter and more certain mode of obtaining relief from hardships and losses, than the usual process of law." The Revolution had thus served to accentuate the medieval court-like character of the American legislatures. Since 1776 the Pennsylvania Assembly, like other state legislatures, had strengthened its control over equity jurisdiction, the amendment of land titles, the absolving of marriage ties, and the remitting of fines. The law books were filled, as never before, with legislation for individuals and with resolves redressing minor grievances. In fact, said the Pennsylvania Censors, American political experience, now being brought to a conspicuous head in the 1780's, had actually changed the meaning of the word "grievances." Formerly grievances had referred to "the excesses and oppressive proceedings of the executive power, and courts of justice" which, "arising from the undue influence of the crown," could not be remedied without the interposition of the people's representatives. In America, however, grievances had become simply the "hardships which will always arise from the operation of general laws," or "even the misdeeds of particular officers, or private men, for which there is an easy and legal remedy," or sometimes even "inconveniences" growing out of the negligence of the sufferer himself. "The assumption of the judicial and executive, into the hands of the legislative branch," concluded the report of the Censors, "doth as certainly produce instances of bad government as any other unwarrantable accumulation of authority." Others in all the states agreed: "The legislature swallowing up all the other powers," as James Wilson put it, was a widespread practice, the proofs of which in all the states, said Madison in *The Federalist*, "might be multiplied without end."[25]

4. DEMOCRATIC DESPOTISM

In the 1780's the Americans' inveterate suspicion and jealousy of political power, once concentrated almost exclusively on the Crown and its agents, was transferred to the various state legislatures. Where once the magistracy had seemed to be the sole source of tyranny, now the legislatures through the Revolutionary state constitutions had become the institutions to be most feared. American "prejudices against the Executive," said James Wilson in 1787, "resulted from a misapplication of the adage that the parliament was the palladium of liberty. Where the Executive was really formidable, *King* and *Tyrant*, were naturally associated in the minds of the people." But where the executive was weak, as in the American constitutions, "*legislature* and *tyranny* . . . were most properly associated." Increasingly, from the outset of the Revolution on through the next decade, the legislatures, although presumably embodying the people's will, were talked of in terms indistinguishable from those formerly used to describe the magistracy. "If it is possible for the legislature to be influenced by avarice and ambition and by either of these extremes to *betray* their country, and abuse the people . . . , then would the state be in danger of being ruined by their *Representatives*."[26] As the supposedly representative legislatures drifted away from the people, men more and more spoke of the legislators' being just other kinds of rulers, liable to the same temptations and abuses rulers through history had shown—all of which made comprehensible the intensifying desire to make the representatives more dependent on the opinion of their constituents and the increasing invocations of "the collective body of the people" to set against the legislatures.

Yet there were some Americans who perceived that the prob-

25. *Calling the Conventions of 1776 and 1790*, 85–86, 92–93, 117; Farrand, ed., *Records of the Federal Convention*, II, 300; *The Federalist*, No. 48. On legislative usurpation see Corwin, "Progress of Political Theory," *Amer. Hist. Rev.*, 30 (1924–25), 517–20.

26. Farrand, ed., *Records of the Federal Convention*, II, 300–01; Charleston *St. Gazette of S.-C.*, Aug. 27, 1783.

lems of the 1780's were not due to the drifting and unrepresentative character of the legislatures, but were rather due to the legislatures' very representativeness. The distresses of the period, in
other words, did not arise because the people-at-large had been
forsaken by their legislatures, "but because their transient and
indigested sentiments have been too implicitly adopted." The
evils and vices of state legislation, said James Madison, were not
based, as some said, on the temporary deceit of a few designing
men who were perverting their representative authority for their
own selfish ends. Such vices actually sprang from the emergent
nature of American society, and therefore brought "into question
the fundamental principle of republican Government, that the
majority who rule in such governments are the safest Guardians
both of public Good and private rights." "According to Republican Theory," said James Madison, "Right and power being both
vested in the majority, are held to be synonimous." But was this
truly the case? asked Madison in a brilliant series of letters and
essays, describing clearly and cogently what he thought was happening to the traditional assumptions of Whig constitutionalism.
"Wherever the real power in a Government lies," he told Jefferson, "there is the danger of oppression. In our Governments the
real power lies in the majority of the Community, and the invasion
of private rights is chiefly to be apprehended, not from acts of
Government contrary to the sense of its constituents, but from
acts in which the Government is the mere instrument of the major
number of the constituents." The people, it seemed, were as
capable of despotism as any prince; public liberty was no guarantee after all of private liberty. At the beginning of the Revolution,
wrote Madison, Americans obviously had not perceived this
danger to the private rights of property from public liberty. "In
all the Governments which were considered as beacons to republican patriots and lawgivers, the rights of persons were subjected
to those of property"; throughout history the poor had always
been sacrificed to the rich. In 1776 Americans had assumed that
their society was unique—so egalitarian that both rights coincided,
so different that "a provision for the rights of persons was supposed to include of itself those of property." And Americans naturally inferred, said Madison, "from the tendency of republican
laws"—like the abolition of primogeniture and entail—"that these
different interests would be more and more identified." But alas!
"experience and investigation" had eventually taught Madison

that America was not different from other societies, that equality
of condition was a chimera. Only a minority, said Madison, "can
be interested in preserving the rights of property." Yet what could
be done? In 1786 a New Jersey critic of this majoritarian tyranny
had argued that there were occasions when the legislature must
ignore the voice of its constituents. "A virtuous legislature will
not, cannot listen to any proposition, however popular, that came
within the description of being *unjust*, impolitic or unnecessary."
"Then we are not a republican government," was the formidable
reply, "for the evident signification thereof is that the people (the
majority of the people) bear rule, and it is for them to determine
wether a proposition is *unjust*, *impolitic*, and *unnecessary* or
not."[27]

Americans thus experienced in the 1780's not merely a crisis of
authority—licentiousness leading to anarchy—which was a comprehensible abuse of republican liberty, but also a serious shattering of older ways of examining politics and a fundamental questioning of majority rule that threatened to shake the foundations
of their republican experiments. It was extremely difficult, however, for most Americans to grasp what was happening and fit
it into their accepted paradigm of politics. Most commentators
were concerned with what they described as the breakdown in
governmental authority, the tendency of the people to ignore
the government and defy the laws by their claims that "a *subordination* to the laws, is always the cant word to enslave the people."
"Every man of sense," said Fisher Ames, "must be convinced
that our disturbances have arisen more from the want of power
than the abuse of it." Yet the pressing constitutional problem was
not really the lack of power in the state legislatures but the excess
of it—popular despotism. Writers, like Noah Webster, cried out
against the evils of the day: "So many legal infractions of sacred
right—so many public invasions of private property—so many
wanton abuses of legislative powers!" Nevertheless, in almost the
same breath, they urged the people to obey their elected legislatures, right or wrong, contending that the only remedy for abuses

27. Boston *Independent Chronicle*, May 10, 1787; Madison, "Vices of the
Political System," Hunt, ed., *Writings of Madison*, II, 366, 363; Madison to
Jefferson, Oct. 17, 1788, Boyd, ed., *Jefferson Papers*, XIV, 19; Madison's Observa-
tions on Jefferson's Draft of a Constitution for Virginia, 1788, *ibid.*, VI, 310;
Elizabethtown *Political Intelligencer*, Jan. 4, 25, 1786, quoted in McCormick,
New Jersey in the Critical Period, 72–73.

was new elections. Somehow the people were both licentious and tyrannical, but ironically the remedy for one was the source of evil for the other.[28]

Shays's Rebellion in western Massachusetts was received with excited consternation mingled with relief by many Americans precisely because it was an anticipated and understandable abuse of republican liberty. Liberty had been carried into anarchy and the throwing off of all government—a more comprehensible phenomenon to most American political thinkers than legislative tyranny. The rebels, announced the town of Boston, must obey the majority. "Let the majority be ever so much in the wrong," it was the only remedy for grievances "compatible with the ideas of society and government!" The insurgents, argued a publicist, must rely on their elected representatives for the redress of wrongs: "Can human wisdom devise a more effectual security to our liberties?"[29] So relieved by the rebellion were many social conservatives that some observers believed the Shaysites were fomented by those who wanted to demonstrate the absurdity of republicanism.[30]

Nothing so insidious has been proved, but many social conservatives did see the rebellion as encouraging the move for constitutional reform. It was both a confirmation of their worst fears —hence their horror, and a vindication of their desires for stronger government—hence their relief. It fitted nicely into the traditional pattern of political thinking and thus cleared the air of much of the confusion which had hung over the 1780's. Yet Shays's Rebellion was irrelevant to the major constitutional difficulty experienced in the Confederation period—the problem of legal tyranny, the usurpation of private rights under constitutional cover. Connecticut had no violence like that of Massachusetts, said Noah Webster, "because the Legislature wear the complexion of the people." Only "the temporizing of the legislatures in refusing legal protection to the prosecution of the just rights of creditors," remarked David Ramsay, freed the southern states from similar disturbances. Within a few months, however, observers noted

28. Charleston *St. Gazette of S.-C.*, June 13, 1785; Boston *Independent Chronicle*, Mar. 1, 1787, in Ames, ed., *Works of Fisher Ames*, II, 106; Webster, "Government," *American Magazine*, 1 (1787–88), 75, 206.

29. Boston *Independent Chronicle*, Sept. 14, Oct. 12, Nov. 2, 1786.

30. See Robert A. East, "The Massachusetts Conservatives in the Critical Period," in Morris, ed., *Era of the Revolution*, 379–80; Main, *Antifederalists*, 59–64.

that the Shaysites were trying their strength in another way, "that is," said James Madison, "by endeavoring to give the elections such a turn as may promote their views under the auspices of constitutional forms." Merely subduing the rebels and calling upon them to obey the authority of the legislature did not go to the heart of the Americans' predicament. With "a total change of men" in the legislature, wrote Webster, "there will be, therefore, no further insurrection, because the Legislature will represent the sentiments of the people." Hence some Americans in the 1780's could come to believe that "sedition itself will sometimes make laws."[31]

The classical political spectrum did not make sense to a perceptive and probing mind trying to understand American politics. "It has been remarked," wrote Madison to Jefferson, "that there is a tendency in all Governments to an augmentation of power at the expense of liberty." But for Madison the statement now seemed ill founded. There seemed little danger in the American republics that the tyranny of the rulers would subvert liberty. No doubt, said Madison, governmental power, when it attained a certain degree of energy and independence, went on to expand itself. "But when below that degree, the direct tendency is to further degrees of relaxation, until the abuses of liberty beget a sudden transition to an undue degree of power." Licentiousness, in other words, led not to anarchy, but to a new kind of popular despotism. Only in this sense, said Madison, was the traditional spectrum of power "applicable to the Governments in America." America had little to fear from the traditional abuse of power by the few over the many. "It is much more to be dreaded that the few will be unnecessarily sacrificed to the many."[32]

5. POLITICAL PATHOLOGY

This fear by the few of the power of the many, as crucial as it was in shaping a new understanding of politics and in promoting the desire for a new central government, did not go to the heart

31. Ramsay to Jefferson, Apr. 7, 1787, Madison to Jefferson, Apr. 23, 1787, Jay to Jefferson, Apr. 24, 1787, Boyd, ed., *Jefferson Papers*, XI, 279, 307, 313; [Noah Webster], "To the Public," May 8, 1787, in Warfel, ed., *Letters of Webster* (N. Y., 1953), 64–65; Boston *Independent Chronicle*, May 10, 1787. See also East, "Massachusetts Conservatives," Morris, ed., *Era of the Revolution*, 378.

32. Madison to Jefferson, Oct. 17, 1788, Boyd, ed., *Jefferson Papers*, XIV, 20.

of the pervasive sense of anxiety in the 1780's. The crisis was not confined to any one economic or social group, although the evidence of alarm is clearly weighted on those who were most articulate, that is, on those who considered themselves the established social leaders and who were most likely to write for the press and to preserve their correspondence. Indeed, it seems that it was precisely the actions of those least liable to be aware of the social and moral significance of what they were doing that so frightened American intellectuals in the 1780's. Yet the period was truly critical not solely because members of the social and economic elite felt themselves and their world threatened, but because anyone who knew anything of eighteenth-century political science could not help believing that the American republics were heading for destruction even as they were being created.

The crisis was therefore of the most profound sort, involving no limited political or economic problems but the success of the republican experiment itself. Indeed no more appropriate term than "crisis" could have been used to describe what was happening. Viewing the state as analogous to the human body, Americans saw their country stricken by a serious sickness. The 1780's seemed to mark the point in the life of the young nation where a decisive change had to occur, leading either to recovery or death. It was a "crisis of moral and national reputation." "The reputation of America is at stake. . . . The fate of (perhaps it may be said without exaggerating) mankind depends upon the issue of American councils at this crisis!" The writings of Americans in the eighties became a series of self-diagnoses, an intensive examination of the sources of political decay characteristic of the age of Gibbon. Writers from Montesquieu to Edward Wortley Montagu were ransacked in a continuing search to understand what was called "political pathology."[33] All the lessons that had been learned from the analysis of Britain's fate in the 1760's and seventies were now brought home to Americans with a renewed vividness. While virtue was advantageous for any kind of government, it was, as a group of New Hampshire ministers affirmed in

---

33. Charleston *S.-C. Gazette and General Advertiser*, Aug. 9, 1783; *Providence Gazette*, Aug. 12, 1786; "On the Present State of Affairs," *American Museum*, 2 (1787), 170. For references to Edward Wortley Montagu's work see Warren, *Oration, Delivered July 4th, 1783*, 18; Gardiner, *Oration, Delivered July 4, 1785*, 8; Butterfield, ed., *Diary of Adams*, III, 444n. See Gerald J. Gruman, " 'Balance' and 'Excess' as Gibbon's Explanation of the Decline and Fall," *History and Theory*, 1 (1960–61), 75–85.

1784, "absolutely necessary to the existence of a republick." "In a Republic," declared Samuel West in 1786, "the people are not only the source of authority, but the exercise of it, is in a great measure, lodged in their hands. Corruption therefore among the people at large, must be immediately felt, and if not seasonably prevented, proves fatal in the end." However uncritical the conditions of the 1780's may seem in retrospect, to those imbued with eighteenth-century assumptions about the nature of the social hierarchy and the signs of health and sickness in the body politic, those conditions took on a dreadful significance. American society seemed to possess all the symptoms of the most destructive diseases that could afflict a republic. As early as 1779 it had become "undeniably evident . . . that some malignant disorder has seized upon our body politic, and threatens at least an interruption of our advances to manhood, if not a political dissolution." The American people apparently did not possess and were unwilling to acquire the moral and social character necessary to sustain republican governments.[34]

Since "the individual conduct of those who compose a community, must have an intimate and extensive connection with all our public measures, it is from the nature and tendency of that conduct that our public character must receive its complexion." The war with Britain had scarcely begun before the nature and tendency of American behavior were frighteningly revealed. The self-sacrifice and patriotism of 1774–75 soon seemed to give way to greed and profiteering at the expense of the public good. Perhaps, it was suggested, that peculiar expression of virtue in those few years before Independence had been simply the consequence of a momentary sense of danger. At one time public spirit had been "the governing principle and distinguishing characteristic of brave Americans. But where is it now? Directly the reverse. We daily see the busy multitude engaged in accumulating what they fondly call riches, by forestalling, extortioning and imposing upon each other." Men returning from abroad in the early eighties found "the sentiments of the people of this country . . . surprisingly altered" since they had left. "They were no longer governed by that pure, disinterested patriotism, which distinguished the Infancy of the Contest." Everywhere "Private Interest seemed to

34. Boston *Independent Chronicle*, Dec. 16, 1784; Samuel West, *A Sermon Preached before His Excellency James Bowdoin* . . . (Boston, 1786), 21. Trenton *N.-J. Gazette*, Mar. 17, 1779, Nelson *et al.*, eds., *New Jersey Archives*, 2d Ser., III, 140.

predominate over every Consideration that regarded the public weal."[35]

Throughout all the states orators and writers warned of the vicious effects of wealth and prosperity. "The great body of the people, smote by the charms and blandishments of a life of ease and pleasure, fall easy victims to its fascinations." The great increase of private and public credit and the paper money and debtor-favoring legislation stemming from it, it was widely argued, were not actually the result of a scarcity of specie and the peculiar economic problems of the 1780's. They were rather a consequence and a symptom of the degenerate character of the people. All men, rich and poor, northerners and southerners, were living "in a manner much more expensive and luxurious, than they have Ability to support," borrowing heavily on the promises of the future, captivated by *an immoderate desire of high and expensive living.* "Our citizens," said a Carolinian, "seem to be seized with a general emulation to surpass each other in every article of expence. Those who possess affluent fortunes lead the way, and set the example. Others, whose estates are not sufficient to bear them out, madly adopt the same expensive system, and in order to support it, contract debts which they have no rational prospect of discharging. All they seem to wish, is to obtain credit, to figure away, and to make a brilliant appearance at the expence of others."[36] The end of the war saw only a scramble to purchase long-denied European luxuries. America's commerce seemed to have become almost exclusively importation. It was a strange sight—a young undeveloped country acting the part of a mature one. Indeed, said a New Yorker, "we are affected in a quite a different manner from all the other nations upon earth, for, with others, wealth is the mother of luxury, but with us poverty has the same effect."[37]

By 1780 Patrick Henry "feared that our Body politic was

35. Boston *Independent Chronicle*, Aug. 31, 1786; John Brooks, *An Oration Delivered to the Society of the Cincinnati in the Commonwealth of Massachusetts, July 4th 1787* (Boston, 1787), 8; Phila. Pa. *Gazette*, Mar. 31, 1779; William Bingham to John Jay, July 1, 1780, Johnston, ed., *Papers of Jay*, I, 364.

36. Thomas Welsh, *An Oration, Delivered March 5, 1783 . . .* (Boston, 1783), in Niles, ed., *Principles*, 76; Stephen Higginson to John Adams, July 1786, J. Franklin Jameson, ed., "Letters of Stephen Higginson, 1783–1804," Amer. Hist. Assoc., *Annual Report, 1896*, I, 740; Thomas Reese, *An Essay on the Influence of Religion, in Civil Society* (Charleston, 1788), 69.

37. William Findley (1786), in Carey, ed., *Debates of the General Assembly of Pennsylvania*, 67; *N.-Y. Journal*, May 5, 1788, quoted in Spaulding, *New York in the Critical Period*, 15. The luxuries, as in the case with all empires on the

dangerously sick." The signs of disease spread everywhere. Merchants and farmers were seeking their own selfish ends; hucksters were engrossing products to raise prices. Even government officials, it was charged, were using their public positions to fill their own pockets.[38] The fluctuation in the value of money was making "every kind of commerce and trade precarious, and as every individual is more or less interested in it," was putting a premium on selfishness. Everyone was doing "what was right in his own eyes," and "thus the whole of that care and attention which was given to the public weal is turned to private gain or self preservation."[39] That benevolence among the people had not grown as a result of the Revolution was measured in the frightening increase in litigation, to as many as eight hundred cases in a single New England county court during a year, most of which were actions of debt for only five or six pounds.[40] Vices now seemed more prevalent than before the war. Virtue was being debased by "the visible declension of religion, . . . the rapid progress of licentious manners, and open profanity." Such symptoms of degeneracy threw the clergy especially into confusion. Instead of bringing about the moral reformation they had anticipated from victory, the Revolution had only aggravated America's corruption and sin. The Americans, they said in sermon after sermon throughout the eighties, could only be an ill-tempered and unrighteous people, so soon forgetting the source of their deliverance from British tyranny. Such ingratitude and sinfulness could only bring upon them God's terrible and just vengeance—a Providential penalty that marvelously coincided with the dreadful calamity predicted by the political scientists for a corrupted people.[41]

---

verge of destruction, came from the East—a point that did not go unnoticed. Sylvius, "Letter III, on Frugality and Industry . . . ," Amicus, "Letter I . . . ," Tench Coxe, "An Address to an Assembly of the Friends of American Manufactures . . . ," *American Museum*, 2 (1787), 116, 217, 253.

38. Patrick Henry to Jefferson, Feb. 15, 1780, Boyd, ed., *Jefferson Papers*, III, 293; Madison, *Sermon Preached in Botetourt*, 14–18; Charleston *S.-C. and American Gazette*, Feb. 19–26, 1778; Nathan Williams, *A Sermon, Preached in the Audience of the General Assembly of the State of Connecticut* . . . (Hartford, 1780), 21, 37. See the discussion of the mingling of business and government in the 1780's in Ferguson, *Power of the Purse*, 70–105.

39. Trenton *N.-J. Gazette*, Apr. 7, 1779, in Nelson *et al.*, eds., *New Jersey Archives*, 2d Ser., III, 208–12; [Cooper], *Enquiry into Public Abuses*, 16; Cumings, *Sermon Preached May 28, 1783*, 39.

40. Hartford *Conn. Courant*, Sept. 30, 1783; Taylor, *Western Massachusetts*, 127.

41. Charleston *S.-C. and American Gazette*, Jan. 21, 1779. For examples of the clergy's concern see John Murray, *Jerubbaal, or Tyranny's Grove Destroyed, and the Altar of Liberty Finished* (Newburyport, 1784), 8, 32, 55; Macclintock,

Throughout all the secular and religious jeremiads of the eighties the key term was "luxury," that important social product and symptom of extreme selfishness and pleasure-seeking. Over and over men emphasized "the destructive tendency of luxury," so much so that it had become by 1788 "a beaten topic." But still "the history of the world points to this, as the rock on which the state vessel hath most commonly split." The success of the war had taught the effete British "that the savage wilds of America could produce a barrier to their attempts" to erect a tyranny. But now a more insidious enemy was sapping America's strength and liberty from within. "LUXURY, LUXURY, the great source of dissolution and distress, has here taken up her dismal abode; infectious as she is, she is alike caressed by rich and poor" and was thus destroying "that simplicity of manners, native manliness of soul, and equality of station, which is the spring and peculiar excellence of a free government."[42] Associations sprang up to combat all the increased displays of extravagance, and writers debated over the kinds of art and theater permissible in a republic. These were not simply the legacies of some old puritanical fever, for, as Joel Barlow said in 1787, "It is for existence that we contend." "Whenever democratic states degenerate from those noble republican virtues which constitute the chief excellency, spring, and even basis of their government, and instead of industry, frugality, and economy, encourage luxury, dissipation and extravagance," Americans were warned, "we may justly conclude that ruin is near at hand." "No virtue, no Commonwealth." It was that simple.[43]

Like Puritanism, of which it was a more relaxed, secularized version, republicanism was essentially anti-capitalistic, a final attempt to come to terms with the emergent individualistic society that threatened to destroy once and for all the communion and

Sermon, June 3, 1784, 9–10; William Symmes, *A Sermon Preached before His Honor Thomas Cushing* . . . (Boston, [1785]), 7; Wales, *Dangers of National Prosperity,* 5–10. See Miller, "From the Covenant to the Revival," in Smith and Jameson, eds., *Shaping of American Religion,* 343–50.

42. Reese, *Essay on the Influence of Religion,* 71; Boston *Independent Chronicle,* Aug. 24, 1786; "An Oration Delivered at Petersburgh, Virginia, on the 4th of July, 1787 . . . ," *American Museum,* 2 (1787), 420.

43. Phila. *Pa. Journal,* Feb. 14, 1784; *American Museum,* 2 (1787), 165–66; *Providence Gazette,* Apr. 7, 21, May 26, June 9, 23, July 14, 1787; Joel Barlow, "An Oration, Delivered . . . in Hartford . . . July the Fourth, 1787 . . . ," "Oration Delivered at Petersburgh," *American Museum,* 2 (1787), 138, 420; Boston *Independent Chronicle,* June 21, 1787.

benevolence that civilized men had always considered to be the ideal of human behavior. Right from the beginning of the Revolution there had been some Americans who had doubted the ability of any people, including the Americans, to surrender their individual interests for the good of the whole. The questioning of American virtue begun by men like Livingston and Jay of New York during the prerevolutionary debates in the Continental Congress was broadened during the critical years of the war.[44] Throughout the seventies all the discussions of the Continental Congress on the issues of economic regulation or moral and sumptuary controls tended to hinge on the capacity of the public law to control vice and individual behavior. For those at the very outset of the Revolution who had discounted American virtue, at least among the mass of the society, the scrambling of the people to satisfy private wants and aspirations became a vindication of their doubts. A merchant, or anyone for that matter, it was increasingly said by such men, could not be expected for the sake of some nebulous public good "to quit the line which interest marks out for him." "It is inconsistent with the principles of liberty," said Robert Morris, "to prevent a man from the free disposal of his property on such terms as he may think fit."[45] With the movement of people with these kinds of thoughts into positions of influence and authority once the war was underway, it was inevitable that the old patriots who had thrived on the spirit of 1774–75 should have become alarmed. The issue between them was brought to a head in the Continental Congress over the Lee-Deane affair.

On the surface the split in Congress in the late seventies assumed sectional lines, New England favoring Arthur Lee against the South favoring the Yankee merchant Silas Deane, with the middle states divided. Yet beneath this sectional division was a more complicated disagreement among American leaders that transcended state interests. The Lee-Deane imbroglio was not simply a quarrel provoked by personal or family pique or even by the conduct of American diplomacy. It went to the heart of the fundamental disagreement rapidly emerging among American leaders over the virtuous character of the American people and the nature of the republican society being formed. The Lees of

---

44. See above, 95–96.
45. Silas Deane to Jonathan Williams, Sept. 24, 1781, quoted in Ferguson, *Power of the Purse*, 74*n*; Robert Morris, quoted in *ibid.*, 120.

Virginia and the Adamses of Massachusetts saw in Silas Deane and in the connections and support he mustered a serious threat to the success of the Revolution, even to the point, wrote John Adams, of "endangering a civil War in America." In the eyes of strict republicans like the Lees, the Adamses, and Henry Laurens of South Carolina, Deane's cause was the cause of all the "avaricious and ambitious men" who sought to reverse the Revolution and to establish an aristocratic and mercantile society that would allow full play to private interests.[46] The American Revolution, said John Adams, "had not been sustained by such characters" as Gouverneur Morris and John Jay, those "Tory friends and Mercantile Abettors" of Deane, as Richard Henry Lee called them, who represented so many "Mandevilles . . . who laugh at virtue, and with vain ostentatious display of words will deduce from vice, public good"—these men were "much fitter to be Slaves in the corrupt, rotten despotisms of Europe, than to remain citizens of young and rising republics." Although Deane was a Yankee, said Samuel Adams, his principles were not those of New England; they were "commercial and interested." If allowed to flourish they would eventually destroy America's experiment in republicanism, since, as even the retired and redeemed merchant Henry Laurens said, the "bane of patriotism" was "commerce."[47]

By the late seventies the old patriots, embodied in the Adams-Lee junto, saw a "Design" afoot, "a joynt Combination of political and Commercial Men" centering in New York and the South, which aimed to exclude from power all "those who took an early active Part and have continued consistent in Support of the Liberties of America" in order "to get the Trade, the Wealth, the Power and the Government of America into their own Hands." It increasingly seemed to these old patriots "that the Principles and Manners of New England," the manners, said Richard Henry Lee, of a "wise, attentive, sober, dilligent and frugal" people, had

---

46. John Adams, entry, Feb. 12, 1779, Butterfield, ed., *Diary of Adams*, II, 353; R. H. Lee to William Shippen, Jr., Apr. 18, 1779, Ballagh, *Letters of R. H. Lee*, II, 45, see also 31. The best discussion of the Lee-Deane affair and of continental congressional politics in general is in Herbert James Henderson, Party Politics in the Continental Congress, 1774–1783 (unpubl. Ph.D. diss., Columbia University, 1962), Chaps. III–IX.

47. Adams, entry, June 22, 1779, Butterfield, ed., *Diary of Adams*, II, 390; R. H. Lee to Purdie's Wmsbg. *Va. Gazette*, Jan. 1779, R. H. Lee to Henry Laurens, June 6, 1779, both in Ballagh, ed., *Letters of R. H. Lee*, II, 5, 62–63; Samuel Adams to Samuel Cooper, Jan. 3, 1779, Cushing, ed., *Writings of Samuel Adams*, IV, 112; David Duncan Wallace, *The Life of Henry Laurens* (N. Y., 1915), 335.

"produced that Spirit which finally has established the Independence of America."[48] As the southern fears of eastern Presbyterianism and leveling tendencies and the New Englanders' dislike of the aristocratic and luxurious manners of the South—an antagonism implicit from the beginning— became more and more exposed, Lee's and Laurens's alliance with New England became increasingly anomalous. If individual and state interests were to reign supreme, then, men believed, southerners had no business supporting New England. By the early 1780's many New Englanders saw themselves as the last bastion of devout republicanism standing against the torrent of aristocratic vice and luxury that was sweeping America.[49]

But, as these strict republicans knew only too well, New England itself was not free of the baneful influences of luxury and aristocracy. When a friend wrote to Samuel Adams in 1777 telling him that self-denial was now a rare virtue in Boston, Adams was shocked. "God forbid," said Adams, that the people of Boston "should so soon forget their own generous Feelings for the Publick and for each other as to set private Interests in Competition with that of the great Community." Yet Adams's beloved Boston—his hope for a "Christian Sparta"—never seemed capable of recapturing the patriotism of those wonderful years of 1774 and 1775. By 1778 new merchants and a "Spirit of Avarice" had taken over; by 1781 Adams was questioning "whether there is not more Parade among our Gentry than is consistent with sober republican Principles." By the mid-1780's Boston was wallowing in luxury and amusement. Adams could only express sorrow and indignation over "the Equipage, the Furniture and expensive Living of too many, the Pride and Vanity of Dress which pervades thro every Class, confounding every Distinction between the Poor and the Rich."[50] As evidence Adams could point

48. Samuel Adams to Samuel Cooper, Dec. 25, 1778, and Jan. 3, 1779, to James Warren, Jan. 6, 1779, and Feb. 12, 1779, all in Cushing, ed., *Writings of Samuel Adams*, IV, 105, 113, 115, 105, 115, 124; R. H. Lee to Arthur Lee, Feb. 11, 1779, Ballagh, ed., *Letters of R. H. Lee*, II, 33.

49. Stephen Higginson to John Adams, Dec. 30, 1785, Jameson, ed., "Letters of Higginson," Amer. Hist. Assoc., *Annual Report, 1896*, I, 728–29; Mass. Delegates to the Governor of Mass., Sept. 3, 1785, Burnett, ed., *Letters of Congress*, VIII, 208.

50. Adams to John Scollay, Mar. 20, 1777, to Francis Lightfoot Lee, 1778, to Scollay, Dec. 30, 1780, to Mrs. Adams, Feb. 1, 1781, to John Adams, July 2, 1785, all in Cushing, ed., *Writings of Samuel Adams*, III, 365, IV, 19–20, 236–38, 248, 315–16.

to what was the confirmation of his worst fears, the establishment in Boston in 1785 of, of all things, a tea club.

The Tea Assembly, or "Sans Souci Club" as it was labeled, seems innocuous enough—meeting every other week for dancing and card-playing. But because the club was to be the exclusive domain of the newly parading gentry, like Harrison Gray Otis, it was immediately and viciously attacked in the press, creating a frenzied public uproar that is inexplicable, and indeed ludicrous, unless viewed within the terms in which contemporaries described social character. The club, wrote an "Observer" (probably Samuel Adams), represented another example of effeminate refinement, another symptom of the dissipation of the day, another amusement designed "to lull and enervate these minds already too much softened, poisoned and contaminated by idle pleasures, and foolish gratifications." The republic was truly in grave danger. "We are prostituting all our glory, as a people, for new modes of pleasure, ruinous in their expences, injurious to virtue, and totally detrimental to the well being of society." The Tea Assembly, declared "Candidus" (probably Benjamin Austin), was considered by most of the people at this very critical time "as a very *dangerous* and *destructive institution*," suitable perhaps for "the long, established Courts of *Europe*," but fatal to the infant republics of America.[51]

It was not simply the public encouragement of gaming that bothered these severe republicans; it was more the social pretensions of the club's subscribers, their efforts to use the Tea Assembly to promote "decent manners and polite attentions." In a republican government "when all the individuals of a State are so nearly on an equality," said one critic, everyone tried to keep up public appearances by being fashionable and thus pursued such public amusements even to the ruin of fortune and family. The "*politeness* and *gentility*" of the Tea Assembly were powerful allurements; the "*etiquette* and *stile*" of the club were "*more inticing*," more destructive of republican character "than an evening spent in a *back chamber* of a tavern, among a group of wretches."[52]

This was no trivial debate. The issue at stake was nothing less than the nature of American society. "We, my countrymen," de-

51. Charles Warren, "Samuel Adams and the Sans Souci Club in 1785," Mass. Hist. Soc., *Proceedings*, 3d Ser., 60 (1926–27), 322–23, 328.
52. Boston *Independent Chronicle*, Jan. 27, 1785.

clared "Candidus," "have a character to establish." What kind of people were Americans anyhow? This was the fundamental question that ran through the thought of the 1780's. Supporters of the Sans Souci Club charged that its enemies were eaten with "envy and malice," pining for pleasures that they were "not qualified to enjoy." The club was no orgy, but rather a company "observant of the nicest and most scrupulous laws of delicacy," encouraging only the purest and highest manners as benefiting the best kind of republic. One defender was bold enough to state that the club had been drawn from the example of America's French ally, the model of manners for the world. For America to imitate France was to display "delicacy of taste" and "a genius for what is elegant and sublime." And Americans needed such refinement. Already foreign states thought Americans were "a rude, imbecile people, inspired with antipathy to the very name of gentlemen and adverse to the innovations of taste." Another writer even attempted a tentative defense of luxury. Without it, he said, Americans must abandon commerce, refuse all connections with the arts and sciences, live in savage simplicity, and end up cutting one another's throats. For "Candidus," however, this was the strangest doctrine he had ever heard broached—the idea that luxury was a communal blessing! "Rome, Athens, and all ye cities of reknown, whence came your fall?"[53]

Americans could not rid themselves of this compelling and frightening analogy with the ancient world. "Every page of the history of the great revolution of Rome shows some instances of the degeneracy of Roman virtue, and of the impossibility of a nation's continuing free after its virtue is gone." And so the writings went: essays, sermons, pamphlets, throughout the Confederation period—all pointing to the fate of states which had died because their people had become corrupted. And America seemed equally fated. "While we are pleasing and amusing ourselves with Spartan constitutions on paper, a very contrary spirit reigns triumphant in all ranks. . . . Spartan constitutions and Roman manners, peculiar to her declining state, never will accord." One or the other must give way. Apparently the revolution from the infection of the mother country had not been in time after all. "In emancipating ourselves from British tyranny, we expected to

53. Warren, "Sans Souci Club," Mass. Hist. Soc., *Proceedings*, 3d Ser., 60 (1926–27), 325–26; Boston *Independent Chronicle*, Jan. 20, 27, 1785; Boston *Mass. Centinel*, Jan. 10, 1785.

escape from that torrent of corruption which deluges their land, preys upon the labor and industry of its best citizens, and reduces them to little better than slaves." But the expectation was vain. The child seemed to be going the way of the parent, dissipated and corrupted even as it got on its feet, rushing through its life in a matter of years. "In other countries," said Aedanus Burke, "governments, like the human body, have had their growth, perfection and decay: but ours, like an untimely birth, suffered an abortion before it was in maturity fit to come into the world."[54]

It was this fear of premature death for their country that made the 1780's truly critical for American intellectuals. By 1787 correspondents were writing Jefferson in Paris that America was "marked by symptoms . . . truly alarming, which have tainted the faith of the most orthodox republicans." The American people were no longer uniquely virtuous. They were "a Luxurious Voluptuous indolent expensive people without Economy or Industry." "Instead of finding general proofs of industry, economy, temperance, and other republican virtues," some Americans now saw themselves as "a nation that was more luxurious, more indolent, and more extravagant, than any other people on the face of the earth." Such a people could not possess the proper character for republican government. America was not to be another Sparta or Rome after all. Americans had hoped to establish "great, wholesome equal republics," but the "high expectations," as James Wilson called them, seemed smashed. "We are not," said Charles Lee, "materials for such divine manufacture." The war, Robert Livingston told Gouverneur Morris in 1779, had not produced the effect "expected from it upon the manners of the people." It had not "rendered them more worthy, by making them more virtuous, of the blessings of free government." The people had been given an extraordinary amount of power in the 1776 constitutions but apparently were not qualified to wield it. "The idea of liberty has been held up in so dazzling colours," declared the *Essex Result* as early as 1778, "that some of us may not be willing to submit to that subordination necessary in the freest States." The people were not as self-sacrificing as had been hoped. "Shall we alone boast an exemption from the general fate of mankind?" was the ominous question. "Are not our manners becoming soft and luxurious, and have not our vices began to shoot?" "Too

54. Phila. *Pa. Packet*, Aug. 8, 1786; Boston *Independent Chronicle*, June 3, 1779; Phila. *Pa. Packet*, Aug. 20, 1778; [Burke], *Considerations on the Cincinnati*, 28.

much," said John Jay, "has been expected from the Virtue and good Sense of the People." Americans, concluded William Livingston in the common reckoning of 1787, "do not exhibit the virtue that is necessary to support a republican government."[55]

In 1776 America had seemed the fittest place in the world for the republican experiment, wrote Jeremy Belknap in 1784. Let the republican system "have fair play" in the New World, Americans had urged, "and it will be seen that men can live together on a plan of equality, and govern themselves without foreign connections or domestic usurpation." All this was "very pretty," said Belknap, but all chimerical. Republicanism could not work unless the foundations of the state were laid as deep as Lycurgus had driven them. The state must prevent men from rising one above the other. All foreign commerce must be stopped. All men must eat together at one table and their labor be put into common stock—"in short, let *individuals be poor and the State rich*, and then set off in your republican career: but if you attempt it on any other plan," warned Belknap, "you may be sure it will come to nothing." "If 'Equality is the soul of a republic' then we have no soul." America's property was not equally distributed. The individuals were rich and the state was poor. The farmers of New England were the most equal in the country, yet they lacked any semblance of public virtue: they were mean and selfish, and were as greedy for land as the merchants were for cash. Was this not sufficient evidence then, concluded Belknap, "that the people of this country are not destined to be long governed in a democratic form?"[56]

6. The Continuance of Hope

For all of the expressions of pessimism in the 1780's, it is clear that not all American intellectuals had lost their confidence in the republican experiment. Jefferson, viewing the new republics

55. Madison to Jefferson, Mar. 19, 1787, William Hay to Jefferson, Apr. 26, 1787, James Currie to Jefferson, May 2, 1787, all in Boyd, ed., *Jefferson Papers*, XI, 219, 318–19, 328–29; Sylvius, "Letter III," *American Museum*, 2 (1787), 114–15; Charles Lee to Benjamin Rush, Apr. 30, 1780, *Lee Papers*, III, 427; Wilson, in McMaster and Stone, eds., *Pennsylvania and the Federal Constitution*, 228; Dangerfield, *Livingston*, 108; *Essex Result*, Parsons, *Memoir*, 364, 378; Jay to Jefferson, Feb. 9, 1787, Boyd, ed., *Jefferson Papers*, XI, 129; Theodore Sedgwick, *A Memoir of the Life of William Livingston* (N. Y., 1833), 403.

56. Jeremy Belknap to Ebenezer Hazard, Mar. 3, 1784, *Belknap Papers*, 312–14.

while standing amidst the pomp and debauchery of Paris, remained calm and sanguine. America—by contrast—still seemed the land of happy frugal yeomen. "With all the defects of our constitutions, whether general or particular, the comparison of our governments with those of Europe are like a comparison of heaven and hell." Send those gentry, he urged, who had forsaken the American republics "here to count the blessings of monarchy." "The best schools for republicanism," Jefferson concluded, "are London, Versailles, Madrid, Vienna, Berlin etc." It was absurd, admonished Benjamin Rush in 1787, for Americans to "cry out, after the experience of three or four years, that we are not proper materials for republican government. Remember, we assumed these forms of government in a hurry, before we were prepared for them." The American Revolution, declared Rush, was not yet over. "We have changed our forms of government, but it remains yet to effect a revolution in our principles, opinions, and manners so as to accommodate them to the forms of government we have adopted." Rush had no doubt of the present vice-ridden character of the American people, but he was sure that the vices could be eradicated. "Let us have patience. Our republican forms of government will in time beget republican opinions and manners. All will end well." Others agreed. Americans were expecting too much too soon. It took time to eliminate ancient prejudices.[57]

The most obvious republican instrument for eliminating these prejudices and inculcating virtue in a people was education. "Wisdom and knowledge, as well as virtue, diffused generally among the body of the people, being necessary for the preservation of their rights and liberties," declared the Massachusetts Constitution of 1780, it was imperative that the government spread "the opportunities and advantages of education in the various parts of the country, and among the different orders of the people." Jefferson was not the only American concerned with erecting a hierachy of educational institutions from grammar schools to universities. "The spirit and character of a republic," said the Pennsylvania Council of Censors in 1784, 'is very different from

---

57. Jefferson to Joseph Jones, Aug. 14, 1787, to George Washington, Aug. 14, 1787, to John Rutledge, Aug. 6, 1787, all in Boyd, ed., *Jefferson Papers*, XI, 34, 38, 701; Rush, "On the Defects of the Confederation" (1787), Runes, ed., *Writings of Rush*, 30–31; Rush to Horatio Gates, Sept. 5, 1781, to Richard Price, May 25, 1786, both in Butterfield, ed., *Rush Letters*, I, 265, 388; James Campbell, "An Oration," *American Museum*, 3 (1788), 22.

that of a monarchy, and can only be imbibed by education." It seemed increasingly clear to many, like Benjamin Rush, that if Americans were not naturally virtuous they must be taught to be. "It is possible," said Rush, "to convert men into republican machines." They must be instructed that their lives were not their own. The republican pupil must "be taught that he does not belong to himself, but that he is public property."[58]

The clergy, of course, offered religion as the major instrument of salvation for a corrupted people. Religion was "the source of liberty, the soul of government and the life of a people." Christianity fostered benevolence, a love of one's fellow man and of the community. Religion was the strongest promoter of virtue, the most important ally of a well-constituted republic. It not only suppressed vice, but it added "the weight of divine authority to him who is the minister of God for good to his people."[59] Indeed, so pronounced was the encouragement of religion in the critical period that Virginia's 1786 act for the establishment of religious freedom, declaring "that our civil rights have no dependence on our religious opinions any more than on opinions in physics or geometry," became something of an anomaly.[60] No state in the 1780's was willing to go so far in the search for religious liberty; and in fact religious freedom and the multiplicity of denominations were coming to seem to some Americans actually incompatible with republicanism. The dilemma was fully exposed in the bitter controversy over Article III of the Massachusetts Constitution of 1780. "As the happiness of a people, and the good order and preservation of civil government, essentially depend upon piety, religion and morality," the article gave the legislature the right to establish and promote public worship and religious train-

---

58. Mass. Constitution (1780), Pt. 2, Chap. V, Sec. II; *Calling the Conventions of 1776 and 1790*, 121; Rush, "On the Defects of the Confederation" (1787), "Of the Mode of Education Proper in a Republic" (1798), "Education Agreeable to a Republican Form of Government" (1786), in Runes, ed., *Writings of Rush*, 31, 91–92, 98–99. See also Frederick Rudolph, ed., *Essays on Education in the Early Republic* (Cambridge, Mass., 1965).

59. Jonas Clark, *A Sermon Preached before His Excellency John Hancock...* (Boston, 1781), 37; Adams, *Sermon Preached May 29, 1782*, 47; Symmes, *Sermon Preached before Thomas Cushing*, 16; Williams, *Sermon Preached in the General Assembly*, 9–10, 14, 28.

60. For a trenchant attack on the Virginia Assembly for destroying "the most powerful seeds of that very virtue it must be supposed they wish to see flourish in the state they represent," see [John Swanwick], *Considerations on an Act of the Legislature of Virginia, Entitled an Act for the Establishment of Religious Freedom* (Phila., 1786), 6, and *passim*.

ing—a right that in the eyes of many seemed contradictory to the Constitution's profession of the liberty of religious conscience.[61] In South Carolina William Tennent turned this powerful argument for a religious establishment in a republic against itself, arguing that it was not the presence of several denominations but rather "inequality that excites jealousy and dissatisfaction." Following Tennent's advice, South Carolina reconciled a multiplicity of sects with the republic's need for harmony and unanimity by declaring the "Christian Protestant religion . . . the established religion of this State." Many in Maryland in the mid-eighties began to have second thoughts about too rigid a separation of church and state and likewise moved toward a multiple establishment, the House of Delegates declaring that since *religion* hath the most powerful influence upon *manners*, and . . . has such an intimate connection with government," it was the duty of the legislature to make "permanent provision" for its "administration and support."[62]

Other Americans, however, were less sure of the efficacy of religion and education in infusing virtue into the American character. Indeed, a long-existing split in the American mind between what has been called the evangelical scheme and the legal scheme was now conspicuously revealed.[63] Although many Americans in 1776 had blended and continued to blend both schemes in an uneasy combination, the events of the 1780's were forcing a separation between those who clung to moral reform and the regeneration of men's hearts as the remedy for viciousness and those who looked to mechanical devices and institutional contrivances as the only lasting solution for America's ills. It was a basic division that separated "unenlightened" from "enlightened," Calvinist from Liberal, and ultimately Antifederalist from Federalist.

61. Mass. Constitution (1780), Pt. 1, Art. III, See the discussion in Handlin, eds., *Popular Sources*, 29–33.

62. Newton B. Jones, ed., "Writings of the Reverend William Tennent, 1740–1777," *S. C. Hist. Mag.*, 61 (1960), 194–209; S. C. Constitution (1778), XXXVIII; Baltimore *Md. Journal*, Jan. 18, Feb. 8, May 20, 1785. Webster, in his "Comparative Study of the State Constitutions," Amer. Acad. of Pol. and Soc. Sci., *Annals*, 9 (1897), 403, was impressed with "the striking contrast between facts and pretensions" characterizing the religious clauses of nearly all of the Revolutionary constitutions. Although liberty of conscience was proclaimed and the establishment of a single denomination disavowed in most of the state constitutions, few Americans were willing "to carry the idea of religious liberty so far, as . . . to rob civil government of one of its main supports." Cumings, *Sermon Preached May 28, 1783*, 47.

63. Heimert, *Religion and the American Mind*.

"No government under heaven," said Benjamin Austin in a bold enunciation of the moral outlook, "could have prevented a people from ruin, or kept their commerce from declining, when they were exhausting their valuable resources in paying for superfluities, and running themselves in debt to *foreigners*, and to *each other* for articles of folly and dissipation." As long as men were morally corrupt, "we may contend about forms of government, but no establishment will enrich a people, who wantonly spend beyond their income." But for others, despairing of any such inner regeneration, something more external was necessary. If the people were as corrupt and vicious, as permeated by a commercial spirit as the eighties seemed to indicate, then it was foolish to rely on religion and education alone to curb America's passions and to maintain viable republican societies. "Whenever any disorder happens in any government," declared those committed to a legalistic remedy, "it must be ascribed, to a fault in some of the institutions of it."[64] Only the institutions of government arranged in a certain manner could manage an unvirtuous people. If men's souls could not be redeemed then their governments must be adjusted to their sinfulness. Monarchy, of course, could control a corrupt society, but it was out of the question for most.[65] Only republicanism was "reconcilable with the genius of the people of America" and "with the fundamental principles of the Revolution." The American dilemma was to make "such an arrangement of political power as ensures the existence and security of the government, even in the absence of political virtue," without, however, at the same time destroying republicanism. The task was a formidable and original one: to establish a republican government even though the best social science of the day declared that the people were incapable of sustaining it. Somehow, as Madison put it, Americans must find "a republican remedy for the diseases most incident to republican government."[66]

64. Boston *Independent Chronicle*, Dec. 6, 1787; Phila. *Pa. Packet*, Oct. 25, 1786.
65. See Louise B. Dunbar, *A Study of "Monarchical" Tendencies in the United States, from 1776 to 1801* (Urbana, Ill., 1922).
66. *The Federalist*, No. 39; Boston *Independent Chronicle*, Nov. 2, 1786; *The Federalist*, No. 10.

CHAPTER XI

Republican Remedies

1. CONSTITUTIONAL REFORM

Apparently the Americans of 1776 had not fully understood the science of politics after all. "We were, at the commencement of the late war, but novices in politics," wrote Thomas Tudor Tucker of South Carolina in 1784, "and it is to be wished that we may not now be too indolent to correct our mistakes." After lopping off "the monarchical part" of the English constitution, "we vainly imagined that we had arrived at perfection, and that freedom was established on the broadest and most solid basis that could possibly consist with any social institution. That we have in some points been mistaken, is too evident to be denied." "Although we understood perfectly the principles of Liberty," said Benjamin Rush in 1787, "yet most of us were ignorant of the forms and combinations of power in republics." Looking back, 1776 now seemed to be a very unfavorable time for constitution-making. The war and the threats of invasion had been too unsettling, and hatred of the British had been so intense that Americans "unfortunately refused to copy some things in the administration of justice and power, in the British government, which have made it the admiration and envy of the world."[1] Americans soon began telling themselves that their early constitutions were "hasty productions on the spur of exigency," ill adapted to the nature of the society. "Our government should in

---

1. [Tucker], *Conciliatory Hints*, 20; Rush, "On the Defects of the Confederation" (1787), Runes, ed., *Writings of Rush*, 26; [Oliver Ellsworth], "The Landholder, XII," Mar. 17, 1788, in Ford, ed., *Essays on the Constitution*, 197.

some degree be suited to our manners and circumstances," John Jay said to Washington early in 1787, "and they, you know, are not strictly democratical." By 1787 it had become a common opinion among many that "the source of all evils of which we complain, and of all those which we apprehend" lay in their "political systems." Indeed, to some the American states possessed "some of the weakest and most inefficient governments . . . that ever nations were afflicted with." There could be no doubt, as Washington put it, that "we have errors to correct." If the American character was not capable of sustaining the popular nature of the Revolutionary constitutions, then the structure of those governments must be changed.[2]

"When by some violent convulsion a revolution has been effected," governments would obviously be unsettled. "Some time must always intervene before new ideas can be received, new forms established, and the machine of government brought back to a regular motion. . . . Defects appear which time only could bring to view; many things require amendment, and some must undergo a total alteration." Yet the ink on the Revolutionary constitutions of 1776 was scarcely dry before defects were appearing and reforms were being proposed. Within even a few months some of those states which had delayed their constitution-making were beginning to entertain doubts about the capacity of their people to maintain extremely popular governments. And it was not long before men in other states which had quickly adopted popular constitutions in 1776 were reconsidering their earlier assumptions. The Pennsylvania Constitution of 1776, it was widely pointed out, had paid no attention "to the ancient habits and customs of the people of Pennsylvania in the distribution of the supreme power of the state. . . . It supposes perfect equality, and equal distribution of property, wisdom and virtue, among the inhabitants of the state." The people of Massachusetts, declared the Essex County Convention in 1776, were in danger of committing similar errors. Perhaps the people in 1775 had dismissed parts of their old colonial government too brusquely.[3] In

2. Phila. *Pa. Journal*, Sept. 3, 17, 1783; Jay to Washington, Jan. 7, 1787, Johnston, ed., *Papers of Jay*, III, 227; Henry Knox to Mercy Warren, May 30, 1787, Ford, ed., *Warren-Adams Letters*, II, 294; Baltimore *Md. Journal*, June 26, 1787; Washington to Jay, Aug. 15, 1786, Johnston, ed., *Papers of Jay*, III, 208–09.

3. Charleston *St. Gazette of S.-C.*, Feb. 22, 1787; [Rush], *Observations on the Government of Pennsylvania*, in Runes, ed., *Writings of Rush*, 55; *Essex Result*, Parsons, *Memoir*, 364, 378; John Adams to James Warren, June 11, 17, 1777, Ford, ed., *Warren-Adams Letters*, I, 329, 331–32.

New York fear of a government too popular for the society was especially acute in 1776, and some of the gentry were even reluctant to leave the state for the Continental Congress out of fear of surrendering the framing of the constitution to those who would create a government, as Robert Livingston put it, "without that influence that is derived from respect to old families wealth age etc."[4] Everywhere reformation seemed to be in tandem with the formation of the Revolutionary constitutions.

Since the "unsteadiness of the people" was the complaint most commonly made, the kinds of governmental reforms needed soon became obvious. "We have been guarding against an evil that old States are most liable to, *excess of power* in the rulers," said Benjamin Franklin; "but our present danger seems to be *defect of obedience* in the subjects." The liberty of the people in the traditional mixed government must be lessened, and the power of the monarchical and aristocratical elements must be strengthened. In other words, power had to be taken from the houses of representatives and given to the senates and particularly to the governors. "At the commencement of the revolution," Americans were telling themselves in the eighties, "it was supposed that what is called the executive part of a government was the only dangerous part; but we now see that quite as much mischief, if not more, may be done, and as much arbitrary conduct acted, by a legislature." The early state constitutions had rendered government too feeble. "The principal fault," constitutional reformers agreed, "seems to be, a want of energy in the administration of government." In nearly all of the states there were growing demands that the libertarian bias of 1776 be corrected, that the apparent licentiousness of the people be offset by an increase of magisterial power in order to provide for the "execution of the laws that is necessary for the preservation of justice, peace, and internal tranquility."[5]

By the middle eighties Franklin could write to correspondents abroad that whatever faults there were in the Americans' constitutions were being rapidly corrected. "We are, I think, in the

4. Livingston to Edward Rutledge, Oct. 10, 1776, quoted in Dangerfield, *Livingston*, 87; Timothy Pickering, Jr., to John Pickering, Jr., Apr. 26, 1778, Pickering Papers, V, 76, Mass. Hist. Soc.; William Duer to President of the N. Y. Congressional Delegation, and to the President of the N. Y. Convention, Apr. 21, 29, 1777, Burnett, ed., *Letters of Congress*, II, 331, 337, 344.

5. Boston *Independent Chronicle*, May 10, 1787; Franklin to Charles Carroll, May 25, 1789, Smyth, ed., *Writings of Franklin*, X, 7; Phila. *Pa. Packet*, Sept. 21, 1786; Hartford *Conn. Courant*, Sept. 16, 1783; Boston *Independent Chronicle*, May 20, 1779.

right Road of Improvement, for . . . we are daily more and more enlightened."⁶ But the reforms were not easily made, for they flew in the face of much of what the American Whigs had learned from their colonial experience under the British monarchy. The problem was conspicuously revealed at the outset in the drafting of the New York Constitution of 1777. The New York constitution-makers, meeting in the spring of 1777, continually found themselves in dilemmas. Torn in two directions—between the inherited dread of magisterial despotism and a fear of popular disorder which was greater than that of any state at that time—the New York Convention was repeatedly obliged to resort to unusual and intricate expedients in order to avoid the extremes. The executive veto, both feared and desired, was eventually transformed into the ingenious Council of Revision, made up of the governor, chancellor, and Supreme Court judges. The power of appointment, the crucial power in the Whig scheme of politics, was the most confused and hotly debated issue; it deadlocked the Convention and was only settled by another unique invention, a Council of Appointment, made up of the governor and four senators chosen by the Assembly, thus resolving the problem of lodging the power of appointment exclusively with either the governor or the legislature. The result was a Constitution in tension—one which members of the same social standing could describe quite differently. For some it savored too much of "the leveling principle," while for others it was "the best system which has as yet been adopted, and possibly as good as the temper of the times would admit of." For constitutional reformers outside of New York, however, the Constitution of 1777, with its strong Senate and its independent governor elected directly by the people for a three-year term, seemed to be a great victory for energy and order. It pointed the direction constitutional reform would take.⁷

6. Franklin to Ferdinand Grand, Mar. 5, 1786, and to Jonathan Shipley, Feb. 24, 1786, both in Smyth, ed., *Writings of Franklin*, IX, 493, 489.

7. *Journals of the Provincial Congress of New York*, I, 834, 836, 843, 853, 860, 862, 874, 891; Dangerfield, *Livingston*, 97; R. R. Livingston and Gouverneur Morris to John Jay, Apr. 26, 1777, and William Duer to Jay, May 28, 1777, both in Johnston, ed., *Papers of Jay*, I, 128–29, 138; William Smith, entry, Apr. 11, 1777, Sabine, ed., *Memoir of Smith*, 109–10; Hamilton to the N. Y. Committee of Correspondence, May 7, 1777, and Gouverneur Morris to Hamilton, May 16, 1777, both in Syrett and Cooke, eds., *Hamilton Papers*, I, 248, 253–54. See J. M. Gitterman, "The Council of Appointment in New York," *Pol. Sci. Qtly.*, 7 (1892), 80–115; Hugh M. Flick, "The Council of Appointment in New York State . . . ," *New York History*, 15 (1934), 253–80; Alfred B. Street, *The Council of Revision of the State of New York* (Albany, 1859).

It was the Massachusetts Constitution of 1780, adopted by the state after a long and embarrassing delay and the defeat by the towns of one proposed Constitution in 1778, that eventually came to stand for the reconsidered ideal of a *"perfect constitution."* Only the partial limitation on the governor's veto authority and the popular election of the militia officers, said Theophilus Parsons in 1780, marred its perfection. The Constitution seemed to many to have recaptured some of the best elements of the British constitution that had been forgotten in the excitement of 1776. It alone of all the American constitutions had happily found the true mixture. "It in some measure inculcates the doctrine of *equality*, so far as is consistent with the present state of humanity, and tho' it makes *virtue* its principal pillar, it has not rested itself on that single foundation. It inspires with the principles of *honour and dignity*, which attach to its interest a most valuable class of citizens; and like a *despot* it may stamp dread upon those, who can be governed by no other motive." The legislature was balanced between a House of Representatives embodying the people and a Senate of forty whose membership was proportioned to districts in accord with the amount of public taxes paid by the inhabitants. The members of the three branches of the legislature, the House of Representatives, the Senate, and the governor, were qualified by an ascending scale of property-holding and residence. A lengthy bill of rights preceded the Constitution and spelled out the principle of separation of powers in repetitious detail. Although the governor was circumscribed by a Council, selected by both houses from those chosen to be senators, he still represented the most powerful magistrate of all of the states. Like the New York governor, he was elected directly by the people. But unlike the New York governor, the Massachusetts chief magistrate could alone veto all acts of the legislature, except those repassed by a two-thirds majority of both houses. Together with the Council, the governor was granted much of the power his royal predecessor had held, in particular the power to appoint the judicial and leading civil officers, and was given a fixed salary so that "the governor should not be under the undue influence of any of the members of the general court, by a dependence on them for his support."[8]

8. Parsons to Francis Dana, Aug. 3, 1780, Taylor, ed., *Massachusetts Constitution*, 159; Boston *Independent Chronicle*, Nov. 2, 1786; Mass. Constitution (1780), Pt. 2, Chap. II, Sec. I, Art. XIII.

The Massachusetts Constitution of 1780 not only had a direct influence on the New Hampshire Constitution adopted in 1784 but it seemed to many in the 1780's to climax the second wave of state constitutional construction. In its structure at least, it came to represent much of what reformers in other states desired for their own constitutions—a strengthening of the governor at the expense of the legislature, particularly the lower house. The executive power, as the New Hampshire Convention of 1781 declared in defense of its proposed Constitution, had become "the active principle in all governments: It is the soul, and without it the body-politic is but a dead corpse." The governor, as Jefferson's draft in the early eighties for a new Virginia Constitution stated, must be granted those powers "which are necessary to execute the laws (and administer the government) and which are not in their nature either legislative or judiciary," their precise extent being "left to reason." Reformers sought to center magisterial responsibility in the governors by making the executive councils more advisory than they were in the early Revolutionary constitutions. They also sought to make the governors less dependent on the legislatures, especially in election. Election of the governors by the legislature, said Madison, "not only tends to faction intrigue and corruption, but leaves the Executive under the influence of an improper obligation to that department." Election by the people-at-large, as in New York and Massachusetts, or by some system of indirect election, "or indeed by the people through any other channel than their legislative representatives, seems to be far preferable." Critics of the early constitutions now saw that vesting the power of appointment to offices, so much feared in 1776, in the legislatures destroyed "all responsibility" and created "a perpetual source of faction and corruption."[9] Election of the militia officers by the soldiers rather than magisterial appointment from above "not only renders every superior officer dependent on his inferior, but opens a dangerous avenue to division, discord and animosity in every corps." It now seemed unquestionable that the governor should participate in legislation through some sort of revisionary power, such as a council of revision as in New York, or through a limited veto as

9. Address of the N. H. Convention (1781), Bouton *et al.*, eds., *State Papers of N. H.*, IX, 849; Jefferson, *Notes on Virginia*, ed. Peden, 214; Madison's Observations on Jefferson's Draft of a Constitution for Virginia (1788), Boyd, ed., *Jefferson Papers*, VI, 311–12.

in Massachusetts, if there were to be "a check to precipitate, to unjust, and to unconstitutional laws."[10]

Since it was the power of the houses of representatives in particular that had to be checked, the constitutional reformers urged that the upper branches of the legislatures be made more stable, if they were, as Madison said, "to withstand the occasional impetuosities of the more numerous branch." This meant longer terms for senators and some distinct means of qualification which would "supply the defect of knowledge and experience incident to the other branch." Jefferson in his proposal of 1783 for a new Virginia Constitution favored an indirect method of electing senators and the elimination of all restrictions on the senate's power to originate or amend any bill.[11] Only a strong senate, the Virginia reformers believed, could "maintain that system and steadiness in public affairs without which no Government can prosper or be respectable." The judiciary as well must be freed of all dependence on any branch of the government. Only appointment by the governors during good behavior would make the judges "*wholly* independent of the Assembly—of the Council—nay more, of the people." And to ensure that the best men be maintained in office, rotation, which had been such a cardinal principle in 1776, was now openly attacked as leading to instability and confusion. Although even the reactionary *Essex Result* had admitted a need for rotating the governor in 1778, by 1780 the members of the Massachusetts Convention wanted no restrictions on the governor's tenure.[12]

While the magisterial power was to be invigorated, the authority of the legislatures, which, as many now saw, had become "wholly undefined and unlimited, so that neither the people know the extent of their privileges, nor the legislatures the bounds of their power," was to be correspondingly reduced. In his draft for a new Virginia Constitution Jefferson explicitly denied the

10. Address of the N. H. Convention (1782), Bouton *et al.*, eds., *State Papers of N. H.*, IX, 880; Madison's Observations, Boyd, ed., *Jefferson Papers*, VI, 315. For the amendment of the Vermont Constitution in 1786, enabling the governor and Council to review all bills and propose amendments with the power to suspend their passage until the next session of the legislature, see Carroll, *Legislature of Vermont*, 14.

11. Madison's Observations, Boyd, ed., *Jefferson Papers*, VI, 308; Jefferson, *Notes on Virginia*, ed. Peden, 211.

12. Madison's Observations, Boyd, ed., *Jefferson Papers*, VI, 308; Phila. *Pa. Journal*, Mar. 27, 1784; *Essex Result*, in Parsons, *Memoir*, 398–99; Adams, ed., *Works of John Adams*, IV, 250–51.

legislature "the power to infringe this constitution," "to abridge the civil rights of any person on account of his religious beliefs," and to pass certain specified acts, including bills of attainder and *ex post facto* laws. The constitutions themselves, reformers argued, must be made more fundamental, drawn directly by the people and thus rendered unalterable by ordinary legislatures. But higher laws and executive vetoes were not enough. If unjust and foolish laws were to be prevented from even being enacted, the character of the lower houses themselves must be changed, largely, the reformers argued, by decreasing the number of the members by as much as one-half. A smaller house, it was claimed, would be more orderly and energetic and more devoted to the public good. The New Hampshire Convention of 1781 even went so far as to propose a system of indirect election for a fifty-member House of Representatives. The mode of "being twice sifted," the Convention declared, would result in a higher proportion of suitable legislators.[13]

Because these proposals for constitutional reform attempted to reverse the democratic tendencies of the early constitutions, that is, because they sought to lessen the power of the representatives of the people in the legislatures, and conversely to strengthen the magisterial power, they were bitterly resisted, on the very formidable ground that such reforms were antagonistic to the spirit of 1776 and all that the Revolution was politically about. The constitutional changes, like those embodied in the Massachusetts Constitution of 1780, it was charged, "will introduce (at Least) as Many Evils as Could have Been feared from the British power in Case They had Succeeded in Their first attempts against This Continent." It seemed to many that the proposed reforms were but insidious devices to return to the aristocratic and monarchical tones of the former colonial governments. To enhance the rulers' power and to diminish the power of the houses of representatives was precisely what British officials had attempted on the eve of the Revolution. Americans had been indoctrinated too long in the Whig fear of governmental power to consent readily to its aggrandizement at the expense of liberty.[14]

13. *Political Establishments of the United States*, 22; Jefferson, *Notes on Virginia*, ed. Peden, 213; Hartford *Conn. Courant*, June 12, Nov. 13, 1786, June 17, 1787; Address of the N. H. Convention (1781), Bouton *et al.*, eds., *State Papers of N. H.*, IX, 848.
14. Address of Middleborough, Aug. 21, 1780, in Mass. Hist. Soc., *Proceedings*, 50 (1917), 58; Charleston *St. Gazette of S.-C.*, June 13, 1785.

Yet the changes in constitutionalism that were advocated in the years after Independence never seemed quite as unpopular or as unwhiggish as opponents made them out to be. For the Americans' ideas of what constituted governmental power and what constituted popular liberty were not frozen in 1776. Indeed, as has been seen, they were constantly in flux, continually adapting and adjusting to ever-shifting political and social circumstances. Involved in the midst of these changes and contributing to them, the constitutional reformers soon found themselves developing arguments against the construction of the early state constitutions that seemed to be elaborations and extensions rather than repudiations of what Americans had fought for. All of the developments in political thought taking place in the decade after 1776—the changes in the character of representation, in the nature of the senate and the magistracy, in the conception of a constitution and the institution of a convention, in the growing discrepancy between the power of the people out-of-doors and their delegates in the legislatures—all of these developments were both furthered and used by those who in the late seventies and early eighties sought to amend the state constitutions drafted in 1776. By the 1780's such had been the evolution of political ideas that it was no longer self-evident, as it would have been a decade earlier, that the Massachusetts Constitution of 1780 was less popular, less libertarian, less democratic, than the Pennsylvania Constitution of 1776.

2. WHIGGISM AGAINST ITSELF

Because the Pennsylvania Constitution of 1776 was the most radical and most democratic of the Revolutionary constitutions, the attempts to reform or replace it are especially illustrative of the way ideas were developing under pressure in these years after Independence. Amidst all the party strife among Pennsylvanians in the seventies and eighties—over the test oaths, the College of Philadelphia, the Bank of North America, the incorporation of Philadelphia—the future of the radical Constitution of 1776 remained a basic issue. However much the antagonists, the Constitutionalists and Republicans, may have temporarily shifted tactics and accepted or abused the Constitution for their partisan purposes, the ultimate worth and durability of the Constitution was never long lost from debate. As the faction-torn Council of Censors lamented in 1784, this "question whether the constitution should be continued or altered," "this unhappy question . . . has lain at the bottom of all our disputes." From the moment of its inception, despite the fact that many who were at first violently opposed eventually came to terms with it, the Constitution of 1776 was marked for revision by a group of Pennsylvanians calling themselves Republicans, centered in Philadelphia and led by James Wilson and Robert Morris.[15]

It soon became clear from the numerous criticisms voiced in the press and pamphlets of the late seventies what kind of constitution these Republicans or anti-Constitutionalists wanted. If there were any doubts, the first session of the Council of Censors meeting in the winter of 1783–84 and dominated by the Republicans made the many scattered proposals for change official. Foremost, the legislative power was to be "vested in two separate and distinct bodies of men" and brought into similarity with most of the other American republics. "In order to prevent a too numerous representation, which would be expensive and burthensome," the membership in the lower house was to be limited to one hundred, the upper house to fifty. Residence requirements for the electors were to be increased. The upper house was to hold office for a three-year staggered term. "A principal executive magistrate" was to replace the Executive Council of twelve and was to be elected, as the councilors had been, directly by the people for a three-year term. The new governor was to appoint all judicial officers and leading civil officers and was to possess a limited veto of all legislation. Rotation of the various offices was to be abolished, since, among other objections to rotation, "the privilege of the people in elections, is so far infringed as they are thereby deprived of the right of choosing those persons whom they would prefer." Judges were no longer to be elected, but were to hold office during good behavior and were to have fixed salaries, since "the liberties of the state are evidently connected with their independence." The notorious Section 15 of the 1776 Constitution, which provided for all bills to be referred to the people-at-large before they became law—a practice which the Republicans conceived "was always delusory"—would be "rendered unnecessary" by the establishment of a second branch in the legislature. Finally the Republican-dominated Council of

15. *Calling the Conventions of 1776 and 1790*, 125–26. On Pennsylvania politics in the 1780's see Robert L. Brunhouse, *Counterrevolution in Pennsylvania 1776–1790* (Harrisburg, 1942).

Censors recommended that their own body be abolished. The proposed constitution, as one sympathetic observer noted, thus bore a strong resemblance to the recently established Massachusetts Constitution of 1780, which had been "composed by some of the wisest men, and greatest friends to democratical government, in the United States."[16]

The Constitutionalists, composed largely of Scotch-Irish Presbyterians led by George Bryan, William Findley, and John Smilie, could scarcely agree that such proposed changes were friendly to democratical government. As a substantial minority of the first session of the Council of Censors in 1784, the Constitutionalists immediately published dissents to the Republicans' proposals in terms that had become familiar to Pennsylvanians. The Constitution of 1776, they said, had carried the state through the most trying times and thus should "not be lightly changed." The submitted reforms were not only "expensive, burthensome and complicated," but more important, "they tend to introduce among the citizens new and aristocratic ranks, with a chief magistrate at their head, vested with powers exceeding those which fall to the ordinary lot of kings." The Republicans, the people were told in angry tones, were really attempting "to establish and fill an upper House of *Lords* amongst you, that they may thereby more effectually teach you submission to your *betters*," for the obvious design of the suggested second house was "to accommodate the *better sort of people*, and to vest them with full power to prevent any law from passing, which a number of honest farmers from the country may judge to be salutary and beneficial to the state." And to prevent the people from getting even a single law enacted "which does not comport with the views of your new lords and masters" the new "Governor or King (for it matters not by what name you may call him)" was to be granted an "absolute power to put a negative" on any bill of the legislature "unless he be so poor, or avaricious as not to be able to bribe one third of either House to adhere to the alterations he may be pleased to make." In short, declared the Constitutionalists, "the grand objection to our present Constitution is, that it retains too much power in the hands of the people, who do not know how to use it, so well as gentlemen of fortune, whose easy circumstances give them leisure, to contrive how to spend your money to the best advantage; and that it gives no advantage to the rich over the poor, inasmuch as they must sit in the same House with the ill-dressed farmers from the country, if they would have any share in the Legislature." It seemed to the supporters of the 1776 Constitution that every proposed change, from the abolition of rotation in office to the elimination of the Council of Censors, was designed so that "no check may be left against the encroachments of power." Such proposals only represented "the ambitious views of a restless aristocracy."[17]

From the beginning of the Revolution the opponents of the Pennsylvania Constitution had been compelled time and again to face this kind of popular, anti-aristocratic rhetoric, and they had quickly learned how best to deal with it. They were at once aware that they could never deny the grand principle of the Revolution—"that the government should be founded *on the authority of the people.*" And indeed they soon became foremost advocates of the authority of the people. Such was the development of ideas in the years after 1776 that the Republicans could intelligibly claim that, far from being the most libertarian constitution of the Revolution, the Pennsylvania Constitution was actually "inconsistent with the true principles of Liberty." "Can it be believed," they asked, "that any reasonable creature, will think it the great bulwark of equal liberty? is it not, what we have truly represented it? the most complete system of aristocratic tyranny, that has appeared in the world." The Republicans soon came to represent in their own minds and in their language the real party of the people and the authentic defenders of Revolutionary Whiggism.[18]

The premise on which the opponents of the Pennsylvania Constitution based their stand was the common Whig fear of political power. "Absolute power should never be trusted to man," wrote Benjamin Rush in 1777 in terms no good Whig could deny. "It has perverted the wisest heads, and corrupted the best hearts in the world." In the Pennsylvania Constitution "the supreme, absolute, and uncontrolled power of the State is lodged in the hands of *one body* of men." No matter that this body was not magisterial but in fact representative of the people. Had the supreme power

17. *Calling the Conventions of 1776 and 1790*, 78–79; Phila. *Pa. Gazette*, Jan. 28, 1784.
18. Phila. *Pa. Packet*, June 3, 1777; Phila. *Pa. Journal*, May 21, 1777; *Calling the Conventions of 1776 and 1790*, 107.

"been lodged in the hands of one man," declared Rush in an extraordinary distortion of Whiggism, "it would have been less dangerous to the safety and liberties of the community." Indeed, because the Pennsylvania Constitution vested all the legislative power in a single Assembly "without any controul," it had peculiarly violated the principles of the Revolution. "In every free state," the opponents of the Constitution contended over and over, "the sovereign power should be watched with a jealous eye, and every abuse of it, which infringes the right of the subject, instantly opposed. Whether that power is lodged in the hands of one or many, the danger is equally great."[19]

Although some polemicists continued to talk in conventional terms of imposing a barrier to the *"unbounded* liberty" of the Assembly "to prevent its degenerating into licentiousness," most opponents of the Constitution soon grasped that the Assembly's power, although supposedly representative of the people, was best described in the way Crown or magisterial power had formerly been described—not as the extension but as the antithesis of liberty, not as leading to anarchy but as leading to despotism. "We have been so long habituated to a jealousy of tyranny from monarchy and aristocracy," some even dared to say, "that we have yet to learn the dangers of it from *democracy*." Despotism had to be opposed "whether it came from Kings, Lords or the people."[20] Yet so directly ascribing tyranny to the people themselves was rare and confined mostly to private correspondence. Besides, there was no need to, for the power of the Assembly could be attacked, it was soon seen, without in any way impugning the authority of the people-at-large, so much was a discrepancy between the people and their representatives emerging in American thought. This distinction between the people and their representatives was quickly pounced on and widened by those who were continually hard put to defend their populism and their adherence to the egalitarian principles of the Revolution.

In the spring and summer of 1776 those opposed to the radical Presbyterian group that sought to call a Revolutionary convention had argued that the old proprietary Assembly was fully capable of carrying out the May 15 resolution of the Continental Congress to frame a new government for the colony. Even after

19. [Rush], *Observations on the Government of Pennsylvania*, Runes, ed., *Writings of Rush*, 57; Phila. *Pa. Packet*, June 3, 1777, Oct. 8, 1778.
20. Phila. *Pa. Packet*, Sept. 24, 1776; Phila. *Pa. Journal*, June 30, 1784.

the establishment of the new government in the early fall of 1776, many of its opponents, now faced with a Constitution that by its own terms could presumably not be changed for seven years, continued to argue that the ordinary legislature "ought to have full powers to make such alterations and amendments in the Constitution" as it should judge proper. Yet when confronted with the emergent and imposing Constitutionalist contention that the Constitution, if it were truly a fundamental constitution, could not be tampered with by the legislature, the anti-Constitutionalists began shifting their position. They soon perceived the significance of the newly defined conception of a constitution as a set of fundamentals immune from legislative violation and turned it against its radical creators, who were now in control of the legislature and busy trying to secure their revolution. The Presbyterian-dominated Assembly, with its test oaths, suffrage requirements, and enlarged fees for offices, the anti-Constitutionalists charged, was repeatedly violating all that the radicals had formerly stood for. Such acts against the Constitution, the Republicans argued, were mere nullities, passed against the true authority of the people. "Wherever the Assembly assume the exercise of powers not granted them, they act arbitrarily and without authority." This in fact was what the Revolution was all about, and James Burgh was quoted by the anti-Constitutionalists to prove it. When the Constitutionalists urged the people to obey the acts of this new Assembly they were using the same language that had been formerly used by Lord North and "every *tory, non-resisting* minion of power in Great Britain . . . in the face of *arbitrary* and unconstitutional acts of Parliament." The new Pennsylvania Assembly was no more free to violate the Constitution than Parliament had been.[21]

Although those who made up the anti-Constitutionalist party had strongly resisted the calling of the Revolutionary convention that eventually drafted the Constitution in 1776, they rapidly became the foremost advocates of the convention principle. If the Assembly could not change the Constitution, as the Constitutionalists had earlier argued and as the anti-Constitutionalists had eventually conceded, then surely a convention, such as had originally created the Constitution, could. And the Republicans soon began to clamor for a new convention, through which "a better judgment will be formed of the opinions of the majority, than

21. Phila. *Pa. Gazette*, Oct. 23, 1776; Phila. *Pa. Packet*, Sept. 26, Oct. 8, 13, 1778.

by any other method that can be suggested." Even though they were now willing to admit the authority of the 1776 Convention in framing a constitution, the Republicans said, "does it follow from this, that the people did not reserve to themselves the power of approving or disapproving of the constitution, after it was framed?" The radicals, it was increasingly charged, actually lacked the confidence of the people, which explained their resort to test oaths and suffrage restrictions. In their rhetoric the anti-Constitutionalists were soon outpopularizing the most popular party of the Revolution. "It is because we esteem the sacred POWER of the PEOPLE to be above all OTHER power," the anti-Constitutionalists declared, "that we have appealed to them" beyond any existing political body. Only a new convention, it seemed clear by 1777, could clarify the people's will. "Let the Majesty and authority of the PEOPLE determine as it shall please them."[22]

Although, as the Constitutionalists protested, the Constitution had provided for a septennial revision of the Constitution in Section 47 through the Council of Censors, the increased pressure of the Republicans' arguments and political strength was too great to be resisted, and the legislature on June 17, 1777, agreed to test the wishes of the people on the issue of a convention. After Howe's invasion disrupted this plan, the Assembly on November 28, 1778, once again resolved to give the people an opportunity in the early spring of 1779 to vote on the convocation of a convention to revise the Constitution. A flood of opposing petitions allowed the legislature once more to renege on the promise of a referendum on the calling of a convention. The convention issue continued to divide the Republicans and Constitutionalists on through the septennial meetings of the Council of Censors in 1783–84, where the Republicans were unable to secure the necessary two-thirds majority required to convene a convention. Throughout all the maneuvering the Republicans continued to assume the popular mantle, claiming that the people had "an inherent right, as freemen, to demand an opportunity of declaring their sentiments upon the subject" of the Constitution. Why were the Constitutionalists opposed to a convention? the Republicans taunted. "Who will compose this convention? Men

22. Phila. *Pa. Packet*, June 3, 1777; Phila. *Pa. Journal*, May 14, June 4, 1777; Broadside, *Address to the Inhabitants of the City and Liberties of Philadelphia*, Nov. 2, 1776 (Phila., 1776); Phila. *Pa. Journal*, Oct. 16, 1776, May 21, 1777.

chosen by the whole state. They will be the breath of our nostrils. Why then should you be afraid of them?" Since the Council of Censors was unrepresentative of the state, influenced by passions and cabals, and required a two-thirds majority to convoke a convention, it was ill-equipped to gauge the people's will. Only the people themselves, "the sovereigns of Pennsylvania," the Republicans said, could "call a convention, when and in what manner" they pleased. But the Constitutionalists, clinging to "the sweets of office," were afraid. "That is—you are afraid to trust the people with their *own* power. . . . The people (you seem to say by your conduct) are such a set of stupid creatures, that they will chuse improper men to make a constitution for them." Before the decade of the eighties was out and the next septennial meeting of the Council of Censors convened, the Republicans with the help of this kind of popular rhetoric would have their convention and their new constitution.[23]

Even more significant for the development of political thought in the 1780's than this use and expansion of the sovereignty of the people were the arguments the Republicans employed to justify the changes they intended to make in the Constitution of 1776—a Constitution, they said, which "contains principles subversive of political liberty and equal government." Far from introducing an aristocracy by the erection of two houses in the legislature, as the Constitutionalists charged, bicameralism, or "a different distribution of power," the Republicans declared, would prevent "the danger to liberty from an aristocracy" by compelling designing men to control two bodies instead of one. By the 1780's, as has been seen, the proposed upper house was being explained entirely as a division of mistrusted legislative power and as a double representation of the people.[24] The proposed single magistrate was also defended in expanded Whiggish terms. Fear of executive usurpation and the compensatory favor given the legislature in the appointment of officers and other responsibilities made sense under the British government when the governors derived their authority from the Crown or the proprietor. But

23. Meader, "Council of Censors," *Pa. Mag. of Hist. and Biog.*, 22 (1898), 286; Phila. *Pa. Journal*, Feb. 3, 1779; Phila. *Pa. Gazette*, Mar. 24, 1779; Phila. *Pa. Journal*, June 23, 1784; *Calling the Conventions of 1776 and 1790*, 81–82; Phila. *Pa. Gazette*, Mar. 24, 1779; Phila. *Pa. Journal*, June 23, 1784.

24. Phila. *Pa. Gazette*, Feb. 11, 1784; Phila. *Pa. Journal*, July 7, 1784. On the explanation of the upper house as another kind of representation of the people see above, Chap. VI, Sec. 8.

this was no longer true. "The executive and legislative powers draw their authority from the *same source*," from the sovereign people. "Let the political existence of every person in the Legislative and Executive branches," the people were told, "depend upon yourselves." An independent governor would not be a king over the people but would instead be an "umpire raised to the supreme power by their own suffrages." Such a popularly elected governor would focus, not cloud responsibility; unlike the president of the existing Council, who was selected by the legislature, the new executive "will be the creature not of the Assembly, but of the people. He will be the right hand of *their* power and majesty." It was not too much now to say that he would be another kind of representative of the people. In fact, a major objection made by the Republicans to the plural Executive Council was "that it consists of one member from the city and each county, without the least regard to 'Representation in proportion to the number [of] taxable inhabitants,' though this is expressly declared in our constitution to be 'the only principle which can at all times secure liberty.' " A single executive chosen by the people-at-large, it was argued, would be more equally representative of the people. Benjamin Rush, together with others seeking to justify executive appointment of officials, carried the logic of this thinking to an extreme. The local district elections of petty magistrates, Rush argued, could often result in a man's being bound by decisions and acts of magistrates whom he had no hand in choosing, that is, "bound contrary to the principles of liberty (which consist in a man being governed by men chosen by himself)." But if all the magistrates were appointed by a governor who was elected by all of the people, said Rush in a remarkable perversion of the traditional conception of representation, then it would be impossible for anyone "to appear before the bar of a magistrate any where who did not derive his power *originally*" from all of the people.[25]

3. THE REVISION OF SEPARATION OF POWERS

Such arguments, refined and expanded by the early eighties, were made possible by a subtle but profound shift in the Ameri-

25. Phila. *Pa. Packet*, June 3, 1777; Phila. *Pa. Gazette*, Feb. 11, 1784; Phila. *Pa. Journal*, June 30, Mar. 27, July 7, 1784, Jan. 29, 1785; [Rush], *Observations on the Government of Pennsylvania*, Runes, ed., *Writings of Rush*, 70.

cans' understanding of political power and the people's relationship to the government that was taking place in these years. Wherever there were pressures to strengthen the magisterial elements at the expense of the legislature without doing violence to the popular principles of the Revolution, men developed new lines of thought to justify and explain the constitutional changes they proposed. Because these developments grew out of what was firmly established and acceptable, because they seemed to be extensions rather than repudiations of what Americans of 1776 believed, and because they were really inextricable parts of a broad intellectual front that was emerging in these years after Independence, few sensed any deviation or newness in what they were saying. Political power still seemed to be the conventional Whig object of fear. "The love of Power is so alluring . . . ," declared the New Hampshire Convention of 1781, "that few have ever been able to resist its bewitching influence." Only now it did not matter which part of the government wielded it. "Wherever power is lodged there is a constant propensity to enlarge its boundaries." One tyrant or sixty tyrants, any government like that of New Hampshire since 1776 which vested all power in a single body was a tyranny. "A despotic government is that where any man, or set of men, have the power of making what laws they think proper, or executing them in their own way. . . . Is it possible that Europe, or even Asia itself, can present a more perfect tyranny?" In the eyes of those who favored a new constitution for New Hampshire in the early eighties, the old government had lost whatever representativeness of the people it had presumably possessed.[26]

Because of what was being done to the concept of representation in these years—the breakdown of the mutuality of interests between the people and their delegates and the consequent reliance on suffrage as the main criterion of representation—it was becoming entirely comprehensible to regard the electoral process itself as the foundation and measure of representation. Therefore all elected officials, not just the houses of representatives, were in some way representatives of the people, "other depositaries of the devolved sovereignty of the people." There seemed now to be no essential distinction separating the lower houses of the legislature from the other elected parts of the government. Like the

26. Address of the N. H. Convention (1781), Bouton *et al.*, eds., *State Papers of N. H.*, IX, 846; Portsmouth *N.-H. Gazette*, Mar. 1, 1783.

Pennsylvania Republicans, other constitutional reformers were contending that once the governor was chosen by the whole community, he would become, as the 1781 New Hampshire Convention put it, through "the manner of his choice . . . the most perfect representative of the people." "The Governor," declared the Massachusetts Convention of 1780, "is emphatically the Representative of the whole People, being chosen not by one Town or County, but by the People at large." In fact, it was now widely claimed, "as all the powers of government are derived from the people, and as government is itself instituted for their benefit, every person to whom the power is delegated should feel himself dependent on the people, and be accountable to them for his political conduct." It was impossible now, men argued, to "suppose the Governor a servant, and the Council and branches of the Legislature his masters, when they *all* equally derive their power from the same source." "All power residing originally in the people, and being derived from them," declared the new Massachusetts Constitution, "the several magistrates and officers of government, vested with authority, whether legislative, executive, or judicial, are their substitutes and agents, and are at all times accountable to them."[27]

Once this homogenization of all political power was grasped, once all governmental officials whether executive, judicial, or even legislative were regarded, in Jefferson's words, as "three branches of magistracy," important implications for constitutional reform inevitably followed. If all parts of the government regardless of their former denotations were now considered to be equal servants of the people because of their common derivation of authority, then it seemed obvious that "no peculiar prerogatives should be allowed to one branch, or particular rights to another, lest as in Britain; the seeds of a political warfare should be sowed in the constitution. . . . Though every person holding any part of the powers of government should be dependent on the people; yet it by no means follows that all the authority may be lodged with any particular set of men, more than in the hands of an individual." Legislative power was essentially no different from

27. *Calling the Conventions of 1776 and 1790*, 117; Address of the N. H. Convention (1781), Bouton *et al.*, eds., *State Papers of N. H.*, IX, 850; Address of the Mass. Convention (1780), Handlin, eds., *Popular Sources*, 437; Portsmouth *N.-H. Gazette*, Feb. 22, 1783; Boston *Independent Chronicle*, May 26, 1785; Mass. Constitution (1780), Pt. i, Art. V. See also [Burke], *Address to South-Carolina*, 13–14.

magisterial power. If government were truly to promote the happiness of the people, its several powers, legislative, executive, and judicial, "must be so divided and guarded as to prevent those given to one from being engrossed by the other; and if properly separated, the persons who officiate in the several departments become centinels in behalf of the people to guard against every possible usurpation."[28]

Separation of powers, as has been described earlier, had been invoked occasionally during the imperial debate and had actually been written into several of the state constitutions. In 1776 it had generally been used to justify an isolation of the legislature and the judiciary from what was believed to be the corrupting influence of executive power. The governors' power of appointment was clipped, and magisterial and administrative officials were prohibited from sitting in the legislatures, all in the name of Montesquieu's principle of the separation of powers.[29] Yet if the use of separation of powers had been confined to this experience in 1776, it is difficult to see how the doctrine would have acquired the important place it eventually did in American constitutionalism. It was in fact only in the years after 1776, when the problems of politics seemed new and different from what had been expected, that the idea of separation of powers assumed major significance. Only in these years was the separation as stated in the early constitutions—"that the legislative, executive, and judiciary departments, ought to be forever separate and distinct from each other"—made truly reciprocal by those seeking new justifications for strengthening the magisterial parts of the government at the expense of the legislature. Seizing upon this relatively minor eighteenth-century maxim, the constitutional reformers in the years after 1776 exploited it with a sweeping intensity and eventually magnified it into the dominant principle of the American political system.

Almost immediately upon the adoption of the Pennsylvania Constitution of 1776, critics and reformers saw that the principle of separation of powers mentioned in the Constitution could be used interchangeably against any part of the new government, whatever its presumed representativeness of the people. The new Constitution, declared a meeting of the citizens of Philadelphia

28. Jefferson, *Notes on Virginia*, ed. Peden, 121; Portsmouth *N.-H. Gazette*, Feb. 22, 1783.
29. See above, Chap. IV, Sec. 4.

on October 21–22, 1776, had violated the advice of the Continental Congress in their address to the inhabitants of Canada, and "the sentiments of the most distinguished writers on the subject of government," including Montesquieu and Addison. By making the judiciary dependent on the legislature for their salaries and behavior, by permitting the legislature to elect the president and vice-president of the Executive Council, and by providing for only a single legislative body, the Constitution of 1776 had failed to achieve what the Continental Congress had declared to be the only effective mode ever invented to promote freedom—having the several powers of government "*separated* and *distributed* into *different* hands, for *checks one upon another.*" The Constitution as framed had "no '*distribution* of power into *different* hands, that *one may check another.*' On the contrary, the *executive* and *judicial* powers are made unduly dependent on a *single legislative* body, the Assembly: So that in truth the *legislative, executive* and *judicial* powers may be said to be *united* in *one* body, the Assembly." Indeed, the fact that the Pennsylvania legislature was only one body made this unity of power particularly dangerous. Without being fully aware of the significance of what they were doing, the opponents of the new Constitution mingled Addison's defense of mixed government with Montesquieu's reference to separation of powers as the most authoritative indictment of the unicameralism of the Pennsylvania legislature they could find. Since the Assembly was no less to be feared than the English ministry had been, power seemed to have lost all connection with its function or social constituency.[30]

These confused arguments and criticisms of the Pennsylvania Constitution, thrown up in the passion of the moment in 1776, were soon expanded and reiterated, so much so that within a few years the separation and distribution of power had become the major justification for all the constitutional reforms the Republicans proposed. "The most celebrated writers upon government agree," it was repeatedly argued, "that the *legislative, executive* and *judicial* powers should be so separated, as not to be dependent one upon another." Only two branches in the legislature, "who might mutually restrain and inform each other," a strong chief magistrate appointing all executive officials, and an independent judiciary could form a "well-constituted government, consisting of *legislative, executive* and *judicial* powers duly disposed," a

30. Phila. *Pa. Gazette*, Oct. 23, 1776.

government of laws where "the legislative, executive and judicial departments may, uninterrupted by one another, exercise their several powers." By the 1780's separation of powers had emerged as such an imposing doctrine that both parties, Constitutionalists as well as Republicans, sought to use it against each other.[31]

Wherever in the years after 1776 there was concern with the effects of legislative sovereignty and the unanticipated excesses of the Revolutionary constitutions, men invoked the principle of the separation of powers in order to unscramble what seemed to be a dangerous blurring of the three major functions of government. "If the three powers are united," declared the 1778 report of the Essex County Convention, "the government will be absolute, *whether these powers are in the hands of one or a large number.*" "One great design of the proposed form," argued a defender of the new New Hampshire Constitution in 1783, "is to render the three essential powers of government independent of each other, without which liberty cannot exist." "The Union of powers" in the Virginia Constitution, said Madison in 1784, was, as Montesquieu had written, nothing less than "tyranny." The absorption of "all the powers of government, legislative, executive, and judiciary," by the legislature, wrote Jefferson in his *Notes on the State of Virginia*, was one of the capital defects of the Virginia Constitution. The declaration of separation in the 1776 Constitution had been an ineffective barrier between the departments. "The judiciary and executive members were left dependent on the legislature, for their subsistence in office, and some of them for their continuance in it. If therefore the legislature assumes executive and judiciary powers, no opposition is likely to be made; nor, if made, can it be effectual; because in that case they may put their proceedings into the form of an act of assembly, which will render them obligatory on the other branches. They have accordingly, in many instances, decided rights which should have been left to judiciary controversy: and the direction of the executive, during the whole time of their session, is becoming habitual and familiar." Unintended as it may have been, said Jefferson, this concentration of the three powers "in the same hands is precisely the definition of despotic government." It was no comfort that these powers would be exercised by a plurality of hands instead of a single hand. "173 despots would surely be as

31. Phila. *Pa. Journal*, July 7, June 19, 1784; *Calling the Conventions of 1776 and 1790*, 117.

oppressive as one." Nor did it matter that the assemblies were chosen by the people. "An *elective despotism* was not the government we fought for."[32]

Nearly all of the proposals for constitutional change being put forward in these years could be explained as a means of separating these three functions of government. "That the three essential powers of government ought ever to be kept totally independent of each other" became the one standard by which all constitutions could be measured. Judges who relied on the legislature for appointment and salary were "liable to be tossed about by every veering gale of politicks" and could hardly possess "dignity and independence." Legislatures must now be prevented from doing what they had done for over a century, exercising judicial functions, or else, as the *Essex Result* declared, "the maker of law will also interpret it." Only election of the governor by "the people at large," it was increasingly claimed, could render the executive authority properly independent of the legislature. Appointment of military and magisterial officials must be taken away from the legislature and put back in the hands of the governors in the name of separation of powers. "The power of the Legislature to appoint any other than their own officers," said Madison, "departs too far from the Theory which requires a separation of the great Departments of Government."[33]

Even the proposal for a limited veto by the governor was being described as a way of maintaining the necessary separation of powers, as "a check upon the legislature" to prevent it from encroaching upon the executive "and stripping it of all it's rights." The governors were now to be granted a share in the lawmaking not because, as in England, the magistracy was a social entity which must consent and thus bind itself to all laws, but rather because, as the Massachusetts Convention of 1780 explained, "a due balance may be preserved in the three capital powers of Government." Since two-thirds of the legislature could override the governor's negative, it was not an absolute but a suspensive veto, which, as some noted, was "exceedingly different" and an indication of its new significance. The governor was not so much

32. *Essex Result*, Parsons, *Memoir*, 373; Portsmouth *N.-H. Gazette*, Mar. 8, 1783; Madison, Notes of Speech, June 1784, Hunt, ed., *Writings of Madison*, II, 54; Jefferson, *Notes on Virginia*, ed. Peden, 120.

33. Address of the N. H. Convention (1781), Bouton *et al.*, eds., *State Papers of N. H.*, IX, 846–47; Phila. *Pa. Gazette*, Mar. 24, 1779; *Essex Result*, Parsons, *Memoir*, 373, 382; Madison's Observations, Boyd, ed., *Jefferson Papers*, VI, 311.

assenting to legislation as checking it. "It is an appeal to the people who are and forever ought to be the dernier resort."[34]

This new interpretation of the governor's voice in legislation, together with the explanation of bicameralism as simply a division of mistrusted legislative power, was tending to blur the once distinct theory of balanced government among social orders with the doctrine of separation of governmental departments. The "proper Balance in the three Capital powers of Government" that men now spoke of was not always that of monarchical, aristocratic, and democratic elements of a mixed polity, but often that of the executive, legislative, and judicial functions.[35] The assumption behind this remarkable elaboration and diffusion of the idea of separation of powers was that all governmental power, whether in the hands of governors, judges, senators, or representatives, was essentially indistinguishable; that is, power in the hands of the people's "immediate representatives" in the lower houses of the legislatures was basically no different, no less dangerous, than power in the hands of the governors, senators, and judges. Only the great changes taking place in these years in the Americans' understanding of representation and the people's relationship to the government—all culminations of a century and a half of experience in the New World brought to a head by the anomalies inherent in the constitution-making experiments and summed up in the new meaning given to the idea of the sovereignty of the people—made this assumption possible. By the 1780's many had come to believe that the principle of separation of powers was "the basis of all free governments," the most important attribute of the kinds of governments they had fought for— one, in Jefferson's words, "in which the powers of government should be so divided and balanced among several bodies of magistracy, as that no one could transcend their legal limits, without being effectually checked and restrained by the others."[36]

4. The Enhancement of the Judiciary

The department of government which benefited most from

34. *Essex Result,* Parsons, *Memoir,* 397; Address of the Mass. Convention (1780), Handlin, eds., *Popular Sources,* 437; Phila. *Pa. Gazette,* Feb. 11, 1784; Portsmouth *N.-H. Gazette,* Mar. 15, 1783.
35. Brennan, *Plural Office-Holding,* 159.
36. Portsmouth *N.-H. Gazette,* Mar. 15, 1783; Jefferson, *Notes on Virginia,* ed. Peden, 120.

this new, enlarged definition of separation of powers was the judiciary. At the time of Independence, with the constitution-makers absorbed in the problems of curtailing gubernatorial authority and establishing legislative supremacy the judiciary had been virtually ignored or considered to be but an adjunct of feared magisterial power. Only the experience of the following years gave the judicial department the position of respect and independence as one of "the three capital powers of Government" that is so characteristic of later American constitutionalism. Once the reaction to legislative supremacy had set in, once legislative interference in judicial matters had intensified as never before in the eighteenth century, a new appreciation of the role of the judiciary in American politics could begin to emerge. "When the assembly leave the great business of the state, and take up private business, or interfere in disputes between contending parties," men now increasingly argued, "they are very liable to fall into mistakes, make wrong decisions, and so lose that respect which is due to them, as the Legislature of the State." The evils of this legislative meddling were "heightened when the society is divided among themselves; —one party praying the assembly for one thing, and the opposite party for another thing. . . . In such circumstances, the assembly ought not to interfere by any exertion of legislative power, but leave the contending parties to apply to the proper tribunals for a decision of their differences." Out of just this kind of experience a growing recourse to judicial settlement was bred and nurtured. By 1787 Hamilton was arguing in the New York Assembly that the terms of the New York Constitution prohibited anyone from being deprived of his rights but by due process of law—terms, he said, which were applicable only to the proceedings of courts of justice; "they can never be referred to an act of the legislature." With this kind of fear of legislative power it is not surprising that some had even come to believe that the very "existence" of America's elective governments depended on the judiciary. "That is the only body of men who will have an effective check upon a numerous Assembly."[37]

By the 1780's the judiciary in several states, New Jersey, Virginia, New York, Rhode Island, and North Carolina, was gingerly and often ambiguously moving in isolated but important cases

37. Address of Mass. Convention (1780), Handlin, eds., *Popular Sources*, 437; Phila. *Pa. Packet*, Sept. 2, 1786; Hamilton, Debates in the N. Y. Assembly, Feb. 6, 1787, Syrett and Cooke, eds., *Hamilton Papers*, IV, 35; William Plumer to William Coleman, May 31, 1786, in Lynn W. Turner, *William Plumer of New Hampshire, 1759–1850* (Chapel Hill, 1962), 34–35.

to impose restraints on what the legislatures were enacting as law, attempting in effect to say to the legislature, as George Wythe of Virginia did in 1782, "Here is the limit of your authority; and, hither, shall you go, but no further." Yet tentative and cautious as they were, such attempts by the judiciary "to declare the nullity of a law passed in its forms by the legislative power, without exercising the power of that branch," were not easily justified, for they raised, in the words of Judge Edmund Pendleton, "a deep, important, and . . . a tremendous question, the decision of which might involve consequences to which gentlemen may not have extended their ideas." Judicial review was in truth a question, said James Monroe, "calculated to create heats and animosities that will produce harm." To many, desirous as they may have been to find some way of checking encroaching legislatures, the judiciary's pronouncing of a law enacted by the legislature, particularly a law enacted over a governor's veto by a two-thirds majority, as unconstitutional and invalid seemed inconsistent with free popular government. To vest the judges with the "authority to declare a law void" ran too directly counter to the Blackstonian theory of legislative sovereignty and to the Americans' intense fear of judicial discretion. As late as 1787 many like John Dickinson were convinced that "no such power ought to exist." Yet Dickinson, like others concerned with legislative usurpations in the 1780's, "was at the same time at a loss what expedient to substitute."[38]

Some experimented with proposals for councils of revision, in effect giving the executive and judiciary together a limited but not final veto over those "unwise and unjust measures" of the legislatures "which constituted so great a portion of our calamities."[39] Others in the growing enthusiasm for separation of powers contended that some sort of judicial voice in legislation was

38. *Commonwealth of Va.* v. *Caton and others* (Nov. 1782), Peter Call, ed., *Reports of Cases Argued and Decided in the Court of Appeals of Virginia* (Richmond, 1833), IV, 8, 17–18; James Monroe to James Madison, Nov. 22, 1788, Stanislaus M. Hamilton, ed., *The Writings of James Monroe* . . . (N. Y., 1898–1903), I, 196; Farrand, ed., *Records of the Federal Convention*, II, 298–99. On judicial review in the 1780's see Charles G. Haines, *The American Doctrine of Judicial Supremacy* (Publications of the University of California at Los Angeles in Social Science, 1 ([Berkeley, 1932]), 88–121; and Crosskey, *Politics and the Constitution*, II, 938–75. For an extensive bibliography on the subject of judicial review see Charles A. Beard, *The Supreme Court and the Constitution*, intro. and bibliog. by Alan F. Westin (Englewood Cliffs, N. J., 1962, first published 1912), 133–46.

39. Madison's Observations, Boyd, ed., *Jefferson Papers*, VI, 315; Farrand, ed., *Records of the Federal Convention*, II, 73–74.

necessary to guarantee the judges' independence and integrity.[40]
Yet all of these arguments in the eighties for enhanced judicial
authority and discretion would have made little headway if it had
not been for the fundamental changes in American attitudes toward politics and law taking place in these years. The growing mistrust of the legislative assemblies and the new ideas rising
out of the conception of the sovereignty of the people were weakening legislative enactment as the basis for law. The legislatures
seemed to many to be simply another kind of magistracy, pro-
mulgating decrees to which the collective people, standing outside the entire government, had never really given their full and
unqualified assent. Thus all the acts of the legislature, it could now
be argued, were still "liable to examination and scrutiny by the
people, that is, by the Supreme Judiciary, their servants for this
purpose; and those that militate with the fundamental laws, or
impugn the principles of the constitution, are to be judicially set
aside as void, and of no effect."[41]

With the questioning of legislative enactment as the foundation
of law, other criteria were more easily emphasized. It seemed increasingly clear "that sound policy and strict justice are inseparably connected; and that nothing ever was *politically right*,
that was *morally wrong*." As Trenchard and Gordon had written,
the essence of law, of right and wrong, did "not depend upon
words and clauses, inserted in a code or statute book, much less
upon the conclusions and explications of lawyers; but upon reason
and the nature of things, antecedent to all laws." The result was
a growing discussion in pamphlets and press of the morality and
equity that presumably made law what it was. The "imaginary
omnipotence" of the legislatures, "that whatever is ordained must
be law, without any exception of right or wrong," wrote a North
Carolinian in 1787, "must be restrained within the bounds of
reason, justice, and *natural equity*." "WILL and LAW" were not
synonymous in free governments. "Any acts therefore which are
contrary to nature, justice, morality, benevolence, are contrary
to reason," and, "notwithstanding the authority of Kings, Lords
and Commons, or to speak more in place, of the Senate and
House of Commons," were "null, and void, being mere corrup-

40. See Andrew C. McLaughlin, *The Courts, the Constitution and Parties:
Studies in Constitutional History and Politics* (Chicago, 1912), 38–39; Edward
S. Corwin, "The Establishment of Judicial Review," *Michigan Law Review,* 9
(1910), 118.

41. *Providence Gazette,* May 12, 1787.

tions, and not laws."[42] Equity jurisdiction, once so much feared, now seemed increasingly necessary "to soften the rigour of Written Law, and to act upon such parts of natural Law, as have not been rendered Sufficiently clear and plain in their Statutes." Under the deluge of litigation in the eighties state courts were more and more resorting to referees and equitable judgments, particularly in debt cases. A Pennsylvania judge now argued that since the state lacked chancery courts "the judges here, are, therefore to determine causes according to equity, as well as positive law" in order "to prevent a failure of justice." In fact, said another Pennsylvanian in 1787, in "these more enlightened days" law should be nothing but justice, since "there cannot be anything more absurd than a distinction between *law* and *equity*." In this atmosphere law seemed to be rapidly reverting to what it had been for Coke in the seventeenth century—something that had to be in accord with "common right and natural equity" in order to have judicial force.[43] In no court decision of the 1780's was this Cokean conception more clearly expressed than in the famous case of *Rutgers v. Waddington*.[44]

The case, tried in the Mayor's Court of New York City in 1784, involved a suit brought by Elizabeth Rutgers under a recent New York statute against Joseph Waddington, agent for British merchants who had occupied and used Rutgers's abandoned property during the British occupation of New York. Although the law of nations, considered part of the common law adopted by the 1777 New York Constitution, allowed the use of abandoned

42. Phila. *Pa. Journal*, Mar. 28, 1781; *Providence Gazette*, July 22, 1786; *The Independent Citizen* (n.p., 1787), in Boyd, ed., *Eighteenth Century Tracts*, 471, 475, 472, 475.

43. Return of Braintree, June 5, 1780, Handlin, eds., *Popular Sources*, 766; "Law Report in the Supreme Court of Pennsylvania," *American Museum*, 2 (1787), 471–73; Charleston *S.-C. Gazette and General Advertiser*, Jan. 3–6, 1784; Bancroft, *Formation of the Constitution*, I, 229, 233; Phila. *Pa. Packet*, Oct. 23, 1787, in McMaster and Stone, eds., *Pennsylvania and the Federal Constitution*, 153. The morality of law perhaps has more to do with the development of judicial review than the fundamentality of law; "for," as J. W. Gough has pointed out, "while (largely as a result of modern American practice) fundamental law has come to be associated with judicial review, the two are not essentially connected, as is evident from the part played by the idea of fundamental law at its hey-day in seventeenth-century England." Gough, *Fundamental Law*, 206. See also Corwin, "Progress of Political Theory," *Amer. Hist. Rev.*, 30 (1924–25), 522. For the sources of this American emphasis on the morality of law see above, Chap. VII, Sec. 5.

44. The best discussion of the case with many of the relevant documents is in Goebel, ed., *Hamilton's Law Practice*, I, 282–543.

property in wartime when authorized by the local military commander, the New York Trespass Act of 1783 had specifically refused any justification by military authorization for such appropriations of property. Thus the new state law was put in direct conflict with the law of nations and the Treaty of Peace, which had mutually renounced all claims to damages resulting from the war. The case therefore seemed to possess great constitutional and political significance, setting legislative law against the common law or law of nations, and the authority of the New York legislature against the authority of Congress. Underlying all was the basic question whether the court had the right at all to refer to any other source of law in order to control the authority of the legislature which was supposedly the supreme lawgiving body of the state.

The opinion of the court, which was apparently written mainly by Chief Judge James Duane, carefully avoided any direct confrontation between the court and the legislature, or between legislative law and any other law. "The supremacy of the Legislature," said Duane, "need not be called into question; if they think fit *positively* to enact a law, there is no power which can controul them. When the main object of such a law is clearly expressed, and the intention manifest, the Judges are not at liberty, altho' it appears to them to be *unreasonable*, to reject it: for this were to set the *judicial* above the legislative, which would be subversive of all government." But, continued Duane, in words that Coke would have endorsed, when the legislature enacted a general statute whose effect in a particular case is "*unreasonable*," then "the Judges are in decency to conclude, that the consequences were not foreseen by the Legislature; and therefore they are at liberty to expound the statute by *equity*, and only *quoad hoc* to disregard it. When the judicial make these distinctions, they do not controul the Legislature; they endeavour to give their *intention* it's proper effect."[45] The Court thus decided that since the Trespass Act of 1783 had not expressly repealed the law of nations, the common law or law of nations could be used to construe the statute in this specific case so as to arrive at an equitable result, largely in favor of Waddington. Duane had set for the court precisely that kind of interpretative role that James Otis had so

45. *Arguments and Judgment of the Mayor's Court of the City of New York, in a Cause between Elizabeth Rutgers and Joshua Waddington* (N. Y., 1784), in Goebel, ed., *Hamilton's Law Practice*, I, 415.

vehemently contended for in the 1760's—a role that depended mainly on an equation of law with justice.

Like Otis's writings in the 1760's, Duane's opinion in 1784 was considered by many to be a flagrant violation of the theory of legislative sovereignty and was immediately attacked as a judicial assumption of the power "to set aside an Act of the State," an assumption that marked a "revolution in the spirit and genius of our Government." "The design of Courts of Justice, in our Government. from the very nature of their institution, is to *declare* laws, not to *alter* them." If the judges "are to be invested with a power to overrule a plain law, though expressed in *general words*, as all general laws are and must be: when they may judge the law unreasonable, because not consonant to the Law of Nations or to the opinion of ancient or modern civilians and philosophers, for whom they may have a greater veneration than for the solid statutes and supreme Legislative power of the State: we say," declared opponents of the decision, "if they are to assume and exercise such a power, the probable consequence of their independence will be the most deplorable and wretched dependency of the People." Not only would the law no longer be "absolute," but the lawmaking power would be transferred to the judges, "who are independent of the People."[46] Yet because of what was happening to the Americans' understanding of politics and the people's relationship to the legislative authority, Duane's opinion seemed much more comprehensible than similar views expressed by Otis had two decades earlier.

As strong as the conviction was becoming that law must be inherently reasonable and just in order to be law, it could not by itself sustain judicial review of legislation, as was revealed in Rhode Island in 1786–87 by the arguments of James Varnum, attorney for the defense, in the case of *Trevett* v. *Weeden*. In a published version of his brief, Varnum argued that the act enforcing recent paper money bills under which Weeden was indicted had provided for no jury trial or right of appeal and was therefore "unconstitutional and void." In developing his argument Varnum moved in several directions at once. On one hand, with quotations from Bacon and Coke he contended, as Otis and Duane had done, that acts contrary to common right and reason were not

46. *New York Packet and American Advertiser*, Nov. 4, 1784, in Henry B. Dawson, *The Case of Elizabeth Rutgers versus Joshua Waddington . . . with an Historical Introduction* (Morrisania, N. Y., 1866), xxix, xl, xxxiii, xxxvi.

law and "that the power of construing a statute is in the Judges; for they have authority over all laws, more especially over statutes, to mold them according to reason and convenience to the best and truest use." On the other hand, Varnum also resorted to a more modern distinction between the fundamental law of the constitution and ordinary statutory law, arguing that the legislature could never make a law contrary to the principles of the constitution, not simply because such a law was inherently unjust but because the principles of the constitution "were ordained by the people anterior to and created the powers of the General Assembly." Indeed, said Varnum, in an argument that nicely expressed the clarifying American conception of politics, "the powers of legislation, in every possible instance, are derived from the people at large, are altogether fiduciary, and subordinate to the association by which they are formed." When the people entered into civil society, the charter or constitution being "conclusive evidence of the compact of the people," they surrendered some of their natural rights to the government. "The aggregate of this surrender forms the power of government," including the power to make laws. "Consequently the Legislature cannot intermeddle with the retained rights of the people," even though the legislature presumably represented the people. It was the duty of the judiciary, said Varnum, to measure the laws of the legislature against the constitution and the rights of the people. Such fundamental laws were created and hence could be changed only by the people-at-large, not by the legislatures, which were no longer considered uniquely representative of the people. The judges were in a sense as much agents of the people as the legislators; neither could overleap the bounds of their appointment. The judiciary's special task was to "reject all acts of the Legislature that are contrary to the trust reposed in them by the people."[47]

Because Rhode Island, as opponents of Varnum's position contended, lacked a written constitution comparable to those of other states, the argument that Varnum presented was left to be more fully developed elsewhere, particularly by James Iredell of North Carolina. Iredell, later a justice of the United States Supreme Court and recently attorney for the plaintiff in the 1787 case of *Bayard* v. *Singleton*, in which the North Carolina Supreme Court

47. James M. Varnum, *The Case, Trevett against Weeden . . . Tried before the Honorable Superior Court in the County of Newport, September Term, 1786 . . .* (Providence, 1787), 33, 29, 21, 22, 21, 27, 29.

declared an act of the legislature void, saw with remarkable clarity the direction American constitutionalism was taking. That it was difficult for many in the 1780's to accept the newly emerging conception of the judiciary's role in government, even when they were sympathetic with efforts to restrain rampaging legislatures, is vividly revealed in an exchange of correspondence between Richard Spraight and Iredell over the Bayard decision. As much as Spraight agreed with Iredell that the legislative act in question was unjust and unconstitutional, he could not understand how the judiciary could presume to declare it void. Such judicial usurpation, said Spraight, echoing the conventional thinking of mid-century Englishmen, was "absurd" and "operated as an absolute negative on the proceedings of the Legislature, which no judiciary ought ever to possess." Instead of being governed by their representatives in the general assembly, the people would be subject to the will of three individuals in the court, "who united in their own persons the legislative and judiciary powers"— a despotism more insufferable than that of the Roman decemvirate or of any monarchy in Europe. It might be wise to restrict the legislative authority, conceded Spraight, but in a free government this could only be done by the people themselves through the annual election of the legislators.

But declaring unconstitutional laws void was not judicial usurpation, answered Iredell. The constitution had become something unique in America. It was not only "a fundamental law" but it was as well a "law in writing" created specially by the people, a law "limiting the powers of the Legislature, and with which every exercise of those powers, must necessarily, be compared." The judges were not, as was sometimes thought, "appointed arbiters" of the Constitution "to determine as it were upon any application, whether the Assembly have or have not violated the Constitution." Rather they were simply judicial officials fulfilling their duty of applying the proper law. When faced with a decision between "the *fundamental unrepealable* law" made by the people and an act inconsistent with the Constitution, "founded on an authority not given by the people, and to which, therefore, the people owe no obedience," they must simply determine which law was superior. The exercise of this power, said Iredell, was "unavoidable," for the Constitution was not "a mere imaginary thing, about which ten thousand different opinions may be formed, but a written document to which all may have recourse, and to which, therefore, the judges cannot witfully blind themselves."[48]

The Americans, as Iredell pointed out, had rejected the conventional British "theory *of the necessity of the legislature being absolute in all cases*" and had been willing to run the risk of conducting their government on other principles, principles best described by the doctrine of separation of powers.[49] Separation of powers, wrote Alexander Hamilton in *The Federalist,* Number 78, the most concise and frank defense of judicial review in the 1780's, required that the weakest department in what had become the tripartite division of American government be given the power to defend its independence against the encroachments of other departments. But since the American governments were limited, the judiciary must also defend the constitution against violations by the other departments, particularly the legislature. Without this power of judicial review of legislation, "all the reservations of particular rights or privileges" by the people and the several departments of government "would amount to nothing." What made such a judicial power comprehensible, Hamilton acutely realized, was the changed relation that had taken place between the people and their supposed representatives in the legislature. The representatives of the people were not really the people, but only the servants of the people with a limited delegated authority to act on behalf of the people. Americans, said Hamilton, had no intention of enabling "the representatives of the people to substitute their *will* to that of their constituents." It was in fact "far more rational to suppose, that the courts were designed to be an intermediate body between the people and the legislature, in order, among other things, to keep the latter within the limits assigned to their authority." The decisive assumption in the development of this judicial agency and authority was the real and ultimate sovereignty of the people. Judicial review did not "by any means suppose a superiority of the judicial to the legislative power. It only supposes that the power of the people is superior to both; and that where the will of the legislature declared in its statutes, stands in opposition to that of the people, declared in the constitution, the judges . . . ought to regulate their decisions by the fundamental laws, rather than by those which are not fundamental." With these kinds of arguments constitu-

48. Richard Spraight to James Iredell, Aug. 12, 1787, Iredell to Spraight, Aug. 26, 1787, and "To the Public," Aug. 17, 1786, all in McRee, *Life of Iredell,* II, 169–70, 172–76, 148.
49. "To the Public," Aug. 17, 1786, *ibid.,* 146.

tional reformers in the 1780's were preparing the way for a more radical reconstruction of their political system than anyone had conceived possible a few years earlier.[50]

5. THE ABANDONMENT OF THE STATES

As vigorously as the constitutional reforms of the states were urged and adopted in the 1780's, they never seemed sufficient. Despite the remedies embodied in the New York, Massachusetts, and New Hampshire constitutions and the probability of reform in the other states, the disillusionment with American politics in the 1780's only grew more intense. Although some could admit that "many of the state constitutions we have chosen, are truly excellent," possessing in theory the necessary powers to act vigorously, it seemed increasingly evident that such powers were not being implemented. In the politics of the various states "it often happens, that those who are appointed to manage the affairs of the State, are extremely averse to exercise those powers with which they are invested. . . . While they feel themselves so frequently dependent on the breath of the people for a continuance in their elevated stations, many will . . . court the favour of the multitude and basely violate the most solemn obligations rather than hazard their own popularity." Only by shifting the arena of reform to the federal level, it seemed, could the evils of American politics be finally remedied. "It is very extraordinary . . . ," some were saying as early as 1783, "that so much pains have been taken to form and organize the constitutions of the several individual governments, and so little has been taken, in that which respects the whole nation of America, and which is superiorly important, that all our greatness, and our greatest concerns rest upon it." While some like Charles Carroll of Maryland were still convinced as late as 1787 that "a Reform of our State Constitutions or Governments should accompany, if not precede the reformations of the federal Government," most reformers by that date were looking to some sort of modification of the structure of the central government as the best, and perhaps the only, answer to America's problems.[51]

50. *The Federalist*, No. 78. See James Wilson, "Lectures on Law," Wilson, ed., *Works of Wilson*, I. 455–62.

51. Hartford *Conn. Courant*, Nov. 19, 1787; Boston *Independent Chronicle*, Sept. 7, 1786; Phila. *Pa. Journal*, July 2, 1783; Philip A. Crowl, ed., "Charles Carroll's Plan of Government," *Amer. Hist. Rev.*, 46 (1941), 592.

The central government had never been entirely ignored. Right from the beginning of the war a continental-minded minority centered in the middle Atlantic states had sought to strengthen the authority of the Confederation at the expense of the states. By the early eighties the nationalist program of men like Robert Morris and Alexander Hamilton had gathered a substantial amount of support from various groups. The war was dragging on, and the value of the paper money issued to finance it was sinking fast. The attempts of the states to prevent the depreciation of currency by legal-tender laws, price-fixing, and anti-monopoly legislation only aggravated discontent among business interests. Both the army and the public creditors of the Confederation were clamoring for help. It seemed for a moment in 1780–81 that the weakness of the central government was actually threatening the victory against Britain. Yet despite such pressure even the nationalists' proposals for a limited federal impost and a restricted congressional commercial power could not overcome the Revolution's commitment to the separate sovereignty of the states. And with the end of the war and the reassertion of state authority, expressed most explicitly in the states' absorption of the congressional debt, the nationalist program rapidly dissipated. The reputation of Robert Morris, as the superintendent of finance, became clouded with suspicion. The army grumbled but disbanded, and most of the nationalist delegates in Congress completed their three-year terms and retired. By the middle eighties Congress had virtually collapsed. The danger of the Union's falling to pieces, however great, meant little in the face of most Americans' deeply rooted mistrust of central power. As urgent as the need for some sort of revision of the Articles had become by 1785, many creditors and merchants like Theodore Sedgwick, Stephen Higginson, and the entire Massachusetts delegation in Congress still hesitated to subject the Confederation to "a *chance of alteration*" for fear of giving "birth to new hopes of an aristocratical faction which every community possesses." In the opinion of the Massachusetts delegates there were too many Americans with "artfully laid, and vigorously pursued" plans afoot which aimed at transforming "our republican Governments into balefull Aristocracies."[52]

---

52. Theodore Sedgwick to Caleb Davis, Jan. 31, 1786, quoted in Welch, *Sedgwick*, 38; Elbridge Gerry, Samuel Holton and Rufus King to Gov. Bowdoin, Sept. 3, 1785, Charles R. King, *The Life and Correspondence of Rufus King* (N. Y., 1894–1900), I, 63. The nationalists' program of the early eighties is most fully analyzed in Ferguson, *Power of the Purse*, Chaps. VI–VII.

In the end it was not pressure from above, from the manifest debility of the Confederation, that provided the main impulse for the Federalist movement of 1787; it was rather pressure from below, from the problems of politics within the separate states themselves, that eventually made constitutional reform of the central government possible.

By early 1787 with the experience of Shays's rebellion and its aftermath Sedgwick, Higginson, and other New England men like them had altered their thinking and reinterpreted their fears. Not only the fact of the rebellion itself but the eventual victory of the rebels at the polls brought the contradictions of American politics to a head, dramatically clarifying what was taking place in nearly all the states. Urging the people to obey the laws of their state governments as a cure for the anarchical excesses of the period seemed to be backfiring, resulting in evils even worse than licentiousness. If the elected representatives in the state legislatures were likely, as they increasingly seemed to be, "to establish iniquity by Law," then obedience to these unjust laws was no solution to the evils of the day. Orators and writers, struggling with the consequences, admitted, on the one hand, that legislators in the enactment of "private views" could be "tyrannical" and warned that "statutes contradictory and inconsistent are to be expected, and even such as might invert the order of things, and substitute vice, in the room of virtue." Yet, on the other hand, they realized at the same time that the need for authority and "our social obligations require us to be subject to laws which we may think very inconvenient." Although the legislatures were daily committing acts of "injustice" and were violating "the most simple ties of common honesty," still "while we pretend to be governed by our Representatives in General Court assembled, let not each man foolishly assume the reins of government, and attempt to enforce his sentiments against the majority." State governments, however well structured, no longer seemed capable of creating virtuous laws and citizens. Had not the Massachusetts Constitution of 1780, asked Thomas Dawes in a Fourth of July oration of 1787, been acclaimed as the model of political perfection? "But if our constitution is the perfect law of liberty, whence those mighty animosities which have so lately distracted the bosom of peace, and stained the first pages of our history with civil blood?" Actually, said Dawes, in an opinion that others had reached by this time, the structure of the Massachusetts Constitution was not at fault. "Our sufferings have arisen from a *deeper fountain* than the deficiency of a single constitution." Even if Massachusetts had possessed a more perfect and more exalted government, its citizens, declared Dawes, would continue to experience evils, "should our *National Independence* remain deprived of its proper *federal authority.*" "In vain," said Stephen Higginson in 1787, "must be all our exertions to brace up our own Government without we have a better federal System than the present."⁵³

By 1786–87 the reconstruction of the central government had become the focal point of most of the reform sentiment that had earlier been concentrated on the states. The continental-minded of the early eighties now found their efforts to invigorate the national government reinforced by the support of hitherto suspicious state-minded men. What had formerly been considered advisable for the functioning of the Confederation was fast becoming essential for the future of republicanism itself. It was no longer simply a matter of cementing the union or of satisfying the demands of particular creditor, mercantile, or army interests. The ability of America to sustain any sort of republican government seemed to be the issue. As long as the revision of the Articles was based solely on the need to solve specific problems of finance, commerce, and foreign policy, its support was erratic and fearful. But once men grasped, as they increasingly did in the middle eighties, that reform of the national government was the best means of remedying the evils caused by the state governments, then the revision of the Articles of Confederation assumed an impetus and an importance that it had not had a few years earlier. The desire for reform of the states now came together with national reform opinion to create a new and powerful force. As Benjamin Rush told Richard Price in June of 1787, "the same enthusiasm *now* pervades all classes in favor of *government* that actuated us in favor of *liberty* in the years 1774 and 1775, with this difference, that we are more *united* in the former than we were in the latter pursuit."⁵⁴

53. Theodore Sedgwick to Gov. Bowdoin, Apr. 8, 1787, quoted in Welch, *Sedgwick*, 54; David Parsons, *A Sermon, Preached before His Excellency, John Hancock . . . May 28, 1788 . . .* (Boston, [1788]), 26–29; Boston *Independent Chronicle*, Jan. 11, 1787; Thomas Dawes, Jr., *An Oration, Delivered July 4, 1787 . . .* (Boston, 1787), 13–15; Higginson to Nathan Dane, June 16, 1787, Jameson, ed., "Letters of Higginson," Amer. Hist. Assoc. *Annual Report, 1896*, I, 759–60.
54. Rush to Price, June 2, 1787, Butterfield, ed., *Rush Letters*, I, 418–19.

The move for a stronger national government thus became something more than a response to the obvious weaknesses of the Articles of Confederation. It became as well an answer to the problems of the state governments. It was "the vile State governments," rather than simply the feebleness of the Confederation, that were the real "sources of pollution," preventing America from "being a nation." It was "the corruption and mutability of the Legislative Councils of the States," the "evils operating in the States," that actually led to the overhauling of the federal government in 1787. These vices coming out of the state governments, said Madison, "so frequent and so flagrant as to alarm the most stedfast friends of Republicanism, . . . contributed more to that uneasiness which produced the Convention, and prepared the public mind for a general reform, than those which accrued to our national character and interest from the inadequacy of the Confederation to its immediate objects." The federal Constitution became the culmination of a decade's efforts by Americans to readjust their constitutional structures to fit what Hamilton called "the commercial character of America" and what Jay called "manners and circumstances" that were "not strictly democratical."[55] The calling of the Philadelphia Convention in 1787 was the climax of the process of rethinking that had begun with the reformation of the state constitutions in the late seventies and early eighties, a final step "taken from the fullest conviction that there was not a better, perhaps no other, which could be adopted in this crisis of our public affairs." The federal Convention, Americans told themselves repeatedly, was to frame a constitution that would "decide forever the fate of republican government."[56]

55. Henry Knox to Rufus King, July 15, 1787, King, *Life of King*, I, 228; John Francis Mercer and Hamilton in Farrand, ed., *Records of the Federal Convention*, II, 288, I, 291; Madison to Jefferson, Oct. 24, 1787, Boyd, ed., *Jefferson Papers*, XII, 276; *The Federalist*, No. 11; Jay to Washington, Jan. 7, 1787, Johnston, ed., *Papers of Jay*, III, 227. See also R. H. Lee to Francis Lightfoot Lee, July 14, 1787, Ballagh, ed., *Letters of R. H. Lee*, II, 423–24; Phila. *Pa. Journal*, June 30, 1787; Farrand, ed., *Records of the Federal Convention*, I, 466–67, II, 47–48; Robert A. Rutland, *The Ordeal of the Constitution: The Antifederalists and the Ratification Struggle of 1787–1788* (Norman, Okla., 1966), 27, 51.

56. Boston *Independent Chronicle*, Sept. 20, 1787; Madison, quoted in Charles Warren, *The Making of the Constitution* (Cambridge, Mass., 1947), 82.

PART FIVE

The Federal Constitution

It will be considered, I believe, as a most extraordinary epoch in the history of mankind, that in a few years there should be so essential a change in the minds of men. 'Tis really astonishing that the same people, who have just emerged from a long and cruel war in defence of liberty, should now agree to fix an elective despotism upon themselves and their posterity.

—RICHARD HENRY LEE, 1788

CHAPTER XII

The Worthy against the Licentious

1. THE FEDERALIST REVOLUTION

Nearly everyone in 1787 conceded "the weakness of the Confederation." All "men of reflection," even "the most orthodox republicans," said Madison, were alarmed by "the existing embarrassments and mortal diseases of the Confederacy." "It is on all hands acknowledged," said Thomas Tredwell, a New York opponent of the Constitution, "that the federal government is not adequate to the purpose of the Union." It had become, said Samuel Bryan, "the universal wish of America to grant further powers" to Congress, "so as to make the federal government adequate to the ends of its institution." But what men like Madison had in mind for America "was not," as the Antifederalists soon perceived, "a mere revision and amendment of our first Confederation, but a compleat System for the future government of the United States." "All parties" had admitted "the propriety of some material change" in the federal government, but they had hardly expected what they got—a virtual revolution in American politics, promising a serious weakening, if not a destruction, of the power of the states.[1]

1. James Galloway (N.C.), in Elliot, ed., *Debates*, IV, 25; Madison to Edmund Pendleton, Feb. 24, 1787, to Jefferson, Mar. 18, 1787, to James Madison, Apr. 1, 1787, Hunt, ed., *Writings of Madison*, II, 318, 326, 335; Tredwell (N.Y.), in Elliot, ed., *Debates*, II, 358; [Samuel Bryan], "Letters of Centinel, No. III," Nov. 8, 1787, McMaster and Stone, eds., *Pennsylvania and the Federal Constitution*, 594; "Letters of John De Witt," Oct. 27, 1787, Cecelia M. Kenyon, ed., *The Antifederalists* (Indianapolis, 1966), 96; James Monroe to Thomas Jefferson, July 12, 1788, Hamilton, ed., *Writings of Monroe*, I, 186. On the willingness of

Given America's experience with central power, it is easy to see how the erection of a national government represented a political revolution as great as the revolution of a decade earlier, when the British monarchy had been overthrown and new state governments formed. Those earlier ventures, said George Mason during the meeting of the Philadelphia Convention, "were nothing compared to the great business now before us," mainly because Americans were now without the former enthusiasm for liberty "which inspired and supported the mind." This was indeed a more desperate revolution, bred from despair and from the sense of impending failure of the earlier revolution; for, as Madison put it, "men of reflection" were "much less sanguine as to the new than despondent as to the present System." "*We have, probably,*" wrote Washington with emphasis, "*had too good an opinion of human nature in forming our confederation.*" Only the profoundest disillusionment with the great hopes of the Revolution of 1776 could have led someone like Madison to make the extraordinary kinds of proposals he made to his Virginia correspondents in the spring of 1787—proposals that were soon embodied in the Virginia plan that formed the basis for the new federal Constitution.[2]

No one was better prepared for the Philadelphia Convention than Madison. Returning home from Congress in the winter of 1785–86, Madison at once began an intensive study of ancient and modern confederacies in search of an understanding of "the science of federal government" which Americans direly needed. Later embodied in *The Federalist*, Numbers 18, 19, and 20, Madison's studies pointed up the fundamental weaknesses of mere confederations composed of independent states, forming a nerveless whole that was threatened from without and torn by popular convulsions from within. All history, wrote Madison, unequivocally demonstrated that "a sovereignty over sovereigns, a government over governments, a legislation for communities, as contradistinguished from individuals," was "subversive of the order and

the Antifederalists to reform the Confederation see Main, *Antifederalists*, 113–14, and Linda G. De Pauw, *The Eleventh Pillar: New York State and the Federal Constitution* (Ithaca, N. Y., 1966), esp. 58–60, 69, 173, 176, 201, 264.
  2. George Mason to George Mason, Jr., June 1, 1787, Farrand, ed., *Records of the Federal Convention*, III, 32–33; Madison to Pendleton, Feb. 24, 1787, Hunt, ed., *Writings of Madison*, II, 318; Washington to Jay, Aug. 15, 1786, Johnston, ed., *Papers of Jay*, III, 208.

ends of civil polity." By 1787 Madison, like others, had become a thorough nationalist, intent on subordinating the states as far as possible to the sovereignty of the central government. Both trade conventions of the two previous years, at Mount Vernon and at Annapolis, were but devices to be used in the move to change the central government. Even the unanimity among Americans in 1786–87 in favor of some sort of reform of the Confederation, desirable as it once was, now became for the nationalists simply a means towards a much larger end; for it seemed evident that no mere tinkering with the Articles, no mere expedients, would suffice. In truth Madison's ideas of reform, as he himself realized, struck "so deeply at the old Confederation, and lead to such a systematic change, that they scarcely admit of the expedient." To Madison in 1787 it seemed to be "a fundamental point, that an individual independence of the States is utterly irreconcilable with the idea of an aggregate sovereignty." While "a consolidation of the States into one simple republic" was impractical and politically unattainable, still some "middle ground" might be found "which will at once support a due supremacy of the national authority, and leave in force the local authorities so far as they can be subordinately useful." There was no doubt in Madison's mind, as in the minds of many other reformers in 1787, that the new federal government should be "clearly paramount" to the state governments. Not only should the national government have "a positive and complete authority in all cases where uniform measures are necessary," as in finance, commerce, and foreign policy, but it should have "a negative, in all cases whatsoever, in the Legislative acts of the States, as the King of Great Britain heretofore had." This negative on all state legislation, said Madison, seemed "absolutely necessary," and "the least possible encroachment on the State jurisdictions" that should be established. No proposal better indicated the nature of Madison's anxieties about the eighties than this federal veto. Without it, the whole purpose of the constitutional revision of 1787 would be defeated. The states would continue to ignore or evade federal authority and the society would continue to be plagued by "the internal vicissitudes of State policy" where "interested majorities" trampled "on the rights of minorities and individuals." What was needed, said Madison, was "some disinterested and dispassionate umpire" that would control "disputes between different passions and interests in the State," but that at the same time "would itself be sufficiently restrained from the pursuit of interests adverse to those of the whole Society."[3]

Like the reformers of the state constitutions in the decade after 1776 the Federalists were filled with "an enlightened zeal for energy and efficiency of government" to set against "the turbulence and follies of democracy" as expressed by the lower houses of the state legislatures, "the democratic parts of our constitutions." If the proposed central government that Madison and other nationalists had in mind in the spring of 1787 were to play the impartial role of neutralizer of interested majorities within the states, something more than simple amendment of the Articles was required. No longer would the granting of "*any* further degree of power to Congress do the business." The people of America, as John Jay said, had to become "one nation in every respect," and their separate state legislatures had to stand in relation to the Confederacy "in the same light in which counties stand to the State, of which they are parts, viz., merely as districts to facilitate the purposes of domestic order and good government." Thus the new general government could not remain a confederation of independent republics but had to be in its own right "a stable and firm Government organized in the republican form," divided into three distinct departments and somehow superimposed on the state republics, "a government," declared Oliver Ellsworth, "capable of controlling the whole, and bringing its force to a point," in order to enable, in James Iredell's words, "justice, order and dignity" to take the place "of the present anarchical confusion prevailing almost everywhere."[4]

Such a government had to be founded "on different principles" and "have a different operation" from the Articles because its purpose was truly radical. The new national government was not simply a response to the domestic problems of credit, commerce,

3. Madison, "Of Ancient and Modern Confederacies," Hunt, ed., *Writings of Madison*, II, 369–90; *The Federalist*, No. 20; Madison to Edmund Randolph, Apr. 8, 1787, to Jefferson, Mar. 18, 1787, and to Washington, Apr. 16, 1787, Hunt, ed., *Writings of Madison*, II, 337–38, 326, 338, 346, 347.

4. *The Federalist*, No. 1; Randolph, in Farrand, ed., *Records of the Federal Convention*, I, 51, 26; Jay to Washington, Jan. 7, 1787, Jay to John Adams, May 4, 1786, Johnston, ed., *Papers of Jay*, III, 226, 195; Madison, in Farrand, ed., *Records of the Federal Convention*, I, 219; [Oliver Ellsworth], "A Landholder, No. III," Nov. 19, 1787, Ford, ed., *Essays on the Constitution*, 146–47; James Iredell, *Answers to Mr. Mason's Objections to the New Constitution* . . . (Newburn, N. C., 1788), in Paul L. Ford, ed., *Pamphlets on the Constitution of the United States* . . . (Brooklyn, 1888), 370.

and interstate rivalries, or to the foreign problems of a confederated republic in a hostile monarchical world. It was not, in short, meant merely to save the Union, for strengthening the Confederation along the lines of the New Jersey plan could have done that. The Federalists of the late eighties wanted and believed they needed much more than the nationalists of the early eighties had sought. Their focus was not so much on the politics of the Congress as it was on the politics of the states. To the Federalists the move for the new central government became the ultimate act of the entire Revolutionary era; it was both a progressive attempt to salvage the Revolution in the face of its imminent failure and a reactionary effort to restrain its excesses. Only a new continental republic that cut through the structure of the states to the people themselves and yet was not dependent on the character of that people could save America's experiment in republicanism. In some way or other this new republican government had to accommodate itself to the manners and habits of a people which experience in the past few years had demonstrated were incapable of supporting republican government. Believing with Washington that virtue had "in a great degree taken its departure from our land" and was not to be easily restored, the Federalists hoped to create an entirely new and original sort of republican government—a republic which did not require a virtuous people for its sustenance. If they could not, as they thought, really reform the character of American society, then they would somehow have to influence the operation of the society and moderate the effects of its viciousness. The supporters of the new federal Constitution thus aimed to succeed where the states, not the Confederation, had failed, in protecting, in John Dickinson's phrase, "the worthy against the licentious."[5]

2. THE SEPARATION OF SOCIAL AND POLITICAL AUTHORITY

How the Federalists expected a new central government to remedy the vices the individual states had been unable to remedy is the central question, the answer to which lies at the heart of their

5. Madison to Jefferson, Oct. 24, 1787, Boyd, ed., *Jefferson Papers*, XII, 274; Washington to Jay, May 18, 1786, Johnston, ed., *Papers of Jay*, III, 196; [John Dickinson], *The Letters of Fabius, in 1788, on the Federal Constitution . . .* (Wilmington, Del., 1797), in Ford, ed., *Pamphlets*, 188.

understanding of what was happening in the critical period. In the minds of the Federalists and of "men of reflection" generally, most of the evils of American society—the atmosphere of mistrust, the breakdown of authority, the increase of debt, the depravity of manners, and the decline of virtue—could be reduced to a fundamental problem of social disarrangement. Even the difficulties of the United States in foreign affairs and its weakness as a nation in the world, as Jay argued in *The Federalist*, Number 3, could be primarily explained by what the Revolution had done to America's political and social hierarchy. More than anything else the Federalists' obsession with disorder in American society and politics accounts for the revolutionary nature of the nationalist proposals offered by men like Madison in 1787 and for the resultant Federalist Constitution. Only an examination of the Federalists' social perspective, their fears and anxieties about the disarray in American society, can fully explain how they conceived of the Constitution as a political device designed to control the social forces the Revolution had released.

The most pronounced social effect of the Revolution was not harmony or stability but the sudden appearance of new men everywhere in politics and business. "When the pot boils, the scum will rise," James Otis had warned in 1776; but few Revolutionary leaders had realized just how much it would rise. By the end of the war men like Governor James Bowdoin of Massachusetts could "scarcely see any other than new faces," a change almost "as remarkable as the revolution itself." The emigration of thousands of Tories, the intensification of interest in politics, the enlargement of the legislatures and the increase in elections, the organization of new militia and political groups, the breakup of old mercantile combinations and trade circuits, the inflation and profiteering caused by the war—all offered new opportunities for hitherto unknown but ambitious persons to find new places for themselves. As John Adams noted, his own deep resentment of his supposed social superiors was being echoed throughout various levels of the society. For every brilliant provincial lawyer ready to challenge the supremacy of the imperial clique in the colonial metropolis, there were dozens of lesser men, not so brilliant but equally desirous of securing a local magistracy, a captaincy of the militia, some place, however small, of honor and distinction. With the elimination of Crown privilege and appointment men were prepared to take the republican emphasis on equality seriously. The result, as one Baltimore printer declared as early as 1777, was "Whiggism run mad." "When a man, who is only fit 'to patch a shoe,' attempts 'to patch the State,' fancies himself a *Solon* or *Lycurgus*, . . . he cannot fail to meet with contempt." But contempt was no longer enough to keep such men in their place.[6]

Everywhere "*Specious, interested designing* men," "men, respectable neither for their property, their virtue, nor their abilities," were taking a lead in public affairs that they had never quite had before, courting "the suffrages of the people by tantalizing them with improper indulgences." Thousands of the most respectable people "who obtained their possessions by the hard industry, continued sobriety and economy of themselves or their virtuous ancestors" were now witnessing, so the writings of nearly all the states proclaimed over and over, many men "*whose fathers they would have disdained to have sat with the dogs of their flocks*, raised to immense wealth, or at least to carry the appearance of a haughty, supercilious and luxurious spendthrift." "Effrontery and arrogance, even in our virtuous and enlightened days," said John Jay, "are giving rank and Importance to men whom Wisdom would have left in obscurity."[7] Since "every new election in the States," as Madison pointed out in *The Federalist*, Number 62, "is found to change one half of the representatives," the newly enlarged state legislatures were being filled and yearly refilled with different faces, often with "men without reading, experience, or principle." The Revolution, it was repeatedly charged (and the evidence seems to give substance to the charges), was allowing government to fall "into the Hands of those whose ability or situation in Life does not intitle them to it."[8] Everywhere in the 1780's the press and the correspondence of those

6. Otis quoted by John Eliot to Jeremy Belknap, Jan. 12, 1777, *Belknap Papers*, 104; James Bowdoin to Thomas Pownall, Nov. 20, 1783, quoted in Paul Goodman, *The Democratic-Republicans of Massachusetts: Politics in a Young Republic* (Cambridge, Mass., 1964), 8; John Adams, entry, Feb. 4, 1772, Butterfield, ed., *Diary of Adams*, II, 53; William Goddard, *The Prowess of the Whig Club* . . . (Baltimore, 1777), 7, 12.

7. Charleston *Columbian Herald*, Sept. 23, 1785; "Sober Citizen," *To the Inhabitants of the City and County of New-York, Apr. 16, 1776* (N. Y., 1776); Baltimore *Md. Journal*, Mar. 30, 1787; Phila. *Pa. Gazette*, Mar. 31, 1779; Jay to Hamilton, May 8, 1778, Syrett and Cooke, eds., *Hamilton Papers*, I, 483.

8. *The Federalist*, No. 62; Samuel Johnston to James Iredell, Dec. 9, 1776, quoted in Jones, *Defense of North Carolina*, 288; Coleman, *Revolution in Georgia*, 85. For the infusion of new men in the Revolutionary legislatures see Main, "Government by the People," *Wm. and Mary Qtly.*, 3d Ser., 23 (1966), 391–407.

kinds of men whose letters are apt to be preserved complained that "a set of unprincipled men, who sacrifice everything to their popularity and private views, seem to have acquired too much influence in all our Assemblies." The Revolution was acquiring a degree of social turbulence that many, for all of their knowledge of revolutions, had not anticipated. Given the Revolutionary leaders' conventional eighteenth-century assumption of a necessary coincidence between social and political authority, many could actually believe that their world was being "turned upside down."[9]

Beginning well before the Revolution but increasing to a fever pitch by the mid-eighties were fears of what this kind of intensifying social mobility signified for the traditional conception of a hierarchical society ("In due gradation ev'ry rank must be, Some high, some low, but all in their degree")—a conception which the Revolution had unsettled but by no means repudiated. In reaction to the excessive social movement accelerated by the Revolution some Americans, although good republicans, attempted to confine mobility within prescribed channels. Men could rise, but only within the social ranks in which they were born. Their aim in life must be to learn to perform their inherited position with "industry, economy, and good conduct." A man, wrote Enos Hitchcock in his didactic tale of 1793, must not be "elevated above his employment." In this respect republicanism with its emphasis on spartan adversity and simplicity became an ideology of social stratification and control.[10] Over and over writers urged

9. James Hogg to Iredell, May 17, 1783, McRee, *Life of Iredell,* II, 46; *Providence Gazette,* Mar. 3, 1787. The Tory, Jonathan Boucher, writing in 1797, reflected in an insightful passage on what he thought was happening in both England and America to the political and social structure. What alarmed Boucher was the growing tendency for "those persons who are probably the least qualified, and certainly (as far as having much at stake in the welfare of a State can make it proper for any persons to take a lead in the direction of it's public affairs) the least proper exclusively to become public men. . . . O that the people, seeing their error, and their misfortune in thus submitting to be dupes of those who in general are their superiors only in confidence, would at length have the resolution (the ability they already have) to assert their undoubted right—and no longer bear to be the marketable property of a new species of public men, who study the arts of debate, and pursue politics merely as a gainful occupation!" The emergence of this "new species of public men," and not the extension of the suffrage, was to Boucher the essence of democratic politics. Boucher, *View of the Causes,* lxxvi.

10. Robert Proud, "On the Violation of Established and Lawful Order, Rule or Government—Applied to the Present Times in Penna in 1776," quoted in Selsam, *Pennsylvania Constitution,* 210; Enos Hitchcock, *The Farmer's Friend,*

that "the crosses of life improve by retrenching our enjoyments," by moderating "our expectations," and by giving "the heart a mortal disgust to all the gaudy blandishments of sense." Luxury was such a great evil because it confounded "every Distinction between the Poor and the Rich" and allowed "people of the very meanest parentages, or office, if fortune be but a little favourable to them" to "vie to make themselves equal in apparel with the principal people of the place." "Dissipation and extravagance" encouraged even "country-girls in their market carts, and upon their panniered horses," to ride "through our streets with their heads deformed with the plumes of the ostrich and the feathers of other exotick birds." Although many, especially in the South, had expected the Revolution to lessen this kind of social chaos, republicanism actually seemed only to have aggravated it.[11]

Most American leaders, however, were not opposed to the idea of social movement, for mobility, however one may have decried its abuses, lay at the heart of republicanism. Indeed, many like John Adams had entered the Revolution in order to make mobility a reality, to free American society from the artificial constraints Britain had imposed on it, and to allow "Persons of obscure Birth, and Station, and narrow Fortunes" to make their mark in the world. Republicanism represented equality of opportunity and careers open to talent. Even "the reins of state," David Ramsay had said at the outset, "may be held by the son of the poorest man, if possessed of abilities equal to that important station." Ramsay's qualification, however, was crucial to his endorsement of mobility. For all of its emphasis on equality, republicanism was still not considered by most to be incompatible with the conception of a hierarchical society of different gradations and a unitary authority to which deference from lower to higher should be paid. Movement must necessarily exist in a republic, if talent alone were to dominate, if the natural aristocracy were to rule. But such inevitable movement must be into and out of clearly discernible ranks. Those who rose in a republic, it was assumed, must first acquire the attributes of social superiority —wealth, education, experience, and connections—before they

---

or the History of Mr. Charles Worthy. Who, from Being a Poor Orphan, Rose, through Various Scenes of Distress and Misfortune, to Wealth and Eminence, by Industry, Economy and Good Conduct . . . (Boston, 1793), 40.

11. *Providence Gazette*, Nov. 12, 1785; Samuel Adams to John Adams, July 2, 1785, Cushing, ed., *Writings of Samuel Adams*, IV, 316; Charleston *Columbian Herald*, Oct. 7, 1785; Gardiner, *Oration, Delivered July 4, 1785,* 33.

could be considered eligible for political leadership. Most Revolutionary leaders clung tightly to the concept of a ruling elite, presumably based on merit, but an elite nonetheless—a natural aristocracy embodied in the eighteenth-century ideal of an educated and cultivated gentleman. The rising self-made man could be accepted into this natural aristocracy only if he had assimilated through education or experience its attitudes, refinements, and style. For all of their earlier criticism of "the better sort of People" in the name of "real Merit," few of the Revolutionary leaders were prepared to repudiate the idea of a dominating elite and the requisite identity of social and political authority.[12]

Perhaps no one developed the theme of abused social mobility more fully than did Hugh Henry Brackenridge of Pennsylvania in his famous novel, *Modern Chivalry*, the first part of which was published in 1792. Brackenridge, as the son of a poor Scottish immigrant farmer, had every reason to believe in the promise of the American Revolution. Liberty, he wrote in 1779, would "call forth the powers of human genius," and "a honest husbandman" like himself could "rapidly improve in every kind of knowledge" and thus would eventually "be capable of any office to which the gale of popularity amongst his countrymen may raise him." His own experience, rising from obscurity through self-cultivation and training at the College of New Jersey to election to the Pennsylvania Assembly in 1786, seemed to vindicate his faith in the people and the mobility of American society. Yet the electors of western Pennsylvania were not sending to the legislature just husbandmen who had become college-educated men of letters but husbandmen who were without any of the proper marks of cultivation and distinction. Brackenridge's electoral defeat by one of these uneducated parvenus, the ex-weaver William Findley, dramatically exposed for him the crucial difference between orderly and disorderly social mobility. His insight became the basis for his lengthy satire on the popular folly of precipitantly raising the ignorant and unqualified—weavers, brewers, and tavern-keepers—into public office. "To rise from the cellar to the senate

12. John Adams, entry, Nov. 5, 1760, Butterfield, ed., *Diary of Adams*, I, 167; Ramsay, *Oration on the Advantages of American Independence*, in Niles, ed., *Principles*, 375; Adams, entry, Dec. 24, 1766, Butterfield, ed., *Diary of Adams*, I, 326. For explicit avowals of the compatibility of social distinctions and republicanism see *Observations on "Considerations upon the Cincinnati*," 21; Elizur Goodrich, *The Principles of Civil Union and Happiness Considered and Recommended . . .* (Hartford, 1787), 20–22. See also John G. Cawelti, *Apostles of the Self-Made Man* (Chicago, 1965), 34.

house, would be an unnatural hoist. To come from counting threads, and adjusting them to the splits of a reed, to regulate the finances of a government, would be preposterous; there being no congruity in the case. . . . It would be a reversion of the order of things." It was obvious to Brackenridge as to other Americans that social and political standing must coincide. Indeed, to bring social and political superiority into harmony had been for many a major aim of the Revolution.[13]

Yet the Revolution seemed to be having precisely the opposite effect: enabling socially insignificant men, like Brackenridge's character, the servant Teague O'Regan, to gain positions of dominance without passing through the social ranks and acquiring the recognizable dignities of social leadership, in short, allowing upstarts to short-circuit the social hierarchy. The Revolution in fact accelerated this kind of movement and gave it an ideological justification that it had never quite had before in America. The same republican ideology that permitted established social leaders to decry the excesses of social mobility also encouraged new men to criticize a hierarchy that strained to resist their premature rising. "It is a very strange thing," Brackenridge had the people in his novel say to his hero and spokesman, Captain Farrago, "that after having conquered Burgoyne and Cornwallis, and got a government of our own, we cannot put in it whom we please." The man whom we elect to office may be a weaver or even a servant, "but if we chuse to make him a delegate, what is that to you. He may not be yet skilled in the matter, but there is a good day a-coming. We will impower him; and it is better to trust a plain man like him, than one of your high flyers, that will make laws to suit their own purposes." But because Brackenridge's hero was a true Enlightenment figure ("his ideas were drawn chiefly from what may be called the old school; the Greek and Roman notions of things"), and because he was "so unacquainted with the world, as to imagine that jockeys and men of the turf could be composed by reason and good sense," it came to him as something of a surprise, as it had to Brackenridge himself, that "the common people are more disposed to trust one of their own class, than those who may affect to be superior." It began to seem clearer than it had before that "there is a certain pride in man, which leads him to elevate the low, and pull down the high." The people were becoming exultant in their "creating

13. Brackenridge, *Modern Chivalry*, ed. Newlin, xiii–xiv, 14.

power exerted in making a senator of an unqualified person" and were turning upon the entire "patrician class."[14]

Throughout all the states spokesmen for "the poor and middling orders" were directly challenging the eighteenth-century assumption that social authority was a necessary prerequisite to the wielding of political power. "Names, families, and connections," wrote Benjamin Austin of Massachusetts, had no real relation to a man's worth and opinion. "Must the poor man be forever debarred from delivering his mind, lest the inquiry should be concerning his *origin*. Are there no observations worthy our attention, unless they are authorized by *family alliances*?" "Elevation in office, and wealth and titles, and political rank and dignity," said William Paca of Maryland, "have no influence at all in making men *good* or *honest*." Even suggestions of degrees of respectability had aristocratic overtones for the most egalitarian. "A democratic government like ours," said John Smilie of Pennsylvania in terms that bluntly denied the traditional belief in a social hierarchy, "admits of no superiority. A virtuous man, be his situation what it may, is respectable." Americans who used other designations of respectability had no basis for them. All such men really had was "more money than their neighbors," and because of this they claimed they were "therefore more respectable."[15]

In South Carolina these kinds of sentiments became particularly pronounced in the eighties; the planters found themselves confronted with widespread challenges to their authority that they had never anticipated in 1776, challenges that came from a new kind of politician, one who, as a defender proudly pointed out, "had no relations or friends, but what his money made for him." In the tense atmosphere of the mid-eighties the case of William Thompson, an unfortunate tavern-keeper who was threatened with banishment from the state by the legislature for allegedly insulting John Rutledge, became a *cause célèbre* and a focal point for the political and social animosities released and aggravated by the Revolution. Thompson's address to the public in April 1784 is a classic expression of American resentment against social superiority, a resentment voiced, as Thompson said, not on behalf of himself but on behalf of the people, or "those more especially, who go at this day, under the opprobrious appel-

14. *Ibid.*, 16, 53, 11, 19.
15. [Austin], *Observations on the Pernicious Practice of the Law*, 44; Baltimore *Md. Journal*, Feb. 20, 1787; Carey, ed., *Debates of the General Assembly of Pennsylvania*, 21.

lation of, the *Lower Orders of Men*." Thompson was not simply attacking the few aristocratic "Nabobs" who had humiliated him, but was actually assaulting the entire conception of a social hierarchy ruled by a gentlemanly elite. In fact he turned the prevailing eighteenth-century opinion upside down and argued that the natural aristocracy was peculiarly unqualified to rule. Rather than preparing men for political leadership in a free government, said Thompson, "signal opulence and influence," especially when united "by intermarriage or otherwise," were really "calculated to subvert *Republicanism*." The "persons and conduct" of the South Carolina "Nabobs" like Rutledge "in *private* life, may be unexceptionable, and even amiable, but their pride, influence, ambition, connections, wealth and political principles, ought in *public* life, ever to exclude them from *public confidence*." All that was needed in republican leadership was "being *good, able, useful*, and *friends to social equality*," for in a republican government "consequence is from the *public opinion*, and not from *private fancy*." In sardonic tones Thompson recounted how he, a tavern-keeper, "a *wretch* of no higher rank in the Commonwealth than that of Common-Citizen," had been debased by "those *self-exalted* characters, who affect to compose the *grand hierarchy* of the State, . . . for having dared to dispute with a *John Rutledge*, or any of the NABOB *tribe*." The experience had been degrading enough to Thompson as a man, but as a former officer in the army it had been "insupportable"—indicating how Revolutionary military service may have affected the social structure. Undoubtedly, said Thompson, Rutledge had "conceived me his inferior." But Thompson like many others in these years— tavern-keepers, farmers, petty merchants, small-time lawyers, former military officers—could no longer "comprehend the *inferiority*."[16] The resultant antagonism between those who conceived of such men as their inferiors, unfit to hold public positions, and those who would not accept the imputation of inferiority lay beneath the social crisis of the 1780's—a social crisis which the federal Constitution of 1787 brought to a head.

3. ARISTOCRACY AND DEMOCRACY

The division over the Constitution in 1787–88 is not easily analyzed. It is difficult, as historians have recently demonstrated, to

16. Charleston *Gazette of the St. of S.-C.*, May 13, Apr. 29, 1784.

equate the supporters or opponents of the Constitution with particular economic groupings. The Antifederalist politicians in the ratifying conventions often possessed wealth, including public securities, equal to that of the Federalists.[17] While the relative youth of the Federalist leaders, compared to the ages of the prominent Antifederalists, was important, especially in accounting for the Federalists' ability to think freshly and creatively about politics, it can hardly be used to explain the division throughout the country.[18] Moreover, the concern of the 1780's with America's moral character was not confined to the proponents of the Constitution. That rabid republican and Antifederalist, Benjamin Austin, was as convinced as any Federalist that "the luxurious living of all ranks and degrees" was "the principal cause of all the evils we now experience." Some leading Antifederalist intellectuals expressed as much fear of "the injustice, folly, and wickedness of the State Legislatures" and of "the usurpation and tyranny of the majority" against the minority as did Madison. In the Philadelphia Convention both Mason and Elbridge Gerry, later prominent Antifederalists, admitted "the danger of the levelling spirit" flowing from "the excess of democracy" in the American republics.[19] There were many diverse reasons in each state why men supported or opposed the Constitution that cut through any sort of class division. The Constitution was a single issue in a complicated situation, and its acceptance or rejection in many states was often dictated by peculiar circumstances—the prevalence of Indians, the desire for western lands, the special interests of commerce—that defy generalization. Nevertheless, despite all of this confusion and complexity, the struggle over the Constitution, as the debate if nothing else makes clear, can best be understood as a social one. Whatever the particular constituency of the antagonists may have been, men in 1787–88 talked as if they were representing distinct and opposing social elements. Both the proponents

17. See especially Forrest McDonald, *We the People: The Economic Origins of the Constitution* (Chicago, 1958).

18. On the relative youth of the Federalists see Charles Warren, "Elbridge Gerry, James Warren, Mercy Warren and the Ratification of the Federal Constitution in Massachusetts," Mass. Hist. Soc., *Proceedings*, 64 (1930–32), 146; Stanley Elkins and Eric McKitrick, "The Founding Fathers: Young Men of the Revolution," *Pol. Sci. Qtly.*, 76 (1961), 203; but cf. Main, *Antifederalists*, 259.

19. Boston *Independent Chronicle*, Dec. 6, 1787; R. H. Lee to Francis Lightfoot Lee, July 14, 1787, Ballagh, ed., *Letters of R. H. Lee*, II, 424; [James Winthrop], "Letters of Agrippa, XVIII," Feb. 5, 1788, Ford, ed., *Essays on the Constitution*, 117; Farrand, ed., *Records of the Federal Convention*, I, 48, II, 647.

and opponents of the Constitution focused throughout the debates on an essential point of political sociology that ultimately must be used to distinguish a Federalist from an Antifederalist. The quarrel was fundamentally one between aristocracy and democracy.

Because of its essentially social base, this quarrel, as George Minot of Massachusetts said, was "extremely unequal." To be sure, many Antifederalists, especially in Virginia, were as socially and intellectually formidable as any Federalist. Richard Henry Lee was undoubtedly the strongest mind the Antifederalists possessed, and he sympathized with the Antifederalist cause. Like Austin and other Antifederalists he believed that moral regeneration of America's character, rather than any legalistic manipulation of the constitutions of government, was the proper remedy for America's problems. "I fear," he wrote to George Mason in May 1787, "it is more in vicious manners, than mistakes in form, that we must seek for the causes of the present discontent."[20] Still, such "aristocrats" as Lee or Mason did not truly represent Antifederalism. Not only did they reject the vicious state politics of the 1780's which Antifederalism, by the very purpose of the Constitution, was implicitly if not always explicitly committed to defend, but they could have no real identity, try as they might, with those for whom they sought to speak. Because, as Lee pointed out, "we must recollect how disproportionately the democratic and aristocratic parts of the community were represented" not only in the Philadelphia Convention but also in the ratifying conventions, many of the real Antifederalists, those intimately involved in the democratic politics of the 1780's and consequently with an emotional as well as an intellectual commitment to Antifederalism, were never clearly heard in the formal debates of 1787–88.[21]

The disorganization and inertia of the Antifederalists, especially in contrast with the energy and effectiveness of the Federalists, has been repeatedly emphasized.[22] The opponents of the Constitution lacked both coordination and unified leadership;

20. Minot, quoted in Rutland, *Ordeal of the Constitution*, 113; Lee to Mason, May 15, 1787, Ballagh, ed., *Letters of R. H. Lee*, II, 419.

21. [Richard Henry Lee], *Observations Leading to a Fair Examination of the System of Government, Proposed by the Late Convention . . . in a Number of Letters from the Federal Farmer . . .* ([N. Y.], 1787), in Ford, ed., *Pamphlets*, 285; Main, *Antifederalists*, 172–73, 177.

22. On the political effectiveness of the Federalists in contrast to the ineptness of the Antifederalists see John P. Roche, "The Founding Fathers: A Reform Caucus in Action," *Amer. Pol. Sci. Rev.*, 55 (1961), 799–816; Main, *Antifederalists*, 252–53; and above all, Rutland, *Ordeal of the Constitution*, 66, 76–77, 113, 165, 210, 236, 243–44, 309, 313.

"their principles," wrote Oliver Ellsworth, "are totally opposite to each other, and their objections discordant and irreconcilable." The Federalist victory, it appears, was actually more of an Antifederalist default. "We had no principle of concert or union," lamented the South Carolina Antifederalist, Aedanus Burke, while the supporters of the Constitution "left no expedient untried to push it forward." Madison's description of the Massachusetts Antifederalists was applicable to nearly all the states: "There was not a single character capable of uniting their wills or directing their measures. . . . They had no plan whatever. They looked no farther than to put a negative on the Constitution and return home." They were not, as one Federalist put it, "good politicians."[23]

But the Antifederalists were not simply poorer politicians than the Federalists; they were actually different kinds of politicians. Too many of them were state-centered men with local interests and loyalties only, politicians without influence and connections, and ultimately politicians without social and intellectual confidence. In South Carolina the up-country opponents of the Constitution shied from debate and when they did occasionally rise to speak apologized effusively for their inability to say what they felt had to be said, thus leaving most of the opposition to the Constitution to be voiced by Rawlins Lowndes, a low-country planter who scarcely represented their interests and soon retired from the struggle. Elsewhere, in New Hampshire, Connecticut, Massachusetts, Pennsylvania, and North Carolina, the situation was similar: the Federalists had the bulk of talent and influence on their side "together with all the Speakers in the State great and small." In convention after convention the Antifederalists, as in Connecticut, tried to speak, but "they were browbeaten by many of those Cicero'es as they think themselves and others of Superior rank." "The presses are in a great measure secured to *their* side," the Antifederalists complained with justice: out of a hundred or more newspapers printed in the late eighties only a dozen supported the Antifederalists, as editors, "afraid to offend the great men, or Merchants, who could work their ruin," closed their

---

23. [Ellsworth], "The Landholder, VIII," Dec. 24, 1787, Ford, ed., *Essays on the Constitution*, 176; Aedanus Burke to John Lamb, June 23, 1788, quoted in Rutland, *Ordeal of the Constitution*, 165; Madison to Jefferson, Feb. 19, 1788, Hunt, ed., *Writings of Madison*, V, 101–02; Tobias Lear to Washington, June 2, 1788, in *Documentary History of the Constitution* (Washington, 1894–1905), IV, 676.

columns to the opposition. The Antifederalists were not so much beaten as overawed.[24] In Massachusetts the two leading socially established Antifederalists, Elbridge Gerry and James Warren, were defeated as delegates to the Ratifying Convention, and Antifederalist leadership consequently fell into the hands of newer, self-made men, of whom Samuel Nasson was perhaps typical—a Maine shopkeeper who was accused of delivering ghostwritten speeches in the Convention. Nasson had previously sat in the General Court but had declined reelection because he had been too keenly made aware of "the want of a proper Education I feel my Self So Small on many occasions that I all most Scrink into Nothing Besides I am often obliged to Borrow from Gentlemen that had advantages which I have not." Now, however, he had become the stoutest of Antifederalists, "full charged with Gass," one of those grumblers who, as Rufus King told Madison, were more afraid of the proponents of the Constitution than the Constitution itself, frightened that "some injury is plotted against them" because of "the extraordinary Union in favor of the Constitution in this State of the Wealthy and sensible part of it."[25]

This fear of a plot by men who "talk so finely and gloss over matters so smoothly" ran through the Antifederalist mind. Because the many "new men" of the 1780's, men like Melancthon Smith and Abraham Yates of New York or John Smilie and William Findley of Pennsylvania, had bypassed the social hierarchy in their rise to political leadership, they lacked those attributes of social distinction and dignity that went beyond mere wealth. Since these kinds of men were never assimilated to the gentlemanly cast of the Livingstons or the Morrises, they, like Americans earlier in confrontation with the British court, tended to view with suspicion and hostility the high-flying world of style and connections that they were barred by their language and tastes, if by nothing else, from sharing in. In the minds of these socially inferior politicians the movement for the strengthening of the central government could only be a "conspiracy" "planned and set to work" by a few aristocrats, who were at first, said

24. Rogers, *William Loughton Smith*, 150; Rutland, *Ordeal of the Constitution*, 211, 55, 98, 118–19, 212, 253, 85, 211, 165. Rutland's book is particularly important in demonstrating the political and social inferiority of the Antifederalists.
25. Harding, *Ratification in Massachusetts*, 64; Rufus King to James Madison, Jan. 20, 27, 1788, King, *Life of King*, I, 314, 316–17. See also John Brown Cutting to Jefferson, July 11, 1788, Boyd, ed., *Jefferson Papers*, XIII, 331; Welch, *Sedgwick*, 64–65.

Abraham Yates, no larger in number in any one state than the cabal which sought to undermine English liberty at the beginning of the eighteenth century. Since men like Yates could not quite comprehend what they were sure were the inner maneuverings of the elite, they were convinced that in the aristocrats' program, "what was their view in the beginning" or how "far it was Intended to be carried Must be Collected from facts that Afterwards have happened." Like American Whigs in the sixties and seventies forced to delve into the dark and complicated workings of English court politics, they could judge motives and plans "but by the Event."[26] And they could only conclude that the events of the eighties, "the treasury, the Cincinnati, and other public creditors, with all their concomitants," were "somehow or other, . . . inseparably connected," were all parts of a grand design "concerted by a few *tyrants*" to undo the Revolution and to establish an aristocracy in order "to lord it over the rest of their fellow citizens, to trample the poorer part of the people under their feet, that they may be rendered their servants and slaves." In this climate all the major issues of the Confederation period—the impost, commutation, and the return of the Loyalists—possessed a political and social significance that transcended economic concerns. All seemed to be devices by which a ruling few, like the ministers of the English Crown, would attach a corps of pensioners and dependents to the government and spread their influence and connections throughout the states in order "to dissolve our present Happy and Benevolent Constitution and to erect on the Ruins, a proper Aristocracy."[27]

Nothing was more characteristic of Antifederalist thinking than this obsession with aristocracy. Although to a European, American society may have appeared remarkably egalitarian, to many Americans, especially to those who aspired to places of consequence but were made to feel their inferiority in innumerable, often subtle, ways, American society was distinguished by its inequality. "It is true," said Melancthon Smith in the New York Ratifying Convention, "it is our singular felicity that we

26. Amos Singletary (Mass.), in Elliot, ed., *Debates*, II, 102; Staughton Lynd, ed., "Abraham Yates's History of the Movement for the United States Constitution," *Wm. and Mary Qtly.*, 3d Ser., 20 (1963), 232, 231.

27. Samuel Osgood to Stephen Higginson, Feb. 2, 1784, Burnett, ed., *Letters of Congress*, VII, 435; Phila. *Independent Gazetteer*, Feb. 7, 1788, in Kenyon, ed., *Antifederalists*, 71; Farmington Records, May 6, 1783, quoted in Main, *Antifederalists*, 108–09, see also 76–77.

have no legal or hereditary distinctions . . . ; but still there are real differences." "Every society naturally divides itself into classes. . . . Birth, education, talents, and wealth, create distinctions among men as visible, and of as much influence, as titles, stars, and garters." Everyone knew those "whom nature hath destined to rule," declared one sardonic Antifederalist pamphlet. Their "qualifications of authority" were obvious: "such as the dictatorial air, the magisterial voice, the imperious tone, the haughty countenance, the lofty look, the majestic mien." In all communities, "even in those of the most democratic kind," wrote George Clinton (whose "family and connections" in the minds of those like Philip Schuyler did not "entitle him to so distinguished a predominance" as the governorship of New York), there were pressures—"superior talents, fortunes and public employments"—demarcating an aristocracy whose influence was difficult to resist.[28]

Such influence was difficult to resist because, to the continual annoyance of the Antifederalists, the great body of the people willingly submitted to it. The "authority of names" and "the influence of the great" among ordinary people were too evident to be denied. "Will any one say that there does not exist in this country the pride of family, of wealth, of talents, and that they do not command influence and respect among the common people?" "The people are too apt to yield an implicit assent to the opinions of those characters whose abilities are held in the highest esteem, and to those in whose integrity and patriotism they can confide; not considering that the love of domination is generally in proportion to talents, abilities and superior requirements." Because of this habit of deference in the people, it was "in the power of the enlightened and aspiring few, if they should combine, at any time to destroy the best establishments, and even make the people the instruments of their own subjugation." Hence, the Antifederalist-minded declared, the people must be awakened to the consequences of their self-ensnarement; they must be warned over and over by popular tribunes, by "those who are competent to the task of developing the principles of

28. Smith (N.Y.), in Elliot, ed., *Debates*, II, 246; *The Government of Nature Delineated; Or an Exact Picture of the New Federal Constitution* (Carlisle, Pa., 1788), 7; [George Clinton], "Cato, VI," Dec. 16, 1787, Ford, ed., *Essays on the Constitution*, 273; Philip Schuyler to John Jay, July 14, 1777, Johnston, ed., *Papers of Jay*, I, 147. De Pauw, *Eleventh Pillar*, 283–92, questions Clinton's authorship of the "Cato" letters and suggests that Abraham Yates may have written them.

government," of the dangers involved in paying obeisance to those who they thought were their superiors. The people must "not be permitted to consider themselves as a grovelling, distinct species, uninterested in the general welfare."[29]

Such constant admonitions to the people of the perils flowing from their too easy deference to the *"natural aristocracy"* were necessary because the Antifederalists were convinced that these "men that had been delicately bred, and who were in affluent circumstances," these "men of the most exalted rank in life," were by their very conspicuousness irreparably cut off from the great body of the people and hence could never share in its concerns nor look after its interests. It was not that these "certain men exalted above the rest" were necessarily "destitute of morality or virtue" or that they were inherently different from other men. "The same passions and prejudices govern all men." It was only that circumstances in their particular environment had made them different. There was "a charm in politicks"; men in high office become habituated with power, "grow fond of it, and are loath to resign it"; "they feel themselves flattered and elevated," enthralled by the attractions of high living, and thus they easily forget the interests of the common people, from which many of them once sprang. By dwelling so vividly on the allurements of prestige and power, by emphasizing again and again how the "human soul is affected by wealth, in all its faculties, . . . by its present interest, by its expectations, and by its fears," these ambitious Antifederalist politicians may have revealed as much about themselves as they did about the "aristocratic" elite they sought to displace.[30] Yet at the same time by such language they contributed to a new appreciation of the nature of society.

In these repeated attacks on deference and the capacity of a

---

29. [Bryan], "Centinel, No. I," Oct. 5, 1787, McMaster and Stone, eds., *Pennsylvania and the Federal Constitution*, 566–67; Smith (N. Y.), in Elliot, ed., *Debates*, II, 246–47; *Rudiments of Law and Government*, 26; Main, *Antifederalists*, 203.

30. *Government of Nature Delineated*, 8; Smith (N. Y.), in Elliot, ed., *Debates*, II, 246; Bernard Steiner, "Connecticut's Ratification of the Federal Constitution," Amer. Antiq. Soc., *Proceedings*, 25 (1915), 77; "Address and Reasons of Dissent of the Minority of the Convention of the State of Pennsylvania," Dec. 18, 1787, McMaster and Stone, eds., *Pennsylvania and the Federal Constitution*, 472; Smith (N. Y.) and Patrick Henry (Va.), in Elliot, ed., *Debates*, II, 260, 247, III, 54; "John De Witt," Nov. 5, 1787, Kenyon, ed., *Antifederalists*, 105; Carey, ed., *Debates of the General Assembly of Pennsylvania*, 66; Robert Lansing and Smith (N. Y.), in Elliot, ed., *Debates*, II, 293, 13, 247, 260.

conspicuous few to speak for the whole society—which was to become in time the distinguishing feature of American democratic politics—the Antifederalists struck at the roots of the traditional conception of political society. If the natural elite, whether its distinctions were ascribed or acquired, was not in any organic way connected to the "feelings, circumstances, and interests" of the people and was incapable of feeling "sympathetically the wants of the people," then it followed that only ordinary men, men not distinguished by the characteristics of aristocratic wealth and taste, men "in middling circumstances" untempted by the attractions of a cosmopolitan world and thus "more temperate, of better morals, and less ambitious, than the great," could be trusted to speak for the great body of the people, for those who were coming more and more to be referred to as "the middling and lower classes of people."[31] The differentiating influence of the environment was such that men in various ranks and classes now seemed to be broken apart from one another, separated by their peculiar circumstances into distinct, unconnected, and often incompatible interests. With their indictment of aristocracy the Antifederalists were saying, whether they realized it or not, that the people of America even in their several states were not homogeneous entities each with a basic similarity of interest for which an empathic elite could speak. Society was not an organic hierarchy composed of ranks and degrees indissolubly linked one to another; rather it was a heterogeneous mixture of "many different classes or orders of people, Merchants, Farmers, Planter Mechanics and Gentry or wealthy Men." In such a society men from one class or group, however educated and respectable they may have been, could never be acquainted with the "*Situation and Wants*" of those of another class or group. Lawyers and planters could never be "adequate judges of tradesmens concerns." If men were truly to represent the people in government, it was not enough for them to be for the people; they had to be actually of the people. "Farmers, traders and mechanics . . . all ought to have a competent number of their best informed members in the legislature."[32]

31. William Heath (Mass.), Lansing (N. Y.), Smith (N. Y.), and Henry (Va.), in Elliot, ed., *Debates*, II, 13, 293, 247, 260.

32. Samuel Chase quoted in Philip A. Crowl, "Anti-Federalism in Maryland, 1787–1788," *Wm. and Mary Qtly.*, 3d Ser., 4 (1947), 464; Walsh, *Charleston's Sons of Liberty*, 131–32; "Dissent of the Minority," McMaster and Stone, eds., *Pennsylvania and the Federal Constitution*, 472.

Thus the Antifederalists were not only directly challenging the conventional belief that only a gentlemanly few, even though now in America naturally and not artificially qualified, were best equipped through learning and experience to represent and to govern the society, but they were as well indirectly denying the assumption of organic social homogeneity on which republicanism rested. Without fully comprehending the consequences of their arguments the Antifederalists were destroying the great chain of being, thus undermining the social basis of republicanism and shattering that unity and harmony of social and political authority which the eighteenth century generally and indeed most Revolutionary leaders had considered essential to the maintenance of order.

Confronted with such a fundamental challenge the Federalists initially backed away. They had no desire to argue the merits of the Constitution in terms of its social implications and were understandably reluctant to open up the character of American society as the central issue of the debate. But in the end they could not resist defending those beliefs in elitism that lay at the heart of their conception of politics and of their constitutional program. All of the Federalists' desires to establish a strong and respectable nation in the world, all of their plans to create a flourishing commercial economy, in short, all of what the Federalists wanted out of the new central government seemed in the final analysis dependent upon the prerequisite maintenance of aristocratic politics.

At first the Federalists tried to belittle the talk of an aristocracy; they even denied that they knew the meaning of the word. "Why bring into the debate the whims of writers—introducing the distinction of *well-born* from others?" asked Edmund Pendleton in the Virginia Ratifying Convention. In the Federalist view every man was "*well-born* who comes into the world with an intelligent mind, and with all his parts perfect." Was even natural talent to be suspect? Was learning to be encouraged, the Federalists asked in exasperation, only "to set up those who attained its benefits as butts of invidious distinction?" No American, the Federalists said, could justifiably oppose a man "commencing in life without any other stock but industry and economy," and "by the mere efforts of these" rising "to opulence and wealth." If social mobility were to be meaningful then some sorts of distinctions were necessary. If government by a natural aristocracy, said Wilson, meant "nothing more or less than a government of the best men in the community," then who could object to it? Could the Antifederalists actually intend to mark out those "most noted for their virtue and talents . . . as the most improper persons for the public confidence?" No, the Federalists exclaimed in disbelief, the Antifederalists could never have intended such a socially destructive conclusion. It was clear, said Hamilton, that the Antifederalists' arguments only proved "that there are men who are rich, men who are poor, some who are wise, and others who are not; that indeed, every distinguished man is an aristocrat."[33]

But the Antifederalist intention and implication were too conspicuous to be avoided: all distinctions, whether naturally based or not, were being challenged. Robert Livingston in the New York Convention saw as clearly as anyone what he thought the Antifederalists were really after, and he minced no words in replying to Smith's attack on the natural aristocracy. Since Smith had classified as aristocrats not only "the rich and the great" but also "the wise, the learned, and those eminent for their talents or great virtues," aristocrats to the Antifederalists had in substance become all men of merit. Such men, such aristocrats, were not to be chosen for public office, questioned Livingston in rising disbelief in the implications of the Antifederalist argument, "because the people will not have confidence in them; that is, the people will not have confidence in those who best deserve and most possess their confidence?" The logic of Smith's reasoning, said Livingston, would lead to a government by the dregs of society, a monstrous government where all "the unjust, the selfish, the unsocial feelings," where all "the vices, the infirmities, the passions of the people" would be represented. "Can it be thought," asked Livingston in an earlier development of this argument to the Society of the Cincinnati, "that an enlightened people believe the science of government level to the meanest capacity? That experience, application, and education are unnecessary to those who are to frame laws for the government of the state?" Yet strange as it may have seemed to Livingston and others in the 1780's, America was actually approaching the point where ability, education, and wealth were becoming liabilities, not assets, in the attaining of public office. "Envy and the ambition of the unworthy" were robbing respectable men of the rank they merited. "To these

33. Edmund Pendleton (Va.), in Elliot, ed., *Debates*, III, 295, 296; Wilson, in McMaster and Stone, eds., *Pennsylvania and the Federal Constitution*, 335; Hamilton (N. Y.), in Elliot, ed., *Debates*, II, 256.

causes," said Livingston, "we owe the cloud that obscures our internal governments."[34]

The course of the debates over the Constitution seemed to confirm what the Federalists had believed all along. Antifederalism represented the climax of a "war" that was, in the words of Theodore Sedgwick, being "levied on the virtue, property, and distinctions in the community." The opponents of the Constitution, despite some, "particularly in Virginia," who were operating "from the most honorable and patriotic motives," were essentially identical with those who were responsible for the evils the states were suffering from in the eighties—"narrowminded politicians . . . under the influence of local views."[35] "Whilst many *ostensible* reasons are assigned" for the Antifederalists' opposition, charged Washington, "the real ones are concealed behind the Curtains, because they are not of a nature to appear in open day." "The real object of all their zeal in opposing the system," agreed Madison, was to maintain "the supremacy of the State Legislatures," with all that meant in the printing of money and the violation of contracts.[36] The Antifederalists or those for whom the Antifederalists spoke, whether their spokesmen realized it or not, were "none but the horse-jockey, the mushroom merchant, the running and dishonest speculator," those "who owe the most and have the least to pay," those "whose dependence and expectations are upon changes in government, and distracted times," men of "desperate Circumstances," those "in Every State" who "have Debts to pay, Interests to support or Fortunes to make," those, in short, who "wish for scrambling Times." Apart from a few of their intellectual leaders the Antifederalists were thought to be an ill-bred lot: "Their education has been rather indifferent—they have been accustomed to think on the small scale." They were often blustering demagogues trying to push their way into office—"men of much self-importance and supposed skill in politics, who are not of sufficient consequence to obtain public employment." Hence they were considered to be

34. Livingston (N. Y.), in Elliot, ed., *Debates*, II, 276–78; Robert Livingston, "An Oration Delivered July 4, 1787 . . . ," *American Museum*, 3 (1788), 109–10.

35. Sedgwick to King, June 18, 1787, King, *Life of King*, 1, 224; Madison to Jefferson, Oct. 17, 1788, Boyd, ed., *Jefferson Papers*, XIV, 18; Washington to Hamilton, July 10, 1787, Syrett and Cooke, eds., *Hamilton Papers*, IV, 225.

36. Washington to Bushrod Washington, Nov. 10, 1787, *Documentary History of the Constitution*, IV, 373–74; Madison to Tench Coxe, July 20, 1788, quoted in Rutland, *Ordeal of the Constitution*, 172; Madison to Jefferson, Oct. 17, 1788, Boyd, ed., *Jefferson Papers*, XIV, 18.

jealous and mistrustful of "every one in the higher offices of society," unable to bear to see others possessing "that fancied blessing, to which, alas! they must themselves aspire in vain."[37] In the Federalist mind therefore the struggle over the Constitution was not one between kinds of wealth or property, or one between commercial or noncommercial elements of the population, but rather represented a broad social division between those who believed in the right of a natural aristocracy to speak for the people and those who did not.

Against this threat from the licentious the Federalists pictured themselves as the defenders of the worthy, of those whom they called "the better sort of people," those, said John Jay, "who are orderly and industrious, who are content with their situations and not uneasy in their circumstances." Because the Federalists were fearful that republican equality was becoming "that *perfect equality* which deadens the motives of industry, and places Demerit on a Footing with Virtue," they were obsessed with the need to insure that the proper amount of inequality and natural distinctions be recognized. "Although there are no nobles in America," observed the French minister to America, Louis Otto, in 1786, "there is a class of men denominated 'gentlemen,' who, by reason of their wealth, their talents, their education, their families, or the offices they hold, aspire to a preeminence which the people refuse to grant them." "How idle . . . all disputes about a technical aristocracy" would be, if only the people would "pay strict attention to the natural aristocracy, which is the institution of heaven. . . . This aristocracy is derived from merit and that influence, which a character for superiour wisdom, and known services to the commonwealth, has to produce veneration, confidence and esteem, among a people, who have felt the benefits. . . ." Robert Morris, for example, was convinced there were social differences—even in Pennsylvania. "What!" he exclaimed in scornful amazement at John Smilie's argument that a republic admitted of no social superiorities. "Is it insisted that there is no distinction of character?" Respectability, said Morris with conviction, was not confined to property. "Surely persons possessed

---

37. *Providence Gazette*, Feb. 26, 1785; Boston *Independent Chronicle*, Aug. 31, 1786; Francis Hopkinson to Jefferson, Apr. 6, 1788, Boyd, ed., *Jefferson Papers*, XIII, 38–39; Hartford *Conn. Courant*, Nov. 20, 1786; [Ellsworth], "A Landholder, II," Nov. 12, 1787, Ford, ed., *Essays on the Constitution*, 144; [Alexander C. Hanson], *Remarks on the Proposed Plan of a Federal Government* . . . (Annapolis, [1788]), in Ford, ed., *Pamphlets*, 232.

of knowledge, judgment, information, integrity, and having extensive connections, are not to be classed with persons void of reputation or character."[38]

In refuting the Antifederalists' contention "that all classes of citizens should have some of their own number in the representative body, in order that their feelings and interests may be the better understood and attended to," Hamilton in *The Federalist*, Number 35, put into words the Federalists' often unspoken and vaguely held assumption about the organic and the hierarchical nature of society. Such explicit class or occupational representation as the Antifederalists advocated, wrote Hamilton, was not only impractical but unnecessary, since the society was not as fragmented or heterogeneous as the Antifederalists implied. The various groups in the landed interest, for example, were "perfectly united, from the wealthiest landlord down to the poorest tenant," and this "common interest may always be reckoned upon as the surest bond of sympathy" linking the landed representative, however rich, to his constituents. In a like way, the members of the commercial community were "immediately connected" and most naturally represented by the merchants. "Mechanics and manufacturers will always be inclined, with few exceptions, to give their votes to merchants, in preference to persons of their own professions or trades. . . . They know that the merchant is their natural patron and friend; and . . . they are sensible that their habits in life have not been such as to give them those acquired endowments, without which in a deliberative assembly, the greatest natural abilities, are for the most part useless." However much many Federalists may have doubted the substance of Hamilton's analysis of American society, they could not doubt the truth of his conclusion. That the people were represented better by one of the natural aristocracy "whose situation leads to extensive inquiry and information" than by one "whose observation does not travel beyond the circle of his neighbors and acquaintants" was the defining element of the Federalist philosophy.

It was not simply the number of public securities, or credit outstanding, or the number of ships, or the amount of money pos-

---

38. Jay to Washington, June 27, 1786, Johnston, ed., *Papers of Jay*, III, 204–05; Thomas Dawes, Jr., *Oration, Delivered July 4, 1787*, 10; Otto to Vergennes, Oct. 10, 1786, in Bancroft, *Formation of the Constitution*, II, 399–400; Goodrich, *Principles of Civil Union*, 20–22; Carey, ed., *Debates of the General Assembly of Pennsylvania*, 38.

sessed that made a man think of himself as one of the natural elite. It was much more subtle than the mere possession of wealth: it was a deeper social feeling, a sense of being socially established, of possessing attributes—family, education, and refinement—that others lacked, above all, of being accepted by and being able to move easily among those who considered themselves to be the respectable and cultivated. It is perhaps anachronistic to describe this social sense as a class interest, for it often transcended immediate political or economic concerns, and, as Hamilton's argument indicates, was designed to cut through narrow occupational categories. The Republicans of Philadelphia, for example, repeatedly denied that they represented an aristocracy with a united class interest. "We are of different occupations; of different sects of religion; and have different views of life. No factions or private system can comprehend us all." Yet with all their assertions of diversified interests the Republicans were not without a social consciousness in their quarrel with the supporters of the Pennsylvania Constitution. If there were any of us ambitious for power, their apology continued, then there would be no need to change the Constitution, for we surely could attain power under the present Constitution. "We have already seen how easy the task is for *any character* to rise into power and consequence under it. And there are some of us, who think not so meanly of ourselves, as to dread any rivalship from those who are now in office."[39]

In 1787 this kind of elitist social consciousness was brought into play as perhaps never before in eighteenth-century America, as gentlemen up and down the continent submerged their sectional and economic differences in the face of what seemed to be a threat to the very foundations of society. Despite his earlier opposition to the Order of the Cincinnati, Theodore Sedgwick, like other frightened New Englanders, now welcomed the organization as a source of strength in the battle for the Constitution. The fear of social disruption that had run through much of the writing of the eighties was brought to a head to eclipse all other fears. Although state politics in the eighties remains to be analyzed, the evidence from Federalist correspondence indicates clearly a belief that never had there occurred "so great a change in the opinion of the best people" as was occurring in the last few years of the

39. *The Federalist*, No. 35; Phila. *Pa. Gazette*, Mar. 24, 1779.

decade. The Federalists were astonished at the outpouring in 1787 of influential and respectable people who had earlier remained quiescent. Too many of "the better sort of people," it was repeatedly said, had withdrawn at the end of the war "from the theatre of public action, to scenes of retirement and ease," and thus "demagogues of desperate fortunes, mere adventurers in fraud, were left to act unopposed."[40] After all, it was explained, "when the wicked rise, men hide themselves." Even the problems of Massachusetts in 1786, noted General Benjamin Lincoln, the repressor of the Shaysites, were not caused by the rebels, but by the laxity of "the good people of the state." But the lesson of this laxity was rapidly being learned. Everywhere, it seemed, men of virtue, good sense, and property, "almost the whole body of our enlighten'd and leading characters in every state," were awakened in support of stronger government. "The scum which was thrown upon the surface by the fermentation of the war is daily sinking," Benjamin Rush told Richard Price in 1786, "while a pure spirit is occupying its place." "Men are brought into action who had consigned themselves to an eve of rest," Edward Carrington wrote to Jefferson in June 1787, "and the Convention, as a Beacon, is rousing the attention of the Empire." The Antifederalists could only stand amazed at this "weight of talents" being gathered in support of the Constitution. "What must the individual be who could thus oppose them united?"[41]

Still, in the face of this preponderance of wealth and respectability in support of the Constitution, what remains extraordinary about 1787–88 is not the weakness and disunity but the political strength of Antifederalism. That large numbers of Americans could actually reject a plan of government created by a body "compossd of the first characters in the Continent" and backed by Washington and nearly the whole of the natural aristocracy of the country said more about the changing character of Amer-

40. Welch, *Sedgwick*, 56; St. John de Crèvecoeur to Jefferson, Oct. 20, 1788, Boyd, ed., *Jefferson Papers*, XIV, 30; Edward Rutledge to Jay, Nov. 12, 1786, Johnston, ed., *Papers to Jay*, III, 216–19; Edward Carrington to Jefferson, June 9, 1787, Boyd, ed., *Jefferson Papers*, XI, 408–09.

41. Parsons, *Sermon Preached May 28, 1788*, 22–23; Taylor, *Western Massachusetts*, 164; John Brown Cutting to Jefferson, July 11, 1788, Boyd, ed., *Jefferson Papers*, XIII, 332; Rush to Richard Price, Apr. 22, 1786, Butterfield, ed., *Rush Letters*, I, 386; Carrington to Jefferson, June 9, 1787, Boyd, ed., *Jefferson Papers*, XI, 408–09; William Nelson to William Short, July 12, 1788, quoted in Rutland, *Ordeal of the Constitution*, 253.

ican politics and society in the eighties than did the Constitution's eventual acceptance.[42] It was indeed a portent of what was to come.

4. THE EXTENDED SPHERE OF GOVERNMENT

Actually the confrontation of sociologies between Federalists and Antifederalists that emerged in 1787 was not as sharp as it logically might have been. By challenging the right of an elite to represent the common people, the Antifederalists without being quite aware of what they were doing had brought into question the traditional hierarchical and organic nature of society that made such elitism comprehensible to the eighteenth century. For, as Hamilton's social analysis in *The Federalist*, Number 35, suggested, what justified elite rule, together with the notion of virtual representation and the idea of the homogeneity and unity of the people's interest, was the sense that all parts of the society were of a piece, that all ranks and degrees were organically connected through a great chain in such a way that those on the top were necessarily involved in the welfare of those below them. Although the Antifederalists were presumably committed by their actual and class-based conception of representation to a quite different view of the nature of society, nevertheless they did not follow out the implications of their attack on elitism. Indeed, in the end they became fervent defenders of the traditional assumption that the state was a cohesive organic entity with a single homogeneous interest at the very time they were denying the consequences of this assumption. Given the extensive size of the proposed national republic, they perhaps had no other choice.

To the Antifederalists the Constitution was "so essentially differing from the principles of the revolution and from freedom" that it was unbelievable that it could have even been proposed. The best political science of the century, as expressed most pointedly but hardly exclusively by Montesquieu, had told them "that so extensive a territory as that of the United States, including such a variety of climates, productions, interests; and so great differences of manners, habits, and customs" could never be a single republican state. "No government formed on the principles

42. Rutland, *Ordeal of the Constitution*, 39.

of freedom can pervade all North America." An extended republic, such as the Federalists proposed, could never be "so competent to attend to the various local concerns and wants, of every particular district, as well as the peculiar governments, who are nearer the scene, and possessed of superior means of information." Southerners and northerners were different peoples with different cultures, and therefore could never constitute a single organic society with a similarity of interest. "It is impossible for one code of laws to suit Georgia and Massachusetts." The idea of a single republic, "on an average one thousand miles in length, and eight hundred in breadth, and containing six millions of white inhabitants all reduced to the same standard of morals, of habits, and of laws, is," said the Antifederalists, "in itself an absurdity, and contrary to the whole experience of mankind." "Nothing would support government, in such a case as that, but military coercion."[43]

It was a very powerful argument, resting as it did on the republican assumptions of 1776. For what gave such an argument force was the belief that a republic, wholly based as it was on the suffrage of the people, had to possess a population homogeneous in its customs and concerns. Otherwise the unitary public good, the collective welfare of the people that made a republic what it was, would be lost in the clashing of "interests opposite and dissimilar in their nature."[44] While the Antifederalists had unwittingly shaken the foundations of this belief with their denial of elite rule, it was actually left to the Federalists, or the most perceptive of them, to expose fully the flimsiness of this assumption and to grasp and exploit the significance of a new conception of society. In doing so, however, they ultimately destroyed whatever remained of the traditional social justification for aristocratic politics.

In the minds of many observers the relatively hierarchical so-

43. "Philadelphiensis," Mar. 8, 1788, Kenyon, ed., *Antifederalists*, 84; Lee to ?, Apr. 28, 1788, Ballagh, ed., *Letters of R. H. Lee*, II, 464; John Dawson (Va.), in Elliot, ed., *Debates*, III, 608; [Bryan], "Centinel, No. I," Oct. 5, 1787, McMaster and Stone, eds., *Pennsylvania and the Federal Constitution*, 573; Joseph Taylor (N. C.), in Elliot, ed., *Debates*, IV, 24; [Winthrop], "Agrippa, IV," Dec. 3, 1787, Ford, ed., *Essays on the Constitution*, 64–65; Samuel Spencer (N. C.), Elliot, ed., *Debates*, IV, 52. See Cecelia M. Kenyon, "Men of Little Faith: The Anti-Federalists on the Nature of Representative Government," *Wm. and Mary Qtly.*, 3d Ser., 12 (1955), 7–8.

44. [George Clinton], "Cato, III," Oct. 25, 1787, Ford, ed., *Essays on the Constitution*, 256; Phila. *Independent Gazetteer*, Apr. 15, 1788, McMaster and Stone, eds., *Pennsylvania and the Federal Constitution*, 536.

ciety of the eighteenth century seemed at last to be breaking up, as more and more groups with broadly based social, economic, and religious interests were emerging in politics, led by obscure men who stimulated and courted their concerns. Farmers, merchants, mechanics, manufacturers, debtors, creditors, Baptists, Presbyterians—all seemed more self-conscious of their special interests than ever before. "Every one must take care of himself— Necessity requires that political opinions should be squared to private views." Not only had "the great objects of the nation" been "sacrificed constantly to local views," but "the general interests of the States had been sacrificed to those of the Counties," lost in the scramble for private advantages and local favors.[45] Such developments had occurred precisely because "the best people" had lost control of politics. "Instead of choosing men for their abilities, integrity and patriotism," the people seemed too prone to "act from some mean, interested, or capricious motive." They "choose a man, because he will vote for a new town, or a new county, or in favour of a memorial; because he is noisy in blaming those who are in office, has confidence enough to suppose that he could do better, and impudence enough to tell the people so, or because he possesses in a supereminent degree, the all-prevailing popular talent of coaxing and flattering." The bulging and fluctuating state assemblies were filled with such narrow-minded politicians who constantly mistook "the particular circle" in which they moved for "the general voice" of the society. Under such circumstances men could ask whether the principles of "the spirit of '75 . . . a glorious spirit for *that period*" still applied "at the present day?"[46]

The Americans of 1776, convinced that a republic could only exist in a small area, wrote Madison from the perspective of a decade, had assumed "that the people composing the Society enjoy not only an equality of political rights; but that they have all precisely the same interests and the same feelings in every

45. Taylor, *Western Massachusetts*, 167; Hartford *Conn. Courant*, Aug. 6, 1787; Gouverneur Morris, in Farrand, ed., *Records of the Federal Convention*, I, 552. See *The Federalist*, No. 46.

46. Hartford *Conn. Courant*, Nov. 27, 1786, Feb. 5, 1787; James Wilson, in Farrand, ed., *Records of the Federal Convention*, I, 253; [Monroe], *Observations upon the Proposed Plan of Federal Government* . . . (Petersburg, Va., 1788), in Hamilton, ed., *Writings of Monroe*, I, 357, 365; Boston *Mass. Centinel*, May 10, 1788, quoted in John C. Miller, *Sam Adams: Pioneer in Propaganda* (Boston, 1936), 387.

respect." The narrow limits of the state were necessary to maintain this social homogeneity and to prevent factionalism. In such
an organic republic "the interest of the majority would be that
of the minority also; the decisions could only turn on mere
opinion concerning the good of the whole of which the major
voice would be the safest criterion; and within a small sphere,
this voice could be most easily collected and the public affairs
most accurately managed." Now, however, such an assumption
seemed "altogether fictitious." No society, no matter how small
(Rhode Island was an object lesson), "ever did or can consist
of so homogeneous a mass of Citizens." "In all civilized Societies,
distinctions are various and unavoidable." There were "rich and
poor; creditors and debtors; a landed interest, a monied interest, a mercantile interest, a manufacturing interest," together with
numerous subdivisions of these economic interests and interests based on differing religious and political opinions. All of this
heterogeneity, it had become increasingly evident, was responsible for the "instability" in the states. "Labouring parties, differing views and jarring Interests," said James Sullivan of
Massachusetts, "were the sum of our politicks." Many were now
prepared to conclude that the great danger to republicanism was
not magisterial tyranny or aristocratic dominance but "faction,
dissension, and consequent subjection of the minority to the
caprice and arbitrary decisions of the majority, who instead of
consulting the interest of the whole community collectively, attend sometimes to partial and local advantages."[47]

Indeed, it was this factious majoritarianism, an anomalous and
frightening conception for republican government, grounded as
it was on majority rule, that was at the center of the Federalist
perception of politics. In the minds of the Federalists the measure
of a free government had become its ability to control factions,
not, as used to be thought, those of a minority, but rather those of
"an interested and overbearing majority." "To secure the public
good and private rights against the danger of such a faction, and
at the same time to preserve the spirit and form of popular government," said Madison, was the "great *desideratum* of republican wisdom."[48]

47. Madison to Jefferson, Oct. 24, 1787, Boyd, ed., *Jefferson Papers*, XII, 277–
78; Madison, in Farrand, ed., *Records of the Federal Convention*, I, 214; James
Sullivan to Rufus King, June 14, 1787, King, *Life of King*, I, 222; Francis Corbin
(Va.), in Elliot, ed., *Debates*, III, 107.
48. *The Federalist*, No. 10. See Gottfried Dietze, *The Federalist: A Classic on
Federalism and Free Government* (Baltimore, 1960), 150.

From the moment, often at the very beginning of the Revolution, that various Americans realized that their separate states were not to be homogeneous units, they sought to adjust their thoughts and their institutions to the diversity. By the 1780's the most common conception used to describe the society was the dichotomy between aristocracy and democracy, the few and the many. The essential struggle of politics was not between the magistracy and the people, as the Whigs had thought, but between two social groups of the people themselves. "All political societies have two contending parties—the majority, whose interest it is to be free, and who have the power to be so—and the minority, whose interest it is to oppress, but who can never succeed, till they have blinded their opponents." As early as the seventies men talked publicly of the struggle between the few and the many, and in some states, particularly in Massachusetts, came to see this struggle embodied in the two houses of the legislature. Instead of merely allowing the natural aristocracy of wisdom and talent a special voice to promote the welfare of the people equally with the lower house, the senates had become for some blatantly self-interested bodies representing the distinct concerns of the propertied or rich of the community set in opposition to the common good of the ordinary people. While most Americans shied away from the implications of what some now saw as an inevitable social division, others were even going so far as to argue that such factions of rich and poor were "the materials of which the most perfect societies are formed. . . . The most opposite interests rightly blended, make the harmony of the State."[49]

By 1787 it seemed evident to Madison and to others that property and persons, the few and the many, were rapidly becoming distinct elements in the society. "In future times," said Madison in the Philadelphia Convention, "a great majority of the people will not only be without landed, but any other sort of, property." Since persons and property were "both essential objects of Government," both should be embodied in and protected by the structure of the government. This could most obviously be done through the bicameral system, in particular by "confining to the holders of property, the object deemed least secure in popular

49. Phila. *Pa. Journal*, Nov. 8, 1783; Boston *Independent Chronicle*, Oct. 18, 1787. On the celebration of the "diversity of tempers and constitutions among men" as "both a spur and check to one another" see Henry Cumings, *A Sermon Preached at Lexington on the 19th of April, 1781* (Boston, 1781), 28–29; Adams, *Sermon Preached May 29, 1782*, 42.

Governments, the right of suffrage for one of the two Legislative branches," as had been attempted in several states, most conspicuously in Massachusetts. Yet this bicameral solution had not really worked in the United States, admitted Madison. Since the senates had too often been composed of the self-same elements as the lower houses, they were ineffectual checks to the thrusts of the common people. America, said Madison, had not yet "reached the stage of Society in which conflicting feelings of the Class with, and the Class without property, have the operation natural to them in Countries fully peopled." But although the revised theory of mixed government made famous by the Massachusetts Constitution was as yet inapplicable to America's immature society, still, said Madison, the difficult problem remained "of so adjusting the claims of the Two Classes as to give security to each, and to promote the welfare of all." If bicameralism could not yet work, then some other constitutional solution would have to be found.[50]

What Madison and other Federalists did was turn all the old assumptions about republicanism around in order to create and justify their enlarged federal republic with its new kind of "mixed character." Seizing on David Hume's radical suggestion that a republican government operated better in a large territory than in a small one, several Federalists and Madison in particular ingeniously developed it. Since experience in America had demonstrated that no republic could be made small enough to contain a homogeneous interest that the people could express through the voice of the majority, the republican state, said Madison, must be so enlarged, "without departing from the elective basis of it," that "the propensity in small republics to rash measures and the facility of forming and executing them" would be stifled. Religion and exhortation had proved ineffective in restraining the rash and overbearing majorities of small republics. "What remedy can be found in a republican Government, where the majority must ultimately decide," argued Madison, "but that of giving such an extent to its sphere, that no one common interest or passion will be likely to unite a majority of the whole number in an unjust pursuit." Another Federalist put it more bluntly. "The ambition of the poor, and the avarice of the rich demagogue can never be restrained upon the narrow scale of state government." Only in the "extensive reservoir of power" of the federal government "will it be impossible for them to excite storms of sedition or oppression."

50. Madison, in Farrand, ed., *Records of the Federal Convention*, II, 204.

Thus the Antifederalist objection to the extended territory of the new national republic was actually its greatest source of strength. "In a large Society," concluded Madison, "the people are broken into so many interests and parties, that a common sentiment is less likely to be felt, and the requisite concert less likely to be formed, by a majority of the whole."[51]

But Madison did not want to be misunderstood. "I mean not by these remarks," he warned Jefferson, "to insinuate that an esprit de corps will not exist in the national Government." Although an impassioned and factious majority could not be formed in the new federal government, Madison had by no means abandoned the idea that the public good was the goal of government, a goal that should be positively promoted. He did not expect the new federal government to be neutralized into inactivity by the pressure of numerous conflicting interests. Nor did he conceive of politics as simply a consensus of the various groups that made up the society. The peculiar advantage of the new expanded national republic for Madison lay not in its inability to find a common interest for such an enlarged territory, but rather "in the substitution of representatives whose enlightened views and virtuous sentiments render them superior to local prejudices and to schemes of injustice." In the new federal scheme power would be "more likely to centre in men who possess the most attractive merit and the most diffusive and established characters," men who would be able to pursue vigorously what they saw to be the true interest of the country free from the turbulence and clamors of "men of factious tempers, of local prejudices, or of sinister designs."[52] Beneath his

51. *The Federalist*, No. 39; Madison, in Farrand, ed., *Records of the Federal Convention*, II, 204; Madison to Jefferson, Oct. 24, 1787, Boyd, ed., *Jefferson Papers*, XII, 277–78; *The Federalist*, No. 10; "To the Freemen of the United States," *American Museum*, 1 (1787), 431. On the advantages of an extensive republic see also [Jonathan Jackson], *Thoughts upon the Political Situation of the United States . . .* (Worcester, 1788), 88–90. For Hume's influence on Madison see Douglass Adair, " 'That Politics May Be Reduced to a Science': David Hume, James Madison and the Tenth *Federalist*," *Huntington Lib. Qtly.*, 20 (1956–57), 343–60. On Madison as a "Republican Savior" see the articles by Neal Riemer, "The Republicanism of James Madison," *Pol. Sci. Qtly.*, 69 (1954), 45–64; and especially "James Madison's Theory of the Self-Destructive Features of Republican Government," *Ethics*, 65 (1954–55), 34–43. Much of the recent interest in Madison has been stimulated or anticipated by the work of Douglass Adair; see his unpublished doctoral dissertation, The Intellectual Origins of Jeffersonian Democracy (Yale, 1943).

52. Madison to Jefferson, Oct. 24, 1787, Boyd, ed., *Jefferson Papers*, XII, 275; *The Federalist*, No. 10, No. 27.

sophisticated analysis of American society and politics, Madison grounded the success of the new Constitution on a common assumption about the social character of the federal government that lay at the heart of the Federalist program.

5. THE FILTRATION OF TALENT

If the new national government was to promote the common good as forcefully as any state government, and if, as the Federalists believed, a major source of the vices of the eighties lay in the abuse of state power, then there was something apparently contradictory about the new federal Constitution, which after all represented not a weakening of the dangerous power of republican government but rather a strengthening of it. "The complaints against the separate governments, even by the friends of the new plan," remarked the Antifederalist James Winthrop, "are not that they have not power enough, but that they are disposed to make a bad use of what power they have." Surely, concluded Winthrop, the Federalists were reasoning badly "when they purpose to set up a government possess'd of much more extensive powers . . . and subject to much smaller checks" than the existing state governments possessed and were subject to. Madison for one was quite aware of the pointedness of this objection. "It may be asked," he said, "how private rights will be more secure under the Guardianship of the General Government than under the State Governments, since they are both founded in the republican principle which refers the ultimate decision to the will of the majority."[53] What, in other words, was different about the new federal Constitution that would enable it to mitigate the effects of tyrannical majorities? What would keep the new federal government from succumbing to the same pressures that had beset the state governments? The answer the Federalists gave to these questions unmistakably reveals the social bias underlying both their fears of the unrestrained state legislatures and their expectations for their federal remedy. For all of their desires to avoid intricate examination of a delicate social structure, the Federalists' program itself demanded that the discussion of the Constitution would be in essentially social terms.

53. [Winthrop], "Agrippa, XVII," Jan. 20, 1788, Ford, ed., *Essays on the Constitution*, 113; Madison to Jefferson, Oct. 24, 1787, Boyd, ed., *Jefferson Papers*, XII, 276. See also [Ellsworth], "A Landholder, III," Nov. 19, 1787, Ford, ed., *Essays on the Constitution*, 147.

The Federalists were not as much opposed to the governmental power of the states as to the character of the people who were wielding it. The constitutions of most of the states were not really at fault. Massachusetts after all possessed a nearly perfect constitution. What actually bothered the Federalists was the sort of people who had been able to gain positions of authority in the state governments, particularly in the state legislatures. Much of the quarrel with the viciousness, instability, and injustice of the various state governments was at bottom social. "For," as John Dickinson emphasized, "*the government will partake of the qualities of those whose authority is prevalent.*" The political and social structures were intimately related. "People once respected their governors, their senators, their judges and their clergy; they reposed confidence in them; their laws were obeyed, and the states were happy in tranquility." But in the eighties the authority of government had drastically declined because "men of sense and property have lost much of their influence by the popular spirit of the war." "That exact order, and due subordination, that is essentially necessary in all well appointed governments, and which constitutes the real happiness and well being of society" had been deranged by "men of no genius or abilities" who had tried to run "the machine of government." Since "it cannot be expected that things will go well, when persons of vicious principles, and loose morals are in authority," it was the large number of obscure, ignorant, and unruly men occupying the state legislatures, and not the structure of the governments, that was the real cause of the evils so much complained of.[54]

The Federalist image of the Constitution as a sort of "philosopher's stone" was indeed appropriate: it was a device intended to transmute base materials into gold and thereby prolong the life of the republic. Patrick Henry acutely perceived what the Federalists were driving at. "The Constitution," he said in the Virginia Convention, "reflects in the most degrading and mortifying manner on the virtue, integrity, and wisdom of the state legislatures; it presupposes that the chosen few who go to Congress will have more upright hearts, and more enlightened minds, than those who are members of the individual legislatures." The new Constitution was structurally no different from the constitutions of some of the

54. [Dickinson], *Letters of Fabius*, Ford, ed., *Pamphlets*, 188; Hartford *Conn. Courant*, Nov. 27, 1786; Charleston *Gazette of the St. of S.-C.*, Jan. 3, 1785; Josiah Whitney, *A Sermon, Preached in the Audience of His Excellency Samuel Huntington* . . . (Hartford, 1788), 23.

states. Yet the powers of the new central government were not as threatening as the powers of the state governments precisely because the Federalists believed different kinds of persons would hold them. They anticipated that somehow the new government would be staffed largely by "the worthy," the natural social aristocracy of the country. "After all," said Pelatiah Webster, putting his finger on the crux of the Federalist argument, "the grand secret of forming a good government, is, to put good men into the administration: for wild, vicious, or idle men, will ever make a bad government, let its principles be ever so good."[55]

What was needed then, the Federalists argued, was to restore a proper share of political influence to those who through their social attributes commanded the respect of the people and who through their enlightenment and education knew the true policy of government. "The people commonly intend the PUBLIC GOOD," wrote Hamilton in *The Federalist*, but they did not "always *reason right* about the *means* of promoting it." They sometimes erred, largely because they were continually beset "by the wiles of parasites and sycophants, by the snares of the ambitious, the avaricious, the desperate, by the artifices of men who possess their confidence more than deserve it, and of those who seek to possess rather than to deserve it." The rights of man were simple, quickly felt, and easily comprehended: in matters of liberty, "the mechanic and the philosopher, the farmer and the scholar, are all upon a footing." But to the Federalists matters of government were quite different: government was "a complicated science, and requires abilities and knowledge, of a variety of other subjects, to understand it." "Our states cannot be well governed," the Federalists concluded, "till our old influential characters acquire confidence and authority." Only if the respected and worthy lent their natural intellectual abilities and their natural social influence to political authority could governmental order be maintained.[56]

Perhaps no one probed this theme more frenziedly than did Jonathan Jackson in his *Thoughts upon the Political Situation of the United States*, published in 1788. For Jackson the problems of the eighties were not merely intellectual but personal. Although

55. Corbin and Henry (Va.), in Elliot, ed., *Debates*, III, 107, 167; [Pelatiah Webster], *The Weakness of Brutus Exposed* . . . (Phila., 1787), in Ford, ed., *Pamphlets*, 131. See also John Francis Mercer's insight into the social basis of government in Farrand, ed., *Records of the Federal Convention*, II, 289.

56. *The Federalist*, No. 71; "To the Freemen of the United States," *American Museum*, 1 (1787), 429; Hartford *Conn. Courant*, Nov. 20, 1786.

at the close of the Revolution he had been one of the half-dozen richest residents of Newburyport, Massachusetts, by the end of the eighties not only had his wealth been greatly diminished but his position in Newburyport society had been usurped by a newer, less well-educated, less refined group of merchants.[57] His pamphlet, expressing his bitter reaction to this displacement, exaggerated but did not misrepresent a common Federalist anxiety.

Although differences of rank were inevitable in every society, wrote Jackson, "there never was a people upon earth . . . who were in less hazard than the people of this country, of an aristocracy's prevailing—or anything like it, dangerous to liberty." America possessed very little "inequality of fortune." There was "no rank of any consequence, nor hereditary titles." "Landed property is in general held in small portions, even in southern states, compared with the manors, parks and royal demesnes of most countries." And the decay of primogeniture and entail, together with the "diverse" habits and passions between fathers and sons, worked to retard the engrossing of large estates. The only kind of aristocracy possible in America would be an "*aristocracy of experience, and of the best understandings*," a "*natural aristocracy*" that had to dominate public authority in order to prevent America from degenerating into democratic licentiousness, into a government where the people "would be directed by no rule but their own will and caprice, or the interested wishes of a very few persons, who *affect* to speak the sentiments of the people." Tyranny by the people was the worst kind because it left few resources to the oppressed. Jackson explicitly and heatedly denied the assumption of 1776: "that large representative bodies are a great security to publick liberty." Such numerous popular assemblies resembled a mob, as likely filled with fools and knaves as wise and honest men. Jackson went on to question not only the possibility that the general good of the people would be expressed by such large assemblies, but also the advisability of annual elections and rotation of office. The people, Jackson even went so far as to say, "are nearly as unfit to choose legislators, or any of the more important publick officers, as they are in general to fill the offices themselves." There were in fact too many examples in the eighties of men from the people gaining seats in America's public assemblies, men "of good natural abilities and sound understanding, but

57. Benjamin W. Labaree, *Patriots and Partisans: The Merchants of Newburyport, 1764–1815* (Cambridge, Mass., 1962), 87, 96–97.

who had had little or no education, and still less converse with the world." Such men were inevitably suspicious of those "they call the *gentle folks*," those who were bred in easier circumstances and better endowed with education and worldly experience. Yet without the dominance of these "gentle folks" in the legislatures, the good of the whole society could never be promoted. The central problem facing America, said Jackson, was to bring the natural aristocracy back into use and to convey "authority to those, and those only, who by nature, education, and good dispositions, are qualified for government." It was this problem that the federal Constitution was designed to solve.[58]

In a review of Jackson's pamphlet Noah Webster raised the crucial question. It was commendable, he wrote, that only the wise and honest men be elected to office. "But how can a constitution ensure the choice of such men? A constitution that leaves the choice entirely with the people?" It was not enough simply to state that such persons were to be chosen. Indeed, many of the state constitutions already declared "that senators and representatives *shall* be elected from the *most wise*, *able*, and *honest* citizens. . . . The truth is, such declarations are *empty things*, as they require *that* to be *done* which cannot be *defined*, much less *enforced*." It seemed to Webster that no constitution in a popular state could guarantee that only the natural aristocracy would be elected to office. How could the federal Constitution accomplish what the state constitutions like Massachusetts's and Connecticut's had been unable to accomplish? How could it insure that only the respectable and worthy would hold power?[59]

The evils of state politics, the Federalists had become convinced, flowed from the narrowness of interest and vision of the state legislators. "We find the representatives of counties and corporations in the Legislatures of the States," said Madison, "much more disposed to sacrifice the aggregate interest, and even authority, to the local views of their Constituents" than to promote the general good at the expense of their electors. Small electoral districts enabled obscure and designing men to gain power by practicing "the vicious arts by which elections are too often carried." Already observers in the eighties had noticed that a governmental official "standing, not on local, but a general election of the whole

58. [Jackson], *Thoughts upon the Political Situation*, 54, 55, 56, 57, 55, 58, 59, 61–62, 69, 76–79, 98, 117–18, 57.

59. Review of "Thoughts upon the Political Situation of the United States of America . . . ," *American Magazine*, 1 (1787–88), 804.

body of the people" tended to have a superior, broader vision by "being the interested and natural conservator of the universal interest." "The most effectual remedy for the local biass" of senators or of any elected official, said Madison, was to impress upon their minds "an attention to the interest of the whole Society by making them the choice of the whole Society." If elected officials were concerned with only the interest of those who elected them, then their outlook was most easily broadened by enlarging their electorate.[60] Perhaps nowhere was this contrast between localism and cosmopolitanism more fully analyzed and developed than in a pamphlet written by William Beers of Connecticut. Although Beers wrote in 1791, not to justify the Constitution, his insight into the workings of American politics was precisely that of the Federalists of 1787.

"The people of a state," wrote Beers, "may justly be divided into two classes": those, on one hand, "who are independent in their principles, of sound judgments, actuated by no local or personal influence, and who understand, and ever act with a view to the public good"; and those, on the other hand, who were "the dependent, the weak, the biassed, local party men—the dupes of artifice and ambition." While the independent and worthy were "actuated by a uniform spirit, and will generally unite their views in the same object," they were diffused throughout the whole community. "In particular districts, they bear not an equal proportion to the opposite party, who tho incapable of extending their views throughout the state, find in their particular communities similar objects of union." Thus the best people were often overpowered in small district elections, where "the success of a candidate may depend in a great degree on the quantity of his exertions for the moment," on his becoming "popular, for a single occasion, by qualities and means, which could not possibly establish a permanent popularity or one which should pervade a large community," on his seizing "the occasion of some prevailing passion, some strong impression of separate interest, some popular clamor against the existing administration, or some other false and fatal prejudice"—all the arts which were "well known, by the melancholy experience of this and other nations,

60. Madison to Jefferson, Oct. 24, 1787, Boyd, ed., *Jefferson Papers*, XII, 275; *The Federalist*, No. 10; Stiles, *United States Elevated*, in Thornton, ed., *Pulpit*, 420; Madison's Observations on Jefferson's Draft of a Constitution for Virginia (1788), Boyd, ed., *Jefferson Papers*, VI, 308–09.

to have met, in small circles of election, but too often with triumphant success." But an entire state could not be so deluded. "No momentary glare of deceptive qualities, no intrigues, no exertions will be sufficient to make a whole people lose sight of those points of character which alone can entitle one to their universal confidence." With a large electorate the advance toward public honors was slow and gradual. "Much time is necessary to become the object of general observation and confidence." Only established social leaders would thus be elected by a broad constituency. Narrow the electorate, "and you leave but a single step between the lowest and the most elevated station. You take ambition by the hand, you raise her from obscurity, and clothe her in purple." With respect to the size of the legislative body, the converse was true. Reduce the number of its members and thereby guarantee a larger proportion of the right kind of people to be elected, for "the more you enlarge the body, the greater chance there is, of introducing weak and unqualified men."[61]

Constitutional reformers in the eighties had continually attempted to apply these insights to the states, by decreasing the size of the legislatures and by proposing at-large elections for governors and senators in order to "make a segregation of upright, virtuous, intelligent men, to guide the helm of public affairs." Now these ideas were to be applied to the new federal government with hopefully even more effectiveness. The great height of the new national government, it was expected, would prevent unprincipled and vicious men, the obscure and local-minded men who had gained power in the state legislatures, from scaling its walls. The federal government would act as a kind of sieve, extracting "from the mass of the society the purest and noblest characters which it contains." Election by the people in large districts would temper demagoguery and crass electioneering and would thus, said James Wilson, "be most likely to obtain men of intelligence and uprightness." "Faction," it was believed, "will decrease in proportion to the diminution of counsellors." It would be "transferred from the state legislatures to Congress, where it will be more easily controlled." The men who would sit in the federal legislature, because few in number and drawn from a broad electorate, would be "the best men in the country." "For," wrote John Jay in *The Federalist*, "although town or county, or other contracted influence, may place men in State assemblies, or sen-

61. [Beers], *Address to Connecticut*, 18–23, 29.

ates, or courts of justice, or executive departments, yet more general and extensive reputation for talents and other qualifications will be necessary to recommend men to offices under the national government." Only by first bringing these sorts of men, the natural aristocracy of the country, back into dominance in politics, the Federalists were convinced, could Americans begin to solve the pressing foreign and domestic problems facing them. Only then, concluded Jay, would it "result that the administration, the political counsels, and the judicial decisions of the national government will be more wise, systematical, and judicious than those of individual States, and consequently more satisfactory with respect to other nations, as well as more *safe* with respect to us." The key therefore to the prospects of the new federal government, compared to the experience of the confederation of sovereign states, declared Francis Corbin of Virginia in words borrowed from Jean Louis De Lolme, the Genevan commentator on the English constitution, lay in the fact that the federal Constitution "places the remedy in the hands which *feel* the disorder; the other places the remedy in those hands which *cause* the disorder."[62]

In short, through the artificial contrivance of the Constitution overlying an expanded society, the Federalists meant to restore and to prolong the traditional kind of elitist influence in politics that social developments, especially since the Revolution, were undermining. As the defenders if not always the perpetrators of these developments—the "disorder" of the 1780's—the Antifederalists could scarcely have missed the social implications of the Federalist program. The Constitution was intrinsically an aristocratic document designed to check the democratic tendencies of the period, and as such it dictated the character of the Antifederalist response. It was therefore inevitable that the Antifederalists should have charged that the new government was "dangerously adapted to the purposes of an immediate *aristocratic tyranny*." In state after state the Antifederalists reduced the issue to those social terms predetermined by the Federalists themselves: the Constitution was a plan intended to "raise the fortunes and respectability

62. *Providence Gazette*, Aug. 12, 1786; Madison, "Vices of the Political System," Hunt, ed., *Writings of Madison*, II, 369; Wilson, in Farrand, ed., *Records of the Federal Convention*, I, 154; Corbin (Va.), in Elliot, ed., *Debates*, III, 107–08; *The Federalist*, No. 3. For De Lolme's expression of the difference between "a *representative*" and "a *popular*" constitution see Jean Louis De Lolme, *The Constitution of England* . . . (London, 1788), 271.

of the *well-born few*, and oppress the plebians"; it was "a continental exertion of the *well-born* of America to obtain that darling domination, which they have not been able to accomplish in their respective states"; it "will lead to an aristocratical government, and establish tyranny over us." Whatever their own particular social standing, the Antifederalist spokesmen spread the warning that the new government either would be "in practice a *permanent* ARISTOCRACY" or would soon "degenerate to a compleat Aristocracy."[63] Both George Mason and Richard Henry Lee, speaking not out of the concerns of the social elite to which they belonged but out of a complicated sense of alienation from that elite, expressed as much fear of a "consolidating aristocracy" resulting from the new Constitution as any uncultivated Scotch-Irish upstart. While Lee privately revealed his deep dislike of "the hasty, unpersevering, aristocratic genius of the south" which "suits not my disposition," Mason throughout the duration of the Philadelphia Convention acted as the conscience of an old republicanism he thought his Virginia colleagues had forgotten and continually reminded them of what the Revolution had been about. "Whatever inconveniency may attend the democratic principle," said Mason repeatedly, "it must actuate one part of the Government. It is the only security for the rights of the people." As the Constitution seemed to demonstrate, the "superior classes of society" were becoming too indifferent to the "lowest classes." Remember, he warned his fellow delegates pointedly, "our own children will in a short time be among the general mass." The Constitution seemed obviously "calculated," as even young John Quincy Adams declared, "to increase the influence, power and wealth of those who have it already." Its adoption would undoubtedly be "a grand point gained in favor of the aristocratic party."[64]

Aristocratic principles were in fact "interwoven" in the very

---

63. [Mercy Warren], *Observations on the New Constitution* . . . ([Boston, 1788]), in Ford, ed., *Pamphlets*, 6; *Providence Gazette*, Jan. 5, 1788; [Bryan], "Centinel, No. IX," Jan. 8, 1788, "Centinel, No. I," Oct. 5, 1787, McMaster and Stone, eds., *Pennsylvania and the Federal Constitution*, 627, 575; William Goudy (N. C.), in Elliot, ed., *Debates*, IV, 56; "John De Witt," Nov. 5, 1787, Kenyon, ed., *Antifederalists*, 104.

64. [Lee], *Letters from the Federal Farmer*, Ford, ed., *Pamphlets*, 285, 295; George Mason, *Objections . . . to the Proposed Federal Constitution* (n.p., n.d.), *ibid.*, 332; Lee to John Adams, Oct. 8, 1779, Ballagh, ed., *Letters of R. H. Lee*, II, 155; Mason, in Farrand, ed., *Records of the Federal Convention*, I, 359, 49, 56; John Quincy Adams, *Life in a New England Town: 1787-1788* . . . (Boston, 1903), 46.

fabric of the proposed government. If a government was "so constituted as to admit but few to exercise the powers of it," then it would "according to the natural course of things" end up in the hands of "the natural aristocracy." It went almost without saying that the awesome president and the exalted Senate, "a compound of *monarchy* and *aristocracy*," would be dangerously far removed from the people. But even the House of Representatives, the very body that "should be a true picture of the people, possess a knowledge of their circumstances and their wants, sympathize in all their distresses, and disposed to seek their true interest," was without "a tincture of democracy." Since it could never collect "the interests, feelings, and opinions of three or four millions of people," it was better understood as "an Assistant Aristocratical Branch" to the Senate than as a real representation of the people.[65] When the number of representatives was "so small, the office will be highly elevated and distinguished; the style in which the members live will probably be high; circumstances of this kind will render the place of a representative not a desirable one to sensible, substantial men, who have been used to walk in the plain and frugal paths of life." While the ordinary people in extensive electoral districts of thirty or forty thousand inhabitants would remain "divided," those few extraordinary men with "conspicuous military, popular, civil or legal talents" could more easily form broader associations to dominate elections; they had family and other connections to "unite their interests." If only a half-dozen congressmen were to be selected to represent a large state, then rarely, argued the Antifederalists in terms that were essentially no different from those used by the Federalists in the Constitution's defense, would persons from "the great body of the people, the middle and lower classes," be elected to the House of Representatives. "The Station is too high and exalted to be filled but [by] the *first Men* in the State in point of Fortune and Influence. In fact no order or class of the people will be represented in the House of Representatives called the Democratic Branch but the rich and wealthy."[66]

65. [Clinton], "Cato, VI," Dec. 16, 1787, Ford, ed., *Essays on the Constitution*, 273; Smith (N. Y.), in Elliot, ed., *Debates*, II, 246, 245; "Philadelphiensis," Feb. 7, 1788, Kenyon, ed., *Antifederalists*, 72; [Lee], *Letters from the Federal Farmer*, Ford, ed., *Pamphlets*, 295; "John De Witt," Nov. 5, 1787, Kenyon, ed., *Antifederalists*, 108.

66. "Dissent of the Minority," McMaster and Stone, eds., *Pennsylvania and the Federal Constitution*, 471; Smith (N. Y.), in Elliot, ed., *Debates*, II, 246; Boston *Independent Chronicle*, Dec. 13, 1787; Samuel Chase, quoted in Crowl, "Anti-Federalism in Maryland," *Wm. and Mary Qtly.*, 3d Ser., 4 (1947), 464.

The Antifederalists thus came to oppose the new national government for the same reason the Federalists favored it: because its very structure and detachment from the people would work to exclude any kind of actual and local interest representation and prevent those who were not rich, well born, or prominent from exercising political power. Both sides fully appreciated the central issue the Constitution posed and grappled with it throughout the debates: whether a professedly popular government should actually be in the hands of, rather than simply derived from, common ordinary people.

Out of the division in 1787–88 over this issue, an issue which was as conspicuously social as any in American history, the Antifederalists emerged as the spokesmen for the growing American antagonism to aristocracy and as the defenders of the most intimate participation in politics of the widest variety of people possible. It was not from lack of vision that the Antifederalists feared the new government. Although their viewpoint was intensely localist, it was grounded in as perceptive an understanding of the social basis of American politics as that of the Federalists. Most of the Antifederalists were majoritarians with respect to the state legislatures but not with respect to the national legislature, because they presumed as well as the Federalists did that different sorts of people from those who sat in the state assemblies would occupy the Congress. Whatever else may be said about the Antifederalists, their populism cannot be impugned. They were true champions of the most extreme kind of democratic and egalitarian politics expressed in the Revolutionary era. Convinced that "it has been the principal care of free governments to guard against the encroachments of the great," the Antifederalists believed that popular government itself, as defined by the principles of 1776, was endangered by the new national government. If the Revolution had been a transfer of power from the few to the many, then the federal Constitution clearly represented an abnegation of the Revolution. For, as Richard Henry Lee wrote in his *Letters from the Federal Farmer*, "every man of reflection must see, that the change now proposed, is a transfer of power from the many to the few."[67]

Although Lee's analysis contained the essential truth, the Federalist program was not quite so simply summed up. It was true that through the new Constitution the Federalists hoped to resist

67. Smith (N. Y.), in Elliot, ed., *Debates*, II, 247; [Lee], *Letters from the Federal Farmer*, Ford, ed., *Pamphlets*, 317.

and eventually to avert what they saw to be the rapid decline of the influence and authority of the natural aristocracy in America. At the very time that the organic conception of society that made elite rule comprehensible was finally and avowedly dissolving, and the members of the elite were developing distinct professional, social, or economic interests, the Federalists found elite rule more imperative than ever before. To the Federalists the greatest dangers to republicanism were flowing not, as the old Whigs had thought, from the rulers or from any distinctive minority in the community, but from the widespread participation of the people in the government. It now seemed increasingly evident that if the public good not only of the United States as a whole but even of the separate states were to be truly perceived and promoted, the American people must abandon their Revolutionary reliance on their representative state legislatures and place their confidence in the highmindedness of the natural leaders of the society, which ideally everyone had the opportunity of becoming. Since the Federalists presumed that only such a self-conscious elite could transcend the many narrow and contradictory interests inevitable in any society, however small, the measure of a good government became its capacity for insuring the predominance of these kinds of natural leaders who knew better than the people as a whole what was good for the society.

The result was an amazing display of confidence in constitutionalism, in the efficacy of institutional devices for solving social and political problems. Through the proper arrangement of new institutional structures the Federalists aimed to turn the political and social developments that were weakening the place of "the better sort of people" in government back upon themselves and to make these developments the very source of the perpetuation of the natural aristocracy's dominance of politics. Thus the Federalists did not directly reject democratic politics as it had manifested itself in the 1780's; rather they attempted to adjust to this politics in order to control and mitigate its effects. In short they offered the country an elitist theory of democracy. They did not see themselves as repudiating either the Revolution or popular government, but saw themselves as saving both from their excesses. If the Constitution were not established, they told themselves and the country over and over, then republicanism was doomed, the grand experiment was over, and a division of the confederacy, monarchy, or worse would result.

Despite all the examples of popular vice in the eighties, the Federalist confidence in the people remained strong. The letters of "Caesar," with their frank and violent denigration of the people, were anomalies in the Federalist literature.[68] The Federalists had by no means lost faith in the people, at least in the people's ability to discern their true leaders. In fact many of the social elite who comprised the Federalist leadership were confident of popular election if the constituency could be made broad enough, and crass electioneering be curbed, so that the people's choice would be undisturbed by ambitious demagogues. "For if not blind to their own interest, they choose men of the first character for wisdom and integrity." Despite prodding by so-called designing and unprincipled men, the bulk of the people remained deferential to the established social leadership—for some aspiring politicians frustratingly so. Even if they had wanted to, the Federalists could not turn their backs on republicanism. For it was evident to even the most pessimistic "that no other form would be reconcilable with the genius of the people of America; with the fundamental principles of the Revolution; or with that honorable determination which animates every votary of freedom, to rest all our political experiments on the capacity of mankind for self-government." Whatever government the Federalists established had to be "strictly republican" and "deducible from the only source of just authority—the People."[69]

68. The "Caesar" letters are reprinted in Ford, ed., *Essays on the Constitution*, 283–91. It now appears that Hamilton did not write them. See Jacob E. Cooke, "Alexander Hamilton's Authorship of the 'Caesar' Letters," *Wm. and Mary Qtly.*, 3d Ser., 17 (1960), 78–85.

69. Hartford *Conn. Courant*, Feb. 5, 1787; *The Federalist*, No. 39; Jay to Washington, Jan. 7, 1787, Johnston, ed., *Papers of Jay*, III, 229. See Martin Diamond, "Democracy and *The Federalist*: A Reconsideration of the Framers' Intent," *Amer. Pol. Sci. Rev.*, 53 (1959), 52–68.

CHAPTER XIII

The Federalist Persuasion

1. THE REPUDIATION OF 1776

There could be little doubt that the federal Constitution was intended to be, as Oliver Ellsworth said, "a creation of power," which meant a corresponding reduction of those kinds of liberty "which enervate a necessary government." Although the most extreme nationalists in the Philadelphia Convention questioned whether the Constitution that emerged would "effect our purpose," being "nothing more than a combination of the peculiarities of two of the State Governments which separately had been found insufficient," most Federalists realized that it was probably the strongest government that could have been formed under the circumstances. Certainly in its creation of power, that is, in its creation of an independent executive and an upper house with a six-year term, it went well beyond what many Americans had anticipated. Even some ardent Federalists, whose greatest apprehensions were "from the inroads of the democracy," conceded privately that there was "a preposterous combination of powers in the President and Senate, which may be used improperly."[1]

If even some Federalists were startled by the proposed combination of power in the new government, it is not surprising that the Antifederalists, however much they agreed that "some reform in our government must take place," were profoundly shocked at the revolutionary nature of the plan, "calculated," as

1. [Ellsworth], "A Landholder, III," Nov. 19, 1787, Ford, ed., *Essays on the Constitution*, 146–47; Madison, in Farrand, ed., *Records of the Federal Convention*, II, 291; Edward Carrington to Jefferson, Oct. 23, 1787, Boyd, ed., *Jefferson Papers*, XII, 255.

Richard Henry Lee said, "totally to change, in time, our condition as a people." "From a well-digested, well-formed democratic," warned James Lincoln of South Carolina, "you are at once rushing into an aristocratic government." Far from being a mere copy of some of the state constitutions and hence insufficiently vigorous to remedy the vices of American society, as many Federalists believed, the Constitution if established, it seemed clear to the Antifederalists, would result in "an immediate *aristocratic tyranny*; that from the difficulty, if not the impracticability of its operation, must soon terminate in the most *uncontrouled despotism*."[2]

Throughout all of their speeches and writings the Antifederalists expressed a pervasive mistrust of the new government that has earned them the title of "men of little faith," a title they would not have disavowed. It was true that they were "jealous of their rulers." "They ought to be so; it was just they should be so; for jealousy was one of the greatest securities of the people in a republic." An Antifederalist, it was claimed, was "so far an enthusiast in favor of liberty" that he "never will trust the sacred deposit to other hands." Yet the Antifederalists' lack of faith was not in the people themselves, but only in the organizations and institutions that presumed to speak for the people. Jealousy and suspicion of all bodies set above the people was a cardinal principle of radical Whiggism. Since it was the extension of this Whig principle, enhancing the people out-of-doors as it correspondingly disparaged their elected officials, even their supposed representatives, that eventually led to democracy as America came to know it, the Antifederalists can never be considered undemocratic. They were "localists," fearful of distant governmental, even representational, authority for very significant political and social reasons that in the final analysis must be called democratic.[3]

It was out of this localist, eighteenth-century radical Whig tradition of mistrust of governmental authority that the Antifederalists in 1787–88 spoke. For them the decade since 1776 had not essentially altered the problems of politics. Power, that "predominant thirst of domination which has invariably and uniformly prompted rulers to abuse their powers," was on the march again,

2. [Melancthon Smith], *An Address to the People of the State of New York* . . . (N. Y., 1788), in Ford, ed., *Pamphlets*, 99; [Lee], *Letters from the Federal Farmer, ibid.,* 280, 282; Lincoln (S. C.), in Elliot, ed., *Debates,* IV, 313; [Warren], *Observations on the New Constitution,* Ford, ed., *Pamphlets,* 6.

3. W. Bodman (Mass.), and John Dawson (Va.), in Elliot, ed., *Debates,* II, 60, III, 612. Cf. Kenyon, "Men of Little Faith," *Wm. and Mary Qtly.,* 3d Ser., 12 (1955), 3–43.

for there was really nothing new or unprecedented in this latest attempt at usurpation. There were "precedents in abundance . . . drawn from Great Britain." The Antifederalists saw themselves in 1787–88 fighting the good old Whig cause in defense of the people's liberties against the engrossing power of their rulers. "The tyranny of Philadelphia," declared Patrick Henry, one of the most articulate of the opponents of the Constitution, "may be like the tyranny of George III." All the efforts of the Antifederalists aimed at proving "this similitude."[4]

The supreme magistrate was truly awesome. Standing alone, as commander-in-chief of the armed forces unencumbered by an executive council, with power over appointments that few state executives possessed and with a term of office longer than any, the president was a magistrate who could "easily become king." "There is hardly an instance where a republic trusted its executive so long with much power." Indeed, all the offices of the federal government, including the president, were perpetually re-eligible for reelection. Rotation in office, a "truly republican institution," had been abandoned, making the Senate, some feared, "a fixed and unchangeable body of men" and the president "a king for life, like a king of Poland." The members of the upper house of the legislature were so closely allied with the executive in so many important matters that they would become his "counsellors and partners in crime." Together the president and Senate held all the executive and two-thirds of the legislative power; in treaty-making they possessed the whole legislative power, and jointly they appointed all the civil and military officers. It was, as Richard Henry Lee remarked, "a most formidable combination of power" that could only unbalance the Constitution. Beside the president and Senate, the House of Representatives, the supposed "democratic branch" of the government, seemed but a "mere shred or rag" of the people's power, hardly a match for the monarchical and aristocratic branches.[5] "What have you been contending for these ten years past?" the Antifederalists asked. "Liberty! What is liberty? The power of governing yourselves. If you adopt this Constitution, have you this power? No: you give it into the hands of a set of men who live one thousand miles distant from you." Secure in their ten-mile square these men could easily be-

4. Patrick Henry (Va.), in Elliot, ed., *Debates*, III, 436, 314.
5. Henry and William Grayson (Va.), Smith (N. Y.), in Elliot, ed., *Debates*, III, 58, 491, II, 310; Jefferson to William Carmichael, Dec. 15, 1787, Boyd, ed., *Jefferson Papers*, XII, 425; Grayson (Va.), in Elliot, ed., *Debates*, III, 491; Lee to Edmund Randolph, Oct. 16, 1787, Ballagh, ed., *Letters of R. H. Lee*, II, 451–52.

come as dangerous as the court of George III once was, for "Congress will be vested with more extensive powers than ever Great Britain exercised over us; too great . . . to intrust with any class of men, let their talents or virtues be ever so conspicuous, even though composed of such exalted, amiable characters as the great Washington." The elimination of annual elections, rotation, and recall, together with the extensive powers given to Congress, would make "the federal rulers . . . masters, and not servants." "After we have given them all our money, established them in a federal town, given them the power of coining money and raising a standing *army*, and to establish their arbitrary government; what resources have the people left?"[6]

In the eyes of the Antifederalists the whole government, representatives in Congress included, appeared magisterial, that is, composed of rulers or extraordinary men whose interests were distinct from those of the ruled or ordinary men. The president and Senate were clearly detached from the people, and even the supposed "democratic branch," the House of Representatives, was so structured that "men may be appointed who are not representatives of the people." Why then should such so-called representatives be trusted any more than rulers or governors in the past had been? "Will not the members of Congress have the same passions which other rulers have had." Why were members of Congress given the sole power of making and trying impeachments? Who would impeach them? asked Joseph Taylor of North Carolina in a series of queries that plainly revealed this Antifederalist denial of representation in the new government. "If any tyranny or oppression should arise, how are those who perpetrated such oppression to be tried and punished? By a tribunal consisting of the very men who assist in such tyranny. Can any tribunal be found, in any community, who will give judgement against their own actions?" Scornfully North Carolina Federalists answered that impeachment, as in all governments, "extended only to the officers of the United States," that is, only to the magistracy. Never had legislators, never had representatives been impeached. "No member of the House of Commons, in England, has ever been impeached before the Lords, nor any lord, for a legislative misdemeanor." "A representative," the Federalists argued, "is answerable to no power but his constituents." But so great was the Antifederalists' fear of Congress as a magisterial power that this argument only made

6. Lincoln (S. C.), Nathaniel Barrell (Mass.), M. Kingsley (Mass.), in Elliot, ed., *Debates*, IV, 313, II, 159, 62.

congressional immunity from impeachment appear "in a still worse light than before." To be told "that those who are to tax us are our representatives" was no comfort, for there was "no actual responsibility," no real representation of the people's interests. The House of Representatives was no more to be trusted than were the president and Senate.[7]

To the Antifederalists the Constitution represented a repudiation of everything that Americans had fought for. They could not have made a more severe or more accurate condemnation of the new government than to charge that it "departed widely from the principles and political faith of '76." In the context of conventional eighteenth-century political thought the Constitution obviously represented a reinforcement of "*energy*" at the expense of "*liberty*," a startling strengthening of the rulers' power at the expense of the people's participation in the government. For the Antifederalists the same radical Whig terms that earlier had been used against the British monarchy were still applicable, terms that had been incorporated into America's Revolutionary constitutions. "Poor little humble republican maxims have attracted the admiration, and engaged the attention, of the virtuous and wise in all nations, and have stood the shock of ages." Now the Federalists were attempting to deny the validity of these principles that English Whigs had delighted in; they were deserting "those maxims which alone can preserve liberty" in favor of newer, more refined maxims "which tend to the prostration of republicanism." Had the Constitution, the Antifederalists correctly pointed out time and again, "been presented to our view ten years ago, . . . it would have been considered as containing principles incompatible with republican liberty, and therefore doomed to infamy."[8]

Yet by 1787 the intellectual issue was no longer this clear. The Constitution presented no simple choice between accepting or rejecting the principles of 1776. During the intervening years, in newspapers, pamphlets, town meetings, and legislative debates,

7. James Bloodworth (N. C.), Henry (Va.), Taylor, Samuel Johnston (N. C.), and Henry (Va.), in Elliot, ed., *Debates*, IV, 55, III, 437, IV, 33, 34, III, 167. The issue of the impeachment of legislative officials was faced in the trial of Senator William Blount of North Carolina in 1798–99. Blount was acquitted on the ground that as a senator he was not a "civil officer" within the meaning of the impeachment provision of the Constitution. See also [Monroe], *Observations upon the Proposed Plan of Federal Government*, Hamilton, ed., *Writings of Monroe*, I, 361–62.

8. Thomas Tredwell (N. Y.), in Elliot, ed., *Debates*, II, 431; Theodore Bland to Arthur Lee, June 13, 1788, quoted in Rutland, *Ordeal of the Constitution*, 231; Henry and Dawson (Va.), in Elliot, ed., *Debates*, III, 137, 607; see also *ibid.*, II, 101.

the political assumptions of 1776 had been extended, molded, and perverted in ways that no one had clearly anticipated. Under the severest kinds of political and polemical pressures old words had assumed new meanings, and old institutions had taken on new significance. By 1787 it was entirely possible for the Federalists to turn the Whiggism of 1776 against itself without any sense of intellectual violence. The Federalists, far from seeing themselves as rejecters of populism and the faith of 1776, could now intelligibly picture themselves as the true defenders of the libertarian tradition of Whiggism. "The supporters of the Constitution," said John Marshall in the Virginia Convention, "claim the title of being firm friends of the liberty and the rights of mankind." The Federalists were the real protectors of the people; they "idolize democracy." They admired the Constitution precisely because they "think it a well-regulated democracy." The principle of democracy, declared James Wilson, permeated the Constitution, "in its terms and in its consequences."[9] Such Federalist statements required no conscious wrenching and distortion of ideas, no hypocrisy, because so many piecemeal changes in thought had occurred in the decade since Independence that, without anyone's being fully aware of what was happening, the whole intellectual world of 1776 had become unraveled. Now, under the pressure of the debate over the Constitution, these scattered strands of Whig thought, used disconnectedly for years but never before comprehended as a whole, were picked up and brought together by the Federalists and woven into a new intellectual fabric, a new explanation of politics, of whose beauty and symmetry the Federalists themselves only gradually became aware. In the process those who clung to the principles of 1776 could only stand amazed with confusion, left holding remnants of thought that had lost their significance. The Antifederalists could never offer any effective intellectual opposition to the Constitution because the weapons they chose to use were mostly in their opponents' hands.

2. CONSOLIDATION OR CONFEDERATION

Before they were through with the debate over the Constitution the Federalists had not only turned their opponents' thought

---

9. Marshall (Va.), in Elliot, ed., *Debates*, III, 222; Wilson, in McMaster and Stone, eds., *Pennsylvania and the Federal Constitution*, 340, 344.

on its head, but they had transformed the Americans' understanding of politics. At the heart of this transformation was the Federalists' conception of the flow and structure of political authority to which they gave their name. Yet as crucial as the idea of federalism was to the Federalists in explaining the operation of their new system, it seems clear that few of them actually conceived of it in full before the Constitution was written and debated. In fact, the leading Federalists had at first thought of the Constitution that emerged from the Philadelphia Convention as something of a failure. The Constitution, Madison told Jefferson in September 1787, "will neither effectually answer its *national object*," nor "prevent the local *mischiefs* which everywhere *excite disgusts* against the State Governments." While most Federalists had no intention of doing away with the states entirely (although some would have), many undoubtedly desired, as William Grayson charged, to establish "a very strong government" in order "to prostrate all the state legislatures, and form a general system out of the whole." Edmund Randolph proposed the Virginia plan, as he candidly confessed, to create not "a federal government" but rather "a strong *consolidated* union, in which the idea of states should be nearly annihilated." The Virginia plan envisioned, said Gouverneur Morris, a "*national, supreme*, Government . . . having a compleat and *compulsive* operation" on individuals, not states, and resting on the principle that "in all communities there must be one supreme power, and one only."[10] The evidence is very strong that the leading nationalists in the Convention inevitably expected a substantial degree of consolidation. As late as the spring of 1787 Madison, for example, showed little comprehension of a political system in which the national and state governments would coexist as equal partners. His "middle ground" in 1787 was not the federalism of 1788, but meant rather "a due supremacy of the national authority" with "the local authorities" left to exist only in "so far as they can be subordinately useful." Both Madison and James Wilson fought hard in the Convention to prevent both equal representation of the states in the Senate and elimination of the congressional veto of all state laws that Congress deemed unjust and unconstitutional. Both proportional representation and the congressional veto, they believed, would deny any recognition of state sover-

10. Madison to Jefferson, Sept. 6, 1787, Boyd, ed., *Jefferson Papers*, XII, 103; William Grayson to James Monroe, May 29, 1787, Farrand, ed., *Records of the Federal Convention*, III, 30; Randolph and Morris, in *ibid.*, I, 24, 34.

eignty in the Constitution, and thus prevent a reversion to the evils of the Confederacy. Concerning the equal representation of the states in the Senate, Rufus King even thought it would be better "to submit to a little more confusion and convulsion, than to submit to such an evil." Yet others in the Convention feared that the states under the Virginia plan would become more insignificant than corporations were in the states. Although James Wilson warned that "we talk of states, till we forget what they are composed of," the nationalists' plan ran too counter to the diverse interests of the country and to the attachments to state integrity to be acceptable, and compromise, or concession as the nationalists saw it, became inevitable.[11]

Nevertheless, however much the most extreme Federalists thought they were surrendering the principle of consolidation in the Constitution that came out of the Philadelphia Convention, the Antifederalists hardly saw it that way. They had no doubt that it was precisely an absorption of all the states under one unified government that the Constitution intended, and they therefore offered this prospect of an inevitable consolidation as the strongest and most scientifically based objection to the new system that they could muster. "The question turns, sir," said Patrick Henry at the opening of the Virginia Convention, "on that poor little thing—the expression, We, the *people,* instead of the *states,* of America." "States," said Henry, "are the characteristics and the soul of a confederation. If the states be not the agents of this compact, it must be one great, consolidated, national government, of the people of all the states." "I confess, as I enter the Building," said Samuel Adams, "I stumble at the threshold. I meet with a National Government, instead of a Federal Union of Sovereign States." If the phrase, "We, the people," said Samuel Nasson of Massachusetts, "does not go to an annihilation of the state governments, and to a perfect consolidation of the whole Union, I do not know what does." "Instead of being thirteen republics, under a federal head," wrote Richard Henry Lee, the Constitution "is clearly designed to make us one consolidated government." "Instead of securing the sovereignty of the states," said William Lenoir of North Carolina, "it is calculated to melt them down into one solid empire"—an empire that from its very extent would be

11. Madison to Randolph, Apr. 8, 1787, Hunt, ed., *Writings of Madison*, II, 336–40; King and Wilson, in Farrand, ed., *Records of the Federal Convention*, II, 7, I, 483.

oppressive. All political authorities had declared "that no extensive empire can be governed upon republican principles, and that such a government will degenerate to a despotism, unless it be made up of a confederacy of smaller states, each having the full powers of internal regulation." The reason was obvious. "In large states the same principles of legislation will not apply to all the parts." Different interests, different climates, different habits, would require different laws and regulations. For a single legislature to control the whole country it would be necessary to cramp and to mold groups of the population. The great empires thus had always been despotic. Tyranny would surely result "if we should submit to have the concerns of the whole empire managed by one legislature." When British theorists had suggested that Americans should be represented in Parliament, recalled the Antifederalists, "we uniformly declared that one legislature could not represent so many different interests for the purposes of legislation and taxation. This was the leading principle of the revolution," the Antifederalists concluded, "and makes an essential article in our creed."[12]

What gave substance to this Antifederalist claim that the proposed federal government would inevitably end in a consolidation was the conventional eighteenth-century theory of legislative sovereignty. The same logic that the English had used against the Americans in the late sixties and that most Americans had finally accepted in 1774–75 was now relentlessly thrown back at the Federalists by the opponents of the Constitution. There could be but one supreme legislative power in every state, the Antifederalists said over and over, and any proposition to the contrary was inconsistent with the best political science of the day. "I never heard of two supreme co-ordinate powers in one and the same country before," said William Grayson. "I cannot conceive how it can happen. It surpasses everything that I have read of concerning other governments, or that I can conceive by the utmost exertions of my faculties." The logic of the doctrine of sovereignty required either the state legislatures or the national Congress to predominate. Since, as the Pennsylvania Antifederalists argued,

12. Henry (Va.), in Elliot, ed., *Debates*, III, 44, 22; Adams to R. H. Lee, Dec. 3, 1787, Cushing, ed., *Writings of Samuel Adams*, IV. 324; Nasson (Mass.), in Elliot, ed., *Debates*, II, 134; [Lee], *Letters from the Federal Farmer*, Ford, ed., *Pamphlets*, 282; Lenior (N. C.), in Elliot, ed., *Debates*, IV, 202; [Winthrop], "Agrippa, IV," Dec. 3, 1787, Ford, ed., *Essays on the Constitution*, 64–65. See above, 499–500.

"two co-ordinate sovereignties would be a solecism in politics, . . . it would be contrary to the nature of things that both should exist together—one or the other would necessarily triumph in the fulness of dominion." It was impossible, wrote Robert Yates, that the "powers in the state constitution and those in the general government can exist and operate together." The Constitution, said Samuel Adams, established an "Imperia in Imperio justly deemed a solecism in Politicks." A "divided sovereignty"—"not knowing whether to obey the Congress or the State"—was a horrible absurdity to James Winthrop. "We shall find it impossible to please two masters." There could be no compromise: "It is either a federal or a consolidated government, there being no medium as to kind."[13] Like the disputants in the imperial debate of 1774–75, the Antifederalists could not conceive of "a sovereignty of power existing within a sovereign power." "These two concurrent powers cannot exist long together," warned George Mason; "the one will destroy the other." And the Antifederalists had no doubt that the federal government with its great sweeping power and its "supreme law of the land" authority "must eventually annihilate the independent sovereignties of the several states." How long, it was asked, would the people "retain their confidence for two thousand representatives who shall meet once in a year to make laws for regulating the height of your fences and the repairing of your roads?" Once the Constitution was established, "the state governments, without object or authority, will soon dwindle into insignificance, and be despised by the people themselves."[14]

It was a formidable position directly related to the Anglo-American debate that had led to the Revolution. When the Antifederalists asked, "How are two legislatures to coincide, with powers transcendent, supreme and omnipotent?" they were raising the fundamental issue on which the British empire had broken, an issue that the Federalists could no more avoid in 1787 than American Whigs could a decade and a half earlier. Although

13. Grayson (Va.), in Elliot, ed., *Debates*, III, 281; "Dissent of the Minority," Dec. 18, 1787, McMaster and Stone, eds., *Pennsylvania and the Federal Constitution*, 467–68; [Robert Yates], "Sidney, I," June 13, 1788, Ford, ed., *Essays on the Constitution*, 304; Adams to R. H. Lee, Dec. 3, 1787, Cushing, ed., *Writings of Samuel Adams*, IV, 324; [Winthrop], "Agrippa, V," Dec. 11, 1787, Ford, ed., *Essays on the Constitution*, 68; Phila. *Independent Gazetteer*, Apr. 15, 1788, in McMaster and Stone, eds., *Pennsylvania and the Federal Constitution*, 535.

14. E. Pierce (Mass.), and Mason (Va.), in Elliot, ed., *Debates*, II, 77, III, 29; Robert Whitehill, in McMaster and Stone, eds., *Pennsylvania and the Federal Constitution*, 284; Smith (N. Y.), in Elliot, ed., *Debates*, II, 312–13.

some Federalists shared the Antifederalist assumption that "two sovereignties can not co-exist within the same limits" and probably welcomed, as did Benjamin Rush, "the eventual annihilation of the state sovereignties," most soon realized that this problem of sovereignty was the most powerful obstacle to the acceptance of the new Constitution the opponents could have erected. Under this Antifederalist pressure most Federalists were compelled to concede that if the adoption of the Constitution would eventually destroy the states and produce a consolidation, then the "objection" was not only "of very great force" but indeed "insuperable." Both sides in the debate over the Constitution soon came to focus on this, "the principal question," "the source of the greatest objection, which can be made to its adoption"—"whether this system proposes a consolidation or a confederation of the states."[15]

The Federalists groped to explain the new system and to make sense of the "concurrent jurisdiction" of two legislatures over the same people. They stressed that the new government in many of its provisions was so "dependent on the constitution of the state legislatures for its existence" that it could never "swallow up its parts." Each state was only "giving up a portion of its sovereignty" in order "better to secure the remainder of it." Some talked of a dual allegiance, "two governments to which we shall owe obedience," while many others emphasized that "the sphere in which *the states* moved was of a different nature" from that of the federal government. "The two governments act in different manners, and for different purposes," said Edmund Pendleton in a common argument, "the general government in great national concerns, in which we are interested in common with other members of the Union; the state legislature in our mere local concerns. . . . They can no more clash than two parallel lines can meet." The truth was, said Madison, the Constitution was "not completely consolidated, nor is it entirely federal." It was "of a mixed nature," made up "of many coequal sovereignties."[16]

15. Grayson (Va.), in Elliot, ed., *Debates*, III, 281; Hamilton and Morris, in Farrand, ed., *Records of the Federal Convention*, I, 287, 34, 43; Rush, in McMaster and Stone, eds., *Pennsylvania and the Federal Constitution*, 300; Wilson in *ibid.*, 264; William Davie (N. C.), in Elliot, ed., *Debates*, IV, 58; Madison, in *ibid.*, III, 93–94; John Smilie, in McMaster and Stone, eds., *Pennsylvania and the Federal Constitution*, 267.

16. R. R. Livingston (N. Y.), Davie (N. C.), James Bowdoin (Mass.), James Iredell (N. C.), Livingston (N. Y.), Pendleton (Va.), Madison (Va.), in Elliot, ed., *Debates*, II, 385, IV, 160, 59, II, 129, IV, 35, II, 323, III, 301, 94, 381.

But none of these arguments about "joint jurisdictions" and "coequal sovereignties" convincingly refuted the Antifederalist doctrine of a supreme and indivisible sovereignty. The Federalists, like American Whigs in the late sixties, sought to refine, to evade, even to deny the doctrine, but it remained, as it had earlier, an imposing, scientific conception that could not be put down. It was left to James Wilson in the Pennsylvania Ratifying Convention to deal most effectively with the Antifederalist conception of sovereignty. More boldly and more fully than anyone else, Wilson developed the argument that would eventually become the basis of all Federalist thinking. He challenged the Antifederalists' use of the concept of sovereignty not by attempting to divide it or to deny it, but by doing what the Americans had done to the English in 1774, by turning it against its proponents.

"In all governments, whatever is their form, however they may be constituted, there must be a power established from which there is no appeal, and which is therefore called absolute, supreme, and uncontrollable. The only question," said Wilson, "is where that power is lodged?" Blackstone had placed it in the will of the legislature, in the omnipotence of the British Parliament. Some Americans, said Wilson, had tried to deposit this supreme power in their state governments. This was closer to the truth, continued Wilson, but not accurate; "for in truth, it remains and flourishes with the people." Those Antifederalists who argued that "there can not exist two independent sovereign taxing powers in the same community" had misplaced the sovereignty. The supreme power, Wilson emphasized, did not rest with the state governments. "It *resides* in the PEOPLE, as the fountain of government." "They have not parted with it; they have only dispensed such portions of power as were conceived necessary for the public welfare." The sovereignty always stayed with the people-at-large; "they can delegate it in such proportions, to such bodies, on such terms, and under such limitations, as they think proper." Unless the people were considered as vitally sovereign, declared Wilson with some exasperation, "we shall never be able to understand the principle on which this system was constructed." Only then would it be possible to comprehend how the people "may take from the subordinate governments powers with which they have hitherto trusted them, and place these powers in the general government. . . . They can distribute one portion of power to the more contracted circle called State governments; they can also furnish another proportion to the government of the United States." Therefore under the new Constitution neither the state legislatures nor the Congress would be sovereign. "The power both of the general government, and the State governments, under this system, are acknowledged to be so many emanations of power from the people." The state legislatures could therefore never lose their sovereignty under the new Constitution, as the Antifederalists claimed, because they never possessed it. A consolidated government could never result unless the people desired one. For only the people-at-large could decide how much power their various governments should have. "Who will undertake to say as a state officer," taunted Wilson, "that the people may not give to the general government what powers and for what purposes they please? how comes it . . . that these State governments dictate to their superiors?—to the majesty of the people?"[17]

Although no Federalist grasped and wielded "this leading principle" of the Constitution with more authority than Wilson, others in the ratification debates were inevitably led to invoke the same principle. Faced with the Antifederalists' persistent references to consolidation and with their intense mistrust of Congress, the Federalists were repeatedly pressed to ask in exasperation: "But what is the sovereignty, and who is Congress?" In the Virginia Convention, Henry, for example, would not leave the issue of federal taxing power alone and continually denied the possibility of concurrent jurisdiction between the states and the national government. Without effect Madison argued that the tax collections between the general government and the states would be similar to those between the states and the various counties and petty corporations within their boundaries. "The comparison," retorted Henry, "will not stand examination." The taxes collected within the state, whether from the state, county, or parish level, all "radiate from the same center. They are not coequal or coextensive. There is no clashing of power between them. Each is limited to its own particular objects, and all subordinate to one supreme, controlling power—the legislature." All right, answered Madison. If there had to be one supreme, controlling power over the tax collections of the general and state governments, then one could be found. "To make use of the gentleman's own terms, the concurrent collections under the

17. Wilson and Findley, in McMaster and Stone eds., *Pennsylvania and the Federal Constitution*, 229, 301, 316, 301–02, 316, 317, 302, 389, 302.

authorities of the general government and state governments all radiate from the people at large. The people is their common superior."[18]

Relocating sovereignty in the people by making them "the fountain of all power" seemed to make sense of the entire system. Once the Federalists perceived "the great principle of the primary right of power in the people," they could scarcely restrain their enthusiasm in following out its implications. One insight seemed to lead to another, until the Federalists were tumbling over each other in their efforts to introduce the people into the federal government, which they had "hitherto been shut out of." "The people of the United States are now in the possession and exercise of their original rights," said Wilson, "and while this doctrine is known and operates, we shall have a cure for every disease."[19]

3. The Primal Power of the People

Even before the Philadelphia Convention met in the summer of 1787 some Federalists had perceived the political and constitutional importance of founding the new structure directly on the people rather than on the state governments. The very idea of calling a convention to change the Articles attested to the advantages of avoiding the states. As early as 1780 Hamilton had urged the calling of a national convention because the states individually could never agree on reform. By 1787 men who hitherto had shied away from such a convention because of the illegal proliferation of conventions within their own states in opposition to the state legislatures now saw that the authority of a convention would give the new system a stronger foundation than the Congress had possessed. Madison saw clearly that the new national government, if it were to be truly independent of the states, must obtain "not merely the assent of the Legislatures, but the ratification of the people themselves." Only "a higher sanction than the Legislative authority" could render the laws of the federal government "paramount to the acts of its members." If the Federalists were to accomplish their revolution, they would necessarily have to circumvent the Articles of Confederation whose amendment

18. Archibald Maclaine (N. C.), Henry (Va.), and Madison (Va.), in Elliot, ed., *Debates*, IV, 181, III, 306, 326–27, 332.

19. Pendleton (Va.), in Elliot, ed., *Debates*, III, 298; Wilson, in McMaster and Stone, eds., *Pennsylvania and the Federal Constitution*, 302, 341.

legally required the unanimous consent of the state legislatures. By appealing over the heads of the states directly to the people, who were "the supreme authority, the federal compact may be altered by a *majority of them*; in like manner as the Constitution of a particular State may be altered by a majority of the people of the State." As Madison put it, "the people were in fact, the fountain of all power, and by resorting to them, all difficulties were got over. They could alter constitutions as they pleased."[20]

At once the nationalist-minded in the Philadelphia Convention saw that "all the considerations which recommended this Convention in preference to Congress for proposing the reform were in favor of State Conventions in preference to the Legislatures for examining and adopting it." Not only would the Constitution more easily pass through the single body of a convention than through the two branches of the state legislatures, but a state convention was more apt to be "composed in part at least of other men" than those who sat in the state legislatures and was "the most likely means of drawing forth the best men in the States to decide on it." The very revolutionary nature of the new system, moreover, required popular ratification, for, in Madison's words, "the true difference" "between a *league* or *treaty*, and a *Constitution*" was the difference between "a system founded on the Legislatures only, and one founded on the people." Despite the objections of some delegates at Philadelphia fearful of this "new sett of ideas," it had become clear to most by 1787 that legislatures were no longer competent to change constitutions. By resorting to ratifying conventions the Federalists hoped to avoid "all disputes and doubts concerning the legitimacy of the new Constitution." If the Constitution were to be considered a truly fundamental law against which ordinary statutory law could be declared by judges to be "null and void," then it must be "ratified in the most unexceptionable form, and by the supreme authority of the people themselves."[21]

Those who criticized the revolutionary proceedings of the

20. Hamilton to James Duane, Sept. 3, 1780, Syrett and Cooke, eds., *Hamilton Papers*, II, 407; Stephen Higginson to Henry Knox, Feb. 8, 1787, Jameson, ed., "Letters of Higginson," Amer. Hist. Assoc., *Annual Report, 1896*, I, 746–48; Madison to Pendleton, Apr. 22, 1787, Hunt, ed., *Writings of Madison*, II, 355; Gouverneur Morris and Madison in Farrand, ed., *Records of the Federal Convention*, II, 92, 476.

21. Madison, Nathaniel Gorham, Rufus King, Hugh Williamson, Gouverneur Morris, in Farrand, ed., *Records of the Federal Convention*, II, 93, 90–92, I, 123, II, 476, 92, 93, 92, 93, I, 123.

Philadelphia Convention soon found themselves in the embarrassing position of seeming to deny the voice of the people. "Strange it is," remarked James Sullivan, that the critics of the Constitution "should suppose it unjustifiable for the people to alter or amend, or even entirely abolish, what they themselves have established." "Who but the people," asked Edmund Pendleton, "can delegate powers? Who but the people have a right to form government?" "All power," the Federalists said, "is in the people, and not in the state governments." If the Antifederalists "will not deny the authority of the people to delegate power to agents, and to devise such a government as a majority of them thinks will promote their happiness," then they could not logically object to the formation of the present Constitution. The "transcendent power" of the people "is competent to form this or any other government which they think promotive of their happiness." Every attempt by the Antifederalists to oppose the calling of the ratifying conventions was met with Federalist charges that the Antifederalists were trying "to take away from the people the power of judging and determining for themselves. Their language amounts to this—we are better judges [of] what suits the people than they are—we are acquainted with government—we think this a bad form, and will not even submit it to the people." The Constitution, the Federalists increasingly emphasized, was truly intended, as the Confederation had not been, to be "the scheme of the people." Why else, asked Oliver Ellsworth, would the framers have "determined State Conventions as the tribunal of ultimate decision?"[22] Indeed, what did it matter if the Constitution were a violation of the Articles, since the Confederation had been "adopted and confirmed without being submitted to the great body of the people for their approbation." The Confederation, it was now possible to argue, had never rested on "the principle of free governments" and had been defective and inferior to the state constitutions because it had never been a real constitution, never having obtained "a higher ratification, than a resolution of assembly in the daily form." The Constitution, the Federalists could now point out, "is more a government of the people, than the present Congress ever was" and thus was "more in favour of lib-

22. [James Sullivan], "Cassius, IV," Nov. 23, 1787, Ford, ed., *Essays on the Constitution*, 16; Pendleton (Va.), Maclaine (N. C.), in Elliot, ed., *Debates*, III, 37, IV, 161; One of the People, "To the Freemen of Pennsylvania," *American Museum*, 2 (1787), 373–74; [Ellsworth], "A Landholder, II," Nov. 12, 1787, Ford, ed., *Essays on the Constitution*, 145.

erty." The Constitution was in fact a reassertion of the first principles of Whiggism. The Declaration of Independence had expressed "the inherent and unalienable right of the people" to form
whatever kind of government they wanted. "This is the broad
basis on which our independence was placed. On the same certain
and solid foundation this system is erected."[23]

The more the Federalists stressed the foundation of the new
Constitution in the people, the more excited they became with the
spectacular significance of the whole constitution-making process. "What is the object exhibited to our contemplation?" exulted the poet, Francis Hopkinson. "A WHOLE PEOPLE exercising
its first and greatest power—performing an act of SOVEREIGNTY,
ORIGINAL, and UNLIMITED." Americans, said Edmund Pendleton
in the Virginia Ratifying Convention, had finally showed the
world how to form a real constitution. If their governments were
defective, Americans had no need to resort crudely to revolution
in the traditional Whig fashion, "conveying an idea of force."
"No, we will assemble in Convention; wholly recall our delegated powers." Then, "we, the people, possessing all power,
form a government, such as we think will secure happiness." The
ratifying conventions, said Wilson, were meeting "under the
practical influence of this great truth . . . that in the United States
the people retain the supreme power." "Under its operation, we
can sit as calmly, and deliberate as cooly in order to change a constitution, as a legislature can sit and deliberate under the power
of a constitution in order to alter or amend a law." Through the
conventions the people vest some of their supreme power in
the general government, some in the state governments, but "the
fee simple continues, resides and remains with the body of the
people."[24]

With this kind of understanding of the constitution-making
process, the nature of the constitution itself had to change. In

23. *An Impartial Address, to the Citizens of the City and County of Albany:
Or, the Thirty-five Anti-Federal Objections Refuted* (Albany, [1788]), 4–5;
Wilson, in McMaster and Stone, eds., *Pennsylvania and the Federal Constitution*,
318; Edmund Randolph, *Letter on the Federal Constitution, October 16, 1787*
([Richmond, 1787]), in Ford, ed., *Pamphlets*, 267; "Objections to the Constitution, Answers to the Objections . . . ," *American Museum*, 2 (1787), 423; Wilson,
in McMaster and Stone, eds., *Pennsylvania and the Federal Constitution*, 317.

24. [Francis Hopkinson], *Account of the Grand Federal Procession, Philadelphia, July 4, 1788* . . . ([Phila., 1788]), 14; Pendleton (Va.), in Elliot, ed., *Debates*, III, 37; Wilson, in McMaster and Stone, eds., *Pennsylvania and the Federal
Constitution*, 318, 340, 318.

fact, because the concept of a constitution was central to the Federalists' emerging comprehension of the character of the system
they were creating, it became the source of heated contention
during the ratification debates, particularly as it related to the
omission of a bill of rights in the federal Constitution.

4. THE IRRELEVANCE OF A BILL OF RIGHTS

A bill of rights had scarcely been discussed in the Philadelphia
Convention. As Wilson remarked, it had "never struck the mind
of any member," until George Mason almost as an afterthought
in the last days of the Convention brought the issue up, when it
was defeated by every state. Even what semblances there were
in the Constitution of a bill of rights, such as the prohibition
against *ex post facto* laws, had been opposed by some delegates
as irrelevant and useless provisions that would only bring "reflections on the Constitution." Even to some eager Federalists, the
new central government, as much of a consolidation as it may
have been, still seemed to be concerned with "objects of a general
nature" and calculated to leave the preservation of individual
rights to the states. Given their desire to establish a strong central
government, the only rights and powers the delegates emphasized
and feared were those of the states, Rufus King going so far as
to suggest that "as the fundamental rights of individuals are secured by express provisions in the State Constitutions; why may
not a like security be provided for the Rights of the States in the
National Constitution?"[25]
Yet once the Antifederalists grasped the consolidating aspects
of the new Constitution, particularly with its supreme law and
necessary and proper clauses, they rose in defense of a declaration
of rights to "serve as a barrier between the general government
and the respective states and their citizens." "Why was not this
Constitution ushered in with the bill of rights?" the Antifederalists asked over and over. "Where is the security? Where is the
barrier drawn between the government and the rights of the
citizens, as secured in our own state government." Probably nothing made the Constitution more vulnerable to criticism than the

25. Wilson in McMaster and Stone, eds., *Pennsylvania and the Federal Constitution*, 253; Farrand, ed., *Records of the Federal Convention*, II, 375–76, 378–79,
I, 492–93.

omission of this traditional Whig means of protecting the people's liberties against governmental power—"the polar star and great support of American liberty." A government could be founded on true Whig principles, wrote Robert Yates, only "by expressly reserving to the people such of their essential rights, as are not necessary to be parted with." The experience of all ages had confirmed that the rulers were always eager to enlarge their powers and to abridge the public liberty. "This has induced the people in all countries, where any sense of freedom remained, to fix barriers against the encroachments of their rulers." Most of the state constitutions, the Antifederalists emphasized, were prefaced by bills of rights or were interwoven with certain express reservations of rights. Jefferson, who gave a qualified approval of the new government, was right when he said that the absence of a bill of rights was a major drawback to the acceptance of the Constitution. "A bill of rights is what the people are entitled to against every government on earth, general or particular, and what no just government should refuse, or rest on inference." Above all, said Jefferson, revealing much of the character and manner of his thought, "the enlightened part of Europe have given us the greatest credit for inventing this instrument of security for the rights of the people, and have been not a little surprised to see us so soon give it up."[26]

Because the Federalists believed that the frenzied advocacy of a bill of rights by most Antifederalists masked a basic desire to dilute the power of the national government in favor of the states, they were determined to resist all efforts at amendment. A bill of rights, some Federalists said, was not necessary. "It is but a paper check." Such declarations of rights had been violated time and again by the states. Besides, too precise an enumeration of the people's rights was dangerous "because it would be implying, in the strongest manner, that every right not included in the exception might be impaired by the government without usurpation." Seizing upon the latest thinking about the role of the judiciary

---

26. Luther Martin's Reply to the Landholder, Mar. 19, 1788, Farrand, ed., *Records of the Federal Convention*, III, 290; Lincoln (S.C.), Mason (Va.), and Monroe (Va.), in Elliot, ed., *Debates*, IV, 315, III, 266, 217; Boston *Independent Chronicle*, Nov. 30, 1787; Jefferson to Madison, July 31, 1788, to Francis Hopkinson, Mar. 13, 1789, to David Humphreys, Mar. 18, 1789, Boyd, ed., *Jefferson Papers*, XIII, 442, XIV, 650–51, 678; Main, *Antifederalists*, 158–59. On the orthodoxy of Jefferson's Whiggism see Robert R. Palmer, "The Dubious Democrat: Thomas Jefferson in Bourbon France," *Pol. Sci. Qtly.*, 72 (1957), 388–404.

and the nature of law, other Federalists argued that the courts, as "in all well-regulated communities," would protect the common law liberties of the people and determine "the extent of legislative powers" even in the absence of a specific bill of rights. "No power," said Theophilus Parsons of Massachusetts, "was given to Congress to infringe on any one of the natural rights of the people by this Constitution; and, should they attempt it without constitutional authority, the act would be a nullity and could not be enforced." "If the United States go beyond their powers," said Oliver Ellsworth, "if they make a law which the Constitution does not authorize, it is void; and the judicial power, the national judges, who, to secure their impartiality, are to be made independent, will declare it to be void."[27]

But the Antifederalists, as Mercy Warren later wrote, were men of 1776, men "jealous of each ambiguity in law or Government, or the smallest circumstance that might have a tendency to curtail the republican system." As the Revolution had demonstrated, all natural and common law rights not specified and codified, not set down in documents "that were clear and unequivocal," were hopelessly insecure. The proposed Constitution, the Antifederalists complained, "secures no right; or, if it does, it is in so vague and undeterminate a manner, that we do not understand it." "A legislative assembly," wrote James Winthrop in a direct denial of judicial interpretation, "has an inherent right to alter the common law, and to abolish any of its principles, which are not particularly guarded in the constitution. Any system therefore which appoints a legislature, without any reservation of the rights of individuals, surrenders all power in every branch of legislation to the government." "The truth is," said John Smilie of Pennsylvania, "that unless some criterion is established by which it could be easily and constitutionally ascertained how far our governors may proceed, and by which it might appear when they transgress their jurisdiction," the principles of the Declaration of Independence endorsing the people's right of resistance were "mere sound without substance."[28]

27. George Nicholas (Va.), Iredell (N.C.), Parsons (Mass.), and Ellsworth (Conn.), in Elliot, ed., Debates, III, 459, IV, 167, III, 443, II, 162, 196.

28. Mercy Warren, History of the . . . American Revolution . . . (Boston, 1805), III, 360; Timothy Bloodworth (N. C.), and Lenoir (N. C.), in Elliot, ed., Debates, IV, 68, 202; [Winthrop], "Agrippa, XIII," Jan. 14, 1788, Ford, ed., Essays on the Constitution, 95; Smilie, in McMaster and Stone, eds., Pennsylvania and the Federal Constitution, 250–51. See the discussion in Alpheus Thomas Mason, The States Rights Debate: Antifederalism and the Constitution (Englewood Cliffs, N. J., 1964), 76–88.

The more the Antifederalists referred to the ideas of 1776 and the bills of rights written then, the more the Federalists realized that the new national Constitution was based on a fundamentally different principle from that of the earlier state constitutions, that, indeed, the very nature of the new Constitution obviated the need for a bill of rights. "When the Confederation was made, we were by no means so well acquainted with the principles of government as we are now. We were then jealous of the power of our rulers, and had an idea of the British government when we entertained that jealousy." Bills of rights had possessed a relevance in England "where there is a king and a House of Lords, quite distinct with respect to power and interest from the rest of the people." Since the English kings had "claimed all power and jurisdiction," bills of rights like the Magna Carta had been "considered by them as grants to the people." "A bill of rights was used in England to limit the king's prerogative; he could trample on the liberties of the people in every case which was not within the restraint of the bill of rights."[29] But many Americans had come to realize that their political power was differently organized. As the Federalists were increasingly compelled to explain the absence of a bill of rights, they were ultimately driven into elaborating and developing what they were coming to realize was the unique character of the new system.

Again it was James Wilson, in the Pennsylvania Ratifying Convention and in a widely-circulated speech given out-of-doors, who most forthrightly set down what was to become the central Federalist explanation for a lack of a bill of rights. Wilson at once focused on what he now saw to be an important difference between the Revolutionary state constitutions and the new federal Constitution. When the people established their state governments in 1776, "they invested their representatives with every right and authority which they did not in explicit terms reserve." These reservations were embodied in their declarations of rights. In the new federal government, however, the delegation of powers was clearly limited: "The congressional power is to be collected . . . from the positive grant expressed in the instrument of the union." Therefore in the federal Constitution there was manifestly no need for a conventional bill of rights, since every power

29. Maclaine (N. C.), in Elliot, ed., *Debates*, IV, 161; Thomas McKean, in McMaster and Stone, eds., *Pennsylvania and the Federal Constitution*, 377; [Ellsworth], "The Landholder, VI," Dec. 10, 1787, Ford, ed., *Essays on the Constitution*, 163; Randolph (Va.), in Elliot, ed., *Debates*, III, 191.

that was not expressly delegated to the general government was reserved in the people's hands. Given Wilson's understanding that the federal government resulted from a partial delegation of the people's supreme power, a declaration reserving specific rights belonging to the people was both superfluous and absurd.[30]

Others elsewhere repeated and expanded Wilson's argument. The proposed Constitution, it was claimed, "goes on the principle that all power is in the people, and that rulers have no powers but what are enumerated in that paper." "It would be very extraordinary to have a bill of rights, because the powers of Congress are expressly defined. . . . We retain all those rights which we have not given away to the general government." Hence, to list the people's rights might actually imply "we had delegated to the general government a power to take away such of our rights as we had not enumerated." In America, the Federalists said with mounting enthusiasm, "all power is in the people, and immediately derived from them," and "whatever portion" of this power the people "did not transfer to the government, was still reserved and retained by the people." Therefore, wrote Hamilton in *The Federalist*, it had become evident that bills of rights, "according to their primitive signification, . . . have no application to constitutions, professedly founded upon the power of the people, and executed by their immediate representatives and servants. Here, in strictness, the people surrender nothing; and as they retain every thing they have no need of particular reservations." Although Madison later told Jefferson he was not so insistent on the uselessness of a bill of rights as Wilson had been, in the Virginia Convention nothing had seemed to Madison to be "a more positive and unequivocal declaration of the principle" underlying the Constitution than the view "that the powers granted by the proposed Constitution are the gift of the people, and may be resumed by them when perverted to their oppression, and every power not granted thereby remains with the people, and at their will."[31]

Unable to grasp the sweeping significance the Federalists were attributing to the sovereignty of the people, the Antifederalists

---

30. Wilson, in McMaster and Stone, eds., *Pennsylvania and the Federal Constitution*, 143–44, 313–14.

31. Henry Lee (Va.), Maclaine (N. C.), C. C. Pinckney (S. C.), in Elliot, ed., *Debates*, III, 186, IV, 140–41, 316, 161; Thomas Hartley, in McMaster and Stone, eds., *Pennsylvania and the Federal Constitution*, 290–91; *The Federalist*, No. 84; Madison to Jefferson, Oct. 17, 1788, Boyd, ed., *Jefferson Papers*, XIV, 18–19; Madison (Va.), in Elliot, ed., *Debates*, III, 620.

stood amazed at the Federalists' effrontery. No other country in the world, said an increasingly perplexed Patrick Henry, looked at government as a delegation of express powers. "All nations have adopted this construction—that all rights not expressly and unequivocally reserved to the people are impliedly and incidentally relinquished to rulers. . . . It is so in Great Britain; for every possible right, which is not reserved to the people by some express provision or compact, is within the king's prerogative. . . . It is so in Spain, Germany, and other parts of the world." And it was so in America at the time of the Revolution. George Mason for one could not see any difference between the state constitutions with their bills of rights and the new Constitution. "They are both," said a Massachusetts Antifederalist, "a compact between the Governors and the Governed." And precisely because any constitution was "a great political compact between the governors and the governed," said John Smilie, "a plain, strong, and accurate criterion by which the people might at once determine when, and in what instance their rights were violated, is a preliminary, without which, this plan ought not to be adopted."[32]

Repeatedly the Antifederalist arguments kept coming back to this idea that "government is a compact between the rulers and the people," a contract by which "liberty ought not to be given up without knowing the terms." "Whether it be called a *compact, agreement, covenant, bargain,* or what," a constitution to the Antifederalists represented in traditional Whig terms "a concession of power, on the part of the people to their rulers," a mutual bargain between two hostile interests, between power and liberty. Since it was so crucial to the Antifederalist thinking, the nature of this contract quickly became a focal point of Federalist arguments over the lack of a bill of rights.[33]

"A compact between the rulers and the ruled, which gentlemen compare the government with," said James Iredell, "is certainly not the principle of our government." "In other countries, where the origin of government is obscure, and its formation different from ours, government may be deemed a contract between the rulers and the people." But "our government is founded on much

32. Henry (Va.) and Mason (Va.), in Elliot, ed., *Debates*, III, 445, 149–50, 316–17, 444; "John De Witt," Oct. 27, 1787, Kenyon, ed., *Antifederalists*, 98; Smilie, in McMaster and Stone, eds., *Pennsylvania and the Federal Constitution*, 255.

33. David Caldwell (N. C.), John Tyler (Va.), and Goudy (N. C.), in Elliot, ed., *Debates*, IV, 9, III, 641, IV, 10.

nobler principles. The people are known with certainty to have originated it themselves. Those in power are their servants and agents; and the people, without their consent, may new-model their government whenever they think proper." Hence governmental power in America was not pre-existing; the people did not have to contract to gain their liberties. Indeed, said Oliver Ellsworth, "government is considered as originating from the people, and all the power government now has is a grant from the people. The constitution they establish with powers limited and defined, becomes now to the legislator and magistrate, what originally a bill of rights was to the people." A traditional bill of rights was unnecessary because this power was never surrendered by the people. "The people divest themselves of nothing; the government and powers which the Congress can administer, are the mere result of a compact made by the people with each other, for the common defence and general welfare." Whatever other contractual image may have been still applicable, it had become clear to the Federalists that an American constitution could no longer be truthfully called a contract or bargain between two parties, between the rulers and the people. "If we admit it," said James Wilson, "we exclude the idea of amendment; because a contract once entered into between the governor and governed becomes obligatory, and cannot be altered but by the mutual consent of both parties." A constitution in America "where the people are avowedly the fountain of all power" must therefore be solely a creation of the people, a creation like the federal Constitution where all power was partially and tentatively delegated and which required no explicit reservation of rights.[34]

The desire for a bill of rights was too strong, however, for the Federalists arguments to overcome. Jefferson thought that most of the people in the country, including even a respectable number of Federalists, agreed with him on the need for a written declaration of the people's liberties. By the fall of 1788 Madison surrendered to the pressure, telling Jefferson that he had never really been opposed to a bill of rights, but that he actually favored it now only because "it is anxiously desired by others." But by early 1789 Madison had come to see that a bill of rights might serve the

34. Iredell (N. C.), in Elliot, ed., *Debates*, IV, 10, 9; [Ellsworth], "The Landholder, VI," Dec. 10, 1787, Ford, ed., *Essays on the Constitution*, 163; Parsons (Mass.), in Elliot, ed., *Debates*, II, 89; Wilson, in McMaster and Stone, eds., *Pennsylvania and the Federal Constitution*, 384–85; Iredell, in Elliot, ed., *Debates*, IV, 11.

"double purpose of satisfying the minds of well meaning opponents, and of providing additional guards in favour of liberty." As Jefferson and others pointed out and as Madison was later to emphasize in pressing for congressional adoption of the first ten amendments to the Constitution, a bill of rights put "a legal check ... into the hands of the judiciary" which it could take hold of in protecting the people's liberties. Because the Antifederalists in their demand for amendments and a bill of rights had actually been more concerned with weakening the power of the federal government in its relation to the states in matters such as taxation than with protecting "personal liberty alone," they found even this, the strongest of their objections to the Constitution, eventually turned against them.[35]

5. THE ALLIANCE OF POWER AND LIBERTY

The quarrel over the bill of rights, if it did nothing else, served to expose dramatically the gulf in assumptions between Federalists and Antifederalists, a gulf that some had perceived right at the beginning of the debates. The opposition to the Constitution, said Edmund Pendleton in the Virginia Convention, rested on "mistaken apprehensions of danger, drawn from observations on government which do not apply to us." Most of the governments of the world had been "dictated by a conqueror, at the point of the sword," or had sprung out of "confusion, when a great popular leader, restores order at the expense of liberty, and becomes the tyrant over the people." From the very beginning such governments had necessarily bred hostility between "the interest and ambition of a despot" and "the good of the people," thus creating "a continual war between the governors and governed." Inevitably libertarian writers had considered "the two parties (the people and tyrants) as in a state of perpetual warfare," and in their Whiggish literature had "sounded the alarm to the people, to regain that liberty which circumstances have thus deprived them of." These alarms raised by "the friends of liberty," said Pendle-

35. Jefferson to Hopkinson, Mar. 13, 1789, Boyd, ed., *Jefferson Papers*, XIV, 650–51; Madison to Jefferson, Oct. 17, 1788, *ibid.*, 18; Madison to George Eve, Jan. 2, 1789, Hunt, ed., *Writings of Madison*, V, 320; Jefferson to Madison, Mar. 15, 1789, Boyd, ed., *Jefferson Papers*, XIV, 659; Farrand, ed., *Records of the Federal Convention*, II, 376–79; William Grayson to Patrick Henry, June 12, 1789, in Henry, *Patrick Henry*, III, 391; Mason, *States Rights Debate*, 88–97.

ton, were being "misrepresented and improperly applied to this government." These false alarms were responsible for the Anti-federalists' demand for a bill of rights and for their other mistaken fears of the Constitution.

By 1787 the Federalists had come to believe that the century-old maxims of radical English Whiggism (which saw the great danger to liberty in an encroaching Crown and an aristocratic House of Lords, and the major safeguards for liberty in checks on executive power and in a free, equal, and uncorrupted participation of the people in the government) were no longer relevant for the American republics. In America the rulers and people were no longer "contending interests." "There is no quarrel between government and liberty." Indeed, Federalists like Pendleton now argued, government was "the shield and protector" of liberty. Because "government and liberty were friends and allies" set against "turbulence, faction, and violence," there could be no danger in America from "making the ligaments of government firm" and establishing "a rigid execution of the laws." In a republic "regular government" was even "more necessary, than in a monarchy, to preserve the virtue . . . which all declare to be the pillar on which the government and liberty, its object, must stand." "The friends of the Constitution are as tenacious of liberty as its enemies," said John Marshall. "They wish to give no power that will endanger it. They wish to give the government powers to secure and protect it." Government was so essential to liberty, declared James Iredell, that "we must run the risk of the abuse" of its power. It was not, said Madison, that the people must "place unlimited confidence" in the new general government and "expect nothing but the most exalted integrity and sublime virtue." But it must be assumed (and this was a crucial Federalist assumption reinforced by the extended sphere of the government) that the people will at least have sufficient "virtue and intelligence to select men of virtue and wisdom," or "no theoretical checks, no form of government, can render us secure."[36]

Precisely because the Federalists realized that the Antifederalist "distrust does not arise so much from the nature of the institution, as from the characters, or conduct of those who have or do composed the Congress," they were repeatedly driven into emphasizing and exaggerating the limited and representative nature

36. Pendleton (Va.), Marshall (Va.), Iredell (N. C.), and Madison (Va.), in Elliot, ed., *Debates*, III, 36–37, 293–95, 226, IV, 95, III, 536–37.

of the new national government. "The federal representatives will represent *the people*; they will be *the people*; and it is not *probable* they will abuse themselves." They will be "ourselves; the men of our own choice, in whom we can confide; whose interest is inseparably connected with our own. Why is it, then, that gentlemen speak of Congress as some foreign body, as a set of men who will seek every opportunity to enslave us?" The opponents of the Constitution, said the Federalists, threaten us "with the loss of our liberties by the possible abuse of power, notwithstanding the maxim, that those who give may take away. It is the people that give power, and can take it back. What shall restrain them? They are the masters who give it, and of whom their servants hold it." Thus there could be no real difference between the Congress and the state legislatures. "Are they not both the servants of the people? Are not Congress and the state legislatures the agents of the people, and are they not to consult the good of the people?" "Congress can have no other power than the states had." "To whom do we delegate these powers?" the Federalists asked over and over. "To our own representatives. Why should we fear so much greater dangers from our representatives there, than from those we have here. Why make so great a distinction between our representatives here, and in the federal government, where every branch is formed on the same principle—preserving throughout the representative, responsible character?"[37]

Such radical arguments were made possible and comprehensible by the Federalists' particular understanding and use of the sovereignty of the people. Their belief that "the people hold all powers in their own hands, and delegate them cautiously, for short periods, to their servants, who are accountable for the smallest mal-administration" became the key to the workings of the entire system. Only by making the people themselves, and not their representatives in any legislature, the final, illimitable, and incessant wielders of all power, could the Federalists explain their emerging doctrine of federalism, where, contrary to the prevailing thought of the eighteenth century, both the state and federal legislatures were equally representative of the people at the same time, "both possessed of our equal confidence—both chosen in

37. Charleston *St. Gazette of S.-C.*, Nov. 7, 1785; J. C. Jones (Mass.), Samuel Stillman (Mass.), Marshall (Va.), Johnston (N. C.), and Pendleton (Va.), in Elliot, ed., *Debates*, II, 29, 167, III, 233, IV, 56, III, 299–300.

the same manner, and equally responsible to us." "The federal and state governments," wrote Madison in *The Federalist*, "are in fact but different agents and trustees of the people, constituted with different powers, and designed for different purposes." Therefore the power given to the Congress by the Constitution was not granted by the people in a wholesale fashion to some detached and alien legislature but was parceled out in a partial and tentative way to responsible and limited servants, no longer confined to the lower houses of the state legislatures.[38]

Once the people were regarded as the supreme and continuing repository of all political power, distributing some of it to their agents in the state governments, some to their agents in the federal government, and reserving the rest, then it followed that all governmental power, whatever its nature or function, was something of a delegation by the people, essentially indistinguishable in its character. Since the people obviously could not "exercise the powers of government personally," they "must trust to agents." And to the Federalists, using and broadening the connotations of actual representation that had developed in the years since 1776, the entire government, president as well as Congress, became a responsible agency of the people. For the Federalists the historic distinction between rulers and people, governors and representatives, was dissolved, and all parts of the government became rulers and representatives of the people at the same time. "The proposed Government," said John Jay, "is to be the government of the people—all its offices are to be their offices, and to exercise no rights but such as the people commit to them." By the Constitution all members of the government were delegated part of the people's power to manage, "not for themselves and as their own, but as agents and overseers for the people to whom they are constantly responsible, and by whom only they are to be appointed." The Constitution, wrote John Dickinson, gave "*the will of the people* a decisive influence over the whole, and over all of the parts." It was indeed surprising that some critics had declared that the Constitution was not founded on a broad enough bottom, even "though the *whole people* of the United States are to be *trebly* represented in it in *three different modes* of representation." Every office, said Tench Coxe, will either be "the immediate gift" of the people, "or it will come from them through the

38. Marshall (Va.) and Pendleton (Va.), in Elliot, ed., *Debates*, III, 232, 301; *The Federalist*, No. 46.

hands of their servants." Since the Federalists were equating representation with the mere flow of authority, every officer would be in some way a representative of the people. Even "the President of the United States," declared Hamilton in the New York Ratifying Convention, "will be himself the representative of the people." "Whatever of dignity or authority he possesses," declared the Federalists, "is *a delegated part of their Majesty and their political omnipotence, transiently vested in him by the people themselves for their own happiness.*" With this understanding of the delegation of authority firmly in the Federalist grasp, all the Antifederalists' "rage for democracy, and zeal for the rights of the people" could be turned back upon them, and the Federalists could argue "with truth" that the supporters of the Constitution were "true republicans, and by no means less attached to liberty than those who oppose it."[39]

6. THE CHECKING AND BALANCING OF POWER

In a crucial sense the Antifederalists had lost the struggle over the Constitution when the New Jersey plan, embodying the essential character of the Articles of Confederation, was rejected in the Philadelphia Convention in favor of a national republic stemming mostly from and operating on individuals. Faced with this national republic instead of a league of independent states, the Antifederalists in the ratification debates were compelled to argue its merits on Federalist terms. Many who wanted changes in the federal structure now found themselves forced, as Richard Henry Lee said, to accept "this or nothing."[40] The question could no longer really be the one the Antifederalists would have liked: should America have a national republic or a confederated system? but necessarily had to be the one the Philadelphia Convention had dictated: what should be the structure and powers of this proposed national government? Once the question was posed in this way all the polemical advantages lay with the Federalists. If

39. Marshall (Va.), in Elliot, ed., *Debates*, III, 225; [John Jay], *An Address to the People of the State of New York* . . . (N. Y., [1788]), in Ford, ed., *Pamphlets*, 77; [Dickinson], *Letters of Fabius, ibid.*, 173, 178; [Tench Coxe], *An Examination of the Constitution for the United States* . . . (Phila., 1788), in *ibid.*, 147; Hamilton (N. Y.), in Elliot, ed., *Debates*, II, 253; Boston *Independent Chronicle*, Oct. 11, 1787; H. Lee (Va.), in Elliot, ed., *Debates*, III, 177.
40. Lee to Mason, Oct. 1, 1787, Ballagh, ed., *Letters of R. H. Lee*, II, 438.

they could establish that the new federal government was essentially similar to the various state republics and hence was to be judged in accord with the way those state republics were structured, then the Antifederalists' reliance on the principles underlying the old Confederation became irrelevant. In vain did the Antifederalists protest that the Constitution was in principle the wrong kind of government to be established. All they could do was attack the federal government in those mechanical Enlightenment terms most agreeable to the thought of the Federalists: the division and balancing of political power.

"Instead of checks in the formation of the government, to secure the rights of the people against the usurpations of those they appoint to govern," the Antifederalists could only "see all important powers collecting in one centre, where a few men will possess them almost at discretion." Over and over the Antifederalists denied their confidence in the new government and lamented that "no constitutional checks were provided—such checks as would not leave the exercise of government to the operation of causes which, in their nature, are variable and uncertain." "It is wise," said Melancthon Smith, "to multiply checks to a greater degree than the present state of things requires." Antifederalists from Massachusetts, Pennsylvania, and Virginia all emphasized that it was "now generally understood that it is for the security of the people that the powers of the government should be lodged in different branches." "That the legislative, executive, and judicial powers should be separate and distinct, in all free governments, is a political fact so well established" that it could not be questioned. Although the various states had declared themselves in favor of a proper separation of powers, the new Constitution, said the Antifederalists, clearly contained an "undue and dangerous mixture of the powers of government; the same body possessing legislative, executive and judicial powers." The president and Senate, in their appointive and treaty-making powers, seemed especially united, thereby forming "a combination that cannot be prevented by the representatives. The executive and legislative powers thus connected," concluded George Mason, "will destroy all balances."[41]

41. [Lee], *Letters from the Federal Farmer*, Ford, ed., *Pamphlets*, 318; Smith (N. Y.), in Elliot, ed., *Debates*, II, 259, 315; [Winthrop], "Agrippa, XVIII," Feb. 5, 1788, Ford, ed., *Essays on the Constitution*, 116; Dawson (Va.), in Elliot, ed., *Debates*, III, 608; "Dissent of the Minority," McMaster and Stone, eds., *Pennsylvania and the Federal Constitution*, 475; Mason (Va.), in Elliot, ed., *Debates*, III, 493–94.

By 1787 the doctrine of separation of powers, as the various debates over reforming the state constitutions revealed, had become something far more important than what it had been in 1776, becoming in fact for many Americans an "essential precaution in favor of liberty." Therefore it was perhaps inevitable that the Antifederalists would invoke the notion of separation of powers in opposition to the Constitution. But it was equally inevitable that the Federalists would respond with the same doctrine, and because of the peculiar way they had come to view governmental power, would be able to wield it with a comprehensiveness and effectiveness that left their opponents bewildered. Precisely because the Federalists considered "every branch of the constitution and government to be popular" and regarded the president, Senate, and even the judiciary as well as the House of Representatives as somehow all equal agents of the people's will, they could more easily than their opponents justify the separation and protection of each branch "by the strongest provisions, that until this day have occurred to mankind." The framers of the Constitution, said John Jay, "not only determined that it should be erected by, and depend on the people; but remembering the many instances in which governments vested solely in one man, or one body of men, had degenerated into tyrannies, they judged it most prudent that the three great branches of power should be committed to different hands."[42]

The Federalists were particularly adept in contrasting the new Constitution with the Confederation, a comparison that was plausible only because they had transformed political power into an indistinguishable agency of the people, dissolving what once would have been an important distinction between the delegates to the Continental Congress and the members of the new federal government. The Confederation Congress, it was now argued, was dangerous exactly because it was "a single body of men possessed of legislative, executive and judicial powers." Thus merely granting more powers to the existing Congress was no solution to the problems of the eighties, since reason and experience had taught that "tyranny" was "the natural and certain consequence" of joining the executive, legislative, and judicial powers in the same hands. "Hence," concluded Edmund Pendleton, the Philadelphia Convention had rightly recognized "the necessity of a

42. *The Federalist*, No. 47; [Dickinson], *Letters of Fabius*, Ford, ed., *Pamphlets*, 195; [Jay], *Address, ibid.*, 75.

new organization and distribution of these powers." The new government was thus even more republican than the Confederation. "From all the public servants responsibility is secured, by their being representatives, mediate or immediate, for short terms, and their powers defined." One of the excellent features of the new system, argued Wilson, was that "in it the legislative, executive and judicial powers are kept nearly independent and distinct." In fact, said Wilson, "in no constitution for any country on earth is this great principle so strictly adhered to or marked with so much precision and accuracy as in this."[43]

In the state constitutions, wrote Madison, "notwithstanding the emphatical and, in some instances, the unqualified terms in which this axiom has been laid down, there is not a single instance in which the several departments of power have been kept absolutely separate and distinct," largely because the state constitution-makers had relied on a "mere demarcation on parchment of the constitutional limits of the several departments." In no case had "a competent provision been made for maintaining in practice the separation delineated on paper." In the new system, however, said Madison, the very structure of the government was designed to prevent "those encroachments which lead to a tyrannical concentration of all the powers of government in the same hands," particularly in those of the legislature, which had become to the Federalists "the real source of danger to the American Constitutions." Since "experience in all the States had evinced a powerful tendency in the Legislature to absorb all power into its vortex," the Federalists, like the constitutional reformers in the states, had become convinced of "the necessity of giving every defensive authority to the other departments that was consistent with republican principles." Because the Federalists regarded the people as "the only legitimate fountain of power," the single source from which under the Constitution "the several branches of government hold their power," no department was theoretically more popular and hence more authoritative than any other. "The several departments being perfectly coordinate by the terms of their common commission, none of them, it is evident, can pretend to an exclusive or superior right of settling the boundaries between their respective powers." This being the case, it was not inconsistent

43. Wilson, in McMaster and Stone, eds., *Pennsylvania and the Federal Constitution*, 319, 341, 391; Randolph (Va.) and Pendleton (Va.), in Elliot, ed., *Debates*, III, 83, 39.

with republican theory for the people through their constitution to strengthen the executive and judicial departments at the expense of the legislative. Indeed, to the Federalists "the true policy of the axiom [of separation of powers] is that legislative usurpation and oppression may be obviated."[44]

The first great object of the Convention, therefore, was (as Madison summed it up for Jefferson in Paris) "to unite a proper energy in the Executive and a proper stability in the Legislative departments, with the essential characters of Republican Government." Not only was the president to be made independent of the legislature, but he was to be granted an extraordinary amount of power. "The questions concerning the degree of power," Madison told Jefferson, "turned chiefly on the appointment to offices, and the control on the Legislature." It seemed to be taken for granted in the Convention, said George Mason, that all offices would be "filled by the executive"; and some delegates even went so far as to justify the need for "influence" by the president, that is, the right to appoint members of the legislature to executive offices, even though all Whigs knew this was "the great source" from which flowed the "great venality and corruption" of Great Britain. "We have been taught," said Hamilton, "to reprobate the danger of influence in the British government, without duly reflecting how far it was necessary to support a good government." While Elbridge Gerry protested in 1776 terms that presidential appointment of legislators to executive offices would destroy the attempts "to keep distinct the three great branches of government," the Federalists argued that the real source of the blurring of powers came from legislatures' having the authority to make magisterial appointments. "The proper cure ... for corruption in the Legislature was to take from it the power of appointing to offices." The appointment and payment of executive offices, said Madison in the Virginia Convention, was "the most delicate part in the organization of a republican government" and "the most difficult to establish on unexceptionable grounds." The Constitution compromised the issue, on one hand, by allowing the president power to appoint members of Congress to executive positions whose salaries were fixed by Congress, and, on the other, by requiring members of Congress to "fill no new offices created by

44. *The Federalist*, No. 47; Madison, in Farrand, ed., *Records of the Federal Convention*, II, 74; *The Federalist*, No. 49; Mercer, in Farrand, ed., *Records of the Federal Convention*, II, 298.

themselves, nor old ones of which they increased the salaries."[45]

The judiciary department also required strengthening. Many of the delegates expected that the judiciary's function of measuring laws against the Constitution and declaring unconstitutional laws void would be a sufficient check to legislative encroachments. Others, however, thought that such a power in the hands of the judges would be confined mostly to "defending their constitutional rights," and they thus urged that the judges "have an opportunity of remonstrating against projected encroachments on the people as well as on themselves." For, as Madison and Wilson pointed out, although the judges could declare an unconstitutional law void, they would probably be compelled by the nature of their office to uphold all other laws, "however unjust, oppressive or pernicious" they may be. In order then to restrain not only the "unconstitutional" but "the unwise and unjust measures" of the legislatures, the judges needed to be joined with the president in a council of revision (modeled on the New York plan). However, despite Madison's plea that this executive and judicial co-operation was in no way a violation of the doctrine of separation of powers but was "on the contrary . . . an auxiliary precaution in favor of the maxim," for most of the delegates the proposed council of revision was too much of an alliance against the legislature.[46]

With the rejection of a revisionary council the presidential veto became the major bulwark against legislative encroachment and the chief means of maintaining executive independence—a veto that to the most ardent Federalists had to be absolute, since "without such a Self-defence" in the hands of the executive "the Legislature can at any moment sink it into non-existence." An absolute negative was in fact "the only possible mean of reducing to practice, the theory of a free government which forbids a mixture of the Legislative and Executive powers." Although the Convention, following the experience of the states, confined the president to a limited veto, the Federalists soon found such a qualified negative even more defensible in terms of separation of powers than an ab-

45. Madison to Jefferson, Oct. 24, 1787, Boyd, ed., *Jefferson Papers*, XII, 271, 273; Mason, Pierce Butler, Gerry, Wilson, in Farrand, ed., *Records of the Federal Convention*, I, 380, 379, 393, 387; Madison, in Elliot, ed., *Debates*, III, 374. See F. William O'Brien, S. J., "The Executive and the Separation Principle at the Constitutional Convention," *Md. Hist. Mag.*, 55 (1960), 201–20.

46. Wilson, Mason, Madison, in Farrand, ed., *Records of the Federal Convention*, II, 73, 78, 77, also I, 109–10.

solute negative would have been. The limited negative did not grant, as critics were charging, legislative power to the executive, thus violating the doctrine of separation of powers. The president, the Federalists argued, was not a part of the legislature and therefore "possesses no legislative authority." The president's assent was not essential for a bill to become a law. Whether a law passes by a bare or a two-thirds majority, "what gives active operation to it is, the will of the senators and representatives," not the will of the president. "His power extends only to cause it to be reconsidered." The veto was thus only a check on the legislature—a device to maintain the proper separation of powers.[47] Such a description of the executive veto was a perversion of the ancestral English Crown's role in legislation, and of the traditional theory of mixed government. It coincided with the changing function being proposed for the Senate.

7. The Redefinition of Bicameralism

Once the Philadelphia Convention had decided to establish a real legislature in place of a congress of independent states, the division of the legislature into two houses was "agreed to without debate." In fact, said George Mason, as unsettled as the American mind was in many things, it was firmly established in its "attachment to Republican Government" and its "attachment to more than one branch in the Legislature." The larger branch, the House of Representatives, was "to be the grand depository of the democratic principle of the Government" and thus was to be elected directly by the people. The upper house, the Senate, was expected to be a body that would act "with more coolness, with more system, and with more wisdom, than the popular branch." Its members would be older and fewer in number, and somehow refined through a filtration process of election to ensure that the wisest and most experienced in the society were selected. Yet the precise nature of the upper house was not at all clear to the delegates.[48]

The resemblance to the aristocratic House of Lords or to the patrician Senate of ancient Rome was never lost, and men con-

47. Wilson and Madison, in *ibid.*, I, 98, 139; Madison to Jefferson, Oct. 24, 1787, Boyd, ed., *Jefferson Papers*, XII, 273; Wilson, in McMaster and Stone, eds., *Pennsylvania and the Federal Constitution*, 334–35.

48. Mason and Madison, in Farrand, ed., *Records of the Federal Convention*, I, 339, 48, 151.

tinued to invoke the rapidly disintegrating theory of mixed government to explain the character of the Senate. Some delegates frankly wanted to reproduce the social balance of the British constitution. John Dickinson desired the Senate "to consist of the most distinguished characters, distinguished for their rank in life and their weight of property, and bearing as strong a likeness to the British House of Lords as possible"—a Senate that would combine "the families and wealth of the aristocracy" in order to "establish a balance that will check the Democracy." In Hamilton's opinion every community divided itself into the hostile interests of the few and the many, the rich and well-born against the mass of the people. If either of these interests possessed all the power, it would oppress the other. Hence both must be given power "that each may defend itself against the other." Everyone, said Hamilton, warned that "we need to be rescued from the democracy." But what was the remedy proposed? "A democratic assembly is to be checked by a democratic senate, and both these by a democratic chief magistrate." "Nothing," he concluded, "but a permanent body"—a senate for life—"can check the imprudence of democracy." It was a candid speech, more honest perhaps than Gouverneur Morris's proposal of an upper house for life, which, said Morris, was designed not only to restrain the passions of the many but also to set apart the aristocracy "into a separate interest" so it could be better controlled. The influence of the rich was to be greatly feared, said Morris, and they therefore must be kept "within their proper sphere." Similar justifications for an independent and stable upper house were increasingly voiced by others like Morris in the 1780's, and seem to represent more of a subtle, perhaps even unconscious, concession to the egalitarian sentiments of republican America than a real fear of the rich and well-born. These proposals of Dickinson, Hamilton, and Morris were the closest approximations to the classical theory of the mixed constitution made in the Convention.[49] But because other Federalists, in their pressing desire to establish a national senate that would be free of state influence, argued the case for the upper house in newer, more popular terms, this classical theory was rapidly undermined.

Under the need to justify proportional representation of the people in the Senate in order to avoid any reference to the sov-

---

49. Dickinson, Hamilton, and Morris, in Farrand, ed., *Records of the Federal Convention*, I, 150, 158, 288, 310, 299, 512–14.

ereignty of the states, the nationalists in the Convention were led into emphasizing the egalitarian nature of American society and the consequent irrelevance of the British constitutional model. "We have no materials for a similar one," said Wilson. "Our manners, our laws, the abolition of entails and of primogeniture, the whole genius of the people, are opposed to it." There was "but one great and equal body of citizens composing the inhabitants of this country," said Charles Pinckney of South Carolina in the most extensive rejection of the social basis for a mixed polity made in the Convention. In America there were no aristocratic orders, no separate social interests, like that of the English peers, "which could only be represented by themselves." Thus, said Pinckney, Americans could never possess an aristocratic senate: "we neither have nor can have the members to compose it, nor the rights privileges and properties of so distinct a class of Citizens to guard." Yet significantly Pinckney had no desire to eliminate the Senate, even though he believed there was no order in American society for which it stood. He made his lengthy speech not to destroy the rationale for an upper house but only to justify the proportional representation of the people in the Senate desired by the nationalists and the spokesmen for large state interests. But these kinds of arguments only made the question of what the Senate embodied more glaring than ever.[50]

The long wrangle in the Convention involving the Senate's authority over money bills helped to clarify the direction American thinking about the upper house was taking, but it did not resolve the issue. Some delegates in the Convention, as well as some Antifederalists in the ratifying conventions, equated the Senate with the House of Lords and thus opposed granting the Senate any power at all to meddle with money bills, since "it was a maxim that the people ought to hold the purse-strings."[51] Others, however, rejected the comparison with the House of Lords. "We were always following the British Constitution," said Pierce Butler of South Carolina, "when the reason of it did not apply. There was no analogy between the House of Lords and the body proposed to be established." "The Senate," urged Madison, "would be the representatives of the people as well as the 1st. branch." "The Senate," added Roger Sherman of Connecticut, "bear their

50. Wilson and Pinckney, in *ibid.*, I, 153, 398–404, 412.

51. Gerry in *ibid.*, I, 233; see also *ibid.*, II, 224, 273–74, and Elliot, ed., *Debates*, III, 376.

share of the taxes, and are also the representatives of the people."
The money bill restriction placed on the upper house thus seemed
to make no sense in America. "With us both houses are appointed
by the people, and both ought to be equally trusted." In fact, argued some delegates, if either branch were to be granted exclusive
control over money bills, better to give it to the Senate, as the
smaller body was generally regarded as the wiser and more suitable for deliberation. The restrictions on the senates in the state
constitutions, said John Rutledge, "had been put in through a
blind adherence to the British model. If the work was to be done
over now, they would be omitted." The discrimination between
the two houses, declared Wilson, was without significance in
America, "a trifle light as air." It had only led to useless squabbling between the two houses in the state legislatures, and all sorts
of subterfuges to avoid the letter of the constitutions. In fact, said
Wilson, both houses ought to be elected directly by the people so
that both would clearly rest on the same foundation, thus making
serious dissensions between them less likely. Precisely because of
this fear of contention between the two houses, as had occurred
in Maryland, others thought that "two such opposite bodies" as
Morris, Dickinson, and Hamilton had suggested "could never
long co-exist." Heated conflict would lead to appeals to the people, resulting in commotions which "would involve the whole in
ruin."[52]

The Senate, it seemed to many, could not and should not represent any sort of social interest distinct from that of the lower
house and was therefore not to play the social role the House of
Lords did in the English constitution. "As to balances," said Oliver Ellsworth in a common reaction to Pinckney's egalitarian
analysis of American society, "where nothing can be balanced, it
is a perfect *utopian* scheme. But still"—and it was an exception that
most Americans fully agreed with—"great advantages will result
in having a second branch endowed with the qualifications . . .
[of] weight and wisdom [which] may check the inconsiderate
and hasty proceedings of the first branch." The Senate, said Madison, would protect the people both from their representatives
(whom Madison significantly called "their rulers") and themselves. The danger of the legislature's betraying its trust would be

52. Butler, Madison, Sherman, Wilson, Hugh Williamson, Rutledge, Daniel
Carroll, and Randolph, in Farrand, ed., *Records of the Federal Convention*, I,
233–34, 238, 544, II, 275–76, 279–80, I, 151, 514–15.

mitigated by dividing "the trust between different bodies of men, who might watch and check each other," much as power was separated among the other departments of government. Yet Madison, like others in the Convention, could not fully forget the social significance of the Senate. Pinckney, he said, was generally right about the egalitarian nature of American society at the present. However, the society could not be regarded "even at this time, as one homogeneous mass, in which every thing that affects a part will affect in the same manner the whole. In framing a system which we wish to last for ages, we should not lose sight of the changes which ages will produce." The future to Madison, probably even more than to his colleagues, appeared ominous. Time and social maturation would accentuate distinctions in the society; the gap between a rich minority and a poor majority would widen. The Senate could then play the role of guarding the wealthier minority against a future "levelling spirit" in the majority.[53] Faced with all these varying interpretations, complicated by the eventual representation of the states in the Senate, the Convention could never be sure of just what kind of upper house it was creating. This Federalist confusion and uncertainty was carried over into the ratification debates.

"Permanency," "steadiness and wisdom," "stability and energy," the need for "knowledge" and "more extensive information than can be acquired in a short time" were all stressed by the Federalists in the ratifying debates as the qualities a Senate would bring to the government. Yet the Federalists generally shied away from any suggestion that the upper house resembled a House of Lords. Although the Senate should "not be at the mercy of every popular clamor" and would occasionally "prevent factious measures taking place, which may be highly injurious to the real interests of the public," the senators, it was clear, said James Iredell, were "not to hold estates for life in the legislature, nor to transmit them to their children." They would be under no temptation "to forget the interest of their constituents." While some Federalists came close to the traditional explanation of a mixed polity, only Hamilton in the New York Convention boldly emphasized it, in defending "the establishment of some select body" to give "*strength* and *stability*" to the government. "There are few positions more demonstrable," he said, "than that there should be, in every republic, some permanent body to correct the prejudices,

53. Ellsworth and Madison, in *ibid.*, I, 414, 421–23.

check the intemperate passions, and regulate the fluctuations, of a popular assembly." But this body, said Hamilton, unable to shed the ideas that had led him to propose a senate for life in the Philadelphia Convention, "must be so formed as to exclude, as much as possible, from its own character, those infirmities, and that mutability, which it is designed to remedy." It should thus be much smaller and hold office longer than the lower house. As the House of Representatives would be "peculiarly endowed with sensibility," the Senate would be endowed "with knowledge and firmness." Through the opposition of these "two distinct bodies," the Constitution would arrive at that "certain balance and mutual control indispensable to a wise administration." Too many of the states, concluded Hamilton, had failed to create this balance, and were therefore "either governed by a single democratic assembly, or have a senate constituted directly upon democratic principles."[54]

Actually it was the defeat of the proposed national Senate in the Virginia plan, where the senators were to be elected by the House of Representatives in proportion to either wealth or population of the states, that offered the Federalists a ready explanation of the Senate that avoided the aristocratic connotations of the traditional theory of mixed government. With the "Connecticut compromise," which provided for two senators from each state, the Federalists found a justification for the upper house that they had not anticipated. "The people will be represented in one house, the state legislatures in the other," the Federalists said time and again in explanation of the establishment of bicameralism in the new Congress. The Senate now became a means of restraining *"the large states from having improper advantages over the small ones."* Indeed, many Federalists could now argue, precisely because "the *senators* represent the *sovereignty of the states,"* the consolidation predicted by the Antifederalists could never result. By this mixture of states and people, some Federalists claimed, the Convention had actually created a new kind of balanced government. "It is in a manner unprecedented; we cannot find one express example in the experience of the world." Since the two branches "have different constituents, and as they are designed as mutual checks upon each other, and to balance the legislative powers," said Theophilus Parsons, "there will be frequent strug-

---

54. Davie (N. C.), Pendleton (Va.), Iredell (N. C.), and Hamilton (N. Y.), in Elliot, ed., *Debates*, IV, 21, III, 298, IV, 41, 40, II, 301, 302, 316, 302, 317.

gles and contentions between them," which to Parsons, one of the great architects of the Massachusetts constitutional balance between persons and property, was the very purpose of a bicameral system. Even Madison, who had fought longest and hardest in the Convention to avoid the "Connecticut compromise," argued in the Virginia Ratifying Convention that the federal government could only have been called "completely consolidated" if the Senate had been "chosen by the people in their individual capacity, in the same manner as the members of the other house"—an electoral process which would have destroyed "the dissimilarity in the genius of the two bodies" that, wrote Madison in *The Federalist*, Number 62, lay at the heart of the bicameral principle.[55]

Yet amidst all of the jumble of explanations presented during the ratification debates there was one that the Federalists repeatedly came back to: the need to distribute and separate mistrusted governmental power. "A division of the power in the legislative body itself," said Wilson, was "the most useful restraint upon the legislature, because it operates constantly." The danger that the people's interest might be betrayed by their own representatives, argued Madison in *The Federalist*, was "evidently greater where the whole legislative trust is lodged in the hands of one body of men, than where the concurrence of separate and dissimilar bodies is required in every public act." In order to have "a power in the legislature sufficient to check every pernicious measure," wrote Noah Webster, it was necessary to divide "the powers of legislation between the two bodies of men, whose debates shall be separate and not dependent on each other." Bicameralism was thus increasingly defended as simply another means of restraining and separating political power. In a single sentence Alexander Hanson linked the separation of the executive from the legislature and the division of the legislature into two branches as the Convention's perceptive achievement in preventing all power from concentrating in a single body—a concentration which the Federalist had come to call "the very definition of tyranny."[56]

55. Iredell, in *ibid.*, IV, 38; "To the Impartial of All Denominations in the United States," *American Museum*, 2 (1787), 376; Fisher Ames (Mass.), Madison (Va.), and Parsons (Mass.), in Elliot, ed., *Debates*, II, 46, III, 94, 95, II, 26; *The Federalist*, No. 62.

56. Wilson, in McMaster and Stone, eds., *Pennsylvania and the Federal Constitution*, 304–05; *The Federalist*, No. 63; [Noah Webster], *An Examination into the Leading Principles of the Federal Constitution . . .* (Phila., 1787), in Ford, ed., *Pamphlets*, 31; [Hanson], *Remarks on the Proposed Plan of a Federal Government*, in *ibid.*, 225; *The Federalist*, No. 47.

Although the Federalists realized that "the design of the senate is not merely to check the legislative assembly, but to collect wisdom and experience," the more they equated the division of the legislature with the separation of executive, legislative, and judicial powers, the more they obscured the aristocratic basis of the upper house and denied the conventional wisdom of the mixed constitution. Out-of-doors few Federalists dared to ascribe any sort of aristocratic character to the Senate, but were continually pressed to emphasize that the senators were "elective and rotative, to the mass of the people." The very division of the legislature into separate branches, said Alexander Hanson, had made talk of an aristocracy farcical. Even someone like John Dickinson who had favored a reproduction of the House of Lords in Philadelphia now publicly denied that the Constitution balanced social interests. Most Federalists, like James Iredell, stressed that the Senate was as "nearly a popular representative" of the people as the lower house, an argument that was comprehensible only because of the Federalists' equating of all popularly delegated power. The Constitution, explained Christopher Gadsden of South Carolina, "in all respects, takes its rise, where it ought, from the people; its President, Senate and House of Representatives, are sufficient and wholesome checks on each other, and at proper periods are dissolved again into the common mass of the people." Most Federalists were now willing to accept and even to glorify what Hamilton had scornfully called "a democratic senate" and "a democratic chief magistrate."[57]

Under such circumstances it was not surprising that some Antifederalists, guardians of the Whiggism of 1776, should have emerged in the debates as forthright apologists of the British constitution and the traditional conception of the mixed polity—admirers, the Federalists taunted, "of that king and Parliament over the Atlantic!" The new Constitution, the Antifederalists discovered, was not properly mixed or balanced. It blended the various powers "in a manner entirely novel and unknown, even in the

57. [Webster], *Examination*, Ford, ed., *Pamphlets*, 31; [Ellsworth], "The Landholder, VI," Dec. 10, 1787, Ford, ed., *Essays on the Constitution*, 165; [Hanson], *Remarks on the Proposed Plan of a Federal Government*, Ford, ed., *Pamphlets*, 256; [Dickinson], *Letters of Fabius, ibid.*, 182; [Iredell], *Answers to Mr. Mason's Objections, ibid.*, 340; [Christopher Gadsden], "A Steady and Open Republican," May 5, 1788, Ford, ed., *Essays on the Constitution*, 413. Ford's identification of the author of this last essay as Charles Pinckney seems to be in error, since "A Steady and Open Republican" was the pseudonym used by Gadsden throughout the 1780's.

constitution of Great Britain." "Is it like the model of Tacitus or Montesquieu?" asked William Grayson. "Are there checks in it, as in the British monarchy?" Since "even the king of England, circumstanced as he is, has not dared to exercise" his negative on the Parliament "for near a century past," would not the president, asked Samuel Bryan of Pennsylvania, be too weak "to exercise his prerogative of conditional control" upon the Congress? And, added Bryan, would not the bicameral check on the Senate be "rendered nugatory for want of due weight in the democratic branch?" The division and balancing of power of all other governments, ancient and modern, declared James Monroe, "was founded on different principles from those of this government." The ancient Roman and modern British constitutions both contained "a composition or mixture of aristocracy, democracy, and monarchy, each of which had a repellent quality which enabled it to preserve itself from being destroyed by the other two; so that the balance was continually maintained." But America possessed no distinct orders. "What is the object of the division of power in America? Why is the government divided into different branches? . . . Where is there a check?" There were no repellent qualities, no balance of interests in this Constitution, said Patrick Henry. "The President, senators, and representatives, all, immediately or mediately, are the choice of the people." The Federalists, their critics charged, had thus created an artificial mixture. "In the British government there are real balances and checks: in this system there are only ideal balances."[58]

But such arguments were not to be refuted by most Federalists, but instead were to be endorsed and expanded. The Americans, the Federalists increasingly emphasized, were different from the English. "Our President is not a King, nor our Senate a House of Lords." "No lords strut here with supercilious hautiness, or swell with emptiness. . . . All dignities flow from the people: those indeed of the judicial kind, not so immediately." Political power was seen to be similar, and the new government became one "consisting of three branches elected by the people, and having checks on each other," a government with "three different chambers, . . . all

58. Lee (Va.), in Elliot, ed., *Debates*, III, 177; Phila. *Independent Gazetteer*, Nov. 6, 1787, in McMaster and Stone, eds., *Pennsylvania and the Federal Constitution*, 181; Grayson (Va.), in Elliot, ed., *Debates*, III, 376, 279–80; [Bryan], "Centinel, No. II," Oct. 24, 1787, in McMaster and Stone, eds., *Pennsylvania and the Federal Constitution*, 586; Monroe and Henry (Va.), in Elliot, ed., *Debates*, III, 218–19, 164, 165.

equally competent to the subject and equally governed by the same motives and interests, viz., the good of the great commonwealth, and the approbation of the people." Through this kind of perversion of the ancient theory of balanced government the Federalists could even conclude that the new Constitution, like all American constitutions, had created "a perfectly democratical form of government."[59]

8. The Triumph and End of American Ideology

Considering the Federalist desire for a high-toned government filled with better sorts of people, there is something decidedly disingenuous about the democratic radicalism of their arguments, their continual emphasis on the popular character of the Constitution, their manipulation of Whig maxims, their stressing of the representational nature of all parts of the government, including the greatly strengthened executive and Senate. In effect they appropriated and exploited the language that more rightfully belonged to their opponents. The result was the beginning of a hiatus in American politics between ideology and motives that was never again closed. By using the most popular and democratic rhetoric available to explain and justify their aristocratic system, the Federalists helped to foreclose the development of an American intellectual tradition in which differing ideas of politics would be intimately and genuinely related to differing social interests. In other words, the Federalists in 1787 hastened the destruction of whatever chance there was in America for the growth of an avowedly aristocratic conception of politics and thereby contributed to the creation of that encompassing liberal tradition which has mitigated and often obscured the real social antagonisms of American politics. By attempting to confront and retard the thrust of the Revolution with the rhetoric of the Revolution, the Federalists fixed the terms for the future discussion of American politics. They thus brought the ideology of the Revolution to consummation and created a distinctly American political theory but only at the cost of eventually impoverishing later American political thought.

59: Richard Law (Conn.), in Elliot, ed., *Debates*, II, 200; Charleston *St. Gazette of S.-C.*, Oct. 22, 1787; Joseph Varnum (Mass.), in Elliot, ed., *Debates*, II, 79; [Pelatiah Webster], *Remarks on the Address of Sixteen Members of the Assembly . . .* (Phila., 1787), in McMaster and Stone, eds., *Pennsylvania and the Federal Constitution*, 96; Gorham (Mass.), in Elliot, ed., *Debates*, II, 69.

Actually, given the nature and pressures of American society in 1787, the Federalists had little choice in the matter. For they were not detached intellectuals free from the constraints of power and the demands of an electorate; they were public officials and social leaders fully immersed in the currents of American politics —a politics that would no longer permit the members of an elite to talk only to each other. Because of the increasing emergence of a broader popular audience, the Federalists could not ignore George Mason's warning that the genius of the American people was in favor of democracy, "and the genius of the people must be consulted." It was the realities of republican politics more than the analogies to the House of Lords that led to the eventual acceptance by the Convention of the prohibition on the Senate's right to originate money bills. Gerry's prediction that "the plan will inevitably fail, if the Senate be not restrained from originating Money bills" was undoubtedly exaggerated but not without truth. "When the people behold in the Senate, the countenance of an aristocracy," said Randolph, "and in the president, the form at least of a little monarch, will not their alarms be sufficiently raised without taking from their immediate representatives, a right which has been so long appropriated to them." The Federalists knew, as John Dickinson said, that "when this plan goes forth, it will be attacked by the popular leaders. Aristocracy will be the watchword; the Shibboleth among its adversaries."[60]

Precisely because the Antifederalists, as Hamilton observed in the New York Convention, did talk "so often of an aristocracy," the Federalists were compelled in the debates to minimize and eventually to deny the resemblance of their new government to the English constitution. And precisely because the Constitution seemed so contrary to the faith of 1776, its supporters were forced over and over to explain how and why the new system was "strictly republican." Yet in these debates the Federalists were never free to use whatever ideas they wished. They could not push and pull thought into any shape they desired. They could employ only those ideas that were available and consistent with what Americans had learned about politics. They had not, as they realized, been "obliged to look abroad for assistance" in creating their new Constitution. "Many approved models were to be found

60. Mason, Gerry, Randolph, and Dickinson, in Farrand, ed., *Records of the Federal Convention*, II, 263, 275, 278–79, 278. On the Federalists' ability to work within a democratic framework see Roche, "Founding Fathers," *Amer. Pol. Sci. Rev.*, 55 (1961), 799–816.

at home, the excellencies and deficiencies of which experience had already discovered."[61] Indeed, it was out of this experience in the formation and reformation of the state constitutions during the previous decade that the Federalists found the intellectual materials for the explanation of their new system. Because new ideas had grown often imperceptibly out of the familiar, the arguments the Federalists used in 1787–88 never really seemed disruptive or discontinuous. Americans had been prepared for a mighty transformation of political thought by a century and a half of political experience telescoped into the rapid intellectual changes that had taken place in the three decades of the Revolutionary era. The Federalists' achievement was not in creating a totally new set of ideas, for this they could never have done. Rather their achievement lay in their ability to bring together into a comprehensive whole diffuse and often rudimentary lines of thought, to make intelligible and consistent the tangles and confusions of previous American ideas. Only as the debates over the Constitution unfolded and the pieces gradually fell into place did the Federalists themselves become conscious of just how revolutionary and how unique the new system they had created was.

61. Hamilton, in Elliot, ed., *Debates*, II, 256; Charleston *St. Gazette of S.-C.*, Oct. 22, 1787.

PART SIX

The Revolutionary Achievement

The introduction of this new principle of representative democracy has rendered useless almost everything written before on the structure of government.

—THOMAS JEFFERSON, 1816

CHAPTER XIV

The Relevance and Irrelevance of John Adams

1. THE ENSNARING OF THE ENLIGHTENMENT

Not all of those who eventually supported the new federal Constitution understood the Federalist persuasion or shared in the assumptions that made it meaningful. Only a few perhaps saw in an instant the momentous implications the Constitution had for the Americans' traditional understanding of politics. Many only stumbled into fragments in the heat of debate and struggled to fit them into some larger conception; some of those who became Federalists never really comprehended the newness of the system at all. Of these undoubtedly the most notable was John Adams. Indeed, it was Adams's unfortunate fate to have missed the intellectual significance of the most important event since the Revolution.

It is ironic that Adams, of all people, should have misunderstood the meaning of the Constitution, for no American was more deeply involved in the constitutionalism of the American Revolution. Certainly no one took the Revolution and its significance for politics more seriously, and no one identified his whole life and career with the Revolution and its success more completely. Politics for Adams was always the supreme science. At the beginning of and throughout his career he continually admonished himself into intellectual activity. "Keep your Law Book or some Point of Law in your mind at least 6 Hours in a day. . . . Aim at an exact Knowledge of the Nature, End, and Means of Government. Compare the different forms of it with each other and each of them with their Effects on public and private Happiness. Study Seneca, Cicero, and all other good moral Writers. Study Montesque, Bolinbroke, . . . and all other good, civil Writers, etc."[1] No one read more and thought more about law and politics. As much as any of the Revolutionaries Adams represented the political side of the American Enlightenment. At the outset of the constitution-making period his pamphlet, *Thoughts on Government*, became the most influential work guiding the framers of the new republics; and in the late seventies he took an important hand in drafting the Massachusetts Constitution of 1780, widely regarded as the most consequential state constitution of the Revolutionary era. He never tired of investigating politics and advising his countrymen, and he came to see, with more speed and insight than most, the mistaken assumptions about their character on which the Americans of 1776 had rested their Revolution. At the height of the intellectual crisis of the 1780's he attempted, while in England, to translate what he thought he and other Americans had learned about themselves and their politics into basic principles of social and political science that were applicable to all peoples at all times. The result was the only comprehensive description of American constitutionalism that the period produced—the finest fruit of the American Enlightenment, the bulky, disordered, conglomeration of political glosses on a single theme, his *Defence of the Constitutions of Government of the United States*.

If only because of these significant contributions to American constitutionalism, Adams deserves to be singled out for consideration. But, more important, he merits special attention because of the contrasting character of his ideas with those of other Americans in these years. For all of his intense involvement in constitutionalism and for all of his insight into his own and America's character, Adams never really comprehended what was happening to the fundamentals of political thought in the years after 1776. Throughout his life he remained the political scientist par excellence, and in the end it was the very intensity of his devotion to the science of politics as he understood it that played him false.

1. John Adams, entry, Jan. 1759, Butterfield, ed., *Diary of Adams*, I, 72–73. There have been many studies of Adams's political thought. See Correa M. Walsh, *The Political Science of John Adams* . . . (N. Y., 1915); Joseph Dorfman, "The Regal Republic of John Adams," in his *Economic Mind in American Civilization* (N. Y., 1946–59), I, 417–33; Zoltán Haraszti, *John Adams and the Prophets of Progress* (Cambridge, Mass., 1952), esp. Chap. III; Edward Handler, *America and Europe in the Political Thought of John Adams* (Cambridge, Mass., 1964); and above all, John R. Howe, Jr., *The Changing Political Thought of John Adams* (Princeton, 1966).

Perhaps he read and remembered too much; perhaps he was too honest, too much the scientist and too little the politician. At any rate amidst the intellectual turmoil of the 1780's Adams clung ever more tightly to the truths of enlightened politics as he had learned them: government bore an intimate relation to society and unless the two were reconciled no state could long remain secure. There was never anything disingenuous about Adams. He refused to pervert the meaning of language, and he could not deny or disguise, without being untrue to everything he felt within himself, the oligarchic nature of American politics. He correctly saw that no society, including America, could ever be truly egalitarian, and he attempted, as no other Revolutionary quite did, to come to terms with this fact of social and political life. But he paid a high price for his honesty. For by defending more comprehensively and stridently than anyone else the traditional conception of eighteenth-century politics at the very moment of its disintegration, Adams steadily and perversely moved in a direction that eventually left him isolated from the main line of American intellectual development.

2. No Special Providence for Americans

Like other Americans, Adams began the Revolution filled with excitement and enthusiasm for the future. "America," he had written as early as 1765, "was designed by Providence for the Theatre, on which Man was to make his true figure, on which science, Virtue, Liberty, Happiness and Glory were to exist in Peace." The Revolution, he said in 1776, would be "an Astonishment to vulgar Minds all over the World, in this and in future Generations." No one was as much attuned as Adams to the hopefulness and promise of the best Enlightenment thought of the day. Yet at the same time no Revolutionary leader punctured the faith of 1776 with so many doubts and so many misgivings. He had no illusions in 1776 about the difficulties that lay ahead. There would be "Calamities" and "Distresses," he predicted on the eve of Independence, "more wasting" and "more dreadfull" than any yet experienced by Americans. Such affliction, however, would have "this good Effect, at least: it will inspire Us with many Virtues, which We have not, and correct many Errors, Follies, and Vices, which threaten to disturb, dishonour, and destroy Us."[2] Adams

2. Adams, unpubl. newspaper communication, Dec. 1765, Butterfield, ed., *Diary of Adams*, I, 282; Adams to James Warren, Mar. 31, 1777, Ford, ed.,

knew full well the dependence of republicanism on the character of the people. History had taught that "public Virtue is the only Foundation of Republics." No republican government could last, he said, unless there was "a positive Passion for the public good, the public Interest, . . . established in the Minds of the People, . . . Superiour to all private Passions." Yet could America attain this spartan sense of sacrifice? "Is there in the World a Nation, which deserves this Character?" Americans, Adams noted, possessed as much public spirit as any people in the modern world. Nevertheless, he had seen all through his life "Such Selfishness and Littleness even in New England" that the cause seemed doubtful, not for lack of power or wisdom, but for lack of virtue. The Revolution had unleashed a bundle of passions—"Hope, Fear, Joy, Sorrow, Love, Hatred, Malice, Envy, Revenge, Jealousy, Ambition, Avarice, Resentment, Gratitude," creating a whirlwind up and down the continent. There was, he told Mercy Warren in January 1776, "so much Rascallity, so much Venality and Corruption, so much Avarice and Ambition such a Rage for Profit and Commerce among all Ranks and Degrees of Men" that republicanism seemed indeed a precarious experiment. It was as if Adams was carrying in his own mind all of the promise and all of the anxiety engendered by the Revolution.[3]

More so perhaps than any other Revolutionary in 1776 Adams rested his hopes for the future on the regenerative effects of republican government and on the emergence of politicians who could mold the character of the people, extinguishing their follies and vices and inspiring their virtues and abilities. As early as 1765 he had observed that Americans alone among the peoples of the world had learned that liberty could not be preserved without "knowledge diffused generally through the whole body of the people." In the excitement of the early days of the Revolution, Adams, like others, clung to this trust in the capacity of education to curb the violent passions of men, to the expectation that a republican form of government would somehow give a "decisive Colour to the Manners of the People," and thereby produce "Strength, Hardiness Activity, Courage, Fortitude and Enterprise," along with a pervasive belief in the principle "that all

---

Warren-Adams Letters, I, 308; Adams to Abigail Adams, July 3, 1776, Butterfield, ed., *Family Correspondence*, II, 28.

3. Adams to Mercy Warren, Jan. 8, Apr. 16, 1776, Ford, ed., *Warren-Adams Letters*, I, 201–02, 222; Adams to Abigail Adams, Apr. 28, 1776, Butterfield, ed., *Family Correspondence*, I, 401.

Things must give Way to the public." If "pure Virtue," "the only foundation of a free Constitution . . . ," he explained in June 1776, "cannot be inspired into our People, in a greater Measure, than they have it now, They may change their Rulers, and the forms of Government, but they will not obtain a lasting Liberty. —They will only exchange Tyrants and Tyrannies." Such reliance as Adams placed on the ameliorative power of republicanism may have been an empty dream, but given his deep apprehension of the American character, an apprehension that sprang from his knowledge of himself, he had little choice. The Revolution had to result in a reformation or it could not succeed.[4]

Within a few years after Independence, however, whatever optimism Adams had had for the refinement of the American character was gone. The American people could no more change than he himself could. By the 1780's what he had feared all along was too evident to deny: Americans had "never merited the Character of very exalted Virtue," and it was foolish to have "expected that they should have grown much better." He now saw and expressed more vividly than anyone that if the new republics were to rely simply on the virtue of the people they were destined, like every previous republic, for eventual destruction. By the time he came to write his *Defence* this conviction of the viciousness of his countrymen was obstinately established in his mind. Unlike Jefferson's, Adams's long stay in Europe had only confirmed his anxiety about the American character. Whereas to Jefferson Europe only made American simplicity and virtue appear dearer in contrast, to Adams Europe seemed to represent what America was fast becoming. It was now clear that there was "no special providence for Americans, and their nature is the same with that of others." Once the hopes of 1776 were dissipated, Adams set for himself the formidable task of convincing his countrymen that they were after all "like all other people, and shall do like other nations." In effect he placed himself not only in the path of the American Revolution but in the course of the emerging American myth of exceptionalism.[5]

4. [Adams], "Dissertation on the Canon and Feudal Law" (1765), Adams, ed., *Works of John Adams*, III, 455–57; Adams to Mercy Warren, Jan. 8, Apr. 16, 1776, Ford, ed., *Warren-Adams Letters*, I, 202, 201, 223; Adams to Zabdiel Adams, June 21, 1776, Butterfield, ed., *Family Correspondence*, II, 21.

5. Adams to James Warren, Jan. 9, 1787, Ford, ed., *Warren-Adams Letters*, II, 280; Adams, *Defence of the Constitutions*, in Adams, ed., *Works of John Adams*, IV, 401; Mercy Warren to Adams, July 28, 1807, recalling a comment of Adams made in 1788, Mass. Hist. Soc., *Colls.*, 5th Ser., 4 (1878), 361.

Americans, Adams now believed, were as driven by the passions for wealth and precedence as any people in history. Ambition, avarice, and resentment, not virtue and benevolence, were the stuff of American society. Those who argued that Americans were especially egalitarian were blind to reality. "Was there, or will there ever be," asked Adams, "a nation, whose individuals were all equal, in natural and acquired qualities, in virtues, talents, and riches?" Every people, contended Adams, possessed inequalities "which no human legislator ever can eradicate." Such inequalities did not have to be legal or artificial—hereditary dignities symbolized by titles or ribbons—in order to be real. They were rooted in nature, in wealth, in birth, or in merit. Because of greater industry or because of a bountiful legacy, some were richer than others. Some were better born than others, inheriting from their families position and prestige in the community. And some were wiser, more talented, more bold than others, displaying courage or learning in such a way as to command respect. All such distinctions produced inequality in the society; and all were "common to every people, and can never be altered by any, because they are founded in the constitution of nature."[6]

The inevitability of these distinctions lay at the heart of Adams's image of society. All life, he believed, was a scramble for them, for wealth, for power, for social eminence, that hopefully would be immortal, passed on to one's descendants. "We may call this desire of distinction childish and silly," said Adams; "but we cannot alter the nature of men." The desires of man were unlimited and consuming, especially those which Adams called the "aristocratical passions." "The love of gold grows faster than the heap of acquisition." The love of praise so magnified itself that "man is miserable every moment when he does not snuff the incense." And ambition so intensified that it "at last takes possession of the whole soul so absolutely, that a man sees nothing in the world of importance to others or himself, but in his object."[7]

Only a handful made their way to the top in this struggle for superiority; but unfortunately there was little guarantee that these few would be only men of talent and virtue. The republican hope that only real merit should govern the world was laudable but hollow. How could it be arranged, asked Adams, "that men ought

---

6. Adams, *Defence of the Constitutions*, Adams, ed., *Works of John Adams*, IV, 392, 397.
    7. *Ibid.*, V, 488, IV, 406.

to be respected only in proportion to their talents, virtues, and services . . . ? How shall the men of merit be discovered? . . . Who shall be the judge?" The republican reliance on elections had hardly worked out. The voters had repeatedly been deceived by the chicanery and falsehoods of pretended merit. The numbers who thirsted for respect and position were "out of all proportion to those who seek it only by merit." Men thus disguised their lack of talent "by displaying their taste and address, their wealth and magnificence, their ancient parchments, pictures, and statues, and the virtues of their ancestors," any artifice, any hypocrisy, that would convince others that they were designed to rule. "What chance has humble, modest, obscure, and poor merit in such a scramble?"[8]

It seemed therefore that there was nothing meritorious in those who reached the pinnacle of the society except their ability to get there. And once on top the few would seek only to stabilize and aggrandize their position by oppressing those below them. Those on the bottom of the society, meanwhile, driven by the most ambitious, would seek only to replace and to ruin the social leaders they hated and envied. Those especially "whose fortunes, families, and merits, in the acknowledged judgment of all" seemed closest to those on the top "will be much disposed to claim the first place as their own right." No matter that the few were not happy in their superiority. Men were driven by inscrutable passions to supplant those above them. "To better their condition, to advance their fortunes, without limits, is the object of their constant desire, the employment of all their thoughts by day and by night." They want to share in that pleasure "which they presume those enjoy, who are already powerful, celebrated, and rich."[9]

Hence arose, concluded Adams, that inevitable social division between "the rich and the poor, the laborious and the idle, the learned and the ignorant"—a division neither rigid nor secure, grounded in the irrationalities of men, a division, moreover, from which America, however republican, however egalitarian, could never escape. "Perhaps it may be said," remarked Adams, "that in America we have no distinctions of ranks, and therefore shall not be liable to those divisions and discords which spring from them." But this was a futile hope. "All that we can say in America

8. [Adams], "Discourses on Davila" (1790), *ibid.*, VI, 249–50.
9. Adams, *Defence of the Constitutions, ibid.*, IV, 399–400; [Adams], "Discourses on Davila," *ibid.*, VI, 257.

is, that legal distinctions, titles, powers, and privileges, are not he-reditary." The desire for distinction—rooted in all human nature—still prevailed. Were not in America, asked Adams, the slightest differences of rank and position, between laborers, yeomen, and gentlemen, for example, "as earnestly desired and sought, as titles, garters and ribbons are in any nation of Europe?"[10]

In fact, argued Adams, almost a half century before Tocque-ville made the same penetrating observation, the urge for distinc-tion was even stronger in America than elsewhere. "A free people are the most addicted to luxury of any." Americans would in-evitably seek to set themselves off one from another, yet their republicanism would give them no sanctions for such distinctions. In a democratic society "there can be no subordination." A man would see his neighbor "whom he holds his equal" with a better coat, hat, house, or horse. "He cannot bear it; he must and will be upon a level with him." Following the war, noted Adams, Amer-ica "rushed headlong into a greater degree of luxury than ought to have crept in for a hundred years." Indeed, because America was "more Avaricious than any other Nation that ever existed," it would be madness, concluded Adams, to expect the society to be free of luxury and the desire for distinction. The Crown was not, as many had believed, the source of corruption and factional-ism after all. Social struggle and division were endemic to every society, and America possessed no immunity.[11]

3. THE BALANCED CONSTITUTION

This then was the America John Adams felt and saw, a cease-less scrambling for place and prestige, a society without peace, contentment, or happiness, a society in which "the awful feeling of a mortified emulation" ate at everyone's heart and made failure unbearable: Adams gave Americans as grim and as dark a picture of themselves as they have ever been offered. Indeed, so pessi-

10. *Ibid.*, 280; Adams, *Defence of the Constitutions, ibid.*, V, 488.
11. *Ibid.*, VI, 95, 97, 95, 96; Adams to Benjamin Rush, Apr. 4, 1790, Alexander Biddle, ed., *Old Family Letters*, Ser. A (Phila., 1892), 57. The Adams-Rush cor-respondence has been recently republished in dialogue in John A. Schutz and Douglass Adair, eds., *The Spur of Fame: Dialogues of John Adams and Benjamin Rush, 1805–1813* (San Marino, 1966). For a discussion of the connection between Adams's personality and his political and social attitudes see Bailyn, "Butterfield's Adams," *Wm. and Mary Qtly.*, 3d Ser., 19 (1962), 238–56.

mistic was Adams's conception of American society that despair seemed inevitable. What possibly could keep this restless society from tearing itself to pieces? What could restrain these brutal passions that threatened to destroy their possessors? Nature had "wrought the passions into the texture and essence of the soul," and man could never destroy them. "To regulate and not to eradicate them," said Adams, "is the province of policy." But how to regulate them? By the 1780's Adams had lost his former faith in the inspirational and ameliorating qualities of republicanism. Education, in which Americans like Jefferson and Benjamin Rush had the highest hopes, no longer seemed to Adams capable of disciplining the emotions of men, of compelling the people to submerge their individual desires into a love for the whole. No nation could so educate its people. "Millions must be brought up, whom no principles, no sentiments derived from education, can restrain from trampling on the laws." It was impossible, said Adams, to reconcile the "diversity of sentiments, contradictory principles, inconsistent interests, and opposite passions" of America "by declamations against discord and panegyrics upon unanimity." Neither education, religion, superstition, nor oaths could control human appetites. "Nothing," he told Jefferson, "but Force and Power and Strength can restrain them." Nothing "but three different orders of men, bound by their interests to watch over each other, and stand the guardians of the laws" could maintain social order.[12]

A balanced constitution—only such a scheme could restrain the irrationalities of men and keep the society together. The political solution Adams offered was essentially the classic mixed polity, the traditional eighteenth-century English constitution, which Adams called "the most stupendous fabric of human invention," refined and refurbished in the manner of the Swiss observer, John Louis De Lolme, "whose book," said Adams, "is the best defence of the political balance of three powers that ever was written." It was not, however, the English constitution as most eighteenth-century Englishmen had understood it. By the 1780's Adams's balance was no longer that between the monarchy and the people, the equipoise of the Glorious Revolution which pitted the ever encroaching power of the Crown against the liberty of the people,

12. [Adams], "Discourses on Davila," Adams, ed., *Works of John Adams*, VI, 247, 246; Adams, *Defence of the Constitutions, ibid.,* IV, 557, V, 431; Adams to Jefferson, Oct. 9, 1787, Boyd, ed., *Jefferson Papers*, XII, 221; Adams, *Defence of the Constitutions*, Adams, ed., *Works of John Adams*, IV, 557.

mediated by a nobility which had in the Whig scheme of history interceded on the side of the people as much as it had aided the King. Adams, like other Americans in these years, reconstructed this traditional Whig balance to fit what seemed to be a new social situation, a new appraisal of the nature of American society.[13]

It was not a jumbling of diverse passions that Adams pictured. Society was not for Adams the hodgepodge of various interests and factions that it was for Madison in *The Federalist*, Number 10. The passions may have been varied but there was no doubt in Adams's mind that the interests in the society could be reduced to a duality, the few and the many, those who had attained superiority and those who aspired to it—a conclusion that was by no means unique. Others too in the 1780's were increasingly describing politics as a contest between "men of some, but small property, much embarrassed and devoured by the interest of their debts," and "men of large estates, especially those which consist in money," in short, between the democracy and the aristocracy. In Massachusetts especially references to this social polarity attained an intensity that was not duplicated elsewhere in the 1780's. As early as 1778 Theophilus Parsons in the *Essex Result* had suggested a legislature that would represent in separate houses the persons and the property of the state—a stark distinction later embodied in the Massachusetts Constitution of 1780. No other state in the period so boldly interpreted the bicameral principle in this way. By the middle eighties the Massachusetts press was filled with talk of the struggle between the rich and the poor, the patricians and the plebians; and some radicals were even urging that the stronghold of property, the Senate, be abolished. In 1784–86 Benjamin Lincoln, in a series of articles in the *Boston Magazine* and the *Independent Chronicle*, explained the natural and historical basis of the Massachusetts Constitution, and in doing so anticipated John Adams's *Defence* at every major point. Although Adams abroad may not have been directly influenced by these writings, he was certainly familiar with the intellectual and po-

---

13. Adams, ed., *Works of John Adams*, IV, 358. De Lolme's book, *The Constitution of England*, was published first in French at Amsterdam in 1771, followed by numerous London editions in English beginning in 1775. On De Lolme see Palmer, *Age of the Democratic Revolution*, I, 145–48. On Adams's "systematic reevaluation of American society and of the American political order" in the 1780's see Howe, *Changing Political Thought*, 133, and Chaps. IV–VI.

litical atmosphere which produced them. His *Defence* grew out
out of his Massachusetts experience.[14]

"A balance," Lincoln had written in 1785, "supposes three
things, the two scales, and the hand that holds it." Adams himself
could not have put it more nicely. Only "orders of men, watching
and balancing each other," could preserve the constitution. The
legislature must provide separate chambers for those on the top
and those on the bottom of the society, for the aristocracy and for
the people, an organizing, segregating, and a balancing of the war-
ring social elements, mediated by an independent executive who
shared in the law-making. The perfect constitution, said Adams,
was "the tripartite balance, the political trinity in unity, trinity
of legislative, and unity of executive power, which in politics is
no mystery."[15]

The aristocracy, "the rich, the well-born, and the able," with
their heightened sense of avarice and ambition, were especially
dangerous; yet Adams also believed that they generally represented the best the society could offer in honor and wisdom.
How then, asked Adams, "shall the legislator avail himself of their
influence for the equal benefit of the public? and how, on the
other hand, shall he prevent them from disturbing the public happiness?" Only by arranging this natural aristocracy, or the most
conspicuous of them, together in a separate house, isolating them
from the rest of the nation, would the state "have the benefit of
their wisdom, without fear of their passions."[16]

In a like manner the mass of the society must also be restrained.
Just as Adams feared the overweening passions of the aristocracy
because he experienced them in his own tormented soul, so too did
he perceive the voracious character of the people because he once
had been one of them. The many were just as dangerous to liberty
and the public good as the few: "they are all of the same clay;
their minds and bodies are alike." "The people will not bear a

14. Boston *Independent Chronicle*, Oct. 18, 1787. For discussion of the Massachusetts Constitution and Lincoln's articles see above, 219–20.

15. Boston *Independent Chronicle*, Dec. 8, 1785; Adams, *Defence of the Constitutions*, Adams, ed., *Works of John Adams*, IV, 557, VI, 128. What mattered
for Adams was the equilibrium of the democratic, aristocratic, and monarchical
elements of the classic mixed constitution, not the separation of the executive,
legislative, and judicial functions of government. See Haraszti, *John Adams and
the Prophets of Progress*, 27–28, 310.

16. Adams, *Defence of the Constitutions*, Adams, ed., *Works of John Adams*,
IV, 290, 414.

contemptuous look or disrespectful word." Indeed, the aristocracy had at least the advantage of wisdom derived from education
and breeding, while the people were generally inconstant and
ignorant. Unchecked, the people would not only turn on the
aristocracy, robbing them and ruining them without hesitation,
but they would also despoil and plunder among themselves. All
history, said Adams, offered irrefutable proof that the people, unrestrained, "have been as unjust, tyrannical, brutal, barbarous,
and cruel, as any king or senate possessed of uncontrollable power." Yet without the people's representation in the constitution
the government would surely be oppressive. "There can be no
free government," wrote Adams, "without a democratical branch
in the constitution." In fact, the absence of the people's voice in
the governments of Europe had rid the Continent of liberty. The
people's passions must also be institutionalized in order to counter
the wiles and greed of the aristocracy. Their houses of representatives thus became the bulwark against the exploitation of the
many by the few.[17]

However, a balance between these two social elements was not
enough, indeed, "in the nature of things, could be no balance at
all," but only a perpetually swinging pendulum. Only an independent executive power, the one, the monarchical element of the
society, could mediate these clashing passions of the democracy
and the aristocracy. The executive with a negative on all legislation could then throw its weight against the irrational and oppressive measures of either branch of the legislature, particularly,
said Adams, against the usurpations of the aristocracy. "If there
is one certain truth to be collected from the history of all ages,"
argued Adams, it was "that the people's rights and liberties, and
the democratical mixture in a constitution, can never be preserved without a strong executive." The executive for Adams, as
for De Lolme and for Lincoln, was the mainstay of the entire
mechanism, the indispensable balancer, "the essence of government," that kept the social forces in equilibrium. The only alternative means of controlling the passions and parties of a society
to the balance he proposed, declared Adams, was an absolute
monarchy with a standing army.[18]

No aspect of Adams's ideas in his *Defence* more pointedly

17. *Ibid.*, VI, 10, 89, 10, IV, 289; see also *ibid.*, IV, 290, 480, VI, 109–10.
18. *Ibid.*, IV, 285, 290, 585, 588.

characterized the changes that had taken place in his thought since 1776 than this new appreciation of the role of the executive. In the decade since Independence the principal antagonists of politics had significantly shifted for Adams. In his *Thoughts on Government* Adams, like most Whigs in 1776, had assumed that politics was essentially a struggle between the ruler or chief magistrate and the people in which the aristocracy sitting in an upper house would act as mediator. Now, in the *Defence*, Adams described the basic struggle as one between the people and the aristocracy in which the magistracy or executive assumed the function of balancer. Where earlier Adams, like other Americans, had conceived of the aristocracy as constituting the ablest and wisest men of the state, different from the people but by no means opposed to the people's welfare, he now saw the aristocratic interest set in opposition to the people's or the democratic interest. Between these two antagonistic social elements stood the magistracy as an independent social entity representing the monarchical interest and as such obliged to share in the lawmaking of the state.

"Among every people, and in every species of republics," said Adams, "we have constantly found *a first magistrate, a head, a chief*, under various denominations, indeed, and with different degrees of authority." Yet for all of their differences of titles and power these single magistrates were fundamentally similar: they all sprang from the basic need of every society to realize its monarchical impulse. Hereditary and elective rulers were essentially alike; the American governors, despite their elective dependency and their lack of hereditary sacrosanctity, fulfilled the same social role in politics as did the King of England. Therefore to Adams most states could never be categorized intelligibly as either monarchies or republics. Massachusetts was actually as much a monarchy as England was a republic. The only meaningful classification of governments was by their degree of mixture, and the only good government was a properly mixed one, a regal republic.

For Adams this balancing of the forces inevitable in every society was the Enlightenment fulfilled: a principle of political science discovered to be applicable to all times and all peoples. Only by "combining the great divisions of society in one system," only by forming an "equal, independent mixture" of the three classic kinds of government, "monarchy, aristocracy, and democracy," could order in any state be achieved. These "three branches of power have an unalterable foundation in nature. . . . If all of them are not acknowledged in any constitution of government, it will be found to be imperfect, unstable, and soon enslaved."[19]

4. THE ANOMALY OF THE *Defence of the Constitutions*

It was this remedy of the mixed constitution, this constitutional overlay on the ferocious social scramble he described, that makes Adams's political theory so contrary to the central thrust of constitutional thought in 1787. Too immersed in the climate of opinion of his own state of Massachusetts, too involved in Europe out of the whirling broader currents of American thinking, Adams never quite perceived what polemics were doing to the Americans' understanding of politics and to the assumptions underlying the theory of the mixed polity. He aimed in his *Defence*, he said, "to lay before the public a specimen of that kind of reading and reasoning which produced the American constitutions," particularly the Massachusetts Constitution of 1780. As a result he was initially uninterested in the Federalist attempts to create a new national government. As late as 1787 the states remained for Adams the source of American salvation, "whatever Imperfections may remain incurable in the Confederation." While he was cautiously willing to grant some additional powers to the Congress, he believed, as he wrote in the *Defence*, that the American people had decided "that a single assembly was every way adequate to the management of all their federal concerns; and with very good reason, because congress is not a legislative assembly, nor a representative assembly, but only a diplomatic assembly."[20]

However, when the new federal Constitution was created, Adams at once saw the similarity of its internal structure to his own proposals for balance and immediately became a fervent advocate of it. But because he remained unaware of the originality of the newly emergent American thought, he was convinced that the Constitution necessarily had created a "wholly national" gov-

19. *Ibid.*, IV, 379; Adams to Abigail Adams, Mar. 14, 1788, quoted in Howe, *Changing Political Thought*, 166; [Adams], "Discourses on Davila," Adams, ed., *Works of John Adams*, VI, 272; Adams, *Defence of the Constitutions, ibid.*, IV, 579. See also *ibid.*, IV, 358–60, 462, 474, V, 108, VI, 108.

20. Adams, *Defence of the Constitutions*, Adams, ed., *Works of John Adams*, IV, 293–94; Adams to Philip Mazzei, June 12, 1787, quoted in Howe, *Changing Political Thought*, 67; Adams, *Defence of the Constitutions*, Adams, ed., *Works of John Adams*, IV, 579–80.

ernment. "Foederal," he said, was an "improper Word" to describe it. Sovereignty, "the Summa imperii," he had learned from both "history and experience," was "indivisible." The doctrine "that imperium in imperio is a solecism, a contradiction in tčrms," inevitably made the new government "not a confederation of independent Republicks" but "a monarchical republic." Perhaps nothing was more symptomatic of Adams's divergence from the mainstream of American thought than his inability to understand what the Federalists were doing to this concept of sovereignty. It was a divergence that the debates over the Constitution exposed and that was never closed. Even as Adams was writing his book he perceived his fate and sensed the eccentric character of his ideas. The *Defence*, he said to Benjamin Franklin in 1787, "contains my confession of political faith, and, if it is heresy, I shall, I suppose, be cast out of communion. But it is the only sense in which I am or ever was a Republican." "Popularity," he told James Warren, "was never my Mistress, nor was I ever, or shall I ever be a popular Man. This Book will make me unpopular."[21]

It did not, however, at least not immediately. Adams's advocacy of a two-house legislature with an independent executive sharing in the lawmaking power coincided with the Federalist remedy for the constitutional problems of the 1780's and so obscured the obsolescence of the reasoning behind his scheme. The response to his three-volume work was thus confused. Because of the seeming identity of his system with that proposed by the Philadelphia Convention, the *Defence* was generally warmly praised as proof "that a people cannot long be free under a government that consists of a single legislature." After only a cursory reading of the first volume Jefferson told Adams that it would "do a great deal of good." Many commended the work as further support for the Federalist cause. Joel Barlow thought it would "do infinite service, by correcting thousands of erroneous sentiments arising from our inexperience." Benjamin Rush informed Richard Price that Adams's book had "diffused such excellent principles among us, that there is little doubt of our adopting a vigorous and compounded federal legislature." The timing of the first volume was fortunate; and although it was actually an apology for America's

21. Adams to William Tudor, June 28, 1789, and Adams to James Lovett, June 4, 1789, in Adams Papers Microfilm, Reel 115; Adams to Franklin, Jan. 27, 1787, John Bigelow, ed., *The Works of Benjamin Franklin* (N. Y., 1904), XI, 298–99; Adams to Warren, Jan. 9, 1787, Ford, ed., *Warren-Adams Letters*, II, 281.

balanced state constitutions, the book and the new federal Constitution became linked in men's thinking.[22]

Those who took the time to probe Adams's reasoning, however, soon found many contradictions with radical American thought as it had developed by 1787. Some even in their admiration saw that the book was "rather an encomium on the British Constitution than a defence of American systems." "Men of learning," said Madison, "find nothing new in it, Men of taste many things to criticize." Instead of explaining the principles of the American constitutions, critics observed, Adams seemed to be "insidiously attempting, notwithstanding now and then a saving clause, to overturn our Constitutions, or at least to sow the seeds of discontent." Perhaps, it was said, Adams's "optics have been too weak to withstand the glass of European Courts." It was not long before the *Defence* was being "squibbed at in almost every paper," and being called "one of the most deep wrought systems of political deception that ever was penned by the ingenuity of man."[23] Everywhere critics pounced on Adams's talk "of the awful distance which should be maintained between some and others," and on his declamations "upon the necessity of one of his three balancing powers, consisting of the *well born*, or of those who are distinguished by their descent from a race of illustrious ancestors. In what part of America are those *well born* to be found? or, if there are any, did they come into the world with coronets upon their heads, or with any other marks of preeminence above the poorest of our species?" In every society, and particularly in America, said Samuel Bryan of Pennsylvania, there existed "so great a disparity in the talents, wisdom and industry of mankind" that no "corresponding weight in the community" with distinct views and interests could be isolated so as to allow Adams's three orders "to exercise their several parts" in the government. Even in England, said Bryan, where there was "a powerful hereditary nobil-

22. *Providence Gazette*, June 23, 1787; Jefferson to Adams, Sept. 28, 1787, Boyd, ed., *Jefferson Papers*, XII, 189; Joel Barlow, *An Oration Delivered . . . at the Meeting of the . . . Cincinnati, July 4, 1787* (Hartford, 1787), 13; Rush to Richard Price, June 2, 1787, Farrand, ed., *Records of the Federal Convention*, III, 33.

23. William Davie to James Iredell, Aug. 6, 1787, McRee, *Life of Iredell*, II, 168; Madison to Jefferson, June 6, 1787, Boyd, ed., *Jefferson Papers*, XI, 401–02; Rev. James Madison to Madison, June 11, 1787, James McClurg to Madison, Aug. 22, 1787, and the Richmond *Virginia Independent Chronicle*, Aug. 15, 1787, all quoted in Warren, *Making of the Constitution*, 816–18.

ity, and real distinctions of rank and interests," such a balanced scheme as Adams proposed had not worked.[24]

None of these criticisms, however, was as fully developed as that of John Stevens, a prominent New Jersey "Farmer." Like others, Stevens was particularly bothered by Adams's obsession with aristocracy. America, he argued, was peculiar in its equality. "We have no such thing as orders, ranks, or nobility; and . . . it is almost impossible they should ever gain any footing here." Only immense accumulations of wealth in a few hands could breed an aristocracy. Yet because of America's republican laws of descent, its prohibitions on monopolies and privileges in any one set of men, and its extensive commercial and social mobility, "there is little danger to be apprehended from this source of wealth being confined to a few places, or to a few persons: in all probability it will be diffused every where." Of course, Stevens admitted, Adams had denied that America possessed at this time different orders of men. But Stevens quite correctly realized that Adams was at bottom arguing for the recognition of an aristocracy in America, however inchoate. There could in fact be no mistaking Adams's meaning: despite the absence of an hereditary nobility, America was no freer of aristocracy than Europe; and the only way to control and to use this aristocracy properly was to ostracize it in a separate house of the legislature. It was the classic theory of mixed government—orders of government derived from constituents of the society—that Stevens rightly saw as the basis of Adams's writing. And Stevens, no doubt less well read in political theory but more attuned to current American thinking than Adams, would have nothing to do with this superannuated idea. "Not a single scruple of this universal and so much boasted political nostrum," said Stevens, "is to be found in any one of the governments of the United States." If Adams's arguments were correct, then, declared Stevens, America's grand experiment in republicanism was not unique after all, and "we have hitherto been only in pursuit of a phantom." Yet Stevens was convinced that Adams was wrong. The American republics were different, and were not mere copies of the English constitution. They were, emphasized Stevens, all "democratic forms of government."[25]

24. Baltimore *Md. Journal*, July 6, 1787; [Samuel Bryan], "Centinel, No. I," Oct. 5, 1787, McMaster and Stone, eds., *Pennsylvania and the Federal Constitution*, 568–69.
25. [Stevens], *Observations on Government*, 46–47, 4–7.

And they were democracies, said Stevens, even though they balanced powers and possessed upper houses and independent executives. At least one historian has been confused by Stevens's criticism of Adams's balanced government, since Stevens himself apparently favored the same kind of government.[26] Yet Stevens was not quarreling with the structure of government that Adams defended; he was actually contesting Adams's reasoning and his justifications. For Stevens the purpose of instituting an upper house was not to confine or embody the aristocracy, but rather to mitigate the inconvenience of having only a single house of representatives. To prevent these inconveniences, said Stevens, "another representative branch is added: these two separate houses form mutual checks upon each other." As a further means of curbing legislative inconstancy and usurpation, added Stevens, other checks were to be placed in the executive and judiciary, which should be made as independent as possible from the legislature. Adams's analogy of government as a set of two scales held by a third hand, said Stevens, was inapplicable for America. He suggested a more appropriate mechanical analogy: a jack which represented the machinery of government, controlled by a weight, which was the people, "the power from which the motion of all parts originates." For Stevens no part of the government existed alongside of the people; indeed the people were not really a part of the government at all. Government was not a balancing of people and aristocracy, but only the distribution and delegation of the people's political power. "The several component powers of government should be so distributed that no one man, or body of men, should possess a larger share thereof than what is absolutely necessary for the administration of government." Stevens's balance of powers was not designed to embody and confine the major constituents of the society, but was intended only to separate, diffuse, and check a mistrusted political authority delegated by the people. For Stevens the parts of the government had lost their social roots. All had become more or less equal agents of the people. Thus the institutions of government for both Adams and Stevens were identical, but the rationale was quite different.[27]

Other Americans kept stumbling over Adams's statements, bewildered by the contradiction between his political structure, which appeared so consonant with the American governments, and his reasoning, which seemed so inconsistent with what many

26. See Palmer, *Age of the Democratic Revolution*, I, 280–81.
27. [Stevens], *Observations on Government*, 39–40, 30–32, 14.

Americans had gradually and often imperceptibly come to believe by 1790. Adams accepted the axiom of the Revolution that all political authority stemmed from the people; yet he remained so wrapped up in the traditional categories of political theory that he could not grasp what his countrymen had done to the relationship between the people and the government. For Adams the people may have been the source of all authority, yet the people themselves still only participated directly as a constituent element of the society in one part of the government. They merely partook of the sovereignty (as they did in England through the House of Commons), and they could exercise the whole sovereignty only in a single-house legislature like that of Pennsylvania. "Whenever I use the word *republic* with approbation," he told Samuel Adams, "I mean a government in which the people have collectively, or by representation, an essential share in the sovereignty." Samuel Adams, like most Americans by 1790, accepted wholeheartedly the desirability of a two-house legislature; yet he had no doubt in his mind that the entire sovereignty of government remained in the people, "a political doctrine which I have never heard an American politician seriously deny." He just could not make sense of his cousin's statement that the people only shared in the supreme power of government. "Is not the *whole sovereignty*, my friend, essentially in the people?" The people had the power to amend or even to abolish their forms of government whenever they pleased. They exerted their sovereignty continually, said Samuel, by electing their representatives, senators and governors: "they delegate the exercise of the powers of government to particular persons, who, after short intervals, resign their powers to the people, and they will reelect them, or appoint others, as they think fit."[28]

It was as if Adams were speaking a language different from that of other Americans. "How it is possible," he lamented, "that whole nations should be made to comprehend the principles and rules of government, until they shall learn to understand one another's meaning by words?" Roger Sherman, for example, was thoroughly perplexed by Adams's statements. He could not comprehend Adams's unusual definition of a republic as "*a government whose sovereignty is vested in more than one person*," a definition which made England as much a republic as America,

28. John Adams to Samuel Adams, Oct. 18, 1790, and Samuel Adams to John Adams, Nov. 20, 1790, Adams, ed., *Works of John Adams*, VI, 415, 420–21.

"a monarchical republic it is true, but a republic still; because the sovereignty, which is the legislative power . . . is equally divided, indeed, between the one, the few, and the many, or in other words, between the natural division of mankind in society,—the monarchical, the aristocratical, and democratical." For Sherman a republic was the antithesis of a monarchy, a commonwealth without a king, a government under the authority of only the people, consisting of a legislature, with one or more branches which, together with an executive, were elected by the people. What especially denominated a state "a *republic*," said Sherman, "is its dependence on the *public* or *people at large*, without any hereditary powers."[29]

Yet to Adams this definition was just another example of the "peculiar sense in which the words *republic, commonwealth, popular state*" were being used by men "who mean by them a democracy, or rather a representative democracy." Adams could not understand that in America by 1787 the magistracy and senates had become somehow as representative of the people as the houses of representatives, and that therefore government wholly in the hands of the people, or a democracy, did not for many Americans necessarily signify, as Adams thought, a government in "a single assembly, chosen at stated periods by the people, and invested with the whole sovereignty." To Adams, thinking in old-fashioned terms, the mere presence of a governor and a senate inevitably made the government something other than a democracy. Since the governor of Massachusetts was "a limited monarch," so "the Constitution of the Massachusetts is a limited Monarchy." So too, said Adams, was the new national government "a limited Monarchy" or "a monarchical republic" like that of England. While many Americans by 1787 had moved away from the implications of the assumptions behind the mixed commonwealths of 1776, Adams had sought for ten years to bring those implications into bold relief and to reconcile them with the English conception of a mixed monarchy, recently made most famous by De Lolme. "The duration of our president," he told Sherman, "is neither perpetual nor for life; it is only for four years; but his power during those four years is much greater than that of an avoyer, a consul, a podestà, a doge, a stadtholder; nay, than a king of Poland; nay, than a king of Sparta." And because America was a monar-

29. Adams, *Defence of the Constitutions, ibid.,* V, 453; Adams to Roger Sherman, July 17, 1789, and Sherman to Adams, July 20, 1789, *ibid.,* VI, 428, 437.

chical republic, its president being a kind of elective king and an embodiment of the "one" in the society, "it is essential to a monarchical republic, that the supreme executive should be a branch of the legislature, and have a negative on all the laws." Without a proper share in the legislature by the monarchical order, he told Sherman, the desired balance of the state "between the one, the few, and the many" could not be preserved.[30]

By 1790 this explanation of the executive veto was totally out of touch with American thinking. An absolute veto, said Sherman, may have been meaningful in England where the rights of the people and the rights of the nobility had to be balanced by a complete negative in the Crown. But the American republics "wherein is no higher rank than that of common citizens" had no such interests to balance. The veto in America had nothing to do with representing the magisterial element in the society; the qualified negative given to American executives was designed "only to produce a revision" of the laws and to prevent hastily drawn legislation. In fact, the more Sherman thought about it, the more Adams's ideas seemed to be unrelated to the new government. To say, as Sherman did, that he saw "no principles in our constitution that have any tendency to aristocracy" was to point up with a vengeance the obsolescence of Adams's political theory. "As both branches of Congress are eligible from the citizens at large, and wealth is not a requisite qualification, both will commonly be composed of members of similar circumstances in life." There could be no real struggle then between the several branches of the government; all were equal agents of the people, "directed to one end, the advancement of the public good."[31]

5. AN INQUIRY INTO THE PRINCIPLES AND POLICY OF THE GOVERNMENT OF THE UNITED STATES

As most Americans shifted the justifications for their forms of government, Adams, seemingly immune to the new thought around him, moved back into history and grasped the classical theory of the mixed polity even more firmly. His friends' reserva-

30. Adams, *Defence of the Constitutions, ibid.,* V, 454; Adams to Benjamin Lincoln, June 19, 1789, Adams Papers Microfilm, Reel 115; Adams to Sherman, July 18, 17, 1789, Adams, ed., *Works of John Adams,* VI, 430, 428–29.

31. Sherman to Adams, July 20, ?, 1789, Adams, ed., *Works of John Adams,* VI, 438, 441.

tions and objections were no match for his vitriolic and gushing passion. For every statement of conventional American republicanism timidly offered by Benjamin Rush, Adams had a fiery retort that left Rush aghast. In Rush's opinion Americans were different from other people, freer of faction, and peculiarly qualified for republicanism, which, said Rush, had never before in history had a fair trial. For Adams this was absurd. Boston, New York, and Philadelphia were as vicious and profligate as London. "How can you say," he demanded of Rush, "that Factions have been few in America? . . . Have not our Parties behaved like all Republican Parties? is not the History of Hancock and Bowdoin, the History of the Medici and Albizi?" To Rush's horror Adams even praised hereditary institutions as not only possessing "admirable wisdom and exemplary Virtue in a certain stage of Society in a great Nation," but also "as the hope of our Posterity," to which Americans must eventually resort "as an Asylum against Discord, Seditions and Civil War, and that at no very distant Period of time." Even titles and symbols of distinction now seemed necessary, indeed beneficial, for America. The widening separation from his countrymen frightened and frustrated him, but only compelled him to proclaim his diverging beliefs more shrilly than ever. He saw himself as a Promethean figure, cast aside and punished for his knowledge, while his fellow Americans went on "bawling about a Republicanism which they understand not."[32]

Old age brought no rest. At seventy-nine Adams had to contend with the most penetrating and devastating attack ever written on his *Defence of the Constitutions of the United States*. No one perceived more acutely how Adams had diverged from the mainstream of American Revolutionary thinking than John Taylor, in his *Inquiry into the Principles and Policy of the Government of the United States*. Fortunately perhaps for Adams and unfortunately surely for Taylor the criticism was too long delayed. Although the *Inquiry* was not published until 1814, the book really belonged to the previous century, both in time and in thought. Taylor admittedly had devoted at least twenty years to its composition and had deferred publication until time had abated the polemical passions—a tragic mistake which helps to account for the book's awkward position in American political literature. By 1814 Taylor's refutation of Adams had lost its point, making the book, as Taylor himself put it, "almost letters from the

32. Adams to Rush, Feb. 8, June 9, 19, July 5, 24, 1789, Biddle, ed., *Old Family Letters*, 31, 37, 39, 40, 44, 46.

dead."[33] Nevertheless, Taylor's book, although burdened with a heavy style, brilliantly expressed the conception of American politics that had emerged from the Revolutionary era; and Taylor exposed, as no one else ever so candidly did, the intellectual chasm that separated John Adams from his countrymen.

Taylor grounded his assault on Adams in the assumption that the American polities were different from any previous forms of government in history. The American Revolution, declared Taylor, had finally freed men's minds from the "numerical analysis" of politics—the classification of governments into the one, few, and many, into monarchy, aristocracy, and democracy—which had inhibited political thinking since antiquity. At the outset of the Revolution, America had observed only the elevation of the mixed British constitution; yet "through the telescope, necessity, new principles were discovered," a new way of looking at politics was found. America, declared Taylor, had moved more rapidly in twenty years toward an understanding of political science than the world had in twenty centuries.[34]

Yet Adams seemed unaccountably oblivious of these break-throughs in political thinking. His "very language" was "strange" to Americans. He did not appear to understand the new basis of the American states, and considered American society as made up of orders created by nature. He had arranged "men into the one, the few and the many" and had attempted to bring the political system of America within the pale of this tripartite classification "by modifying our temporary, elective, responsible governors, into monarchs; our senates into aristocratical orders; and our representatives, into a nation personally exercising the functions of government." But the American governments had nothing to do with these ancient categories of politics. Aristocracy, said Taylor, that is, the kind of aristocracy that was "capable of being collected into a legislative chamber," was impracticable in America, where education and commerce had diffused knowledge and wealth among so many. Inequalities and distinctions of superiority, Taylor admitted, would inevitably exist; but in America, he argued, they were so numerous and fluctuating that they could never be gathered together and confined in the upper houses of the legislatures.[35]

33. John Taylor, *An Inquiry into the Principles and Policy of the Government of the United States* (New Haven, 1950, first published 1814), 34.

34. *Ibid.*, 32, 37, 118, 158–59.

35. *Ibid.*, 372, 101, 37, 51, 54.

The people, moreover, were no longer the kind of social element that Adams assumed. Adams, said Taylor, had in effect retained the British conception of virtual representation and had thereby transplanted the whole people into the lower houses of the legislatures. Adams thus still "considers the people as an order, electing only one branch of the legislature," the democracy, standing alongside and checking the other two orders of monarchy and aristocracy. But this old-fashioned notion of democracy had lost its significance and had been replaced by a new American version, by "the right of the people to institute a government," and by "the responsibility of magistrates to the people." The American constitutions, said Taylor, did not consider society as made of orders encompassed by the government, but "as made of individuals," existing outside all governments, distributing pieces of power "into a multitude of hands." "It is our policy," said Taylor, "to consider the people as retaining a vast share of political power, and as only investing their government with so much as they deem necessary for their own benefit." The distribution was endless: "Power is first divided between the government and the people, reserving to the people, the control of the dividend allotted to the government. The dividend allotted to the government, is subdivided between its two branches, federal and state." Then these two portions were further broken up and "distributed in quotas still more minute" to the various departments and branches of government, all rigidly controlled by the people.[36]

There was nothing then in this multitude of division "to justify the hypothesis of three natural orders"; it was only intended to prevent any dangerous accumulation of power and, aided by the frequency of elections and the use of instructions, "to defend the sovereignty of the people against all." And it was a real sovereignty the people possessed, a sovereignty of which suffrage and representation were but the most superficial and transitory expressions. In the English constitution, the model of the mixed polity favored by Adams, "the nation and the government is considered as one, and the passive obedience denied to the king conceded to the government . . . ; whereas, by ours, the nation and the government are considered as distinct." A government of orders was believed sovereign "because the orders composing it, consider themselves as composing the society." In England, the concept of complete, virtual representation assumed by Adams "helps to take

36. *Ibid.*, 114, 99, 101, 176, 170, 363.

sovereignty from the people, and bestows it upon the government." But the American governments were not full embodiments of the society. Indeed, said Taylor, "all our governments are limited agencies." "Power is divided by our policy," asserted Taylor, "that the people may maintain their sovereignty; by the system of orders, to destroy the sovereignty of the people." Once a society was divided into the three hostile interests in the manner Adams had proposed, there remained no outside body, no national will, that could bring the government to account or alter the form of the constitution. In fact, said Taylor, the entire conception of mixed government arose out of the ancient belief that the power of a government was unlimited and therefore must be split into three balancing and interacting parts in order to preserve liberty. The American Revolution, however, had laid bare a new policy. "A nation, possessed of a mountain of gold, which should bestow the whole upon three ministers, trusting to their broils for its liberty, would pursue the old policy; by keeping the mass of its mountain, and entrusting agents with occasional sums, to be employed for its use, the new."[37]

In Taylor's opinion Adams had been hopelessly wrong, his system antiquated. The New World had rejected the alternatives of a suffocating tyranny and a jarring mixture, "both the calm despotism of one order, and the turbulent counterpoise of several," and had constructed a unique system of politics—a system founded on the self-interest of its members. While Adams was carrying on in a timeworn manner about the principles of honor and virtue infusing the social constituents of the government, the Americans, said Taylor, were showing how republican governments could be sustained with the members of the society possessed of neither quality, how in fact "an avaricious society can form a government able to defend itself against the avarice of its members" by enlisting "the interest of vice . . . on the side of virtue." "If virtue, as a basis of government, be understood to mean, not that the principles of government, but that the individuals composing the nation must be virtuous, the republicks would be founded in . . . the evanescent qualities of individuals" and thus doomed to destruction. The American governments through their moral constitutions and pervasion of responsibility had demonstrated that "the principles of a society may be virtuous, though the individuals composing it are vicious." Because Adams had

37. *Ibid.*, 364, 171, 33, 150, 422, 200, 356, 393, 374.

never comprehended any of these new virtuous principles and had made the "radical errour" of confounding "our division of power . . . with his balance of orders," his work, concluded Taylor, was in no way a defense of the American constitutions; it was "a caricature or travesty" of them.[38]

What could the old man reply? Adams had clung too long to his political principles to allow one more attack, however powerful, to shake them loose. For Adams the "analysis of antiquity" was still the "eternal, unchangeable truth." He answered Taylor of course—in over thirty letters. But age had mellowed his passion; and the correspondence, he told Taylor, was "intended for your amusement and mine." He only reiterated his deep-felt belief in the inevitability of inequality in society and showed little indication that he had read, let alone comprehended, the entirety of Taylor's book. The gulf separating him from his countrymen was saddening. He felt misunderstood and persecuted, and it seemed it had been so from the beginning. "From the year 1761, now more than Fifty years," he lamented to Benjamin Rush in 1812, "I have constantly lived in an enemies Country."[39] For too long and with too much candor he had tried to tell his fellow Americans some truths about themselves that American values and American ideology would not admit.

38. *Ibid.*, 373, 461, 460, 355, 356, 355.
39. Adams to Taylor, no dates, Adams, ed., *Works of John Adams*, VI, 464, 463, 482–83, 514; Adams to Rush, Jan. 8, 1812, Biddle ed., *Old Family Letters*, 369.

CHAPTER XV

The American Science of Politics

1. DEMOCRATIC REPUBLICS

Undoubtedly John Taylor was right about the source of the new principles of politics discovered during the Revolutionary era. The creation of a new political theory was not as much a matter of deliberation as it was a matter of necessity. The blending of diverse views and clashing interests into the new federal system, Madison told Jefferson in October 1787, was nothing "less than a miracle." Although no one person had done so much to create the Constitution, Madison generously but rightly stressed to the end of his life that it was not "the offspring of a single brain" but "the work of many heads and many hands." The formation of the new government, as Franklin observed to a European correspondent in 1788, was not like a game of chess, methodically and consciously played. It was more like a game of dice, with so many players, "their ideas so different, their prejudices so strong and so various, and their particular interests, independent of the general, seeming so opposite, that not a move can be made that is not contested." Yet somehow out of all these various moves the Constitution had emerged, and with it had emerged not only "a wonder and admiration" among the members of the Convention themselves, but also a growing awareness among all Americans that the Constitution had actually created a political system "so novel, so complex, and intricate" that writing about it would never cease.[1]

1. Madison to Jefferson, Oct. 24, 1787, Boyd, ed., *Jefferson Papers*, XII, 272; Madison (1834), quoted in Brant, *Madison*, III, 154–55; Benjamin Franklin to Du Pont de Nemours, June 9, 1788, Smyth, ed., *Writings of Franklin*, IX, 659;

The Constitution had become the climax of a great revolution. "Till this period," declared Aaron Hall of New Hampshire in a 1788 oration, "the revolution in America has never appeared to me to be completed; but this is laying on the cap-stone of the great American Empire." It was not the revolution that had been intended but it was a real revolution nonetheless, marked by a momentous upheaval in the understanding of politics where the "collected wisdom of ages" was "interwoven in this form of government." "The independence of America considered merely as a separation from England, would have been a matter but of little importance," remarked Thomas Paine, "had it not been accompanied by a revolution in the principles and practise of governments." "There are some great eras," said James Wilson, "when important and very perceptible alterations take place in the situation of men and things." And America, added David Ramsay, was in the midst of one of those great eras.[2]

Americans now told themselves with greater assurance than ever that they had created something remarkable in the history of politics. "The different constitutions which have been adopted by these states," observed John Stevens in 1787, "are experiments in government entirely new; they are founded upon principles peculiar to themselves." Admittedly they had not fully understood politics at the outset of the Revolution; but within a decade they believed that most of the defects of their early state constitutions had been discovered and were on the way to being remedied. And the new federal Constitution expressed all they had learned. "The government of the United States," wrote Nathaniel Chipman of Vermont in 1793, "exhibits a new scene in the political history of the world, . . . exhibits, in theory, the most beautiful system, which has yet been devised by the wisdom of man." With their governments the Americans had placed the science of politics on a footing with the other great scientific discoveries of the previous century. Their governments, said William Vans Murray, repre-

Wilson, in McMaster and Stone, eds., *Pennsylvania and the Federal Constitution*, 224; James Sullivan, *Observations upon the Government of the United States of America* (Boston, 1791), v.

2. Aaron Hall, *An Oration . . . to Celebrate the Ratification of the Federal Constitution by the State of New-Hampshire* (Keene, N. H., 1788), 6, 7; Paine, *Rights of Man*, in Foner, ed., *Writings of Paine*, I, 354; James Wilson, "Lectures on Law," Wilson, ed., *Works of Wilson*, II, 40; Ramsay, *American Revolution*, I, 356.

sented "the most finished political forms" in history and had "deservedly attracted the attention of all speculative minds." It was therefore important for "the cause of liberty all over the world, that they should be understood." And by the end of the 1780's and the early nineties Americans increasingly felt compelled to explain to themselves and to the world the uniqueness of what they had discovered.[3]

Their governments were so new and so distinctive that they groped for political terms adequate to describe them. By the late 1780's Americans generally were calling their governments democracies, but peculiar kinds of democracies. America, said Murray, had established governments which were "in their principles, structure, and whole mass, purely and unalterably Democratic." The American republics, remarked John Stevens, approached "nearer to perfect democracies" than any other governments in the world. Yet democracy, as eighteenth-century political scientists generally understood the term, was not, they realized, a wholly accurate description of their new governments. They were "Democratic Republics," as Chipman called them, by which was "meant, a Representative Democracy." In *The Federalist*, Number 10, Madison called the American governments republics, as distinct from a "pure democracy" in which a small number of citizens assembled and administered the government in person. For Madison a republic had become a species of government to be classed alongside aristocracy or democracy, a distinctive form of government "in which the scheme of representation takes place." Representation—that was the key conception in unlocking an understanding of the American political system. America was, as Hamilton said, "a *representative democracy*." Only the American scheme, wrote Thomas Paine, was based "wholly on the system of representation," and thus it was "the only real republic in character and practise, that now exists." The American polity was "representation ingrafted upon democracy," creating "a system

3. [Stevens], *Observations on Government*, 51; Nathaniel Chipman, *Sketches of the Principles of Government* (Rutland, Vt., 1793), 239, 277; [Murray], *Political Sketches*, 1. With the adoption of the new federal Constitution pressure was placed on the states to bring their constitutions, as one writer put it, into "closer harmony" with that of the national government. By 1790 Pennsylvania, South Carolina, and Georgia had done so; New Hampshire, Delaware, and Vermont followed in the early nineties. Hartford *Conn. Courant*, Oct. 8, 1787; Nevins, *American States*, 196–205. See also Elizabeth K. Bauer, *Commentaries on the Constitution, 1790–1860* (N. Y., 1952).

of government capable of embracing and confederating all the various interests and every extent of territory and population."[4]

2. THE PERVASIVENESS OF REPRESENTATION

It was representation then—"the delegation of the government . . . ," said Madison, "to a small number of citizens elected by the rest"—that explained the uniqueness of the American polities. "The *principle* on which all the American governments are founded," wrote Samuel Williams of Vermont, "is *representation.*" No other nation, said Charles Pinckney of South Carolina, so enjoyed the right of self-government, "where the true principles of representation are understood and practised, and where all authority flows from and returns at stated periods to, the people." Representation, said Edmund Randolph, was "a thing not understood in its full extent till very lately." Neither the Israelites nor the ancients had properly comprehended the uses of representation—"a very excellent modern improvement in the management of republics," said Samuel Langdon of New Hampshire. "It is surprising, indeed," said Wilson, "how very imperfectly, at this day, the doctrine of representation is understood in Europe. Even Great Britain, which boasts a superior knowledge of the subject, and is generally supposed to have carried it into practice, falls far short of its true and genuine principles." Representation, remarked Wilson, barely touched the English constitution, since it was not immediately or remotely the source of executive or judicial power. Even in the legislature representation was not "a pervading principle," but actually was only a check, confined to the Commons. The Lords acted either under hereditary right or under an authority granted by the prerogative of the Crown and hence were "not the representatives of the people." The world, it seemed, had "left to America the glory and happiness of forming a government where representation shall at once supply the basis and the cement of the superstructure."[5] "In America," said

4. [Murray], *Political Sketches*, 5; [Stevens], *Observations on Government*, 50; Chipman, *Principles of Government*, 102; *The Federalist*, No. 10, No. 14; Hamilton, Notes for a Speech of July 12, 1788, in the N. Y. Ratifying Convention, Syrett and Cooke, eds., *Hamilton Papers*, V, 150; Paine, *Rights of Man*, Foner, ed., *Writings of Paine*, I, 370–71. On the confusion of terms, see Robert W. Shoemaker, " 'Democracy' and 'Republic' as Understood in Late Eighteenth-Century America," *American Speech*, 41 (1966), 83–95.

5. *The Federalist*, No. 10; Williams, *History of Vermont*, 342; Pinckney (S.

Williams, "every thing tended to introduce, and to complete the system of representation." America, wrote Madison, had created the first example of "a government wholly popular, and founded at the same time, wholly on that principle [of representation]." Americans had made their entire system from top to bottom representative, "diffusing," in Wilson's words, "this vital principle throughout all the different divisions and departments of the government." Since Americans, influenced by the implications of the developing conception of actual representation, now clearly believed that "the right of representing is conferred by the act of electing," every part of the elective governments had become representative of the people. In truth, said Madison, representation was "the pivot" on which the whole American system moved.[6]

Although the members of the houses of representatives were perhaps the more "immediate representatives," no longer were they the full and exclusive representatives of the people. "The Senators," said Nathaniel Chipman, "are to be representatives of the people, no less, in fact, than the members of the other house." Foreigners, noted William Vans Murray, had mistaken the division of the legislatures in America as some sort of an embodiment of an aristocracy. Even in Maryland and in the federal Constitution where the senates were indirectly elected, the upper house was derived mediately from the people. "It represents the people. It represents no particular order of men or of ranks." To those who sought to comprehend fully the integrity of the new system the senate could only be a weight in the powers of legislative deliberation, not a weight of property, of privileges, or of interests. Election by the people, not the number of chambers in the legislature, declared John Stevens, had made "our governments the most democratic that ever existed anywhere." "With us," concluded Wilson, "the power of magistrates, call them by whatever name you please, are the grants of the people."[7]

C.) and Randolph (Va.), in Elliot, ed., *Debates*, IV, 331, III, 199; Samuel Langdon, *The Republic of the Israelites an Example to the American States . . .* (Exeter, N. H., 1788), 7; Wilson, in McMaster and Stone, eds., *Pennsylvania and the Federal Constitution*, 222–23.

6. Williams, *History of Vermont*, 343; *The Federalist*, No. 14; Wilson, "Lectures on Law," Wilson, ed., *Works of Wilson*, I, 430, II, 57; *The Federalist*, No. 63.

7. Chipman, *Principles of Government*, 150; [Murray], *Political Sketches*, 52–53; [Stevens], *Observations on Government*, 51; Wilson, "Lectures on Law," Wilson, ed., *Works of Wilson*, I, 445. By 1823 Jefferson, who in 1776 in his desire to establish an aristocratic senate free from popular dictation had even been

Therefore all governmental officials, including even the executive and judicial parts of the government, were agents of the people, not fundamentally different from the people's nominal representatives in the lower houses of the legislatures. The Americans
of 1776, observed Wilson, had not clearly understood the nature
of their executives and judiciaries. Although the authority of
their governors and judges became in 1776 as much "the child of
the people" as that of the legislatures, the people could not forget
their traditional colonial aversion to the executive and judiciary,
and their fondness for their legislatures, which under the British
monarchy had been the guardians of their rights and the anchor
of their political hopes. "Even at this time," Wilson noted with
annoyance, "people can scarcely devest themselves of those opposite prepossessions." The legislatures often were still called "the
people's representatives," implying, "though probably, not
avowed upon reflection," that the executive and judicial powers
were not so strongly or closely connected with the people. "But
it is high time," said Wilson, "that we should chastise our prejudices." The different parts of the government were functionally
but not substantively different. "The executive and judicial powers are now drawn from the same source, are now animated by
the same principles, and are now directed to the same ends, with
the legislative authority: they who execute, and they who administer the laws, are so much the servants, and therefore as much
the friends of the people, as those who make them." The entire
government had become the limited agency of the sovereign
people.[8]

The pervasive Whig mistrust of power had in the years since
Independence been increasingly directed not only against the traditional rulers, but also against the supposed representatives of
the people, who now seemed to many to be often as distant and
unrepresentative of the people's interests as Parliament once had
been. "The representatives of the people, in a popular assembly,"

---

willing to have it elected for life, was suggesting to European constitution-makers
that in order "to avoid all temptation to superior pretensions of the one over the
other House, and the possibility of either erecting itself into a privileged order,
might it not be better to choose at the same time and in the same mode, a body
sufficiently numerous to be divided by lot into two separate Houses, acting as in-
dependently as the two Houses in England, or in our governments, and to shuffle
their names together and re-distribute them by lot, once a week for a fortnight?"
Jefferson to A. Coray, Oct. 23, 1823, Andrew A. Lipscomb and Albert E. Bergh,
eds., *The Writings of Thomas Jefferson* (Washington, 1905), XV, 485–86.
   8. Wilson, "Lectures on Law," Wilson, ed., *Works of Wilson*, I, 398–99.

said Hamilton, "seem sometimes to fancy that they are the people themselves." The constitutional reformers seized on the people's growing suspicion of their own representatives and reversed the perspective: the houses of representatives, now no more trusted than other parts of the government, seemed to be also no more representative of the people than the other parts of the government. They had lost their exclusive role of embodying the people in the government. In fact the people did not actually participate in the government any more, as they did, for example, in the English House of Commons. The Americans had taken the people out of the government altogether. The "true distinction" of the American governments, wrote Madison in *The Federalist*, "lies *in the total exclusion of the people, in their collective capacity*, from any share" in the government. Or from a different point of view the Americans could now argue that the people participated in all branches of the government and not merely in their houses of representatives. "The whole powers of the proposed government," said Hamilton in *The Federalist*, "is to be in the hands of the representatives of the people." All parts of the government were equally responsible but limited spokesmen for the people, who remained as the absolute and perpetual sovereign, distributing bits and pieces of power to their various agents.[9]

Confrontation with the Blackstonian concept of legal sovereignty had forced American theorists to relocate it in the people-at-large, a transference that was comprehensible only because of the peculiar experience of American politics. "Sovereignty," said James Sullivan, "must in its nature, be absolute and uncontrollable by any civil authority. . . . A subordinate sovereignty is nonsense: A subordinate, uncontrolable power is a contradiction in terms." In America this kind of sovereignty could only exist in the people themselves, who "may invest the exercise of it in whom they please; but where the power delegated by them is subordinate, or controlable by any other delegated civil power, it is not a sovereign power." Thus it was obvious that in America "there is no supreme power but what the people themselves hold." "The supreme power," said Wilson, "is in them; and in them, even when a constitution is formed, and government is in operation, the supreme power still remains." The powers of the people were thus never alienated or surrendered to a legislature. Representation, in other words, never eclipsed the people-at-large, as

9. *The Federalist*, No. 71, No. 63, No. 28.

apparently it did in the English House of Commons. In America the people were never really represented in the English sense of the term. "A portion of their authority they, indeed, delegate; but they delegate that portion in whatever manner, in whatever measure, for whatever time, to whatever persons, and on whatever conditions they choose to fix." Such a delegation, said Sullivan, was necessarily fragmentary and provisional; "it may extend to some things and not to others or be vested for some purposes, and not for others." Only a proper understanding of this vital principle of the sovereignty of the people could make federalism intelligible. The representation of the people, as American politics in the Revolutionary era had made glaringly evident, could never be virtual, never inclusive; it was acutely actual, and always tentative and partial. "All power whatever," said John Stevens, "is vested in, and immediately derived from, the people only; the rulers are their deputies merely, and at certain short periods are removable by them: nay," he added, "the very government itself is a creature formed by themselves, and may, whenever they think it necessary, be at any time new modelled."[10]

3. THE EQUATION OF RULERS AND RULED

This conception of the sovereignty of the people used to create the new federal government had at last clarified the peculiar American idea of a constitution. A constitution, as James Iredell said, was "a declaration of particular powers by the people to their representatives, for particular purposes. It may be considered as a great power of attorney, under which no power can be exercised but what is expressly given." A constitution for Americans, said Thomas Paine, was "not a thing in name only; but in fact. . . . It is the body of elements, to which you can refer, and quote article by article; and which contains . . . every thing that relates to the complete organization of a civil government, and the principles on which it shall act, and by which it shall be bound." A constitution was thus a "thing *antecedent* to a government, and a government is only the creature of a constitution." It was truly, said Wilson, the act of the people, and "in their hands it is clay in the hands of the potter: they have the right to mould,

10. Sullivan, *Observations upon the Government*, 22, 23; Wilson, "Lectures on Law," Wilson, ed., *Works of Wilson*, I, 439–40; [Stevens], *Observations on Government*, 50.

to preserve, to improve, to refine, and to furnish it as they please."
Only by conceiving of a constitution as a written delimitation
of the grant of power made by the people to the government was
"the important distinction so well understood in America, between a Constitution established by the people and unalterable
by the government, and a law established by the government and
alterable by the government" rendered truly comprehensible.[11]

In America a constitution had become, as Madison pointed out,
a charter of power granted by liberty rather than, as in Europe,
a charter of liberty granted by power. Magna Carta and the English Bill of Rights were not constitutions at all. They "did not,"
said Paine, "create and give powers to Government in the manner
a constitution does." They were really only "restrictions on assumed power," bargains "which the parts of the government
made with each other to divide powers, profits and privileges."
"The far famed social compact between the people and their
rulers," declared David Ramsay, "did not apply to the United
States." "To suppose that any government can be a party in a
compact with the whole people," said Paine, "is to suppose it to
have existence before it can have a right to exist." In America, said
Ramsay, "the sovereignty was in the people," who "deputed certain individuals as their agents to serve them in public stations
agreeably to constitutions, which they prescribed for their conduct." Government, concluded Paine, "has of itself no rights;
they are altogether duties."[12]

Yet if the ancient notion of a contract was to be preserved in
American thinking, then it must be a Lockean contract, one
formed by the individuals of the society with each other, instead
of a mutual arrangement between rulers and ruled. In most countries, declared Charles Backus in 1788, the people "have obtained
a partial security of their liberties, by extorted concessions from
their nobles or kings. But in America, the *People* have had an opportunity of forming a compact *betwixt themselves*; from which
alone, their rulers derive all their authority to govern." This image
of a social contract formed by isolated and hostile individuals was
now the only contractual metaphor that comprehended American

11. Iredell (N. C.), in Elliot, ed., *Debates*, IV, 148; Paine, *Rights of Man*, Foner,
ed., *Writings of Paine*, I, 278; Wilson, "Lectures on Law," Wilson, ed., *Works
of Wilson*, I, 417–18; *The Federalist*, No. 53.

12. [Madison], Phila. *National Gazette*, Jan. 19, 1792, Hunt, ed., *Writings of
Madison*, VI, 83–85; Paine, *Rights of Man*, Foner, ed., *Writings of Paine*, I, 382–
88, 379; Ramsay, *American Revolution*, I, 355–56.

social reality. Since an American constitution could no longer be regarded as a contract between rulers and people, representing distinct and unified interests, considerations like protection and allegiance lost their relevance. "Writers on government have been anxious on the part of the people," observed Nathaniel Chipman in 1793, "to discover a consideration given for the right of protection.... While government was supposed to depend on a compact, not between the individuals of a people, but between the people and the rulers, this was a point of great consequence." But not any longer in America, where government was based on a compact only among the people. Obedience to the government in America followed from no such traditional consideration. The flow of authority itself was reversed, and "*consent*," which had not been the basis of magisterial authority in the past, now became "the sole obligatory principle of human government and human laws." Because of the pervasiveness of representational consent through all parts of the government, "the judgments of our courts, and the commissions constitutionally given by our governor," said John Jay, "are as valid and as binding on all our persons whom they concern, as the laws passed by our legislature." The once important distinction between magisterial authority and representative legislative authority was now obliterated. "All constitutional acts of power, whether in the executive or in the judicial department, have as much legal validity and obligation as if they proceeded from the legislature." No more revolutionary change in the history of politics could have been made: the rulers had become the ruled and the ruled the rulers.[13]

4. The Parceling of Power

The American governments, wrote Samuel Williams in his *Natural and Civil History of Vermont* of 1794, "do not admit of sovereignty, nobility, or any kind of hereditary powers; but only of powers granted by the people, ascertained by written constitutions, and exercised by representation for a given time." Hence such governments "do not admit of monarchy, or aristocracy; nor do they admit of what was called democracy by the ancients." The old classification of politics by the number and

13. Backus, *Sermon Preached at Long Meadow*, 8; Chipman, *Principles of Government*, 110–11; Wilson, "Lectures on Law," Wilson, ed., *Works of Wilson*, I, 221; *The Federalist*, No. 64. See Andrew C. McLaughlin, "Social Compact and Constitutional Construction," *Amer. Hist. Rev.*, 5, (1899–1900), 467–90.

character of the rulers no longer made sense of American practice where "all is transacted by representation" expressed in different ways. The government in the several states thus "varies in its form; committing more or less power to a governor, senate, or house of representatives, as the circumstances of any particular state may require. As each of these branches derive their whole power from the people, are accountable to them for the use and exercise they make of it, and may be displaced by the election of others," the liberty and security of the people, as Americans had thought in 1776, no longer came from their participation in one part of the government, as the democracy balanced against the monarchy and aristocracy, "but from the responsibility, and dependence of each part of the government, upon the people."[14]

In slightly more than two decades of polemics the Americans had destroyed the age-old conception of mixed government and had found new explanations for their polities created in 1776, explanations that rested on their expansion of the principle of representation. America had not discovered the idea of representation, said Madison, but it could "claim the merit of making the discovery the basis of unmixed and extensive republics." And their republics were now peculiarly unmixed, despite the presence of senates and governors. They could in fact intelligibly be considered to be democracies, since, as James Wilson said, "in a democracy" the supreme power "is inherent in the people, and is either exercised by themselves or their representatives." Perhaps no one earlier or better described the "new and rich discoveries in jurisprudence" Americans had made than did Wilson. The British constitution, he said, had attempted to combine and to balance the three different forms of government, but it had obviously failed. And it was left to the Americans to realize that it was "not necessary to intermix the different species of government" in order to attain perfection in politics. "We have discovered, that one of them—the best and purest—that, in which the supreme power remains with the people at large, is capable of being formed, arranged, proportioned, and organized in such a manner, as to exclude the inconveniences, and to secure the advantages of all three." The federal Constitution, said Wilson, was therefore "purely democratical," even though in its outward form it resembled the conventional mixed government: "all authority of every kind *is derived by* REPRESENTATION *from the* PEOPLE *and the* DEMOCRATIC *principle is carried into every part of*

14. Williams, *History of Vermont*, 342, 343.

the government." The new government was in fact, incongruous as it sounded, a mixed or balanced democracy.[15]

Americans had retained the forms of the Aristotelian schemes of government but had eliminated the substance, thus divesting the various parts of the government of their social constituents. Political power was thus disembodied and became essentially homogeneous. The division of this political power now became (in Jefferson's words) "the first principle of a good government," the "distribution of its powers into executive, judiciary, and legislative, and a sub-division of the latter into two or three branches." Separation of powers, whether describing executive, legislative, and judicial separation or the bicameral division of the legislature (the once distinct concepts now thoroughly blended), was simply a partitioning of political power, the creation of a plurality of discrete governmental elements, all detached from yet responsible to and controlled by the people, checking and balancing each other, preventing any one power from asserting itself too far. The libertarian doctrine of separation of powers was expanded and exalted by the Americans to the foremost position in their constitutionalism, premised on the belief, in John Dickinson's words, that "government must never be lodged in a single body." Enlightenment and experience had pointed out "the propriety of government being committed to such a number of great departments"—three or four, suggested Dickinson—"as can be introduced without confusion, distinct in office, and yet connected in operation." Such a "repartition" of power was designed to provide for the safety and ease of the people, since "there will be more obstructions interposed" against errors and frauds in the government. "The departments so constituted," concluded Dickinson, "may therefore be said to be balanced." But it was not a balance of "any intrinsic or constitutional properties," of any social elements, but rather only a balance of governmental functionaries without social connections, all monitored by the people who remained outside, a balanced government that worked, "although," said Wilson, "the materials, of which it is constructed, be not an assemblage of different and dissimilar kinds."[16]

Abuse of governmental power, especially from the legislature,

15. *The Federalist*, No. 14; Wilson, in McMaster and Stone, eds., *Pennsylvania and the Federal Constitution*, 230, 231, 344; Wilson, "Lectures on Law," Wilson, ed., *Works of Wilson*, I, 416–17.

16. Jefferson to John Adams, Sept. 28, 1787, Boyd, ed., *Jefferson Papers*, XII, 189; [Dickinson], *Letters of Fabius*, Ford, ed., *Pamphlets*, 182–83; Wilson, "Lectures on Law," Wilson, ed., *Works of Wilson*, I, 435.

was now best prevented, as Madison put it in *The Federalist*, Number 51, one of the most significant expressions of the new political thinking, "by so contriving the interior structure of the government as that its several constituent parts may, by their mutual relations, be the means of keeping each other in their proper places." Perhaps the most rigorous separation of powers could be attained, suggested Madison in a revelation of the assumptions behind the new conception of government, by having all the departments of government drawn directly from the same fountain of authority, the people, "through channels having no communication whatever with one another." However, since such a plan was probably impractical, some deviations from "the principle" were necessary. Yet every effort, emphasized Madison, should be made to keep the separate departments independent, or else they could not effectively check and balance each other. The legislature must be divided and the executive fortified with a veto in order to distribute power and guard against encroachments. Moreover, continued Madison with mounting enthusiasm, the new federal government—with its new kind of "mixed character" —possessed an immense advantage over the conventional single republics which were limited in the amount of separating and dividing of powers they could sustain. "In the compound republic of America," said Madison, "the power surrendered by the people is first divided between two distinct governments, and then the portion allotted to each subdivided among distinct and separate departments." Furthermore, the partitioning of power in America would be intensified by "the extent of country and number of people comprehended under the same government," so that "the society itself will be broken into so many parts, interests and classes of citizens, that the rights of individuals, or of the minority, will be in little danger from interested combinations of the majority."[17]

It was an imposing conception—a kinetic theory of politics— such a crumbling of political and social interests, such an atomization of authority, such a parceling of power, not only in the governmental institutions but in the extended sphere of the society itself, creating such a multiplicity and a scattering of designs and passions, so many checks, that no combination of parts could hold, no group of evil interests could long cohere. Yet out of the clashing and checking of this diversity Madison believed the public good, the true perfection of the whole, would somehow arise. The

17. *The Federalist*, No. 51.

impulses and passions would so counteract each other, so neutralize their potencies, as America's contending religious sects had done, that reason adhering in the natural aristocracy would be able to assert itself and dominate.

5. THE END OF CLASSICAL POLITICS

The Americans had reversed in a revolutionary way the traditional conception of politics: the stability of government no longer relied, as it had for centuries, upon its embodiment of the basic social forces of the state. Indeed, it now depended upon the prevention of the various social interests from incorporating themselves too firmly in the government. Institutional or governmental politics was thus abstracted in a curious way from its former associations with the society. But at the same time a more modern and more realistic sense of political behavior in the society itself, among the people, could now be appreciated. This revolution marked an end of the classical conception of politics and the beginning of what might be called a romantic view of politics. The eighteenth century had sought to understand politics, as it had all of life, by capturing in an integrated, ordered, changeless ideal the totality and complexity of the world—an ideal that the concept of the mixed constitution and the proportioned social hierarchy on which it rested perfectly expressed. In such an ideal there could be only potential energy, no kinetic energy, only a static equilibrium among synthetic orders, and no motion among the particular, miscellaneous parts that made up the society. By destroying this ideal Americans placed a new emphasis on the piecemeal and the concrete in politics at the expense of order and completeness. The Constitution represented both the climax and the finale of the American Enlightenment, both the fulfillment and the end of the belief that the endless variety and perplexity of society could be reduced to a simple and harmonious system. By attempting to formulate a theory of politics that would represent reality as it was, the Americans of 1787 shattered the classical Whig world of 1776.

Americans had begun the Revolution assuming that the people were a homogeneous entity in society set against the rulers. But such an assumption belied American experience, and it took only a few years of independence to convince the best American minds that distinctions in the society were "various and unavoidable," so much so that they could not be embodied in the government.[18] Once the people were thought to be composed of various interests in opposition to one another, all sense of a graduated organic chain in the social hierarchy became irrelevant, symbolized by the increasing emphasis on the image of a social contract. The people were not an order organically tied together by their unity of interest but rather an agglomeration of hostile individuals coming together for their mutual benefit to construct a society. The Americans transformed the people in the same way that Englishmen a century earlier had transformed the rulers: they broke the connectedness of interest among them and put them at war with one another, just as seventeenth-century Englishmen had separated the interests of rulers and people and put them in opposition to each other.

As Joel Barlow noted in 1792, the word "*people*" in America had taken on a different meaning from what it had in Europe. In America it meant the whole community and comprehended every human creature in the society; in Europe, however, it meant "something else more difficult to define." "Society," said Enos Hitchcock in 1788, "is composed of individuals—they are parts of the whole." And such individuals in America were the entire society: there could be nothing else—no orders, no lords, no monarch, no magistrates in the traditional sense. "Without the distinctions of titles, families, or nobility," wrote Samuel Williams, "they acknowledged and reverenced only those distinctions which nature had made, in a diversity of talents, abilities, and virtues. There were no family interests, connexions, or estates, large enough to oppress them. There was no excessive wealth in the hands of a few, sufficient to corrupt them." The Americans were thus both equal and unequal at the same time.

They all feel that nature has made them equal in respect to their rights; or rather that nature has given to them a common and an equal right to liberty, to property, and to safety; to justice, government, laws, religion, and freedom. They all see that nature has made them very unequal in respect to their original powers, capacities, and talents. They become united in claiming and in preserving the equality, which nature has assigned to them; and in availing themselves of the benefits, which are designed, and may be derived from the inequality, which nature has also established.[19]

18. Madison to Jefferson, Oct. 24, 1787, Boyd, ed., *Jefferson Papers*, XII, 277.
19. Joel Barlow, *Advice to the Privileged Orders in the Several States of Europe Resulting from the Necessity and Propriety of a General Revolution in the*

Politics in such a society could no longer be simply described as a contest between rulers and people, between institutionalized orders of the society. The political struggles would in fact be among the people themselves, among all the various groups and individuals seeking to create inequality out of their equality by gaining control of a government divested of its former identity with the society. It was this disembodiment of government from society that ultimately made possible the conception of modern politics and the eventual justification of competing parties among the people. Those who criticized such divisive jealousy and opposition among the people, said William Hornby of South Carolina in 1784, did not understand "the great change in politics, which the revolution must have necessarily produced.... In these days we are equal citizens of a DEMOCRATIC REPUBLIC, in which jealousy and opposition must naturally exist, while there exists a difference in the minds, interests, and sentiments of mankind." While few were as yet willing to justify factionalism so blatantly, many now realized with Madison that "the regulation of these various and interfering interests forms the principal task of modern legislation, and involves the spirit of party and faction in the necessary and ordinary operations of the government." Legislation in such a society could not be the transcending of the different interests but the reconciling of them. Despite Madison's lingering hope, the public good could not be an entity distinct from its parts; it was rather "the general combined interest of all the state put together, as it were, upon an average."[20]

Under the pressure of this transformation of political thought old words and concepts shifted in emphasis and took on new meanings. Tyranny was now seen as the abuse of power by any branch of the government, even, and for some especially, by the traditional representatives of the people. "The accumulation of all powers," said Madison, "legislative, executive, and judiciary, in the same hands, whether of one, a few, or many, and whether hereditary, self-appointed, or elective, may justly be pronounced the very definition of tyranny." The separation of this governmental power, rather than simply the participation of the people in a part of the government, became the best defense of liberty.

Principles of Government (Ithaca, N. Y., 1956, first published London, 1792), 17; Hitchcock, Oration, Delivered July 4, 1788, 18; Williams, History of Vermont, 344, 330.

20. Charleston Gazette of the St. of S.-C., July 29, 1784; The Federalist, No. 10; Charleston Gazette Extra. of the St. of S.-C., July 17, 1784.

Therefore liberty, as the old Whigs had predominantly used the term—public or political liberty, the right of the people to share in the government—lost its significance for a system in which the people participated throughout.[21]

The liberty that was now emphasized was personal or private, the protection of individual rights against all governmental encroachments, particularly by the legislature, the body which the Whigs had traditionally cherished as the people's exclusive repository of their public liberty and the surest weapon to defend their private liberties. Such liberties, like that of freedom of the press, said both Madison and Paine, were now in less danger from "any direct attacks of Power" than they were from "the silent awe of a predominant party" or "from a fear of popular resentment." The assumptions behind such charges were radically new and different from those of the Whigs of 1776: men now began to consider "the interests of society and the rights of individuals as distinct," and to regard public and private liberty as antagonistic rather than complementary. In such circumstances the aim of government, in James Iredell's words, became necessarily twofold: to provide "for the security of every individual, as well as a fluctuating majority of the people." Government was no longer designed merely to promote the collective happiness of the people, but also, as the Tories had urged in the early seventies, "to protect citizens in their personal liberty and their property" even against the public will. Indeed, Madison could now say emphatically, "Justice is the end of government. It is the end of civil society." Unless individuals and minorities were protected against the power of majorities no government could be truly free.[22]

21. *The Federalist*, No. 47, No. 48.

22. Madison's Observations on Jefferson's Draft of a Constitution for Virginia (1788), Boyd, ed., *Jefferson Papers*, VI, 316; Paine, *Letter to Raynal*, in Foner, ed., *Writings of Paine*, II, 250; *Rudiments of Law and Government*, v; James Iredell, "To the Public" (1786), McRee, *Life of Iredell*, II, 146; *Providence Gazette*, Nov. 7, 1789; *The Federalist*, No. 51. For a new definition of liberty similar to that being formed by the Americans see De Lolme, *Constitution of England* (London, 1788), 244–46: Liberty was not, as men used to think, the establishing of a governmental order or the participating in legislation through voting for representatives; for "these are functions, are acts of Government, but not constituent parts of Liberty." "To concur by one's suffrage in enacting laws, is to enjoy a share, whatever it may be, of Power," while liberty, "so far as it is possible for it to exist in a Society of Beings whose interests are almost perpetually opposed to each other, consists in this, that, *every Man, while he respects the persons of others, and allows them quietly to enjoy the produce of their industry, be certain himself likewise to enjoy the produce of his own industry, and that his person be also secure.*"

Because of this growing sense of discrepancy between the rights of the society and the rights of individuals and because the new federal government was designed to prevent the emergence of any "common passion" or sense of oneness among large numbers of persons "on any other principles than those of justice and the general good," comprehensible only by a natural elite, the older emphasis on public virtue existing throughout the society lost some of its thrust; and men could now argue that "*virtue*, patriotism, or love of country, never was nor never will be till men's natures are changed, a fixed, permanent principle and support of government." The problem was, as Charles Thompson lamented in 1786, that most Americans had no other "Object" than their own "individual happiness." While Thompson still hoped that the people would eventually become "sufficiently impressed with a sense of what they owe to their national character," others began recasting their thinking. As early as 1782 Jefferson told Monroe that it was ridiculous to suppose that a man should surrender himself to the state. "This would be slavery, and not that liberty which the bill of rights has made inviolable, and for the preservation of which our government has been changed." Freedom, said Jefferson, would be destroyed by "the establishment of the opinion that the state has a *perpetual* right to the services of all it's members." The aim of instilling a spartan creed in America thus began to seem more and more nonsensical. By 1785 Noah Webster was directly challenging Montesquieu's opinion that public virtue was a necessary foundation for democratic republics. Such virtue or patriotism, said Webster, could never predominate. Local attachments would always exist, self-interest was all there ever was. But under a democracy, argued Webster, a self-interested man must court the people, thus tending to make self-love coincide with the people's interest.[23]

William Vans Murray devoted an entire chapter of his *Political Sketches*, published in 1787, to a denial of the conventional view that republicanism was dependent upon virtue. The compulsion for such arguments was obvious. America, as Murray ad-

23. *The Federalist*, No. 50, No. 51; *Providence Gazette*, Dec. 29, 1787; Thompson to Jefferson, Apr. 6, 1786, Boyd, ed., *Jefferson Papers*, IX, 380; Jefferson to Monroe, May 20, 1782, *ibid.*, VI, 185–86; Webster, *Sketches of American Policy*, 25. For Hamilton's disavowal of "the necessity of disinterestedness in republics" and his ridiculing of the seeking "for models in the simple ages of Greece and Rome" see "The Continentalist No. VI," July 4, 1782, Syrett and Cooke, eds., *Hamilton Papers*, III, 103.

mitted, was "in a state of refinement and opulence," and was increasingly being permeated by "luxurious habits"—characteristics which time-honored writers on politics had declared incompatible with republican virtue and simplicity, and thus foreboding signs of an inevitable declension of the state. Yet the political scientists who spouted these maxims of republicanism had never known America. "The truth is," said Murray, "Montesquieu had never study'd a free Democracy." All the notions of these "refining speculists" had come from impressions of the ancient republics which possessed only "undefined constitutions, . . . constructed in days of ignorance." The republics of antiquity had failed because they had "attempted to force the human character into distorted shapes." The American republics, on the other hand, said Murray, were built upon the realities of human nature. They were free and responsive to the people, framed so as to give "fair play" to the actions of human nature, however unvirtuous. They had been created rationally and purposefully—for the first time in history—without attempting to pervert, suppress, or ignore the evil propensities of all men. Public virtue—the "enthusiasm," as Murray called it, of a rude and simple society, the public proscription of private pursuits for luxury—had at last "found a happy substitution in the energy of true freedom, and in a just sense of civil liberty." The American governments possessed "the freedom of Democracy, without its anarchy."[24]

Although they were "so extremely popular," wrote John Stevens, "yet the checks which have been invented (particularly in some of them) have rendered these governments capable of a degree of stability and consistency beyond what could have been expected, and which will be viewed with surprise by foreigners." Undoubtedly virtue in the people had been an essential substitute for the lack of good laws and the indispensable remedy for the traditional defects of most democratic governments. But in America where the inconveniences of the democratic form of government had been eliminated without destroying the substantial benefits of democracy—where there was introduced, said James Wilson, "into the very form of government, such particular checks and controls, as to make it advantageous even for bad men to act for the public good"—the need for a society of sim-

24. [Murray], *Political Sketches*, Chap. II, "Virtue," 24, 25, 28–30, 47, 43, 38, 10. On Murray and the circumstances of the writing of his pamphlet see Alexander DeConde, "William Vans Murray's *Political Sketches*: A Defense of the American Experiment," *Miss. Valley Hist. Rev.*, 41 (1954–55), 623–40.

ple, equal, virtuous people no longer seemed so critical. America alone, wrote Murray, had united liberty with luxury and had proved "the consistency of the social nature with the political happiness of man."[25]

Such depreciations of public virtue were still sporadic and premature, yet they represented the beginnings of a fundamental shift in thought. In place of individual self-sacrifice for the good of the state as the bond holding the republican fabric together, the Americans began putting an increasing emphasis on what they called "public opinion" as the basis of all governments. Montesquieu in his *Spirit of the Laws*, wrote Madison in 1792, had only opened up the science of politics. Governments could not be divided simply into despotisms, monarchies, and republics sustained by their "operative principles" of fear, honor, and virtue. Governments, suggested Madison, were better divided into those which derived their energy from military force, those which operated by corrupt influence, and those which relied on the will and interest of the society. While nearly all governments, including the British monarchy, rested to some extent on public opinion, only in America had public consent as the basis of government attained its greatest perfection. No government, Americans told themselves over and over, had ever before so completely set its roots in the sentiments and aims of its citizens. All the power of America's governments, said Samuel Williams, was "derived from the public opinion." America would remain free not because of any quality in its citizens of spartan self-sacrifice to some nebulous public good, but in the last analysis because of the concern each individual would have in his own self-interest and personal freedom. The really great danger to liberty in the extended republic of America, warned Madison in 1791, was that each individual may become insignificant in his own eyes—hitherto the very foundation of republican government.[26]

Such a total grounding of government in self-interest and consent had made old-fashioned popular revolutions obsolete. Establishments whose foundations rest on the society itself, said

25. [Stevens], *Observations on Government*, 51; Wilson, "Lectures on Law," Wilson, ed., *Works of Wilson*, I, 393; [Murray], *Political Sketches*, 47–48. See also [Jackson], *Thoughts upon the Political Situation*, 22–24; Taylor, *Inquiry into the Principles*, 386, 390, 461–62.

26. [Madison], Phila. *National Gazette*, Feb. 20, Jan. 19, 30, 1792, Dec. 19, 1791, Hunt, ed., *Writings of Madison*, VI, 93–94, 85, 87, 70; Williams, *History of Vermont*, 206–07, 344–45; Wilson, "Lectures on Law," Wilson, ed., *Works of Wilson*, II, 125.

Wilson, cannot be overturned by any alteration of the government which the society can make. The decay and eventual death of the republican body politic now seemed less inevitable. The prevailing opinion of political writers, noted Nathaniel Chipman, had been "that man is fatally incapable of forming any system which shall endure without degeneration," an opinion that appeared "to be countenanced by the experience of ages." Yet America had lighted the way to a reversal of this opinion, placing, as David Ramsay put it, "the science of politics on a footing with the other sciences, by opening it to improvements from experience, and the discoveries of future ages." Governments had never been able to adjust continually to the operations of human nature. It was "impossible," said Chipman, "to form any human institution, which should accommodate itself to every situation in progress." All previous peoples had been compelled to suffer with the same forms of government—probably unplanned and unsuitable in the first place—despite extensive changes in the nature of their societies. "The confining of a people, who have arrived at a highly improved state of society, to the forms and principles of a government, which originated in a simple, if not barbarous state of men and manners," was, said Chipman, like Chinese foot-binding, a "perversion of nature," causing an incongruity between the form of government and the character of the society that usually ended in a violent eruption, in a forceful effort to bring the government into accord with the new social temperament of the people.[27]

However, the American republics possessed what Thomas Pownall called "a *healing principle*" built into their constitutions. Each contained "within itself," said Samuel Williams, "the means of its own *improvement*." The American governments never pretended, said Chipman, to perfection or to the exclusion of future improvements. "The idea of incorporating, in the constitution itself, a plan of reformation," enabling the people periodically and peacefully to return to first principles, as Machiavelli had urged, the Americans realized, was a totally new contribution to politics. The early state constitutions, David Ramsay admitted, possessed many defects. "But in one thing they were all perfect. They left the people in the power of altering and amending them, when-

27. Wilson, "Lectures on Law," Wilson, ed., *Works of Wilson*, I, 384; Chipman, *Principles of Government*, 282, 286, 288–89; Ramsay, *American Revolution*, I, 357.

ever they pleased." And the Americans had demonstrated to the world how a people could fundamentally and yet peaceably alter their forms of government. "This revolution principle—that, the sovereign power residing in the people, they may change their constitution and government whenever they please—is," said James Wilson, "not a principle of discord, rancour, or war: it is a principle of melioration, contentment, and peace." Americans had in fact institutionalized and legitimized revolution. Thereafter, they believed, new knowledge about the nature of government could be converted into concrete form without resorting to violence. Let no one, concluded Chipman, now rashly predict "that this beautiful system is, with the crazy empires of antiquity, destined to a speedy dissolution; or that it must in time, thro' the degeneracy of the people, and a corruption of its principles, of necessity give place to a system of remediless tyranny and oppression." By actually implementing the old and trite conception of the sovereignty of the people, by infusing political and even legal life into the people, Americans had created, said Wilson, "the great panacea of human politics."[28] The illimitable progress of mankind promised by the Enlightenment could at last be made coincident with the history of a single nation. For the Americans at least, and for others if they followed, the endless cycles of history could finally be broken.

The Americans of the Revolutionary generation believed that they had made a momentous contribution to the history of politics. They had for the first time demonstrated to the world how a people could diagnose the ills of its society and work out a peaceable process of cure. They had, and what is more significant they knew they had, broken through the conceptions of political theory that had imprisoned men's minds for centuries and brilliantly reconstructed the framework for a new republican polity, a reconstruction that radically changed the future discussion of politics. The Federalists had discovered, they thought, a constitutional antidote "wholly popular" and "strictly republican" for the ancient diseases of a republican polity—an antidote that did not destroy the republican vices, but rather accepted, indeed en-

---

28. Pownall, *Memorial to America*, 53; Williams, *History of Vermont*, 345; Chipman, *Principles of Government*, 289–90, 291–92; Ramsay, *American Revolution*, I, 357; Wilson, "Lectures on Law," Wilson, ed., *Works of Wilson*, I, 21, 420; Jefferson to David Humphreys, Mar. 18, 1789, Boyd, ed., *Jefferson Papers*, XIV, 678; Wilson, in McMaster and Stone, eds., *Pennsylvania and the Federal Constitution*, 230.

dorsed and relied upon them. The Federalist image of a public good undefinable by factious majorities in small states but somehow capable of formulation by the best men of a large society may have been a chimera. So too perhaps was the Federalist hope for the filtration of the natural social leaders through a federal sieve into political leadership. These were partisan and aristocratic purposes that belied the Federalists' democratic language. Yet the Federalists' intellectual achievement really transcended their particular political and social intentions and became more important and more influential than they themselves anticipated. Because their ideas were so popularly based and embodied what Americans had been groping towards from the beginning of their history, the Federalists' creation could be, and eventually was, easily adopted and expanded by others with quite different interests and aims at stake, indeed, contributing in time to the destruction of the very social world they had sought to maintain. The invention of a government that was, in James Sullivan's words, "perhaps without example in the world" could not long remain a strictly Federalist achievement. "As this kind of government," wrote Samuel Williams, "is not the same as that, which has been called monarchy, aristocracy, or democracy; as it had a conspicuous origin in America, and has not been suffered to prevail in any other part of the globe, it would be no more than just and proper, to distinguish it by its proper name, and call it, *The American System of Government*."[29]

So piecemeal was the Americans' formulation of this system, so diverse and scattered in authorship, and so much a simple response to the pressures of democratic politics was their creation, that the originality and the theoretical consistency and completeness of their constitutional thinking have been obscured. It was a political theory that was diffusive and open-ended; it was not delineated in a single book; it was peculiarly the product of a democratic society, without a precise beginning or an ending. It was not political theory in the grand manner, but it was political theory worthy of a prominent place in the history of Western thought.

29. Sullivan, *Observations upon the Government*, 38; Williams, *History of Vermont*, 346.

A Note on Sources

PRIMARY

Of all the mammoth publication programs presently underway in early American history perhaps none is more important than Clifford K. Shipton's preparation under the auspices of the American Antiquarian Society of microcard reprints of all the titles in Charles Evans's *American Bibliography*. Through the use of this "Early American Imprint" series I have been able to gain access to and to read and reread nearly every pamphlet, sermon, and tract concerned with politics that was written in the Revolutionary era. It is probably not too much to say that this project has contributed as much as anything else to the recent renewed interest in the intellectual character of the American Revolution.

It came as something of a surprise to find how little of the public literature of the Revolutionary era was available in modern letterpress editions. While some of the Revolutionary tracts can be located in the collected writings of prominent individuals, there are only a few collections of the pamphlets of lesser men. William K. Boyd, ed., *Some Eighteenth Century Tracts concerning North Carolina* (Raleigh, 1927), has some of the Regulator writings and one selection from the Confederation period. Hezekiah Niles, ed., *Principles and Acts of the Revolution in America* (New York, 1876), contains many important pieces, including the Boston Massacre orations. Many of the significant Revolutionary sermons can be found in John W. Thornton, ed., *The Pulpit of the American Revolution . . .* (Boston, 1860), and in Frank Moore, ed., *The Patriot Preachers of the American Revolution, 1750–1776* (N. Y., 1862). Peter Force, ed., *American Archives*, 4th Ser., 5th Ser. (Washington, 1837–56), is a mine of miscellaneous information—letters, newspaper clippings, and some pamphlets—for the years 1774–76. While Bernard Bailyn, ed., *Pamphlets of the American Revolution, 1750–1776* (Cambridge, Mass., 1965–), is helping to remedy the deficiency of printed tracts in the decades of the imperial controversy preceding the Declaration of Independence, most writings of the decade after 1776 are still unavailable in print. The Confederation period in particular has been neglected, since it seems to fall between publication programs that end with the colonial era or the Revolutionary War on the one hand and those that begin with the establishment of the new federal government in 1787 on the other. For much of the twentieth century even the creation of the federal Constitution has been slighted. Until the National History Publications Commission completes its project under the direction of Robert E. Cushman of publishing the Documentary History of the Ratification of the Constitution and the First Ten Amendments, we have to rely essentially on Jonathan Elliot, ed., *The Debates in the Several State Conventions, on the Adoption of the Federal Constitution . . .* (Washington, 1854), and on Paul L. Ford's two editions, *Pamphlets on the Constitution of the United States . . .* (Brooklyn, 1888), and *Essays on the Constitution of the United States* (Brooklyn, 1892). In the meantime, however, there have been several recent collections of Antifederalist writings, the most important and useful being Cecelia M. Kenyon, ed., *The Antifederalists* (Indianapolis, 1966).

Since legislative debates were not generally transcribed in the Revolutionary period, official public records have only a limited use for a study of political thought. A valuable exception is Mathew Carey, ed., *Debates and Proceedings of the General Assembly of Pennsylvania* (Phila., 1786), which focuses on the controversy over the rechartering of the Bank of North America. Recording of legislative debates went further in Pennsylvania than in any other state, and some debates can be found in the columns of the Pennsylvania newspapers of the 1780's. Many of the records of the states are published; others are available either through the "Early American Imprint" series or on microfilm. See William S. Jenkins, ed., *Guide to the Microfilm Collection of Early State Records* (Washington, 1950). Some of the published collections of state papers, particularly those of New Jersey and New Hampshire, contain a wide range of unofficial documents, including newspaper clippings and pamphlets. *The Proceedings Relative to Calling the Conventions of 1776 and 1790 . . .* (Harrisburg, 1825) has much important Pennsylvania material, particularly that relating to the meeting of the Council of Censors in 1784. Since court decisions were usually not published as yet, the notion of precedents in judicial development has to be handled with great caution. Unofficial means of communication—newspapers and pamphlets—were beginning to make important judicial decisions more widely known.

Particularly frustrating for an analysis of constitutional thinking is the lack of any record of the official debates accompanying the adoption of the Revolutionary state constitutions. For the states in 1776, in other words, there is nothing remotely resembling Madison's, Yates's, or even Pierce's notes at the Philadelphia Convention or the record of the ratification debates of 1787–88. Such a discrepancy of material between 1776 and 1787—which itself is an interesting commentary on the developments of the period—has inhibited work on the early state constitutions and has given a somewhat false picture of the relative importance of the state constitutions and the later federal Constitution. As a result ideas richly expressed in 1787–88 have sometimes been attributed indiscriminately to the entire Revolutionary era, leading to an anticipating and telescoping of intellectual developments that were only haltingly worked out. A notable exception to the lack of official debates over the Revolutionary state constitutions is the Massachusetts town returns concerning the constitutions of 1778 and 1780, now conveniently published in Oscar and Mary Handlin, eds., *The Popular Sources of Political Authority: Documents on the Massachusetts Constitution of 1780* (Cambridge, Mass., 1966).

Because of the meagerness of the official records before 1787, I necessarily relied heavily on other kinds of public sources—pamphlets, magazines, and newspapers—and on private correspondence. Since newspaper essays offered the closest approximation of the give and take of personal debate, I have tried to read most of the available papers. Nearly every state—New York and South Carolina are conspicuous exceptions—has at least one newspaper during the Confederation period on microfilm. Some of the most significant issues of the decade after 1776—the problem of mobbing and extra-legislative associations in South Carolina, the role of the upper house in Maryland—can be discovered only through the press. What such newspaper polemics lose in continuity and development of argument, they gain in immediacy and unself-consciousness. Newspaper essays are sometimes more revealing of what is happening intellectually than longer pamphlets because of their very brevity and lack of deliberateness. Collections of the important newspaper debates would be especially helpful.

Private correspondence has to be used with care, for it is obvious that our interpretations of the period can be easily influenced by the disproportionate amount of elitist correspondence published in contrast with the scarcity of the letters of less well-known men. Nevertheless, private correspondence did prove to be an important supplement to the record of the public mind throughout, but especially in the 1780's as a serious gap began to emerge between public and private thought among the elite. With the growing publication of legislative debates and the increase in the number of newspapers the nature of the political audience began to change, and political figures were more and more forced in public discussions to concede to the popular and egalitarian ideology of the Revolution. It is important to recall that the debates in the Philadelphia Convention were deliberately kept secret, for this crucial decision in 1787—a decision that apparently never really had to be made a decade earlier, because it was taken so much for granted—accounts for the kind of candid discussion of aristocracy and the frank expressions of a fear of popular power in the Convention that is missing from the ratification debates. The emerging distinction between public and private views is itself an important part of the historical record and needs further exploration in the context of the changes occurring in the latter part of the eighteenth century in the role of the press and of other devices for influencing a wider public.

SECONDARY

Serious interest in the constitutional history of the Revolutionary era dates back to the latter part of the nineteenth century when writers began to approach the institutions of the period not as strokes of political genius or as inheritances from Europe but as products of American political experience. Since most historians in the first half of the twentieth century have been absorbed in a scientific and behavioral approach to the Revolutionary era, much of the best work on Revolutionary thought has been left to nonbehaviorists in government departments and others with a traditional approach to political theory —scholars like Andrew C. McLaughlin, Walter F. Dodd, Edward S. Corwin, William S. Carpenter, Charles McIlwain, Charles Warren, and more recently Benjamin F. Wright, Alpheus T. Mason, Clinton Rossiter, Adrienne Koch, and Cecelia M. Kenyon. Although most of these writers are not, strictly speaking, historians, they have an historian's sensitivity to time and to the avoidance of anachronism, which makes their books and articles indispensable to an understanding of the political thought of the period. A necessary recent supplement by a historian to the work of these political scientists, indeed, a prerequisite to any sort of refined comprehension of the problem of political theory in the eighteenth-century Anglo-American world, is Richard Buel, Jr., "Democracy and the American Revolution: A Frame of Reference," *William and Mary Quarterly*, 3d Ser., 21 (1964), 165–90.

The present interest of historians in the intellectual character of the Revolution was stimulated by Edmund S. and Helen M. Morgan, *The Stamp Act Crisis: Prologue to Revolution* (Chapel Hill, 1953), which focused attention on those problems of parliamentary sovereignty which the older constitutional historians had long considered crucial. This growing concern with early American constitutionalism and ideology has been invigorated by some superb studies of seventeenth and eighteenth-century English political thought, namely, the work of Peter Laslett, Michael Walzer, J. G. A. Pocock, Zera Fink, Charles Blitzer, C. B. Macpherson, W. H. Greenleaf, Christopher Hill, W. B. Gwyn, Betty Kemp, Caroline Robbins, Corinne C. Weston, and J. W.

Gough. I found Gough's *Fundamental Law in English Constitutional History* (Oxford, 1961) particularly valuable. Although Douglass Adair, and Clinton Rossiter in his sprawling study, *Seedtime of the Republic: The Origin of the American Tradition of Political Liberty* (N. Y., 1953), had some time ago minimized Locke and stressed the importance of lesser-known radical Whigs in the development of American political ideology, further development of the connection of this radical Whig tradition to America had to await the publication of Caroline Robbins's monumental study, *The Eighteenth-Century Commonwealthman: Studies in the Transmission, Development, and Circumstances of English Liberal Thought from the Restoration of Charles II until the War with the Thirteen Colonies* (Cambridge, Mass., 1959). With studies like H. Trevor Colbourn, *The Lamp of Experience: Whig History and the Intellectual Origins of the American Revolution* (Chapel Hill, 1965), and Richard M. Gummere, *The American Colonial Mind and the Classical Tradition: Essays in Comparative Culture* (Cambridge, Mass., 1963), recent work on American Revolutionary thought seems to be reverting to an older nineteenth-century emphasis on America's debt to Europe's intellectual heritage. It has been left, however, to Bernard Bailyn, *Ideological Origins of the American Revolution* (Cambridge, Mass., 1967), to develop and exploit most fully the relationship between American Revolutionary thought and European traditions, in particular, the libertarian heritage of English radical Whiggism. Bailyn's book has now become the starting point for any further study of the political and constitutional ideas of the Revolutionary decades.

Several older books on eighteenth-century English thought—Herbert Butterfield, *The Statecraft of Machiavelli* (London, 1940), and Frank T. H. Fletcher, *Montesquieu and English Politics, 1750–1800* (London, 1939)—together with an excellent study of eighteenth-century French thought—Henry Vyverberg, *Historical Pessimism in the French Enlightenment* (Cambridge, Mass., 1958)—helped to clarify my thinking about the Enlightenment's obsession with political health and sickness. It is amazing that so little has been written about the American Enlightenment. Gilbert Chinard's studies are perhaps the best we have. It is to be hoped that Peter Gay's first of a two-volume study, *The Enlightenment: An Interpretation: The Rise of Modern Paganism* (N. Y., 1966), together with his healthy intrusion into early American history, *A Loss of Mastery: Puritan Historians in Colonial America* (Berkeley, 1966), will provoke a thorough analysis of eighteenth-century American thought.

A clarification of the place of American Protestantism in the Enlightenment is especially needed. The involvement of the "black regiment" of Protestant clergy in the American Revolutionary movement was investigated by Alice M. Baldwin, *The New England Clergy and the American Revolution* (N. Y., 1958, first published 1928), but hardly explained until the whole problem was laid open by Alan Heimert, *Religion and the American Mind: From the Great Awakening to the Revolution* (Cambridge, Mass., 1966). In putting the pieces together we will need to find out much more about the divisions among the Calvinist clergy and the complicated connections of the liberal ministry and left-wing sects to the Revolution. On these points I found two recent biographies, Charles W. Akers, *Called unto Liberty: A Life of Jonathan Mayhew, 1720–1766* (Cambridge, Mass., 1964), and William C. McLoughlin, *Isaac Backus and the American Pietistic Tradition* (Boston, 1967), very suggestive. Although the work of Perry Miller is not substantively concerned with the Revolutionary era, except for a provocative essay, "From the Covenant to the Revival," originally published in James Ward Smith and A. Leland Jameson, eds., *The Shaping of American Religion*, in *Religion in American Life* (Princeton, 1961), reprinted in Miller's *Nature's Nation* (Cambridge, Mass., 1967), I was deeply influenced by his conception of the way ideas interact with society and change through time.

Work on the Revolutionary state constitutions is surprisingly limited. Detailed comparative study is confined to two nineteenth-century articles: William C. Morey, "The First State Constitutions," American Academy of Political and Social Science, *Annals*, 4 (1893), 201–32, and William C. Webster, "Comparative Study of the State Constitutions of the American Revolution," *ibid.*, 9 (1897), 380–420. Fletcher M. Green, *Constitutional Development in the South Atlantic States, 1766–1860* (Chapel Hill, 1930), surveys the important constitutional events for the five southern colonial states. Elisha P. Douglass, in his *Rebels and Democrats: The Struggle for Equal Political Rights and Majority Rule during the American Revolution* (Chapel Hill, 1955), although often disconcertingly partisan and ahistorical, seems to me to be more right than not in the thrust of his interpretation of state constitution-making in the Revolution. Allan Nevins, *The American States during and after the Revolution, 1775–1789* (N. Y., 1924), is a good antidote to Douglass's biases and is still the best account of state politics and constitutionalism of the period; it badly needs reprinting. The state constitutions can most conveniently be found in Francis N. Thorpe, ed., *The Federal and State Constitutions . . .* (Washington, 1909).

Politics in many of the states in the Revolution, particularly the southern states, requires further study. There is a special need for the investigation of the period 1774–76 and the emergence of extralegal governments. Considering the novelty and the significance of the American constitutional convention, there is very little on its origins. Walter F. Dodd, "The First State Constitutional Conventions, 1776–1783," *American Political Science Review*, 2 (1908), 545–61, largely incorporated into his *Revision and Amendment of State Constitutions* (Johns Hopkins University Studies in Historical and Political

Science, New Ser., 1 [Baltimore, 1910]), is perhaps the best account. Robert J. Taylor, *Western Massachusetts in the Revolution* (Providence, 1954), has some good material on conventioneering and extra-legislative associations. The entire subject should probably be viewed in the context of similar English developments at the end of the eighteenth century, revealed in the work of Herbert Butterfield, Eugene C. Black, Ian Christie, and George Rudé. Many of the late nineteenth and early twentieth-century examinations of early American constitutionalism, particularly those in the Johns Hopkins University Studies in Historical and Political Science, e.g., Charles C. Thach, *The Creation of the Presidency, 1775–1789: A Study in Constitutional History* (Baltimore, 1922), are still very valuable; yet nearly all the constitutional problems of bicameralism, representation, executive power, etc., in the colonial period could benefit from modern treatment in the way, say, that Mary P. Clarke, *Parliamentary Privilege in the American Colonies* (New Haven, 1943), has been supplemented by Jack P. Greene, *The Quest for Power: The Lower Houses of Assembly in the Southern Royal Colonies, 1689–1776* (Chapel Hill, 1963). What is particularly needed is the relating of constitutional ideas to their political and social circumstances. An excellent recent example of writing in "the borderland between political ideas and the history of politics" is Jack R. Pole's comparative study, *Political Representation in England and the Origins of the American Republic* (London, 1966). The colonial judiciary has been especially neglected, as has the subject of early American law. Edward S. Corwin has the best material on the development of judicial review, but the topic, for all that has been written about it, remains perplexing. Its resolution requires less work on the Supreme Court and more work in colonial jurisprudence.

Corwin's article, "The Progress of Constitutional Theory between the Declaration of Independence and the Meeting of the Philadelphia Convention," *American Historical Review*, 30 (1924–25), 511–36, is the best study of political thought in the Confederation period. Merrill Jensen, "The Idea of a National Government during the American Revolution," *Political Science Quarterly*, 58 (1943), 356–79, and E. James Ferguson, *The Power of the Purse: A History of American Public Finance, 1776–1790* (Chapel Hill, 1961), have excellent accounts of the nationalist movement in the early 1780's that needs to be more fully distinguished from and related to the Federalist movement in the late 1780's. Forrest McDonald's survey of the period, *E Pluribus Unum: The Formation of the American Republic, 1776–1790* (Boston, 1965), is often perverse, but enlightening on financial dealings during these years.

The several recent studies of the Philadelphia Convention—Clinton Rossiter, *1787: The Grand Convention* (New York, 1966), and Catherine Drinker Bowen, *Miracle at Philadelphia: The Story of the*

Constitutional Convention, May to September 1787 (Boston, 1966) —have not replaced Charles Warren, *The Making of the Constitution* (Cambridge, Mass., 1947). Staughton Lynd's collection of pieces, *Class Conflict, Slavery, and the United States Constitution* (Indianapolis, 1968), has important material on social and economic groups in New York and their relationship to the Revolution and the Constitution, but Lynd's argument about the influence of slavery in the forming of the Constitution seems anachronistic and overdrawn. I found the appropriate chapters in Irving Brant's multivolumed biography of James Madison the most sure-footed of the various accounts of the debates in the Philadelphia Convention. Alpheus T. Mason's brief essays in *The States Rights Debate: Antifederalism and the Constitution* (Englewood Cliffs, N.J., 1964), are also illuminating; they nicely capture the tone and purpose and the "ambiguous interplay" of the polemics out of which developed a document no one clearly anticipated or was satisfied with. Much of the recent work on the Constitution has focused on the Antifederalists, largely as a result of Cecelia Kenyon's provocative article "Men of Little Faith: The Anti-Federalists on the Nature of Representative Government," *William and Mary Quarterly*, 3d Ser., 12 (1955), 3–43. While I agree with Kenyon that the Antifederalists had little faith in the representative structure of the federal government, and hence wanted more checks and balances in the Constitution, I have tried to suggest in Chapters XII and XIII the substantial basis of their mistrust and the intellectual dilemma the Constitution posed for their political thinking.

Partly as a consequence of the devasting criticism by Robert E. Brown, *Charles Beard and the Constitution: A Critical Analysis of "An Economic Interpretation of the Constitution"* (Princeton, 1956), and by Forrest McDonald, *We the People: The Economic Origins of the Constitution* (Chicago, 1958), we seem to be gradually escaping from the particular problem of interpreting the Constitution posed by Charles Beard. It seems obvious by now that Beard's notion that men's property holdings, particularly personalty holdings, determined their ideas and their behavior was so crude that no further time should be spent on it. Yet while Beard's interpretation of the origins of the Constitution in a narrow sense is undeniably dead, the general interpretation of the Progressive generation of historians— that the Constitution was in some sense an aristocratic document designed to curb the democratic excesses of the Revolution—still seems to me to be the most helpful framework for understanding the politics and ideology surrounding the Constitution. What is needed is not a restrictive economic interpretation but rather, as Lee Bensen in *Turner and Beard: American Historical Writing Reconsidered* (New York, 1960) has suggested, a broad social interpretation in which the struggle over the Constitution is viewed as the consequence of opposing ideologies rooted in differing social circumstances.

Many of the difficulties of interpreting the period seem to stem from an oversimplified conception of the social structure. Jackson Turner Main's argument in *The Antifederalists: Critics of the Constitution, 1781–1788* (Chapel Hill, 1961) for a commercial-noncommercial division, for example, does not account for the obvious commercial character of many of the Antifederalists. Although the rhetoric of the debate over the Constitution split along an aristocratic-democratic seam, American society in 1787 does not appear to have been sharply or deeply divided into two coherent classes corresponding to the Federalists and Antifederalists. Nevertheless, while the prevalent talk of aristocracy versus democracy in 1787 cannot be taken literally, it undoubtedly reflected a feeling of social distinction between the Federalist and Antifederalist spokesmen that has to be explained. Robert A. Rutland, *The Ordeal of the Constitution: The Antifederalists and the Ratification Struggle of 1787–1788* (Norman, Okla., 1966), seems helpful in this respect, as does the recent work of Paul Goodman and Alfred F. Young on the emergence of Democratic-Republican parties. The problem seems to be not one of class warfare, but one of social and political antagonism between elites or would-be elites often representing the same but differently established interests competing for the support of what Richard Henry Lee called "the weight of the community." In this connection I found Main's recent work in the social composition of the Revolutionary legislatures, "Government by the People: The American Revolution and the Democratization of the Legislatures," *William and Mary Quarterly*, 3d Ser., 23 (1966), 391–407, and *The Upper House in Revolutionary America, 1763–1788* (Madison, Wis., 1967), especially enlightening and corroborative of what many contemporaries thought was happening to Revolutionary state politics. His findings are sure to stimulate further studies of politics in the 1780's and beyond, as we try to assess the immense consequences of the social forces released by the Revolution.

No note on books about the constitutionalism of the Revolution would be complete without mentioning R. R. Palmer's magnificent study, *The Age of the Democratic Revolution: A Political History of Europe and America 1760–1800* (Princeton, 1959, 1964). In a few brief chapters on America it captures more of the political and constitutional significance of the American Revolution than many volumes have. There are of course many other articles and books, too numerous to mention, that I have used; I have tried to indicate at appropriate places in the notes those that I found most valuable.

Select List of Full Titles

ADAMS, ZABDIEL, *A Sermon Preached . . . May 29, 1782 . . .* [Boston, 1782]

An Affectionate Address to the Inhabitants of the British Colonies in America (Philadelphia, 1776)

The Alarm: Or, an Address to the People of Pennsylvania on the Late Resolve . . . (Phila., 1776)

[AUSTIN, BENJAMIN], *Observations on the Pernicious Practice of the Law* (Boston, 1786)

BACKUS, CHARLES, *A Sermon Preached at Long Meadow, April 17th . . .* (Springfield, Mass., 1788)

BALDWIN, EBENEZER, *The Duty of Rejoicing under Calamities and Afflictions . . .* (New York, 1776)

BARLOW, JOEL, *An Oration Delivered . . . at the Meeting of the . . . Cincinnati, July 4, 1787* (Hartford, 1787)

[BEERS, WILLIAM PITT], *An Address to the Legislature and People of . . . Connecticut* (New Haven, 1791)

BERNARD, FRANCIS, *Select Letters on the Trade and Government of America . . .* (London, 1774)

BLAND, RICHARD, *An Inquiry into the Rights of the British Colonies . . .* (Williamsburg, Va., 1766)

BOUCHER, JONATHAN, *A View of the Causes and Consequences of the American Revolution . . .* (London, 1797)

BRACKENRIDGE, HUGH HENRY, *Six Political Discourses . . .* (Lancaster, Pa., 1778)

BUELL, SAMUEL, *The Best New-Year's Gift for Young People: Or, the Bloom of Youth Immortal by Piety and Glory* (New London, 1775)

[BURKE, AEDANUS], *An Address to the Freemen of the State of South-Carolina . . .* (Phila., 1783)

[BURKE, AEDANUS], *Considerations on the Society or Order of Cincinnati . . .* (Charleston, 1783)

[*629*]

CARMICHAEL, JOHN, *A Self-Defensive War Lawful* . . . (Phila., 1775)

[CHALMERS, JAMES], *Plain Truth;* . . . *Containing, Remarks on a Late Pamphlet, Entitled Common Sense* . . . (Phila., 1776)

CHAMPION, JUDAH, *Christian and Civil Liberty* . . . (Hartford, 1776)

CHIPMAN, NATHANIEL, *Sketches of the Principles of Government* (Rutland, Vt., 1793)

[COOPER, DAVID], *An Enquiry into Public Abuses, Arising for Want of a Due Execution of Laws* (Phila., 1784)

The Crisis, Number I . . . (N. Y., [1775])

The Crisis, Number XI (N. Y., [1775])

CUMINGS, HENRY, *A Sermon Preached in Billerica, on the 23d of November 1775* . . . (Worcester, 1776)

CUMINGS, HENRY, *A Sermon Preached* . . . *May 28, 1783* (Boston, 1783)

DALRYMPLE, JOHN, *The Address of the People of Great-Britain to the Inhabitants of America* (London, 1775)

DEMOPHILUS [pseud.], *The Genuine Principles of the Ancient Saxon, or English Constitution* . . . (Phila., 1776)

DOUGLASS, WILLIAM, *A Summary, Historical and Political,* . . . *of the British Settlements in North-America* (Boston and London, 1755)

[DRAYTON, WILLIAM HENRY], *A Letter from Freeman of South-Carolina* . . . (Charleston, 1774)

DUCHÉ, JACOB, *The American Vine, A Sermon, Preached* . . . *before the Honourable Continental Congress, July 20th, 1775* (Phila., 1775)

An Essay of a Frame of Government for Pennsylvania (Phila., 1776)

An Essay upon Government, Adopted by the Americans, Wherein, the Lawfulness of Revolutions, are Demonstrated in a Chain of Consequences from the Fundamental Principles of Society (Phila., 1775)

FITCH, ELIJAH, *A Discourse, the Substance of Which Was Delivered at Hopkinton, on the Lord's Day, March 24th, 1776* . . . (Boston, 1776)

FOSTER, DAN, *A Short Essay on Civil Government* . . . (Hartford, 1775)

Four Letters on Interesting Subjects (Phila., 1776)

[GALE, BENJAMIN], *Brief, Decent, but Free Remarks and Observations, on Several Laws Passed by the Honorable Legislature of the State of Connecticut, since the Year 1775* (Hartford, 1782)

GARDINER, JOHN, *An Oration Delivered July 4, 1785* . . . (Boston, 1785)

GOODRICH, ELIZUR, *The Principles of Civil Union and Happiness Considered and Recommended* . . . (Hartford, 1787)

GORDON, WILLIAM, *A Sermon Preached before the Honorable House of Representatives* . . . (Watertown, Mass., 1775)

The Government of Nature Delineated; Or an Exact Picture of the New Federal Constitution (Carlisle, Pa., 1788)

GREEN, JACOB, *Observations: On the Reconciliation of Great Britain, and the Colonies* ... (Phila., 1776)

HART, LEVI, *Liberty Described and Recommended* (Hartford, 1775)

HEMMENWAY, MOSES, *A Sermon, Preached before His Excellency John Hancock* ... (Boston, 1784)

[HULME, OBADIAH], *An Historical Essay on the English Constitution* (London, 1771)

HUNTINGTON, ENOCH, *A Sermon Delivered at Middleton, July 20th, A.D. 1775* ... (Hartford, [1775])

HURT, JOHN, *The Love of Our Country* ... (Phila., 1777)

[INGLIS, CHARLES], *The True Interest of America* ... (Phila., 1776)

[JACKSON, JONATHAN], *Thoughts upon the Political Situation of the United States* ... (Worcester, 1788)

[JENYNS, SOAME], *The Objections to the Taxation of Our American Colonies, by the Legislature of Great Britain, Briefly Consider'd* (London, 1765)

LEIGH, SIR EGERTON, *Considerations on Certain Political Transactions of the Province of South Carolina* ... (London, 1774)

[LIVINGSTON, PHILIP], *To the Inhabitants of the City and County of New-York, March 4, 1775* ([N. Y., 1775])

LYMAN, JOSEPH, *A Sermon Preached at Hatfield December 15th, 1774* ... (Boston, 1775)

MACAULAY, CATHARINE, *An Address to the People of England, Scotland, and Ireland, on the Present Important Crisis of Affairs*, 3d ed. (N. Y., 1775)

MACCLINTOCK, SAMUEL, *A Sermon Preached June 3, 1784 On the Commencement of the New Constitution* ... (Portsmouth, 1784)

MADISON, JAMES, *A Sermon Preached in the County of Botetourt* ... (Richmond, 1781)

[MATHER, MOSES], *America's Appeal to the Impartial World* ... (Hartford, 1775)

MATHER, MOSES, *Sermon, Preached in the Audience of the General Assembly* ... *on the Day of Their Anniversary Election, May 10, 1781* (New London, 1781)

[MURRAY, WILLIAM VANS], *Political Sketches, Inscribed to His Excellency John Adams* (London, 1787)

NOBLE, OLIVER, *Some Strictures upon the Sacred Story Recorded in the Book of Esther* ... (Newburyport, 1775)

Observations on a Late Pamphlet, Entitled, "Considerations upon the Society or Order of the Cincinnati" ... (Phila., 1783)

PARSONS, DAVID, *A Sermon, Preached before His Excellency, John Hancock* ... *May 28, 1788* ... (Boston, [1788])

PARSONS, JONATHAN, *A Consideration of Some Unconstitutional Mea-*

sures, Adopted and Practiced in This State (Newburyport, 1784)

PERRY, JOSEPH, *A Sermon, Preached before the General Assembly of the Colony of Connecticut, at Hartford, on the Day of Their Anniversary Election, May 11, 1775* (Hartford, 1775)

The Political Establishments of the United States (Phila., 1784)

POWNALL, THOMAS, *A Memorial Addressed to the Sovereigns of America* (London, 1783)

PRICE, RICHARD, *Additional Observations on the Nature and Value of Civil Liberty, and the War with America* (London, 1778, first pub. 1777)

PRICE, RICHARD, *Observations on the Nature of Civil Liberty* ... (London, 1778, first pub. 1776)

The Proceedings Relating to Calling the Conventions of 1776 and 1790 ... (Harrisburg, 1825)

[RAYNAL, GUILLAUME THOMAS FRANÇOIS], *The Sentiments of a Foreigner on the Disputes of Great-Britain with America* (Phila., 1775)

REESE, THOMAS, *An Essay on the Influence of Religion, in Civil Society* (Charleston, 1788)

RITTENHOUSE, DAVID, *An Oration, Delivered February 24, 1775, before the American Philosophical Society, Held at Philadelphia, for Promoting Useful Knowledge* (Phila., 1775)

ROSS, ROBERT, *A Sermon, in Which the Union of the Colonies Is Considered* ... (N.Y., 1776)

Rudiments of Law and Government, Deduced from the Law of Nature ... (Charleston, 1783)

[SEABURY, SAMUEL], *A View of the Controversy between Great-Britain and Her Colonies* (N. Y., 1774)

SENTINEL [pseud.], *To the Inhabitants of the City and County of New-York, Apr. 13, 1776* (N. Y., 1776)

STEARNS, JOSIAH, *Two Sermons, Preached at Epping in the State of New Hampshire, January 30th, 1777* (Newburyport, 1777)

STEARNS, WILLIAM, *A View of the Controversy Subsisting between Great Britain and the American Colonies* ... (Watertown, 1775)

[STEVENS, JOHN], *Observations on Government, Including Some Animadversions on Mr. Adams' Defence of the Constitutions* ... (N. Y., 1787)

SULLIVAN, JAMES, *Observations upon the Government of the United States of America* (Boston, 1791)

SYMMES, WILLIAM, *A Sermon Preached before His Honor Thomas Cushing* ... (Boston, [1785])

[THACHER, OXENBRIDGE], *Considerations on Election of Counsellors, Humbly Offered to the Electors* ([Boston], 1761)

TUCKER, JOSIAH, *The True Interest of Britain* ... (Phila., 1776)

[TUCKER, THOMAS TUDOR], *Conciliatory Hints, Attempting by a Fair State of Matters, to Remove Party Prejudice* (Charleston, 1784)

WALES, SAMUEL, *The Dangers of Our National Prosperity* ... (Hartford, 1785)

WARREN, JOHN, *An Oration, Delivered July 4th, 1783* ... (Boston, 1783)

WEBSTER, NOAH, *Sketches of American Policy* (Hartford, 1785)

WEBSTER, PELATIAH, *A Dissertation on the Political Union and Constitution of the Thirteen United States* (Phila., 1783)

[WELLS, RICHARD], *The Middle Line: Or, an Attempt to Furnish Some Hints for Ending the Differences Subsisting between Great-Britain and the Colonies* (Phila., 1775)

[WHATELEY, THOMAS], *The Regulations Lately Made concerning the Colonies and the Taxes Imposed upon Them, Considered* (London, 1765)

WHITAKER, NATHANIEL, *An Antidote against Toryism* ... (Newburyport, 1777)

[WHITING, WILLIAM], *An Address to the Inhabitants of the County of Berkshire* ... (Hartford, 1778)

WHITNEY, JOSIAH, *A Sermon, Preached in the Audience of His Excellency Samuel Huntington* ... (Hartford, 1788)

WILLIAMS, NATHAN, *A Sermon, Preached in the Audience of the General Assembly of the State of Connecticut* ... (Hartford, 1780)

WILLIAMS, SAMUEL, *A Discourse on the Love of Our Country* ... (Salem, 1775)

WILLIAMS, SAMUEL, *The Natural and Civil History of Vermont* ... (Walpole, N.H., 1794)

[ZUBLY, JOHN JOACHIM], *An Humble Enquiry into the Nature of the Dependency of the American Colonies* ... ([Charleston], 1769)

ZUBLY, JOHN JOACHIM, *The Law of Liberty* ... (Phila., 1775)

Index

A

Act of Settlement (1701), 295

Adams, John: and political science, 6, 8, 567–68; on British constitution, 11, 206, 575, 579, 582, 586; on Great Britain, 35–36, 39, 82n, 136n, 137; on demagoguery, 39; on the people, 39, 62, 329, 577–78; on history, 44, 49; on republicanism, 48–49, 53, 56, 92, 131; on virtue, 49, 105, 570–71; on aristocracy, 67, 71, 572–74, 577, 578, 582, 583, 588; on American society, 67, 75, 147, 569–70, 571–74, 575, 576n; on American Revolution, 74, 78, 105, 106, 117, 121, 569–70, 571; personality of, 75, 79–80, 82n, 123, 574, 588, 592; on Carter Braxton, 97, 97n; describes republic, 119–20, 121, 123, 585–86; on U. S. government, 128, 356, 357, 358, 580–81; on executive, 136n, 137, 141, 207, 578–79; on impeachment, 141–42; on fine arts, 105; as "Humphrey Ploughjogger," 106; on creation of new governments, 127, 129, 130, 131, 132, 134; and Thomas Hutchinson, 146; on judiciary, 159, 161, 294–95; on law, 162, 261, 299n; on *Political Disquisitions* (James Burgh), 165; on representation, 165, 170, 180, 182; on democracy, 182, 201–02; on mixed government, 198, 203, 204, 206, 208–09, 577, 579, 586–87; on colonial councils, 211, 212–13; on the British empire, 211, 212, 352, 353; compared with Benjamin Lincoln, 220, 576, 577; on mobs, 321; on sovereignty, 345, 351, 581, 585; and Lee-Deane affair, 420; on social mobility, 476, 479; works about, 568n; and Enlighten-

ment, 568, 569, 579; on education, 570, 575; disillusionment of, 571, 575; on separation of powers, 577n; and Benjamin Rush, 588; and John Taylor, 588–92

Writings of: *Thoughts on Government*, 131, 134, 141, 161, 203, 208, 568, 579; *Defence of the Constitutions*, 568, 571, 576–82 *passim*, 588

Adams, John Quincy, 393, 514

Adams, Samuel: on British constitution, 11; on republicanism, 58, 61, 118, 121n; on government, 58, 129–30, 205, 317, 363; on democracy, 67, 168, 202, 324, 327; on popular excesses, 67, 327; on equality, 70; on Enlightenment, 99; on "the Christian Sparta," 118, 421; on luxury, 124, 131, 421; on Revolutionary movement, 129, 131, 317; on suffrage, 168; on the nature of a constitution, 266, 267; on conventions, 327; on sovereignty, 352, 353, 526, 528, 585; on Society of the Cincinnati, 400; on Lee-Deane affair, 420; on U. S. Constitution, 526, 528

Adams, Zabdiel, 375

Addison, Joseph, 14, 450

Africa, 30

Agrarian laws, 64, 89

Alarm, The (anon., Phila.), 337

Albany, 174

Albemarle County, Va., 240–41, 272, 363, 366

Allen, Thomas, 285

Amendment, constitutional, 307–09, 613. *See also* Conn., constitution; Del. Constitution (1776); Ga. Constitution (1777); Md. Constitution (1776); Mass. Constitution (1780);

[635]

D